STATE LIABILITY IN INVESTMENT TREATY ARBITRATION

Today there are more than 2,800 bilateral investment treaties (BITs) and more than 300 other international investment agreements around the world. Most of these investment protection treaties offer foreign investors a direct cause of action to claim damages against host-states before international arbitral tribunals. This procedure, together with the requirement of compensation in indirect expropriations and the fair and equitable treatment standard, have transformed the way we think about state liability in international law.

We live in the BIT generation, a world where BITs define the scope and conditions according to which states are economically accountable for the consequences of regulatory change and administrative action. Investment arbitration in the BIT generation carries new functions which pose unprecedented normative challenges, such as the arbitral bodies established to resolve investor / state disputes defining the relationship between property rights and the public interest. They also review state action for arbitrariness, and define the proper tests under which that review should proceed.

State Liability in Investment Treaty Arbitration is an interdisciplinary work, aimed at academics and practitioners, which focuses on five key dimensions of BIT arbitration. First, it analyses the past practice of state responsibility for injuries to aliens, placing the BIT generation in historical perspective. Second, it develops a descriptive law-and-economics model that explains the proliferation of BITs, and why they are all worded so similarly. Third, it addresses the legitimacy deficits of this new form of dispute settlement, weighing its potential advantages and democratic shortfalls. Fourth, it gives a comparative overview of the universal tension between property rights and the public interest, and the problems and challenges associated with liability grounded in illegal and arbitrary state action. Finally, it presents a detailed legal study of the current state of BIT jurisprudence regarding indirect expropriations and the fair and equitable treatment clause.

Volume 26 in the series Studies in International Law

Studies in International Law

Volume 1: Between Light and Shadow: The World Bank, the International Monetary Fund and International Human Rights Law *Mac Darrow*

Volume 2: Toxics and Transnational Law: International and European Regulation of Toxic Substances as Legal Symbolism *Marc Pallemaerts*

Volume 3: The Chapter VII Powers of the United Nations Security Council *Erika de Wet*

Volume 4: Enforcing International Law Norms Against Terrorism *Edited by Andrea Bianchi*

Volume 5: The Permanent International Criminal Court *Edited by Dominic McGoldrick, Peter Rowe and Eric Donnelly.*

Volume 6: Regional Organisations and the Development of Collective Security *Ademola Abass* Volume 7: Islamic State Practices, International Law and the Threat from Terrorism: A Critique of the 'Clash of Civilizations' in the New World Order *Javaid Rehman*

Volume 8: Predictablity and Flexibility in the Law of Maritime Delimitation *Yoshifumi Tanaka*

Volume 9: Biotechnology and International Law *Edited by Francesco Francioni and Tullio Scovazzi*

Volume 10: The Development of Human Rights Law by the Judges of the International Court of Justice *Shiv Bedi*

Volume 11: The Environmental Accountability of the World Bank to Third Party Non-State Actors *Alix Gowlland-Gualtieri*

Volume 12: Transnational Corporations and Human Rights *Edited by Olivier De Schutter*

Volume 13: Biotechnologies and International Human Rights *Edited by Francesco Francioni*

Volume 14: Human Security and International Law: Prospects and Problems *Barbara Von Tigerstrom*

Volume 15: The Arms Trade and International Law *Zeray Yihdego*

Volume 16: Africa: Mapping New Boundaries in International Law *Edited by Jeremy Levitt*

Volume 17: Forced Migration, Human Rights and Security *Edited by Jane McAdam*

Volume 18: The Use of Nuclear Weapons and the Protection of the Environment during International Armed Conflict *Erik Koppe*

Volume 19: The Shifting Allocation of Authority in International Law: Considering Sovereignty, Supremacy and Subsidiarity *Edited by Tomer Broude and Yuval Shany*

Volume 20: Counterterrorism: Democracy's Challenge *Edited by Andrea Bianchi and Alexis Keller*

Volume 21: Amnesty, Human Rights and Political Transitions *Louise Mallinder*

Volume 22: Property Rights and Natural Resources *Richard Barnes*

Volume 23: Human Dignity and the Foundations of International Law *Patrick Capps*

Volume 24: Sovereignty and the Stateless Nation: Gibraltar in the Modern Legal Context *Keith Azopardi*

Volume 25: The International Court of Justice and Self-Defence in International Law *James A Green*

State Liability in Investment Treaty Arbitration

Global Constitutional and Administrative Law in the BIT Generation

Santiago Montt

OXFORD AND PORTLAND, OREGON
2012

Published in North America (US and Canada) by
Hart Publishing
c/o International Specialized Book Services
920 NE 58th Avenue, Suite 300
Portland, OR 97213-3786
USA
Tel: +1-503-287-3093 or toll-free: (1)-800-944-6190
Fax: +1 503 280 8832
E-mail: orders@isbs.com
Website: www.isbs.com

First published in 2009. Reprinted in paperback in 2012

Hart Publishing, 16C Worcester Place, Oxford, OX1 2JW
Telephone: +44 (0)1865 517530 Fax: +44(0)1865 510710
E-mail: mail@hartpub.co.uk
Website: http://www.hartpub.co.uk

British Library Cataloguing in Publication Data
Data Available

ISBN: 978-1-84113-856-5 (Hardback)
978-1-84946-213-6 (Paperback)

Typeset by Hope Services, Abingdon, Oxon
Printed and bound in Great Britain by
TJ International Ltd, Padstow, Cornwall

For Alejandra, Violeta, and Matilde

Foreword

The international investment regime has changed dramatically in recent decades. Emerging economies throughout the world are attracting foreign direct investment (FDI) that goes beyond the traditional concentration on natural resources and agricultural products. Infrastructure projects and manufacturing for export and for the domestic market account for an important share of FDI. Furthermore, a growing share involves contracts or joint ventures between multinational corporations (MNCs) and domestic firms, rather than the state. Although the global economic slowdown has had an important negative impact on emerging economies worldwide, a key role for foreign capital and, in particular, for FDI will remain. In the face of overall declines in investment spending, competition for the remaining private funds will be intense.

Multi-national investors can no longer view emerging economies as passive recipients of whatever benefits investors wish to bestow or as dominated by corruptible leaders willing to make deals for personal gain. Of course, corruption and self-dealing remain in some quarters and are facilitated by long-standing MNC business practices. However, the strengthening of democratic regimes worldwide acts as a check on unfettered deal-making and has introduced demands for political accountability into the international investment environment. These demands, however, are rising to prominence just as more and more investment projects are essentially private arrangements that require state acquiescence but no direct state financial participation. The state may give tax breaks, low-interest loans, and regulatory exemptions, but it does not have an ownership stake. Even when the FDI is part of a counter-part investment surrounding a military contract, it nominally may be a private deal. Even when the state has an ownership stake, it may be unable to control management decisions.

The tension between rising democratic demands and growing private FDI comes into focus in Santiago Montt's major study of Bilateral Investment Treaties (BITs). Montt argues that the rise of BITs to over 2500 worldwide represents a major shift in investor-state relations in developing and emerging economies worldwide.

BITs and the investment chapters of free trade agreements govern the relationships between investors from wealthy countries and host states. They are most commonly signed between wealthy countries and developing or emerging economies where investors believe that the host countries' legal regimes lack key protections. Many low income countries have also signed BITs with each other, but they account only for a small share of world FDI volume. Although firms' contractual relations are increasingly with private firms, BITs frame that relationship by imposing obligations on host states that limit their ability to interfere with investors' expectations. A key aspect of most BITs is the ability of private firms to trigger their enforcement by bringing cases before the World Bank's arbitration facility, the International Center for the Settlement of International Disputes (ICSID). Hence, private firms can initiate actions to enforce these treaties even if the MNCs' home countries are not supportive. This feature provides extra benefits to MNCs and can encourage them to invest in otherwise risky environments, but it also can challenge the political independence of host countries struggling to create modern, democratic states. For a state that is both an emerging economy and an emerging democracy conflicts may arise between investors' interest in preserving a favorable status quo and popular demands for more effective regulation; better, increased tax-financed infrastructure and social services; and investments that generate and preserve jobs.

Montt's ambitious and wide-ranging study of Bilateral Investment Treaties takes on these fundamental issues and recommends a balanced resolution. He links important issues in international investment law with the domestic political legitimacy of an accountable administrative law system. Montt asks whether international treaties, especially Bilateral Investment Treaties (BITs), limit the ability of emerging democracies to make domestic policy that may impose costs on international investors. He makes empirical claims about the way in which the BIT's regime operates, in practice, and develops his own normative arguments about how the BIT's regime ought to develop in order to balance concerns for state sovereignty and regulatory reform against the encouragement of international investment. Montt draws on a deep and extensive knowledge of the way the BIT's regime operates and the way disputes are resolved through arbitration.

Montt claims that the growing BIT's regime is creating bandwagon or network effects. As experience with BITs grows, a specialized bar has arisen to deal with disputes. These lawyers, acting as both advocates and arbitrators, are playing a key role in interpreting poorly defined terms that recur in many treaties, most of which originate in model treaties drafted by countries whose firms are prominent source of FDI. Over time, this developing expertise encourages more and more countries to sign BITs and enhances their value by removing a source of uncertainty. At the same time, the increasing coverage of BITs means that a country that signs a treaty does not stand out as an especially attractive locale for investment because all if its competitors also have signed BITs. True, those outside the regime are disadvantaged, but those in the regime are in an increasingly competitive situation. Nevertheless, if Montt is correct that learning over time lowers costs for investors, the regime has the character of a focal point that will be stable even in the face of serious problems with the way it operates in practice.

In this regard, Montt worries that ICSID arbitral tribunals will interpret the treaties in a way that is too close to the rules of private contract law. The arbitrator may not take account of the character of BITs as treaties between sovereign states that ought to be accountable to their citizens over time. He argues that international investors should not be protected against broad-based domestic policy shifts. His standard is the operation of takings law in wealthy, developed countries; in his view, international investors should have no greater protections abroad than they have at home. This seems an eminently sensible position, but one that would require arbitral tribunals to move beyond a focus on international law jurisprudence to examine domestic constitutional texts. Perhaps it is also a call for broadening the personnel of such tribunals to include some who specialize in constitutional law, especially with respect to the protection of property rights and role of the state as regulator and taxing authority. States with constitutionally mandated takings clauses, which require compensation for the expropriation of private property, nevertheless, both regulate and tax. Laws limit discharges of pollutants, control workplace health and safety, and affect the risk of products. The law requires businesses to comply without obtaining compensation for lost profits. There is no constitutional right to impose risks and other costs on society. Similarly, taxes are constitutionally permitted that reduce profits and raise prices. In Montt's view arbitrators' interpretations of BITs needs to recognize and accept constitutionally-permitted policymaking and use the more well-developed jurisprudence of MNCs home countries as a guideline or benchmark. This observation is particularly important once one recognizes that emerging democracies often must engage in massive amounts of law reform to bring their systems up to date. Thus FDI will often occur in a very dynamic environment, and investors would be naïve to suppose that the current inherited pattern of laws will remain frozen in place. They will likely benefit from some legal reforms that improve the operation of courts and bureaucracies and that clarify the rules, but they can also expect other reforms to impose costs. Investors should not be able to use BITs to pick and choose—benefiting from some reforms and gaining exemption from others.

Mont argues that international investment law can and should have an impact on the domestic legal and political systems in host countries. He is optimistic about the 'halo effect' of international investment law insofar as it can equalize the position of foreign and domestic investors by improving the status of the latter. International investment law should help emerging economies develop their own regulatory takings jurisprudence without imposing rigid rules that could prevent policy innovation in such countries. It should aim to improve the position of domestic investors consistent with democratic values, not undermine local initiative and local democracy.

Montt's study is a comprehensive and thoughtful contribution to the ongoing debates over foreign direct investment and bilateral investment treaties in particular. Practitioners in the field will add to their knowledge of the area and find many issues to debate. In addition, Montt has opened up a new area of study and concern for those interested in the development of constitutional and administrative law in emerging democracies worldwide. Henceforth, comparative constitutional and administrative law will need to take account of the way the international investment regime interacts with domestic political and policy imperatives.

Susan Rose-Ackerman
Yale University
New Haven CT
July 15, 2009

Preface to the Paperback Edition

Investment Treaty Arbitration and Global Public Law Two Years Later

More than two years have passed since I sent the manuscript of *State Liability in Investment Treaty Arbitration* for publication. Although we have not observed any revolutionary development since then, the steady evolution continues. Today, investment treaty arbitration is an established area of international law, here with us to stay.

In the 2009-10 period, investment treaty tribunals and reviewing courts have issued at least 84 new decisions, including 25 on jurisdiction, 40 on liability, 10 on annulment, and 5 on challenges before domestic courts[1]. The vast majority of these cases had either a Latin American or an Eastern European state as the defendant party.

The public law paradigm of investment treaty arbitration, namely, the understanding of this area of the law as a form of review of arbitrariness of state conduct akin to domestic constitutional and administrative law—on a global level—is gaining momentum. No doubt awards issued during the 2009-10 period indicate that the investment treaty arbitration community is becoming increasingly aware of the analytical complexities of the process required to reach a decision that a government must pay damages for the implementation of public policy reforms or administrative interventions in the market.

In my view, new awards confirm one of the central assertions of this book: from a substantive perspective, the key standard in investment treaty arbitration is one of fair and equitable treatment (FET). In the vast majority of cases in which governments are ordered to pay damages, it is because the FET standard is found to have been breached. Consequently, from a public law paradigm, the FET standard continues to demonstrate that it is the central substantive provision that demands investment treaty arbitration to develop a body of global administrative law that allows investors, states and future arbitrators to determine when a government has acted arbitrarily.

This body of global administrative law is possible because of the positive externalities derived from the fact that bilateral treaties are part of a network of treaties worded in relatively similar terms. That is, in fact, one of the main positive claims of this book, explored from a socio-legal perspective in Chapter 2.

[1] Based on the list of cases published on http://italaw.com

I would here like to add a normative claim: the future of investment arbitration—this experiment of global governance that emerged in the last quarter of the 20th century —depends on the development of a coherent and moderate common body of global administrative law that defines what is arbitrary government conduct. The development of such a *common* body of law is one of the legitimate pillars of investment treaty arbitration. Without that rule of law form of legitimacy, the institutional future of investment arbitration seems at least unstable and uncertain.

One of the main threats to the legitimacy and, therefore, future of investment treaty arbitration is the development of two different FET standards: a lax FET-customary international law and a highly demanding FET-autonomous standard. In Chapter 6, I argue extensively against the possibility of an FET-autonomous standard as a matter of treaty interpretation. Here, I would like to include a new normative argument against such a dual system of investment treaty arbitration: two FET standards—where, statistically speaking, one tends to be applied to the US and Canada, and the other to developing countries in general—cast doubt on the legitimacy of the investment treaty protection system.

As a professor of administrative law, I am highly skeptical that the interpretative methods of international law may determine, with precision, the manner in which to assess arbitrary state conduct. As the comparative history of administrative law demonstrates, assessing arbitrariness with precision can only result from a sufficiently dense flux of case law. Therefore, only a relatively coherent body of precedents can help future decision makers determine the proper levels of review and intrusiveness that constitute the relevant standard to be applied. History teaches us that administrative law is a jurisprudential art, not a textual-interpretative one.

Having two FET standards, therefore, disrupts one of the main legitimacy pillars of investment treaty arbitration because it slows down, and even places at risk, the formation of the necessary precedential reserves.

But it also introduces a dual form of assessment of facts and bureaucratic practices that is extremely difficult to reconcile with rule of law legitimacy. In recent cases, political interference and political changes of proper courses of action have been interpreted as legitimate expressions of the people's right to transparency and participation under the FET-international law standard, while they are almost automatically equated to treaty breaches under the FET-autonomous standard. A climate of adversity in a local community has seemed to constitute a circumstance that investors need to factor in under the former standard, but it would surely be the root of a government's unfair and unequal treatment under the latter standard. While for a government to take nine years in a permitting process is considered an acceptable practice under the lax standard, the very same practice would be found as an unacceptable delay under the stricter one. And this merely illustrative list can prove to be much longer.

Ultimately, one of the worse scenarios for investment treaty arbitration is one in which developed countries win cases they should lose, and developing countries lose cases they should win. The dual FET system facilitates this illegitimate scenario becoming a reality. Certainly a one-FET standard system cannot prevent this situation from occurring, but at least it would rule out a lax standard that allows developed states to win cases by exempting improper government behaviour that seriously unsettles investors' expectations, but which does not amount to extremely outrageous conduct assessed under an old-fashion mindset (ie, à la *Neer*).

Again, as an administrative law scholar, I consider that investment treaty arbitration should produce a coherent and moderate *common* body of global law that defines what is arbitrary government conduct. Thirty years ago US judge Harold Leventhal provided a key insight of judicial review in administrative law, one that is fully applicable to investment treaty arbitration:

> The substantive review of administrative action is modest, but it cannot be carried out in a vacuum of understanding. Better no judicial review at all than a charade that gives the imprimatur without the confirmation that the agency is not acting unreasonably… On issues of substantive review, on conformance to statutory standards and requirements of rationality, the judges must act with restraint. Restraint, yes, abdication, no[2].

A unique and balanced FET standard—not too lax, not too strict—should strive to achieve this difficult balance mentioned by Leventhal between restraint and abdication, creating a body of precedents that give valuable indications on how to conduct the assessment. Such a unique FET standard will allow investment treaty arbitration to protect investors' investments against arbitrary state conduct, without creating what Harlow and Rawlings refer to as a 'red light theory' of public law, where it becomes 'a brake on state action'[3].

Santiago Montt
Santiago, Chile
October 2011

[2] *Ethyl Corp v EPA*, 541 F2d 1, 69 DC Cir 1977.

[3] Carol Harlow and Richard Rawlings, *Law and Administration* 3rd edn (Cambridge University Press, Cambridge, 2009) 6.

Acknowledgements

This book is a revised and updated version of the JSD dissertation that I wrote at Yale Law School between 2004 and 2006. I came to Yale in 2003, to pursue a Masters' and Doctorate in administrative law and regulation. Prior to this, I had practised law in Chile, where my work primarily involved defending domestic and foreign companies against government measures, particularly in the fishing industry, which was one of the most heavily regulated industries in the country.

During my first semester as an LLM, I stumbled across the *Metalclad* award.[1] Being completely ignorant at that time on the subject of investment treaties and their system of investor–state arbitration, I was stunned. My immediate reaction was to realise that several of the disputes that I previously handled in Chilean courts—and, of course, many similar ones—would now be litigated before arbitral tribunals pursuant to investment treaty standards.

In addition, the administrative legal scholar in me reacted with deep shock at the reasoning and tone of the award. Although I did not disagree with the outcome itself, many of the arguments adopted by the Tribunal would not have been remotely possible for plaintiffs suing government under any Western public law tradition. Moreover, the Tribunal tended to disregard domestic law, effectively downplaying the importance it deserved in this case. More importantly, in the award, I could not find the deferential and modest attitude normally displayed by public law judges who review decisions made by the political branches of government.

I am neither 'pro-state' nor 'pro-investor'. Instead, I would like to describe myself as 'pro-appropriate equilibrium'. In fact, in terms of my background if anything I would be more on 'pro-investor' side: just before beginning my graduate studies at Yale, I wrote a book on administrative law, galvanised by the consistently poor treatment that a foreign investor, in whose defence I participated, received at the hands of a public entity. This book was designed with the purpose of clarifying and resolving several inadequacies that I found in the Chilean legal system.[2]

The important point is that I had the impression, while reading the *Metalclad* award and later confirmed from other decisions, that international investment law was failing to seriously take into account the

[1] *Metalclad Corporation v Mexico*, ICSID Case No ARB(AF)/97/1 (Lauterpacht, Civiletti, Siqueiros), Award (30 August 2000).

[2] Santiago Montt, *El Dominio Público. Estudio de su Régimen Especial de Protección y Utilización* (Santiago de Chile, Conosur-Lexis, 2002).

enormous reservoir of human experience that had accumulated over many decades, at the domestic level. This struck me as a significant oversight, since domestic public law generally possesses a much more refined conceptual framework than international law for dealing with the problems that typically arise in the confrontation between private interests and the public good.

I decided, then, to embark upon a project that would examine investment treaty arbitration against the more well-established background of domestic constitutional and administrative law. My ultimate purpose—which I hope the reader may appreciate throughout the present book—was and continues to be to contribute to the development of an investment treaty jurisprudence characterised by moderation and deference, in which the interests and expectations of foreign investors will be properly balanced against the regulatory state's exercise of its powers.

Given this agenda, it should come as no surprise that this book does not follow what has become the canon in international investment law. A brief scanning of the table of contents will undoubtedly reveal that the book provides an alternative, multidisciplinary approach to the subject, incorporating historical, economic and legal analysis that places a strong emphasis on issues of constitutional law and expropriations, and of administrative law and arbitrariness.

I had the privilege of working on this project at three of the most intellectually stimulating and vibrant places that a legal scholar can possibly find: Yale Law School, Columbia Law School, and the Woodrow Wilson School of Public and International Affairs at Princeton University. I would like to generally thank all of the people who work at these three institutions, and in particular, their librarians and library personnel.

I am particularly indebted to Yale, my graduated *alma mater*, for deeply changing the way in which I understand the law and its relationship to other social sciences. Professor Susan Rose-Ackerman was the most inspiring and generous supervisor that a JSD student could wish to have, and Professor Michael Reisman served as an endless source of knowledge and wisdom. Professor Michael Levine introduced me to public choice and positive approaches to economic regulation. I am grateful for all the hours spent on this project by such talented people, as well as the voluminous number of insights and perspectives that they offered me.

At Yale, I also wish to thank Professors George Priest, Rudolf Dolzer and Amy Chua; and my classmates and colleagues Mariana Mota, Maciek Kisilowski, Yoon-Ho Alex Lee, Laura Saldivia, and Johanna Kalb. At Columbia Law School, I would like to thank Sylvia T Polo, the Dean of Graduate Legal Studies. At Princeton University, I am indebted to Professors Kim Scheppele, Ingolf Pernice, and George Bustin; and to my classmates and fellows Dan Firger, Matt Jacobs, Nick Poletti, Scott Withrow, Julien Jeanneney, and Mareike Kleine.

I would also like to thank the participants of the New York University GAL project held in Buenos Aires, Professor Richard Stewart, Benedict Kingsbury, and Katrina Wyman; my hosts in Madrid during August, 2005, Professor Gaspar Ariño, and the Fundación de Estudios de la Regulación; Professor Matthew Mirow; my good friend María José Poblete; and two anonymous readers from Hart Publishing. Special thanks to Rachel Turner and Mel Hamill at Hart, for their patience; to Christopher Schuck, my proofreader, who supplied prompt and deft assistance with respect to my limited English; to my former bosses and friends at Weil, Gotshal and Manges, Guillermo Aguilar-Alvarez, Eric Ordway, and Chip Roh, for the many hours spent discussing the various dimensions of investment treaty arbitration; and, finally, to Ramón Vergara Grez for his generosity in authorising me to use his painting 'Carta Abierta a Europa'—undoubtedly one of the most important Chilean artworks of the 20th century—which can be fully appreciated on the back cover of this book.

Writing any book in the midst of other work and study is a selfish act. Without the support of my wife Alejandra, and the inspiration of my daughters Violeta and Matilde, this would have been impossible. If there is any specific *expropriation* which they have come to know while I worked on this project, it is that their husband and dad has been *taken* to the library. In return—though this constitutes far from *prompt, adequate,* and *effective compensation*—I dedicate this book to them, with love.

Of course, in the midst of all this tremendous help and support, all faults and errors are exclusively mine.

Princeton
1 March 2009

Table of Contents

Table of Cases

Anglo–Chilean Tribunal of Arbitration

Canada

Chile

European Court and Commission of Human Rights

European Court of Justice and Court of First Instance

France

Germany

Investment Arbitration

ICSID

LCIA

STOCKHOLM CHAMBER OF COMMERCE

International Court of Justice and Permanent Court of International Justice

Iran–US Claims Tribunal

Permanent Court of Arbitration, Other Ad Hoc Arbitrations and Mixed Claims Commission Cases

United Kingdom

United States

WTO

Table of Legislation

Chile

Ecuador

European Union

France

Germany

Spain

United States

Venezuela

Table of International Agreements and Draft International Agreements

Bilateral Investment Treaties (BITs)

FCN Treaties

Introduction

> [T]akings theory is ultimately about political theory—specifically, about how much faith one has in government.[1]

I WHY THIS BOOK

SINCE GERMANY AND Pakistan signed the first BIT in 1959, the number of concluded bilateral investment treaties (BITs) has grown globally to 2,608.[2] Most of them were signed subsequent to the fall of the USSR, on the understanding that foreign direct investment (FDI) is a key factor for development which should be actively pursued.[3]

BITs, as well as other investment treaties such as free trade agreements (FTAs) containing investment chapters,[4] regulate the admission, treatment and expropriation of foreign investment. This is accomplished, in short, through their dual function of providing a set of open-ended principles that govern state behavior towards foreign investors, and establishing a neutral forum for the resolution of investor–state disputes.

What makes these treaties truly unique is the fact that they are designed to function without the political involvement of either host- or home governments. Indeed, an overwhelming majority of BITs allow foreign investors to file damages actions directly against host states before international arbitral tribunals. Foreign investors are entitled to claim that legislative, administrative or judicial measures have breached the

[1] David A Dana and Tomas W Merrill, *Property. Takings* (New York, Foundation Press, 2002) 57.

[2] Data through the end of 2007. See United Nations Conference on Trade and Development (UNCTAD), *World Investment Report* (New York, United Nations, 2008) 13. A comprehensive list of BITs—although incomplete—can be found at UNCTAD website: http://www.unctadxi.org/templates/DocSearch____779.aspx.

[3] See Kenneth J Vandevelde, 'US Bilateral Investment Treaties: The Second Wave' (1993) 14 *Michigan Journal of International Law* 621, and Jeswald W Salacuse, 'BIT by BIT: The Growth of Bilateral Investment Treaties and Their Impact on Foreign Investment in Developing Countries' (1990) 24 *International Lawyer* 655.

[4] As ironically pointed out by José E Alvarez, 'Critical Theory and the North American Free Trade Agreement's Chapter Eleven' (1997) 28 *University of Miami Inter-American Law Review* 303, 304, NAFTA Chapter 11 is 'a US bilateral investment treaty on steroids'.

substantive principles of these treaties, and they can do so without exhausting local remedies at host states' courts, and without securing authorisation from or endorsement by their own home states. Moreover, under the authority of the New York Convention[5] or ICSID Convention,[6] awards issued by these tribunals are directly enforceable in courts sitting in signatory states throughout the world.

As a consequence of this favourable legal architecture, foreign investors have been filing claims against host states at a pace of 25–45 per year,[7] with a cumulative total of about 300 known cases (up to 2007).[8] These claims have placed and will continue to place, a truly impressive array of regulatory action under the direct and immediate scrutiny of arbitral tribunals. These range from environmental policies, banking sector reforms, implementation of treaty obligations, and responses to economic crises; to revocations of licenses and permits, termination of concession contracts, contractual disagreements of all kinds, and application of tax laws, just to name a few.

One of the most distinctive features of this 'worldwide BIT network',[9] is the degree of similarity to be found among core substantive provisions.[10] As McLachlan et al have noted before, 'this patchwork of interlocking but separate treaties—each the product of its own negotiation—*in fact betrays a surprising pattern of common features*'. (emphasis added)[11]

Notwithstanding difference in wording, from a sociological perspective the language used by BITs' key provisions is sufficiently uniform to have given birth to a *common legal practice*. As a result, since the first arbitral award based on a BIT was rendered in 1990,[12] investment treaty arbitration has become a distinctive field in international law. In Duprey's words, investment treaties have given way to 'the establishment of a genuine arbitration case law specific to the field of investment'.[13] Using

[5] *Convention on Recognition and Enforcement of Foreign Arbitral Awards* (adopted 10 June 1958, entered into force 7 June 1959) 330 UNTS 38 (hereinafter, *New York Convention*).

[6] *Convention on the Settlement of Investment Disputes between States and Nationals of Other States* (adopted 18 March 1965, entered into force 14 October 1966) 575 UNTS 159 (hereinafter *ICSID Convention*).

[7] This pace corresponds to the period 2002–2007, which can be considered to represent the mature equilibrium of the system.

[8] See UNCTAD, n 2, 17.

[9] *Asian Agricultural Products Ltd v Sri Lanka*, ICSID Case No ARB/87/3 (El-Kosheri, Goldman, Asante), Award (27 June 1990) ¶ 49 (hereinafter, *Asian Agricultural Products*).

[10] See eg Rainer Geiger, 'The Multifaceted Nature of International Investment Law' in Karl Sauvant (ed), *Appeals Mechanisms in International Investment Law* (New York, OUP, 2008) 17, 18 (noting that 'the treaty practice of most countries show a certain degree of convergence in investment protection provisions').

[11] Campbell McLachlan et al, *International Investment Arbitration. Substantive Principles* (New York, OUP, 2007) 5–6.

[12] The first award was rendered in *Asian Agricultural Products*.

[13] Pierre Duprey, 'Do Arbitral Awards Constitute Precedents? Should Commercial Arbitration Be Distinguished from Arbitration Based on Investment Treaties' in Emmanuel Gaillard (ed), *Towards a Uniform International Arbitration Law?* (Huntington, Juris Publishing,

the expression coined by Reisman and Sloane, today we live in the 'BIT generation'.[14]

Investment treaty arbitration, also referred to here as investment arbitration, or international investment law, is certainly a new development in international law. While having roots in general international law—particularly in the traditional field of protection of aliens and their property—international investment law confronts challenges so novel, that older precedents, doctrines, and modes of thought, by their very nature, are suddenly of limited value. Indeed, never before has international law enjoyed so much authority over the regulatory state on a permanent basis and without the previous intervention of domestic courts.

The difficulty of the challenges that confront us in investment treaty arbitration derives not only from the novelty of the enterprise, but more importantly, from an absence of guidance provided by the relevant treaties. Indeed, investment treaties do not establish concrete *rules*, but only the most abstract and open-ended *standards*. As a consequence, arbitral tribunals are placed in the position of having to develop concrete norms of state behavior toward foreign investors. In international investment law, '[c]ase law thus plays a fundamental role in developing the scope of treaty obligations'.[15] This effectively converts investment treaty arbitration into a form of global governance, which, moreover, to the extent that there is no central authority but only a constellation of arbitral panels, is private and decentralised.

Today, after 19 years of investment treaty arbitration practice, we are beginning to gain a clearer idea of what BITs' key open-ended provisions actually mean. Although the precise content of these provisions is still far from settled, we are now in the position of determining, to a certain extent, conceptual 'bands' that apply to the potential meaning of those concepts. Stated more formally, to adapt Coe's comment on NAFTA Chapter 11, we may say that '[t]hough a mature jurisprudence has by no means emerged, substantive trends have been established and several of investment treaties' distinctive features, strengths, and weaknesses have been illuminated'.[16]

There is no doubt that, at present, the most pro-investor and the pro-state bounds for possible interpretations of investment treaties' key

2005) 251, 276–77. See also Jeffrey P Commission, 'Precedent in Investment Treaty Arbitration' (2006) 24 *Journal of International Arbitration* 129, 129 (noting that 'the development of an investment treaty case law or jurisprudence is unmistakable').

[14] W Michael Reisman and Robert D Sloane, 'Indirect Takings and its Valuations in the BIT Generation' (2003) 74 *British Ybk of Intl Law* 115.

[15] Andrea K Bjorklund, 'Investment Treaty Arbitral Decisions as *Jurisprudence Constante*' in Colin B Picker et al (eds), *International Economic Law. The State and Future of the Discipline* (Portland, Hart Publishing, 2008) 265, 265.

[16] Jack J Coe Jr, 'Taking Stock of NAFTA Chapter 11 in Its Tenth Year: An Interim Sketch of Selected Themes, Issues, and Methods' (2003) 36 *Vanderbilt Journal of Transnational Law* 1381, 1385.

provisions remain significantly different. Yet, their relative positions are already close enough to allow for an adequate discussion of the goals and functions of international investment law, and to more precisely identify the normative equilibria that should be sought in the process of balancing investors' interests and the regulatory state's powers.

Moreover, to the extent that jurisprudence in the short- and mid- term future will have to adopt various positions within this more narrow and more closely- defined context, international investment law is now entering its most critical phase. I believe that awards to be issued in the next few years will largely determine the future of the BIT generation—either as a successful institutional arrangement of global governance, or as a failed experiment that spawned an illegitimate and conservative system geared toward the excessive protection of investments. Fortunately, because there still exists a reasonable probability that BITs' key provisions will stabilise at appropriate equilibria, I remain optimistic about the future of the BIT generation.

With this general framework in mind, this book attempts to contribute to our general understanding of international investment law; particularly the policy objectives that should guide its development, and the normative equilibria that should be considered to represent its successful achievements. The timing is highly appropriate: we are in the midst of a once-in-a-century financial and economic crisis, which is bringing about globalisation's 'biggest reversal in the modern era',[17] and which will certainly test the soundness of the institutional foundations of the BIT generation (along with other arrangements of global governance).

Following earlier seminal works, investment arbitration is presented here as a form of public law adjudication.[18] This means that the functions of arbitral tribunals do not substantially differ from those of public law courts throughout the Western world. They must review state action for unlawfulness, and ascertain whether the political branches of government have achieved a proper balance between private and public interests.[19] Accordingly, state liability in investment arbitration is understood and explained here as a form of global constitutional and administrative law.

As a Chilean citizen, in this book I have tried to reflect the perspective of developing countries;[20] specifically, those that are seriously committed to democracy, the rule of law, and regulatory capitalism.[21] Given the

[17] *The Economist*, 7–13 February 2009, 'The Return of Economic Nationalism' 9.

[18] See Gus Van Harten and Martin Loughlin, 'Investment Treaty Arbitration as a Species of Global Administrative Law (2006) 17 *European Journal of International Law* 121, 131.

[19] See Gus Van Harten, *Investment Treaty Arbitration and Public Law* (New York, OUP, 2007) 10.

[20] Of course, other views reflecting the perspective of developing countries can disagree with the ideas defended in this book. I do not claim any monopoly over such a perspective.

[21] See eg John Braithwaite, *Regulatory Capitalism. How it Works, Ideas for Making it Work Better* (Edward Elgar, Northampton 2008).

current dimensions of foreign direct investment and its relevance to the developing countries' economies, investment arbitration can make considerable demands in terms of sovereignty and democracy, even more so than international trade regimes.[22] We should not forget that, as Wälde has observed, '[i]nvestment treaties as international law disciplines interfere in domestic regulatory and administrative sovereignty; *that is their very purpose*'. (emphasis added)[23]

Yet, notwithstanding the enormous intrusive potential of this new form of global public law, there has been relatively little analysis of the political and legal consequences to the commitments adopted by developing countries in investment treaties. This book tries to fill in some of these gaps, drawing inspiration from the nineteenth-century Latin American publicists—primarily Andrés Bello—who were active members in the debate concerning state responsibility for injuries to aliens.

Of course, today's challenges are not those of the nineteenth century. Nor are we in need of a Manichean stance favouring developing countries, that disregards investors' expectations and rights as a matter of principle, as was the case during the highly-polarised twentieth century. Instead, the true challenge ahead is the achievement of a proper balance between investors' rights and expectations on the one hand, and valid and legitimate regulatory goals on the other.[24] Only such a compromise can, in the field of investment arbitration, overcome what Keohane has referred to more generally as the 'governance dilemmas' of globalisation:

> I have asked how we can overcome the governance dilemma on a global scale. That is, how can we gain benefits from institutions without becoming their victims? How can we help design institutions for a partially globalized world that performs valuable functions while respecting democratic values? And how can we foster beliefs that maintain benign institutions? . . . [O]ur objective should be to help our students, colleagues, and the broader public understand both the necessity for governance in a partially globalized world and the principles that

[22] See eg Graham Mayeda, 'Playing Fair: The Meaning of Fair and Equitable Treatment in Bilateral Investment Treaties' (2007) 41 *Journal of World Trade* 273, 291, and Joachim Karl, 'International Investment Arbitration: A Threat to State Sovereignty' in Wenhua Shan et al (eds), *Redefining Sovereignty in International Economic Law* (Portland, Hart Publishing, 2008) 225.

[23] Thomas W Wälde, 'Investment Arbitration under the Energy Charter Treaty: An Overview of Selected Key Issues Based on Recent Litigation Experience' in Norbert Horn and Stefan Kröll (eds), *Arbitrating Foreign Investment Disputes* (The Hague, Kluwer Law International, 2004) 193, 210. See also, Jan Paulsson, 'Avoiding Unintended Consequences' in Karl Sauvant (ed), *Appeals Mechanisms in International Investment Law* (New York, OUP, 2008) 241, 245; and, Tai Heng Cheng, 'Power, Authority, and International Investment Law' (2005) 20 *American University International Law Review* 465, 482. Among arbitral decisions, see eg *ADC Affiliate Ltd et al v Hungary*, ICSID Case No ARB/03/16 (Kaplan, Brower, van den Berg), Award (2 October 2006), ¶ 423.

[24] See Rainer Geiger, 'Regulatory Expropriations in International Law: Lessons from the Multilateral Agreement on Investment' (2002) 11 *New York University Environmental Law Journal* 94, 108.

> would make such governance legitimate . . . If global institutions are designed well, they will promote human welfare. But if we bungle the job, the results could be disastrous.[25]

In sum, this book constitutes an effort to answer some of these questions in the context of the global institutional arrangements created for the protection of foreign investment. It takes an interdisciplinary approach which attempts to organise the key normative dimensions of international investment law, and to provide a critical assessment of the various arbitral decisions and academic commentary produced up until the present.

II WHAT THIS BOOK IS ABOUT

In the pages ahead lies an ambitious and novel understanding of state liability in investment arbitration, with an emphasis on the principles of no expropriation without compensation, and fair and equitable treatment (FET), the two most expansive and influential standards contained in investment treaties.

Having already touched upon a general summary of investment treaty arbitration, I will now provide a brief overview of the remaining building blocks of this work, which shape its overall tone and spirit. As the title indicates, this book is about: *State Liability in Investment Treaty Arbitration, Global Constitutional and Administrative law,* and *the BIT Generation*.

A State Liability in Investment Treaty Arbitration

The first major theme of this book is the idea of state liability, or more precisely, regulatory state liability. Because the regulatory state has the power to harm citizens and investors, state liability is explained and justified by a much more complex mixture of corrective and distributive justice rationales than tort liability in private law: not every intentional harm caused by the state is a wrong, not even prima facie; and, the state may be required to pay compensation even in the absence of wrongdoing. The public law nature of state liability deserves then a brief explanation at the outset.

As is well known, the administrative state that emerged in the first half of the twentieth century radically expanded the scope and depth of the public domain. In contrast to the laissez-faire liberal state, this form of

[25] Robert O Keohane, 'Governance in a Partially Globalized World: Presidential Address, American Political Science Association, 2000' (2001) 95 *American Political Science Review* 1, 11–12.

state—as Ackerman observes—'surveys the outcome of market processes and finds them wanting. Armed with a prodigious array of legal tools, it sets about improving upon the invisible hand—taxing here, subsidising there, regulating everywhere'.[26]

Today, throughout Western nations and even beyond, the administrative state has adopted a particular form: the regulatory state.[27] The latter is the result of a transformative process that began with privatisations and deregulations in the 1970s and 1980s, and eventually replaced the previous *dirigiste* version of the administrative state.[28] According to Harlow, this form of state is characterised by having ubiquitous regulatory functions:

> The modern state, in which today I sit and write these words, is characterised above all by its regulatory functions. The regulatory state operates on the risk-averse society, where regulation is pervasive and the routine use of the vocabulary and procedural tools for purposes of social control is both accepted and acceptable.[29]

Regulation's central role at the beginning of the twenty-first century reminds us that the state possesses the constitutional power to redefine and readjust the relationship between private interests and the public interest. Put differently, it has the constitutional duty to allocate burdens and benefits across society in its permanent quest for the public good. The constant upsetting of the status quo, hence, is part of the essence of the regulatory state. As Craig notes, 'legislation is constantly being passed which is explicitly or implicitly aimed at benefiting one section of the population at the expense of another. *It is a matter of conscious legislative policy*'. (emphasis added)[30]

This legitimate power to harm—which may surprise those not trained in public law—constitutes a fundamental aspect of state liability, which any serious approach to the subject in international law must take into

[26] Bruce Ackerman, *Private Property and the Constitution* (New Haven, Yale University Press, 1977) 1.

[27] See David Levi-Faur, 'The Global Diffusion of Regulatory Capitalism' (2005) 598 *Annals of the American Academy of Political and Social Sciences* 12–32 (identifying transitions from *laissez-faire* capitalism, to welfare capitalism, to regulatory capitalism). Some commentators prefer the term 'regulatory capitalism' to 'regulatory state', because it would better capture a new order that is less state-centered. See David Levi-Faur, 'Foreword' in John Braithwaite, *Regulatory Capitalism. How it Works, Ideas for Making it Work Better* (Northampton, Edward Elgar, 2008) viii.

[28] See Giandomenico Majone, 'The Rise of the Regulatory State in Europe' (1994) 17 *West European Politics* 77, 97, and Ferran Pons Cànovas, *La incidencia de las intervenciones administrativas en el derecho de propiedad. Perspectivas actuales* (Madrid, Marcial Pons, 2004) 17.

[29] Carol Harlow, *State Responsibility: Tort Law and Beyond* (New York, OUP, 2004) 6. See also, Levi-Faur, n 27, viii; and Thomas Waelde and Abba Kolo, 'Environmental Regulation, Investment Protection and 'Regulatory Taking' in International Law' (2001) 50 ICLQ 811, 813.

[30] Paul P Craig, 'Compensation in Public Law' (1980) 96 *Law Quarterly Review* 413, 450. Note that *givings*, the opposite of *takings*, have been generally overlooked. See Abraham Bell and Gideon Parchomovsky, 'Givings' (2001) 111 *Yale Law Journal* 547.

account. As Caranta notes, because 'administrative decisions can legally encroach on citizens' rights',[31] '[h]arm alone cannot therefore be sufficient to establish liability'.[32] Something more than a demonstration of economic damages is needed in order to successfully demand that the government pay compensation.

Of course, this does not mean that private interests may always be sacrificed without consequence. There are circumstances in which private rights and expectations should prevail over the public interest, and others in which the affected citizen must at least be compensated. Here lies the dilemma of state liability that Ackerman so accurately sums up in the following words:

> [W]elfare gains can rarely be purchased without social cost—though many may gain, some will lose as a result of the new governmental initiative. And it is the fate of those called upon to sacrifice for the public good that will concern us in this essay: When may they justly demand that the state compensate them for the financial sacrifices they are called upon to make?[33]

It should be noted that defining state liability in the context of the regulatory state is a decidedly new task for international law. As recently as 1983, Judge Higgins commented that such a function was a 'somewhat newer theme',[34] referring specifically to the question that lies at the core of the state liability dilemma: 'do interventions by the State that leave title untouched in the hands of plaintiff, but nonetheless occasion him loss, give rise to a right of compensation?'[35]

Notwithstanding the lack of experience characterising general international law in this area,[36] investment treaty arbitration has been charged with the mission of 'solving' the state liability dilemma.[37] Up until now,

[31] Roberto Caranta, 'Public Law Illegality and Governmental Liability', in Duncan Fairgrieve et al (eds), *Tort Liability of Public Authorities in Comparative Perspective* (London, The British Institute of International and Comparative Law, 2002) 271, 272.

[32] ibid.

[33] Ackerman, n 26, 1. Similarly, Jeremy Paul, 'The Hidden Structure of Takings Law' (1991) 64 *Southern California Law Review* 1393, 1406, poses the following question: 'When do individual contributions to collective welfare cease to be a proper price of communal citizenship and become an unfair sacrifice of the few to the many?'

[34] See Rosalyn Higgins, 'The Taking of Property by the State. Recent Developments in International Law' in *Académie de Droit International*, 176 *Recueil des Cours. Collected Courses of the Hague Academy of International Law, 1982-III* (The Hague, M Nijhoff, 1983) 259, 269.

[35] ibid.

[36] See Ethan Shenkman, 'Could Principles of Fifth Amendment Takings Jurisprudence Be Helpful in Analyzing Regulatory Expropriation Claims under International Law?' (2002) 11 *New York University Environmental Law Journal* 174, 174 (commenting that 'our experience with regulatory expropriation claims under international law is fairly limited').

[37] See Mads Andenas, 'An Introduction to the British Institute of International and Comparative Law's Investment Forum' in Federico Ortino et al (eds), *Investment Treaty Law. Current Issues I* (London, The British Institute of International and Comparative Law, 2006) 7, 7, noting that '[i]nvestment treaty law raises many difficult issues concerning the proper balance to be found between the rights of investors and rights of states'. See also, Kaj Hobér,

traditional views of investment arbitration, which are typically embedded in private law, have not fully grasped the proper scope and extent of this mission.[38] The late professor Thomas W Wälde, to whom the international investment law community will always be in debt, remarked upon this point in at least two separate articles:

> The commercial arbitration community . . . has in fact taken over investment arbitration and runs it as a new form of commercial arbitration business, with little understanding that enforcing disciplines against States is quite different from holding mature and experienced international commercial players to their bargains.[39]
>
> Investment arbitration is not international commercial arbitration. It is essentially a form of international judicial review of governmental (regulatory, administrative and at times fiscal) action, though using the forms of commercial arbitration. This is not always appreciated by lawyers used in the traditions of commercial arbitration [*sic*].[40]

When viewed from a public law adjudication perspective, state liability comprises two different areas: torts and expropriations. Together, they constitute what the Germans referred to as *staatliche Ersatzleistungen* or 'public indemnifications'.[41] This broad category—which I will classify in this work under the general heading of state liability—covers, on the one hand, indemnifications grounded in fault and negligence, including illegality and irrationality; and, on the other hand, indemnifications grounded in proportionality and equality.

Harlow refers to the first group as *liability*—which, to avoid confusion, I will refer to here as liability (*stricto sensu*)—and to the second as *compensation*.[42] Liability (*stricto sensu*) is governed mainly by principles of corrective justice. Generally speaking, this form of justice—which has traditionally lain at the heart of private law, at least of tort law[43]—centers

Investment Arbitration in Eastern Europe. In Search of a Definition of Expropriation (Huntington, JurisNet, 2007) 224.

[38] There are notable exceptions. For instance, in *Wintershall Aktiengesellschaft v Argentina*, ICSID Case No ARB/04/14 (Nariman, Torres, Bernardini), Award (8 December 2008), ¶ 160 No 2, the Tribunal expressly noted that '[t]he ICSID Convention, under which this arbitration case has been registered, *combines a public law system of State liability with private arbitration*' (emphasis added).

[39] Thomas W Wälde, 'The Present State of Research Carried Out by the English-Speaking Section of the Centre for Studies and Research' in Centre for Studies and Research in International Law and International Relations (eds), *New Aspects of International Investment Law* (Leiden, Nijhoff 2006) 63, 114–15.

[40] Wälde, n 23, 211. See also, Van Harten and Loughlin, n 18, 148 ('Rather than being viewed as an offshoot of commercial arbitration, investment arbitration should be treated as a unique, internationally-organized strand of the administrative law systems of states').

[41] See ch 4, 177 n 45.

[42] See Harlow, n 29, 56–68.

[43] See Jules Coleman, *The Practice of Principle. In Defence of a Pragmatic Approach to Legal Theory* (New York, OUP, 2001) 12 and *Risks and Wrongs* (New York, OUP, 1992) 373–74 (arguing that tort law is best explained by corrective justice). See also, Richard W Wright, 'Right, Justice, and Tort Law' in David G Owen (ed), *Philosophical Foundations of Tort Law* (New York,

attention on the direct and immediate relationship between two parties, and the wrongful character of the actions of one of them. Weinrib summarises the concept in the following terms:

> [Corrective justice] focuses on a quantity that represents what rightfully belongs to one party but is now wrongly possessed by another party and therefore must be shifted back to its rightful owner. Corrective justice embraces quantitative equality in two ways. First, because one party has what belongs to the other party, the actor's gain is equal to the victim's loss. Second, what the parties would have held had the wrong not occurred provides the baseline from which the gain and the loss are computed ... A violation of corrective justice involves one party's gain at the other's expense. As compared with the mean of initial equality, the actor now has too much and the victim too little.[44]

In a *Rechtsstaat* or rule-of-law-state, citizens and investors may resist illegal or irrational burdens and harms. Consequently, liability is sometimes imposed in cases of *wrongful* behavior,[45] whereby the decision-maker must review the potentially unlawful character of state action or inaction.[46] As Mashaw has observed more generally, claimants who seek damages 'invariably question the legality of administrative conduct. To that degree, suits against the government and its officials sounding essentially in tort, contract, or property also invite judicial review of administrative action'.[47]

On the other hand, *compensation* is guided by principles of distributive justice.[48] Distributive justice, as Perry observes, is 'most plausibly construed as social justice'.[49] This implies that, in contrast to corrective justice, distributive justice focuses on multilateral considerations, particularly the substantive criteria determining the allocation of burdens and benefits between winners and losers. Wright provides a precise overview of this form of justice:

> Distributive justice claims are multilateral. To determine the resources to which a person is entitled as a matter of distributive justice, we must know both the

OUP, 1995) 159, 182 (arguing that '[t]ort claims, being based on interactional injuries, fall within the domain of corrective justice' and that 'corrective justice ... explains, justifies and illuminates the general structure, content and institutions of tort law'). See also, William Lucy, *Philosophy of Private Law* (New York, OUP, 2007) 268–326.

[44] Ernest J Weinrib, *The Idea of Private Law* (Cambridge, Mass, Harvard University Press, 1995) 62–63.

[45] The standard remedy is the nullification of the wrongful measure.

[46] The extent to which different legal systems view or don't view the principle of legality as the state's individualised duty towards each and every citizen, affects the connection between corrective justice and illegality, and indeed, explains differences in state liability regimes across legal cultures. These differences are explored in ch 4.

[47] Jerry L Mashaw et al, *Administrative Law. The American Public Law System. Cases and Materials*, 5th edn (St Paul, MN, Thomson/West, 2003) 780.

[48] See Harlow, n 29, 3.

[49] Stephen R Perry, 'On the Relationship Between Corrective and Distributive Justice' in Jeremy Horder (ed), *Oxford Essays in Jurisprudence* (New York, OUP, 2000) 237, 239.

> total amount of resources that exist in the community and the person's relative ranking according to the distributive criterion in comparison with all others in the community. All those persons who have too little under the distributive criterion have distributive justice claims against all those who have too much. Thus, proper implementation of distributive justice requires concurrent assessments against all those who have too much and disbursements to all those who have too little.[50]

The distributive justice rationale of state liability dictates that citizens and investors receive compensation when the state harms them disproportionately or unequally, even if the process of burden allocation has been lawfully conducted. Given the anti-redistributive strength that property rights and investments possess in almost all legal cultures,[51] courts and tribunals, to a certain extent, must (and do) control the design and implementation of regulatory programs by the political branches of government.[52]

To take an example, in *Armstrong*, for instance, the United States Supreme Court stated, in a much cited holding, that:

> The Fifth Amendment's guarantee that private property shall not be taken for a public use without just compensation was designed to bar Government from forcing some people alone to bear public burdens which, in all fairness and justice, should be borne by the public as a whole.[53]

As Dagan points out, in this case the Supreme Court placed 'the Aristotelian notion of distributive justice—which requires that recipients of benefits and burdens receive their share according to *some* criterion—at the heart of takings jurisprudence'.[54]

In short, this work analyses state liability in investment treaty arbitration, within the framework of public law adjudication. The key propositions put forth are that the regulatory state has the power to harm citizens and investors, but only if acting diligently and legitimately, and only if the resulting allocation of burdens and benefits complies with the

[50] Wright, n 43, 177. In the same vein, according to Weinrib, n 44, 62: '[D]istributive justice divides a benefit or burden in accordance with some criterion. An exercise of distributive justice consists of three elements: the benefit or burden being distributed, the persons among whom it is distributed, and the criterion according to which it is distributed. The criterion determines the parties' comparative merit for a particular distribution. The greater a particular party's merit under the criterion of distribution, the larger the party's share in the thing being distributed.'

[51] See Frank I Michelman, 'Possession vs Distribution in the Constitutional Idea of Property' (1987) 72 *Iowa Law Review* 1319, 1319 (noting that 'we primarily understand property in its constitutional sense as an antiredistributive principle, opposed to governmental interventions into the extant regime of holdings for the sake of distributive ends').

[52] See Hanoch Dagan, 'Takings and Distributive Justice' (1999) 85 *Virginia Law Review* 741.

[53] *Armstrong v US* (1960) 364 US 40, 49.

[54] Dagan, n 52, 742. See also, David A Dana and Thomas W Merrill, *Property: Takings* (New York, Foundation Press, 2002) 33–34, and Nestor M Davidson, 'The Problem of Equality in Takings' (2008) 102 *Northwestern University Law Review* 1, 20–28.

constraints imposed by the anti-distributive strength of property rights and investments.

B Global Constitutional and Administrative Law

A second core idea explored in this book is the claim that investment treaty tribunals are involved in the process of developing a new form of global constitutional law (GCL), and of global administrative law (GAL). Investment treaties were deliberately designed to constrain sovereignty,[55] and arbitral tribunals' concrete expressions of those constraints can be usefully understood as matters of constitutional and administrative law character.

Indeed, by redefining the scope and limits of the rules for state liability, investment tribunals are currently creating a new body of law that trumps domestic constitutional law within the state's own territory, as *lex specialis* applicable to foreign investors.[56] This means that, since investment treaties delegate jurisdiction of constitutional character to arbitral tribunals, constitutional adjudication no longer resides exclusively in domestic supreme or constitutional courts.[57]

In this regard, international investment law clearly demonstrates that, in the current era of global law, as Walter notes, domestic constitutional law 'loses its claim to regulate comprehensively the exercise of public authority within the territorial limits of the state'.[58] It also proves, in Cottier and Hertig's words, that:

> The Constitution itself can no longer pretend anymore to provide a comprehensive regulatory framework of the state on its own . . . [T]he national Constitution today and in the future is to be considered a 'partial constitution,' which is completed by the other levels of governance.[59]

I am aware that the terms *constitution* and *constitutionalization* have proven difficult and controversial when trying to relate them to inter-

[55] See Paulsson, n 23, 245; and Van Harten and Loughlin, n 18, 146.

[56] See David Schneiderman, *Constitutionalizing Economic Globalization. Investment Rules and Democracy's Promise* (New York, CUP, 2008) 3 (commenting that 'the investment rules regime can be seen as disciplining and reshaping the constitutional law of various states across the globe').

[57] In strict terms, domestic constitutional law remains intact. The constitutional nature of the delegation of jurisdiction is only 'philosophical', not of a domestic law character. International investment law presents an alternative forum for foreign investors, that is, a substitute for domestic constitutional (and administrative) law. To the extent that these are indeed substitutes, and given what it is a stake in the decision of these disputes—for the reasons provided below—they share the same basic 'constitutional' nature.

[58] Christian Walter, 'Constitutionalizing (Inter)national Governance—Possibilities for and Limits to the Development of an International Constitutional Law' (2001) 44 *German Yearbook of International Law* 170, 194.

[59] Thomas Cottier and Maya Hertig, 'The Prospects of 21st Century Constitutionalism' (2003) 7 *Max Planck Yearbook of United Nations Law* 261, 303–4.

national law and institutions, particularly in the absence of a relevant global polity. The lack of a democratic foundation for global governance mechanisms presents a formidable obstacle to any attempt to give a constitutionalised account of post-Cold War international law. The absence of any relevant political community, or global *demos*, renders most charged visions of what constitutional law is and should be, completely incompatible with the new phenomena that presently face us.

Several authors have tried to determine whether these notions can be expanded—or at least a minimum threshold recognised—so that they can be applied to global governance arrangements.[60] Drawing upon some of those efforts, I have arrived at the opinion that the idea of constitutional law at the global level remains attractive.[61] In all, there are five pragmatic reasons for insisting upon the notion that the BIT generation is a global constitutional phenomenon.

First, the key substantive provisions contained in investment treaties constitute a clear limit to states' police powers within their own territory.[62] This represents an external redefinition of the domestic equilibrium and boundaries between property rights and regulatory powers. To use Bruce Ackerman's nomenclature, this redefinition has the functional status of *higher lawmaking*, because it transcends ordinary politics.[63] In this sense, it would not be an exaggeration to say that investment treaties create a new 'economic constitution' favouring a relevant set of actors, as is the case with foreign investors in developing countries.[64]

[60] See eg Joel P Trachtman, 'The Constitutions of the WTO' (2006) 17 *European Journal of International Law* 623; Ingolf Pernice, 'The Global Dimension of Multilevel Constitutionalism: A Legal Response to the Challenges of Globalisation' in Pierre-Marie Dupuy et al (eds), *Common Values in International Law. Essays in Honour of Christian Tomuschat* (Kehl, NP Engel Verlag, 2006) 973; Deborah Z Cass, *The Constitutionalization of the World Trade Organization. Legitimacy, Democracy, and Community in the International Trading System* (New York, OUP, 2005); Robert Howse and Kalypso Nicolaidis, 'Legitimacy through 'Higher Law'? Why Constitutionalizing the WTO is a Step Too Far' in Thomas Cottier and Petros C Mavroidis (eds), *The Role of the Judge in International Trade Regulation. Experiences and Lessons for the WTO* (Ann Arbor, University of Michigan, 2003) 307; Neil Walker, 'The EU and the WTO: Constitutionalism in a New Key' in Gráinne de Búrca and Joanne Scott (eds), *The EU and the WTO. Legal and Constitutional Issues* (Portland, Hart Publishing, 2001) 31.

[61] See Miguel Poiares Maduro, 'Legal Travels and the Risk of Legal Jet-Lag. The Judicial and Constitutional Challenges of Legal Globalisation' in Mario Monti et al (eds), *Economic Law and Justice in Times of Globalization. Festschrift for Carl Baudenbacher* (Baden Baden, Nomos Verlagsgesellschaft, 2007) 175.

[62] See Schneiderman, n 56, 37 (noting that, '[a]t bottom, the investment rule regime represents a form of constitutional precommitment binding across generations that unreasonably constrains the capacity of self-government'). *See also*, Cheng, n 23, 482 (commenting that '[i]nternational investment law diminishes the authority and power of a state by restraining its internal decision-makers').

[63] See Bruce Ackerman, 1 *We the People* (Cambridge, Mass, Belknap Press of Harvard University Press, 1991) 9 ff, and 266 ff. I state that this global law carries the 'functional status' of higher law because it does not fulfill the normative elements that Ackerman requires of constitutional moments in a well-ordered dualist society.

[64] See Stephan W Schill, *Fair and Equitable Treatment under Investment Treaties as an Embodiment of the Rule of Law*, IILJ Working Paper 2006/6. Global Administrative Law Series

The second reason—observable from the EU's institutional experience—is already a classical one that involves the elements of direct effect, supremacy, and judicial review, all characteristics observed in investment treaty law.[65] Although for Anglo-American lawyers those elements may be descriptively insufficient and normatively unacceptable, for continental lawyers—who are presumably more accustomed to, and therefore more afraid of non-democratic regimes—they represent a relatively standard approach to constitutional law.[66] From this more formalistic perspective, international investment law would clearly qualify as GCL. Investment treaties possess direct effect and confer causes of actions to foreign investors, prevail over domestic law in the case of conflict, and charge arbitral tribunals with the function of reviewing state action and inaction.[67]

Third, constitutional law is also a methodology for approaching certain types of political and legal problems. Weiler has taken this view before in defending the idea of constitutional law and constitutionalisation in supranational contexts:

> [Constitutionalism is also] a prism through which one can observe a landscape in a certain way, an academic artifact with which one can organize the milestones and landmarks within the landscape (indeed, determine what is a

4 (2006) (noting that the FET standard plays 'a quasi-constitutional function that serves as a yardstick for the exercise of host states' administrative, judicial or legislative activitiy vis-à-vis foreign investors').

[65] See eg Alec Stone Sweet, *The Judicial Construction of Europe* (OUP, Oxford 2004) 65, who explains *constitutionalization* in the EU context in the following terms: 'The *constitutionalization of the EC* refers to the process by which the Rome Treaty evolved from a set of legal arrangements binding upon sovereign states into a vertically integrated legal regime conferring judicially enforceable rights and obligations on legal persons and entities, public and private, within EC territory. The phrase thus captures the transformation of an intergovernmental organization governed by international law into a multi-tiered system of governance founded on higher-law constitutionalism'.

[66] See Jed Rubenfeld, 'Unilateralism and Constitutionalism' (2004) 79 *New York University Law Review* 1971, 1974–75, who explains this difference in the following terms: 'American constitutionalism differs in certain fundamental respects from contemporary European constitutionalism . . . On this view [the American], which I will call "democratic constitutionalism", a constitution is, first and foremost, supposed to be the foundational law a particular polity has given itself through a special act of popular lawmaking. A very different account sees constitutionalism not as an act of democracy, but as a set of checks or restraints on democracy. These restraints are thought to be entitled to special authority because they express universal rights and principles, which in theory transcend national boundaries, applying to all societies alike. From this universalistic perspective, constitutional law is fundamentally antidemocratic; one of its central purposes is to put limits on democratic self-government'. See also, Christoph Möllers, ' "We are (afraid of) the People": Constituent Power in German Constitutionalism' in Martin Loughlin and Neil Walker, *The Paradox of Constitutionalism. Constituent Power and Constitutional Form* (New York, OUP, 2007) 87.

[67] Following the classification proposed by Neil Walker, 'Beyond Boundary Disputes and Basic Grids: Mapping the Global Disorder of Normative Orders' (2008) 6 *International Journal of Constitutional Law* 373, 379, investment treaty arbitration seems to fit the category of 'institutional incorporation', the closest 'institutional embrace' in his framework, whereby 'the host normative order makes general provision for the normative decisions of an external agency to be incorporated and, to that extent, to be treated as authoritative within the host normative order'.

landmark or milestone), an intellectual construct by which one can assign meaning to, or even constitute, that which is observed.[68]

In the case of BITs, constitutional law traditions around the world have created different techniques and methodologies with which to assess state liability as well as the protective scope of property rights and investments. It is a generally accepted fact that there exists a constitutional law practice whose main objective is to identify the conditions and requirements by which citizens and investors are permitted to claim damages when they have been harmed by state action or inaction.

Fourth, investment treaties replace domestic public law remedies with international remedies. At the domestic level, the legal architecture of public law remedies—a combination of judicial review and state liability—is clearly a matter of constitutional law. It reflects, operatively and procedurally, sensitive considerations about the proper balance of power between the judiciary, executive and legislature.[69] Therefore, by providing foreign investors with a completely new remedial 'toolkit'—which is, incidentlly, in the *Eastern Sugar* Tribunal's words, 'the most essential provision of Bilateral Investment Treaties'[70]—investment treaty law can be characterised as global constitutional law.

Fifth, from a structural perspective, the standards of review adopted by arbitral panels directly reflect—or more precisely, define—the distribution of powers that must inevitably exist between those tribunals and the national bodies under control. This structural issue is a classic constitutional law topic, demarcating the boundary between the political and judicial branches of government.[71]

These five factors build a case for conceptualising investment treaty law as a form of global constitutional law. In this regard, I should be particularly explicit in clarifying *what is not intended here when characterising this field as global constitutional law*. Investments frequently clash with legitimate

[68] JHH Weiler, 'Introduction: The Reformation of European Constitutionalism', in JHH Weiler, *The Constitution of Europe* (New York, CUP, 1999) 221, 223.

[69] For example, in the UK, the impact of EU law has led Harlow, n 29, 62, to assert that '[l]iability is, after all, a highly intrusive remedy, with considerable impact on national constitution'.

[70] *Eastern Sugar BV v The Czech Republic*, UNCITRAL Ad-Hoc Arbitration (Karrer, Volterra, Gaillard), Partial Award (27 March 2007), ¶ 165. See also *Gas Natural SDG, SA v Argentine*, ICSID Case No ARB/03/10 (Lowenfeld, Alvarez, Nikken), Decision on Jurisdiction (17 June 2005), ¶ 29.

[71] See Cottier and Hertig, n 59, 317 (stating that '[i]n a multilayered system, defining the relationship and the boundaries between the different levels of governance are essential constitutional functions'). See also, Deborah Z Cass, 'The 'Constitutionalization' of International Trade Law: Judicial Norm-Generation as the Engine of Constitutional Development in International Trade' (2001) 12 *European Journal of International Law* 39, 42. Standard of review issues have been the focus of attention by WTO commentators, but not by investment treaty ones; see eg Matthias Oesch, *Standards of Review in WTO Dispute Resolution* (New York, OUP, 2003), and Steven P Croley and John H Jackson, 'WTO Disputes Procedures, Standards of Review, and Deference to National Governments' (1996) 90 AJIL 193.

regulatory goals (that is, economic or non-economic public interests). The idea of GCL, in this context, does not imply that the concept of investments is a super-value overriding all competing values in the set of '*investment and* . . .' dichotomies. Nor does it suggest that investment treaty adjudication is legitimate per se, simply because it provides judicial review according to a set of rights that had been predefined as constitutional in nature.[72]

Again, global constitutionalism refers here to the terms of the contest, the mere form of judicial review; not to the alleged trumping power of investments with respect to the outcome. It is a methodology that inquires about the conditions which, according to corrective justice rationales, demand the payment of damages in cases of *wrongful* state action, and, according to distributive justice rationales, demand payment in cases of proper and lawful state action. Ultimately, treating this field as GCL serves to increase awareness in the international investment law community of the serious and delicate nature of cases that involve state liability pursuant to investment treaties.

In addition, this book claims that international investment law constitutes a form of global administrative law. Those who agree with the characterisation of investment treaty law as a form of public law adjudication, but reject the idea of global constitutional law, may easily expand the concept of GAL to encompass this new field of international law. In this regard, the same reasons provided earlier in favour of investment treaty law as a form of GCL apply to the GAL thesis.

Not many commentators have recognised the GAL character of investment treaty arbitration. Van Harten and Loughlin deserve special recognition for being among the first to connect investment arbitration with the nascent concept of global administrative law:

> [T]he regime of international investment arbitration which has been rapidly developing since the 1990s provides not simply a singularly important and under-appreciated manifestation of an evolving system of global administrative law but that, owing to its unique features, it may in fact offer the only exemplar of global administrative law, strictly construed, yet to have emerged . . . [I]t is precisely because of the potential of these internationally generated adjudicative norms and mechanisms to exert a strong disciplinary influence over domestic administrative programmes that investment arbitration should be seen to constitute a powerful species of global administrative law.[73]

[72] I am following Mattias Kumm, 'The Legitimacy of International Law: A Constitutionalist Framework of Analysis' (2004) 15 *European Journal of International Law* 907, 930, who warns about this possible danger in the use of constitutional language.

[73] Van Harten and Loughlin, n 23, 122. See ibid 149: 'Indeed, if one adopts a strict definition of global administrative law—as a system akin to domestic judicial review in that it keeps public authorities within the bounds of legality and provides enforceable remedies to individuals harmed by unlawful state conduct—then investment arbitration would appear to be the *only* case of global administrative law in the world today'.

Here, I follow a continental law approach, which conceptualises administrative law, to recall Werner's classic phrase, as 'constitutional law concretized'.[74] By this understanding, GAL should not be regarded as opposing GCL, but rather, as a specific manifestation of it. The somewhat arbitrary line adopted here divides the global public law 'pie' into the following two portions: one slice, GCL, covers the protection of the core of investments in more or less absolute terms, representing fixed limits that the regulatory state cannot cross; and the other slice, GAL, covers the protection of the periphery of property rights and investments in relative terms, and subject to different types of arbitrariness tests.

In other words, the principle of no expropriation without compensation, and its corresponding focus on the scope of property rights and investments, is defined here as the 'centre of gravity' of GCL; and the FET standard, with its focus on arbitrariness, as the corresponding center of GAL. This perspective is consistent with traditional domestic public law views, where questions posed by expropriation clauses and the protective scope of property rights are usually matters to be settled within the realm of constitutional law, and questions of arbitrariness, within the realm of administrative law.

C The BIT Generation

The narrative of this book is deeply rooted in the sociological concept of the BIT generation. This concept, as used here, refers to the emergence of a *common legal practice*, addressing a distinctive set of legal and normative problems, which have resulted from having a network of thousands of investment treaties all worded in similar terms while simultaneously waiving the customary rule of exhaustion of local remedies.

Probably the best way of grasping the most critical aspects of the BIT generation is to contrast it with the previous *legal practice* that existed before investment treaties became predominant. In this regard, the most distinctive feature of that previous era, referred to in this work as the 'denial of justice age', was that state responsibility could only emerge or, at least, be claimed at the international level, once domestic courts had acted on the case under dispute.[75]

Given the rule of exhaustion of local remedies, international law generally had to assess the judicial system of defendant states or, more

[74] Werner, cited by Luciano Parejo Alfonso, *Derecho Administrativo: Instituciones Generales: Bases, Fuentes, Organización y Sujetos, Actividad y Control* (Barcelona, Ariel, 2003) 64.

[75] The legal literature on this point is extensive. The classic texts are, among other, the following: Edwin M Borchard, *The Diplomatic Protection of Citizens Abroad* (New York, The Banks Law Publishing Co, 1916); Clyde Eagleton, *The Responsibility of States in International Law* (New York, New York University Press, 1928); and, Alwyn Freeman, *The International Responsibility of States for Denial of Justice* (New York, Longmans, Green and Co, 1938).

precisely, the domestic legal system as applied by domestic courts.[76] In the words of the Commission of Arbitration in the *Ambatielos* case, '[i]t is the whole system of legal protection, as provided by municipal law, which must have been put to the test before a State, as the protector of its nationals, can prosecute the claim on the international plane'.[77] Or, as Judge Morelli expressed in his separate opinion in the *Barcelona Traction* case, '[t]he conduct which international law renders incumbent upon a State with regards to the rights which the same State confers on foreign nationals within its own municipal order *consists, in the first place, in the judicial protection of those rights*'. (emphasis added)[78]

Consequently, in this earlier era, international law was essentially concerned with the proper administration of justice and adequate maintenance of the *ordre publique*, both central functions of the nineteenth century 'night-watchman' state. State responsibility for injuries to aliens was conceived as the obligation of states 'to maintain and operate a machinery for protecting the rights of aliens'.[79] In Freeman's words, 'the proper scope of the concept [denial of justice] is one bound up with the operation of the machinery for the vindication and enforcement of rights: the mechanism by which justice is administered'.[80]

During the denial of justice age, the technical term *denial of justice*—that is, the 'failure of redress in the prosecution of local remedies'[81]—was the most important legal category in the area of state responsibility for injuries to aliens and their property.[82] As indicated by one of the main publicists,

[76] In the words of Eagleton, n 75, 113, exhaustion of remedies and denial of justice were then 'interlocking and inseparable'. See also Borchard, n 75, 179–180 ('Again, before the international responsibility of the state may be invoked, the alien must under normal conditions exhaust his local remedies and establish a denial or undue delay of justice, *which in last analysis is the fundamental basis of an international claim*') (emphasis added).

[77] *Ambatielos* Claim (*Greece v UK*) (3 March 1956) (2006) 12 RIAA 83, 120 (2006) (available at http://www.un.org/law/riaa/). See Campbell McLachlan QC, 'Investment Treaties and General International Law' (2008) 57 ICLQ 361, 366, commenting precisely that: 'In practice, save in cases of a refusal to investigate or prosecute, the cases on the international minimum standard and denial of justice were almost always concerned with alleged failures in the judicial system of the host State. Any failures in the administrative decision-making would not give rise themselves to an international claim, since they would first have had to be tested by the investor in the local courts'.

[78] Separate Opinion of Judge Morelli in *Barcelona Traction, Light & Power Co Ltd* (*Belgium v Spain*) (Second Phase) [1970] ICJ Rep 4, 39, 233–34.

[79] Freeman, n 75, 45.

[80] ibid 162.

[81] Edwin M Borchard, 'Theoretical Aspects of the International Responsibility of States' (1929) 1 *Zeitschrift für ausländisches öffentliches Recht und Völkerrecht* 242, 245. As GG Fitzmaurice, 'The Meaning of the Term "Denial of Justice"' (1932) 13 *British Ybk of Intl Law* 93, 108–09, explains, a denial of justice may consist in 'a failure to redress a previous wrong [by the Executive or the Congress], or in an original wrong committed by the court or other organ itself'. See also Charles Cheney Hyde, 1 *International law: Chiefly as Interpreted and Applied by the United States* (Boston, Little, Brown, 1922) 547.

[82] In fact, denial of justice was so important, that in one of its meaning it was equated with the idea of state responsibility for injuries to aliens in its entirety. See 1 Hyde, n 81, 491.

Edwin Borchard, '[p]erhaps no concept and term in the law of state responsibility is more important than that of "denial of justice" '[83]. This was certainly true statistically speaking: most cases of state responsibility involved denial of justice allegations[84].

In the denial of justice age, international law was characterised by a strong respect for state sovereignty. International courts and tribunals were reluctant to interfere with the ways in which domestic policy and law were created and implemented by the political branches of government.[85] Domestic law and its application were considered matters of domestic jurisdiction[86], forming part of the *domaine réservé.*[87] A pronounced dualism, in which national and international law were kept completely separate, was considered to best describe the proper relationship between the two legal orders[88].

The BIT generation presents a stark contrast to the denial of justice age. Today, the primary object of scrutiny for investment treaty tribunals is not judicial decisions, but regulatory action or inaction. As Reisman and Sloane explain, BITs require governments to 'establish and maintain an appropriate legal, administrative, and regulatory framework, the legal environment that modern investment theory has come to recognise as a *conditio sine qua non* of the success of private enterprise,'[89] which includes an 'efficient and legally restrained bureaucracy'.[90] As a result of the waiver of the rule of exhaustion of local remedies, international investment law today is in charge of controlling the regulatory state.

As noted, the idea of the BIT generation as a common legal practice critically depends on the existence of a system that contains thousands of investment treaties, all having substantive provisions worded in closely similar terms. This system of treaties has given way to a common vocabulary, framework of argumentation, and epistemic community. Courses on investment arbitration are taught in elite law schools, seminars on the topic are conducted throughout the world, and groups specialising in this area

[83] Borchard, n 81, 242.

[84] See Fitzmaurice, n 81, 93.

[85] As noted by Karl Joseph Partsch, 'International Law and Municipal Law' in Rudolf Bernhard (ed), 2 *Encyclopedia of Public International Law* (North-Holland, New York 1992) 1183, 1185, international law has traditionally been 'extremely reticent as regards to the competence of States to govern their internal affairs'.

[86] See Humphrey Waldock, 'General Course on Public International Law' in *Académie de Droit* International, 106 *Recueil des Cours—1962-II* (Leyde, AW Sijthoff, 1963) 1, 123 ('Nor can there be any doubt that the internal law of a State and the administration of its internal law are, in principle, matters of domestic jurisdiction').

[87] See ibid 191. Still today, Ian Brownlie, *Principles of Public International Law*, 6th ed (New York, OUP, 2003) 39, affirms that '[i]nternational tribunals cannot declare the internal invalidity of rules of national law since the international legal order must respect the reserved domain of domestic jurisdiction'.

[88] See Partsch, n 85, 1184.

[89] Reisman and Sloan, n 14, 117.

[90] ibid 117.

are included in law firms. Books that give a *comprehensive* treatment of this subject-matter—among others the recent *Law and Practice of Investment Treaties*,[91] *Principles of International Investment Law*,[92] *The Oxford Handbook of International Investment Law*,[93] *Standards of Investment Protection*,[94] and *International Investment Arbitration. Substantive Principles*[95]—are indeed, some of the best examples of what I mean here by a common legal practice. Ultimately, as McLachlan et al have recently observed, we are witnessing the emergence of a 'common law of investment protection'[96]:

> [W]hat is emerging is a common law of investment protection, with a substantially shared understanding of its general tenets. This still depends for the most part on the existence of a treaty forming the basis for the enforceable rights. It will always yield to particular provisions of a treaty which diverge from the general rule, or to other contrary indications resulting from the application of the rules of treaty interpretation. But the differences between treaties, and indeed between treaty and the substantive rights in custom, may be less than the common elements.[97]

Chapter 2 will take this idea even further, envisioning the BIT generation as a network of treaties in a more precise technical sense. The substantive similarity of wording among the treaties' main provisions—particularly the expropriation and FET clauses—is such, that case law developed under one treaty influences the future interpretation of all other treaties. This occurs because, even in the absence of a formal concept of precedent, the international investment community, to a certain extent, takes previous decisions seriously, and cares about the coherence and consistency of the system. This constitutes a true 'network externality'—a positive demand-side externality, growing in magnitude with the number of existing treaties—which, effectively, defines the BIT generation as a virtual network.

[91] Andrew Newcombe and Lluís Paradell, *Law and Practice of Investment Treaties. Standards of Treatment* (Alphen Aan Den Rijn, Kluwer Law and Business, 2009). Unfortunately, this excellent book was published just a few weeks before I sent the manuscript for publication.

[92] Rudolf Dolzer and Christoph Schreuer, *Principles of International Investment Law* (New York, OUP, 2008).

[93] Peter Muchlinski et al (eds), *The Oxford Handbook of International Investment Law* (New York, OUP, 2008).

[94] August Reinisch (ed), *Standards of Investment Protection* (New York, OUP, 2008).

[95] McLachlan et al, n 11.

[96] ibid 19. See also, Thomas W Wälde, 'The Present State of Research Carried Out by the English-Speaking Section of the Centre for Studies and Research' in Centre for Studies and Research in International Law and International Relations, *New Aspects of International Investment Law* (Leiden, Nijhoff, 2006) 63, 120 (observing the emergence of a 'common law of world investment . . . with an increasingly dense and increasingly similar and sometimes in the core identical treaty network as foundation').

[97] McLachlan et al, n 11, 19.

III THE BOOK'S MAIN NORMATIVE CLAIMS

Because this book adopts a critical position with respect to several developments within international investment law, it is important at the outset to summarise some of the main normative claims that underpin the entire work. To be clear, this book does not adopt a pro-state stance, nor is it a blatant critique of investment treaty arbitration from the perspective of developing countries' sovereignty. At the same time, no sentimental reminiscences of the new international economic order (NIEO) and its various doctrines of lack of responsibility in international law will be found in these pages.

Instead, it is claimed here that state liability in investment treaty arbitration, as a form of global constitutional and administrative law, should be concerned with the development of a balanced and prudent system of protection of foreign investment. Such a system, as stated by McLachlan et al, would be one characterised by 'an appropriate balance between protection of the rights of foreign investors on the one hand, and recognition of the legitimate sphere of operation of the host State on the other'.[98]

This means that the objective of international investment law should not be the *super-protection* of investments and property rights.[99] By contrast, following the reasoning of the Mexican–United States General Claims Commission, in the BIT generation, states should only be liable for the 'failure to maintain the *usual order* which it is the duty of every state to maintain within its territory'. (emphasis added)[100] In other words, as observed in the very first award based on a BIT, a 'reasonably well organized modern State'[101] should not be liable. In sum, when applying the key common substantive standards of BITs, investment treaty tribunals must limit themselves to defining minimum thresholds of what is expected from a 'reasonably well-behaved regulatory state'.

Note that these minimum thresholds do not pose an obstacle to those investors who may wish to secure more demanding commitments; they remain free to conclude tailor-made concession contracts and investment

[98] ibid, 21.

[99] In the extreme, as the ICJ held in *Barcelona Traction, Light, and Power Company, Limited* (Second Phase) (*Belgium v Spain*) [1970] ICJ *Rep 3*, ¶ 87: 'When a State admits into its territory foreign investments or foreign nationals it is, as indicated in paragraph 33, bound to extend to them the protection of the law. However, it does not thereby become an insurer of that part of another State's wealth which these investments represent. Every investment of this kind carries certain risks'.

[100] *George Adams Kennedy (USA) v United Mexican States* (1927) 4 RIAA 194, 198, ¶ 7 (available at http://www.un.org/law/riaa/).

[101] *Asian Agricultural Products*, ¶ 77. The Tribunal took the concept from Alwyn V Freeman, 'Responsibility of states for unlawful acts of their armed forces' in *Académie de Droit International*, 88 *Recueil des Cours—1955 II* (AW Sijthoff, Leyde 1956) 263, 277–78 (who refers to the concept of 'well-administered government').

agreements with host states. There is no question of states' obligation to honor those agreements in accordance with the rules and principles of the applicable law, and the right of investors to enforce them before the proper fora.[102]

A critical requirement for the development of such a balanced system of protection of investments is that the necessary 'attitude' dominate among arbitral tribunals. International investment law, understood as global constitutional and administrative law, demands that arbitral tribunals be guided by a principle of 'judicial restraint'.[103] Justice Breyer's words, crafted in the context of constitutional adjudication, fit the case of investment arbitration equally well:

> A judge, when interpreting such open-ended provisions, must avoid being 'willful, in the sense of enforcing individual views.' A judge cannot 'enforce what he thinks best.' 'In the exercise of' the 'high power' of judicial review, says Justice Louis Brandeis, 'we must be ever on our guard, lest we erect our prejudices into legal principles'.[104]

This, indeed, constitutes one of the most important normative claims of this book: arbitral tribunals, when reviewing whether the state has behaved in accordance with the standards of a reasonably well-behaved regulatory state, should demonstrate deference and respect toward governments. In short, the BIT generation should place a special premium maintaining a jurisprudence of 'modesty'.[105]

Only such a reasonable and well-balanced international investment jurisprudence, guided by judicial modesty, can achieve one of the structural conditions for minimal legitimacy of the BIT generation which this work refers to as the updated Calvo Doctrine. The Doctrine states that BIT jurisprudence should not crystallise rules of protection of investments that are more demanding than those which *developed* countries' courts apply in favour of their own national investors.

It is shocking to consider that a United States investor may lose a case against its government in the United States Supreme Court, a German

[102] In the absence of umbrella clauses or broad jurisdictional clauses, investment treaty tribunals are not competent to entertain contract claims. This is, of course, without prejudice of the treaty claims that investors may have in such situations.

[103] Stephen Breyer, *Active Liberty. Interpreting Our Democratic Constitution* (New York, Knopf, 2005) 17.

[104] ibid 18–19 (internal citations omitted).

[105] See Stephen Breyer, 'Our Democratic Constitution', The Fall 2001 James Madison Lecture New York University Law School New York, New York October 22, 2001 (available at http://www.supremecourtus.gov/publicinfo/speeches/sp_10-22-01.html), who explains judicial modesty in the following terms: 'That modesty embodies an understanding of the judges' own expertise compared, for example, with that of a legislature. It reflects the concern that a judiciary too ready to "correct" legislative error may deprive "the people" of "the political experience and the moral education that come from . . . correcting their own errors." It encompasses that doubt, caution, prudence, and concern—that state of not being "too sure" of oneself—that Learned Hand described as the "spirit of liberty". In a word, it argues for traditional "judicial restraint"'. (internal citations omitted).

investor may lose the same case in the *Bundesverfassungsgericht* (Constitutional Court), and a French investor may lose it in the *Conseil d'État*, but, nevertheless, that any of them may win it against a Sri Lanka or Bolivia on the basis of such open-ended BIT principles as no expropriation without compensation or FET.

There is no major Western legal tradition today in which property rights and economic liberties receive the strongest possible protection against the public interest. In the United States, such a tradition existed during the early twentieth century, and was made possible by a 'singular lack of [judicial] modesty'.[106] Yet today, such a commitment to the status quo is deemed incompatible with larger goals that transcend the maximisation of wealth.[107] In simple terms, most capital exporting countries have long been committed to broader collective goals such as the protection of health, safety and the environment, and more generally, the self-determination and welfare of their citizens.

Note that this updated Calvo Doctrine does not defend the old Latin American idea of equality, defined as 'national treatment is the maximum'. International investment law can certainly provide higher protection than domestic law. By contrast, the most problematic scenario today, as noted, is that the general and open-ended standards of investment treaties—which should be interpreted in the proper context of general international law, international minimum standards, general principles of the law, and comparative law[108]—may end up being more protective of investors' rights than *developed* countries' own legal systems. The idea of equality—the key normative element of the Calvo Doctrine in the nineteenth century—is updated and defended here as that of '*developed countries' standards as the maximum*'.

[106] According to Justice Breyer, n 103, 41, the failing of *Lochner*—the case that represents those times of heightened judicial scrutiny of economic regulation—was due to a 'singular lack of modesty'.

[107] Such a commitment to the status quo is not even justified on efficiency grounds. For law and economics approaches to expropriations, *see* Lawrence Blume and Daniel L Rubinfeld, 'Compensation for Takings: An Economic Analysis' (1984) 72 *California Law Review* 569; Lawrence Blume et al, 'The Taking of Land: When Should Compensation Be Paid?' (1984) 99 *Quarterly Journal of Economics* 71 (1984); Louis Kaplow, 'An Economic Analysis of Legal Transitions' (1986) 99 *Harvard Law Review* 509; William A Fischel, 'Introduction: Utilitarian Balancing and Formalism in Takings' (1988) 88 *Columbia Law Review* 1581; William A Fischel and Perry Shapiro, 'Takings, Insurance, and Michelman: Comments on Economic Interpretations of 'Just Compensation' Law' (1988) 17 *Journal of Legal Studies* 269; and Susan Rose-Ackerman, 'Against Ad Hocery: A Comment on Michelman' (1988) 88 *Columbia Law Review* 1697.

[108] For the complete explanation of the 'transmission belt' linking general international law to comparative law, see ch 6, 303–310.

IV THE BOOK'S PLAN

This book is divided into two parts. The First Part addresses the key descriptive and normative questions confronted by the BIT generation: How did developing countries end up as part of this network of treaties, after more than 150 years defending the idea of national treatment as the maximum? Why did they delegate sovereign powers to arbitral tribunals? Are these treaties *convenient* for developing countries? Are they *legitimate*? Chapter 1 situates these questions within a historical timeline. It begins by providing a detailed explanation of the traditional Latin American position against diplomatic protection during the nineteenth century. Then, it proceeds to study the development of state responsibility during the twentieth century. This includes the victories made by developing countries before the Cold War—the definitive prohibition of forcible self-help in diplomatic protection—and later—the advancement of NIEO, according to which expropriations did not require the payment of prompt, adequate, and effective compensation.

One of the main objectives of chapter 1 is to show that the foundations of the Calvo Doctrine—at least, as it was originally conceived by Andres Bello in the first half of the nineteenth century—if properly updated, can help us to establish minimal proper conditions of legitimacy for the BIT generation. After pointing out the potential fallacy of conflating the Calvo Doctrine with NIEO—there are more than 100 years of distance between the two of them—this chapter argues that this Doctrine, with its emphasis on equality, should be interpreted today as establishing the aforementioned principle of '*developed countries' standards as the maximum*'.

Chapter 2 studies the BIT generation descriptively. One of the basic goals of this chapter is to dispute the theory that was recently advanced by Guzman, and later refined by that author together with Elkins and Simmons (EGS). In Guzman's account, the current world order of thousands of BITs is the result of a prisoner's dilemma among developing countries, whereby those countries, competing against each other to attract FDI, have all ended up worse off by signing the treaties. This model of the BIT generation is unsatisfactory; as some commentators on game theory and the law have warned us, the situation has been 'too quickly identified as a prisoner's dilemma'.[109]

Although that theory is correct when identifying a collective action problem that arises from competition, it fails to take into account two highly relevant aspects of this particular 'game' that distinguish it from a prisoner's dilemma: first, its sequential/evolutionary nature, stemming

[109] Douglas G Baird, Robert H Gertner, and Randal C Picker, *Game Theory and the Law* (Chicago, Chicago University Press, 1994) 188.

from the fact that developing countries have been joining (and rejecting) the BIT network at different points in time since 1959; and, second, the positive externalities or network effects of having a system of treaties, nearly all of which share the same key substantive clauses. Once those two factors are taken into consideration, a new theory emerges: the BIT generation as a virtual network.

Chapter 3 develops a framework to analyse the set of normative questions previously identified as the key ones surrounding the BIT generation. It explores the legitimacy deficits that the BIT generation faces as a scheme of global governance, and then assesses alternative sources of legitimacy for the system, which include consent-legitimacy, output-legitimacy, exit-legitimacy, rule of law-legitimacy, and institution building-legitimacy.

In addition, this chapter evaluates the idea of creating an appellate body or international court of investment arbitration. The conclusion is that developing countries should reject such a project; the main concern is the additional danger that investment treaty jurisprudence, under such a regime, could ultimately crystallise standards and rules which are significantly more favourable to investors than those which constitutional courts and supreme courts of developed capitalist countries apply to their own investors (that is, the updated Calvo Doctrine).

The Second Part analyses the current state of investment treaty arbitration jurisprudence, in accordance with the normative framework developed in the First Part. The objective of this part is to determine, from a pragmatic perspective, whether investment treaty jurisprudence is currently ensuring a higher protection of property rights than that provided by the constitutional and administrative courts of developed countries.

Accordingly, chapter 4 analyses, through a comparative approach, the modern regulatory state and its power to harm citizens and investors. The purpose is to show that according to the constitutions of several Western regimes, regulatory reforms will nearly always, by explicit design, harm some groups of citizens and investors. Therefore, legal systems must impose conditions and requirements for the right to claim damages that go substantially beyond the mere fact of harm. Those structural conditions and requirements are the focus of this chapter.

Chapter 5 studies indirect takings in the BIT generation. The focus is on the perennial question of how to distinguish regulation from expropriation. Rather than analyse cases concerning outrageous deprivations, or creeping forms of takings adopted by government that are trying to remove the property of foreign investors—both of which are less frequent

[110] According to Jan Paulsson and Zachary Douglas, 'Indirect Expropriation in Investment Treaty Arbitrations' in Norbert Horn and Stefan Kröll (eds), *Arbitrating Foreign Investment Disputes* (Kluwer Law International, The Hague 2004) 145, 151, '[d]irect expropriations are now overshadowed by the more prevalent paradigm of indirect expropriations'. See also

today[110]—I focus attention here on non-discriminatory and bona fide regulation adopted in the genuine pursuit of the public interest.

One of the key questions of this chapter can be stated in the following terms: Which burdens that are justified by the public interest must, nevertheless, not be borne by foreign investors? Or, in other words, how much anti-redistributive strength does the concept of investments confer to investors' interests? Expressed this way, the scope of indirect takings in investment treaties, and the judicial norm-creation that concretises the precise meaning of those treaties' clauses, are strictly matters of global constitutional law.

Chapter 6 provides a fresh and original approach to the most complex problem touched upon in this work: the FET clause and the quest for operative standards of arbitrariness in the BIT generation. If the expropriation clause is reserved for total or substantial deprivations—as it appears from the analysis of investment treaty jurisprudence—then the most difficult cases, which involve non-destructive state interventions, are left to be resolved by application of the FET clause.

According to the global administrative law approach proposed here, this clause must fulfill two different functions, both included in the general concept of 'arbitrariness'. From a corrective justice perspective, it must recognise the criteria for identifying those wrongful state acts that have caused harm to investors, and which entitle them to damages; namely, 'arbitrariness as illegality' and 'arbitrariness as irrationality'. From a distributive justice perspective, it must define the limits that investment treaties impose upon states in determining which private sacrifices will not be compensated, particularly when those states are genuinely acting in the public interest; that is, 'arbitrariness as special sacrifice' and 'arbitrariness as lack of proportionality'. 'Administrative due process' is another category that is dealt with in this chapter.

Finally, the Conclusions reiterate just how critical it is that the BIT generation achieves a balanced and 'modest' jurisprudence when it comes to investment protection. While I remain optimistic, I also emphasise here that the absence of constraints over the arbitral tribunals' discretion continues to be a source of major concern. Given this concern, the Conclusions insist on the importance of constraints on at least two dimensions. These consist of a vertical dimension, which demands that investment treaty tribunals develop a much richer and more complex view of domestic law's role in investor-state disputes; and, a horizontal dimension, according to which investment treaty tribunals should refrain from leaping to any

Steven R Ratner, 'Regulatory Takings in Institutional Context: Beyond the Fear of Fragmented International Law' (2008) 102 AJIL 475, 477. In *Telenor Mobile Communications AS v Hungary*, ICSID Case No ARB/04/15 (Goode, Allard, Marriott), Award (13 September 2006), ¶ 69, the Tribunal noted that '[n]owadays direct expropriation is the exception rather than the rule'.

conclusion that might simply appear 'equitable', 'just' or 'common sense', without having first taken into consideration the existing public law traditions of developed countries.

I sincerely hope that the following pages will contribute to this debate, and ultimately, that they can enrich our understanding of international investment law as a form of global governance and public law adjudication.

First Part

A Framework of Analysis

The First Part of this work provides a framework of analysis for assessing the BIT generation. The BIT network, a system of more than 2,500 treaties, all having key substantive terms worded in a very similar manner, is hardly a trivial reality to the present world order. There are important descriptive and normative questions regarding it that need to be confronted. How did developing countries end up (or even begin) as part of this network? Or, as Salacuse and Sullivan, pose it, 'why would developing countries enter into such agreements? Why would they constrain their sovereignty by entering into treaties that specifically limit their ability to take necessary legislative and administrative actions to advance and protect their national interests?'[1] Even more important, are these treaties *legitimate* for developing countries? Are they *convenient*?

Chapter 1 provides the necessary historical context to begin answering these questions. It explains the traditional Latin American position that opposed diplomatic protection during the nineteenth century, as well as the development of state responsibility during the twentieth century, presenting ultimately an updated version of the traditional Calvo Doctrine (as originally conceived). Chapter 2 studies the BIT generation descriptively. Its main purpose is to present a new theory which views the BIT generation as the result of competition among developing countries in a sequential/evolutionary game with network effects. Chapter 3 presents some of the main normative problems that challenges the BIT generation, and then advances an assessment of the system's potential sources of legitimacy, including a discussion of the convenience of creating an appellate body or court in international investment law.

[1] Jeswald W Salacuse and Nicholas P Sullivan, 'Do BITs Really Work?: An Evaluation of Bilateral Investment Treaties and Their Grand Bargain' (2005) 46 *Harvard International Law Journal* 67, 77.

1

The Latin American Position on State Responsibility: Looking into the Past for Lessons on the Future

INTRODUCTION: THE LATIN AMERICAN STRUGGLE AGAINST DIPLOMATIC PROTECTION

IT IS DIFFICULT to understand the BIT generation without looking first at the broader historical picture. Any descriptive and normative assessment of the BIT generation—such as the one attempted later in this work—requires, first, a review of the evolution of state responsibility for injuries to aliens under international law during the nineteenth and twentieth centuries.

Latin America has been a major player in the development of rules and principles governing state responsibility; this was particularly true during the nineteenth century. After claiming their independence from the Spanish Empire, the new states found themselves in need of nation-building.[1] An early step taken toward this end was to encourage Europeans to settle the vast and unoccupied territories comprising the new republics. While colonial times had been characterised by the strict prohibition against travel by non-Spanish citizens to the *Indias*—ie, America—the new countries now implemented policies that intensively fostered European immigration and investment.[2]

[1] See Mario Góngora, *Ensayo Histórico sobre la Noción de Estado en Chile en los Siglos XIX y XX* (Santiago de Chile, Editorial Universitaria, 1986) (arguing that, in the case of Chile, the state built the nation).

[2] See Alejandro Alvarez, 'Latin American and International Law' (1909) 3 *American Journal of International Law* 269, 305, who explains that 'Latin America felt a growing need not only of the culture and intellectual material and the commerce of Europe, but also of its capital and population to develop its wealth and populate its territories . . . [I]t is to the interest of the American states, colonizing their own territory, to bring from Europe the greatest possible number of skilled workmen fitted to develop the industries of the country'. In 1832, Andrés Bello, *Principios de Derecho de Jentes*, 1st edn (Santiago de Chile, Imprenta de la Opinion, 1832) 53–54, explained why it was necessary to encourage immigration and why laws and statutes should eliminate all civil differences between nationals and aliens: '*Las restricciones y desventajas a que por las leyes de muchos países están sujetos los estranjeros, se miran jeneralmente como contrarias al incremento de la poblacion y al adelantamiento de la industria y los paises que han hecho*

These Europeans brought great progress to Latin American countries. However, they also brought one of the most serious international political problems to face the continent in more than a century: diplomatic protection. As defined by the Permanent Court of International Justice (PCIJ), diplomatic protection consists of the State's right 'to protect its subjects, when injured by acts contrary to international law committed by another State, from whom they have been unable to obtain satisfaction through the ordinary channels'.[3]

During the nineteenth century and first part of the twentieth century, diplomatic protection—in contrast to today—was not a *peaceful* method of dispute resolution.[4] In fact, the process was usually quite nasty. As Paulsson notes, '[t]he *diplomatic* component of the expression "diplomatic protection" was, in such circumstances, an ironic but hardly subtle fiction'.[5] Indeed, diplomatic protection was a process associated with 'the exercise of military, political or economic pressure by stronger against weaker States'.[6] The option of military self-help transformed diplomatic protection into a 'gunboat diplomacy'.[7]

Undoubtedly, European and US citizens suffered injuries at one time or another in Latin America during this 'organisational' era characterised by civil wars and periods of political unrest.[8] The precarious political conditions of Latin American societies frequently meant levels of justice and law enforcement that fell below international minimum standards

mas progresos en las artes y comercio y se han elevado a un grado mas alto de riqueza y poder, son cabalmente aquellos que han tratado con mas humanidad y liberalidad a los estranjeros'.

[3] *Mavrommatis Palestine Concessions Case* (*Greece v UK*) [1924] PCIJ Rep Series A No 2, 12. The PCIJ, ibid, also noted that '[b]y taking up the case of one of its subjects and by resorting to diplomatic action or international judicial proceedings on his behalf, a State is in reality asserting its own rights—its right to ensure, in the person of its subjects, respect for the rules of international law'.

[4] Today, diplomatic protection is a peaceful method of dispute settlement. See *Ahmadou Sadio Diallo* (*Republic of Guinea v Democratic Republic of the Congo*) (Preliminary Objections) ¶ 39 (available at www.icj-cij.org/docket/files/103/13856.pdf, where the ICJ held that: 'The Court will recall that under customary international law, as reflected in Article 1 of the draft Articles on Diplomatic Protection of the International Law Commission (hereinafter the "ILC"), "diplomatic protection consists of the invocation by a State, through diplomatic action or *other means of peaceful settlement*, of the responsibility of another State for an injury caused by an internationally wrongful act of that State to a natural or legal person that is a national of the former State with a view to the implementation of such responsibility" (Article 1 of the draft Articles on Diplomatic Protection adopted by the ILC at its Fifty-eighth Session (2006), ILC Report, doc A/61/10, p 24)'. (emphasis added)

[5] Jan Paulsson, *Denial of Justice in International Law* (New York, CUP, 2005) 15.

[6] C Wilfred Jenks, *The Prospects of International Adjudication* (Dobbs Ferry, NY, Oceana Publications, 1964) 514–15.

[7] Richard Lillich, 'The Current Status of the Law of State Responsibility for Injuries to Aliens' in Richard Lillich (ed), *International Law of State Responsibility for Injuries to Aliens* (Charlottesville, University Press of Virginia, 1983) 1, 3.

[8] See Alvarez, n 2 above, 273 (noting that the nineteenth century was a period of sudden political change in Latin America, including civil wars, dictatorships and constant modifications of fundamental rules).

(IMS).[9] This fact notwithstanding, the insurmountable military imbalance between European and Latin American countries made diplomatic protection an intrinsically illegitimate process. Both actual military interventions and mere 'credible threats', forced the region to accept many compensation schemes and arbitration agreements which would have been clearly rejected otherwise.

The new Latin American republics fiercely resisted such gunboat diplomacy. As this chapter will show, the regional opposition to the abuses of diplomatic protection was structured through two institutions: the so-called Calvo Doctrine and Calvo Clause.[10] Contrary to what is usually assumed, neither the Doctrine nor the Clause was an ideological or academic invention. They were not even created by their namesake, the Argentine jurist Carlos Calvo. Furthermore, few international law commentators have recognised the true significance of the Calvo Doctrine: it was part of a framework designed to *incentive* foreign investment in the region. Foreign investors were offered and provided full civil (non-political) legal equality, a revolutionary statement for those times. The Doctrine represented the other side of that basic equality created to promote immigration and investment: if investors wanted such a benefit, then they could not ask for more than equality (unless they could prove a denial of justice).

The rather distorted contemporary understanding of the Doctrine maybe due to Marxist and revisionist developments in international law after the Second World War. These much later trends had the effect of obfuscating both the history and content of this institution, particularly during the Cold War, when many developing countries adopted nationalisation and import substitution industrialisation policies. The international agenda sought at that time to minimise the implementation costs of the latter policies.

But that was not the case during the nineteenth century. At the time when the Calvo Doctrine was originally launched, the main international dispute was between 'national standards'—espoused by developing countries—and 'international minimum standards'—espoused by developed countries. This conflict was quite different in nature from the

[9] See Alwyn V Freeman, *The International Responsibility of States for Denial of Justice* 456 (New York, Longmans, Green and Co, 1938), and Frederick Sherwood Dunn, *The Diplomatic Protection of Americans in Mexico* (New York, Columbia University Press, 1933) 55.

[10] See also, FV Garcia-Amador, 'Calvo Doctrine, Calvo Clause' in Rudolph Bernhardt (ed), 2 *Encyclopedia of Public International Law* 521 (New York, North-Holland, 1992) 521 (arguing that the main function of the Calvo Doctrine was to prevent the abuse of diplomatic protection), and Frank Griffith Dawson, 'International Law, National Tribunals and the Rights of Aliens: The Latin American Experience' (1968) 21 *Vanderbilt Law Review* 712, 712 (explaining the difference between the Latin American and the European and African experiences, and how the former developed 'a unique body of law, clustered around the Calvo Doctrine and the principle of national or equal treatment').

more blatant dispute in the second half of the twentieth century between 'expropriation with the compensation deemed appropriate by the host state' or, more simple, 'expropriation without compensation'—espoused by developing countries—and the Hull Rule ('prompt, adequate, and effective compensation'[11])—espoused by developed countries.

The original intent of the Calvo Doctrine was thus far from being a principle of irresponsibility in international law or a standard such as 'expropriation without compensation'. The Doctrine was elaborated and adopted during a time when Latin American republics were under the control of people who believed in liberalism, property rights and individual economic freedom, including the right of foreign investors to come to Latin America and acquire key assets of the national economies.

One of the main claims of this chapter is that the Calvo Doctrine—when correctly understood in its historical light—presents important lessons for developing countries in the BIT generation. A careful historical review of the field of state responsibility for injuries to aliens and their property in the twentieth century demonstrates that by signing investment treaties, developing countries have finally managed to adhere to IMS and the Hull Rule (but not beyond IMS[12]). In other words, history has spiraled full circle, with the result that we now find ourselves in a position somewhat similar to that of the nineteenth century. This permits us to evaluate the BIT generation according to some of the same perspectives and values that were predominant in the region during the nineteenth century, particularly those embodied in the *original* conception of the Calvo Doctrine.

The regulatory capitalist paradigm of the twenty-first century poses several of the same questions that Latin America was trying to resolve in the nineteenth century.[13] In the twenty-first century globalised world, the market-based regulatory state has won general—yet not unanimous—acceptance. With the fall of communism, the ideological tensions of the twentieth century have dissipated substantially, and we find ourselves in a scenario that resembles certain aspects of the liberal nineteenth century.[14] Once

[11] See United States, 'The Secretary of State of the United States (Cordell Hull) to Mexican Ambassador at Washington DC' (1938) 32 *American Journal of International Law Supp* 181.

[12] See ch 6, 298–310, which provides a more complete discussion regarding why the interpretation positing that the 'fair and equitable treatment' clause goes beyond the 'international minimum standards' should be rejected. In this chapter, I will simply show evidence proving why that interpretation is historically unacceptable.

[13] See eg John Braithwaite, *Regulatory Capitalism. How it Works, Ideas for Making it Work Better* (Northampton, Edward Elgar, 2008), and David Levi-Faur, 'The Global Diffusion of Regulatory Capitalism' in David Levi-Faur (ed), *The Rise of Regulatory Capitalism: The Global Diffusion of a New Order* (Thousand Oaks, SAGE Publications, 2005) 12, 12–32.

[14] According to Paul Hirst and Grahame Thompson, 'Globalization and the Future of the Nation State' (1995) 24 *Economy and Society* 408, 428, '[m]ost globalizers have foreshortened memories: they forget that the international economy was in many respects as open between 1870 and 1914 as it is today and that determined efforts were made to recreate it after 1918'. See also, Niall Ferguson, 'Sinking Globalization' (2005) 84(2) *Foreign Affairs* 64 (noting that '[f]rom around 1870 until World War I, the world economy thrived in ways that look

more, we believe in property rights and market-based (though regulated) economies.[15] And, in the field of foreign investment, we are again witnessing a world in which foreign investors own, operate, and exert control over infrastructure, natural resources and other capital-intensive industries.

This chapter proceeds as follows. Section I explores the historical phenomenon of gunboat diplomacy, and analyses the foundation of the Calvo Doctrine and Clause. Section II moves forward to the twentieth century, describing how Latin American countries were able to eliminate forcible self-help and put the problem of gunboat diplomacy to rest. Section III presents the development of state responsibility for injury to aliens after the Second World War, when developing countries defended the so-called New International Economic Order (NIEO), including the new substantive position of expropriation without compensation. Section IV describes how IMS reentered the international law scene in the form of bilateral investment treaties (BITs). Section V puts forth the argument that the similarities between the nineteenth and twenty-first centuries justify our taking lessons from the past in updating the Calvo Doctrine. The conclusions remark upon the value of adopting a normative stance based on equality, which the updated Calvo Doctrine would intend to do.

I THE CALVO DOCTRINE AND CLAUSE: TWO NINETEENTH CENTURY ANTI-DIPLOMATIC PROTECTION INSTITUTIONS

The Calvo Doctrine and Clause have not received sufficient attention among contemporary commentators. Today it is incorrectly assumed that they symbolise state irresponsibility in international law. In order to rectify this misunderstanding, this section presents a brief overview of diplomatic protection during the nineteenth century, an era that—as mentioned—resembles ours in several aspects. It then analyses the Doctrine's and Clause's historical foundations as institutions oriented to fight diplomatic protection.

familiar today'). See also, Harold James, *The End of Globalization: Lessons From the Great Depression* (Harvard Cambridge, CUP, 2002), and Robert O Keohane, 'Governance in a Partially Globalized World. Presidential Address, American Political Science Association, 2000' (2001) 95 *American Political Science Review* 1, 1.

[15] As pointed out by Ian Ayres and John Braithwaite, *Responsive Regulation. Transcending the Deregulation Debate* (New York, OUP, 1992) 12: 'The nineteenth century saw an expansion of markets into traditional domains of pre-existing communities. In the twentieth century, the state asserted itself over domains that had become the prerogative of the market during the nineteenth century. By the late twentieth century, however, strong countercurrents had developed. One was the deregulation push to win back some of the encroachment the state had made on the market'.

A The Practice of Diplomatic Protection in the Nineteenth Century

The Calvo Doctrine and Clause were designed 'to protect the state from the alien, extraordinary though it may sound'.[16] As Mexico once argued, equality of treatment was established to defend 'weak states against the unjustified pretension of foreigners who, alleging supposed international laws, demanded a privileged position'.[17] The objective of these institutions was none other than to combat diplomatic protection and its more threatening manifestation, military self-help. In 1906, when defending the Clause that now bears his name—a clause indeed derived from the Calvo Doctrine[18]—the Argentine diplomat Luis Drago expressed the spirit of the original Latin American stance regarding gunboat diplomacy:

> [I]t was in obedience to that sentiment of common defense . . . that in a critical moment the Argentine Republic proclaimed the impropriety of the forcible collection of public debts by European nations, not as an abstract principle of academic value or as a legal rule of universal application outside of this continent (which is not incumbent on us to maintain), but as a principle of American diplomacy which, whilst being founded on equity and justice, has for its exclusive object to spare the peoples of this continent the calamities of conquest disguised under the mask of financial intervention.[19]

The practice of diplomatic protection constitutes a key dimension of the international law landscape of the nineteenth century. The Great Powers' use of forcible self-help to advance the claims of their citizens living or investing abroad transformed diplomatic protection into an institution well-suited to major abuses. The uneven balance of power between the North Atlantic countries and the new Latin American republics permitted the former to espouse not only legitimate claims but also bogus ones, on the part of their citizens.[20] As Summers remarks, 'the North Atlantic

[16] Andres H Roth, *The Minimum Standard of International Law Applied to Aliens* (Leiden, AW Sijthoff, 1949) 117.

[17] Mexico, 'Translation of Note from the Minister of Foreign Affairs of Mexico to the American Ambassador at Mexico City (2 September 1938)' (1938) 32 *American Journal of International Law Supp* 201, 205.

[18] See Luis M Drago, 'State Loans in their Relation to International Policy' (1907) 1 *American Journal of International Law* 692, and Amos S Hershey, 'The Calvo and Drago Doctrines' (1907) 1 *American Journal of International Law* 26.

[19] Cited in James Brown Scott (ed), 1 *The Hague Peace Conferences of 1899 and 1907. A Series of Lectures Delivered Before the John Hopkins University in the Year 1908* (John Hopkins University, Baltimore 1909) 421.

[20] According to Carlos Calvo, 1 *Derecho Internacional Teorico y Practico de Europa y America*, 1st edn (Paris, D'Amyot, 1869) 188, §91: '[E]*stas indemnizaciones pecuniarias hechas sin exámen alguno de causa y como á la aventura, pero con la amenaza siempre, por parte de los gobiernos européos, de apoyar con la fuerza sus reclamaciones, ha sido la fuente mas copiosa de las intervenciones de dichos gobiernos en America. Pero lo cierto es que en derecho internacional, no se puede admitir como legítimo este motivo de intervencion, y que tampoco lo han admitido en sus relaciones reciprocas los Estados européos. ¿Por qué, pues, se aplica por estos en sus relaciones con los Estados americanos?*'

powers have often intervened diplomatically without a sufficient examination of the facts of the particular case, taking it for granted that their action was justified, when the reverse may have been true'.[21] Neither was Lillich mistaken when concluding that there is 'no doubt' that 'the Great Powers sometimes stretched the substantive standards and abused the diplomatic protection process'.[22]

The writer José María Torres Caicedo—cited by Carlos Calvo in his treatise[23]—provides an interesting description of what was happening in the region during the nineteenth century in this regard:

> *Pero há mucho tiempo que se quiere explotar otra veta, otro filon de esa rica mina de indemnizaciones. Unos ó muchos extranjeros reciben daño á consecuencia de una de esas revoluciones en que es tan fecunda la América latina. Los extranjeros así perjudicados pidem que se les indemnice (si han perdido 1, reclaman 100); el Ministro respectivo apoya su reclamacion; sigue la historia de las escuadras, la protesta del Gobierno injustamente amenazado, y el pago inmediato, ó la promesa de pago hecha por ese Gobierno, al cual se le quita la palabra mostrándole la boca de los cañones.*[24]

Torres did not exaggerate. Just to cite a few examples of military intervention in the region from a very long list: France blocked Argentina's main ports from 1838 to 1840 for the purpose of giving protection to its citizens' property and credits; then England and France intervened in Rio de la Plata from 1843 to 1850. Similarly, France invaded Mexico in 1838 in the so-called 'pastry war' (among the injured was a French restaurant owner who suffered an assault on his supply of pastry). Once again, between 1861 and 1867, France, with the help of Spain and England, not only attacked Mexico but also established the Austrian Archduke Maximilian as the Emperor there. Another well-documented case is the German, British and Italian blockage of the Venezuelan coast in 1902–1903. After the three countries bombed Puerto Cabello and seised military and merchant ships, they settled upon a peace treaty that included the administration of Venezuelan customs by Belgian officers.[25]

In order to emphasise the unfairness characterising the practice of diplomatic protection at the time, one need not point to actual military interventions. The mere possibility of forcible self-help—a very 'credible

[21] Lionel M Summers, 'The Calvo Clause' (1933) 19 *Virginia Law Review* 459, 459.

[22] Lillich, n 7, 3. See also, Dunn, n 9, 6.

[23] Carlos Calvo, 3 *Le Droit International Théorique et Pratique; Précédé d'un Exposé Historique Des Progrès de la Science du Droit des Gens*, 5th edn (Paris, Arthur Rousseau, 1896) 148, §1290.

[24] JM Torres Caicedo, 2 *Mis Ideas y Mis Principios* (Paris, Imprenta Nueva, 1875) 262.

[25] See Miguel Cruchaga Tocornal, 1 *Nociones de Derecho International*, 3rd edn (Madrid, Reus, 1923) 212 ff, and Luis A Podesta Costa, '*La Responsabilidad Internacional del Estado*' in 2 *Cursos Monográficos* (La Habana, Academia Interamericana de Derecho Comparado e Internacional, 1952) 171–93. Calvo provides a more detailed history of interventions during the nineteenth century; see 1 Calvo, n 23, 281–355, §§145–209. For a more recent account of the interventions suffered by Argentina, see Horacio A Grigera Naón, 'Arbitration in Latin America: Progress and Setbacks' (2004) 21 *Arbitration International* 127.

threat', using the language of game theory[26]—deeply altered the relative positions of the parties at the bargaining table.[27] Confronting this reality, Latin America fought strongly against diplomatic protection as well as one of its legal manifestations, the so-called international minimum standards. Nor was it fond of arbitration,[28] which was frequently imposed as the sole alternative to undesirable intervention—including invasions, bombings, and the seizure of customs.[29]

B The Calvo Doctrine

The Calvo Doctrine constitutes perhaps the finest legal / political product to be developed in this regional crusade against diplomatic protection.[30] At its core lay equality:[31] among nations,[32] but more importantly, between

[26] See Jon Hovi, *Games, Threats and Treaties. Understanding Commitments in International Relations* (Pinter, Washington 1998) 11 ('[A] threat is contingent assertion signaling an intention to hurt somebody—physically, economically or otherwise—unless that somebody acts in the way prescribed by the thereatener'). Indeed, as Hovi remarks, ibid 33: '[O]ne of the most fundamental international legal principles [developed in the twentieth century] is that the use of force is prohibited, except in self-defence ... [Therefore] it was probably easier for Western leaders in the nineteenth century to make credible threats of violence than it is for their present-day successors'.

[27] See eg Frank Griffith Dawson and Ivan L Head, *International Law, National Tribunals, and the Rights of Aliens* (Syracuse, Syracuse University Press, 1971) 44–45 ('Although, in fact, the use of forcible self-help to secure conforming behavior was the exception and not the rule, the possibility of its invocation in a variety of situations in earlier times must have been continuously present in the minds of decision-makers').

[28] See Alvarez, n 3, 299, n 36. According to Lionel M Summers, 'Arbitration and Latin America' (1972) 3 *California Western International Law Journal* 1, 6–7, between 1794 and 1938 Latin American countries participated in nearly 200 arbitration arrangements, and in almost all of these cases, arbitration was a less harmful alternative as compared with military intervention. See also Guillermo Aguilar Alvarez and William W Park, 'The New Face of Investment Arbitration: NAFTA Chapter 11' (2003) 28 *Yale Journal of International Law* 365, 367 (explaining how '[d]uring the late nineteenth and early twentieth centuries, developing countries often perceived investment arbitration as little more than an extension of gunboat diplomacy').

[29] As W Michael Reisman, 'International Arbitration and Sovereignty' (2002) 18 *Arbitration International* 231, 232, points out, '[i]f foreign governments did violate what Europe and the United States considered commercial law or market morality, gunboats could seize the customs houses of the violators and manage them until debts were discharged'.

[30] Grigera Naón, n 26, 131, captured this idea earlier: '[T]he Calvo Doctrine is a response to the menace of foreign European intervention in South America, epitomised by the utterances of Thiers, the minister of Napoleon III, who considered Latin American countries as imperfect, bankrupted republics, which because of social and political instability and unrest, their failure to honour their debts, ensure personal security and provide proper police protection, and their inefficient and slow court system, were not to be considered equal to the countries of Europe'.

[31] See Donald Richard Shea, *The Calvo Clause: A Problem of Inter-American and International Law and Diplomacy* (Minneapolis, University of Minnesota Press, 1955) 19, and Denise Manning-Cabrol, 'The Imminent Death of the Calvo Clause and the Rebirth of the Calvo Doctrine: Equality of Foreign and National Investors' (1995) 26 *Law and Policy in International Business* 1169, 1172.

[32] See, Calvo, n 20, 396–97, §294, who insists on this point: '*En derecho internacional hay que recordar ante todo que los Estados soberanos son independientes é iguales, principio olvidado completamente por los que sostienen la necesidad de las convenciones extranjeras* [*demandas de in-*

foreigners and nationals.[33] This equality consisted of two sides, one positive and one negative, that were each part of the same conceptual framework. First, in order to foster foreign immigration and foreign investment in the region—both important public policies in Latin American during the nineteenth century[34]—equality dictated that aliens establishing themselves in Latin America were to receive the same treatment as nationals; that is, they would enjoy the same rights and the same protection in domestic courts as those given to indigenous people. It should be noted that this positive component was 'a great advance for the times, not only in limiting the territorial sovereignty of the State, but also in promoting human rights'.[35] In fact, even today such a principle has not been fully accepted in customary international law.[36]

At the same time—far from being a 'perversion of their early laudable attempts' to give foreigners the same rights as nationals[37]—equality was understood according to the phrase 'equality is the maximum'.[38] As Carlos Calvo explains, 'the responsibility of governments toward foreigners cannot be greater than the responsibility of governments toward their own citizens'.[39] Accepting more extensive responsibility one the part of

demnización] ó de la aplicación de la regla inglesa [empleo de la fuerza] á los Estados americanos. Entre estos y los de Europa no cabe mas que una relacion de derecho, que debe estar fundada en su completa igualdad'.

33 As Calvo, ibid 393, §294, explains: '[*L*]*a regla que en mas de un caso han tratado imponer las primeras* [*las potencias Europeas*] *á los segundos* [*los Estados Americanos*] *es, que los extranjeros merecen mas consideracion y mayores respetos y privilegios que los mismos naturales del país en que residen. Este principio, cuya aplicación es notoriamente injusta y atentatoria á la ley de la igualdad de los Estados, y cuyas consideraciones son esencialmente perturbadoras, no constituye regla de derecho aplicable en las relaciones internacionales de los de Europa, y siempre que se ha exigido por alguno, la contestacion del otro ha sido absolutamente negativa. Y debia ser así, porque de lo contrario los pueblos relativamente débiles estarian a merced de los poderosos, y los ciudadanos de un país tendrían menos derechos y garantías que los residentes extranjeros*'.

34 British investors were the leaders in the region. See Robert E Grosse, *Multinationals in Latin America* (New York, Routledge, 1989) 7–10. (Ch 1, 'A History of MNE [Multi National Enterprises] in Latin America', provides an overview of the history of foreign direct investment in the region). See also, J Fred Rippy, 'The British Investment "Boom" of the 1880s in Latin America' (1949) 29(2) *The Hispanic-American Historical Review* 281 (describing the large sums that British capitalists invested in the region during the period from 1880–1890).

35 Dawson and Head, n 28, 7. According to Lillich, n 8, 5, Latin American countries, 'laudably' went 'beyond then-existing international law' by 'granting aliens equality of treatment with nationals'. See also, Alvarez, n 3, 344.

36 As Campbell McLachlan QC et al, *International Investment Arbitration. Substantive Principles* (New York, OUP, 2007) 212–13, explain, 'the non-contingent standards of national treatment and MFN treatment . . . have always developed exclusively through express grants by treaty. Customary international law does not require that States accord either form of treatment to aliens'. See also, Ian Brownlie, *Principles of Public International Law*, 6th edn (New York, OUP, 2003) 498.

37 Lillich, n 8, 5.

38 Freeman, n 10, 468.

39 3 Calvo, n 23, 138, §1276. In the original: '*La responsabilité des gouvernements envers les étrangers ne peut être plus grande que celle que ces gouvernements ont à l'égard de leurs propres citoyens. On ne saurait prétendre, en effet, que les droits d'hospitalité puissent restreindre le droit qui appartient à un gouvernement d'user de tous les moyens légaux pour pourvoir à la conservation de l'Etat, ou que les étrangers puissent obtenir une position privilégiée*'.

the state toward foreigners would be '*souverainement injuste*'.[40] Hence, if aliens were to reside in those countries and take full advantage of the equality being offered, they should accept their legal systems 'as is': 'aliens who establish in a country are entitled to the same rights to protection enjoyed by nationals; they cannot expect to have a more extended protection'.[41]

These two dimensions of equality reflect the equilibrium that Latin America tried to strike between the goals of fostering foreign immigration and investment, and confronting the abuses that diplomatic protection of those same aliens and investments would create in the future. In any case, as an instrument designed to combat abusive diplomatic protection but not to oppose foreign investors and their investments, the Calvo Doctrine 'was never a bar to those international claims based on breaches of well-established international obligations regarding the treatment of aliens'.[42] Indeed, the Doctrine recognised that, in cases of *denial of justice* construed in more or less narrow terms, aliens could have recourse to diplomatic protection.[43] As Garcia-Amador explains:

> [A]dvocates of the doctrine—both governmental officials and learned publicists, beginning with Calvo himself—have always admitted that, in cases of denial of justice and other well-established wrongful or arbitrary acts and omissions under international law, the State of residence is responsible whether or not the nationals have sustained injuries from those acts or omissions.[44]

A clear demonstration of this proposition can be found in Article 3 of the Convention Relative to the Rights of Aliens, accorded during the Second Panamerican Conference (1902), a provision that embodied the Calvo Doctrine and the denial of justice exception:

> Whenever an alien shall have claims or complaints of a civil, criminal or administrative order against a State, or its citizens, he shall present his claims to a

[40] ibid 140, §1278.

[41] 6 Calvo, n 23, 231, §256 (*'Il est certain que les étrangers qui se fixent dans un pays ont au même titre que ses nationaux droit à la protection, mais ils ne peuvent prétendre à une protection plus étendue'*). See also, 3 Calvo, n 24, 140, §1278.

[42] Garcia-Amador, n 11, 521. See ibid 522 ('[T]he doctrine cannot be characterized as an absolute ban to the exercise of diplomatic protection'). See also, Alwyn V Freeman, 'Recent Aspects of the Calvo Doctrine and the Challenge to International Law' (1946) 40 *American Journal of International Law* 121, 132–33 ('The plea [of Carlos Calvo], in other words, was for recognition of the general principle of submission of foreign subjects to the local law—a thoroughly reasonable demand. But *it did not go to the extent of maintaining that equality with nationals under that law was in itself a bar to any international inquiry*'.) (emphasis added)

[43] The concept of denial of justice was at the centre of the North–South conflict. Not surprisingly, according to Freeman, n 9, 460–61, Latin American States would have wanted to define diplomatic protection as being available only in cases where denial of justice was narrowly defined according to municipal law. See also, Summers, n 21, 460.

[44] FV Garcia-Amador, 1 *The Changing Law of International Claims* (New York, Oceana Publications, 1984) 56.

competent Court of the country and such claims shall not be made through diplomatic channels, *except in the cases where there shall have been on the part of the Court, a manifest denial of justice, or unusual delay, or evident violation of the principles of international law.* (emphasis added)[45]

The most solid proof that the Calvo Doctrine was not designed to immunise Latin American countries from aliens, or to justify the abuses committed against them, can be found in the intellectual and political background of the scholar, jurist, and statesman who first envisioned this institution. Contrary to what is usually assumed, Carlos Calvo did not create the Doctrine.[46] Even learned contemporary commentators incorrectly attribute its authorship to the Argentinean jurist and diplomat. The real author was the Venezuelan jurist Andrés Bello, one of the greatest intellectuals that the region ever produced.[47]

Among other impressive achievements, Bello was the first Latin American internationalist—having written the first treatise on the subject in the region—the drafter of the Chilean Civil Code of 1855, the founder of Universidad de Chile (and its first President), and the author of a Spanish (Castilian) language grammar. More importantly, in Chile and several other Latin American countries, Andrés Bello is considered a symbol of the rule of law. Far from being a revisionist or ideologue of any sort, he was a strong supporter of property rights.[48]

[45] See James Brown Scott, *The International Conferences of American States 1889–1928: A Collection of the Conventions, Recommendations, Resolutions, Reports, and Motions Adopted By the First Six International Conferences of the American States, and Documents Relating to the Organization of the Conferences* (New York, OUP, 1931) 90–91.

[46] Almost all sources provide an inaccurate historical explanation, depicting Calvo as the founder of the Calvo Doctrine. See eg Rudolf Dolzer and Christoph Schreuer, *Principles of International Investment Law* (New York, OUP, 2008) 12; Oscar M Garibaldi, 'Carlos Calvo Redivivus: The Rediscovery of the Calvo Doctrine in the Era of Investment Treaties' (2006) 3(5) *Transnational Dispute Management* 4; Paulsson, n 6, 20; Grigera Naón, n 25, 131; Bernardo Cremades, 'Disputes Arising Out of Foreign Direct Investment in Latin America: A New Look at the Calvo Doctrine and Other Jurisdictional Issues' (2004) 59 *Dispute Resolution Journal* 78, 80; Donald Shea, 'Calvo, Carlos' in 5 *The Encyclopedia Americana. International Edition* (Danbury, Grolier, 1997) 242; Dunn, n 9, 56; FV García-Amador, 'Draft Articles on the Responsibility of the State for Injuries Caused in Its Territory to the Person or Property of Aliens' in FV Garcia-Amador, Louis B Sohn and RR Baxter (eds), *Recent Codification of the Law of State Responsibility for Injuries to Aliens* (Dobbs Ferry, NY, Oceana Publications, 1974) 1, 3.

[47] There are scores of biographies of Andrés Bello. An extraordinary insightful and well researched work can be found in Ivan Jaksić, *Andrés Bello: Scholarship and Nation-Building in Nineteenth-Century Latin America* (New York, CUP, 2001), and Ivan Jaksić, *Andrés Bello: La pasión por el orden* (Santiago de Chile, Editorial Universitaria, 2001).

[48] See eg Pedro Lira Urqueta, *El Código Civil Chileno y Su Epoca* (Santiago de Chile, Editorial Jurídica, 1956) 67–70 (explaining how private property was one of the central normative axes of the Chilean Civil Code of 1855). For instance, Lira, ibid 67, quotes the following words of Bello: '*La propiedad ha vivificado, extendido, agrandado nuestra propia existencia; por medio de la propiedad la industria del hombre, este espíritu de progreso y de vida que todo lo anima, ha hecho desarrollar en los más diversos climas todos los gérmenes de riqueza y de poder*'.

This is not the first time that Bello's authorship over the Doctrine has been claimed.[49] Dawson noted earlier that Bello was 'the first publicist to express the doctrine [of non-intervention] in Spanish, thereby shaping the thoughts of generations of Latin-American jurists and statesmen'.[50] Indeed, in the first Latin American international law treatise—*Derecho de Jentes*, published in 1832—Bello strongly defended the principles of non-intervention and equality among nations. This treatise—a highly influential work that all regional commentators deeply admired, including Calvo himself[51]—was written 36 years before the first edition of Calvo's *Derecho Internacional Teórico y Práctico de Europa y América* (1868), and more than half a century before the augmented French fifth edition of the same work—*Le droit international théorique et pratique; précédé d'un exposé historique des progrès de la science du droit des gens* (1896, six vols).

As Bello explained in 1832, the alien entering a foreign state 'agrees tacitly to be subject to the local laws and jurisdiction'.[52] He also acknowledged that States must apply their laws to aliens in a just manner,[53] and protect them against abuses at the hands of indigenous people.[54] Diplomatic protection could be requested, but only in the event of a denial of justice.[55] In the 1844 Edition of his Treatise, this time titled *Principios de*

[49] Historical mismatches between authors and theories occur not only in the social sciences, but also in mathematics and natural science. According to Roger Penrose, *The Road to Reality. A Complete Guide to the Laws of the Universe* (New York, AA Knopf, 2004) 45, 'there are other instances in mathematics where the mathematician(s) whose name(s) are attached to a result did not even know of the result in question'.

[50] Frank Griffith Dawson, 'The Influence of Andres Bello on Latin-American perceptions of the non-intervention and State Responsibility' (1986) 57 *British Ybk of Intl Law* 253, 273. Then, ibid 287, he explains that 'the alien's obligation to submit to local laws and jurisdiction which was to be an important constituent of the late nineteenth century Calvo Doctrine thus was first expressed by Bello as early as 1832'. See ibid 307.

[51] See 1 Calvo, n 23, 109–10: '*Un des hommes les plus remarquables qu'ait produit l'Amerique latine est sans contredit Andres Bello, né à Caracas (Venezuela) en 1780 et mort en 1863. Bello s'est acquis une juste renommée à la fois comme homme d'État et comme écrivain . . . En 1832, Bello, mettant à profit l'experience des affaires internationales que lui avaient donnée ses fonctions de secrétaire de diverses légations vénézuéliennes en Europe et le poste élevé qu'il occupait dans la direction des relations extérieures du Chili, publia, sous le titre de:* Principios de derecho de gentes *(Principes du droit des gens), un traité élémentaire, dans lequel, quoique en un cadre restreint, sont résolues toutes les questions essentielles sur la matière . . . On peut le considérer comme le précurseur de Wheaton, le publiciste américain, qui lui a emprunté de nombreuses citations. Du reste, les auteurs les plus distingués sont unanimes à parler de l'œvre de Bello avec éloge*'.

[52] Bello, n 2, 55 ('[*A*]*l poner el pié en el territorio de un estado estranjero, contraemos, segun se ha dicho, la obligacion de sometemos a sus leyes, y por consiguiente a las reglas que tienen establecidas para la administracion de justicia*').

[53] ibid 54 ('*El estranjero a su entrada contrae tácitamente la obligacion de sujetarse a las leyes y la jurisdiccion local, y el estado le ofrece de la misma manera la protección de la autoridad pública, depositada en los tribunales*'.)

[54] ibid ('*En fin, es obligacion del soberano que les da acojida atender a su seguridad, haciéndoles justicia en sus pleitos, y protejiéndolos aun contra los naturales, demasiado dispuestos a maltratarlos y vejarlos, particularmente en países de atrasada civilizacion y cultura*'.)

[55] ibid ('*Si éstos* [*los Estados*] *contra derecho rehusaren oir sus quejas, o le hiciesen una injusticia manifiesta, puede entónces interponer la autoridad de su propio soberano*'.)

Derecho Internacional (Principles of International Law), Bello expanded those words to the following set of carefully crafted ideas, which can be considered the first clear and solid formulation of the Calvo Doctrine:

> *[E]s obligación del soberano que les da acogida [a los extranjeros] atender á su seguridad, haciéndoles justicia en sus pleitos, y protegiéndolos aun contra los naturales, demasiado dispuestos á maltratarlos y vejarlos, particularmente en paises de atrasada civilizacion y cultura. El estranjero á su entrada contrae tácitamente la obligacion de sujetarse á las leyes y á la jurisdiccion local, y el Estado le ofrece de la misma manera la proteccion de la autoridad pública, depositada en los tribunales. Si estos contra derecho rehusasen oir sus quejas, ó le hiciesen una injusticia manifiesta, puede entónces interponer la autoridad de su propio soberano, para que solicite se le oiga en su juicio, ó se le indemnizen los perjuicios causados. Los actos jurisdiccionales de una nacion sobre los estranjeros que en ella residen, deben ser respetados de las otras naciones; porque al poner el pié en el territorio de un Estado estranjero, contraemos, segun se ha dicho, la obligacion de someternos á sus leyes, y por consiguiente á las reglas que tiene establecidas para la administracion de justicia. Pero el Estado contrae tambien por su parte la obligacion de observarlas respecto del extranjero, y en el caso de una palpable infraccion, el daño que se infiere á este, es una injuria contra la sociedad de que es miembro. Si el Estado instiga, aprueba ó tolera los actos de injusticia ó violencia de sus súbditos contra los estranjeros, los hace verdaderamente suyos, y se constituye responsable de ellos para con las otras naciones.*[56]

Apart from being a prominent scholar, Bello was also a statesman and a diplomat. From 1829 to his death in 1865, Bello lived in Chile, where he held an important position at the Chilean Ministry of Foreign Relations (1830–1852).[57] One can discern traces of the Calvo Doctrine in his work there. For example, when negotiating as a Chilean representative to the United States, Bello signed the 'Additional and Explanatory Convention to the Treaty of Peace, Amity, Commerce and Navigation' (1 September 1833). This convention clarified the meaning of the 'full protection and security' (FPS) clause contained in Article 10 of the Friendship, Commerce and Navigation (FCN) treaty, recently concluded between both nations (16 May 1833). The Doctrine is unmistakably present behind the following words:

> It being agreed by the 10th article of the aforesaid treaty, that the citizens of the United States of America, personally or by their agents, shall have the right of being present at the decisions and sentences of the tribunals, in all cases which may concern them, and at the examination of witnesses and declarations that may be taken in their trials;—and as the strict enforcement of this article may be

[56] Andrés Bello, *Principios de Derecho Internacional*, 2nd edn (Caracas, JM De Rojas, 1847) 77 (The ortography in this citation and previous footnotes—the Bello ortography—is different from modern Castilian ortography).

[57] See Jaksić, *Andrés Bello: La pasión . . .*, n 47, 135.

in opposition of the present due administration of justice, it is mutually understood, that the Republic of Chili [*sic*] is *only bound by the aforesaid stipulation to maintain the most perfect equality in this respect between American and Chilian* [*sic*] *citizens, the former to enjoy all the rights and benefits of the present or future provisions which the laws grant to the latter in their judicial tribunals, but no special favors or privileges.* (emphasis added)[58]

Similarly, many FCN treaties concluded between Chile and other Latin American countries while Bello was at the Ministry of Foreign Affairs included provisions espousing what has been previously referred to as the positive dimension of equality of treatment—ie, the full equality of treatment to foreigners. This is the case, for example, with the Chile–Mexico FCN (7 March 1831),[59] the Chile–Peru FCN (20 January 1835),[60] and the Chile–Nueva Granada (Colombia) FCN (16 February 1844).[61] In addition, there are at least two examples of FCNs concluded between Chile and European Powers that evidence similar clauses. One is the Chile–France FCN (15 September 1846), and the other, the Belgium–Chile FCN (31 August 1858)[62]. Article III of the former provided that:

Les sujets et citoyens respectifs jouiront, dans les deux Etats, d'une complète et constante protection pour leurs personnes et leurs propriété. Ils auront un libre et facile, accès auprès des tribunaux de justice pour la poursuite et la défense de leurs droits. Ils seront maîtres d'employer, dans toutes les circonstances, les avocats, avoués ou agents de toute classe qu'ils jugeront à propos. Enfin, ils joiront sous ce rapport des mêmes droits et privilèges accordés aux nationaux eux-mêmes. (emphasis added)[63]

Furthermore, the Chilean Civil Code (1855), also drafted by Bello, recognised civil equality between aliens and nationals. Its Article 57, which is still in force, provides for this principle: '*La ley no reconoce diferencias entre el chileno y el extranjero en cuanto a la adquisición y goce de los derechos civiles que regla este código*'.[64]

58 William M Malloy (ed), 1 *Treaties, Conventions, International Acts, Protocols and Agreements between the United States of America and Other Powers, 1776–1909* (Washington DC, Government Printing Office, 1910) 171, 182.

59 Clive Parry (ed), 81 *The Consolidated Treaty Series* (Dobbs Ferry, NY, Oceana, 1969) 261. See eg its Art II: 'The Contracting Parties declare that Chilians and Mexicans respectively, immediately upon their entering the territory of either Republic, shall enjoy the same respect, rights and privileges, as are lawfully enjoy in each respective Country by those who obtained letters of naturalization'.

60 Clive Parry (ed), 85 *The Consolidated Treaty Series* (Dobbs Ferry, NY, Oceana, 1969) 35.

61 Clive Parry (ed), 96 *The Consolidated Treaty Series* (Dobbs Ferry, NY, Oceana, 1969) 150.

62 Clive Parry (ed), 119 *The Consolidated Treaty Series* (Dobbs Ferry, NY, Oceana, 1969) 437 ff. See, ibid 440, Art III: '*Dans tous ces actes, les citoyens des deux Parties Contractantes jouiront respectivement de la même protection et de la même sécurité dans leurs personnes, leurs biens et l'exercise de leur industrie, que les nationaux exus-mêmes, suivant les lois des deux pays respectivement*'.

63 Clive Parry (ed), 100 *The Consolidated Treaty Series* (Dobbs Ferry, NY, Oceana, 1969) 175, 178.

64 According to Edwin Borchard, 'The 'Minimum Standard' of Treatment of Aliens' (1940) 38 *Michigan Law Review* 445, 450, equality between foreigners and nationals 'was first introduced into modern civil codes by Andrés Bello, the famous Venezuelan who in 1855 drafted the Chilean Civil Code'.

In summary, the Calvo Doctrine—at least as Andrés Bello originally envisioned it—did not intend to dismantle state responsibility. Neither was it—as Sohn and Baxter affirm—a 'reflection of a fundamental hostility on the part of some nations to the idea of accountability of state for asserted violations of the rights of aliens',[65] or —as expressed by Goebel—a 'repudiation of the theory of responsibility'[66] and 'a final effort to regulate the liability of the state by municipal legislation'.[67] On the contrary, as Wälde notes, 'the Calvo-doctrine, much opposed by Western governments with respect to developing countries, has in fact been—and still is—the dominant maxim of Western countries themselves'.[68]

C The Calvo Clause

If the Calvo Doctrine has been the subject of historical and conceptual misunderstandings, then, the Calvo Clause has suffered a similar fate. The Calvo Clause required foreigners to be subjected exclusively to domestic law and tribunals, and to renounce diplomatic protection.[69] It appeared either as a contractual provision in agreements, or as a provision of Statutes and Constitutions that forced its explicit or implicit incorporation into concession or construction contracts.[70] Like the Doctrine, the Clause was also the product of weak countries' efforts to protect themselves from colonialist Powers.[71]

Despite this shared goal, the Clause is not a mere byproduct of the Doctrine, as sometimes assumed,[72] but reveals at least two important differences. First, it did not operate unilaterally but bilaterally, that is, the investor 'has consented of his own free will to the abandonment of diplomatic protection'[73]. Second, the Clause went further than the Doctrine by attempting to completely forbid diplomatic protection, even in cases

[65] Louis B Sohn and R Baxter, *Convention on the International Responsibility of States for Injuries to Aliens. Preliminary Draft with Explanatory Notes* (Cambridge, Mass, Harvard Law School, 1959) 36.

[66] Julius Goebel Jr, 'The International Responsibility of States for Injuries Sustained by Aliens on Account of Mob Violence, Insurrections, and Civil Wars' (1914) 8 *American Journal of International Law* 802, 832.

[67] ibid.

[68] Thomas W Wälde, 'Investment Arbitration under the Energy Charter Treaty—From Dispute Settlement to Treaty Implementation' (1996) 12 *Arbitration International* 429, 446.

[69] See Freeman, n 9, 456–57.

[70] See eg, Arts 10 and 149 of the Constitution of Venezuela of 1893 and Art 38 of the Constitution of Ecuador of 1897. See Freeman, n 9, 455–90.

[71] See Summers, n 21, 482.

[72] See eg Cremades, n 46, 80 ('The Calvo doctrine gave rise to the Calvo clause, which precluded arbitration and instead required disputes to be resolved in national courts'). See also, Grigera Naón, n 25, 137.

[73] Summers, n 21, 465.

where there was a denial of justice.[74] Note that, in principle, the Clause was not an arbitrary attempt to unilaterally eliminate state responsibility in international law; in the liberal nineteenth century, the Clause specifically invoked the freedom of contract as its basis of legitimacy.

As was the case with the Doctrine, Carlos Calvo did not invent the Clause.[75] The earliest evidence for a Calvo Clause of which I am aware is a decree that Peru issued in 1846 (as noted before, the first edition of Calvo's treatise is from 1868).[76] In Chile, one of the most stable and foreign-investor friendly countries in Latin America during the nineteenth century,[77] the first observable Clause appeared in the construction contract for completion of the most important railroad line in the nation.[78] That contract, concluded between the Chilean government and US citizen Henry Meiggs on 14 September 1861—at a time when Bello was a highly influential statesman—regulated the construction of what would become the second line in Chile's history, linking its two main cities (Santiago and Valparaiso).

The Latin American *praxis* of incorporating Calvo Clauses in contracts and concessions can be observed throughout the nineteenth century.[79] To

[74] See FV García-Amador, *El Derecho Internacional del Desarrollo. Una Nueva Dimensión del Derecho Internacional Económico* (Madrid, Civitas, 1987) 212.

[75] The conventional wisdom is that Calvo invented the Clause. See eg Edwin M Borchard, *The Diplomatic Protection of Citizens Abroad; or, The Law of International Claims* (New York, The Banks Law Publishing Co, 1915) 792, and AH Feller, *The Mexican Claims Commissions 1923–1934; A Study In the Law and Procedure of International Tribunals* (New York, The Macmillan Co, 1935) 185.

[76] Cited by Alexander Alvarez, *Le Droit International Américain, Son Fondement—Sa Nature D'Après L'Histoire Diplomatique Des États du Nouveau Monde et Leur Vie Politique et Économique* (Paris, A Pedone, 1910) 120.

[77] According to *The Times* (London 22 April 1880), Chile was 'the model republic of South America', cited by Harold Blakemore, *British Nitrates and Chilean Politics, 1886–1896: Balmaceda and North* (London, Athlone Press, 1974) 1.

[78] See Emilio Jofré, 1 *Boletín de Leyes y Decretos sobre Ferrocarriles dictados por la República de Chile desde 1848 hasta 1890* (Santiago de Chile Imprenta 'Santiago', 1891) 71–76. The Clause provided that: '*El contratista don Enrique Meiggs, se somete desde luego a las autoridades y tribunales del país, en todo lo que concierna a la ejecución del fallo que pronuncien los árbitros y a los efectos del presente contrato, renunciando de la manera más formal y solemne al derecho que las prácticas, usos internacionales y tratados ó convenciones diplomáticas acuerdan a los extranjeros, para invocar la protección de los Ministros y Agentes Diplomáticos o Consulares de sus respectivos países, siempre que se vean vejados o perjudicados por las autoridades del Estado, en cuyo territorio residen; pues es su voluntad ponerse para todos y cada uno de los efectos de este contrato, en cualquier tiempo que se produzcan, a la par de los ciudadanos chilenos, sin que pueda hacer uso de otras prerrogativas, exenciones o derechos que los que les competen a dichos ciudadanos chilenos; y si de otros derechos o privilegios quisiere hacer uso, conviene desde ahora en que no se le oiga y permita el ejercicio de ellos, facultando a las autoridades de Chile para que hagan valer esta formal renuncia contra las reclamaciones que pudiera entablar por la vía diplomática; y para que en consecuencia se excusen de admitirlas y contestarlas, como si no se hubieren elevado nunca o como si después de elevados, el interesado mismo conviniere voluntariamente en retractarlas*'.

[79] As Shea, n 31, 9–10, observed in 1955: 'The Calvo Clause has existed as a legal and diplomatic problem for about eighty years. It is closely related to, and a result of, the development and exploitation of the natural resources in the underdeveloped regions of the world that occurred in the latter part of the nineteenth century and the early part of the twentieth . . .

continue with Chile as a case study, the Clause was commonly used in railroad construction contracts in the 1860s,[80] and finally included in a more general regulation passed by the Ministry of Industries and Public in 1888.[81] In railway concession contracts (BOTs), it made its appearance in the 1880s.[82] The later date for BOTs may be explained by the fact that most initial concessions were given to Chilean citizens. By 1886, as part of what seems to have been a general trend in Latin America during the last three decades of the nineteenth century,[83] the Congress passed a general Statute requiring the incorporation of a Calvo Clause into every concession contract.[84]

Another early example is the Calvo Clause appearing in the case *Nitrate Railways Co Ltd (UK) v Chile*.[85] Here, a British investor acquired three railroad concessions from *Montero Hermanos*, a Peruvian partnership that had in turn obtained them from the Peruvian government between 1869 and 1871 (Chile annexed the territories where the railroad was located as a consequence of the War of the Pacific, 1879–1884). In this case, the Tribunal upheld the Calvo Clause—a somewhat rare instance in the practice of nineteenth century claims commissions—seeming to find the following Chilean defense persuasive:

> *Los Gobiernos americanos han procurado poner coto a una situación tan molesta, por lo menos en los casos en que hacían concesiones a extranjeros o contrataban con ellos. Para este efecto, han consignado en las leyes, decretos y contratos, la condición de que el contratista o concesionario extranjero renunciaría al derecho de ocurrir a la vía diplomática, sometiendo sus cuestiones con el Gobierno a la jurisdicción de la justicia ordinaria o de jueces árbitros designados por las partes. Tal es el origen de la cláusula que contiene cada uno de los tres contratos celebrados con Montero Hermanos para la construcción de las*

[T]he exploitation generally came in the form of large foreign investment and a consequent migration of foreigners to these countries to supervise and direct the development of their natural resources'. See also ibid 121–193 (ch VI, 'Arbitral Decisions Involving Calvo Clauses up to 1926'), where Shea refers to several Calvo Clauses agreed upon during the nineteenth century.

[80] One example of this trend in Chile is the '*Licitación ramal desde San Felipe a la línea central, 1869*', authorised by Decree of November 24, 1869, and by Statute of January 7, 1869. Its Art 15 provides that: '*El contratista o contratistas si fueren extranjeros, se considerarán para los efectos del contrato como ciudadanos chilenos. En consecuencia, renunciarán a la protección que pudieran implorar de sus respectivos gobiernos o que éstos pudieran oficiosamente prestarles en apoyo de sus pretensiones*'. (1 Jofré, n 78, 82–85).

[81] 1 Jofré, n 78, 232–33.

[82] See eg Chilean Statute of 23 October 1884, Statute of 11 September 1884, Statute of 18 December 1885, Statute of 28 August 1886 and Statute of 7 August 1885.

[83] See Dawson, n 50, 307–11.

[84] Chilean Statute of 28 August 1886: '*Artículo único: Siempre que se otorguen permisos o concesiones para la construcción de una obra o trabajo público, o para el goce de algún derecho a una persona o empresa particular, ellas o quienes sus derechos representen, aun cuando sean extranjeras y no residan en Chile, se considerarán como domiciliadas en la República, y quedarán sujetas a las leyes del país, como si fueran chilenas, para la resolución de todas las cuestiones que se susciten con motivo de la obra para el cual se otorgan el permiso o las concesiones*'.

[85] Anglo–Chilean Tribunal of Arbitration, 2 *Reclamaciones presentadas al Tribunal Anglo-Chileno* (Santiago de Chile, Imprenta i libreria Ercilla, 1896) 220 ff.

diversas líneas férreas de Tarapacá, por la cual no se permite la transmisión a extranjeros de los derechos conferidos a esos señores, sin poder hacer uso de ningún recurso diplomático.[86]

In sum, the Calvo Doctrine and Clause embodied the principle of national treatment as an attempt to curb the excesses of diplomatic protection. The Doctrine did not deny aliens and foreign investors' their rights under international law,[87] and the Clause did so only under the authority vested in the free will and freedom of contract of those aliens and foreign investors. When viewed in a proper historical light, the Calvo Doctrine and Clause illustrate the tensions inherent in Latin American policy between the priorities of fostering foreign immigration and investment on the one hand, and avoiding military self-help on the other.

II THE END OF GUNBOAT DIPLOMACY

Latin American countries fought a long and organised battle against the use of forcible self-help as the extreme form of diplomatic protection. As this section will show, throughout the nineteenth century and during the first part of the twentieth century, they strongly defended the national treatment standard—as opposed to IMS, the legal key opening the door to military self-help—as well as exhaustion of local remedies, equality of states, and, in general, the Calvo Doctrine.[88] Although it took a long time, they were eventually to succeed in converting diplomatic protection into a peaceful dispute resolution mechanism.

Latin American countries typically pursued this agenda at the International Conferences of the American States. In nearly all the Conferences, there were references to the Calvo Doctrine, as well as attempts to establish rules and principles that would embody it.[89] Eventually, after

[86] ibid, n 85, 282.

[87] As García-Amador, n 74, 212, explains, the Calvo Doctrine was not an instrument of international irresponsibility: '*Dado su verdadero y único propósito —esto es, el de evitar el abuso del derecho a la protección diplomática—, la Doctrina Calvo no es incompatible con la responsabilidad internacional en que puede incurrir el Estado con motivo del incumplimiento de sus obligaciones hacia los extranjeros*'.

[88] See Freeman, n 10, 466 (explaining how Latin American countries continually fought for their doctrines).

[89] See Scott, n 46. During the First International Conference (1889–1890), ibid 45, the majority of states passed—against US opposition—the following *Recommendation*: 'The International American Conference recommends to the Governments of the countries therein represented the adoption, as principle of American international law, of the following: (1) Foreigners are entitled to enjoy all the civil rights enjoyed by natives; and they shall be accorded all the benefits of said rights in all that is essential as well as in the form or procedure, and the legal remedies incident thereto, absolutely in like manner as said natives. (2) A nation has not, nor recognizes in favor of foreigners, any other obligations or responsibilities than those which in favor of the natives are established, in like cases, by the constitutions and the laws'.

The Second Conference (1902) adopted the *Convention Relative to the Rights of Aliens* (ibid 90–91), which prescribed, among other things, the following principles: '*First*: Aliens shall

careful study by an agency established for the codification of international law, the Seventh Montevideo Conference (1933) unanimously—ie, including the US—adopted the Calvo Doctrine.[90] Article 9 of the Convention on Rights and Duties of States provided that: 'The jurisdiction of states within the limits of national territory applies to all the inhabitants. Nationals and foreigners are under the same protection of the law and the national authorities and the foreigners may not claim rights other or more extensive than those of the nationals'.[91]

These Pan-American conferences primarily represented the position of capital importing countries. European countries were absent, and the US—notwithstanding the treaty adopted at the Seventh Montevideo Conference—opposed almost all anti-diplomatic protection and anti-IMS initiatives. Consequently, Latin America sought wider forums in which to defend its position. In the end, it succeeded in at least one key dimension of its agenda: the proscription of the use of force. Indeed, three international conventions were produced during the first half of the twentieth century with the purpose of preventing forcible self-help in the context of diplomatic protection.

enjoy all civil rights pertaining to citizens, and make use thereof in substance, form or procedure, and in the recourses which result therefrom, under exactly the same terms as the said citizens, except as may be otherwise provided by the Constitution of each country. *Second*: The States do not owe to nor recognize in favor of foreigners any obligation or responsibilities other than those established by their constitutions and laws in favor of their citizens. *Third.* Whenever an alien shall have claims or complaints of a civil, criminal or administrative order against a State, or its citizens, he shall present his claims to a competent Court of the country and such claims shall not be made through diplomatic channels except in the cases where there shall been on the part of the Court, a manifest denial of justice, or unusual delay, or evident violation of the principles of international law'.

Also, in order to avoid forcible self-help, the Conference accorded the *Treaty of Arbitration for Pecuniary Claims* (ibid 100–04), that was later confirmed in the Third Conference (ibid 132–33). In this treaty, the parties agreed to 'submit to arbitration all claims for pecuniary loss or damage which may be presented by their respective citizens' (Art 1), and in particular 'to submit [them] to the decision of the Permanent Court of Arbitration' (Art 2).

During the Third Conference (1906), a *Resolution on Public Debts* was issued that recommended the invitation to the 'the Second Peace Conference, at The Hague, to examine the question of the compulsory collection of public debts, and, in general tending to diminish between Nations conflicts having an exclusively pecuniary origin'. As will be seen below, that Conference at The Hague ended up producing the Porter Convention (ibid 135–36).

The Fourth Conference (1910) included another *Convention on Pecuniary Claims* (ibid 183–85), which gave jurisdiction to the Permanent Court of Arbitration over 'all claims for pecuniary loss or damage which may be presented by their respective citizens and which cannot be amicably adjusted through diplomatic channels' (ibid 184). In the Sixth Conference (1928), a *Convention on the Status of Aliens* was concluded, but, in an exception, did not contain any provision embodying the Calvo Doctrine.

[90] Freeman, n 10, 466 explains the US position in this Conference: 'This resolution was unanimously adopted, not excepting the United States whose acquiescence was probably stimulated by the proviso that "should no agreement on said difference be reached through diplomatic channels, within a reasonable period of time, the matter shall be referred to arbitration" '.

[91] FV García-Amador, 1 *The Inter-American System. Treaties, Conventions and Other Documents* (New York, Oceana, 1983) 82.

The first was the *Convention Respecting the Limitation of the Employment of Force for the Recovery of Contract Debts*—the so-called Porter Convention[92]—concluded at the Second Hague Conference in 1907 (known also as the Second International Peace Conference).[93] According to this Treaty, the use of forcible self-help in the collection of 'contracts debts' was limited to cases in which the involved country did not want to avail itself of arbitration.[94] The second was the *General Treaty for the Renunciation of War* of 1928 (Kellogg-Briand Pact).[95] The third, and most important, was the UN Charter (1945), which finally banned definitively and unconditionally, the use of force for protecting property of aliens abroad.[96]

With the progressive retirement of military self-help, the confrontation between the North and the South became more theoretical than political, as independence and sovereignty were no longer directly threatened. While the central legal conflict between national treatment and IMS was far from over, now, having less at stake, developing countries could defend their position with greater strength, and paralyse all international attempts to produce substantive norms on state responsibility for damage to aliens.

[92] The name refers to General Porter, the US representative, who presented the proposition that ultimately gave birth to the treaty. See A Pearce Higgins, *The Hague Peace Conferences and Other International Conferences Concerning the Laws and Usages of War* (Cambridge, CUP, 1909) 188 ff.

[93] See 1 Scott, n 19, 386–422, and George Winfield Scott's, 'Hague Convention Restricting the Use of Force to Recover Contract Claims' (1908) 2 *American Journal of International Law* 78.

[94] For the text of the *Convention Respecting the Limitation of the Employment of Force for the Recovery of Contracts Debt*, *see* 2 Scott, n 20, 356–62. It may also be found reprinted in (1908) 2 *American Journal of International Law Supp* 1 ff. Art 1 of the Porter Convention, ibid 82, establishes that: 'The contracting powers agree not to have recourse to armed force for the recovery of contracts debts claimed from the government of one country by the government of another country as being due to its nationals. This undertaking is, however, only applicable when the debtor states refuses or neglects to reply to an offer of arbitration, or, after accepting the offer, prevents any 'compromis' from being agreed, or, after the arbitration, fails to submit to the award'.

The French version is clearer: '*Les Puissances contractantes sont convenues de nes pas avoir recours à la force armée le recouvrements de dettes contractuelles réclamées au Gouvernement d'un pays par le Gouvernement d'un autre pays comme dues à ses nationaux. Toutefois, cette stipulation ne pourra être appliquée quand l'Etat débiteur refuse ou laisse sans réponse une offre d'arbitrage, ou, en case d'accèptation, rend impossible l'éstablissement du compromis, ou, après l'arbitrage, manque de se conformer à la sentence rendue*'.

[95] The two relevant Articles of this Convention agreed upon in Paris on 27 August 27 1928, reprinted in (1928) 22 *American Journal of International Law Supp* 171 ff, are the following: 'Article I: The High Contracting Parties solemnly declare in the names of their respective peoples that they condemn recourse to war for the solution of international controversies, and renounce it, as an instrument of national policy in their relations with one another. Article II: The High Contracting Parties agree that the settlement or solution of all disputes or conflicts of whatever nature or of whatever origin they may be, which may arise among them, shall never be sought except by pacific means'.

[96] See Art 2.3 of the *Charter of the United Nations* (adopted 26 June 1945, entered into force 24 October 1945) 59 Stat 1031, TS 993, 3 Bevans 1153: 'All members shall settle their international disputes by peaceful means in such a manner that international peace and security, and justice, are not endangered . . . All Members shall refrain in their international relations from the threat or use of force against the territorial integrity or political independence of any state, or in any other manner inconsistent with the Purposes of the United Nations'.

And, indeed, many efforts were made to reach an agreement in this area of the law. Two such attempts, conducted under the auspices of the League of Nations, deserve special attention. The first, the failed Draft Convention on the Treatment of Foreigners, was expressly inspired by the 'equitable treatment' principle recognised in Article 23(e) of the Covenant of the League of Nations:

> Subject to and in accordance with the provisions of international conventions existing or hereafter to be agreed upon, the Members of the League: . . . (e) will make provision to secure and maintain freedom of communications and of transit and *equitable treatment* for the commerce of all Members of the League. In this connection, the special necessities of the regions devastated during the war of 1914–1918 shall be borne in mind. (emphasis added)[97]

In 1921, the League of Nations passed a Resolution, directing its Economic Committee to 'consider and report upon the meaning and scope of the provision relating to equitable treatment of commerce contained in Article 23(e) of the Covenant'.[98] Then, the following year, the Economic Committee reported four areas to be covered under the norm, three relating to trade matters—unfair competition, customs issues, and unjust discrimination regarding goods or ships—and one relating to what we would refer to today as 'investment': 'The application by any Member of the League of unjust or oppressive treatment in fiscal or other matters to the nationals, firms or companies of other Members of the League exercising their commerce, industry or other occupation in its territories'.[99]

[97] The Covenant entered into force 10 January 1920 (available at www.yale.edu/lawweb/avalon/leagcov.htm. See Theodore Kill, 'Don't Cross the Streams: Past and Present Overstatement of Customary International Law in Connection with Conventional Fair and Equitable Treatment Obligations' (2008) 106 *Michigan Law Review* 853, 859.

[98] League of Nations. *Report presented to the Assembly from the Economic and Financial Organisation in accordance with the Council's resolution of September 16th 1922* (Official No A.59.1922.II.(EFS342b)(EF103b)) in League of Nations, *League of Nations Publications: II: Economic and Financial* (1922) 13.

[99] ibid 14. Also, ibid 16, the Committee explained its understanding of this aspect of Art 23(e) of the Covenant, which implicitly reveals the North–South conflict: 'The Committee realise that this subject is a very wide one and naturally divides itself into two parts, both of great importance: (1) The regime to be applied to foreign persons and organisations who have been duly admitted by law to carry on their occupation within the territories of a State; (2) The conditions governing the admission of such persons and organisations to carry on their occupation in another State. The Committee are strongly of opinion that the principle of equitable treatment ought to apply in both cases. They have so far found it impracticable in the present political and economic conditions of the world to formulate any general rule applicable to the second branch of the subject, namely, the conditions of admission, which they could recommend for general adoption, without such important and numerous exceptions as to deprive the rule of all practical value. They have therefore confined their attention exclusively to the first heading and have endeavoured to formulate principles which should be observed in the treatment of persons, firms and companies from arbitrary fiscal treatment and unjust discrimination. In the course of this examination the Economic Committee have encountered many difficulties, mainly of a technical character, which required a wider and more detailed enquiry to solve. While, therefore, they are agreed as to the general principles

Six years later, in 1928, the same Economic Committee produced the Draft Convention on the Treatment of Foreigners,[100] a document carefully discussed at the International Conference on Treatment of Aliens, held in Paris between 5 November and 5 December 1929.[101] However, because this Draft Convention did not go beyond the principle of national treatment—Articles 1, 2, 3, 4, 6, 7, 9, 10 and 11, for instance, adopted the national treatment standard[102]—and even fell short of that treatment—as in the case of Article 7(2), which permitted important exceptions to it—the proposed text was not adopted.[103]

At the same time, the League of Nations also tried to produce a treaty on the topic as part of a series of efforts to codify international law, but to no avail.[104] First, from 1925 to 1928, a Committee of Experts worked to systematise several areas of international law. In the field of state responsibility for damages to aliens, it produced a Report, which was prepared by the great jurist from El Salvador and later Judge of the PCIJ, José Gustavo Guerrero (the so-called Guerrero Report).[105] In 1929, a Preparatory

which should guide Members of the League in respect of the above mentioned matters, they have been compelled with regret to postpone the submission of a definitive recommendation for practical action until they are in possession of the further detailed information they are now taking steps to collect. They hope, however, to be able to frame a definite proposal on the subject at an early date'.

[100] League of Nations, Economic Committee, 'Draft Convention on the Treatment of Foreigners' (Official No C.174.M.153.1928.II), in League of Nations, *League of Nations Publications: II: Economic and Financial* (1928) 14–37.

[101] League of Nations. *Proceedings of the International Conference on Treatment of Foreigners. First Session, Paris, November 5th—December 5th, 1929* (1930) (Official No C.97.M.23.1930.II). In the First Plenary Meeting held in Paris on 5 November 1929, the President of the Conference, M Devèze, described the mission of the meeting in these terms: 'The preparatory studies of which our Conference is the fruit owe their inception to Article 23 of the Covenant, which lays down that the Members of the League of Nations will ensure the equitable treatment of international commerce in their countries. This text would remain a dead letter if the nationals of the State Members did not enjoy the most extensive guarantees in foreign countries as regards their private rights and economic activities . . . Our ideal will be to elaborate a stable contractual system based on law and equity and embodying the minimum guarantees which will henceforward constitute a charter for foreigners and for international trade'.

[102] In this Draft Convention, even compensation for expropriation was subject to national treatment (see Art 11(5)). According the Economic Committee's official commentaries, n 100, 29, 'the principle of national treatment was finally adopted by the Economic Committee and embodied in the clause contained in Article 11'.

[103] According to Edwin M Borchard, '"Responsibility of States," at the Hague Codification Conference' (1930) 24 *American Journal of International Law* 517, 538, 'the proposed Convention of Paris, November, 1929, . . . broke down on the issue of equality . . . because, it is understood, it would not concede equality to foreigners in municipal law'.

[104] See Green H Hackworth, 'Responsibility of States for Damages Caused in Their Territory to the Person or Property of Foreigners. The Hague Conference for the Codification of International Law' (1930) 24 *American Journal of International Law* 500, 500 ('It was, however, left for the League of Nations to launch upon a world-wide effort to place in code form those rules which are regarded as the body of law').

[105] See Guerrero Report, League of Nations, 'Report of the Sub-Committee of the Committee of Experts for the Progressive Codification of International Law' (1926) 20 *American Journal of International Law Spec Supp* 177, 182. For the history, minutes and documents of this Committee

Committee drew up the 'Bases for Discussion', which included 31 Bases on the topic of 'Responsibility of States for Damages caused in their Territory to the Person or Property of Foreigners'.[106]

Those Bases were later discussed at The Hague Codification Conference held from 13 March to 12 April 1930.[107] However, the Third Committee of the Conference—which was charged with producing a draft on state responsibility for damages to aliens—failed to reach an agreement.[108] As expected, Latin America and other developing countries[109] strongly defended the principle of national treatment and the Calvo Doctrine.[110] In this regard, the Guerrero Report played a key role in articulating the position of capital importing countries' at the Conference (according to Borchard, this Report was one of the key causes of the Conference's failure[111]). Among its main assertions, one can find a clear defense of the national treatment standard:

> [I]t [international law] does not thereby recognise the right to claim for the foreigner more favourable treatment than is accorded to nationals. The maximum that may be claimed for a foreigner is civil equality with nationals . . . [A] State

of Experts, see Shabtai Rosenne (ed), *League of Nations. Committee of Experts for the Progressive Codification of International Law [1925–1928]* (Dobbs Ferry, NY, Oceana, 1972).

[106] See League of Nations, 'Conference for the Codification of International Law: III: Responsibility of States for Damages caused in their Territory to the Person or Property or Foreigners' (Official Document No C.75.M.69.1929.V), in Shabtai Rosenne (ed), 2 *League of Nations Conference for the Codification of International Law [1930]* (Dobbs Ferry, NY, Oceana, 1975) 423–702.

[107] See its history, minutes and documents in Rosenne, n 106 (4 vols). The two representatives of the US, Green H Hackworth and Edwin M Borchard of the Committee on Responsibility of States, reported their observations in two articles published by the American Journal of International Law. See Hackworth, n 104, and Borchard, n 103.

[108] Because of the lack of two thirds majority required to reach an agreement, the Committee on Responsibility of States—the Third Committee—was unable to complete its work, and therefore, no report was sent to the Conference. For the minutes of the Third Committee, see 4 Rosenne, n 106, 1427–61.

[109] The Latin American countries—Brazil, Chile, Uruguay, Colombia, Cuba, Nicaragua, Mexico, and El Salvador—were joined by China, the Free City of Danzig, Hungary, Persia, Poland, Portugal, Rumania, Czechoslovakia, Turkey and the Kingdom of Yugoslavia.

[110] For example, in its general observations submitted in relation to the Bases of Discussion, Chile—who clearly supported the Calvo Doctrine—noted that: '[I]t is inadmissible and impossible to reach conclusions which would grant more favourable treatment to foreigners than to nationals. When institutions of the State place foreigners on the same footing as nationals in respect of individual guarantees, the acquisition and enjoyment of civil rights, and the right to bring judicial actions before the courts of the country—as is the case in Chile—actions for damages which foreigners may desire to bring against the State, its officials or private individuals, should be brought by these before the competent national authority, and claims through the diplomatic channel are only allowable in the case of a denial of justice'. (2 Rosenne, n 106, 433).

See also, Borchard, n 103, 537–38, who thought that: '[Developing countries] insistence upon a categorical rule that equality of treatment with nationals was, presumably, the maximum that an alien could demand, moved seventeen nations to vote against the due diligence rule as framed, and ultimately served to prevent that two-third vote without which a convention could not be concluded'.

[111] See Borchard, n 103, 517.

> owes nothing more than that to foreigners, and any pretension to the contrary would be inadmissible and unjust both morally and juridically.[112]

The capital exporting countries, meanwhile, were no less organised. They arrived at the Conference with a complete draft prepared by Harvard Law School, which, of course, supported IMS.[113] The following provisions of the Harvard Draft provide a useful overview of these standards, including the definition of state responsibility in accordance with international law,[114] the imposition of minimum standards regarding government conduct— ie, *direct responsibility*—and the 'duty of diligence' regarding the conduct of private individuals—ie, *indirect responsibility*:

> Article 2: The responsibility of a state is determined by international law or treaty, anything in its national law, in the decisions of its national courts, or in its agreements with aliens, to the contrary notwithstanding.
>
> Article 4: A state has a duty to maintain governmental organization adequate, under normal conditions, for the performance of its obligations under international law and treaties . . .
>
> Article 10: A State is responsible if an injury to an alien results from its failure to exercise due diligence to prevent the injury, if local remedies have been exhausted without adequate redress for such failure. The diligence required may vary with the private or public character of the alien and the circumstances of the case.

Such radical divergence between national treatment and IMS made the goal of codifying state responsibility utterly impossible to achieve.[115] As Green Hackworth, the US representative to the Conference, noted, '[o]ne would perhaps not be accused of extravagance of expression if he suggested that a more difficult subject could hardly have been selected for the first Codification Conference'.[116]

The result was that, by the 1940s, developing countries had effectively resolved the primary obstacle of forcible self-help, as well as the secondary problem of arbitration as a last-resort alternative to military interventions. Moreover, they accomplished this without having agreed to any general substantive norm of state responsibility for injuries to aliens, prolonging the irremediable clash between the national standard and IMS. Not

112 See Guerrero Report, n 105, 182.

113 Harvard Law School (Research in International Law Series), *The Law of Responsibility of States for Damage Done in Their Territory to the Person or Property of Foreigners* (Harvard Law School, Cambridge 1929). This Draft can also be found at (1929) 23 *American Journal of International Law Spec Supp* 133.

114 Note that, as Borchard, n 64, 447, explains, '[i]f it is true that the doctrine of equality is the final test of international responsibility, then the source of international responsibility lies in municipal law'. See also, ibid 452.

115 According to Borchard, n 103, 538, 'the proposed Hague Convention on the international responsibility of states arising out of injuries to foreigners . . . broke down on the issue of equality . . . because equality under all circumstances was not deemed by the majority sufficient'.

116 Hackworth, n 107, 516.

surprisingly, arbitration involving state responsibility substantially decreased in the worldwide after the 1940s, and even earlier in Latin America.[117] The reason for this is obvious: without the threat of military intervention, developing countries no longer accepted arbitration as a dispute resolution mechanism. In Vagts' words, '[w]hen the pressure exerted by one state upon another does not involve the use of armed force, the degree of consensus is appreciably lower'.[118]

In consequence, after more than a hundred years of collective efforts by developing countries, diplomatic protection was finally on the ropes. In 1940, the Yale Law School Professor of international law and author of the most complete work ever on diplomatic protection, Edwin Borchard, wrote that '[w]hile at times diplomatic protection in the hands of dominant powers has oppressed weak states, I venture to say that the shoe is now on the other foot'.[119]

III FROM THE CALVO DOCTRINE TO EXPROPRIATION WITHOUT COMPENSATION

This section explores the stance adopted by developing countries during the twentieth century, particularly after the Cold War. This new stance can be summarised in the idea of expropriation without compensation. With the elimination of military self-help, developing countries began to fight for new substantive rules of state responsibility in international law, leaving behind the traditional national standard espoused during the nineteenth century.

We should recall that Latin America advanced and achieved the prohibition of forcible self-help *before* the Cold War's polarisation of the world. The efforts leading to this outcome were rooted in a *regional* concern, not in an ideological stance of any kind. Of course, everything changed with the Cold War. Although the First World War had already marked the beginning of a general abandonment of liberalism and laissez faire,[120] the Cold War 'deformed the traditional international law that had developed

[117] See Clive Parry, 'Some Considerations upon the Protection of Individuals in International Law' in Académie de Droit International, 90 *Recueil des Cours—1956-III* (Leyde, Sijthoff, 1957) 653, 659–60, and Lillich, n 8, 7–8.

[118] Detlev F Vagts, 'Coercion and Foreign Investment Rearrangements' (1978) 72 *American Journal of International Law* 17, 28. See also, Lillich, n 8, 8 (noting that because developing states 'now no longer need contemplate the possibility of being subjected to coercive measures at the end of the diplomatic protection continuum, they naturally have less incentive than in the past to agree to submit such claims to third-party adjudication').

[119] Borchard, n 64, 449.

[120] According to Georg Schwarzenberger, 'The Province and Standards of International Economic Law' (1948) 2 ILQ 402, 403: 'The turning point, however, was the first World War. Then the picture changed rapidly. The disequilibrium caused by the war, the problems of reparations and inter-Allied debt, the growth of economic nationalism and protectionist and last, but certainly not least, the general trend towards control by the State of activities formerly reserved to the individual, deeply affected national and international economies'.

over centuries to facilitate and regulate political, economic and other human relationships across national boundaries'.[121] As Dawson and Head explain, '[the] international legal order, which had developed in the late nineteenth century and had survived well into the twentieth century was destroyed forever by the emergence after the World War II of the two rival superpowers—the United States and the Soviet Union'.[122]

In this new world order, developing countries rapidly and radically changed their expectations concerning the standards of protection to property of aliens, carrying to extremes their previously moderate positions. Beyond defending national treatment against IMS, they moved to significantly alter the substantive law of expropriations. At this point, the standard pursued became the compensation that the state deems appropriate, or more simply, 'expropriation without compensation'.

For example, Mexico famously defended the principle of expropriation without compensation against the US, in a note written on August 3, 1938 (that is, shortly before the Cold War). In that note, the Government of Mexico contested the United States's claim to compensation for land belonging to US citizens, that had been expropriated since 1927:

> My Government maintains, on the contrary, that there is in international law no rule universally accepted in theory nor carried out in practice, which makes obligatory the payment of immediate compensation nor even of deferred compensation, for expropriations of a general and impersonal character like those which Mexico has carried out for the purpose of redistribution of the land.[123]

The famous letter by the US Secretary of State Cordell Hull, which is the origin of the Hull Rule, was written in response to that statement.[124] This demonstrate that the rule of 'prompt, adequate, and effective compensation', which according to many commentators reflected customary international law at the time,[125] had to be formally defended through

[121] W Michael Reisman, 'International Law after the Cold War' (1990) 84 *American Journal of International Law* 859, 860.

[122] Dawson and Head, n 27, 31. See also, García-Amador, n 74, 26.

[123] 'Translation of note from the Minister of Foreign Affairs of Mexico to the American Ambassador at Mexico City (August 3, 1938)' (1938) 32 *American Journal of International Law Supp* 186, 186.

[124] 'The Secretary of State of the United States (Cordell Hull) to Mexican Ambassador at Washington DC' (1938) 32 *American Journal of International Law Supp* 181 ff.

[125] See Rudolf Dolzer, 'New Foundations of the Law of Expropriation of Alien Property' (1981) 75 *American Journal of International Law* 553, 558–59, citing cases in proof of that assertion. See also, Alexander P Farichi, 'International Law and the Property of Aliens' (1929) 10 *British Ybk of Intl Law* 32, 55, who after reviewing several international law cases of the 19th and 20th centuries, concluded that: '[I]t is a general rule of international law that if a state expropriates the physical property of an alien without the payment of full compensation commits a wrong of which the state of the alien affected is entitled to complain, even if the measure of expropriation applies indiscriminately to nationals and aliens'. But see, John Fischer Williams, 'International Law and the Property of Aliens' (1928) 9 *British Ybk of Intl Law* 1, 28, concluding that 'where no treaty or other contractual or quasi-contractual obligation exists by which a state is bound in its relations to foreign owners of property, no general principal of international law compels it not to expropriate except on terms of paying full or "adequate" compensation'.

diplomatic channels for the first time only in 1938, 106 years after the first appearance of the Calvo Doctrine in Andrés Bello's *Derecho de Jentes* (1832).

As Lillich explains, in the second half of the twentieth century, all discussions of minimum standards and the national standard turned out, in reality, to be about expropriation and compensation, and nothing more.[126] Thus, the *classic* claim—the nineteenth century Calvo Doctrine, whose aim had not been to erode the rule of law but to terminate forcible self-help through national treatment—was transmuted into a new and *opportunistic* one: expropriation without compensation.

The new claim was *opportunistic* in the sense of being strategic. Expropriation without compensation dovetailed perfectly with the cycle of nationalisations that developing countries were facing between the 1950s and 1970s.[127] Such a standard minimised the costs of any nationalisation programs being carried out or planned for launch in the near future. Yet, in Latin America, that claim was inconsistent with the nineteenth century republican legal tradition—including the legal thought of Andres Bello[128]—and even with the pre-republican Spanish law tradition. The latter not only speaks to the roots of Latin American legal history, but was also positive law in many of these countries throughout the nineteenth century. This included the famous *Las Siete Partidas* (written between 1256 and 1265),[129] a text that contained explicit rules of expropriation by the king and the compensation due in favour of his subjects:

> *Otrosi dezimos, que quando el Emperador quisiesse tomar heredamiento, o alguna otra cosa a algunos para si, o para darla a otro; como quier que el sea Señor de todos los del Imperio, para ampararlos de fuerza, e para mantenerlos en Justicia, con todo esso non*

[126] See Richard B Lillich, 'Duties of states regarding the civil rights of aliens' in Académie de Droit International, 161 *Recueil des Cours. Collected Courses of The Hague Academy of International Law, 1978-III* (Alphen aan den Rijn, Sijthoff and Noordhoff, 1980) 329, 364–65, and 368–69.

[127] See eg B.A Wortley, *Expropriation in Public International Law* (Cambridge, CUP, 1959) 58–71; Subhash C Jain, *Nationalization of Foreign Property: A Study in North–South Dialogue* (Deep and Deep, New Delhi 1983) 231–41; Stephen J Kobrin, 'Foreign Enterprise and Forced Divestments in LCDs' (1980) 34 *International Organization* 65; and, Amy L Chua, 'The Privatization-Nationalization Cycle: The Link Between Markets and Ethnicity in Developing Countries' (1995) 95 *Columbia Law Review* 223.

[128] See eg, the Chilean Statute of Expropriation of August 14, 1838, surely written by Mariano Egaña under the influence of Andrés Bello, in Ricardo Anguita, 1 *Leyes Publicadas en Chile desde 1810 hasta el 1o de junio de 1912* (Santiago de Chile, Imprenta Barcelona, 1912) 312: '*Artículo 1.° La espropiacion por causa de utilidad pública, a que hubiere lugar, con arreglo a lo dispuesto en el número 5, art. 12 de la Constitucion, solo podrá llevarse a efecto por decreto de la autoridad judicial . . . Art 3.° El juez dispondrá que se proceda en efecto a la tasación, nombrándose para ella por cada una de las partes un tasador, i un tercero para el caso de discordia. Art 4.° No aviniéndose el propietario ni el comprador en el nombramiento del tercero, lo hará el juez de oficio, nombrando a un perito de notoria buena reputación . . . Art 5.° Declarado por el juez el legítimo valor de la especie, con arreglo a la tasación, decretará que éste se cubra por el comprador, i sin su previo y entero cubierto, no mandará dar posesión a éste de la especie sobre que ha recaído la expropiación, a menos que intervenga consentimiento expreso del propietario*'.

[129] See *Las Siete Partidas* in *Los Códigos Españoles Concordados y Anotados* (Madrid, Imprenta de la Publicidad, 1848).

puede el tomar a ninguno de lo suyo sin su plazer, si non fiziesse tal cosa, porque lo deuiesse perder segund ley. E si por auentura gelo oviesse a tomar por razon que el que el Emperador oviesse menester de fazer alguna cosa en ello, que se tornasse a pro comunal de la tierra, tenudo es por derecho de le dar ante buen cambio, que va a tanto a mas, de guisa que el fin que pagado a bien vista de omes buenos.[130]

The claim here is not that what was good in the past would be good in the present or in the future. The point is only to emphasise the very real difference between the Calvo Doctrine and 'expropriation without compensation', in order to show that the Hull Rule is not foreign to the Spanish rule of law that had applied in the region ever since Columbus discovered it in 1491.

As is well known, the new standard of expropriation without compensation was part of a broader agenda, the *new international economic order* (NIEO), that capital importing countries pursued during the second half of the twentieth century.[131] The history of NIEO is well documented in international law, so it will not be repeated here.[132] The important thing to note here is that during the 1960s, developing countries intensified their efforts to implement their values and perspectives. The turning point came in 1973, when the General Assembly adopted Resolution 3171 on Permanent Sovereignty over Natural Resources (17 December 1973),[133]

[130] Partida 2a, Tit I, Ley II, in 2 ibid 320. See also, Partida 3a, Tit. XVIII, Ley XXXI in 3 ibid 200: '*Contra derecho natural non deue dar priuillejo, nin carta, Emperador ni Rey, ni otro Señor. E si la diere, non deue valer: e contra derecho natural seria, si diessen por priuillejo las cosas de un ome a otro, non auiendo fecho cosa, por que los deuiessen perder aquel cuyas eran. Fueras ende, si el Rey las ouiesse menester, por fazer dellas, o en ellas alguna lauor, o como si fuesse alguna heredad, en que oviessen a fazer castillo, o torre, o puente, o alguna otra cosa semajante destas, que tornasse a pro, o a amparamiento de todos, o de algun lugar señaladamente. Pero estos deuen fazer en una destas dos maneras: dandole cambio por ello primeramente, o comprandozelo segun que valiere*'.

See also, F Clemente de Diego, 'Notas sobre la evolución doctrinal de la expropiación forzosa por causa de utilidad pública. Glosadores y Postglosadores' (1922) 9 *Revista de Derecho Privado* 289 ff (1922) (studying expropriation and due compensation in Middle Age's legal culture), and Gaspar Ariño Ortiz, 'Derechos del Rey, Derechos del Pueblo' in Instituto de Estudios Administrativos, *Actas del II Symposium Historia de la Administración* (Madrid, Instituto de Estudios Administrativos, 1971) 41 (analysing expropriation in the *Siete Partidas*).

[131] According to Dolzer, n 125, 556, 'expropriation is in many corners considered to be the (symbolic or real) central issue in the struggle for a new international economic order'.

[132] See eg Rosalyn Higgins, 'The Taking of Property by the State. Recent Developments in International Law' in Académie de Droit International, 176 *Recueil des Cours. Collected Courses of the Hague Academy of International Law, 1982-III* (The Hague, M Nijhoff, 1983) 259, 279–97; see Dolzer, n 125, 553; Detlev F Vagts, 'Foreign Investment Risk Reconsidered: The View from the 1980s' (1980) 2 *Foreign Investment Law Journal* 1; Ian Brownlie, 'Legal Status of Natural Resources in International Law (Some Aspects)' in Académie de Droit International, 162 *Recueil des Cours. Collected Courses of the Hague Acadamy of International Law* (Alphen aan den Rijn, Sijthoff and Noordhoff, 1980) 244, 255–71; and Nico Schrijver, *Sovereignty Over Natural Resources: Balancing Rights and Duties* (New York, CUP, 1997) 82 ff.

[133] GA Res 3171, UN GAOR, 28th Sess, Supp 30, at 52, UN Doc. A/9030 (1974) reprinted in (1974) 13 ILM 238: '[T]he application of the principle of nationalization carried out by States, as an expression of their sovereignty in order to safeguard their natural resources, implies that each State is entitled to determine the amount of possible compensation and the mode of payment, and that any dispute which might arise should be settled in accordance with the national legislation of each State carrying out such measures'.

and one year later with the adoption of the Charter of Economic Rights and Duties of States (12 December 1974) (*CERDS*).[134]

At the same time, to no one's surprise, efforts to codify the law governing state responsibility for injuries to aliens, which continued under the auspices of the United Nations, completely failed to produce an acceptable document. The process that ultimately gave birth to the International Law Commission's (ILC) Draft Articles on State Responsibility in 2002 is a long and detailed one, and has been described elsewhere.[135] I will only provide a short summary, stressing those aspects that are relevant from the perspective of damage to aliens.

This history begins with the General Assembly Resolution 799 (VIII) of 7 December 1953, which ordered the ILC to initiate the task of codifying the field of state responsibility. Its first Special Rapporteur, the Cuban jurist FV Garcia-Amador, tried to obtain state consent on 'primary rules' of behaviour, that is, on rules of state responsibility *regarding* injuries suffered by aliens to their persons or property. Garcia-Amador's project was based on the idea of 'minimum standards', but this time rooted in human rights norms. Notwithstanding his efforts to develop a relevant treaty based on this philosophy of 'noble synthesis'[136]—ie, an amalgam of national treatment and IMS[137]—his draft failed to obtain the consent of developing countries.

[134] Art 2(2)(c) of the Charter of Economic Rights and Duties of States, GA Res 3281, UN GAOR, UN Doc A/9631 (1975), reprinted *in* (1975) 14 ILM 251, establishes that compensation should be 'appropriate' according to the 'domestic law of the nationalizing State and by its tribunals'. For the developed world explanation of CERDS and its impact in international law, see Burns H Weston, 'The Charter of Economic Rights and Duties and the Deprivation of Foreign Owned Wealth' (1981) 75 *American Journal of International Law* 437, and Charles N Brower and John B Tepe Jr, 'The Charter of Economic Rights and Duties of States: A Reflection or Rejection of International Law?' (1975) 9 *International Lawyer* 295, and Andres Rozental, 'The Charter of Economic Rights and Duties of States and the New International Economic Order' (1976) *Virginia Journal of International Law* 309.

[135] See James Crawford (ed), *The International Law Commission's Articles on State Responsibility: Introduction, Text, and Commentaries* (Cambridge, CUP, 2002); Y Matsui, 'The Transformation of the Law of State Responsibility' (1993) 20 *Thesaurus Acroasium* 5 ff; Shabtai Rosenne (ed), *The International Law Commission's Draft Articles on State Responsibility* (M Nijhoff, Boston 1991); and Marina Spinedi and Bruno Simma (eds), *United Nations Codification of State Responsibility* (New York, Oceana, 1987). A summary and table of contents for all actions and documents may be found at http://untreaty.un.org/ilc/guide/9_6.htm.

[136] Garcia-Amador's Draft Articles and Reports, with some minor changes, can be found in Garcia-Amador, n 46.

[137] See Garcia-Amador, n 46, 5: 'Now, both the "international standard of justice" and the principle of equality between nationals and aliens, hitherto considered as antagonistic and irreconcilable, can well be reformulated and integrated into a new legal rule incorporating the essential elements and serving the main purpose of both. The basis of this new principle would be the "universal respect for, and observance of, human rights and fundamental freedoms" referred to in the Charter of the United Nations and in other general, regional and bilateral instruments'.

Simultaneously, the Director of the Codification Division of the Office of Legal Affairs of the United Nations 'suggested'[138] to the Harvard Law School the production of a Draft Agreement on the matter. Between 1959–1961, under the direction of Louis Sohn and Richard Baxter, a Commission produced several versions of a draft entitled 'Convention on the International Responsibility of States for Injuries to Aliens'.[139] Not surprisingly, this Draft Convention recognised rules and principles in accordance with IMS.

From 1969 to 1979, the Italian professor Roberto Ago succeeded García-Amador in the task of codifying state responsibility as Special Rapporteur. His strategy was radically different from that of his predecessor. He sought to 'reconceptualise' the field, setting aside the primary rules of state responsibility for the treatment of aliens, in order to focus exclusively on general and abstract rules of responsibility, particularly those known as 'secondary rules'. These rules dealt with the nature and consequences of breaches to international obligations, across all branches of international law. As a result, the more specific topics of diplomatic protection, as well as damages to aliens and their property, were abandoned to the murky waters of customary international law.[140]

Even these abstract and general principles would encounter a winding road ahead. After forty-five years of debate, the General Assembly of the United Nations in its 85th plenary meeting held on 12 December 2001, *took note* and *welcomed* the Articles that had been prepared by Ago and later completed by Willem Riphagen, Gaetano Arangio-Ruiz and James Crawford.[141] However useful these Articles are in general terms, they did not resolve (nor did they even attempt to resolve) the long-standing conflict between national treatment and IMS. As indicated earlier, they are abstract and doctrinaire in character, and contain nothing in the way of primary rules for state behaviour regarding injuries to aliens.[142]

[138] According to Louis B Sohn and RR Baxter, 'Final Draft with Explanatory Notes. Convention on the International Responsibility of States for Injuries to Aliens', in FV Garcia-Amador, Louis B Sohn and RR Baxter (eds), *Recent Codification of the Law of State Responsibility for Injuries to Aliens* (Dobbs Ferry Oceana Publications, 1974) 133, 135, '[t]his draft Convention was prepared at the suggestion of Dr. Yuen-li Liang ... [who] expressed the view that such a draft Convention would be of considerable usefulness to the International Law Commission'.

[139] ibid 135. For previous versions, see Sohn and Baxter, n 65, and Louis B Sohn and R Baxter, *Convention on the International Responsibility of States for Injuries to Aliens. Draft No 12 with Explanatory Notes* (Cambridge, Mass, Harvard Law School, 1961).

[140] In the words of Richard R Baxter, 'Reflection on Codification in Light of the International Law of State Responsibility for Injuries to Aliens' (1965) 16 *Syracuse Law Review* 745, 746, 'the Commission had decided to drop the subject of State responsibility for injuries to aliens and to take up a new and markedly different subject—the international responsibility of states in general'.

[141] GA Res 83, UN GAOR, 56th Sess, at UN Doc A/56/589 (2002).

[142] Not surprisingly, they have come under criticism from scholars such as McDougal and Lillich. Indeed, according to Myres S McDougal et al, *Human Rights and World Public Order. The Basic Policies of an International Law of Human Dignity* (New Haven, Yale University Press, 1980) 762, these Articles have been defined 'at such a high level of abstraction as to shed but

In any case, it is not an exaggeration to affirm that, by the mid-1970s, developing countries had won crucial aspects of the battle over the definition of substantive law regarding compensation in expropriations.[143] By strenuously advocating the standards embodied in NIEO, they succeeded at introducing enough confusion into the discussion that formerly accepted standards of state responsibility began to resemble unsound law.[144]

Two cases decided in the 1960s and 1970s—at two of the most important world forums—reflect the weakening status of pre-NIEO international minimum standards. In the *Barcelona Traction* case (1970), the ICJ used language that cast doubt upon classic rules and principles of international law:

> Considering the important developments of the last half-century, the growth of foreign investments and the expansion of the international activities of corporations, in particular of holding companies, which are often multinational, and considering the way in which the economic interests of States have proliferated, it may at first sight appear surprising that the evolution of law has not gone further and that no generally accepted rules in the matter have crystallized on the international plane. Nevertheless, a more thorough examination of the facts shows that the law on the subject has been formed in a period characterized by an intense conflict of systems and interests.[145]

a dim light upon specific controversies'. Similarly, Lillich, n 7, 21, notes that 'Ago's work, in marked contrast to García-Amador's, offers little or no guidance to persons concerned with fashioning a contemporary international law governing the treatment of aliens'.

[143] See Andrew T Guzman, 'Why LDCs Sign Treaties That Hurt Them: Explaining the Popularity of Bilateral Investment Treaties' (1998) 38 *Virginia Journal of International Law* 639, 651 ('[D]eveloping countries had won a clear victory. The international rules governing North–South investment were entirely uncertain and individual states were in a position to determine what constituted appropriate compensation').

[144] See eg, Dolzer, n 125, 553 ('The present state of customary international law regarding expropriation of alien property has remained obscure in its basic aspects'). See also, Mark K Neville Jr, 'The Present Status of Compensation by Foreign States for the Taking of Alien-Owned Property' (1980) 13 *Vanderbilt Journal of Transnational Law* 51, 51 (noting that 'no other exercise of the prerogatives of national sovereignty during the past two decades has proven so divisive to the community of nations or created such uncertainty in international commerce as the taking of alien investor's property by host States'); Greta Gainer, 'Nationalization: The Dichotomy Between the Western and Third World Perspectives in International Law' (1983) 26 *Howard Law Journal* 1547, 1554–55, and 1563 (stating that 'there is no global consensus on what constitutes controlling international law in this area [the standard of compensation in cases of expropriations]', including the question of 'whether the nationalizing state is obligated to compensate an alien for expropriated property'); and Oscar Schachter, 'Compensation for Expropriation' (1984) 78 *American Journal of International Law* 121, 121 (observing that no subject of international law has aroused as much debate as the question of the standard for compensation in case of expropriation).

[145] *Barcelona Traction, Light, and Power Co, Ltd* (Second Phase) (*Belgium v Spain*) [1970] ICJ Rep 3, ¶ 89. It also added, ibid, that: 'It is essentially bilateral relations which have been concerned, relations in which the rights of both the State exercising diplomatic protection and the State in respect of which protection is sought have had to be safeguarded. Here as elsewhere, a body of rules could only have developed with the consent of those concerned. The difficulties encountered have been reflected in the evolution of the law on the subject'.

See also, ibid ¶¶ 61–63, which shows how the court sympathises with rules of compensation that do not correspond to the Hull Rule, and how it disregards the jurisprudential value of previous international arbitration awards.

Even more striking, in *Sabbatino* (1964), the US Supreme Court declined, under the act of state doctrine, to review an expropriation that had occurred in Cuba, because among other reasons, '[t]here are a few if any issues in international law today on which opinion seems to be so divided as the limitations on a state's power to expropriate the property of aliens'.[146] The court then went on to say that:

> The disagreement as to relevant international law standards reflects an even more basic divergence between the national interests of capital importing and capital exporting nations and between the social ideologies of those countries that favor state control of a considerable portion of the means of production and those that adhere to a free enterprise system. It is difficult to imagine the courts of this country embarking on adjudication in an area which touches more sensitively the practical and ideological goals of the various members of the community of nations.[147]

The result of all this is that by the end of the 1970s, both the *classic* and *opportunistic* claims made by Latin American and developing countries had been successfully advanced in international law. The first half of the twentieth century witnessed the dominance of the *classic* claim, and during the second half its *opportunistic* counterpart gained enough momentum to wreak havoc on the entire question of state responsibility, by making it hopelessly ambiguous.

IV INTERNATIONAL MINIMUM STANDARDS STRIKE BACK

It was in the midst of this 'dark night' of IMS that bilateral investment treaties began to emerge like small stars, re-enacting pre-NIEO minimum standards (as defended by developed countries) on a country-by-country basis. This section explores the initial years of the BIT generation, a period the proper understanding of which is essential to grasping the essence of BITs and the protection they offer.

The first BIT was concluded between Germany and Pakistan in 1959, and the ICSID Convention came into force on 14 October 1966.[148] Both BITs and the ICSID Convention emerged against the confusing background of customary international law well-described in the previous section.[149]

[146] *Banco Nacional de Cuba v Sabbatino* (1964) 376 US 398, 428.

[147] ibid 430.

[148] It came into force after 20 countries—17 of which were developing nations, mostly African states—ratified the Convention; see Christoph H Schreuer, *The ICSID Convention: A Commentary* (New York, CUP, 2001) 1274.

[149] See Eileen Denza and Shelagh Brooks, 'Investment Protection Treaties: United Kingdom Experience' (1987) 36 ICLQ 908, 910, observing that: 'It was against this background of apparently eroding standards that the UK formulated its first Model Agreement for the Promotion and Protection of Investments. The impetus came from a White Paper published in 1971 in which the government announced its intention of preparing such a draft and

Ironically, it was precisely the relative success of NIEO that made BITs desirable:[150] both developed and developing countries now had solid reasons to adopt 'primary rules' of state responsibility on a bilateral basis.[151] In the words of a BIT Tribunal: '[t]he impressive development of BITs has been a response to the uncertainty of customary international law relating to foreign investment'.[152]

From a historical perspective, there are at least two features of BITs that tend to be overlooked in the usual recounting of the BIT generation's emergence. With respect to procedure, BITs originally relied on state-to-state arbitration as the proper means of dispute resolution. With respect to substance, BITs sought the re-enactment of classical pre-NIEO IMS (that is, IMS as espoused by developed countries).[153]

seeking negotiations with as many developing countries as possible'. See also, Jeswald W Salacuse, 'BIT by BIT: The Growth of Bilateral Investment Treaties and Their Impact on Foreign Investment in Developing Countries' (1990) 24 *International Lawyer* 655, 659 ('Not only did customary international law contain no generally accepted rules on the subject, it also lacked a binding mechanism to resolve investment disputes'); and M Sornarajah, *The International Law on Foreign Investment* (New York, CUP, 1994) 233 ('In this confused state of conflicting norms [referring to customary international law], bilateral investment treaties provided the parties with the opportunity to set out the definite norms that would apply to the investments their nationals make in each other's state').

[150] See Kenneth J Vandevelde, 'The Political Economy of a Bilateral Investment Treaty' (1998) 92 *American Journal of International Law* 621, 628. From the perspective of the US, this author comments how it was in direct response to the United Nations General Assembly debates on the measure of compensation that 'the United States launched its BIT program in 1977'. He also notes, ibid, that '[s]everal other developed states also inaugurated their programs in the 1970s. France concluded its first BIT in 1972, the United Kingdom in 1975, Austria in 1976, and Japan in 1977'. See also, Kenneth J Vandevelde, 'The Bilateral Investment Treaty Program of the United States' (1988) 21 *Cornell International Law Journal* 201, 209, and K Scott Gudgeon, 'Arbitration Provisions of US Bilateral Investment Treaties' (1985) 20 *Studies in Transnational Legal Policy* 41, 42. More recently, Thomas W Wälde, 'The "Umbrella" Clause in Investment Arbitration. A Comment on Original Intentions and Recent Cases' (2005) 6 *Journal of World Investment and Trade* 183, 198–99, has observed that: 'BIT practice can be much explained by its function to provide a legally binding alternative to the advocacy of absolute sovereignty propounded by the NIEO, its legal instruments (mainly UN General Assembly resolutions of 1974) and its proponents . . . BIT practice was then intentionally developed into an instrument to counter these NIEO positions'.

[151] See eg Herman Walker Jr, 'Treaties for the Encouragement and Protection of Foreign Investment: Present United States Practice' (1956) 5 *American Journal of Comparative Law* 229, 243 (explaining that FCN treaties—the US equivalent of BITs during the 1950s—'illustrate also the feasibilities of bilateralism').

[152] *Total SA v Argentina*, ICSID Case No ARB/04/01 (Sacerdoti, Alvarez, Herrera), Decision on Jurisdiction (25 August 2006) ¶ 78.

[153] See David Schneiderman, *Constitutionalizing Economic Globalization. Investment Rules and Democracy's Promise* (New York, CUP, 2008) 62 (commenting that '[t]he post-1989 investment rules regime signals, it is argued, the final universal acceptance of the minimum standard of treatment long espoused by capital-exporting European and European-derived legal systems'). See also, Tom Ginsburg, 'International Substitutes for Domestic Institutions: Bilateral Investment Treaties and Governance' (2005) *International Review of Law and Economics* 107, 111 (stating that BITs 'constituted an attempt, on a bilateral basis, to *restore* the Hull Rule'.) (emphasis added)

The popular conflation of BITs with investor–state arbitration—that is, the assumption that BITs, by definition, permit investors to make claims against states before international arbitral tribunals—is an erroneous generalisation.[154] After a careful survey of the dispute settlement provisions for a large proportion of BITs signed between 1959 and 1989,[155] I have classified these BITs into three groups: first, those that provide only state-to-state arbitration (state-to-state BITs); second, those that allow investors to have recourse to international arbitration for violations of any provision of the treaty (investor–state BITs); and third, those that provide investor–state arbitration, but only in relation to the amount of compensation in cases where states recognise the existence of a formal expropriation (limited investor–state BITs).[156]

State-to-state BITs were most popular during the first historical phase of BIT development. In aggregate terms, they comprised the majority of all BITs concluded until 1986 (inclusive). This proves a relatively obvious but important fact: *BITs were not designed with the purpose of giving direct cause of action to investors*. By contrast, they were intended to function in the traditional state-to-state setting of international law, including the customary rule of exhaustion of domestic remedies.

Investor-state BITs can be regarded as an historical accident, resulting from the combination of three separate institutional experiments: first, the original state-to-state BITs which provided the substantive provisions; second, the ICSID Convention, which expanded the agenda of investor–state arbitration into international investment law, albeit with concession contracts rather than treaties in mind; and third, the 1959 Abs-Shawcross Draft Convention—followed by the 1963–1967 OECD Draft Convention—whose Article 7 first mentioned investor–state arbitration in an investment treaty (though still requiring consent in a separate document).[157]

[154] See Zachary Elkins, Andrew T Guzman and Beth Simmons, 'Competing for Capital: The Diffusion of Bilateral Investment Treaties, 1960–2000' (2006) 60 *International Organization* 811, 822, noting that 'the core terms of the treaties are almost always present: mandatory dispute resolution before an international arbitration body, a private right of action for investors, monetary compensation in the event of a violation, national treatment, and most-favored-nation treatment.

[155] The source of those treaties is the UNCTAD database (available at http://www.unctadxi.org/templates/DocSearch____779.aspx). When the database was incomplete, I referred to the UN treaty series. Still, some treaties mentioned in the ICSID website's BITs lists can be found neither on the UNCTAD database nor on the UN treaty series.

[156] Only 2 treaties from this period do not fit these categories, due to the fact that they provide no dispute resolution mechanism whatsoever.

[157] The Abs-Shawcross Draft Convention, reprinted in 'The Proposed Convention to Protect Private Foreign Investment' (1960) 9 *Journal of Public Law* 115, 117. See also Art 7(b) of the *OECD Draft Convention On the Protection of Property, Adopted by the Council in its 150th Meeting on 12 October 1967* (1968) 7 ILM 117, 132–33 (the 1963 Draft can be found in (1963) 2 ILM 241), including Commentary No 7, 'Acceptance of Jurisdiction', ibid 135.

The first investor–state BIT was concluded between Gabon and Germany in 1969, and the first limited investor–state BIT between France and Morocco in 1975. Yet, as late recently as 1987, both investor–state and limited investor–state BITs (taken together) began to outnumber state-to-state BITs. The limited investor–state BITs were primarily used during the 1980s by communist countries, and peaked in 1989, a year for which they were the most popular investment treaty. Figures 1 and 2 present comprehensive data on the type of BITs concluded between 1959 and 1989.[158]

The state-to-state jurisdiction established in most BITs until the mid-1980s underscores the 'conservative' or non-innovative origin of these

Figure 1: State-to-State BITs (BITs A), Investor–State BITs (BITs B), and Limited Investor–State BITs (BITs C), By Year (1959–1989)

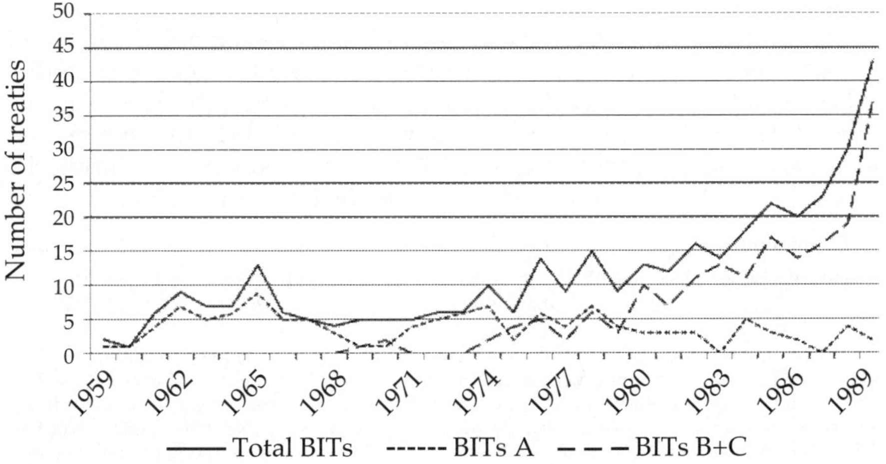

[158] See also the excellent empirical study of Jason Webb Yackee, 'Conceptual Difficulties in the Empirical Studies of Bilateral Investment Treaties', Legal Studies Research Paper No 1053, October 2007 (available at http://ssrn.com/abstract=1015088), in which the author analyses the dispute settlement provisions of nearly 1,000 BITs, observing also that '[t]he majority of BITs in force until the early- to mid-1990s were weak BITs—those containing no trace of investor-state dispute settlement provisions—and BITs with highly imperfect such provisions' (ibid 28).

Figure 2: State-to-State BITs (BITs A), and Investor–State BITs (BITs B) plus Limited Investor–State BITs (BITs C), Cumulative (1959–1989)

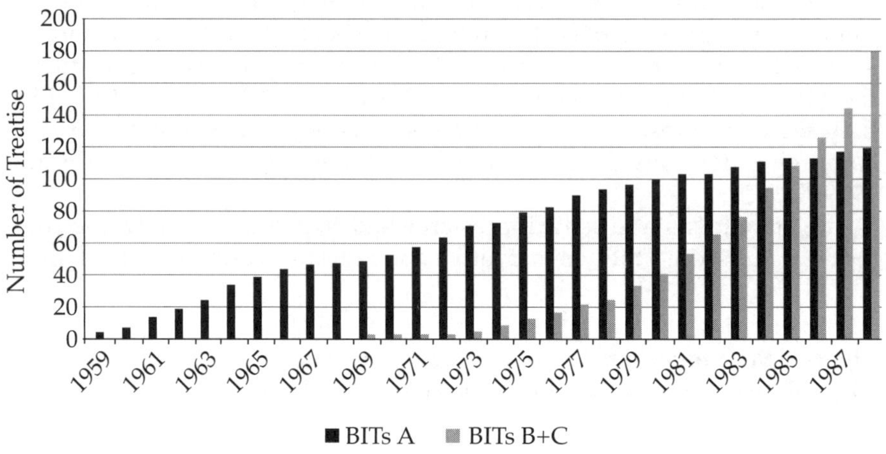

treaties.[159] It also reminds us that, from a substantive perspective, BITs did not attempt to advance anything novel, but merely to re-enact pre-NIEO IMS—including the Hull Rule, the most important provision at the time.[160] The basic *quid pro quo* was none other than IMS for an expected increase in foreign investment. Lord Shawcross, a key player during the early phase of BITs, described this 'deal' in the following terms:

> The *quid pro quo* for the borrowing States' undertakings is, in fact, in the English vernacular the provision of the 'quids,' that the capital importing countries in return for agreeing *to abide by the generally recognised procedures of International*

[159] Commentators usually infer the wrong conclusions as a consequence of believing that BITs were originally designed with investor-state dispute settlement mechanisms, particularly in the context of the IMS *v* FET debate. See eg Ioana Tudor, 'The Fair and Equitable Treatment Standard' in *The International Law of Foreign Investment* (New York, OUP, 2008) 67: 'The main problem with equalizing FET with IMS is that it limits the scope of FET. The IMS provides for action only in extreme cases. In other words, the rights of the foreign Investor have to be violated in a serious manner in order for the Investor to obtain reparation from the host State. In contrast, it appears that FET offers the foreign Investor a type of guarantee which is much more generous and designed to be operational. *Moreover, the IMS was intended to function in a State-to-State type of settlement of dispute organized around the diplomatic protection mechanism not in an Investor-State one, as it is today the case in the existing BITs and agreements*'. (emphasis added)

[160] See eg, Denza and Brooks, n 149, 911–12, explaining that in the UK BIT program the most politically sensitive provision was the expropriation clause. See also, Herman Walker Jr, 'Modern Treaties of Friendship, Commerce and Navigation' (1958) 42 *Minnesota Law Review* 805, 823, a US diplomat who, after reviewing the provisions on 'Protection of Persons and Property' contained in the sixteen FCNs concluded by the US between 1946 and 1958, noted that: '*Most importantly*, any sequestration or expropriation must be accompanied by prompt, just and effective compensation . . . This is an especially valuable right in a day when nationalizations, often entailing great losses to the private owners, has tended to become not uncommon'. (emphasis added)

Law will receive more private investment and with the capital, the benefits of the technical and commercial skills which go with them than would otherwise be the case. (emphasis added)[161]

An individual review of the original provisions proves this assertion. Because there has been a striking *de facto* convergence among BITs toward what game-theory experts call a 'non-cooperative standard',[162] the main provisions we see today in BITs first appeared, worded in closely similar terms, in the earliest German and Swiss BITs concluded between 1959 and 1961. That convergence—amplified by the effect of the MFN clause—justifies paying special attention to the original formulations that thousands of forthcoming BITs would later copy and paste.

The standards of no expropriation without compensation, national treatment, and FPS date from the 1959 Germany–Pakistan treaty (the first BIT).[163] Similarly, the most favoured nation clause (MFN) dates from the 1960 Germany–Malaysia treaty (third BIT),[164] and the fair and equitable treatment standard (FET) from the 1961 Switzerland–Tunisia treaty (seventh BIT).[165]

Yet, none of these provisions were original to those first BITs. No expropriation without compensation, including the Hull Rule, had already been the pre-NIEO customary international law rule on the matter.[166] Full protection and security—including variations such as 'protection and security' and 'the most constant protection and security'—was a recurring clause in the nineteenth century FCN treaties.[167] National treatment was nothing less than the essence of the Calvo Doctrine, and was a usual provision of the FCN treaties. Similarly, the MFN clause has a long tradition in the general history of treaties.[168]

[161] Cited by Earl Snyder, 'Protection of Foreign Investment, Examination and Appraisal' (1961) 10 ICLQ 469, 482.

[162] See ch 2, pp 90–103.

[163] See *Treaty for Promotion and Protection of Investment* (West Germany-Pakistan) (25 November 1959) 457 UNTS 23 (available at www.unctad.org/sections/dite/iia/docs/bits/germany_pakistan.pdf), Arts 1(2), 3(1), (2).

[164] See *Agreement Between the Federal Republic of Germany and the Federation of Malaysia Concerning the Promotion and Reciprocal Protection of Investments* (West Germany–Malaysia) (22 December 1960) (available at www.unctad.org/sections/dite/iia/docs/bits/germany_malaysia.pdf), Art 2(2).

[165] See *Traité entre la Confédération Suisse et la République Tunisienne relatif à la protection et à l'encouragement des investissements de capitaux* (Switzerland–Tunisia) (2 December 1961) (available at www.unctad.org/sections/dite/iia/docs/bits/switzerland_tunisia_fr.pdf). The FET standard was established here as follows: Article 1: '*Les investissements ainsi que les biens, droits et intérêts appartenant à des ressortissants, fondations, associations ou sociétés d'une des Hautes Parties Contractantes dans le territoire de l'autre bénéficieront* d'un traitement juste et équitable, *au moins égal à celui qui est reconnu par chaque Partie à ses nationaux*'. (emphasis added)

[166] See n 125.

[167] See also, Robert R Wilson, 'Property-Protection Provisions in United States Commercial Treaties' (1951) 45 *American Journal of International Law* 83, 92.

[168] ibid 94.

The case of the FET standard is no different. As previously explained, it first appeared in Article 23(e) of the League of Nations Covenants as the 'equitable treatment' standard. Then, the failed Havana Charter of 1948 incorporated a 'just and equitable treatment' into its Article 11(e), although this was not directly applicable for the protection of investors and investments.[169] Later, in 1948, the Ninth International Conference of American States, adopted the Economic Agreement of Bogotá—never ratified and subject to a significant number of reservations at the time of its signature[170]—whose Article 22 established:

> Foreign capital shall receive *equitable treatment*. The States therefore agree not to take unjustified, unreasonable or discriminatory measures that would impair the legally acquired rights or interests of nationals of other countries in the enterprises, capital, skills, arts or technology they have supplied. (emphasis added)[171]

Following the language of the League of Nations Covenant and the Economic Agreement of Bogotá, many US FCNs concluded since 1949 contained an 'equitable treatment' clause.[172] However, several other US

[169] See Art 11(2), reprinted in Clair Wilcox, *A Charter for World Trade* (New York, Macmillan Co, 1949). As Stephen Vasciannie, 'The Fair and Equitable Treatment Standard in International Investment Law and Practice' (1999) 70 British Ybk of Intl Law 99, 108, explains, '[the Havana Charter] did not itself seek to guarantee this standard of treatment for investors. Instead, it merely authorized the International Trade Organization to recommend that this standard be included in future agreements; as such, Article 11(2) was even less than a *pactum de contrahendo*'.

[170] Several countries made reservations to Chapter IV of the Economic Agreement of Bogotá—'Private Investment'—at the time of signature, including Argentina, Cuba, Ecuador, Guatemala, México, Uruguay, and Venezuela. The Mexican reservation—in Secretaría de Relaciones Exteriores (Mexicana), *Conferencias Internacionales Americanas. Segundo Suplemento 1945–1954* (México, Secretaría de Relaciones Exteriores, 1956) 169—is particularly telling: '*Reserva de la Delegación de México a los Artículos 22, 24 y 25 del Convenio Económico de Bogotá :.. 2. Aun estando de acuerdo con el espíritu de equidad en que se inspiran el párrafo tercero del artículo 22 y el primer párrafo del artículo 24, la Delegación de México hace también reserva expresa sobre sus textos, por cuanto, en la forma en que están redactados,* pudieran interpretarse como una limitación al principio según el cual los extranjeros están sujetos, como los nacionales, a las leyes y a los tribunales del país'. (emphasis added)

The excessive number of reservations to Chapter IV of this Agreement was the object of study by a special commission. See Report of the Special Commission on Reservations concerning the Economic Agreement of Bogotá (Pan American Union, Washington, 13 July 1949, Spanish original), cited by Walker, n 151, 241. Furthermore, it is worth noting that, at the time, the main focus of the discussions was the expropriation provision (Art 25). See eg Dardo Regules, *La Lucha por la Justicia y por el Derecho. Apuntes sobre la IX Conferencia reunida en Bogotá durante el mes de abril de 1948* (Montevideo, Barreiro y Ramos, 1949) 88 ('*Este tercero aspecto [expropiación y compensación] fué uno de los más debatidos en la Conferencia*'), and *Ninth International Conference of American States. Bogotá, Colombia, March 30-May 2, 1948. Report of the Delegation of the United States of America With Related Documents* (1948) 64–68.

[171] *Ninth International Conference . . .*, n 170, 207–08.

[172] See eg the *Treaty of Friendship, Commerce and Economic Development signed between the US and Uruguay* (23 November 1949). Its Art IV provided that: 'Each High Contracting Party shall at all times accord equitable treatment to the capital of nationals and companies of the other Party. Neither Party shall take unreasonable or discriminatory measures that would impair the legally acquired rights or interests of such nationals and companies in the

FCNs concluded in the same time period used the slightly different expression of 'fair and equitable treatment'.[173] Note that according to Vandevelde, counsel to the US BIT negotiating teams during the 1980s—both formulations 'equitable treatment' and 'fair and equitable treatment'—are equivalent.[174]

If the historical background is to be taken seriously, then the FET standard, when first used, could not have meant anything higher than IMS. At a time when the opposing North–South legal camps were, respectively, IMS and national treatment, the FET standard could not have referred to either an autonomous standard or to a higher standard than those minima. The League of Nations' equitable treatment standard certainly did not imply something autonomous or higher than IMS; indeed, as we have seen, the Draft Convention that was attempted under its guidance failed even to achieve the national treatment standard. Neither did US negotiators promote such a standard as part of the FCN program.[175] At best, FET originally meant IMS; at worst, something less than that.

Why, then, did negotiators use the expression 'fair and equitable treatment', instead of the more direct 'international minimum standards'?[176] From the perspective of developed countries, there were at least three

enterprises which they have established or in the capital, skills, arts or technology which they have supplied'. (Cited by Wilson, n 167, 102). See also the following FCNs concluded by the US during the 1950s: (1) Ireland (Art V), 21 January 1950, TIAS No 2185; (2) Israel (Art I), 23 August 1951, TIAS No 2948; (3) Nicaragua (Art I), 21 January 1956, TIAS No 4024; (4) France (Art I), 25 November 1959, TIAS No 4625; (5) Pakistan (Art I), 12 November 1959, TIAS No 4683.

[173] See the *Treaty of Amity and Economic Relations between the US and Ethiopia* (7 September 1951) TIAS No 2864. Its Art VIII(1) provided that: 'Each High Contracting Party shall at all times accord fair and equitable treatment to nationals and companies of the other High Contracting Party, and to their property and enterprises; shall refrain from applying unreasonable or discriminatory measures that would impair their legally acquired rights and interests; and shall assure that their lawful contractual rights are afforded effective means of enforcement, in conformity with the applicable laws'. See also the following FCNs, concluded by the US during the 1950s: (1) Germany (29 October 1954) TIAS No 3593, Art I(1); (2) Netherlands, 27 March 1953, TIAS No 3942, Art I(1); (3) Muscat and Oman, 20 December 1958, TIAS No 4530, Art IV(1).

[174] See Vandevelde, n 150, 'The Bilateral Investment . . .', 221 ('[I]nvestments of companies and nationals of the other party must be accorded "fair and equitable treatment", the equivalent of the "equitable treatment" required by the modern FCNs'). See also, United Nations Conference on Trade and Development (UNCTAD), *Fair and Equitable Treatment* (New York, United Nations, 1999) 14.

[175] According to a US diplomat, Walker, n 160, 811–12: '[T]he utility of the approach [of non-contingent or absolute standards] is in fact quite limited . . . [T]he non-contingent standard generally finds its best utility in a few context in which, no contingent standard being adequate, *some recognizable body of applicable international law and terms of art has nevertheless evolved*'. (emphasis added)

[176] In my opinion, UNCTAD, n 174, 13, puts too much emphasis on the textual dimension without giving sufficient consideration to the history of the standard: 'If States and investors believe that the fair and equitable standard is entirely interchangeable with the international minimum standard, they could indicate this clearly in their investment instruments; but most investment instruments do not make an explicit link between the two standards'.

reasons to follow this strategy: first, to avoid using such a politically loaded expression; second, to avoid specifying those standards in further detail (which would have been a deal-breaker);[177] and, third, to expand the limited scope of the nineteenth century full protection and security clause (FPS).

Indeed, the FPS clause—the traditional expression of IMS—corresponded, in essence, to the 'duty of diligence' standard. It mainly covered 'indirect responsibility', that is, failures to maintain the *ordre publique* and to properly operate the criminal law system—both main functions of the nineteenth-century *Nightwatch* State. Due to the explosive expansion of the State's activities and functions during the twentieth century, the FET clause was enacted to ensure coverage of the 'direct responsibility' dimension of IMS, which FPS tended to neglect.[178]

This identification of the FET standard with IMS is less problematic than it might seem because, at the time, IMS were also considered to be dynamic standards,[179] embodying 'nothing more nor less than the ideas which are conceived to be essential to continuation of the existing social and economic order of European capitalistic civilization'.[180] In 1940, writing on IMS, Borchard remarked upon the connection between IMS and general principles of law recognised by civilised nations—principles of indisputably evolutionary nature:

> [International law] is also composed of the uniform practices of the civilized states of the western world who gave birth and nourishment to international law. Long before article 38 of the Statute of the Permanent Court of International Justice made the 'general principles of law recognized by civilized states' a source of common international law, foreign offices and arbitral tribunals had relied on such general principles to work out a loose minimum which they applied constantly in interstate practice.[181] . . . The international standard is compounded of general principles recognised by the domestic law of practically

[177] See Walker, n 160, 811–12: 'There is also a certain margin for the play of non-contingent standards, or "absolute" rules, in the formulation of treaty provisions . . . The scope of these treaties is such that, to be manageable, their content of rules must be stated essentially in a summary or simple fashion. A summary contingent rule has definiteness, because its content is measured against a determinable pole of reference. But a summary non-contingent rule may often be considerably less than so, when reduced to language of agreement between nations of unlike faculties of appreciation and different cultural and juridic backgrounds . . . *An attempt to construct a treaty primarily in non-contingent terms can prove self-defeating because increases in specificity spawn corresponding increases in reservations*'. (emphasis added)

[178] As Schwarzenberger, n 120, 411, explained in 1948, '[t]he last standard which can claim to be of general interest in this field is the standard of *equitable treatment. The special importance of this standard lies in spheres affected by an increase in State planning*'. (emphasis added)

[179] See eg Borchard, n 64, 457–58.

[180] Frederick Sherwood Dunn, 'International Law and Private Property Rights' (1928) 28 *Columbia Law Review* 166, 175.

[181] Borchard, n 64, 448–49.

every civilized country, and it is not to be supposed that any normal state would repudiate it or, if able, fail to observe it.[182]

Before BITs' leap in popularity during the late 1980s—and before Mann's 1981 article initiating the opposite trend[183]—many BIT commentators expressed certainty that the FET standard was equivalent to IMS.[184] One of the most authoritative examples can be found in the official commentary to the *OECD Draft* of 1967.[185] It should be noted that this Draft, though never opened for signature, 'represented the collective view and dominant trend of OECD countries on investment issues and influenced the pattern of deliberations on foreign investment in that period'.[186]

182 ibid 458. In 1965, the American Law Institute also identified IMS with general principles of the law. See *Restatement of the Law, Second: Foreign Relations Law of the United States, as Adopted and Promulgated by the American Law Institute, May 26, 1962* (St Paul, MN, American Law Institute, 1965) 501, ¶ 165.2: 'The international standard of justice . . . is the standard required for the treatment of aliens by: (a) the applicable principles of international law as established by international custom, judicial and arbitral decisions, and other recognized sources or, in the absence of such applicable principles, (b) *analogous principles of justice generally recognized by States that have reasonably developed legal systems*'. (emphasis added) See also, Comments (d) and (e), ibid 503 (for full citation, see ch 6, n 68).

183 See FA Mann, 'British Treaties for the Promotion and Protection of Investments' (1981) 52 British Ybk of Intl Law 241, 244 ('The terms 'fair and equitable treatment' envisage conduct which goes far beyond the minimum standard and afford protection to a greater extent and according to a much more objective standard than any previously employed form of words') (later included also in FA Mann, *Further Studies in International Law* (New York, OUP, 1990)). Following Mann, many modern commentators have adopted this position, including: (1) Rudolf Dolzer and Margrete Stevens, *Bilateral Investment Treaties* (Boston, M Nijhoff, 1995) 60; (2) UNCTAD, n 174, 37–40; (3) Vasciannie, n 169, 144; (4) Christoph H Schreuer, 'Fair and Equitable Treatment in Arbitral Practice' (2005) 6 *Journal of World Investment and Trade* 357, 364; and (5) Tudor, n 159, 65–68. Georg Schwarzenberger, *Foreign Investments and International Law* (New York, Praeger, 1969) 114–15, is sometimes credited for having first advanced this theory, but a careful review of his words does not lead to a clear conclusion. It should be remarked that, in a later book, Mann changed his mind; see F A Mann, *The Legal Aspect of Money*, 5th edn (New York, OUP, 1992) 526 (referring to 'the overriding principle of 'fair and equitable treatment', which, it must be repeated, in turns is perhaps no more than a (welcome) contractual recognition and affirmation of that principle of customary international law which requires States to act in good faith, reasonably, without abuse, arbitrariness, or discrimination'). It should also be noted that, before Mann, at least one commentator advanced the idea of FET as a standard different from IMS: Roy Preiswerk, 'New Developments in Bilateral Investment Protection (With Special Reference to Belgian Practice)' (1967) 3 *Revue Belge du Droit International* 173, 186.

184 That is also the case with FCN commentators. See Walker, n 151, 232 ('It has become settled, also, that he [the alien] and his property shall receive not only equal protection, *but also a certain minimum degree of protection, as under international law,* regardless of a Government's possible lapses with respect to its own citizens'. (emphasis added)). See also, JC Thomas, 'Reflections on Article 1105 of NAFTA: History, State Practice and the Influence of Commentators' (2002) 17 ICSID *Review—Foreign Investment Law Journal* 21, 39–58 (providing an excellent historical overview, including a critical assessment of Mann's article).

185 See n 157.

186 See Organisation of Economic Co-Operation and Development (OECD), *Fair and Equitable Treatment Standard in International Investment Law*, Working Papers on International Investment No 2004/3 (2004) at 4–5 (available at www.oecd.org/dataoecd/22/53/33776498.pdf).

The FET clause of the OECD Draft—which had been taken from the Abs-Shawcross Draft Convention of 1959[187]—came accompanied by the following observation:

> The phrase 'fair and equitable treatment', *customary in relevant bilateral agreements, indicates the standard set by international law for the treatment due by each State with regard to the property of foreign nationals*. The standard requires that—subject to essential security interests [see Article 6(i)]—protection afforded under the Convention shall be that generally accorded by the Party concerned to its own nationals, but, being set by international law, the standard may be more exacting where rules of national law or national administrative practices fall short of the requirements of international law. *The standard required conforms in effect to the 'minimum standard' which forms part of customary international law.* (emphasis added)[188]

Similarly, in 1980, the Swiss Foreign Office—the bureau in charge of the BIT program containing the oldest FET clause—stated that: '*On se réfère ainsi au principe classique du droit de gens selon lequel les États doivent mettre les étrangers se trouvant sur leur territoire et leurs biens au bénéfice du 'standard minimum' international c'est-à-dire leur accorder un minimum de droits personnels, procéduraux et économiques*'.[189]

In 1984, the OECD insisted again that the FET clause 'introduced a substantive legal standard referring to general principles of international law even if this is not explicitly stated'.[190] Explaining the origins of the US BIT program, Pamela B Gann noted in 1985—after working with the USTR Investment Division—that:

> [T]his standard [FET] is meant to supplement the nondiscrimination provisions in paragraphs 1 and 2 [of the US Model BIT] by providing a residual, but absolute minimum, degree of treaty protection to investments, regardless of possible vagaries in the host party's national laws and their administration, or

[187] See n 157. The Abs–Shawcross Draft Convention also reflected the view of capital-exporting countries. See eg Arthur Larson, 'Recipients' Rights Under an International Investment Code' (1960) 9 *Journal of Public Law* 172, 172 ('The principal flaw in the Draft Convention is its one-sidedness. In form it is even-handed . . . In substance, however, the entire concern of the Convention is the protection of the rights of the investor'). Note that, according to Antonio R Parra, 'Applicable Substantive Law in ICSID Arbitration Initiated Under Investment Treaties' (2001) 16 *ICSID Review—Foreign Investment Law Journal* 20, 22, 'the first BITs were made in the period 1959–1969. Much of the inspiration for these and the later treaties came from the 1959 Abs–Shawcross Draft Convention on Investments Abroad and the 1967 OECD Draft Convention on the Protection of Foreign Property'.

[188] See *OECD Draft Convention on the Protection of Property*, n 157, 120, Notes and Comments to Art 1, No 4(a).

[189] *Annuaire suisse de droit international* 178 (1980), cited by Mann, n 183, *Further Studies . . .*, 244. By the early 1980s, scholars in developing countries had a similar understanding. See eg Iván Meznerics, 'Guarantees for Foreign Investors', in Zotan Peteri and Vanda Lamm (eds), *General Reports to the 10th International Congress of Comparative Law* (Budapest, Akadémiai Kiadó, 1981) 331, 350.

[190] OECD, *Intergovernmental Agreements Relating to Investment in Developing Countries* (1984), cited by OECD, n 186, 3.

of a host party's lapses with respect to treatment of its own nationals and companies. *The standard provides, in effect, a 'minimum standard' which forms part of customary international law.* (emphasis added)[191]

Similarly, when commenting generally on the first UK BIT draft, in 1987, Denza and Brooks explained that although there were interest groups strongly advocating for principles that provided 'higher' standards of protection, the most important provisions did not attempt to go further than international law:

> Some of the articles in the draft would of course impose obligations which did not derive from customary international law—for example the provisions for most-favoured-nation treatment and national treatment, on exchange control freedom for investments and returns from them, on subrogation and on compulsory arbitration. *But the most political sensitive provisions—on expropriation,* compensation for damage sustained during armed conflict or revolt and on the nationality of individuals and companies—were drafted in considerable detail *but not so as to go beyond what was thought to reflect international law.*[192] . . . The effect [of nearly 300 treaties] has been to create an infrastructure of agreements based on realistic accommodations rather than political rhetoric, and *to provide important support for those standards of customary international law which had seemed to be slipping away*. (emphasis added)[193]

In one further example, in 1988, the United Nations Centre on Transnational Corporations clearly affirmed that:

> Fair and equitable treatment is a classical international law standard. As such, although not precisely defined, the principle has been shaped by State practice, doctrine and decisions of international tribunals . . . Classical international law doctrine normally considers certain elements to be firm ingredients of fair and equitable treatment, including non-discrimination, *the international minimum standards* and the duty of protection of foreign property by the host State. (emphasis added)[194]

In summary, BITs were launched in response to NIEO and the ambiguous status of customary international law by the second half of the twentieth century. BITs, as originally conceived, were not 'novel' in any relevant sense. They did not provide for investor–state arbitration, but only for traditional state-to-state arbitration. BITs did not embody standards more demanding than IMS, since capital exporting countries during this time were not fighting for such a thing. In the political context of the 1950s and 1960s, it is rather difficult to envision negotiators of capital

[191] Pamela B Gann, 'The US Bilateral Investment Treaty Program' (1985) 21 *Stanford Journal of International Law* 373, 389.

[192] Denza and Brooks, n 149, 911–12.

[193] ibid 913.

[194] United Nations Centre on Transnational Corporations, *Bilateral Investment Treaties* (Graham and Trotman, Boston 1988) 30–31.

exporting countries trying to impose a standard that would delegate to arbitrators the power to decide investment disputes according to whatever 'fair and equitable' could have meant as an 'autonomous' standard. Even more difficult is to envision negotiators of capital importing-countries accepting it.

This step-by-step bilateral plan to re-impose IMS to capital importing countries enjoyed only modest until the late 1980s.[195] However—as chapter 2 will analyse in detail—by then, it eventually began to expand exponentially throughout the world. As a consequence, we live today in an era—the BIT generation—in which IMS, or even more demanding standards according to some, reign once more in international law. More than 2,600 BITs have enabled principles that were long resisted to be accepted today as general and irrefutable truths of the legal landscape.

V UPDATING THE CALVO DOCTRINE IN THE BIT GENERATION

This section represents a move from the descriptive to the normative. It claims that the paradigm shift occurring after the end of the Cold War revisits several of the same questions that Latin American jurists and statesmen were attempting to resolve during the nineteenth century. Although the challenges we face today are very different from those of the nineteenth century, this section seeks to look to the past for lessons on the future. Its central purpose is to update the Calvo Doctrine, and to assess the BIT generation according to the perspectives and values embodied in its original formulation.

What can we say today about the BIT generation as a pillar of the new world order, in light of the *classic* claims made by Bello, Calvo, Guerrero and other Latin American statesmen and jurists? At the core of the Calvo Doctrine was equality between nations, and between aliens and nationals. From this historical perspective, the critical normative question should therefore be whether the BIT generation currently fosters, and will continue to foster, that universal value.

In my opinion, developing countries, have not frustrated the ideal of equality by the mere fact of signing BITs. The abstract principles set down in BITs do not constitute an abdication of Latin America's nineteenth century heritage in this regard. After all, those principles per se are, as

[195] It should be noted, again, how all multilateral efforts failed, including: (1) Draft Convention on the Treatment of Foreigners, Paris (1928–1929); (2) Hague Codification Conference (1930); (3) the Havana Charter (1948); (4) the Economic Agreement of Bogotá (1948); and (5) the 'International Convention for the Mutual Protection of Private Property in Foreign Countries', promoted by the Society to Advance the Protection of Foreign Investments (1957). For this last effort, see Arthur S Miller, 'Protection of Private Foreign Investment by Multilateral Convention' (1959) 53 *American Journal of International Law* 371. See also, Walker, n 151, 239–41.

Reisman and Arsanjani remark, no more than mere 'indulgences'.[196] Indeed, in the absence of military self-help, Bello would certainly have adhered to principles as reasonable as FET/IMS, national treatment, and no expropriation without compensation. And, if international commercial arbitration is able to work as a truly neutral and reliable mechanism for dispute settlement, Bello would have not rejected it.

Although investment treaty provisions are not objectionable in themselves, the concrete jurisprudence resulting from them may easily end up posing a serious threat to developing countries' sovereignty and independence. The point is that by signing BITs, developing countries gave rise to a dynamic process which has the ultimate potential to lead to either equality or inequality. As will be shown in chapters 2 and 3, by adhering to such principles—particularly if they are considered not to be restraint by general international law and IMS—developing countries have institutionalised a process of judicial norm-creation whose final result is still largely uncertain.

If the BIT generation is going to be an instrument of global governance and expansion of the rule of law, rather than a set of privileges created and maintained to the exclusive favour of foreign investors, the regional history tells us that two minimal conditions of legitimacy must be fulfilled: first, BIT jurisprudence on basic substantive standards should not crystallise in more protective terms than those applied by the courts of *developed countries* toward their own national investors; and second, that BIT jurisprudence—if it complies with the first condition—should permeate developing countries' legal systems, with the effect of improving the content of domestic public law. In EU nomenclature, the goal is to avoid any potential *reverse discrimination*,[197] where local citizens receive less favourable treatment than foreigners. This, succinctly, is the updated Calvo Doctrine.

The updated Doctrine is not, in principle, concerned with IMS, but with the process of judicial norm-creation that results from excessively broad and undefined standards. There is, hence, a significant difference between

[196] Michael Reisman and Mahnoush H Arsanjani, 'The Question of Unilateral Governmental Statements as Applicable Law in International Disputes' (2004) 19 *ICSID Review—Foreign Investment Law Journal* 328, 343.

[197] See W van Gerven, 'Mutual Permeation of Public and Private Law at the National and Supranational Level' (1998) 5 *Maastricht Journal of European and Comparative Law* 7, 23–24 (1998), who explains reverse discrimination in these terms: 'Multiple mutual permeation is a good thing. Let us, where possible, promote it . . . [I]n conformity with the principle of equal treatment it is a good thing that persons who are in the same situation, irrespective of the legal area involved, receive equal treatment, first and foremost, in the field of legal protection. It is indeed a matter of principle that equivalent positions, irrespective of the legal area, be judged equally, except where there are objective reasons justifying inequality of treatment'. See also, Miguel Poiares Maduro, *We The Court. The European Court of Justice and The European Economic Constitution. A Critical Reading of Article 30 of the EC Treaty* (Oxford, Hart Publishing, 1998) 71.

the updated and original versions of the Calvo Doctrine. The main threat existing today is that BITs might be interpreted as providing standards higher than IMS and, therefore, higher than those generally applied in developed countries.

Undoubtedly, BITs require from states the creation, implementation, and proper management of functional domestic regulatory systems. They can therefore act as rule-of law-enhancers, a desirable outcome. However, BIT jurisprudence can also end up crystallising concrete rules that protect property rights and economic freedoms to a much greater extent than what constitutional and supreme courts in the US and Europe have traditionally done. It is indeed somewhat shocking—and, once barred by the principle of *allegans contraria non est audiendus*[198]—that a US investor may lose a case against its government in the US Supreme Court, a German investor may lose the same case in the *Bundesverfassungsgericht* (Constitutional Court), and a French investor may lose it in the *Conseil d'État*; but, nevertheless, any of them may win it against a developing country before an investment treaty tribunal.

Speaking very broadly, BIT jurisprudence can crystallise at two different equilibria: one, *the good case* or *BITs-as-developed-countries-constitutional-law-and-no-more*, in which BIT jurisprudence recognises standards of protection of investments no higher than those that state courts in developed countries apply to their own nationals; and at the other extreme, *the bad case* or *BITs-as-gunboat-arbitration*,[199] which corresponds to a jurisprudence that converts investment treaties into a conservative system of overprotection of investments and the status quo, where most diminutions in value resulting from state action give investors the right to be compensated.

The good case or *BITs-as-developed-countries-constitutional-law-and-no-more* constitutes more than an aspiration based on the general principle of equality. It is also a matter of positive law. Unless there is an unambiguous textual provision to the contrary,[200] I see no way to interpret the core

[198] According to Bin Cheng, *General Principles of Law: As Applied by International Courts and Tribunals* (Grotius Publications, Cambridge 1987) 143, in the state-to-state context of diplomatic protection, this has indeed been an application of the principle of *allegans contraria non est audiendus*: 'This principle was also applied by the German-United States Mixed Claims Commission (1922) in the *Life-Insurance Claims Case* (1924) to preclude a State from asserting claims which, on general principles of law, its own courts would not admit, for instance, claims involving damages which its own municipal courts, in similar cases, would consider too remote. Incidentally, this case also shows one of the means whereby general principles of law find their application in the international sphere. *A State may not disregard such principles as it recognises in its own municipal system, except of course where there is a rule of international law to the contrary*'. (emphasis added)

[199] I am following the classic nineteenth century Latin American characterisation of diplomatic protection as gunboat diplomacy.

[200] Of course, other standards such as national treatment, MFN, and free transfer of funds, or specific provisions such as umbrella clauses, go beyond general international law as well as beyond what can be found in comparative law. Yet, this is not the case for the two key standards of no expropriation without compensation and FET.

substantive provisions of BITs, mainly the standards of no expropriation without compensation and FET, as giving foreign investors higher protection than developed legal systems do.[201] BITs's key standards embody IMS, and the latter, as Borchard explains, are essentially 'general principles recognized by the domestic law of practically every civilized country'.[202] Neither developed nor developing countries have domestic legal systems characterised by a *Lochnerian*[203] conception of property rights—that is, a court stance that is 'synonymous with inappropriate judicial intervention in the legislative process'[204]—and, accordingly, they could not have adopted such a strong commitment to the status quo when concluding BITs.

Like all developed legal systems, the BIT network must achieve an acceptable equilibrium between investments and the public interest. Most capital exporting countries have, in fact, been long committed to broader collective goals such as the protection of health, safety and the environment, and more generally, to personal autonomy and human welfare. The jurisprudence of the BIT generation, therefore, cannot adopt a libertarian stance that would generally be deemed incompatible with more progressive goals transcending the maximisation of wealth.[205]

The second condition of legitimacy—equality between aliens and nationals—is of domestic character; thus, developing countries must attain it via their own internal political processes. This condition requires that substantive BIT standards, once they have crystallised at a reasonable

[201] This proposition will be analysed in detail in ch 6.

[202] See n 182.

[203] See *Lochner v New York* (1905) 198 US 45. In that case, the US Supreme Court struck down a New York statute establishing maximum hours of labor for bakers. The right to contract affirmed in *Lochner* was later expanded to cover property rights in *Coppage v Kansas* 236 US 1 (1915).

[204] Kathleen M Sullivan and Gerald Gunther, *Constitutional Law*, 14th edn (New York, Foundation Press, 2001) 463. According to Gregory S Alexander, *The Global Debate over Constitutional Property. Lessons from American Takings Jurisprudence* (The University of Chicago Press, Chicago 2006) 32: 'The conventional story of *Lochner* equates constitutional property with the substantive due process jurisprudence that was antiredistributive, politically motivated, unprincipled, and undemocratic. The term "Lochner", in fact, is a trope signifying judicial activism protecting the property rights of a few at the expense of the democratic will of majorities'. See also, Stephen Breyer, *Active Liberty: Interpreting Our Democratic Constitution* (New York, Knopf, 2005) 10.

[205] Considering the European experience, investment treaty tribunals should conduct a form of 'majoritarian activism'. Poiares Maduro, n 197, 78 devised this concept, explaining it along these lines: 'What the Court [ECJ] does when it considers Article 30 is not to impose a certain constitutional conception of public intervention in the market, but to compensate for the lack of Community harmonisation. This is why the regulatory balance set by the Court normally corresponds to the view of the Commission, *and to the legislation of the majority of Member States*. On the one hand, *the Court is not imposing its own particular economic model of regulation*. On the other hand, the Court does not accept State's different economic models, even if non-protectionist. Its yardstick is what the Court identifies as the European Union majority policy, in this way subjecting States regulation to harmonisation in the Court'. (emphasis added)

level according to the previous condition, must extend to all investors doing business in those territories. Constitutional equal protection provisions in developing countries must be taken seriously; nationals must receive the same treatment as foreigners.[206]

Unlike other commentators, I do not go so far as to claim that the procedural safeguards that BITs confer to foreign investors should also be extended to domestic investors.[207] My claim extends only to the key substantive standards of protection of investment and property rights. Any policy that discriminates between national and foreign investors, on a structural/constitutional level as basic as the standards of protection of property rights and economic freedoms, should be deemed inappropriate. As Been and Beauvais remark, '[t]his discrimination seems objectionable on its face'.[208]

Yet, even provided that standards of protection of property rights under BIT jurisprudence are reasonable, how will these new standards be incorporated by developing countries into their own legal systems? If we do not wish BITs to become 'legal enclaves' for foreign investors,[209] then the mechanisms for internalisation and implementation of these standards remain highly relevant concerns for the updated Calvo Doctrine.

It would be somewhat naive to assume that international law can enhance domestic legal systems—and the rule of law—all by itself. Neither the 'halo effect',[210] the 'desideratum effect',[211] nor the 'signaling effect'[212] possesses sufficient strength to introduce reasonable international standards into a country's internal legal culture. Something more is required in order to fully exploit the BIT generation's *potential* for

[206] In the European context, Søren J Schønberg, *Legitimate Expectations in Administrative Law* (New York, OUP, 2000) 27, does not accept that reverse discrimination breaches the principle of equality.

[207] See eg Wälde, n 150, 188 (noting that the 'aim should be an external governance discipline available to both national and foreign investors—such as Article 1 of the Additional Protocol of the European Convention on Human Rights').

[208] Vicki Been and Joel C Beauvais, 'The Global Fifth Amendment? NAFTA's Investment Protections and the Misguided Quest for an International 'Regulatory Takings' Doctrine' (2003) 78 *New York University Law Review* 30, 129.

[209] The term was coined by Ronald J Daniels, 'Defecting on Development: Bilateral Investment Treaties and the Subversion of the Rule of Law in the Developing World' (Draft) (available at www.unisi.it/lawandeconomics/stile2004/daniels.pdf).

[210] World Bank, *World Development Report* (New York, OUP, 2005) 179 ('While ICSID is designed to encourage foreign investment, domestic firms can benefit from the *halo effect* provided by stronger constraints on arbitrary government action'). (emphasis added)

[211] Sohn and Baxter, n 65, 28 ('By the establishment of an international minimum standard, the law has not only protected aliens but has also suggested a *desideratum* for States in their relationships with their own nationals'). (emphasis added)

[212] Wälde, n 150, 188 ('The example effect of treaty-based contract protection is likely to have an indirect effect also on the treatment of domestic investors, as it signals to the host-State institutions what a proper, international and universal standard of governance is. Such *signaling effect* provides a benchmark for domestic judicial procedures as well'). (emphasis added)

enhancing the rule of law, while successfully avoiding the creation of 'legal enclaves'.

The two cases represented by the internalisation of the international law of human rights, and the 'constitutionalisation' of European Law, provide valuable lessons for the updated Calvo Doctrine. Following those examples, one useful policy might be to recognise BITs as self-executing treaties, that is, as treaties containing norms which are directly applicable to foreign investors before local courts.[213]

Of course, this policy by itself does not directly achieve equality. Even if BITs are self-executing, they continue to be *lex specialis*, applying only to foreign investors. In other words, because national investors are not treaty beneficiaries, they cannot claim any treaty violation before domestic courts. Nevertheless, this policy can produce a significant 'communicating vessels' effect, in which BIT minima are incorporated as 'real domestic law' by domestic tribunals. Foreign investors would then be able to bring causes of action under BITs, in substitution for small and medium-sise cases that otherwise would have been litigated not in international arbitral tribunals, but under domestic constitutional and administrative law schemes.

This solution should not be considered a mere legal technicality. As the history of European law illustrates—albeit in a very different historical, institutional and legal setting—a 'direct effect' policy can have powerful implications for governance in domestic legal systems.[214] Domestic tribunals, working *as* international tribunals, would begin to develop jurisprudence that would inevitably cross-fertilise domestic law with elements and principles of international law.[215] As a result, international law and institutions would no longer be seen to represent esoteric categories divorced from the domestic political and legal process.

[213] For an approach requiring domestic administrative law to 'improve' its internal regime of liability in order to avoid reverse discrimination, see Santiago Montt, 'Aplicación de los tratados bilaterales de protección de inversiones por tribunales chilenos. Responsabilidad del estado y expropiaciones regulatorias en un mundo crecientemente globalizado' (2005) 32 *Revista Chilena de Derecho* 19.

[214] See JHH Weiler, 'The Transformation of Europe' (1991) 100 *Yale Law Journal* 2403, 2413–14, who explains how the doctrine of direct effect played a crucial role in the 'constitutionalization' of the Community Legal Structure. See also, Alex Stone Sweet, *The Judicial Construction of Europe* (New York, OUP, 2004) 64 ff (explaining how supremacy, direct effect, and related constitutional doctrines created by the ECJ 'reconfigured the normative foundations of the Community, thereby upgrading the capacity of the legal system to respond to the demands of transnational society'; ibid 65). For more detailed legal studies of the doctrine of direct effect, see Paul Craig and Gráinne de Búrca, *EC Law. Text, Cases, and Materials* (New York, OUP, 1995) 151 ff, and Brunno de Witte, 'Direct Effect, Supremacy, and the Nature of the Legal Order' in Paul Craig and Gráinne de Búrca (eds), *The Evolution of EU Law* (New York, OUP, 1999) 177.

[215] See Claire L'Heureux-Dube, 'The Importance of Dialogue: Globalization and the International Impact of the Rehnquist Court' (1998) 34 *Tulsa Law Journal* 15, and Anne-Marie Slaughter, 'Judicial Globalization' (2000) 40 *Virginia Journal of International Law* 1103.

But, more importantly, domestic politics will be more effective in its role if BITs are self-executing. Only when domestic tribunals apply two different standards, will domestic constituencies fully realise the need for a serious revision of their own standards in those areas where such gaps disadvantage nationals. Intense pressure will then fall upon the political branches of government to reform the legal system in order to forestall future discrimination against national investors.

In sum, it is essential that we update the Calvo Doctrine to specifically meet the *governance dilemmas* that the BIT generation presents to us. Those dilemmas remind us, as Keohane remarks, that '[a]lthough institutions are essential for human life, they are also dangerous'.[216] As explained, the excessively broad principles contained in BITs can lead to a *Lochnerian* BIT jurisprudence that protects investors to a higher extent than the rules and principles currently in place in mature regulatory capitalist nations. From an international perspective, this is the greatest danger, and it presents a serious risk to the achievement of equality and the rule of law.

CONCLUSIONS: BUILDING A NORMATIVE STANCE BASED ON EQUALITY

This chapter has presented the long history of confrontation between developed and developing countries in the field of protection of aliens and their property. It explored in particular detail the developments of diplomatic protection during the nineteenth century, an era characterised by gunboat diplomacy and military self-help. As shown here, the national treatment standard and Calvo Doctrine defended by Latin American countries at the time, when viewed in their proper historical context, share little in common with the position of no responsibility that became dominant during the revisionist second half of the twentieth century.

Against this nuanced historical background, which distinguishes the realities of the nineteenth and twentieth centuries, the chapter explained the emergence of the BIT generation in terms of a re-establishment of pre-NIEO international minimum standards, as traditionally espoused by developed countries. Given this return to traditional standards, which coincides with a simultaneous abandonment of the more radical NIEO stance, the BIT generation constitutes a new paradigm that, nevertheless, puts forward questions and dilemmas similar to those that preoccupied Andrés Bello and other Latin American jurist statesmen during the nineteenth century—in particular, the potential inequalities that this system of global governance may generate in developing countries.

By taking the nineteenth century Latin American efforts seriously, then, this historical chapter—in addition to correcting various historical

[216] Keohane, n 14, 1.

misperceptions about BITs and their provisions—defended an updated version of the Calvo Doctrine that helps us in confronting these potential inequalities. As explained before, this 'new' Calvo Doctrine demands that the BIT generation meet at least two minimal conditions of legitimacy, if it is to be considered a just and successful instrument of global governance and the rule of law.

First, unless an explicit textual provision to the contrary, investment treaty jurisprudence should not crystallise rules and norms for protection of property rights in terms more rigorous than those generally applied by domestic courts in developed countries. Second, the substantive standards of BITs, if crystallised at a reasonable level, should be extended to nationals and all investors doing business in developing nations. The first condition—the one that we must demand from the investment treaty law jurisprudence, as opposed to the second, which is of domestic nature and depends on the will of developing countries—defines the normative stance from which this work will assess the BIT generation.

The updated Calvo Doctrine differs from the original nineteenth-century version. Instead of arguing that national treatment is the maximum, this updated version claims that BIT minima should be reasonable as compared to domestic public law in developed countries, and if so, should be extended to domestic investors.[217] More than half a century ago, Roth commented that 'South America was and remains the centre of the propaganda which maintains that the alien can have no different nor greater rights than the nationals'.[218] The new Calvo Doctrine intends to rescue that tradition, but this time by leveling the playing field in an upward, and not downward, direction.

A BIT jurisprudence equilibrium like the one envisioned by the updated Calvo Doctrine should not be underestimated. The protection of property rights and economic liberties in developed countries, as practised today, has proven to be a more than sufficient condition for the healthy performance of regulatory capitalist societies. And, imposing a reasonable jurisprudence top-down from the international level—by virtue of the second minimal condition of legitimacy—may be an effective means of bypassing the powerful practices of local elites and special interest groups, who are some of the main culprits responsible for the institutional weaknesses of developing countries.[219] The political process in many of those

[217] As explained by W Michael Reisman and Robert D Sloane, 'Indirect Takings and its Valuation in the BIT generation' (2003) 74 BYIL 115, 118, 'BITs consciously seek to approximate in the developing, capital-importing state the *minimal legal, administrative, and regulatory framework that fosters and sustains investment in industrialized capital-exporting states*'. (emphasis added)

[218] Roth, n 16, 69.

[219] John O McGinnis and Mark L Movsesian, 'The World Trade Constitution' (2000) 114 *Harvard Law Review* 511, make a similar argument in the context of the WTO. They argue, ibid 512, that 'the WTO can be understood as a constitutive structure that, by reducing the power

countries will continue to be slow to enhance the rule of law. The international legal process represents one possible—if admittedly, partial—solution to this problem.

Keohane has noted that '[i]f global institutions are designed well, they will promote human welfare. But if we bungle the job, the results could be disastrous'.[220] The Calvo Doctrine, duly updated, tells us what we should demand from the BIT generation: a commitment to equality and to the rule of law, and ultimately, to personal autonomy and human welfare. Excessive protection of property rights and investments, and the corresponding limitation of the State's power to pursue public interest regulation, represent real threats to these commitments. Again, as Keohane reminds us, '[t]o make a partially globalised world benign, we need not just effective governance, but the *right kind* of governance'.[221]

of protectionist interest groups, can simultaneously promote international trade and domestic democracy'. For the EU case, see Karl-Heinz Ladeur, 'Globalization and the Conversion of Democracy to Polycentric Networks: Can Democracy Survive the End of the Nation State?' in Karl-Heinz Ladeur (ed), *Public Governance in the Age of Globalization* (Burlington, Ashgate, 2004) 89, 117–18 ('In spite of the rhetoric of democratic decision-making, political processes in Member States are increasingly characterized by a dominance of special interest groups. This is due to the fact that the integrative function of representative 'encompassing' groups (Olson) is breaking down, whereas constraints of reciprocity and compliance may exclude narrow short-term interests at the European level').

[220] Keohane, n 14, 12.

[221] ibid 1.

2

The BIT Generation's Emergence as a Collective Action Problem: Prisoner's Dilemma or Network Effects?[1]

INTRODUCTION: WHY DO DEVELOPING COUNTRIES SIGN BITS?

THE BIT GENERATION, that is, the common legal practice of investment arbitration that currently prevails, is possible thanks to the existence of a network containing thousands of investment treaties. The network grew from 245 treaties in 1985 to 422 in 1990, 1,149 in 1995 to 1,916 in 2000, and finally, to the current size of 2,608 treaties by 2007.[2] A quick survey of the treaties that make up this pool reveals two characteristics which, while crucial to understanding the emergence of the BIT generation, have been somewhat overlooked by scholars and commentators.

The first of these is that BITs are written using extremely broad and open-ended terms, particularly concerning their two most important substantive provisions: no expropriation without compensation and fair and equitable treatment. In this regard, investment treaty language resembles constitutional language, and it is no exaggeration to state that the treaties represent the actual *economic constitutions* for foreign investors doing business in those countries that have adopted them.

[1] A previous version of this chapter was awarded the 2007 Cooter–Microsoft Award for scholarship in law and economics, conferred by the Latin American and Caribbean Law and Economics Association, and was published in (2007) 2(1) *Latin American and Caribbean Journal of Legal Studies* (electronic journal available at http://services.bepress.com/lacjls/vol2/iss1/).

[2] The data was obtained from ICSID and UNCTAD (various publications). See also, United Nations Centre on Transnational Corporations, *Bilateral Investment Treaties* (Boston, Graham and Trotman, 1988) 6–7; Rudolf Dolzer and Margrete Stevens, *Bilateral Investment Treaties* (Boston, M Nijhoff, 1995) xii, and 267–326; and, United Nations Conference on Trade and Development, *Bilateral Investment Treaties 1959–1999* (New York, United Nations, 2000) 1 (available at www.unctad.org/en/docs/poiteiiad2.en.pdf); and, United Nations Conference on Trade and Development (UNCTAD), *World Investment Report* (New York, United Nations, 2008) 13.

The second, somewhat under-reported feature of BITs is that their key substantive provisions are worded in closely similar terms.[3] As one French commentator remarks, 'whilst these treaties are signed during different periods of time and with different states, they remain similar in content. Numerous provisions of these treaties are identical. They use specific investment law vocabulary,'[4] citing notions such as 'fair and equitable treatment', 'expropriation', 'measures tantamount to expropriation', 'fork in the road', and 'umbrella clauses'.[5] Given the bilateral nature of most of these treaties, we have witnessed a *de facto standardisation*, in which all countries have adopted the same set of core substantive standards of treatment.[6] As McLachlan et al explain:

> [T]his patchwork quilt of interlocking but separate treaties—each the product of its own negotiation—*in fact betrays a surprising pattern of common features*. No doubt part of the ready success of the investment treaty phenomenon has been the willingness of negotiators to confine their texts, for the most part, to a limited number of rather general guarantees, each expressed in conventional form . . . This means that it is possible to speak of a common lexicon of investment treaty law. (emphasis added)[7]

The combination of these two aspects means that BIT interpretation has given rise to a genuine constitutional jurisprudence, by which I mean a process of judicial norm-creation that gives actual specific content to the overly general provisions of the treaties. Indeed, we can see today how, since the first arbitral award was rendered in 1990,[8] international investment law has gradually become its own distinct field of international law. There is, beyond doubt, 'a genuine arbitration case law specific to the field

[3] Certainly, this is not the first time that the similarity in language between BITs has been noted. See eg Rainer Geiger, 'The Multifaceted Nature of International Investment Law' in Karl Sauvant (ed), *Appeals Mechanisms in International Investment Law* (New York, OUP, 2008) 17, 18; Calvin A Hamilton and Paula I Rochwerger, 'Trade and Investment: Foreign Direct Investment Through Bilateral and Multilateral Treaties' (2005) 18 *New York International Law Review* 1, 8; Pierre Duprey, 'Do Arbitral Awards Constitute Precedents? Should Commercial Arbitration Be Distinguished from Arbitration Based on Investment Treaties' in Emmanuel Gaillard (ed), *Towards a Uniform International Arbitration Law?* (Huntington, Juris Publishing, 2005) 251, 276; Tom Ginsburg, 'International Substitutes for Domestic Institutions: Bilateral Investment Treaties and Governance' (2005) *International Review of Law and Economics* 107, 116; Zachary Douglas, 'The Hybrid Foundation of Investment Treaty Arbitration' (2004) 74 BYIL 151, 159; and, Vaughan Lowe, 'Regulation or Expropriation' (2002) 55 *Current Legal Problems* 447, 451. See also the Introduction to this Work, n 97 and accompanying text.

[4] Duprey, n 3, 276.

[5] Ibid. See also, Geiger, n 3, 18.

[6] See *Industria Nacional de Alimentos SA et al v Peru*, ICSID Case No ARB/03/4 (Danelius, Berman, Giardina), Decision on Annulment (5 September 2007), ¶ 69 (distinguishing between 'boilerplate' provisions and particularised clauses in BITs). See also, Ginsburg, n 3, 116 (observing a 'substantial convergence in the substance of BITs over time').

[7] Campbell McLachlan et al, *International Investment Arbitration. Substantive Principles* (New York, OUP, 2007) 5–6.

[8] See *Asian Agricultural Products Ltd v Sri Lanka*, ICSID Case No ARB/87/3 (El-Kosheri, Goldman, Asante), Award (27 June 1990) (hereinafter, *Asian Agricultural Products*).

of investment'.[9] Again, McLachlan et al have captured this key aspect of the BIT generation when noting that 'the very iterative process of the formulation and conclusion of investment treaties, and the vindication of the rights contained in those treaties in arbitration, is producing a set of general international principles about the meaning of the common substantive clauses'.[10]

This chapter focuses on the descriptive side of the BIT revolution. Salacuse and Sullivan pose the relevant questions in very precise terms: 'why would developing countries enter into such agreements? Why would they constrain their sovereignty by entering into treaties that specifically limit their ability to take necessary legislative and administrative actions to advance and protect their national interests?'[11] These questions are of particular importance for Latin America, a region that defended the Calvo Doctrine and the Calvo Clause for more than 150 years.[12] As one commentator ironically notes, '[n]o region of the world has so completely moved from a principle-based rejection of any international role in the protection of foreign investment, to its near wholesale acceptance as reflected in the signing of investment treaties'.[13]

At present, Andrew Guzman has offered one of the best-articulated explanations for the emergence of the BIT generation, which he later refined in a piece written together with Elkins and Simmons (*hereinafter*, EGS). In Guzman's account, the current situation, in which thousands of BITs exist, is the result of a prisoner's dilemma among developing countries in which these countries, competing against each other to attract foreign direct investment (FDI), have all ended up worse off.[14]

This chapter presents a different theory of what transpired in the last fifty years. While acknowledging the existence of competition between developing countries to attract FDI, as well as the problem of collective action, it disputes the idea that the BIT generation must be explained as a prisoner's dilemma. This work claims, as some legal and game theory experts have also noted more generally, that Guzman has identified the situation too quickly with a prisoner's dilemma.[15]

[9] Duprey, n 3, 276–77.

[10] McLachlan et al, n 7, 20.

[11] Jeswald W Salacuse and Nicholas P Sullivan, 'Do BITs Really Work?: An Evaluation of Bilateral Investment Treaties and Their Grand Bargain' (2005) 46 *Harvard International Law Journal* 67, 77.

[12] See ch 1, 38–55.

[13] Carlos G Garcia, 'All the Other Dirty Little Secrets: Investment Treaties, Latin America, and the Necessary Evil of Investor-State Arbitration' (2004) 16 *Florida Journal of International Law* 301, 318.

[14] Andrew T Guzman, 'Why LDCs Sign Treaties That Hurt Them: Explaining the Popularity of Bilateral Investment Treaties' (1998) 38 *Virginia Journal of International Law* 639, 651; and Zachary Elkins, Andrew T Guzman and Beth Simmons, 'Competing for Capital: The Diffusion of Bilateral Investment Treaties, 1960–2000' (2006) 60 *International Organization* 811.

[15] See Douglas G Baird et al, *Game Theory and the Law* (Cambridge, Mass, CUP, 1994) 188 (noting that '[a] problem is often too quickly identified as a prisoner's dilemma').

In fact, the BIT generation 'game' differs from a prisoner's dilemma in two key respects. First, it has a sequential / evolutionary nature, stemming from the fact that developing countries have been joining (and rejecting) the network at various times since 1959. Indeed, from that point on, developing countries have been constantly confronted with the decision of whether or not to adopt the BIT program.[16] Second, unlike the prisoner's dilemma, the BIT system demonstrates the positive externalities or network effects of having one system of treaties defined in closely similar terms. Taking into account those two differences, a new theory emerges: the BIT generation as a virtual network.[17]

The BIT system bears remarkable similarity to a sequential / evolutionary collective action game. The most notable of these similarities is the fact that the common language contained in BITs has become a de facto standard, and therefore, the group of BITs a virtual network. As stated, over the course of nearly half a century, most countries have adopted treaties containing the same or very similar core substantive provisions. The central claim here is that network externalities—represented, in brief, by the players' anticipation of future BIT-case law created by arbitral tribunals—explain this de facto standardisation. At the same time, these externalities support my most serious contention with Guzman and EGS's theory: that the equilibrium represented by BITs is *not* the worst-case scenario for developing countries.

This new theory intends to address four key questions left unanswered by Guzman's and EGS' account, which any attempt to understand the phenomenon of the BIT generation must consider. First, why did all developing countries adopt more or less the same substantive rules; that is, why did such a high level of uniformity prevail? Secondly, why did developing countries adopt the particular set of rules that we see today in BITs as opposed to others, be they more favourable or unfavourable for host states? Thirdly, why did those rules exist in the 'market' for more than 20 years without being widely adopted? And, fourthly, why did BIT substantive rules constitute a sub-optimal equilibrium, ie, why did states not erode all rents when concluding BITs?

This chapter proceeds as follows. Section I presents theories by Guzman and, to a lesser degree, EGS. Section II summarises the two basic ideas underpinning the new theory presented here: weak competition among countries and network effects. Section III presents a formal model of the

[16] In their own work, EGS, n 14, 821, present evidence that demonstrates that the decision of whether or not to sign BITs is typically the decision of whether or not to adopt the BIT program, that is, the decision to conclude BITs on a systematic basis.

[17] Several authors have used the word 'network' before (in a non-technical sense) to refer to the BIT regime. See eg Americo Beviglia Zampetti and Pierre Sauvé, 'International Investment' in Andrew Guzman and Alan O Sykes (eds), *Research Handbook in International Economic Law* (Northampton, E Elgar, 2007) 211, and 215, and Geiger, n 3, 17–18. See also, *Asian Agricultural Products* ¶ 49, where the Tribunal refers to the 'worldwide BIT network'.

BIT generation as a virtual network. Section IV provides evidence, and section V tries to answer the key questions outlined above. The conclusions remark upon some of the normative implications of this new virtual network theory, which posits—in contrast to the prisoners' dilemma model—that developing countries may actually end up *better* off.

I THE BIT GENERATION AS A PRISONER'S DILEMMA

This section summarises Andrew Guzman's account of the BIT generation's emergence. He explains the present popularity of BITs in terms of a prisoner's dilemma. In this game, developing countries, competing against each other to increase the flow of FDI, bid away all their benefits and, especially, any advantages that could have been secured under a multilateral treaty. For Guzman, the formerly collaborative dynamic among developing countries that had prevailed during the 1960s and 1970s—represented mainly by the Charter of Economic Rights and Duties of States (CERDS), enacted by the General Assembly of the UN in 1974[18]—was destroyed, because it was now in the best interest of each individual state to defect and sign BITs.

The core of his theory is the identification of a collective action problem. In this game, 'an *individual* country has a strong incentive to negotiate with and offer concessions to potential investors—thereby making itself a more attractive location relative to other potential hosts'.[19] At the same time, 'developing countries *as a group* are likely to benefit from forcing investors to enter contracts with host countries that cannot be enforced in an international forum, thereby giving the host a much greater ability to extract value from the investment'.[20] He sees then a frustrated cartel: 'developing countries as a group have sufficient market power in the 'sale' of their resources that they stand to gain more when they act collectively than when they compete against one another'.[21] Hence, the most probable outcome is that 'BITs increase global efficiency, [but] they likely reduce the overall welfare of developing states'.[22]

In Guzman's opinion, less developed countries [LDCs] thus face a prisoner's dilemma. It is in the best interest of LDC, as a group, to reject the Hull Rule—ie, prompt, adequate, and effective compensation—but individually each LDC 'is better off "defecting" from the group by signing a BIT that gives it an advantage over other LDCs in the competition to

[18] The Charter of Economic Rights and Duties of States, GA Res 3281, UN GAOR, UN Doc A/9631 (1975) reprinted in (1975) 14 ILM 251.

[19] Guzman, n 14, 643.

[20] ibid.

[21] ibid.

[22] ibid.

attract foreign investors'.[23] Assuming that the 'market' for FDI is perfect, developing countries compete for larger portions of inflows, and this competition comes at the expense of other developing countries (assuming a fixed pool of capital).[24] In that highly competitive environment, the results are unfavourable because 'the potential hosts will continue to bid against one another until the benefit enjoyed by the host from the investment is zero'.[25]

By contrast, in a world of collective action, all developing countries would be better off by colluding, and adhering to customary international law rules such as those contained in CERDS. In the absence of BITs, host countries can extract value from irreversible investment made by foreign investors by unilaterally changing the conditions under which the firms operate.[26] 'The disadvantage of CERDS, however, is that there will be fewer investments because the inefficiencies of the regime make it more costly to invest'.[27] Whether the net result of moving from CERDS to BITs is positive or negative is uncertain, but the critical issue here is the sensitivity of investment in relation to its costs:

> [I]f the level of investment dropped below a certain point, LDCs would be worse off as a group under the CERDS regime that they would be under a BIT regime. On the other hand, if there is only a small reduction in the overall level of investment, LDCs may be better off under CERDS because they can receive a larger share of the return from investments.[28]

Although Guzman recognises that a definitive answer will require empirical information not yet available,[29] he provides various arguments that make the CERDS case, prima facie, the better scenario for developing countries.[30] In his opinion, developing countries as a group 'may be better off in a regime that leaves them unable to enter binding contracts with investors'.[31] His main argument follows along these lines: As in the case of

[23] ibid 667.

[24] ibid 670, and 674. He states this condition in the following terms: '[The theoretical claims] are true only if the flow of investment into LDCs as a group is relatively insensitive to the terms on which that investment is made as compared to the flow of investment into a single developing country. In economic terms, the demand for resources of LDCs as a group must be relatively inelastic while the demand for the resources of a single country must be relatively elastic'. (ibid 674–75).

[25] ibid 671. He also notes that 'as in any competitive market, the seller—here the host country—will receive no economic profit. The entire profit will be enjoyed by the investor' (ibid 672). Nevertheless, in a footnote, he observes that the winner will not need to bid away all benefits in cases where countries are not identical with each other in nature and characteristics (ibid 672 fn 103).

[26] ibid 673.

[27] ibid.

[28] ibid 673–74.

[29] ibid 674–76.

[30] ibid.

[31] ibid 674. Guzman assumes that without BITs, there are no contracts in international law. One possible explanation is that Guzman considers the New International Economic Order

a cartel, developing countries acting together to support CERDS could have kept all rents, or at least a larger share of them, for themselves.[32] Collective action could have secured monopoly rents by using the market power that is essential to the cartel.[33]

In EGS' later work, the prisoner's dilemma scenario is significantly softened, as they opt just to stress the competitive origins of the BIT generation. The authors, in fact, remain silent on the issue.[34] According to EGS, BITs are signed, most significantly, to 'make credible commitments because they raise the ex post costs of non-compliance above those that might be incurred in the absence of the treaty'.[35] Notwithstanding the tautology of explaining why a contract or treaty is concluded by reference to the idea of a credible commitment device,[36] the use of game theory language permits EGS to highlight the strength of BITs, whose investor–state arbitration clauses serve as the 'teeth' of enforcement. This institutional design, hence, increases the ex post *costs* involved in the violation of BITs, which includes diplomatic costs, arbitration costs, reputation costs, and sovereignty costs.[37]

The collective action problem introduced by Guzman is still present, but depicted in different terms. Acting individually, countries receive reputational advantages that may allow them to attract more FDI (investment which would otherwise have gone to other developing countries). However, signing BITs involves costs for the host government, the majority of which the authors characterise as 'sovereignty costs'. These include 'the political costs of assembling a coalition in support of foreign investors' rights, as well as the costs associated with giving up a broad range of policy instruments relevant to domestic social or developmental purposes (taxation, regulation, performance requirements, property seizure, currency and capital restrictions.)'[38] But most importantly, these costs include

(NIEO) to have been, at some point of time, *jus cogens* in international law. But that is a claim that has been rejected in international law and one which only a very small number of commentators would agree with. See eg FV García-Amador, *El Derecho Internacional del Desarrollo. Una Nueva Dimensión del Derecho Internacional Económico* (Madrid, Civitas, 1987) 251. Moreover, it was expressly rejected in the *Aminoil* case, in *The Government of the State of Kuwait v The American Independent Oil Co*, Final Award (1982) reprinted in (1982) 21 ILM 976, 1021.

32 Guzman, n 14, 683.

33 ibid 677.

34 They say only that, '[c]ollectively, they might be better off resisting the demands of investors (avoiding the sovereignty costs described above), but individually, it is rational to sign, in hopes of stimulating capital inflows' (ibid 825).

35 EGS, n 14, 823.

36 People conclude contracts and states signs treaties because they need to commit themselves credibly in order to overcome a dynamic inconsistency problem. Explaining contracts or treaties as credible commitment devices, then, does not add any new information. The relevant question is why people make credible commitments at certain specific points in time; here, why countries massively concluded BITs during the 1980s and 1990s.

37 See EGS, n 14, 824.

38 ibid 825.

the ones associated with delegating adjudicative authority to international arbitral tribunals.[39]

If developing countries believed that the benefits of signing these treaties outweighed the sovereignty costs, EGS argue, they were wrong: '[i]n many cases, the answer is no'.[40] The writers fail to provide any deeper explanation or empirical justification for the collective action problem. However, Guzman's original account seems to still be present here, at least implicitly. While defection is still a dominant strategy for developing countries, the more of them that sign BITs according to their individual interests, the more that any benefits of defection tend to be cancelled out. Assuming a limited pool of foreign investment, the benefits of defection eventually disappear entirely, and all former members of the cartel are left only with 'sovereignty costs'.

II WEAK COMPETITION AND NETWORK EFFECTS

The theory advanced in this chapter asserts that the success of BITs is better explained using the model of a sequential/evolutionary game, characterised by network effects. It is a well-known fact that network effects create collective action problems.[41] The sequential decisionmaking structure of these games clearly distinguishes them from a prisoner's dilemma, in which non-cooperative forces lead the parties to adopt the worst possible solution. However, before presenting this theory, two ideas that play an important role in explaining the BIT generation's emergence must be reviewed: competition for capital among states, and network externalities.

The model described in this chapter does not assume strong competition among developing countries. States are not and do not behave as firms. Competition for FDI is a highly distorted process, and accordingly, any model based on strong competition is necessarily a flawed representation of reality. As Bell and Parchomovsky remind us in their study of competition between US states in property law, the supply side of government services is far more complicated than any idealised market representation:

> A variety of political institutions, most importantly elected legislative bodies, produce property laws. These bodies, in turn, are staffed by decisionmakers who ideally have no direct pecuniary interest in the legislative outcome, but who often seek to maximize ideological preferences, personal reputation, reelection opportunities, and other political rents, sometimes at the expense of state

[39] ibid.
[40] ibid.
[41] See Baird et al, n 15, 208.

profits or the public welfare. The agency problem that plagues corporate law thus expresses itself even more sharply in the political context.[42]

Therefore, the network theory of the BIT generation explained below does not adopt a strong version of state competition. While accepting the fact that countries have competed for FDI, it depicts this competition as a 'weaker' version of the classic market-based process. Indeed, in this weaker competition model, developing countries that wish to attract FDI are interested in signaling their commitment to property rights and the rule of law, but only up to a certain point, and subject to all the distortions of the political process.[43] In such a context, competition may only partially explain why countries accept rules that, prima facie, are not 'favourable' to them, and that would have never been adopted in the absence of those competitive forces.

In addition to weak competition, the theory developed here relies on the notion of network effects and, more precisely, on that idea's previous application to the field of corporate law, particularly in the context of states' competition for corporate charters in the United States.[44] Network effects—also referred to as 'bandwagon effects'—is an economic concept describing those markets in which the utility derived from the consumption of a good or service increases as more users consume the same good or service.[45] In other words, network effects are positive consumption externalities.[46] They are external demand-side scale economies arising from the fact that the number of users who demand a product or service increases the future number of users.[47] Each consumer who decides to buy

[42] Abraham Bell and Gideon Parchomovsky, 'Of Property and Federalism' (2005) 115 *Yale Law Journal* 72, 98. See also, Robert H Sitkoff and Max M Schanzenbach, 'Jurisdictional Competition for Trust Funds: An Empirical Analysis of Perpetuities and Taxes' (2005) 115 *Yale Law Journal* 356, 363 (analysing state competition with respect to trust funds regulation in the US, and concluding that '[o]ur findings not only contradict the simple, state-revenue-based model but also cast doubt on recent high-profile work that, by showing a lack of tax revenue from attracting new business, questions the existence of the phenomenon').

[43] See United Nations Conference on Trade and Development, *South-South Cooperation in International Investment Arrangements* (New York, United Nations, 2005) 7 (available at www.unctad.org/en/docs/iteiit20053_en.pdf) (observing that '[t]he signing of a BIT has the effect of signaling that a country wishes to provide a stable, transparent and predictable investment environment in which investments can thrive . . . In other words, signing is signaling—enforcing is another matter').

[44] See Michael Klausner, 'Corporations, Corporate Law, and Network of Contracts' (1995) 81 *Virginia Law Review* 757. For a general analysis of network effects and the law, see Mark A Lemley and David McGowan, 'Legal Implications of Network Economic Effects' (1998) 86 *California Law Review* 479.

[45] See Michael Katz and Carl Shapiro, 'Network Externalities, Competition and Compatibility' (1985) 75 *American Economic Review* 424, 424.

[46] See Robert B Ahdieh, 'Making Markets: Networks Effects and the Role of Law in the Creation of Strong Securities Markets' (2003) 76 *Southern California Law Review* 277, 288.

[47] See Jeffrey H Rohlfs, *Bandwagon Effects in High-Technology Industries* (Cambridge, Mass, MIT Press, 2001) 20–21.

the product affects the decision of the rest, increasing the utility that the latter would derive from consuming the same good.[48]

The most typical examples of network products are telephones and faxes, where the individual products lack any inherent value outside the physical network. Yet there are other products—such as computers and their operative systems, as well as typewriter standards (such as QWERTY)—that form 'virtual networks': in those cases the products have inherent value, but their total worth appears only when bound to a group of people using the same standard.

Networks effects produce considerable distortions within standard microeconomic models of competition. They may even lead to market failure. Products that have network effects 'have dynamics that differ from those of conventional products and services. They are quite difficult to get started and often end up in a ditch before they can get under way. Once enough consumers have gotten on a bandwagon, however, it may be unstoppable'.[49] These products are especially prone to 'tipping' or de facto standardisation, 'which is the tendency of one system to pull away from its rivals in popularity once it has gained an initial edge'.[50] For the same reasons, once a product has become the dominant standard in the market, the accrued network externalities lend it an advantage over newly introduced innovations.[51] Changing such a product would be costly 'because new relation-specific investments have to be made. In such a situation, systems that are expected to be popular—and thus have widely available components—will be more popular for that very reason'.[52]

These products display lock-in effects—also called 'inertia'[53] or 'excess inertia'[54]—that enable them to outsell competitors even in the event that those competitors are inherently superior. As Rohlfs explains, 'the best product does not necessarily win the bandwagon effect. On the contrary, if an inferior product for any reason gets an early edge in number of customers, it may well win the race'.[55] That is, 'once one option has enough of a head start, superior technological alternatives may never get the chance to develop'.[56]

[48] See Ahdieh, n 46, 298.

[49] Rohlfs, n 47, 4.

[50] Michael Katz and Carl Shapiro, 'System Competition and Network Effects' (1994) 8 *Journal of Economic Perspectives* 93, 106.

[51] See Klausner, n 44, 791.

[52] Katz and Shapiro, n 50, 94.

[53] See H Peyton Young, *Individual Strategy and Social Structure* (Princeton, Princeton University Press, 1998) 15.

[54] See Joseph Farrell and Garth Saloner, 'Standardization, Compatibility, and Innovation' (1985) 16 *RAND Journal of Economics* 70, 71 ('[Excess inertia] impedes the collective switch from a common standard or technology to a possibly superior new standard or technology'). See also, Baird, n 15, 212 (observing, as well, that consumers 'may reject a new, superior product because a network already exists for the old one').

[55] Rohlfs, n 47, 43.

[56] Avinash Dixit and Barry Nalebuff, *Thinking Strategically* (New York, Norton, 1991) 238.

Alternative products that fail to infiltrate the market may have yielded to a more efficient equilibrium.[57]

One important consequence is that in the presence of network effects, an equilibrium may not exist or multiple equilibria may exist,[58] but regardless, nobody can be assured that the optimal result will be reached.[59] This suggests, as Katz and Shapiro remark, that if someone is trying to explain the actual equilibrium reached by a product with network effects, 'one would like to have a theory that includes the factors that lead to one outcome or the other'.[60] The same idea is endorsed by Peyton, according to whom 'equilibrium can be understood only within a dynamic framework that explains how it comes about (if in fact it does)'.[61] Moreover, as David posits, '[a]ny economist who would explain the particular equilibrium outcome (among the multiplicity of eligible candidates) towards which this system converges *must necessarily have recourse to the historical details of its evolution*'. (emphasis added)[62]

The first detailed application of network effects to the field of law was put forth by Michael Klausner in a ground-breaking article about corporate law's role as a virtual network of contracts.[63] The core concept of Klausner's theory is that corporate contracts, if worded using the same terms, form networks. These contracts 'have network externality qualities, and the firms that use a particular contract term form a "network" analogous to the network of PC users. Unlike a telephone network, where units are physically connected, a contractual network (like a PC network) is linked together by commonly used complementary products'.[64]

According to Klausner, when a contract clause or term is widely-used, many factors contribute to elevate its value, all of which share in common at least one thing: they enhance predictability, one of the core attributes of the rule of law.[65] In his view:

> More judicial precedents can be expected, on average, to enhance the clarity of the term. Common business practices implementing the term may become

[57] See Peyton, n 53, 14.

[58] See Katz and Shapiro, n 50, 94.

[59] See Brett H McDonnell, 'Getting Stuck' (2003) 31 *Hofstra Law Review* 681, 704–05. See also, Paul A David, *Path Dependence, its Critics and the Quest for 'Historical Economics'* 9 (available at http://129.3.20.41/eps/eh/papers/0502/0502003.pdf). See also his seminal work on the subject, Paul A David, 'Clio and the Economics of QWERTY' (1985) 75 *American Economic Review* 332.

[60] Katz and Shapiro, n 50, 96–97.

[61] Peyton, n 53, 4.

[62] Paul A David, *Path Dependence and the Quest for Historical Economics: One More Chorus of the Ballad of Qwerty*, University of Oxford, Discussion Papers in Economic and Social History No 20, November 1997, at 21 (available at www.nuffield.ox.ac.uk/economics/history/paper20/david3.pdf).

[63] Klausner, n 44, 761.

[64] ibid 775.

[65] See also, McDonnell, n 59, 701.

> established, further reducing uncertainty. Legal advice, opinion letters and related documentation will be more readily available, more timely, less costly, and more certain. Finally, firms may find it easier to market their securities.[66]

Network effects are directly tied to the vagueness and ambiguity that is pervasive, and sometimes desirable, in the law.[67] On the one hand, the inherent value of a clause or legal term depends on its autonomous clarity (that is, textual interpretation). On the other hand, network benefits derive from several different sources, the most important of which is the network externalities that reduce uncertainty. The more firms that adopt the same charter term, the more the term will be litigated, and therefore, the more future judicial interpretations will be provided.[68] In other words, 'the expected quantity and frequency of judicial interpretations is positively related to the number of firms that adopt the term. Thus, to the extent that future judicial interpretations are beneficial, they are network benefits associated with particular corporate contract terms'.[69] Hence, a substantial source of value for the term lies in *future* interpretations.[70]

Alec Stone Sweet, in the context of judicial governance, provides valuable insights that help to explain network effects in the law.[71] Stone Sweet argues that legal institutions and adjudication are 'fundamentally conditioned by how earlier legal disputes in that area of the law have been sequenced and resolved'.[72] An essential element of his account is the existence of 'some minimally robust conception of precedent'.[73] Stone Sweet describes his theory in the following terms:

> [H]ow courts typically operate and how legal actors typically behave are likely to provoke and then sustain the path dependent development of litigation and judicial rule-making. Given some underlying notion of precedent, these processes can be expected to exhibit some significant degree of randomness—through the vagaries of sequencing—and non-ergodicity—through the survival of rules announced in past rulings; and judicial rule-making can be expected to provoke positive feedback effects—more litigation and the construction of litigation networks—and to move the law along paths that are relatively inflexible—that is, costly or impossible to reverse.[74]

[66] Klausner, n 44, 761.

[67] See Colin S Diver, 'The Optimal Precision of Administrative Rules (1983) 93 *Yale Law Journal* 65, and Louis Kaplow, 'Rules versus Standards: An Economic Analysis' (1992) 42 *Duke Law Journal* 557.

[68] See Klausner, n 44, 776.

[69] ibid.

[70] ibid 778. Benefits from past decisions are not network effects, but learning effects (where 'past' means with respect to the date of adoption of the term by the party).

[71] See Alec Stone Sweet, 'Path Dependency, Precedent, and Judicial Power' in Martin Shapiro and Alec Stone Sweet, *On Law, Politics, and Judicialization* (New York, OUP, 2002) 112 ff.

[72] ibid 113.

[73] ibid 118.

[74] ibid 120–21.

As shown in Figure 3, Stone Sweet's starting point is that legal norms are essentially indeterminate, and all bodies of law are imperfect and incomplete (point ID in Figure 3).[75] But legal reasoning has the power, through analogy, to create doctrinal or argumentation frameworks, that is, 'discursive structures that organize (1) how parties to a legal dispute ask questions of judges and engage one another's respective arguments, and (2) how courts frame their decisions'.[76] These doctrines and frameworks reduce the degree of indeterminacy among legal norms. According to the author, '[b]y formalizing the results of analogic reasoning into precedents . . . judges give the legal system a measure of "relative determinacy"'.[77] More precisely, '[j]udicial rule-making, being more or less authoritative, should function to reduce uncertainty about the nature and scope of the standard, and also to provoke and reinforce feedback effects'.[78] The outcome is that, over time, we move from ID towards AD (the latter which represents the ideal of absolute determinacy):

Figure 3: Stone Sweet's propagation of argumentation frameworks

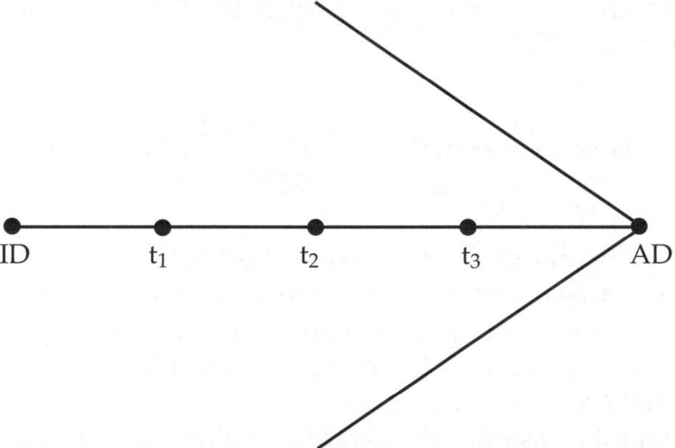

It is precisely this process of judicial rule-making, based on legal provisions commonly adopted by a certain group of users, which constitutes the key network effect observed in the law. In any case, future interpretation of ambiguous language is not the only bandwagon externality that a network of contracts may display. First, certain common business practices also constitute network externalities; as in the case of future precedents, they reduce uncertainty. The assumption here is that the more firms to use a given contract term, 'the larger, and possibly more varied, the base of common practice will be'.[79]

[75] ibid 122.
[76] ibid 124.
[77] ibid.
[78] ibid 117.
[79] Klausner, n 44, 780.

Second, enhancement of legal services and an experienced judiciary are important sources of externalities. '[T]he legal services available for a commonly used term may be superior, either in terms of cost or quality, to those provided for a less commonly used term'.[80] Once a term is adopted, firms need not expend money in drafting and negotiation costs. The costs of research and interpretation of a term are also reduced when the term is widely used.[81] In addition, with a commonly used term, the judiciary will become more experienced and able to decide cases in an expedient and well-considered way.[82] Firms can trust that future decisions will be consistent and correct.

Third, there are marketing externalities. Firms need to attract investors, who must analyse and price the new stocks. A common term may permit investors and securities analysts to estimate the value of the firm's securities through routine financial analysis, at relatively low cost.[83] Meanwhile, an idiosyncratic or uncommon term will be priced in a manner reflecting the uncertainty and lack of knowledge associated with it, leading to higher costs of pricing services. In consequence, 'the cost of capital for firms that use common charter terms may be lower than the cost for those that use uncommon terms'.[84]

III A FORMAL MODEL OF THE BIT GENERATION AS A VIRTUAL NETWORK

The theory of the BIT generation as a virtual network rests on a fairly simple idea: there are economies of scale to having a global regime of treaties worded using closely similar substantive terms, particularly when those terms are as open-ended as the ones contained in BITs. This section provides a formal model for that theory.

The model takes as one of its starting points an important assumption regarding the different credibility and commitment mechanisms available to developing countries. Considering that the latter are reasonably interested in attracting FDI and protecting property rights, I assume here the following ranking of preferences, which are listed in increasing order of sovereignty costs for a given level of investment (following EGS, these costs represents a combination of two factors: loss of governmental regulatory power over internal economic activity, and the loss of jurisdiction by domestic courts):

80 ibid 782.

81 See Roberta Romano, 'Law as a Product' (1985) 1 *Journal of Law, Economic and Organization* 225, 274–75.

82 See McDonnell, n 59, 703–04.

83 See Klausner, n 44, 785.

84 ibid.

a) Only domestic law remedies plus customary international law (state of affairs before the emergence of the BIT generation). This means, essentially, no international forum where to litigate investment disputes, which are therefore left to domestic courts and diplomatic protection under customary international law.[85]
b) BIT-like-*minus* treaties, that is, treaties with substantive standards less convenient to foreign investors, worded in terms different from those commonly used in BITs;
c) BITs as we know them today (that is, treaties containing the key substantive provisions of no expropriation with compensation, fair and equitable treatment, national treatment, full protection and security, most favoured nation, among others);
d) BIT-like-*plus* treaties, that is, treaties with substantive standards more convenient to foreign investors, though worded in terms different from those commonly used in BITs;
e) Tailor-made contracts, containing ICSID arbitration clauses, that fully extract all rents from developing countries. (This category may include BITs that contain umbrella clauses, clearly the type most harmful in terms of sovereignty costs.[86]).

Farrell and Saloner created the formal model of network externalities that I am following here to explain the emergence of the BIT generation, ie, the jump from a) to c). The game has two players (countries). The use of domestic law plus customary international law is the old standard (*X*), and the emergence of BITs with their common substantive terms, the new competing standard (*Y*).

In this game, at time t_1, players can switch to the new standard (an irreversible decision), or stay with the older one; at time t_2, those who stayed with the old standard may decide to switch to the new one. Each player is uncertain of whether the other would follow if the former switches (incomplete information). A particularly important assumption for our purposes is that due to network effects, it is better for both parties to be under the same standard. That is, they are better off together in *X*, or in *Y*, than separately under *X* or *Y*, respectively. If $Bi(a,U)$ is the benefit function of each country—where i represents the type of country according to its political/legal/cultural preferences, and a the number of countries adopting standard *U*, be it *X* or *Y*—then $Bi(2,X) > Bi(1,X)$ and $Bi(2,Y) > Bi(1,Y)$.

[85] In contrast to Guzman, I do not consider CERDS to be the best alternative for developing countries. Instead, I assume that the best option for developing countries in terms of sovereignty costs is for them to simply retain full control over their own domestic legal systems and institutions, signaling their commitment to property rights using domestic public law.

[86] Guzman, n 14, 655, and 680, seems to assume—incorrectly—that all BITs contain umbrella clauses.

This means that even in the case where the first country to sign a BIT captures a higher proportion of FDI, the net benefits captured are smaller than if the two countries had joined the system together. This is due to the presence of network effects. In other words, network benefits are assumed to be higher than the net benefits associated with any extra FDI/sovereignty costs that a country can induce/bear from being the first and lone mover.[87] Underlying this assumption is the idea that the inherent value of BITs is much lower than normally regarded; the first treaty is merely an esoteric document with extremely broad provisions, and nobody knows whether it will work, or how it will work.

As explained before, i reflects the individual country's preferences, where countries with stronger preference (indexed by higher values of i) 'are more eager to switch to Y, both unilaterally and if the other firm [countries] also switches'.[88] Developing countries may therefore be classified according to three different categories of i: first, those that are not interested in attracting foreign investment, including countries that strongly prefer to protect their sovereignty and countries who do not place too much faith in the new standard as a means for attracting FDI (lower values of i, in the extreme $i = 0$);[89] second, countries that urgently need to attract foreign investment and are therefore anxious to signal their commitment to protect foreign property, whatever the sovereignty costs, which includes countries that do not particularly value their sovereignty and countries that have high expectations about the effectiveness of BITs for increasing FDI (higher values of i, in the extreme, $i = 1$); and, third, countries in the intermediate scenario, who value foreign investment, but are at the same time sensitive to the sovereignty costs of signing BITs and reasonably optimistic regarding their efficacy (middle values of i).

Farrell and Saloner make a particularly interesting assumption that suits the BIT model very well; namely, that $B^1(1,Y) > 0$ and that $B^0(2,Y) < B^0(1,X)$. Their explanation is clear:

> Unilateral switching is worthwhile for at least one possible type of firm [country], and (at the other end of the spectrum) there are some types that would rather remain alone with the old technology [legal standard] than join the other firm [country] with the new technology [legal standard]. This assumption also implies that for intermediate values of i, a firm's [country's] decision will at least sometimes depend on its predecessor's decision: this is what makes the model interesting.[90]

[87] In contrast, Ryan Bubb and Susan Rose-Ackerman, 'BITs and Bargains: Strategic Aspects of Bilateral and Multilateral Regulation of Foreign Investment' (2007) 27 *International Review of Law and Economics* 291, 302, begin their analysis from the opposite assumption.

[88] Farrell and Saloner, n 54, 76.

[89] This was the case for countries involved in import substitution industrialisation policies. According to Paul C Szasz, 'The Investment Disputes Convention and Latin America' (1970) 11 *Virginia Journal of International Law* 256, 260, '[i]t must be recognized that not all governments are uniformly eager to attract foreign private investment'.

[90] Farrell and Saloner, n 54, 76.

This model, in other words, includes the realistic assumption that whereas some countries were ready to sign BITs whatever their sovereignty costs, at the same time, there were countries that preferred to preserve the integrity of their domestic legal and political systems and institutions at any price.

Relying upon these assumptions, as well as some more technical ones that do not alter the basic idea explained here, Farrell and Saloner prove that, under certain conditions, there exists a unique 'bandwagon equilibrium'. In our context, this means that there is an equilibrium (that is, a Perfect Bayesian equilibrium) in which each country plays the following 'bandwagon strategy': First, if $i > i^*$, then the country switches at time t_1; second, if $i^* > i \geq \bar{\imath}$, then the country waits until time t_2 and changes only after observing that the other country switched at time t_1; and, third, if $i < \bar{\imath}$, then the country does not move away from standard *X*.[91] This equilibrium, in which each player follows the strategy depicted above, is shown in Figure 4:

Figure 4: An illustration of Farrel and Saloner's derivation of critical levels $\bar{\imath}$, i^0, and i^* ($\tilde{\imath}$ was added for more clarity)

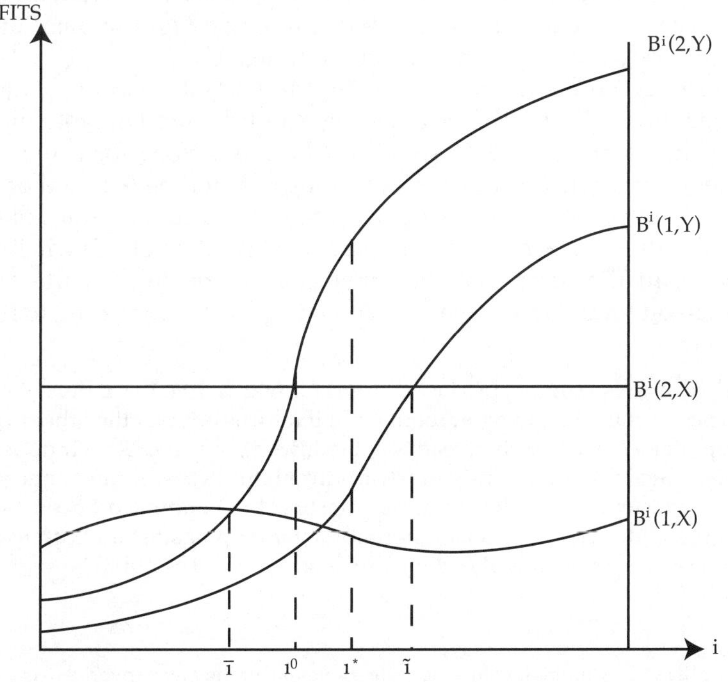

Source: Joseph Farrell and Garth Saloner, 'Standarization, Compatibility, and Innovation' (1985) 16 *RAND J Econ* 70, 78 (the original graph has been simplified and slightly modified).

[91] ibid 76. For a full proof of the value and existence of i*, see Farrell and Saloner, ibid.

The difference between the curves $B^i(1,Y)$ and $B^i(2,Y)$ represents the network effects of standard Y. These benefits will be explained in greater detail in the next section, though for now it can be said that they follow the profile suggested by Klausner in the corporate law field. Similarly, the difference between the curves $B^i(1,X)$ and $B^i(2,X)$ corresponds to the network effects of standard X. The network benefits of domestic law plus customary international law, then, represent the flipside of BITs. Indeed, if a country can gain a larger slice of the FDI pie by signing BITs—even if only slightly larger—then countries abandoning domestic law plus customary international law may impose costs (externalities)—a smaller FDI pie—on countries remaining under those rules.[92]

In this model, it is crucial to understand the relative positions of $\bar{i}$, i^0, i^*, and $\tilde{i}$. First, note that the point $\bar{i}$ corresponds to the country which is indifferent with respect to staying with the old standard or switching to the new one (that is, $B^{\bar{i}}(2,Y) = B^{\bar{i}}(1,X)$). Second, that the point i^* is located above i^0. Here, the intuitive explanation of that relative position is that a country which is thinking of changing at time t_1 needs to obtain substantial benefits from network effects in order to balance the risk that the other country will not change at time t_2 due to having $i < \bar{i}$ (a piece of information inaccessible to the first country at time t_1).[93]

Third, given the assumption of incomplete information, i^* has a lower value than $\tilde{i}$ ($i^* < \tilde{i}$). This is a key aspect of the model. Note that $\tilde{i}$ represents the point where $B^{\tilde{i}}(1,Y) = B^{\tilde{i}}(2,X) = 0$; therefore, for values of i above $\tilde{i}$, the country will be better off switching to Y at time t_1, whether or not the other country follows the lead later at time t_2. Yet, for values of i between i^* and $\tilde{i}$ (that is, $i^* \leq i < \tilde{i}$), the country will take the risk of switching to Y at time t_1, in the hope that the other country belongs to the group that changes at time t_2 (having an i such that $\bar{i} \leq i < i^*$). According to Farrell and Saloner:

> There are also some types just above i^* for which $B^i(1,Y) < 0$ [ie, $i^* \leq i < \tilde{i}$]. These types start the bandwagon rolling, but if it turns out that the other firm was of a type below $\bar{i}$ (so that their lead is not followed), they regret their decision *ex post*. Here, again, there is straightforward intuition. Types in this range sufficiently favor technology Y that they risk starting the bandwagon even though they know with positive probability that they are up against an 'intransigent' with type less than $\bar{i}$ and will end up worse off if this turns out to be so.[94]

[92] If BITs have inherent value—ie, without yet including any network effects—then countries signing BITs (or at least, some of them) may be able to decrease the cost of capital and therefore redirect some portion of FDI from the limited common pool available for all developing countries.

[93] See Farrell and Saloner, n 54, 77. See ibid, where they also formally prove that $Bi^*(1,Y) < 0$ and $Bi^*(2,Y) > 0$.

[94] ibid 79.

Hence, given these values of $\bar{i}$, i^0, i^*, and $\tilde{i}$, developing countries can be classified according to one of the following four types (displayed from left to right in Figure 3). First, from 0 to $\bar{i}$: the country does not change at time t_1 or at time t_2. Second, from $\bar{i}$ to i^0: the country does not change at time t_1 but changes at time t_2 if the other country already did so at time t_1; however, the change represents a negative outcome for this country. Third, from i^0 to i^*: the same scenario exists as the previous one, but the country is better off under the new standard. Fourth, from i^* to $\tilde{i}$: the country changes at time t_1, but does so at a risk because it will be better off only if the other country changes at times t_1 or t_2. Fifth, above $\tilde{i}$: the country changes at time t_1 and is better off whether or not the other country changes to the new standard.

Following this framework, there are several reasons why a country signs a BIT (standard Y). First, if a country has $i > i^*$, then it will join the BIT network at time t_1 simply because it benefits more from the inherent value of BITs than it would by remaining under the old standard ($i > \tilde{i}$), or because it anticipates that future countries will follow its lead ($\bar{i} < i < i^*$). In the former case, the inherent value of BITs is significant enough to justify the change to the new standard. For the latter case, network effects are essential; as noted in the previous extended citation of Farrell and Saloner, '[t]hese types start the bandwagon rolling, but if it turns out that the other firm [country] was of a type below $\bar{i}$ (so that their lead is not followed), they regret their decision ex post'.

Second, a country may join the BIT network at time t_2 after seeing that other countries have joined it ($\bar{i} \leq i < i^*$). Here again, it is possible to identify two different groups. One is comprised of countries that switch to the new standard but would have preferred that everybody stayed with the old one ($\bar{i} \leq i < i^0$); the other is comprised of countries that find themselves better off with the new standard ($i^0 < i < i^*$). The former group is of particular importance because it represents countries that switch if and only if the other country also switches, yet would have preferred that the new standard had not come along.[95]

There is a third simpler explanation exogenous to this model that also should not be rejected. Basic changes in domestic political preferences may increase the value of i to the point that a previously recalcitrant country is willing to sign BITs—from below $\bar{i}$, to above $\bar{i}$, or even above i^*.[96] The experience of China and Eastern Europe in the 1980s proves that a country may jump from $i < \bar{i}$ to $i > i^*$. In fact, as already pointed out, it is difficult to deny that the emergence of the BIT generation during the late 1980s and early 1990s is linked to the fall of the Soviet Union, and consequently,

[95] ibid.

[96] However, as pointed out by David M Kreps, 'Intrinsic Motivation and Extrinsic Incentives' (1997) 87(2) *American Economic Review* 359, 362, '[e]conomists are loathe to rely on this sort of explanation, with good reason: it simply assumes the answer'.

the Communist Bloc. In other words, the values of *i* increased for the entire world.

It must be acknowledged that it is difficult, even impossible, to know which of the previous reasons specifically explains why a particular country began or did not begin to sign BITs. Nevertheless, the bandwagon effects model remains valid. Crucially, it provides an explanation of why countries that would have preferred to remain in full control of their domestic legal systems and institutions—and, therefore, opposed to any change to customary international law and any attempt to create an investment treaty—were forced by circumstances to join the BIT network.

One of the main advantages of this model is its effectiveness in providing answers to efficiency questions. I use the term efficiency in its Kaldor-Hicks sense (the movement away from domestic law plus customary international law toward a BIT network, in order to be considered Pareto-superior, would require that all countries should have $i > i^0$; a condition obviously too strong to hold in reality). The analytic structure devised by Farrell and Saloner demonstrates that this movement might or might not be efficient from the perspective of developing countries. It is certainly possible that winners won more than what losers lost. But it is also possible that losers lost more, and therefore, that it would have been better for the entire group to stay with the old standard. Ultimately, the solution is empirical in nature, and would require us to know the values of *i* for all countries.[97]

It is worth noting that the movement from domestic law plus customary international law to BITs may have been inefficient even without its having resulted from a prisoner's dilemma. In network effect terms, this is a case of 'excess momentum'[98]: 'It is possible that the switch will be made even though the sum of the benefits is negative. This occurs when one of the firms [countries] favours the switch and, although the other opposes it strongly, the latter prefers switching to remaining alone with the old technology'.[99] However, this is only a hypothesis, not a necessary outcome.

Following the same analysis, we can now invert the roles and compare the BIT network—now put as standard *X*—with a potential new standard *Y*. One might envision developing countries meeting around the table (even as a very small group), creating a new BIT-like-*minus* treaty with provisions more favourable to them than actual BITs, and then proposing it to the rest of the world. Why, then, has this not occurred? Aside from the reality that developing countries lack the bargaining capacity to impose such a standard on developed countries, the answer may be in part that

[97] In the model by Bubb and Rose-Ackerman, n 87, 302, and in contrast to the model of Guzman, the prisoner's dilemma result 'is by no means necessary'.

[98] Farrel and Saloner, n 54, 79.

[99] ibid 78–79.

developing countries are prone to 'excess inertia,'[100] defined as a situation 'that impedes the collective switch from a common standard or technology to a possibly superior new standard or technology'.[101]

If two countries belong to the area where $i^0 \leq i < i^*$—where $Bi(2,Y) > 0$—"the switch will not be made, although it would have been made in a world of complete information and although both firms [countries] would then be better off . . . *The intuition is clear. Both firms* [countries] *are fencesitters, happy to jump on the bandwagon if it gets rolling but insufficiently keen to set it rolling themselves*?" (emphasis added)[102]. This result is even more pronounced in the case where one country fits the previous description, but the other is located in the area $\bar{\imath} \leq i < i^0$ —where $Bi(2,Y) < 0$. In this latter scenario, the sum of the benefits may be positive, and therefore the switch—had it occurred—would have been efficient for the group of developing countries.

In other words, countries choose not to abandon a bandwagon treaty, because they are 'reluctant to give up the bandwagon benefits that they currently enjoy'.[103] Uncertainty about whether other users will follow the same path impedes them from changing to a more efficient standard, or even making the effort to do so. Once the extremely high organisational and transactional costs of concluding a new bilateral or multilateral treaty are taken into account (particularly when countries with $i < \bar{\imath}$ are also at the table), the failure to reach such a treaty should be clear.[104]

Setting aside the fact that the OECD Multilateral Agreement on Investment (MAI) failed primarily due to disagreement among developed countries—not due to developing countries' nonparticipation in the negotiations (except a few observers)[105]—excessive inertia point to the fact that it may not be in the best interest of any individual state to advance or ascribe to a new standard, be it bilateral or multilateral, until enough countries have already done so (unless, of course, the new standard has enough substantial inherent benefits). The BIT virtual network displays lock-in effects that explain why countries sign BITs and why, at the same time, fail to make any efforts to reach a new treaty that may be inherently superior.

[100] ibid 78.

[101] ibid 71.

[102] ibid 78.

[103] Rohlfs, n 47, 43.

[104] Bubb and Rose-Ackerman, n 87, 309, reach a similar conclusion: 'Negotiating and concluding an MAI is a costly process. As the surplus achievable by an MAI narrows, it is less likely that countries will be willing to bear the transaction costs of creating an MAI'.

[105] See M Sornarajah, *The International Law on Foreign Investment*, 2nd edn (CUP, Cambridge 2004) 291 ff; Rainer Geiger, 'Regulatory Expropriations in International Law: Lessons from the Multilateral Agreement on Investment' (2002) 11 *New York University Environmental Law Journal* 94; and, David Singh Grewal, 'Network Power and Global Standardization: The Controversy Over the Multilateral Agreement on Investment' (2005) 36 *Metaphilosophy* 128.

IV EVIDENCE OF THE BIT GENERATION AS A VIRTUAL NETWORK

This section presents evidence in favour of the virtual network theory of the BIT generation. First, it advances five structural arguments, that is, general features of virtual networks which can also be found in the BIT system. Then, it identifies the positive externalities of the BIT network, the main one being the fact that interpretations rendered by arbitral tribunals under one BIT affects the content of other BITs.

A Five Structural Arguments

These five structural arguments seek to prove that the BIT system shares many of the typical characteristics of products presenting network externalities. The first is that, as network effects theory dictates, there must exist a 'community of interests' among players.[106] Following the logic of Guzman and EGS, there is undeniable a group of developing countries interested in attracting FDI, which presumably must be obtained from a relatively limited common pool controlled by investors of developed countries. As previously stated, the assumption here is of only 'weak' competition.

In order to illustrate some of the propositions outlined by this section and the following one, I will use Chile as a case study. The Chilean case is particularly interesting because that country was a pioneer in liberalising its economy; by the mid-1980s, it had already become renowned for its demonstrated commitment to property rights and economic liberties through domestic constitutional law. Notwithstanding that fact, Chile joined the BIT system in the early 1990s. Competition to attract FDI indeed played an important role, at least judging from the rhetoric employed by the dominant coalition who pitched the ICSID Convention and initial BITs to congressmen at the beginning of the 1990s. There were special concerns about the movement toward economic liberalisation in formerly Communist European countries, as well as the rest of Latin America;[107] that threatened to erode Chile's competitive edge.

[106] Rohlfs, n 47, 21.

[107] The discussion in the Chilean Congress sheds some light on the importance that both the President of the country and congressmen attached to competition among developing countries. See eg *Mensaje de Su Excelencia el Presidente de la República con el que inicia un proyecto de Acuerdo que aprueba el Convenio sobre Arreglo de Diferencias Relativas a Inversiones entre Estados y Nacionales de Otros Estados, Senado, Sesión 37a, martes 12 de marzo de 1991, Legislatura 321a Extraordinaria*, 3574–5: '[*V*]*arios países de América Latina están tratando de salir de las dificultades económicas y políticas que los afectaron en la década pasada. Estos hechos hacen prever que la competencia internacional por atraer capitales extranjeros se hará cada vez más difícil y que nuestro país deberá esforzarse para mantener los índices de inversión extranjera alcanzados. Una condición básica para continuar atrayendo a los inversionistas es que Chile no pierda ventajas frente a*

However, not all developing countries have been ongoing players in this race, and certainly, not all have displayed the same intensity of preference for attracting FDI over that relevant period. From 1959 to the mid-1980s, and especially during the period when support for CERDS was high, a prominent group of countries displayed a very weak interest in attracting FDI. Instead, they were involved in import substitution industrialisation policies that made them reluctant to have foreigners own and control any fraction of the national economy. Strong ideological and political opposition to liberalisation and FDI—ie, low values of *i* in the formal model—were real barriers that, again, in hindsight, cast into doubt the assumption of strong competition for FDI.

The second structural argument is represented by the notion of de facto standardisation. All BITs signed from 1959 up until today, though not identical, have very similar substantive provisions. As explained in chapter 1, the four most important of these—expropriation with compensation, fair and equitable treatment, national treatment, and most favoured nation—appeared as early as in the first two years of the network's existence (1959–1961), although rooted in previous treaties of the nineteenth and twentieth centuries. We have thus witnessed a clear convergence toward a 'non co-operative standard',[108] or de facto standard, created very early in BIT history.[109]

Indeed, the wording of these provisions remains relatively consistent across treaties.[110] For instance, according to Wälde, the fair and equitable treatment clause is 'a standard that is repeated, more or less identically, in most of the other over 2500 investment treaties in force at present'.[111] Furthermore, any small difference in scope and effect that does exist may end up being erased by the very application of the MFN clause.

Lawyers—whose practice substantially resolves around language nuances—could retort that all BITs are different. Indeed, it is not unusual that BIT awards take the differences among treaties into account. But this critique does not really contradict the idea of the BIT generation as a network. The degree to which all BITs must be similar in order to be able to generate a common professional practice, is a sociological question. Of course, there is a legal component to that sociological question as well:

otros países competidores. En este orden de ideas, el Gobierno ha reestructurado la postura de Chile respecto de tratados que tienen por propósito la protección de inversiones extranjeros entre los Estados signatarios'. See also, *Discusión General, Senado, Sesión 39a, miércoles 20 de marzo de 1991, Legislatura 321a Extraordinaria*, 3850 ff.

108 Farrell and Saloner, n 54, 72 ('One of the clearest features of noncooperative standards setting is its bandwagon quality. When compatibility is an important consideration for a firm setting its product specifications, early movers can influence later movers' decisions'). ibid 72, fn 5.

109 See n 6.

110 See nn 3, 4, and 5.

111 *International Thunderbird Gaming Corporation v Mexico*, UNCITRAL Ad Hoc Arbitration (van den Berg, Wälde, Portal), Award (26 January 2006), Separate Opinion ¶ 25.

legal language must show sufficient commonality if it is to permit that social practice to exist.

In my opinion, the way in which international investment law is practised today in the context of BITs, meets that critical threshold of similarity. Today, we can talk about a international investment law or investment treaty law because there is already a common practice in the process of becoming a new and distinctive legal field. As indicated in the main empirical work currently available on BIT precedents, 'the development of an investment treaty case law or jurisprudence is unmistakable, and has not gone unnoticed in recent times, by treaty tribunals, and by those appearing before them'.[112]

Similarly, one of the best articulated recent treatises on this subject states that we are watching the emergence of a 'common law of investment protection, with a substantially shared understanding of its general tenets'.[113] Wälde also noted that we are witnessing the emergence of a 'common law of world investment . . . *with an increasingly dense and increasingly similar and sometimes in the core identical treaty network as a foundation*' (emphasis added).[114] And, in the same vein, Bishop notes how 'ICSID Tribunals and ad hoc tribunals are carefully reviewing the previous decisions',[115] and how 'they are refining the law from one case to the next . . . seeking to harmonize their decisions with the earlier decisions and not simply ignoring them'.[116]

[112] Jeffrey P Commission, 'Precedent in Investment Treaty Arbitration' (2006) 24 *Journal of International Arbitration* 129, 129. See also, VV Veeder, 'The Necessary Safeguards of an Appellate System' in Federico Ortino et al (eds), *Investment Treaty Law. Current Issues I* (London, The British Institute of International and Comparative Law, 2006) 9, 9, observing that: '[F]or the unsuccessful investor, an adverse final award is obviously adversely final and the result or reasoning of the award can act as a defect of precedent for other investors facing the same issues . . . Likewise for a State, an award's reasoning may also become an important defect of precedent in future disputes under the same or similar investment law or BIT without being a legal precedent at all'.

[113] McLachlan et al, n 7, 19.

[114] Thomas W Wälde, 'The Present State of Research Carried Out by the English-Speaking Section of the Centre for Studies and Research' in Centre for Studies and Research in International Law and International Relations, *New Aspects of International Investment Law* (Leiden, Nijhoff, 2006) 63, 120.

[115] Doak Bishop, 'The Case for an Appellate Panel and Its Scope of Review' in Federico Ortino et al (eds), *Investment Treaty Law: Current Issues I* (London, The British Institute of International and Comparative Law, 2006) 15, 16.

[116] ibid 17. See also, Judith Gill, 'Inconsistent Decisions: An Issue to Be Addressed or a Fact of Life?' in Federico Ortino et al (eds), *Investment Treaty Law. Current Issues I* (London, The British Institute of International and Comparative Law, 2006) 23, 25 ('[O]ne only has to read the awards given in published cases to see the importance that is attributed to previous decisions by investment arbitration tribunals. They are, in practice, treated as "soft precedent" '). Even when tribunals dissent from previous decisions, they tend to discuss those decisions, and to adopt a respectful and considered stance.

At this point in time, arbitral case law is very clear on the existence of network effects. Among scores of decisions proving this point,[117] a representative one can be found in *Bayindir*, where the Tribunal held that:

> In support of their position, both parties relied extensively on previous ICSID decisions or awards, either to conclude that the same solution should be adopted in the present case or in an effort to explain why this Tribunal should depart from that solution . . . The Tribunal agrees that it is not bound by earlier decisions, *but will certainly carefully consider such decisions whenever appropriate*. (emphasis added)[118]

In *Noble Energy*, the Tribunal more strongly stated that:

> The Tribunal considers that it is not bound by previous decisions. At the same time, it is of the opinion that it must give due consideration to earlier decisions of international tribunals. *It believes that, subject to compelling contrary grounds, it should adopt solutions established in a series of consistent cases*. It also believes that, subject to the specific provisions of a given treaty; to the circumstances of the actual case and the evidence tendered, *it should seek to foster the harmonious development of investment law and thereby to meet the legitimate expectations of the community of States and investors towards certainty of the rule of law*. (emphasis added)[119]

Taking the above into account, the case of BITs, and investment treaties in general, can be depicted as indicated in Figure 5. The four circles represent the protection afforded to investors by four different BITs. The BITs are not identical, but they all share an important area (*X*). Moreover, three of these four also share a distinctive area (*Y*). And, of course, there are

[117] See eg *Chevron Corporation (USA) et al v Ecuador*, UNCITRAL Ad Hoc Arbitration (Böckstiegel, Brower, van den Berg), Interim Award (1 December 2008), ¶ 123; *Duke Energy Electroquil Partners and Electroquil SA v Ecuador*, ICSID Case No ARB/04/19 (Kaufmann-Kohler, Gómez, van den Berg), Award (18 August 2008), ¶¶ 116, 117, and 333; *Victor Pey Casado et al v Chile*, ICSID Case No ARB/98/2 (Lalive, Chemloul, Gaillard), Award (8 May 2008), ¶119; *Canadian Cattlemen for Fair Trade v US*, UNCITRAL Ad Hoc Arbitration (Böckstiegel, Bacchus, Low), Award on Jurisdiction (28 January 2008), ¶¶ 51, and 194 ff; *RosInvestCo UK Ltd v The Russian Federation*, SCC Case No V 079/2005 (Böckstiegel, Steyn, Berman), Award on Jurisdiction (October 2007), ¶ 49; *Saipem SpA v Bangladesh*, ICSID Case No ARB/05/07 (Kaufmann-Kohler, Schreuer, Otton), Decision on Jurisdiction and Recommendation on Provisional Measures (21 March 2007), ¶ 67; *ADC Affiliate Ltd et al v Hungary*, ICSID Case No ARB/03/16 (Kaplan, Brower, van den Berg), Award (2 October 2006), ¶ 293; *Fireman's Fund Insurance Co v Mexico*, ICSID Case No ARB(AF)/02/01 (van den Berg, Lowenfeld, Saavedra), Award (17 July 2006), ¶172; *Vladimir Berschader et al v Russian Federation*, SCC Case No 080/2004 (Sjövall, Lebedev, Weiler), Award (21 April 2006), ¶ 97; and, *AES Corporation v Argentine*, ICSID Case No ARB/02/17 (Dupuy, Böckstiegel, Bello), Decision on Jurisdiction (26 April 2005), ¶ 31.

[118] *Bayindir Insaat Turizm Ticaret Ve Sanayi AŞ v Pakistan*, ICSID Case No Arb/03/29 (Kaufmann-Kohler, Berman, Böckstiegel), Decision on Jurisdiction (14 November 2005), ¶¶ 73, and 76.

[119] *Noble Energy Inc and MachalaPower Cia Ltda v Ecuador and Consejo Nacional de Electricidad*, ICSID Case No ARB/05/12 (Kaufmann-Kohler, Cremades, Alvarez), Decision on Jurisdiction (5 March 2008), ¶ 50.

Figure 5: Representation of BITs' similarity

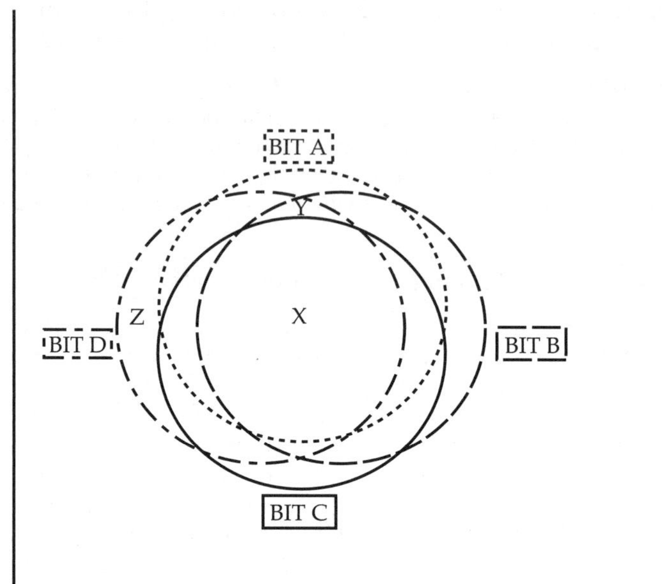

areas specific to each BIT (for example, area *Z* is unique to BIT D). The relevant point is that the four circles must be sufficiently close to one another so that area X be broad enough to permit the development of a common practice. Again, my impression and experience is that this is the case for BITs.[120]

The third structural argument is related to the fact that this 'standard' very much resembles the legal structure of constitutions; it contains *extremely* open-ended and ambiguous provisions that are quite wide in scope, and which do not provide immediate answers for resolving cases. As Klausner observed, this lack of determinacy is an essential condition for the presence of network effects in the law.

Indeed, the two key non-contingent standards in BITs, which have proven to be the most important provisions in practice, are perfect examples of this phenomenon. It is indeed difficult, or even impossible, to envision a broader standard than 'fair and equitable treatment'. One BIT Tribunal has candidly held that 'the exact content of this standard [fair and equitable treatment] is not clear'.[121] The concept of indirect expropriation

[120] See McLachlan et al, n 7, 19, according to whom 'the differences between treaties, and indeed between treaty and the substantive rights in custom, may be less than the common elements'. See also, Campbell McLachlan, 'The Principle of Systemic Integration and Article 31(3)(c) of the Vienna Convention' (2005) 54 ICLQ 279, 283–84.

[121] *Genin v Estonia*, ICSID Case No ARB/99/2 (Fortier, Heth, van den Berg), Award, (25 June 2001), ¶ 367.

is no less indefinite. The conceptual hurdles and corresponding lack of determinacy that characterise regulatory takings and state liability are well-understood throughout the world. In the investment law context, one NAFTA Chapter 11 Tribunal has noted that '[t]he Article 1110 [of NAFTA] language is of such generality [the expropriation clause] as to be difficult to apply in specific cases'.[122]

BITs are, in a sense, concise *economic constitutions* that apply to foreign investors. Because the resolution of cases depends on jurisprudential developments among international arbitral tribunals, the ultimate payoff from BITs depends not so much on the text of treaties already concluded, but on the interpretations adopted among the collection of awards that we are just beginning to see.[123] As with domestic constitutions, which are essentially linked to present and future judicial interpretation, BIT provisions are more likely to have network value than inherent value. This is Wälde's opinion, among others:

> [M]odern international investment law develops now mainly out of cases, and less out of treaties. Treaties may provide a jurisdictional basis, a structure of argument and major concepts to start and categorize the required more detailed line of inquiry, but the way treaty language develops into operative law—i.e. specific principles and rules governing the way tribunals decide—is now mainly a matter of emerging case law.[124]

Of course, as Stone Sweet demonstrates, for this to be the case, previous awards must be at least somewhat valued in international investment adjudication. This is true of BIT practice, as the second structural argument illustrates; almost all awards and parties' briefs contain multiple references to previous decisions. The prior decisions prove to hold a much more important role than that of mere citations: they structure the debate and determine the way in which both the parties and tribunals advance their legal arguments and reasoning. It is certainly worth noting that the absence of a central authority in the BIT system—such as the WTO Appellate Body— though slowing the impact of network effects, does not erase them. In the end, the problem is only one of speed.[125]

[122] *Feldman v Mexico,* Award, ICSID Case No ARB(AF)/99/1 (Kerameus, Covarrubias, Gantz), Award (16 December 2002), ¶ 98.

[123] As mentioned above, n 8, the first BIT award is from 1990.

[124] Wälde, n 114, 66.

[125] See Andrea K Bjorklund, 'Investment Treaty Arbitral Decisions as *Jurisprudence Constante*' in Colin B Picker et al (eds), *International Economic Law: The State and Future of the Discipline* (Portland, Hart Publishing, 2008) 265, 265 (commenting that '[t]he informal and dispersed regime of investment treaty arbitrations is not well suited to developing a system of formal precedent. Eventually, however, an accretion of decisions will likely develop a *jurisprudence constante*—a 'persisting jurisprudence' that secures 'unification and stability of judicial activity''). See also Gill, n 116, 27, who points precisely in this direction when advocating against an appellate system in investment arbitration: 'The second basis on which I would say that an appellate system is not necessary in treaty arbitration is that it may in any event be the case that over time the position in relation to many of the issues that are

The fourth structural argument stems from the fact that BITs did not represent the best institutional alternative for foreign investors. If BITs were the product of competition among developing countries, that competition did not erode all rents for those countries. As seen, there were more preferable alternatives for investors. Those included what I have called 'BIT-like-*plus* treaties', that is, treaties that could have offered more convenient standards to foreign investors—such as the US Friendship, Commerce and Navigation (FCN) program—and tailor-made contracts containing ICSID clauses, that would fully extract all rents. In other words, for investors, BITs did not represent the most convenient outcome of a 'race to the top'. Indeed, in 1990, when there was no BIT jurisprudence, Detlev Vagts commented that tailor-made contracts were quite preferable from the perspective of the investor:

> A priori it would seem that such an agreement [BIT], with a clause providing for resort to the International Court of Justice or an ad hoc international tribunal, would be comforting to the investor. One does have the suspicion that specific investor-host contracts would be better at addressing the specific problems that worry that particular investor.[126]

Therefore, existing BITs are clearly not the consequence of any race to the top. Even taking into account the competition between developing countries, this race has ended up at neither the top nor the bottom. In summary, the history of BITs cannot be compared to a static Bertrand equilibrium in a free market context, where, as a consequence of free market forces, the price ends up equaling marginal costs and eroding all producer's rents.[127]

The fifth and final structural argument is that the historical pattern of BITs perfectly fits the S-shape diffusion curve of network effect products (See Figures 6 and 7).[128]

The period from 1959 to the late 1980s corresponds to the stage at which the network had not yet reached its critical mass. In that period, countries concluding BITs were only those that strongly valued BITs, and for whom the sole inherent benefits outweighed all sovereignty costs.[129] It is worth noting that, during this period, the predominant BIT format did not involve investor–state arbitration (only state-to-state), and therefore, had

currently being debated will become more settled. In other words, the inconsistent decisions themselves will give rise to one approach being generally regarded as more preferable than another and so it will be adopted more frequently thereafter'.

[126] Detlev F Vagts, 'Protecting Foreign Direct Investment: An International Law Perspective' in Cynthia Day Wallace (ed), *Foreign Direct Investment in the 1990s: A New Climate in the Third World* (Boston, M Nijhoff, 1990) 112, 112.

[127] See Guzman, n 14, 672 n 104, who applies the concept of Bertrand equilibrium in his account.

[128] See Dixit and Nalebuff, n 56, 231.

[129] See Rohlfs, n 47, 23–24.

Figure 6: The 'S-Shaped' Diffusion Curve of Network Effect Products

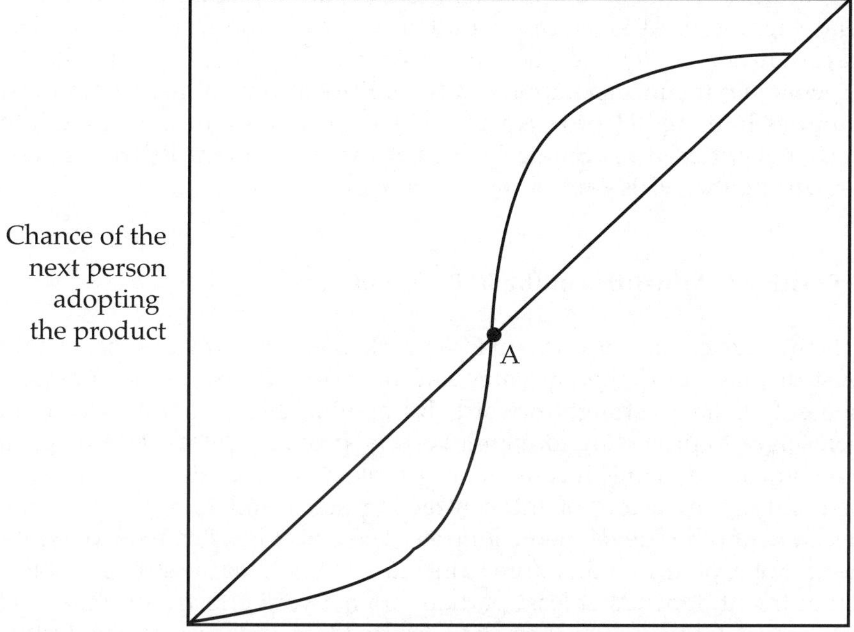

(Source: Dixit and Nalebuff).

Figure 7: The 'S-Shaped' BIT diffusion curve

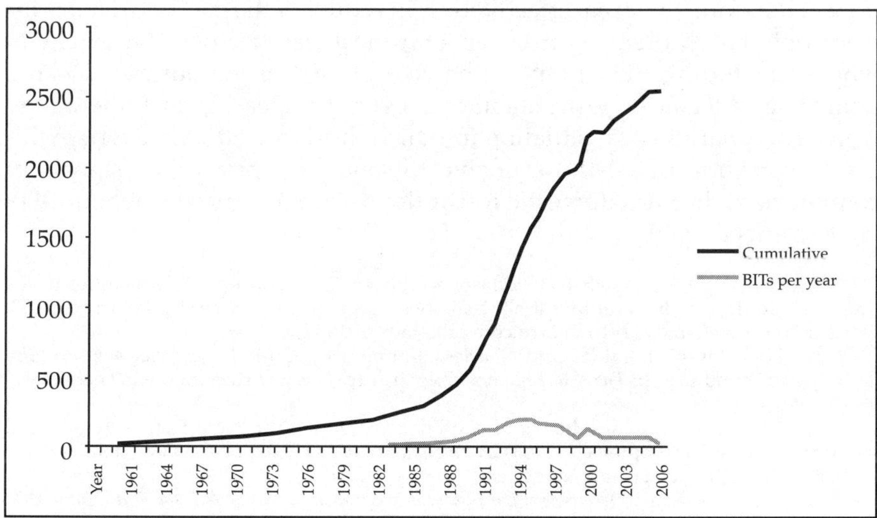

(Source: UNCTAD and ICSID).

much lower sovereignty costs.[130] After reaching the critical point—some time in the late 1980s—BIT development began to display a pronounced bandwagon roll. As is the case for other network products, once a critical mass of users has been reached, the effect may be almost unstoppable.[131] It seems that the incorporation of China, Russia, and former Communist countries into the BIT program played an enormous part in helping it to reach that critical mass. Similarly, the US's adoption of the BIT program—also during the 1980s—must have been relevant.

B Positive Externalities of the BIT System

If the BIT system is really a virtual network, then these treaties' provisions must display both inherent value and network effects. The idea behind inherent value is straightforward. By signing BITs, countries commit themselves to protecting foreign investors' property rights. This helps to overcome the dynamic inconsistency problem and signals the host state's credibility to investors of the contracting state, and to a lesser extent, investors of other developed countries. The object is, of course, to reduce the cost of capital, and therefore to increase FDI.[132] But the strength of this commitment depends at least partially on network effects: investors will rely on BITs only when they have received assurance that the system works, and the reliability of that system depends—as I argue here—on the number of countries joining the system.

With respect to inherent value, it should be noted that—with the exception of domestic courts[133]—BITs do not replace domestic law and institutions. Therefore, their real effectiveness in reducing the cost of capital is far from obvious. Moreover, from an empirical perspective, the extent to which concluding BITs reduces the cost of capital in countries lacking political and legal domestic stability is even less clear. In fact, there may well exist a paradoxical situation in which those countries are more willing to conclude BITs—those unable to send the appropriate signals of commitment through domestic institutions—are the ones for whom BITs are less effective.[134]

[130] See ch 1, Figure 1, pp 65–66. See Jason Webb Yackee, 'Conceptual Difficulties in the Empirical Studies of Bilateral Investment Treaties', Legal Studies Research Paper No 1053, October 2007 (available at http://ssrn.com/abstract=1015088).

[131] See Nicholas Economides and Charles Himmelberg, *Critical Mass and Network Size with Application to the US Fax Market* (available at http://www.stern.nyu.edu/networks/95-11.pdf).

[132] See Guillermo Aguilar Alvarez and William W Park, 'The New Face of Investment Arbitration: NAFTA Chapter 11' (2003) 28 *Yale Journal of International Law* 365, 368.

[133] See ch 3, n 4 and accompanying text.

[134] See Mary Hallward-Driemeier, *Do Bilateral Investment Treaties Attract FDI? Only a Bit ... and They Bite* (June 2003), World Bank Policy Research Working Paper No 3121, 23 (available at http://ssrn.com/abstract=636541); and Eric Neumayer and Laura Spess, *Do Bilateral*

What then, exactly, are the network effects of BITs? As suggested earlier, it is possible to observe the same network externalities that Klausner previously identified in the corporate context. Most of these effects derive from the fact that BITs are worded using *extremely* broad and open-ended terms. The following four are the most important examples.

First, there are interpretative externalities. As previously explained,[135] although arbitral awards applying BITs do not formally carry precedential value for future cases (regarding the same BIT, as well as other BITs), in practice they have strong persuasive force. Even though there is no formal doctrine of stare decisis in international law, in investment treaty arbitration we can properly speak of *soft precedents* or *de facto precedents*.[136] As Wälde points out in his separate opinion in *Thunderbird*, '[w]hile there is no formal rule of precedent in international law, such awards and their reasoning form part of an emerging international investment law jurisprudence'.[137] In the end, future decisions, on the whole, will reduce the high uncertainty of BIT standards.

Note that the beneficial character of these interpretative network effects—at least, from the perspective of developing countries—depends on whether future BIT jurisprudence will stabilise at reasonable levels of protection of investments. More concretely, it depends on whether BIT jurisprudence will crystallise in accordance to what chapter 1 identified as *the good case* or *BITs-as-developed-countries-constitutional-law-and-no-more*, that is, the updated Calvo Doctrine. In this equilibrium, BIT jurisprudence protects investments in terms not higher than those that courts in developed countries apply to their own nationals. Certainly, when developing countries concluded BITs they expected *the good case*, though they might have anticipated *the bad case* as a possible scenario.[138]

A second externality can be found in the same common practices that Klausner identifies in the corporate world. Developing countries will

Investment Treaties Increase Foreign Direct Investment to Developing Countries? (May 2005) 5 (available at http://ssrn.com/abstract=616242). See also, Susan Rose-Ackerman and Jennifer Tobin, 'Do BITs Benefit Developing Countries?', in Roger P Alford and Catherine A Rogers (eds), *The Future of Investment Arbitration* (Oxford, OUP, forthcoming 2009) (noting that 'BITs cannot entirely substitute for a host country's weak political environment for investment. Rather, the marginal impact of BITs is greater in countries that already have moderately effective legal regimes') (see full quotation in n 163).

135 See nn 118–119 and accompanying text.

136 McLachlan et al, n 7, 18 (noting that 'while no *de jure* doctrine of precedent exists in investment arbitration, a *de facto* doctrine has in fact been building for some time'); see also, ibid 72–76. More recently, see Bjorklund, n 125.

137 *Thunderbird*, Separate Opinion, n 111, ¶ 15. See also, ibid ¶ 16: 'While individual arbitral awards by themselves do not as yet constitute a binding precedent, a consistent line of reasoning developing a principle and a particular interpretation of specific treaty obligations should be respected; if an authoritative jurisprudence evolves, it will acquire the character of customary international law and must be respected'.

138 As explained in ch 1, 76–77, *the bad case* or *BITs-as-gunboat-arbitration*, corresponds to a libertarian jurisprudence that is not currently in place in any developed country.

begin to treat investment treaty law as a new layer added to the existing body of law regulating state behaviour. BITs will thus be assumed to be a new form of global constitutional and administrative law, and experts on foreign investment law will be consulted on a daily basis by states and firms about the compatibility of regulatory reform and state behaviour with investment treaty law.

Thirdly, the quality / price ratio of legal services—both during bargaining and implementation of treaties—may be substantially increased by having a single, basic set of key substantive standards of treatment. Consider first the legal cost of bargaining and drafting. It is precisely the network effects of BITs that have enabled countries to sign thousands since 1990, without even discussing their terms. Probably the most dramatic—and amusing—example of this phenomenon is the set of experiments conducted by UNCTAD. The organisation puts several developing and developed countries into the same room for a short period of time, and asks them to conclude treaties.[139] At the end of the meeting, thanks to network effects, they usually conclude a fair number of them.

The cost of research and interpretation is also reduced when a term is widely used. Lawyers can invest in this transaction-specific asset—knowledge of BITs and investment treaty law—and having done so, are equipped to deal with those rules on a long-term basis.[140] More treatises, books and law journal articles are published every year on the topic of BITs. More seminars, professional gatherings, and even comprehensive courses are dedicated to investment law in law schools all over the world. Top law firms are increasingly developing new departments and practices focused on investment arbitration.[141] Meanwhile, there is an increasing number of experienced arbitrators coalescing around a single body of international investment law. The accumulated expertise in that field should help cases to be decided in a more efficient and considered way (with the caveat expressed before, that is, the *good case* vs the *bad case*).

Fourthly, marketing externalities are extremely relevant in the case of BITs. Countries wish to attract foreign investors, and the latter must

[139] See eg www.unctadxi.org/templates/Event____149.aspx, where UNCTAD explains its strategy: 'UNCTAD organized BITs signing ceremonies during UNCTAD X in 2000 and the LDC III Conference in Brussels in 2001. On the occasion of UNCTAD XI, the Secretariat organized a high-level signing ceremony for Bilateral Investment Treaties in Sao Paulo, Brazil on 15 and 16 June 2004. Six bilateral agreements were signed at the ministerial level by seven countries (Benin, Chad, Guinea, Lebanon, Lesotho, Mauritania and Switzerland). The BITs were signed by and between: Benin and Lebanon, Chad and Lebanon, Chad and Guinea, Guinea and Lebanon, Lebanon and Mauritania, Lesotho and Switzerland'. See also, www.unctadxi.org/templates/Event____149.aspx?selected=context.

[140] This argument is taken from Romano, n 81, 275–76, who explains the impact of legal counsel in helping Delaware to dominate the corporate charter competition.

[141] As Alec Stone Sweet, *The Judicial Construction of Europe* (New York, OUP, 2004) 41, has observed, '[w]e have good reasons to think that the development of legal institutions will provoke the development of networks of legal actors specializing in that area of the law. For these actors, existing argumentation frameworks establish the basic parameters for action'.

analyse and price political and regulatory risks. Treaties which are phrased in idiosyncratic terms will be priced higher than those using the generally accepted standards of BITs. Once a certain number of BITs are in existence, the cost of capital may be lower when adopting a BIT rather than a different treaty. This may be true even in the event that some of those idiosyncratic provisions are, on their face, more favourable to investors.

Probably the best example is the case of political risk insurance. It seems that, in some cases, political risk insurance premiums have been priced lower for countries that signed a BIT with the investor's home state.[142] In Chile, this externality was pivotal to its decision to join the BIT network. In the *travaux préparatoires* of the Statute approving the ICSID Convention, the President of the Republic cited it as one of the most important factors:

> [Concluding BITs and the ICSID Convention] will permit foreign investors to obtain lower insurance premiums than those actually obtained in the normal situation [without a BIT]. Therefore, the accession of Chile to this type of treaties would permit the country to keep an advantaged position in order to attract foreign investment.[143]

After interviewing the former chief legal officer (*Fiscal*) of the Chilean Agency that studied and implemented foreign investment policies at the time—*Comité de Inversiones Extranjeras*—I can corroborate the fact that lower premiums were highly relevant to Chile's decision to join the BIT system.[144]

V PROVIDING ANSWERS FOR CRITICAL QUESTIONS

This section attempts to answer the four key questions that any theory of the BIT generation must necessarily confront: First, why did all developing countries adopt more or less the same rules? Second, why did they

[142] There is one international institution, MIGA (Multilateral Investment Guarantee Agency) that provides this kind of insurance. Similarly, several governmental agencies provide insurance to their nationals: OPIC in the US, COFACE in France, CESCE in Spain, UK Trade and Investment in the UK, Netherlands Foreign Investment Agency in the Netherlands, and KfW Bankegruppe in Germany. There are also private insurance companies that provide this service.

[143] *Mensaje de Su Excelencia el Presidente de la República con el que inicia un proyecto de Acuerdo que aprueba el Convenio sobre Arreglo de Diferencias Relativas a Inversiones entre Estados y Nacionales de Otros Estados, Senado, Sesión 37a, martes 12 de marzo de 1991, Legislatura 321a Extraordinaria*, 3574, 3575: '*Los tratados de protección de inversiones tienen dos ventajas para el inversionista: primero, representan una condición para que operen los mecanismos de seguros públicos de inversión de sus respectivos países.* Esto último permite al inversionista acceder a pólizas de seguro para su inversión a un costo menor del que deberían afrontar normalmente. *De este modo, la incorporación de Chile a este tipo de tratados permitiría mantener al país en una situación ventajosa para atraer inversión extranjera. En este aspecto Chile está concediendo actualmente una ventaja en favor de aquellos países que sí han suscrito estos tratados*'. (emphasis added)

[144] Interview with Roberto Mayorga, former *Fiscal* of *Comité de Inversiones Extranjeras* (Santiago de Chile 9 November 2005).

adopt the *specific set of rules* that we see today in BITs, as opposed to others? Third, why did those rules exist in the 'market' for more than 20 years before being widely adopted? And fourth, why do BITs constitute an equilibrium that is neither the worst possible scenario for host states nor the best scenario for investors?

When first presenting the theory of the BIT generation as a virtual network, I answered the first and last of these questions: Developing countries have concluded BITs, all worded in closely similar terms, because of the network effects implicit to a system of such treaties. The movement from domestic law plus customary international law to BITs might or might not have been efficient for the group of developing countries; even if inefficient, however, an excess of momentum would explain such a scenario without our needing to have recourse to a prisoner's dilemma. Moreover, there were institutional arrangements more costly than BITs—tailor-made contracts with ICSID clauses or more demanding treaties, such as the US FCN program—which prove that BITs do not represent the worst possible case for developing countries.

Now I will deal with the two remaining questions. According to the theory of network externalities, this requires an analysis of the history and politics of the system. As explained before, understanding the equilibrium that prevails in the presence of network effects demands that one refer to 'the factors that lead to one outcome or the other'.[145] Indeed, any account trying to explain 'the particular equilibrium outcome (among the multiplicity of eligible candidates) towards which this system converges must necessarily have recourse to the historical details of its evolution'.[146] It is noteworthy, then, that the theory of the BIT generation as a virtual network revisits several classical theories rejected by both Guzman and EGS when presenting their competition model.[147]

Any political-historical account of the BIT system's development requires that we separate the two successive stages of the bandwagon effect: from 1959 to the second half of the 1980s, and then up to the present. Using the language of network externalities theory, during the first phase only a small group of 'initial users' adopted the standard.[148] In our case, only developing countries that were highly interested in attracting FDI, and those that considered the inherent value of BITs to be higher than the sovereignty costs involved, concluded BITs.

[145] See n 60.

[146] See n 62.

[147] See Guzman, n 14, 667–69. See also, EGS, n 14, 826, who label these rejected theories as 'hegemonic, cognitive, or idealistic'.

[148] Rohlfs, n 47, 23 ([the initial user set] corresponds to 'individual entities and small groups (mainly pairs) of entities that that [*sic*] can justify purchasing the service, even if no others purchase it').

During this period, developing countries that joined the BIT system only concluded a small number of BITs.[149] Indeed, they individually signed fewer BITs than developed countries. A comparison of the five developed and developing countries that, in each respective category, signed the most BITs in the first 20 years of the network's history, makes this evident: Germany (45), Switzerland (32), France (19), Netherlands (15), Belgium (9), versus Egypt (12), Korea (7), Romania (7), Singapore (7), Malaysia (6).[150] At the same time, the sovereignty costs of signing BITs were much lower than they are today, since most treaties did not provide investor–state arbitration.

As noted, this first stage fits reasonably well, to various degrees, with several of the theories that Guzman and EGS reject when arguing for their competition model.[151] For example, the cases of Korea and Malaysia may well be explained by 'enlightenment theories', that is, cases of developing countries which understood that they would be better off under an institutional setting of free market and property rights. At the same time, many of the Asian and African countries that signed treaties with Germany and Switzerland from 1959–79 may exemplify 'power-based' or 'coercive' theories, or even more accurately, trade-off theories (in which developing countries sign BITs to obtain specific benefits from developed countries). Indeed, this was an explanation suggested by Rudolf Dolzer in the early 1980s[152], and more recently by Salacuse and Sullivan in 2005.[153]

In addition, there are three specific aspects to the first historical stage of the BIT system that help us to understand its network aspects. First, as already mentioned, for countries concluding BITs, the program might have appeared visibly less expensive in terms of sovereignty costs than its two main competitors: the US FCN program and the original understanding of the ICSID Convention (that is, contracts with ICSID arbitration clauses). Not surprisingly, BITs outperformed both of them.

[149] In the period 1959–79, the following developing countries concluded two or more BITs: Benin (2), Cameroon (3), Central African Republic (2), Chad (3), Congo (2), Cote d'Ivoire (5), Ecuador (2), Egypt (12), Gabon (5), Guinea (3), Indonesia (6), Jordan (4), Korea (7), Liberia (3), Madagascar (4), Malaysia (6), Mali (2), Malta (3), Mauritius (2), Morocco (6), Niger (2), Pakistan (2), Romania (7), Rwanda (2), Senegal (4), Singapore (7), Sudan (5), Syria (3), Tanzania (3), Thailand (3), Togo (2), Tunisia (6), Uganda (3), Yugoslavia (4), and Zaire (4).

[150] When looking at the whole period—1959–2000—due to the impact of what happened during the 1990s, EGS, n 14, 822, arrive at the opposite conclusion: '[I]t is clear that the distribution of BITs over the past forty years is significantly more peaked (less uniform) for the host than it is for home countries . . . The standard deviation of their distributions is also lower for host countries than it is for home . . . suggesting a more clustered pattern of activity for the host. If BITs are driven by home country programs, it is not especially apparent in the data'.

[151] As previously noted, I do not reject these classical theories. Indeed, a network theory is particularly concerned with the history of how one standard overcame the others, and those theories play an important role in this regard.

[152] See Rudolf Dolzer, 'New Foundations of the Law of Expropriation of Alien Property' (1981) 75 *American Journal of International Law* 553, 567.

[153] See Salacuse and Sullivan, n 11, 77–78.

Second, the BIT programs launched by Germany in 1959, and Switzerland in 1960, clearly served as focal points for countries that later wished to launch investment treaty programs, and also signal their commitment to property rights and economic liberalisation. Focal points are extremely relevant to network products. As Klausner explains, 'the factors that make a contract term focal are matters of perception rather than logic'.[154] This includes 'historical accidents' of all types. The original German and Swiss BIT models served as an excellent template: very brief, reasonable and open-ended provisions, and therefore, relatively easy to negotiate. Consequently, countries wishing to pursue property rights and economic liberties—at least, on a bilateral basis—may have found an easy and inexpensive device to pursue that objective, in the form of BITs.[155]

Third, it is a remarkable fact that, by the mid-1980s and as recently as the end of that decade, there were doubts as to whether BITs would survive in the future. This indicates that the critical threshold for the bandwagon effect had not yet been reached at that time, or if so, without anyone's awareness. The following comment made by the UN Centre on Transnational Corporations in 1988 is very telling:

> [I]n spite of their growing popularity, bilateral investment treaties remain a limited phenomenon . . . Nevertheless, it is obvious that the present number of bilateral investment treaties remains far below the number of treaties that could be concluded by all the countries concerned with such investment relations, if they were prepared to do so; and although the number of bilateral investment treaties will no doubt continue to increase in the coming years, it is doubtful whether the gap [between the actual number and the number of treaties and could be signed] will ever be closed.[156]

The second stage of the BIT network development displays the bandwagon effect. The normal pattern with network effect products is that once the critical mass of users has been attained, the effect may be irreversible. With respect to the BIT context, it seems that the addition of China and the former Communist countries provided that critical mass during the 1980s. These countries needed to send a clear signal to the world that, at least in their relations with foreign investors, they had abandoned the communist political and economic models and were now ready to embrace property rights and contracts. In the expectation that the inherent value of BITs would help them to reduce the cost of capital; they began using BITs that contained investor–state arbitration provisions.

[154] Klausner, n 44, 800.

[155] The signaling function of constitutional law for developing countries is studied by Daniel A Farber, 'Rights as Signals' (2002) 31 *Journal of Legal Studies* 83, 83–98, and those arguments can be transposed to international law. In general, for the case of international law, see Beth A Simmons, 'Money and the Law: Why Comply with the Public International Law of Money' (2000) 25 *Yale Journal of International Law* 323.

[156] United Nations Centre on Transnational Corporations, *Bilateral Investment Treaties* (Boston, Graham and Trotman, 1988), 105–06.

After BITs began to be widely accepted, the calculus for developing countries changed. For those seeking to attract FDI, BITs now offered not only the original inherent value of these treaties, but also network benefits. If the network effects were assumed to be positive, as was very probably the case, then for many developing countries the net value of joining the BIT network—BIT inherent value plus network benefits less sovereignty costs—may have began to be positive. For others, even in the absence of that positive net value, it may still have been better to join the BIT network than to remain isolated under the old standard of domestic law plus customary international law.

It should be reiterated that there was and still is great uncertainty regarding the main variable of this network calculus: whether the jurisprudence will crystallise at the equilibrium to which I have referred as *the good case* (*BITs-as-developed-countries-constitutional-law-and-no-more*). Commentators usually overlook the uncertain character of BIT jurisprudence. As noted previously, the first BIT case was decided in 1990. That same year, Vagts commented that 'BITs have not yet been put to the test so that we do not really know how much they enhance the security of foreign investment'.[157] Still eight years later, UNCTAD affirmed that 'it is nevertheless remarkable that, after nearly 40 years of BIT practice, information on the experience with the application of BITs still remains rather sketchy and anecdotal'.[158] Yet, given the apparently reasonable character of the main BIT provisions, capital-importing states during the 1990s might have assumed that the odds favoured *the good case*.

Moreover, during this second stage, countries that did not conclude BITs may have begun to experience two adverse effects. First, they may have started to lose FDI from the common pool, as it was redirected to countries concluding BITs; secondly, they may have been punished for sending the wrong message to the 'market'. As Beth Simmons explains, 'as more countries commit themselves to a rule, non-commitment sends a strong negative signal'.[159] Been and Beauvais recognise the same effect: 'signaling in a competitive market can have a "snowball" effect: As more countries commit themselves to a particular standard, "holdouts" are more likely to develop a negative reputation, making it more difficult to attract investment'.[160] Farber, however, explains this effect with the greatest degree of precision.

[157] Vagts, n 126, 112.

[158] United Nations Conference on Trade and Development, *Bilateral Investment Treaties in the Mid-1990s* (New York, United Nations, 1998) 141. UNCTAD also notes, ibid 140, that 'little is known about how individual protection standards have been applied in practice, and there are few judicial or arbitral authorities to shed light on this aspect'.

[159] Simmons, n 155, 323.

[160] Vicki Been and Joel C Beauvais, 'The Global Fifth Amendment? NAFTA's Investment Protections and the Misguided Quest for an International 'Regulatory Takings' Doctrine' (2003) 78 *New York University Law Review* 30, 120.

Although writing about constitutionalism, he expresses it in terms perfectly applicable to BITs:

> [T]he collective surge by countries toward constitutionalism in regions like eastern Europe is also explainable on the basis of signaling. If no one else has adopted constitutionalism, failure to do so may not be particularly meaningful. When everyone else in a region is adopting constitutionalism, however, failure to do so becomes a sharp negative signal. This signal is particularly important because other countries in the same region are likely to be in competition for the same sources of financial and human capital. Thus, being a holdout against a regional trend can be expensive, and as a result an entire region may shift suddenly into the constitutionalist column once a tipping point is reached.[161]

If this account is correct, then network effects and the concept of excessive inertia would explain one of the greatest mysteries surrounding the BIT generation: why developing countries suddenly rushed to join the BIT network during the second half of the 1980s and early 1990s, more than 20 years after the program was first created (that is, why BITs existed in the 'market' for a long time without being adopted).[162] Similarly, network effects explain why developing countries strongly opposed abandoning the standard of 'domestic law plus customary international law', and why they have rejected the idea of any multilateral investment treaty. More specifically, network effects show why an important group of countries—whose i is such that $\bar{\imath} < i < i^{*}$—may have preferred to stay during time t_1 with the old standard—domestic law plus customary international law—switching to BITs only after a reasonable number of countries have already concluded such treaties. Furthermore, there is an important subgroup of countries that switched—whose i is such that $\bar{\imath} < i < i^{0}$—who would have ideally preferred to have remained permanently with the old standard, rather than switching to the new one.

Finally, an important question must be addressed: how does this model explain the correlation (or lack of) between BITs and FDI? Studies to date have shown contradictory evidence, most of them concluding that there is no correlation, or that it is very weak.[163] But these studies only represent

[161] Farber, n 155, 96.

[162] Bubb and Rose-Ackerman, n 87, 307, recognise that 'the timing of the sudden increase in BIT signings that occurred in the 1990s' is generally an 'an empirical puzzle'.

[163] There are two studies concluding that BITs fulfilled their expected objective: Neumayer and Spess, n 134, 27 (finding that '[d]eveloping countries that sign more BITs with developed countries receive more FDI inflows', particularly in countries with poor institutional quality); and Tim Büthe and Helen V Milner, *The Politics of Foreign Direct Investment into Developing Countries: Increasing FDI through Policy Commitment via Trade Agreements and Investment Treaties?*, Draft (available at http://nathanjensen.wustl.edu/me/files/ButheMilner.pdf) at 35 (finding that 'countries can fruitfully use international investment treaties to induce foreign investment'). But see the following studies that do not conclude a clear positive correlation: (1) Jennifer Tobin and Susan Rose-Ackerman, *Foreign Direct Investment and the Business Environment in Developing Countries: The Impact of Bilateral Investment Treaties*, Yale Law School (May 2005) at 31 (available at http://ssrn.com/abstract=557121) (concluding that the relationship between BITs and FDI is weak: 'BITs, by

early efforts, and as such, their methodologies are subject to debate. Here, I should add the following concerns. Comparing all BITs without controlling for type—ie, whether or not they have investor–state arbitration provisions—could potentially lead to incorrect conclusions. Also, it would be interesting to see what results are obtained if we control for the inherent network benefits of BITs. We still do not know if BITs truly had inherent value, that is, if signing BITs could really reduce the cost of capital and attract FDI for countries with higher values of *i* at a time when the BIT program was not popular (between 1959 and the late 1980s).

Similarly, the correlation between the value of BITs, and the stability of domestic legal systems and institutions, is still not well understood. One thing is clear: it would be false to present BITs as displaying their effects independently of domestic law. BIT legal design does not replace domestic law and institutions, but rather, controls them. As Reisman and Sloane assert, BITs require that developing countries 'establish and maintain an appropriate legal, administrative, and regulatory framework' and an 'efficient and legally restrained bureaucracy'.[164] We therefore need to know which countries with high values of *i* would actually be able to capitalise upon the alleged inherent value of BIT: all of them, or only those with well established legal systems and institutions.[165] Only with more empirical data on inherent value it will be possible to effectively study the second

themselves, appear to have little impact on FDI'); (2) Hallward-Driemeier, n 134 (finding that BITs do not lead to increases in DFI); (3) Salacuse and Sullivan, n 11, 105–06, 120–21 (strictly finding a positive effect, under certain circumstances, for US BITs, but not for those of OECD countries); and, (4) Peter Egger and Micheal Pfaffermayr, 'The Impact of Bilateral Investment Treaties on Foreign Direct Investment' (2004) 32 *Journal of Comparative Economics* 788, 790, and 801 (concluding that 'BITs exert a positive and significant effect on real stocks of outward FDI' but that 'the advantages of simply signing a BIT are inconsequential'). In their most recent article, Rose-Ackerman and Tobin, n 134, 2–3, summarised their conclusions in the following terms: 'Our statistical work provides evidence for three claims. First, the number of BITs signed by a developing host country with wealthy home countries generally has a positive impact on overall FDI in subsequent periods. Second, the marginal impact of a country's own BITs on its ability to attract FDI falls as the global coverage of BITs grows. Although the growing world total of BITs is likely to have stimulated overall FDI to the developing world, countries compete with each other for FDI funds. Hence, the marginal value of BITs as a signal of a strong investment environment in a particular country is dampened by the greater availability of BITs. As the worldwide coverage of BITs increases, the benefit from one's own BITs, although remaining positive, falls. Third, the political-economic environment in a country matters for how BITs affect FDI flows. BITs cannot entirely substitute for a host country's weak political environment for investment. Rather, the marginal impact of BITs is greater in countries that already have moderately effective legal regimes. Furthermore, the general economic environment in a host country interacts with the number of BITs to enhance or dampen BITs' impact on FDI. Overall, the relationship between BITs and FDI is powerfully influenced by both the global and local environments for FDI. The impact of BITs on FDI seems to vary a good deal across time for countries at different levels of development. BITs are not a panacea. Countries with very poor investment environments need to improve domestic conditions before BITs can have an impact on flows of FDI'.

[164] W Michael Reisman and Robert D Sloane, 'Indirect Takings and Its Valuation in the BIT Generation' (2003) 74 BYIL 115, 117.

[165] See nn 134 and 163.

stage of BIT history and network effects, and by implication, the whole BIT system.

I must acknowledge that my virtual network account of the BIT generation may be difficult to either verify or debunk (although, if evidence concerning lower insurance premiums holds, it would be a solid empirical argument in its favour). Among other reasons, this is due to the fact that in network products, a standard may have been adopted given its focal properties, which depend more on perception than on logic. This means that developing countries' *beliefs* about inherent value and network effects may have been the more relevant factor in the adoption of BITs, as opposed to the actual presence of those effects.

CONCLUSIONS: NORMATIVE IMPLICATIONS OF THE VIRTUAL NETWORK THEORY OF THE BIT GENERATION

The theory advanced here demands detailed empirical study. Nevertheless, I hope that I have been able to provide sufficient arguments to support my belief that a prisoner's dilemma model presents an incomplete and incorrect picture of what occurred during the last fifty years of state responsibility for injuries to aliens. There are collective action problems, to be sure, but due to the non-simultaneous timing of the decision to conclude BITs and the presence of network effects, the resultant game varies considerably from the one which Guzman proposes.

The BIT generation is more accurately depicted as a virtual network. Because the treaties' key substantive provisions are worded in such similar terms, investors and countries are able to benefit from a single, relatively unified body of international investment law. As illustrated, it is the anticipation of that future body of law by the relevant players that constitutes the bulk of network effects in this case, lending BITs a particular credibility as compared to more idiosyncratic and lesser-known treaties. This is what ultimately motivated all members of the network to adopt essentially the same standards, rather than negotiate tailor-made provisions.

The descriptive model defended in this chapter has substantial implications for the normative questions raised by the emergence of the BIT generation. A theory in which competition leads capital-importing states to adopt treaties containing standardised substantive provisions, that are open-ended and reasonable in character, appears much more favourable to developing countries than Guzman and EGS's account, where countries erode all benefits in their race to attract investment. The equilibrium in the theory presented here is sub-optimal, and does not reflect a race to the bottom among developing countries.

Undoubtedly, when joining the BIT network, developing countries traded sovereignty for credibility. But as we have seen, this trade-off was made under essential conditions of uncertainty: as to whether the future BIT-case law would crystallise in what chapter 1 has referred to as *the good case—BITs-as-developed-countries-constitutional-law-and-no-more*—or whether it would crystallise in what is referred to as *the bad case—BITs-as-gunboat-arbitration*. Even today, it is not possible to know which scenario will ultimately prevail. Investment treaty law is continuing to evolve, and remains highly dependent upon the specifics of each case. But step-by-step, the jurisprudence is slowly crystallising. The richness and complexity that characterises the legal argumentation today would have been unheard of at the birth of the process almost twenty years ago with the first award.

Under a network effects theory, there is still room for the hope that the BIT generation will go down in history as a valuable experiment in global governance, fostering a fair and just world order; or, in the words of Slaugther, 'a system of global governance that institutionalizes cooperation and sufficiently contains conflict such that all nations and their people may achieve greater peace and prosperity, improve their stewardship of the earth, and reach minimum standards of human dignity'.[166]

[166] Anne-Marie Slaughter, *A New World Order* (Princeton, Princeton University Press, 2004) 15.

3

Trading off Sovereignty for Credibility: Questions of Legitimacy in the BIT Generation

INTRODUCTION: LEGITIMACY IN INTERNATIONAL INVESTMENT LAW

DEVELOPING COUNTRIES DELEGATED sovereign powers when signing BITs and other investment treaties that contained investor–state arbitration provisions.[1] Investment treaties and their arbitral tribunals represent one of the most powerful versions of what Slaughter refers to as *vertical networks*. These treaties form a global governance scheme that has real teeth and whose performance does not depend on the will of foreign affairs ministries and diplomats.[2] From a merely descriptive perspective, BITs represent a movement that transcends democracy and sovereignty.[3]

The delegation of sovereign powers under modern BITs has not been trivial. Although these investment treaties do not replace domestic law and institutions, they do replace domestic tribunals for international arbitration, removing de facto a substantial component of municipal courts' jurisdiction.[4] Investment treaty tribunals entertain claims that

[1] In *Gas Natural SDG, SA v Argentine*, ICSID Case No ARB/03/10 (Lowenfeld, Alvarez, Nikken), Decision on Jurisdiction (17 June 2005), ¶ 29 (hereinafter, *Gas Natural*), the Tribunal noted that 'the provision for independent international arbitration of disputes between investors and host states' is 'a crucial element—indeed perhaps the most crucial element' of BITs. See also, *Eastern Sugar BV v The Czech Republic*, UNCITRAL Ad Hoc Arbitration (Karrer, Volterra, Gaillard), Partial Award (27 March 2007), ¶ 165.

[2] See Anne-Marie Slaughter, *A New World Order* (Princeton, Princeton University Press, 2004) 20.

[3] See Eric Stein, 'International Integration and Democracy: No Love at First Sight' (2001) 95 *American Journal of International Law* 489.

[4] In *Gas Natural* ¶ 29, the Tribunal noted that '[t]he creation of ICSID and the adoption of bilateral investment treaties offered to investors assurances that disputes that might flow from their investments would not be subject to the perceived hazards of delays and political pressures of adjudication in national courts'. According to Guillermo Aguilar Alvarez and William W Park, 'The New Face of Investment Arbitration: NAFTA Chapter 11' (2003) 28 *Yale Journal of International Law* 365, 369, the establishment of arbitration responds to investors' apprehension about 'home town justice'; arbitration provides 'a forum that is more

would otherwise lie within the exclusive province of constitutional and supreme courts in host states.[5]

One of the claims of this work is that BITs create an 'economic constitution' that regulates the economic activities of foreign investors, meaning that the jurisdiction delegated to arbitral tribunals is of constitutional and administrative law character. Investment treaty tribunals have the power to redefine the relationship between property rights and the public interest, and also the authority to review the legitimacy of state actions and omissions according to undefined standards of review. As Van Harten acutely observes, investment treaty arbitration is better understood as 'a unique form of public law adjudication; that is, as a treaty-based regime that uses rules and structures of international law and private arbitration to make governmental choices regarding the regulatory relationship between individuals and the state'.[6]

Until recently, legal scholars debated whether international law was really 'law'.[7] However, now that supra-national organisations have been vested with *real* power, we are faced with the opposite question: where does the legitimacy of international law and institutions of global governance truly lie? The new post-Cold War global order is posing questions of legitimacy which, only a number of years ago, we could not even imagine. Those questions, in a nutshell, refer to issues of authority, justification, and obedience, as well as the rational exercise of power.[8] Legitimacy, and

neutral than host country courts, both politically and procedurally'. Similarly, W Michael Reisman, 'International Arbitration and Sovereignty' (2002) 18 *Arbitration International* 231, 235, observes that '[t]he private actor is generally unwilling to subject itself to the jurisdiction of courts in command economies or economies in transition and even when a local judiciary can boast a degree of independence'. See also, Andreas F Lowenfeld, *International Economic Law* (New York, OUP, 2002) 473–88, and Surya P Subedi, *International Investment Law. Reconciling Policy and Principle* (Portland, Hart Publishing, 2008) 2.

[5] See Horacio A Grigera Naón, 'Arbitration in Latin America: Progress and Setbacks' (2005) 21 *Arbitration International* 127, 182.

[6] Gus Van Harten, *Investment Treaty Arbitration and Public Law* (New York, OUP, 2007) 10.

[7] See Ernest A Young, 'Institutional Settlement in a Globalising Judicial System' (2005) 54 *Duke Law Journal* 1143, 1145–46 (noting that '[t]here was a time when international lawyers had to defend their discipline against the charge that "international law" is an oxymoron . . . These debates seem to be fading now'). See also, Jenny S Martinez, 'Toward an International Judicial System' (2003) 56 *Stanford Law Review* 429, 432 (stating that 'it is no longer possible to dismiss the topic of international adjudication with a version of the cynical critique that "international law is not really law" along the lines that "international courts are not really courts"').

[8] As Mattias Kumm, 'The Legitimacy of International Law: A Constitutionalist Framework of Analysis' (2004) 15 *European Journal of International Law* 907, 908, explains: '[Questions of legitimacy] can be reframed as questions about the moral force of international law or, to use more traditional jurisprudential vocabulary, the *duty to obey international law*. The very idea of legitimacy develops clearer contours when connected to questions of obedience. Only if and to the extent that international law is legitimate is there a moral duty to obey international law'.

how the relevant players perceive it, is also a key factor in the long-term stability and sustainability of any legal regime or institution.[9]

In the legal literature, questions of legitimacy concerning supra-national entities emerged mainly with the process of European integration. Later, during the 1990s, they were extended to the WTO and its institutional arrangement (among other global institutions).[10] Yet, little has been said about the BIT generation in this regard, notwithstanding the fact that its impact on domestic public law and politics, at least from the perspective of developing countries, may be greater than that of the WTO.

This chapter focuses on the major legitimacy deficits of the BIT generation: the lack of democratic pedigree characterising both investor–state arbitral tribunals, and the body of law that those tribunals create through the adjudication of investment disputes.[11] As will be explored below, the essence of these legitimacy problems resides in the use of 'adjudicative law-making' arbitration to control the regulatory state.[12]

Investment treaties limit the political and policy alternatives available to developing countries' governments.[13] These treaties constrain states through highly broad and open-ended substantive standards, particularly those of no expropriation without compensation (including, with special emphasis, indirect expropriations) and fair and equitable treatment (FET). This means that arbitral tribunals are in charge of supervising the states' handling of what Judge Higgins calls the *innate tension* between private property and public powers.[14] Hence, in the present regulatory state era, where all relevant economic sectors are heavily regulated, the BIT generation's legitimacy problem poses a serious concern.[15]

[9] According to Jürgen Habermas, *Between Facts and Norms* (Cambridge, Mass, MIT Press, 1996) 67, this idea belongs to Weber: '[It is] Weber's view that social orders can only be maintained in the long run as legitimate orders'.

[10] See Stein, n 3, 489.

[11] These are, in essence, input-legitimacy or democratic-legitimacy problems. See eg Fritz W Scharpf, *Governing in Europe: Effective and Democratic?* (New York, OUP, 1999) 6 ('Input-oriented democracy thought emphasizes "government *by the people*". Political choices are legitimate if and because they reflect the "will of the people"—that is, if they can be derived from the authentic preferences of the members of a community'). According to Habermas, n 9, 263, '[o]nly the *procedural conditions for the democratic genesis of legal statutes* secures the legitimacy of enacted law'.

[12] See Jose E Alvarez, *International Organizations as Law Makers* (New York, OUP, 2005) 531 ff (explaining the term 'adjudicative law-making').

[13] See Tai Heng Cheng, 'Power, Authority, and International Investment Law' (2005) 20 *American University International Law Review* 465, 482 (2005) ('International investment law diminishes the authority and power of a state by restraining its internal decision-makers').

[14] Rosalyn Higgins, 'The Taking of Property by the State. Decent Developments in International Law' in Académie de Droit International, 176 *Recueil des Cours. Collected Courses of the Hague Academy of International Law, 1982-III* (The Hague, M Nijhoff, 1983) 259, 274.

[15] For a general description of the advances of the regulatory state, see DJ Galligan, 'Judicial Review and the Textbook Writers' (1976) 2 *Oxford Journal of Legal Studies* 257, 257; Giandomenico Majone, 'The Rise of the Regulatory State in Europe' (1994) 17 *West European Politics* 77, 97; and more recently, John Braithwaite, *Regulatory Capitalism: How it Works, Ideas for Making it Work Better* (Northampton, Edward Elgar, 2008).

In joining the BIT system, capital-importing countries traded sovereignty and democracy for credibility. They surrendered a significant amount of jurisdiction on the part of their highest courts, and lost the ability to exert democratic checks and balances—that is, legislative reversals—over the decisions rendered in connection with foreign investment conducted in their territory. That was the cost of seeking additional FDI inflows, and these governments knew and accepted it when they decided to join the BIT network.

This general description alerts us to this chapter's main purpose: to analyse the nature and scope of the legitimacy deficits of the BIT generation. It attempts, indeed, to provide of a realistic understanding and assessment of the normative weaknesses inherent to the BIT generation, taking democratic deficits seriously, but also trying to go beyond simplistic critiques based on sovereignty.[16] Such an analysis is particularly relevant for discussing about institutional reform. The wrong prognosis leads to the wrong remedies, as for example, with the proposal to establish an appellate body or international investment court in the BIT system.

This chapter proceeds as follows. Section I presents the legitimacy problem of the BIT generation, paying special attention to the general context of international law since the end of the Cold War. Section II reviews the potential sources of legitimacy—consent, output, exit, rule of law, and institution-building—and presents a provisional assessment of each. Section III tackles the question of whether the establishment of an appellate body or international investment court represents wise policy. It argues that in the absence of a new and denser investment treaty—one defining the obligations of states in a more specific way—this would not be a good idea. The conclusions revisit the first requirement that the updated Calvo Doctrine imposes on the BIT generation, namely, and as described in chapter 1, that BIT jurisprudence must end up generating proper and reasonable rules of protection of investment.

I THE LEGITIMACY PROBLEM: AD HOC INTERNATIONAL ARBITRAL TRIBUNALS DISCHARGING A PRESERVATIONIST CONSTITUTIONAL FUNCTION

The nature and characteristics of the BIT generation legitimacy problem deserves closer attention. This section provides a descriptive approach, summarised by the idea of *ad hoc international arbitral tribunals discharging a preservationist constitutional function*. However, to avoid any unfair over-

[16] See Aguilar Alvarez and Park, n 4, 398–99 (noting that '[a]ssertions of "sovereignty" may end up being slippery and unhelpful abstractions, serving simply as a justification for the exercise of unfettered government power').

magnification of the legitimacy deficits of investment treaty arbitration, I begin by placing the BIT generation in the more general context of international law as governance.

A International Law as Governance

The BIT generation is not a completely unique case in the history of modern international law and institutions. Such new concepts as 'international law as governance'[17] or 'global governance' reminds us that it is part of a more general trend—a New World Order—dating from the end of the Cold War.[18] An overview of this historical pattern is therefore required in order to fully grasp the legitimacy problems that threaten the BIT generation.

Globalisation is a reality of the current post-Cold War world.[19] The end of the Cold War, as Koh observes, 'initiated the era of global law in which we now live'.[20] One of the most remarkable characteristics of this global law era is the expansion of supra-national governance mechanisms.[21] The degree of interdependence existing in the modern global world, indeed, demands that there be effective supra-national governance mechanisms.[22] These systems of cooperation and coordination require nations to systematically delegate power to international institutions.[23]

[17] Kumm, n 8, 915.

[18] ibid 912–13. See also, Sol Picciotto, 'Constitutionalizing Multilevel Governance' in (2008) 6 *International Journal of Constitutional Law* 457; and Colin Scott, 'Regulation in the Age of Governance: The Rise of the Post-Regulatory State' in Jacint Jordana and David Levi-Faur (eds), *The Politics of Regulation: Institutions and Regulatory Reform for the Age of Governance* (Northampton, Edward Elgar, 2004).

[19] See Thomas W Wälde, 'Investment Arbitration as a Discipline for Good-Governance' in Todd Weiler (ed), *NAFTA Investment Law and Arbitration: Past Issues, Current Practice, Future Prospect* (Ardsley, Transnational Publishers, 2003) 475, 475.

[20] Harold H Koh, 'Review Essay: Why Do Nations Obey International Law?' (1997) 106 *Yale Law Journal* 2599, 2630.

[21] See Laurence R Helfer and Graeme B Dinwoodie, 'Designing Non-National Systems: The Case of the Uniform Domain Name Dispute Resolution Policy' (2001) 43 *William and Mary Law Review* 141, 144–45 nn 1–5; Daniel C Esty, 'Good Governance at the Supranational Scale: Globalizing Administrative Law' (2006) 115 *Yale Law Journal* 1490, 1495; and David Held, 'The Transformation of Political Community: Rethinking Democracy in the Context of Globalization' in Ian Shapiro and Casiano Hacker-Cordón (eds), *Democracy's Edges* (New York, CUP, 1999) 84, 84.

[22] See Stein, n 3, 489–90; Esty, n 21, 1493, and 1500; and, Laurence R Helfer, 'Constitutional Analogies in the International Legal System' (2003) 37 *Loyola Los Angeles Law Review* 193, 194–95.

[23] See Thomas Cottier and Maya Hertig, 'The Prospects of 21st Century Constitutionalism' (2003) 7 *Max Planck Yearbook of United Nations Law* 261, 302. See also Esty, n 21, 1518; Alvarez, n 12, 401 ff; and, the collection of articles published in Thomas M Franck (ed), *Delegating State Powers: The Effect of Treaty Regimes on Democracy and Sovereignty* (Ardsley, Transnational Publishers, 2000).

Such transfers of power, as well as the regulatory outcomes to which they lead, severely erode traditional concepts of sovereignty,[24] democracy,[25] and key public values such as accountability and citizen participation in public affairs. The new post-Cold War international law thus presents us with serious normative puzzles.[26] According to Kumm, we may indeed be witnessing the decline of the liberal constitutional democracy:

> In the 15 years following the end of the Cold War, developments in international law have brought serious legitimacy issues to the fore. The moment of triumph for the post-World War II model of liberal constitutional democracy at the end of the Cold War is increasingly feared to have been the prelude to its decline. This decline is linked to the emergence of an international legal order that increasingly serves—if not as an iron cage—certainly as a firmly structured normative web that makes an increasingly plausible claim to authority. It tends to exert influence on national political and legal processes and often exerts pressure on nations not in compliance with its norms. Actors in constitutional democracies are increasingly engaging seriously with international law's claim to authority. What they find once they seriously engage international law gives rise to concern. Citizens find themselves in a *double bind*: the meaning of participation in the democratic process on the domestic level is undermined as international law increasingly limits the realm in which national self-government can take place.[27]

[24] See Slaughter, n 2, 266–67 ('Theorists, pundits, and policymakers all recognize that traditional conceptions of sovereignty are inadequate to capture the complexity of contemporary international relations. The result is seemingly endless debate about the changing nature of sovereignty: what does it mean? Does it still exist? Is it useful?'). See also, Andrea Hamann and Hélène Ruiz Fabri, 'Transnational Networks and Constitutionalism' (2008) 6 *International Journal of Constitutional Law* 481, 481; Karl-Heinz Ladeur, 'Globalisation and the Conversion of Democracy to Polycentric Networks: Can Democracy Survive the End of the Nation State?' in Karl-Heinz Ladeur (ed), *Public Governance in the Age of Globalization* (Burlington, Ashgate, 2004) 89, 110; Kal Raustiala, 'Rethinking the Sovereignty Debate in International Economic Law' (2003) 6 *Journal of International Economic Law* 841, 843; Koh, n 20, 2631; Stein, n 3, 492; and, John J Jackson, 'Sovereignty-Modern: A New Approach to an Outdated Concept' (2003) 97 *American Journal of International Law* 782, 786.

[25] See Stein, n 3, 490 ('[I]nternationalization almost invariably means a loss of democracy'). See also, Thomas M Franck, 'Can the United States Delegate Aspect of Sovereignty to International Regimes' in Thomas Franck (ed), *Delegating State Powers: The Effect of Treaty Regimes on Democracy and Sovereignty* (Ardsley, Transnational Publishers, 2000) 1, 2–3: 'The general lack of democratic accountability in most [international] regimes, however, has been the subject of intense criticism . . . [T]here can be little disagreement that the lack of direct popular accountability of international regimes creates a constitutional/political problems for American participation in transnational institutions that have acquired significant decision-making power'.

[26] Esty, n 21, 1515, notes how 'many scholars thus see democratic foundations for the exercise of power as the sine qua non of legitimacy. To the extent that this is true, global governance is doomed to illegitimacy'. See also, Martin Shapiro, 'Administrative Law Unbounded: Reflection on Government and Governance' (2001) 8 *Indiana Journal of Global Legal Studies* 369, 374–75 ('Transnational or global governance, however, raises more serious problems for administrative law. Under this form of governance, decision-making processes are relatively new and tend to be elitist and opaque, with few participants and no agreed upon protocol').

[27] Kumm, n 8, 912–13.

From a descriptive perspective, there is one aspect of this new international law of which there is no doubt: the state's monopolistic pretensions with respect to the norms and regulations applying within its own territory have ended.[28] Globalisation as a process 'takes away from individual States the ability to control day-to-day activities within their territories. With globalization, a country is no longer "an island into itself" '.[29]

Governance is an imprecise yet popular concept.[30] On first glance, in the global context, it denotes the ordering and control of both economic and non-economic activity in the absence of a supra-national sovereign authority,[31] and where the traditional limits between the public and the private spheres have become considerably blurred.[32] At the same time, however, governance reminds us that states still figure crucially within the global scenario. They are, indeed, 'pivots between international agencies and sub-national activities . . . [T]hey provide legitimacy as the exclusive voice of a territorially-bounded population'.[33] Even if states have lost their monopoly over the law, they continue to wield substantial 'market power' over it.

The result is that the mechanisms of global governance created by the post-Cold War international law are dramatically changing our views of public law, including constitutional and administrative law. In the past,

[28] See Slaughter, n 24, 262 (citing Wolfgang Reinecket, who notes that 'national governments are losing their ability to formulate and implement national public policy within territorial borders rendered increasingly porous by the forces of globalization, immigration, and the information revolution'). See also, Edward T Hayes, 'Changing Notion of Sovereignty and Federalism in the International Economic System: A Reassessment of WTO Regulation of Federal States and the Regional and Local Governments Within their Territories' (2004) 25 *Northwestern Journal of International Law and Business* 1, 8.

[29] Trevor C Hartley, *European Union Law in a Global Context* (New York, CUP, 2004) *xv*.

[30] See Ladeur, n 24, 110.

[31] See JHH Weiler and Iulia Motoc, 'Taking Democracy Seriously: The Normative Challenges to the International Legal System' in Stefan Griller (ed), *International Economic Governance and Non-Economic Concerns* (New York, Springer, 2003) 47, 69.

[32] See Shapiro, n 26, 369–70, who explains this feature in the following terms: 'In today's public administration and political science literature, however, the word "governance" has largely replaced the word "government." This change in vocabulary announces a significant erosion of the boundaries separating what lies inside a government and its administration and what lies outside them . . . [T]he very distinction between governmental and non-governmental has become blurred, since the real decision-making process now continually involves, and combines, public and private actors'. See also, Gunther Teubner, 'Global Private Regimes: Neo-Spontaneous Law and Dual Constitution of Autonomous Sectors?' in Karl-Heinz Ladeur (ed), *Public Governance in the Age of Globalization* (Burlington, Ashgate, 2004) 71, 73 (referring to the 'cancerous spread of private regulation, agreements and dispute resolution').

[33] Paul Hirst and Grahame Thompson, 'Globalization and the Future of the Nation State' (1995) 24 *Economy and Society* 408, 431. See also, Lawrence M Friedman, 'Frontiers: National and Transnational Order' in Karl-Heinz Ladeur (ed), *Public Governance in the Age of Globalization* (Burlington, Ashgate, 2004) 25, 41 (observing that all international institutions depend, in the last resort, 'on the goodwill of national courts').

domestic public law used to be considered part of the *domaine réservé* of the state.[34] By contrast, the new treaties and institutions, as Helfer remarks, 'exert significant influence on domestic law and politics'.[35] This impact is substantial enough that, in the opinion of one commentator, constitutional law 'loses its claim to regulate comprehensively the exercise of public authority within the territorial limits of the state'.[36] Cottier and Hertig have incisively commented that:

> The Constitution itself can no longer pretend anymore to provide a comprehensive regulatory framework of the state on its own. Of course, there are differences among states, essentially based upon power and might, and graduations exist in different regulatory areas. But conceptually, due to the increasing 'outsourcing of constitutional functions', the national Constitution today and in the future is to be considered a 'partial constitution', which is completed by the other levels of governance.[37]

Today, public law 'also originates from international institutions and bodies, which now "proliferate"'.[38] As a result, the dominant image in continental law of domestic legal systems as a Kelsenian pyramid, no longer holds. The same can be said of another powerful concept introduced by Kelsen: the identification of the state with the law. Both pyramid and equation are broken because the public law produced by global governance institutions 'penetrates national legal systems by dictating principles and criteria that national administrations must respect and that private actors may wield in their own interest'.[39]

[34] See Sabino Cassese, 'Global Standards for National Administrative Procedure' (2005) 68 *Law and Contemporary Problems* 109, 112, who provides a powerful insight into what used to be the traditional perspective: 'Historically, administrative law has sprung from national states. Public administrations belong to a national community, and they depend structurally on national, or state, governments. Because of the principle of legality, these administrations are subjected to laws and regulated by them. Administrative law is thus fundamentally state law . . . [H]istory suggests the impossibility of global governance of national administrative laws, because only within the state can there be an administration that enjoys a monopoly of executive power, and only within the state can there be the authority versus liberty dialectic that characterizes administrative law. A global system governing national administrative law cannot exist, in short, because administrative governance finds its source exclusively in national law. As Otto Mayer, one of the founders of German administrative law, observed, the national public power is the lord in its own domain, to the exclusion of all others'.

[35] Helfer, n 22, 195.

[36] Christian Walter, 'Constitutionalizing (Inter)national Governance—Possibilities for and Limits to the Development of an International Constitutional Law' (2001) 44 *German Yearbook of International Law* 170, 194. See also, Miguel Poiares Maduro, 'Legal Travels and the Risk of Legal Jet-Lag. The Judicial and Constitutional Challenges of Legal Globalization' in Mario Monti et al (eds), *Economic Law and Justice in Times of Globalisation. Festschrift for Carl Baudenbacher* (Baden Baden, Nomos Verlagsgesellschaft, 2007) 175, 176.

[37] Cottier and Hertig, n 23, 303–04.

[38] Giacinto de la Cananea, 'Beyond the State: the Europeanization and Globalisation of Procedural Administrative Law' (2003) 9 *European Public Law* 563, 576.

[39] Cassese, n 34, 110. See also, Picciotto, n 18, 461–63.

In the twenty-first century, the correct picture of the domestic legal systems is that of a pluralist/polycentric legal entity, which resembles a network instead of a pyramid.[40] In this expanded supra-national network, the state is not only constrained by the rules and principles derived from its own norm-creating process—undoubtedly still the *node* of highest relevance—but also by those generated from other points of the network.

International law as governance—the general context for BIT adjudication—raises complicated questions of legitimacy and authority that go well beyond the scope of this work. But, to summarise, if states are constrained by these new rules and principles, then the domestic political process becomes equally limited. As Von Bogdandy explains, 'national politics are now found to be bound by a multiplicity of legal and factual constraints originating outside the nation-state. To the extent that national politics reflect democratic processes, globalization and democracy clash'.[41] Supranational entities can and do impose regulatory solutions, which in many instances supersedes those that had been adopted domestically in accordance with the preferences and values of the people.[42]

B Governing with Judges[43]

Among the various possible global institutional arrangements,[44] the adoption of agreements containing a combination of broad principles and strong dispute settlement mechanisms has been a common strategy. As a result, Lindseth notes, ' "supranational normative power" tends to be

[40] For the idea that we have moved from a pyramid-system to a network-system, see F Ost and M Van der Kerchove, *De la pirámide au réseau? Pour une théorie dialectique du droit* (Brussels, Facultés Universitaires Saint-Louis, 2002), cited by Guy Haarscher, 'Some Contemporary Trends in Continental Philosophy of Law' in Martin Golding and William A Edmundson (eds), *The Blackwell Guide to the Philosophy of Law and Legal Theory* (Malden, Blackwell, 2005) 300 ff. See also, Hamann and Ruiz Fabri, n 24, 482–83.

[41] Armin Von Bogdandy, 'Globalization and Europe: How to Square Democracy, Globalization, and International Law' (2004) 15 *European Journal of International Law* 885, 889.

[42] See Helfer, n 22, 197, according to whom '[w]here treaty obligations are dynamic and evolve through institutional processes outside of any one state's control, compliance with those obligations may clash with domestic preferences and raise trenchant legitimacy concerns'.

[43] The title of this section was taken from Alec Stone Sweet, *Governing with Judges. Constitutional Politics in Europe* (New York, OUP, 2000).

[44] Esty, n 21, 1497–98 provides a comprehensive list of alternatives: 'Supranational governance might therefore refer to any number of policymaking processes and institutions that help to manage international interdependence, including (1) negotiation by nation-states leading to a treaty; . . . (3) rule-making by international bodies in support of treaty implementation; (4) development of government-backed codes of conduct, guidelines, and norms; (5) pre-negotiation agenda-setting and issue analysis in support of treatymaking; (5) [*sic*] technical standard-setting to facilitate trade; (6) networking and policy coordination by regulators; (7) structured public-private efforts at norm creation; (8) informal workshops at which policymakers, NGOs, business leaders, and academics exchange ideas; and (8) [*sic*] private sector policymaking activities'.

adjudicative'.[45] Investment treaty tribunals are, then, just one more example of the number of international institutions with adjudicative powers to have proliferated in the last 16 years.[46]

This speaks, as Helfer and Slaughter point out, to a 'renewed millennial faith in the ability of courts to hold states to their international obligations'.[47] We are, indeed, 'increasingly surrounded by supranational courts'.[48] Yet, these new courts and tribunals fulfill a different function than that traditionally played by international bodies. They are instead performing what Alvarez refers to as 'adjudicative law-making',[49] which 'results from, at least in part, the relative absence of precision in applicable law and from treaty-makers' tendency to use their dispute settlers to 'complete' their treaty contracts'.[50]

In fact, this particular form of adjudication derives directly from the highly open-ended character of treaties' provisions. Instead of concluding detailed treaties or 'dense' binding documents—which, together with other policy alternatives, presuppose a lesser erosion of state sovereignty—state negotiators have typically preferred to agree only on very general principles, leaving the task of concretising them to dispute settlement bodies.[51] This constitutes, as Esty remarks, one of the key forms of global policy-making:

[45] Peter L Lindseth, 'Democratic Legitimacy and the Administrative Character of Supranationalism: The Example of the European Community' (1999) 99 *Columbia Law Review* 628, 631.

[46] See *generally* Martinez, n 8, 430, and Roger P Alford, 'The Proliferation of International Courts and Tribunals: International Adjudication in Ascendance' (2000) 94 *American Society of International Law Proceedings* 160, 160, both noting that 'more than fifty international courts and tribunals are now in existence, with more than thirty of these established in the past twenty years'. See also, Chester Brown, *A Common Law of International Adjudication* (New York, OUP, 2007) 15–34 (analysing the proliferation of international courts and tribunals, and the fragmentation of international law); Poiares Maduro, n 36, 175 (exploring 'the judicialisation of international relations'); and Cesare PR Romano, 'The Proliferation of International Judicial Bodies: The Pieces of the Puzzle' (1999) 31 *New York University Journal of International Law and Policy* 709 (discussing the expanding number of international tribunals). For a complete description of all international tribunals, see the NYU Project on International Courts and Tribunals, available at www.pict-pcti.org.

[47] Laurence R Helfer and Anne-Marie Slaughter, 'Toward a Theory of Effective Supranational Adjudication' (1997) 107 *Yale Law Journal* 273, 387.

[48] Young, n 7, 1146.

[49] Alvarez, n 12, 531 ff.

[50] ibid 523–24. He, ibid 462, also adds that '[t]he level of judicial discretion is all the greater within the context of the rudimentary international legal system as even its most sophisticated and evolved treaty regimes, such as WTO's covered agreements, are replete with substantive and procedural *lacunae* that adjudicators need to fill'.

[51] As Kumm, n 8, 914 explains: 'Treaties today, though still binding only on those who ratify them, increasingly delegate powers to treaty-based bodies with a quasi-legislative or quasi-judicial character. Within their circumscribed subject-matter jurisdiction, these bodies are authorized under the treaty to develop and determine the specific content of the obligations that states are under'. See more generally, Nico Krisch and Benedict Kingsbury, 'Introduction: Global Governance and Global Administrative Law in the International Legal Order' (2006) 17 *European Journal of International Law* 1, 1.

> International policymaking can be carried out through government-to-government negotiations and the contractual exchange of specific commitments in treaties. Alternatively, governments can coordinate policies by mutual recognition of each others' national rules. *But when nation-states agree not on specific substantive outcomes but rather on decision-processes, they create mechanisms of global policymaking or supranational governance.* (emphasis added)[52]

Similarly, Trachtman has observed that the lack of density in treaties results in the delegation of power to international bodies:

> [W]here decision-making authority is allocated to a dispute resolution body, less specific standards are consistent with a transfer of power to an international organization—the dispute resolution body itself—while more specific rules are more consistent with the reservation of continuing power by member states. From a more critical standpoint, it might be argued that allocation of authority to a transnational dispute resolution body by virtue of standards can be used as a method to integrate *sub rosa*, and outside the visibility of democratic controls.[53]

The obvious legitimacy problem raised by this 'governing with judges' form of global governance is that it converts adjudicators—ie, unelected officers—into policymakers. Adjudication that is not based on rules, but on overly broad principles, implicitly places in the hands of courts and tribunals a discretion that is a qualitatively greater than the classic *interstitial* powers they possess at the domestic level.[54] As Stone Sweet notes, 'judges who enforce such [open-ended] standards behave as relatively pure policymakers, in that they use their discretion to evaluate and control the law-making of others?[55]

C Ad Hoc International Arbitral Tribunals Discharging a Preservationist Constitutional Function

Investment treaties perfectly exemplify the 'governing with judges' model of global governance. BITs have at least two basic characteristics that help them to serve as textbook examples. First, the dispute settlement mechanism created by these treaties is truly supra-national; investment treaty tribunals constitute a decentralised institutional arrangement that lacks roots in any particular state.[56] Second, and more importantly, investment

[52] Esty, n 21, 1499.

[53] Joel P Trachtman, 'The Domain of WTO Dispute Resolution' (1999) 40 *Harvard International Law Journal* 333, 335.

[54] See nn 125 and 126, and accompanying text.

[55] Alec Stone Sweet, *The Judicial Construction of Europe* (New York, OUP, 2004) 119. See also, Alvarez, n 12, 473 ('Rules are made by legislators, or, in this case, the treaty drafters. Standards, however, because they rely on adjudicators to apply them, implicitly leave decisions to them').

[56] Strictly speaking, this assertion is only completely true in the case of investment arbitration conducted in accordance with the ICSID Convention, the only international commercial arbitration system that is fully de-nationalised.

treaty tribunals perform 'adjudicative law-making' by interpreting and applying highly open-ended and legally indeterminate norms of public law character.[57]

As already said, BITs define a new economic constitution that applies as *lex specialis* to foreign investors. Following Ackerman's nomenclature, the BIT generation can be envisioned as a (non-democratic) constitutional moment, where the enactment of BITs amounts to 'higher law-making'. The protective content of these treaties has been intentionally left beyond the reach of the domestic political process, functioning in its 'normal law-making' mode.[58] In the institutional architecture of investment treaties, ad hoc arbitral bodies are entrusted 'to discharge [a] preservationist function',[59] and even—to the extent that they perform adjudicative law-making—a constructive function. What we see today in the BIT generation, in other words, is ad hoc international arbitral tribunals discharging a preservationist constitutional function.

It is worth noting that the efficacy of this economic constitution is unprecedented in international law. Investment treaty arbitration replaces public law litigation in host states, and eliminates any possible political intervention on the part of home states. Foreign investors not only can file claims against host states without any form of governmental screening, but they can also enforce arbitral awards in most courts around the world without political scrutiny[60] (thanks to the ICSID Convention[61] and the New York Convention[62]). As stated earlier, this shows the BIT generation to be a clear example of what Slaughter terms 'vertical governmental network'.[63]

The main point here is that entities such as these ad hoc international arbitral tribunals that discharge a preservationist constitutional function

[57] It is also worth noting that investment treaty tribunals' institutional nature is private; international commercial arbitration is, indeed, a typically private form of dispute settlement. This brings to mind Sassen's comments on globalization and privatisation. See Saskia Sassen, 'De-Nationalized State Agendas end Privatized Norm-Making' in Karl-Heinz Ladeur (ed), *Public Governance in the Age of Globalization* (Burlington, Ashgate, 2004) 51, 63: 'Economic globalization has been accompanied by the creation of new legal regimes and legal practices and the expansion and renovation of some older forms that bypass national legal systems. This is evident in the rising importance of international commercial arbitration . . . The emerging privatized institutional framework to govern the global economy has possibly major implications for the exclusive authority of the modern national state over its territory, that is, its exclusive territoriality'.

[58] See Bruce Ackerman, 1 *We the People. Foundations* (Cambridge, Mass, Belknap Press of Harvard, CUP, 1991).

[59] ibid 9, and 266 ff.

[60] See Slaughter, n 2, 21, and Stein, n 3, 490–91.

[61] *Convention on the Settlement of Investment Disputes between States and Nationals of Other States* (adopted 18 March 1965, entered into force 14 October 1966) 17 UST 1270, 575 UNTS 159.

[62] *Convention on Recognition and Enforcement of Foreign Arbitral Awards* (adopted 10 June 1958, entered into force 7 June 1959) 330 UNTS 38.

[63] See n 2 and accompanying text.

are highly problematic for at least four related ways: they are *tribunals* (that is, they adjudicate), they are *international*, they are *arbitral*, and they function on an *ad hoc* basis. The first problem speaks to the fact that these tribunals—given their role as public law adjudicators—face every well-known counter-majoritarian objection received by constitutional judicial review at the domestic level.[64]

Commentators do not always appreciate the judicial review dimension of investment treaty adjudication. They sometimes assume that arbitral tribunals merely award damages against host states. However, anyone trained in public law is aware, as Mashaw observes, that plaintiffs who seek damages 'also invariably question the legality of administrative conduct. To that degree, suits against the government and its officials sounding essentially in tort, contract, or property also invite judicial review of administrative action'.[65]

Besides, it is current matter of debate whether the jurisdiction of investment treaty tribunals does, in fact, include 'pure' judicial review.[66] In an unprecedented decision, the *OEPC* Tribunal not only issued a damage award, but also declared an Ecuadorian tax decree null and void.[67] The English court later upheld the latter portion of the award—the locus of the arbitration was London—but softened it with a confusing *dualist* (that is, non-monist) declaration.[68] Although in my opinion tribunals cannot and

[64] Two classic works on the matter are Alexander Bickel, *The Least Dangerous Branch* (Indianapolis, Bobbs-Merrill, 1962), and John H Ely, *Democracy and Distrust: A Theory of Judicial Review* (Cambridge, Mass, Harvard University Press 1980). More recently, see Jeremy Waldron, *Law and Disagreement* (New York, OUP, 1999).

[65] Jerry L Mashaw et al, *Administrative Law. The American Public Law System. Cases and Materials*, 5th edn (St Paul, Thomson/West, 2003) 780. In the US, the Supreme Court has stated that the judicial review implicitly present in tort cases against the government is the precise reason that Congress chose to ban them. See, *US v SA Empresa de Viacao Aerea Rio Grandense (Varig Airlines)* (1984) 467 US 797, 814: 'This emphasis upon protection for regulatory activities suggest an underlying basis for the inclusion of an exception for the discretionary functions in the Act: Congress wished to prevent judicial "second-guessing" of legislative and administrative decision grounded in social, economic, and political policy through the medium of an action in tort'.

[66] See Christoph Schreuer, 'Non-pecuniary Remedies in ICSID' (2004) 20 *Arbitration International* 325, and before that, Christoph Schreuer, 'Commentary on the ICSID Convention' (1999) 15 *ICSID Review—Foreign Investment Law Journal* 46, 101 (concluding that remedies are not limited to damage awards).

[67] See *Occidental Exploration and Production Co v Ecuador*, LCIA Case No UN 3467 (Orrego, Brower, Barrera), Award (1 July, 2004), ¶ 202: 'The Respondent cannot order the Claimant to return the amounts of VAT refunded by the Granting Resolutions as OEPC had a right to such refunds because no alternative mechanism was included in the Contract as the SRI believed. *The Tribunal accordingly holds that the Claimant is entitled to retain the amounts so refunded and that the SRI Denying Resolutions requiring the return of those amounts are without legal effect*'. (emphasis added) Before *OEPC*, the Tribunal in *Enron Corporation and Ponderosa Assets, LP v Argentina*, ICSID Case No ARB/01/03 (Orrego, Gros, Tschanz), Decision on Jurisdiction (14 January 2004), ¶¶ 75–81, mentioned as obiter dicta that injunctions were an available remedy in the BIT context.

[68] See *Republic of Ecuador v Occidental Exploration and Production Co* [2006] EWHC (Comm) 345, ¶ 124: 'As I read that sentence in paragraph 202 [of the arbitral award], the tribunal is

should not award remedies different from damages, one tribunal recently reached the opposite conclusion, holding that 'under the ICSID Convention, a tribunal has the power to order pecuniary o non-pecuniary remedies, including restitution, i.e., re-establishing the situation which existed before a wrongful act was committed'.[69]

The second problem, the *international* character of investment treaty tribunals, is also a target for legitimacy critiques. Martinez provides a helpful summary, noting that '[i]f the so-called counter-majoritarian difficulty is a central dilemma in defining the judicial role in the United States, the prospect of an international judicial system presents this difficulty multiplied by 10: All the counter-majoritarian features of a court, combined with all the democratic deficit of an international institution'.[70] Yet, as Keohane reminds us, it is unfair to demand too much from international institutions, because they 'will probably never meet the standards of electoral accountability and participation that we expect of domestic democracies, so at best they will be low on a democratic scale'.[71]

This familiar debate in international law is outside the scope of this work. One dimension of it, however, deserves special attention. In contrast to constitutional courts and supreme courts, investment treaty tribunals can and do adopt treaty *interpretations* which democratic institutions cannot control and overturn by proper amendment[72] (as in the case, for instance, of new idea of FET as an autonomous standard[73]). Hence, arbitral tribunals partially deprive *the people* of control over the

declaring the rights of OEPC, as a matter of international law. That is how I read the third and fourth sentences also. The tribunal is declaring that the statements in SRI Resolutions ordering the return to the SRI of VAT that has been reimbursed to OEPC are in breach of OEPC's international law rights. It must be within the powers of the tribunal to declare that the statements by the SRI are in breach of international law, and so, as a matter of international law, "are without legal effect"'.

[69] *Ioan Micula et al v Romania,* ICSID Case No ARB/05/20 (Lévy, Alexandrov, Ehlermann), Decision on Jurisdiction and Admissibility (24 September 2008), ¶ 166.

[70] Martinez, n 8, 461.

[71] Robert O Keohane, 'Governance in a Partially Globalized World. Presidential Address, American Political Science Association, 2000' (2001) 95 *American Political Science Review* 1, 9 (internal citations omitted).

[72] See Armin von Bogdandy, 'Legitimacy of International Economic Governance: Interpretative Approaches to WTO law and the Prospects of its Proceduralization' in Stefan Griller (ed), *International Economic Governance and Non-Economic Concerns* (New York, Springer, 2003) 103, 111, noting that '[i]n fully developed legal systems, *the creative function of the judges is democratically embedded since the legislator can intervene at any given moment.* This possibility of intervention entails political responsibility and, consequently, democratic legitimacy for those developments'. (emphasis added)

[73] In an exceptional occurrence, in the context of NAFTA, the three governments agreed to halt the perpetuation of an erroneous interpretation. See the NAFTA Free Trade Commission, *Notes of Interpretation of Certain Chapter 11 Provisions* (31 July 2001) ¶ B.1 (available at www.sice.oas.org/TPD/NAFTA/Commission/CH11understanding_e.asp: 'Article 1105(1) prescribes the customary international law minimum standard of treatment of aliens as the minimum standard of treatment to be afforded to investments of investors of another Party'.

content of their legal system applicable within the state's territory, and consequently over the policy choices that they would consider to better fit their collective goals and preferences.

Third, the *arbitral* nature of investment treaty tribunals—or more precisely, its *commercial* nature[74]—constitutes an additional normative puzzle. Arbitration has traditionally been considered unacceptable in public law matters. One commentator notes that 'there were areas where the interests of the general public were so intricately interwoven in a dispute that this essentially private form of dispute settlement was considered inappropriate'.[75] From a comparative perspective, a good example can be found in French law. Article 2060 of the French Civil Code prohibits arbitration in *domestic* cases involving the public interest, or involving bodies or juridical persons of public nature: '*On ne peut compromettre . . . sur les contestations intéressant les collectivités publiques et les établissements publics et plus généralement dans toutes les matières qui intéressent l'ordre public*'.[76]

The underlying rationale, at least in continental public law, is that only public authorities can exert public powers. This also applies to the review of the exercise of such powers. Only state courts may nullify, issue injunctions against, and more generally, impose liability on government agencies. From an institutional perspective, state courts are part of a complex system of checks, balances and guarantees—including judicial accountability, openness, and independence[77]—that justifies such monopoly of review. This entire framework is considered to represent a legal conquest of the rule of law—the *Rechtsstaat*, or 'state-law'.[78]

Finally, the *ad hoc* nature of the arbitral process is problematic for the legitimacy of the BIT generation. Ad-hoc adjudication compromises coherence—ie, treating like cases alike—and consistency—that is, applying rules

[74] By contrast, state-to-state arbitration is nothing new in international law. It is well-known that modern arbitration for conflicts dealing with damages to property of aliens, in the form of *mixed commissions,* began in 1794 with the Jay Treaty between the US and Great Britain. It then gained popularity and impetus after the *Alabama Claims* arbitration (1872), also conducted between those two nations. Given its long history in international law and the fact that it is usually constrained by several legal institutions, including denial of justice and exhaustion of local remedies, state-to-state arbitration does not pose a serious question of democratic deficit. See Ian Brownlie, *Principles of Public International Law,* 6th edn (New York, OUP, 2003) 672; John G Collier and Vaugham Lowe, *The Settlement of Disputes in International Law. Institutions and Procedures* (New York, OUP, 1999); Alexander Marie Stuyt, *Survey of International Arbitration, 1794–1989* (Boston, M Nijhoff, 1990); and, John L Simpson and Hazel Fox, *International Arbitration. Law and Practice* (New York, Praeger, 1959) 1 ff.

[75] Shane Spelliscy, 'Burning the Idols of Non-Arbitrability: Arbitrating Administrative Law Disputes with Foreign Investors' (2001) 12 *American Review of International Arbitration* 95, 95.

[76] Code Civil (France), Art 2060.

[77] See Van Harten, n 6, 5. See ibid 152–84.

[78] See Neil MacCormick, *Questioning Sovereignty: Law, State, and Nation in the European Commonwealth* (New York, OUP, 1999) 9.

uniformly in every 'similar' or 'applicable' instance[79]—both of which are 'preconditions for the rationality of any field of knowledge'.[80] A lack of consistency and coherence generates uncertainty, undermining the legitimate expectations of investors and states.[81] We know from Habermas that '*consistent decision making*' is an essential condition of 'the socially integrative function of the legal order and the legitimacy claim of law'.[82] Furthermore, as one commentator notes, consistency and coherence are 'necessary to give the decisions of various [international] institutions the legitimacy that ameliorates domestic opposition'.[83]

A reading of international investment arbitral awards demonstrates that the accusations of incoherence and inconsistency cannot be overlooked.[84] Although a body of case law is currently forming, many of the key BITs clauses have been applied in dissimilar and even contradictory ways, without clear justification in different textual formulations in treaties. In the specific context of investment treaty law, we see what Charney previously noted about international law institutions in general: incoherence and inconsistency are, in part, the price of having a system based on 'a multitude of separate forums without a supreme international court to provide definitive interpretations'.[85] This situation, in Charney's

[79] See Thomas M Franck, *Fairness in International Law* (New York, OUP, 1995) 38. According to Françoise Rigaux, 'The Meaning of the Concept 'Coherence in Law'' in Bob Brouwer and PW Brouwer (eds), *Coherence and Conflict in Law: Proceedings of the 3rd Benelux-Scandinavian Symposium in Legal Theory, Amsterdam, January 3–5, 1991* (Boston, Kluwer Law and Taxation Publishers, 1992) 17, 17: '[C]oherence is a state of peace of the mind, of a logical mind which is disturbed when two competing concepts or rules or two different meanings of the same concept are conflicting. Incoherence also means the intellectual dissatisfaction facing a legal reasoning which is not in concordance with a logical process. *One of the goals of an appropriate method of legal reasoning is to restore to the lawyers that peace of mind which can be called coherence*'. (emphasis added)

[80] Robert Alexy, *A Theory of Constitutional Rights* (New York, OUP, 2002) 10. See also, Aulis Aarnio, *Philosophical Perspectives in Jurisprudence* (Helsinki, Philosophical Society of Finland, 1983).

[81] See Susan D Franck, 'The Legitimacy Crisis in Investment Treaty Arbitration: Privatizing Public International Law through Inconsistent Decisions' (2005) 73 *Fordham Law Review* 1521, 1558. See also, ibid 1584: 'Without the clarity and consistency of both the rules of law and their application, there is a detrimental impact upon those governed by the rules and their willingness and ability to adhere to such rules, which can lead to a crisis of legitimacy. Legitimacy depends in large part upon factors such as determinacy and coherence, which can in turn beget predictability and reliability'. See also, Johanna Kalb, 'Creating an ICSID Appellate Body' (2005) 10 *UCLA Journal of International Law and Foreign Affairs* 179, 200.

[82] Habermas, n 9, 198.

[83] Raj Bhala, 'Symposium: Global Trade Issues in the New Millenium: The Power of the Past: Towards de Jure Stare Decisis in WTO Adjudication (Part Three of a Trilogy)' (2001) 33 *George Washington International Law Review* 873, 894.

[84] See eg Franck, n 81, 1558–82. See also Kalb, n 81, 186–96.

[85] Jonathan I Charney, 'Is international law threatened by multiple international tribunals?' in Académie de Droit International, 271 *Recueil des Cours. Collected Courses of the Hague Academy of International Law, 1998* (The Hague, M Nijhoff, 1999) 101, 117.

words, 'can lead to such diversity of opinion that the coherence of international law and, thus, its legitimacy might be at risk'.[86]

In sum, the BIT generation is fraught with legitimacy problems. *International arbitral tribunals discharging a preservationist function* constitute a serious normative conundrum for any reasonable account that claims to take democratic legitimacy seriously. But this comes at no surprise. Legitimacy questions are brought to the fore when international law and institutions work effectively. In this case, BITs are treaties with teeth, and their arbitral tribunals act as the teeth of the system.

II ASSESSING POTENTIAL SOURCES OF LEGITIMACY

The previous section presented a brief summary of the main legitimacy deficits of the BIT generation. Those deficits were, in essence, the price that developing countries accepted in exchange for the benefits of joining the BIT network, as a trade-off of sovereignty for credibility and, consequently, the expectation of additional FDI. It is time to examine and assess the system's benefits, as well as its other potential sources of legitimacy.

A Consent Legitimacy

The first obvious logical response to legitimacy questions is consent. That is, states voluntarily concluded investment treaties, accepting their open-ended standards as well as investor–state arbitration. However, this explanation is far from satisfactory. It faces at least two serious problems: first, the way in which States gave their consent; and second, the incomplete nature of BITs and the corresponding global governance character of BIT adjudication.

The first of these problems deals with the manner in which developing countries acceded to the BIT network. One striking feature of the BIT generation is that it emerged outside the scope and control of the general public.[87] However, this must be placed in a larger context. The dearth of

[86] ibid. See also, Jonathan I Charney, 'The Impact on the International Legal System of the Growth of International Courts and Tribunals' (1999) 31 *New York University Journal of International Law and Politics* 697, 699, commenting also that, 'if like cases are not treated alike, the very essence of a normative system of law will be lost. Should this develop, the legitimacy of international law as a whole will be placed at risk'.

[87] Commenting on NAFTA Ch 11, Vicki Been and Joel C Beauvais, 'The Global Fifth Amendment? NAFTA's Investment Protections and the Misguided Quest for an International "Regulatory Takings" Doctrine' (2003) 78 *New York University Law Review* 30, 137, mention that 'there was virtually no public awareness of or debate concerning the potential impact of NAFTA's investor protections . . . [T]he specifics of Chapter 11 were negotiated and approved without significant public comment'. See also, Van Harten, n 6, 179.

public information about international relations processes is a well-known fact.[88] Investment treaties represent a clear example of Dahl's observation regarding foreign affairs:

> Yet the weight of elite consensus and the weakness of other citizens' views means that the interests and perspectives of some, possibly a majority, are inadequately represented in decisions. Views that might be strengthened among ordinary citizens if these views were more effectively brought to their attention in political discussion and debate remain dormant. The alternatives are poorly explored among ordinary citizens, if not among the policy elites. Yet if citizens had gained a better understanding of their interests and if their views had then been more fully developed, expressed, and mobilized, the decisions might have gone another way. These conditions probably exist more often on foreign affairs than on domestic issues. Sometimes elites predominantly favor one of the major alternatives; many citizens are confused, hold weak opinions, or have no opinions at all; and those who do have opinions may favor an alternative that the political leaders and activists oppose. So public debate is one-sided and incomplete, and in the end the views and interests of the political leaders and activists prevail.[89]

The political economy of BITs also helps to explain the speed—and consequent lack of opportunity for public discussion—with which developing countries joined the network. Case-by-case dispute mechanisms like the ones established by BITs bear little cost for politicians who adopt them. For each concluded BIT, first claims will presumably arise during the next government; the chances of having a claim *and* an award during the same political period are low.[90]

The informational lag that derived from the complexities of international processes, coupled with the absence of personal costs, granted politicians the necessary 'slack' to join the BIT network without the approval or assessment, not to mention preference, of their constituencies.[91] With the exception of special interest groups that benefited from these treaties—

[88] See Robert A Dahl, 'Can International Organizations Be Democratic? A Skeptic's View' in Ian Shapiro and Casiano Hacker-Cordón (eds), *Democracy's Edges* (New York, CUP, 1999) 19, 21.

[89] ibid 27.

[90] The Tribunal in *Wintershall Aktiengesellschaft v Argentina*, ICSID Case No ARB/04/14 (Nariman, Torres, Bernardini), Award (8 December 2008), ¶ 85, cites the expert opinion of Christoph Schreuer for the proposition that BITs are usually concluded without proper discussion and analysis: '[M]any times, in fact in the majority of times, BITs are among clauses [*sic*] of treaties that are not properly negotiated. BITs are very often pulled out of a drawer, often on the basis of some sort of a model, and are put forward on the occasion of state visits when the heads of states need something to sign, and the typical two candidates in a situation like that are Bilateral Investment Treaties, and treaties for cultural co-operation. In other words, they are very often not negotiated at all, they are just being put on the table, and I have heard several representatives who have actually been active in this Treaty-making process, if you can call it that, say that, "We had no idea that this would have real consequences in the real world"'.

[91] See Michael E Levine and Jennifer L Forrence, 'Regulatory Capture, Public Interest, and the Public Agenda: Toward a Synthesis' (1990) 6 *Journal of Law, Economics and Organization* 167.

mainly foreign investors that, contrary to what is assumed, are highly effective politically, at least in 'normal' times[92]—the general population was unconcerned with the negotiation and ratification of these instruments.[93]

Chile's experience may be of interest on this point. On grounds of sovereign integrity, the Constitutional Court struck down the Congressional Act approving the Rome Statute for the International Criminal Court.[94] The decision followed what in the US would have been an Article III argument, or what John Jackson calls a 'sovereignty argument'.[95] This salient and politically sensitive case—particularly in a country like Chile, with its recent record of human rights violations—contrasts with the 39 BITs concluded by Chile since the early 1990s that are currently in effect, and five FTAs with investment chapters also in effect.[96] Those BITs—particularly the early ones that opened the gates—together with the 1965 Washington (ICISD) Convention, received no serious constitutional attention.[97] This confirms the accuracy of Esty's observation that '[i]t is striking that some supranational governance activities go virtually unnoticed, while others generate great controversy and consternation about limited accountability and lost national sovereignty'.[98]

The second problem with consent as a potential basis for legitimacy is that there is an inversely proportional relationship between consent and incompleteness. That is, the more incomplete an agreement, the less consent serves to justify its legitimacy. Indeed, we know from the millenary wisdom of common law that indefinite agreements are not enforceable. According to Farnsworth, *indefiniteness* as a ground for refusing the enforcement of contracts reminds us of the 'fundamental requirement that the parties must have reached an agreement'.[99]

But more critically, the argument of consent-legitimacy overlooks investment treaties' fundamental nature as a mechanism of global governance.

[92] By contrast, in times of 'crisis', foreign investors are favorite targets for redistribution.

[93] See Weiler and Motoc, n 31, 65, who make a similar argument with respect to certain economic and trade treaties.

[94] *Requerimiento de Diputados con el Objeto de que se Declare la Inconstitucionalidad del Estatuto de Roma de la Corte Penal Internacional, adoptado en dicha ciudad el 17 de julio de 1998*, Case No 346, Tribunal Constitutional de Chile [Constitutional Court of Chile] (8 April 2002), ¶¶ 45–58 (available at www.tribunalconstitucional.cl/index.php/sentencias/download/pdf/274).

[95] See John H Jackson, 'The Great 1994 Debate: United States Acceptance and Implementation of the Uruguay Round Results' (1997) 36 *Columbia Journal of Transnational Law* 157, 157 ff.

[96] Data through the end of 2008.

[97] There was only one instance in which these treaties received constitutional attention. In order to convince the Congress that BITs were constitutional, the Executive Branch asked four very well-known public law professors to write a legal opinion in favor of BITs. See Raul Bertelsen et al, '*Informe en Derecho. Arbitrajes Internacionales por Inversiones Extranjeras en Chile*' in Roberto Mayorga and Luis Montt, *Inversión Extranjera en Chile. Marco Legal General Nacional e Internacional* (Santiago de Chile, Cono-Sur, 1993) 251 ff.

[98] Esty, n 21, 1509.

[99] E Allan Farnsworth, *Contracts*, 4th edn (New York, Aspen Publishers, 2004) 201.

BITs are incomplete agreements. Through the use of highly open-ended principles and standards, they delegate to arbitral tribunals the specific task of creating actual rules of government conduct.[100] Consent therefore functions here at the level of decisionmaking, but not at the level of outcomes. As Kumm explains:

> Treaties today, though still biding only on those who ratify them, increasingly delegate powers to treaty-based bodies with a quasi-legislative or quasi-judicial character . . . *This means that, though states have consented to the treaty as a framework for dealing with a specified range of issues, once they have signed on, the specific rights and obligations are determined without their consent by these treaty-based bodies.* (emphasis added)[101]

So, while States did agree on BITs, consent does not provide a satisfactory answer to the system's legitimacy problems. The manner in which rules of conduct are created through global governance mechanisms 'increasingly attenuates the link between state consent and the existence of an obligation under international law'.[102] In Helfer's words, '[t]he formal rules of state consent to treaties do little to ameliorate these concerns, suggesting the need for alternative sources of legitimacy to support adherence to international agreements and institutions'.[103]

B Output Legitimacy

If *input legitimacy*—that is, democratic legitimacy—connects to the idea of 'government *by the people*', then *output legitimacy* does so with 'government *for the people*'.[104] In this version of legitimacy, 'political choices are legitimate if and because they effectively promote the common welfare of the constituency in question'.[105] In other words, the BIT network, which resulted from a series of trade-offs, exhibits not only *deficits*, but also possible *surpluses*. Countries each reached a deal, and we must assess what has been gained as a result of that deal.

Output-legitimacy in the BIT context translates into the question of whether BITs reduced the cost of capital, and enlarged both the common pool of FDI and the fraction of that pool going to developing countries.

100 See eg Lluís Paradell, 'The BIT Experience of the Fair and Equitable Treatment Standard' in Federico Ortino et al (eds), *Investment Treaty Law: Current Issues II: Nationality and Investment Treaty Claims. Fair and Equitable Treatment in Investment Treaty Law* (London, The British Institute of International and Comparative Law, 2007) 117, 129 (noting that, '[i]n applying the standard to specific circumstances, investment treaty tribunals have given specific content to fair and equitable treatment'). See *more generally,* ch 6, 299–306.

101 Kumm, n 8, 914. See also, Hamann and Ruiz Fabri, n 24, 490–91.

102 Kumm, n 8, 914.

103 Helfer, n 22, 197.

104 See Scharpf, n 11, 6.

105 ibid.

That was the essence of the original deal: sovereignty for extra FDI. As chapter 2 observes, the empirical evidence thus far provides no definitive answer on these points, though it tends not to appear particularly promising for the expectations of developing countries.[106]

C Exit Legitimacy

Apart from *consent* and the *surpluses* that output-legitimacy tries to capture, an additional dimension to consider is *exit*-legitimacy.[107] In this usage, *exit* is, as Weiler explains, 'the mechanism of organizational abandonment in the face of unsatisfactory performance'.[108]

Following Hirschman's nomenclature, 'voice'—that is, democracy—is essential only when members of institutions have long-term attachments ('loyalty'), or when they have no alternative option.[109] But, when competing institutions exist or can be established, then exit may serve as a proper source of legitimacy.[110] In our specific context, '[e]xit mechanisms take the form of denunciation clauses that allow any ratifying state unilaterally to withdraw from a treaty, thereby terminating its obligations'.[111]

The main legitimacy question for us is then whether *exiting* the BIT network is 'prohibitively' costly to developing countries. If it is not, then their actual membership in the network should not necessarily be considered illegitimate. This requires us to assess the nature and magnitude of these exiting costs, an enterprise which can be organised around two different questions. First, how easy is it for developing countries, to exit the BIT network, from a legal perspective;[112] and second, how feasible is it in terms of reputational costs.

Regarding the first question, denunciation of or withdrawal from BITs is usually not possible during the first period in which the treaty is in force (in many instances, ten years). Although this varies on a case-by-case

[106] See ch 2, 120–121.

[107] See Albert O Hirschman, *Exit, Voice, and Loyalty. Responses to Decline in Firms, Organizations, and States* (Harvard, Cambridge, Mass, CUP, 1970).

[108] JHH Weiler, 'The Transformation of Europe' (1991) 100 *Yale Law Journal* 2403, 2411.

[109] See James Tobin, 'A Comment on Dahl's Skepticism' in Ian Shapiro and Casiano Hacker-Cordón (eds), *Democracy's Edges* (New York, CUP, 1999) 37, 37 (noting that '[e]xit is fair when competing institutions or can be established. Equity requires democracy when exit is infeasible or very costly').

[110] ibid.

[111] Helfer, n 22, 228. As Helfer, ibid 230, also notes, '[e]xit can also function as the ultimate check on international institutions, allowing states to influence their actions and, if necessary, create alternative organizations that better serve their interests'.

[112] This is a different question from that concerning the denunciation of the ICSID Convention. Bolivia withdrew from the ICSID Convention in 2007. Yet, its denunciation is merely symbolic; aside from the theoretical discussion of whether the denunciation might affect offers to arbitrate under the ICSID Convention that are currently contained in BITs, BITs generally authorise ad hoc arbitration pursuant to the UNCITRAL Rules.

basis, many BITs are automatically renewed, at which point either party can terminate it. However, even if terminated, BITs' protection of investments already made typically persist for 10 more years beyond the date of termination.[113]

Moreover, in BITs there is no *selective exit*, as opposed to *total exit*. In contrast to the general status of international law—particularly in countries where the doctrine of *dualism* applies—investment treaties have direct effect. This means that investors can bring treaty claims directly before international arbitral tribunals. The result is that governments lack the power to selectively ignore certain BIT provisions. The situation is similar to that of EU law; as Weiler explains it:

> Selective Exit ... [is] the practice of the Member States of retaining membership but seeking to avoid their obligations under the Treaty, be it by omission or commission ... The 'closure of selective Exit' signifies the process curtailing the ability of the Member States to practice a selective application of the *acquis communautaire*, the erection of restraints on their ability to violate or disregard their binding obligations under the Treaties and the laws adopted by Community institutions.[114]

With respect to the second question, a more functional perspective of legitimacy requires that *exiting* BITs be feasible in terms of reputation costs, in particular, in terms of the country's cost of capital. If the network account of the BIT generation presented in chapter 2 is correct, exiting can be expensive for developing countries, particularly for the first-movers. In any case, we have no empirical measure of what these costs might be, though a preliminary analysis suggests that disassociating from the BIT network, while not impossible, may be an onerous policy for developing countries.

D Rule of Law Legitimacy

The rule of law offers another basis of legitimacy, on which treaty makers have relied intensively. As Stein generally observes, 'adjudication procedures have formed the vanguard in the path toward closer integration, offering legitimacy as an aspect of the rule of law'.[115] When compared

[113] See eg the post-termination effectiveness of the following BITs: (1) *Agreement on the mutual promotion and protection of investments* (Estonia–Norway) (15 June 1992) 1748 UNTS 231 (providing for 20 years, Art 13); (2) *Agreement on the mutual promotion and protection of investment* (Chile–France) (14 July 1992) 1928 UNTS 13 (providing for 10 years, Art 13); (3) *Agreement concerning the reciprocal promotion and protection of investments* (Denmark–Turkey) (7 February 1990) 1722 UNTS 251 (providing for 10 years, Art 11); (4) *Agreement for the promotion and protection of investments* (India–UK) (14 March 1993) (providing for 10 years, Art 15); and, (5) *Agreement on the promotion and reciprocal protection of investments* (Mexico–Switzerland) (10 July 1995) 1965 UNTS 269 (providing for 10 years, Art 14).

[114] Weiler, n 108, 2412.

[115] Stein, n 3, 530.

with the unadorned power of rule-making, the norm-application-oriented structure of adjudication makes it appear less damaging to sovereignty.[116]

The idea underlying rule of law legitimacy is none other than the age-old aspiration to live in a world ruled by laws, and not by men. This classic ideal is also embodied by the French term *légalité* and the German *Rechtsstaatlichkeit*, both of which have been just as influential as the Anglo-American *rule of law*. In any case, whichever tradition is followed, the central message is the same: 'a system of objective and accessible commands, law which can be seen to flow from collective agreement rather than from the exercise of discretion or preference by those persons who happen to be in position of authority'.[117]

A key element of the rule of law is the presence of an independent judiciary,[118] which ensure that state powers are 'exercised within a framework of recognized rules and principles'.[119] Rule of law legitimacy demands two critical factors: first, that a higher-ranking authority produces those rules and principles; and, second, that the norms created predate the adjudicative process.[120] When those conditions are fulfilled, the rule of law enables the legitimacy of the adjudication to be shifted to that of the norms being applied.[121]

At first glance, using these criteria, the BIT generation would seem to be legitimate. BITs are treaties that establish an *ex ante* set of standards, and then charge independent adjudicators with the function of applying them. Nevertheless, a closer look reveals that the rule of law legitimacy—like consent-based legitimacy—is severely compromised by the extremely broad and vague nature of the treaties' main clauses, particularly the no expropriation without compensation[122] and FET standards.[123]

[116] See John O McGinnis and Mark L Movsesian, 'The World Trade Constitution' (2000) 114 *Harvard Law Review* 512, 514.

[117] Jerry L Mashaw, *Greed, Chaos, and Governance. Using Public Choice to Improve Public Law* (New Haven, Yale University Press, 1997) 138–39.

[118] See Stein, n 3, 493. Of course, another important dimension is the procedural one. According to Alvarez, n 12, 526–27, who follows here VS Mani, *International Adjudication: Procedural Aspects* (Boston, M Nijhoff, 1980) 25, the following rights must be 'reasonably' fulfilled in international adjudication: 'the right to be heard, the right to due deliberation by a duly constituted tribunal, the right to a reasoned judgment, the right to a tribunal free from corruption, the right to proceeding free from fraud . . . [and] the right to composition of the tribunal'.

[119] Galligan, n 15, 259.

[120] See Habermas, n 9, 261–62.

[121] ibid 238.

[122] This reminds us of the comment that Bruce Ackerman, *Private Property and the Constitution* (New Haven, Yale University Press, 1977) 6, makes in relation to the US Fifth Amendment right to compensation: 'Like many other fundamental provisions, however, the compensation clause is couched *in language of such abstraction as to strike terror in the hearts of the literalists* who imagine that the constitutional text will somehow reveal its secrets without the further intervention of human minds'. (emphasis added)

[123] See eg Stephan W Schill, *Fair and Equitable Treatment under Investment Treaties as an Embodiment of the Rule of Law*, IILJ Working Paper 2006/6, Global Administrative Law Series 5 (2006) (available at http://iilj.org/publications/documents/2006-6-GAL-Schill-web.pdf)

As noted before, investment treaty-makers faced a choice: treaty specification or delegation of power to the dispute resolution bodies. Using open-ended and ambiguous provisions of wide scope, they chose the second alternative, creating arbitral tribunals with 'adjudicate law-making' powers. The point is that the 'adjudicative law-making' that we see in investment treaty adjudication, in turn, erodes the legitimacy of the rule of law.

Undoubtedly, all adjudicative work to a certain extent requires the creation of new law. As Lauterpacht points out, 'judicial law-making is a permanent feature of administration of justice in every society'.[124] However, there is more than a merely quantitative difference between the 'interstitial'[125] powers that judges typically wield in sophisticated legal systems when adjudicating in 'penumbral areas', and 'adjudicative law-making'.[126]

In the case of BITs, arbitral tribunals frequently conduct their affairs in complete obscurity, as opposed to penumbra.[127] The general comments made by Alvarez are perfectly applicable to adjudication under investment treaties:

> Whatever doubts one may have as to the existence of 'pre-existing' law within reasonably developed domestic legal systems, such concern multiply when one moves to the rudimentary international legal system where gaps in the existing

37 (commenting that '[t]he vagueness of the fair and equitable treatment standard constitutes structural problems for the principle's interpretation and construction by arbitral tribunals'); and, *Enron Corporation and Ponderose Assets, LP v Argentina*, ICSID Case No ARB/01/3 (Orrego, van den Berg, Tschanz), Award (22 May 2007), ¶ 256 (holding that '[the] fair and equitable treatment is a standard none too clear and precise'). See also, ch 6, n 60, and accompanying text.

[124] Hersch Lauterpacht, *The Development of International Law by the International Court* (New York, Praeger, 1958) 155.

[125] The idea of 'interstitial' powers comes from Justice Holmes. See *Southern Pac Co v Jensen* 244 US 205, 221 (1917) (Holmes, J, dissenting) ('I recognize without hesitation that judges do and must legislate, but they can do so only interstitially; they are confined from molar to molecular motions'.)

[126] The idea of 'penumbra' comes from HLA Hart, *The Concept of Law*, 1st edn (Oxford, Clarendon Press, 1961) 123, 141–42, and 144. Scott Shapiro, 'HLA Hart' in AP Martinich and David Sosa (eds), *A Companion to Analytic Philosophy* (Malden, Blackwell, 2001) 169, 172, summarises Hart's position: 'Hart, however, was not disturbed by the fact of judicial legislation. He thought that judges should be given free rein to decide some cases, as it enables them to fashion sensible solutions to unforeseen problems. Moreover, given the inherent limitation of natural language, he believed that judicial legislation was unavoidable. According to Hart, all general terms in natural language (e.g. *vehicle*) contained a core of settled meaning (eg *car*) and a penumbra where the reference class is ill-defined (e.g. *tractor*). When a case falls into the core of a general term of the rule, the rule applies and the judge is legally obliged to apply the rule. However, when in the penumbra, the law *runs out* and the judge must exercise his discretion. By necessity, the judge cannot find the law, because there is no law to find, and hence must make new law'. In the end, Hart was not concerned because he implicitly assumed that the core was much larger than the penumbra. See David Dysenhaus, *Legality and Legitimacy. Carl Schmitt, Hans Kelsen and Herman Heller in Weimar* (New York, OUP, 1997) 7.

[127] See Schill, n 123, 5 (noting that '[v]agueness and indeterminacy of fair and equitable treatment are not matter of the penumbra of a rule in the *Hartian* sense . . . but concern the very core of the provision').

> law are manifest on virtually every topic, and where a primary task of international judges . . . is often to interpret vague or contradictory general principles or standards. In other cases, the notion that international judges are charged only with applying pre-existing law seems laughable, given the lack of precision as to relevant choice of law rules.[128]

In investment treaty adjudication, arbitral tribunals must, among other things, define the proper balance between property rights and the public interest—through the expropriation clause—as well as define arbitrariness and unreasonableness in state action—through the FET clause. How are these tribunals going to perform their adjudicative mission in the absence of legal definitions in the relevant treaties? And more importantly, how will they legitimately 'make law' and fill existing gaps in such sensitive areas as those of expropriations and FET?

These questions are particularly relevant from a legitimacy perspective. Franck observes that '[t]he power of a court to do justice depends, rather, on the persuasiveness of the judges' discourse, persuasive in the sense that it reflects not their own, but society's value preferences'.[129] Where, then, are investment treaty tribunals going to find the equivalent of 'society's value preferences'? Given the absence of a global polity, and the thinness of general international law when it comes to controlling the regulatory state, these questions have no simple answer.

Even more worrisome, BIT practice illustrates that many tribunals, confronted with these undefined and ambiguous provisions, are deciding to adjudicate based on their subjective impressions of the case. Indeed, both the no expropriation without compensation and FET standards have been subject to such centrifugal forces, which distance them from the rule of law. For example, it is has been said that expropriation cases are 'to be decided on the basis of its attending circumstances',[130] or 'to be examined on a case-by-case basis',[131] and that '[t]he outcome is a judgment, *i.e.* the product of discernment, and not the printout of a computer programme'.[132]

Similarly, other tribunals have noted that the application of FET clauses is 'a matter of appreciation by the Tribunal in light of all relevant circumstances',[133] or a matter 'to be determined under the specific circumstances

[128] Alvarez, n 12, 523–24.

[129] Franck, n 79, 34. See also, Adrian TL Chua, 'Precedent and Principles of WTO Panel Jurisprudence' (1998) 16 *Berkeley Journal of International Law* 171, 173–74.

[130] *Lauder v Czech Republic*, UNCITRAL Ad Hoc Arbitration (Breiner, Cutler, Klein), Final Award (3 September 2001), ¶ 200.

[131] *Tecnicas Medioambientales Tecmed v Mexico*, ICSID Case N°ARB(AF)/00/2 (Grigera, Fernández, Bernal), Award (29 May 2003), ¶ 114 (hereinafter, *Tecmed*).

[132] *Generation Ukraine, Inc v Ukraine*, ICSID Case No ARB/00/9 (Paulsson, Salpius, Voss), Award (16 September 2003), ¶ 20.29.

[133] *Saluka Investments BV v Czech Republic*, UNCITRAL Ad Hoc Arbitration (Watts, Fortier, Behrens), Partial Award (17 March 2006), ¶ 285 (hereinafter, *Saluka*).

of each specific case'.[134] Two extremes cases are *PSEG* and the *Sempra*. In the former, the Tribunal declared that the FET standard 'changes from case to case ... [y]et, it clearly does *allow for justice to be done* in the absence of the more traditional breaches of international law standards';[135] in the latter, the Tribunal stated that the FET standard 'ensures that even where there is no clear justification for making a finding of expropriation ... there is still *a standard which serves the purpose of justice* and can of itself redress damage that is unlawful and that would otherwise pass unattended'.[136]

It is a truism that all cases need must be decided individually, on their own terms, and in light of all relevant circumstances. So, when tribunals state and highlight these propositions in the context of the treaties' extremely vague language, it may mean something else. Many times, what is really being said is that the tribunal will reach its decision according to its own sense of justice and fairness. Phrases such as '*to allow for justice to be done*' and the '*servicing the purpose of justice*' are extreme manifestation of this phenomenon. Note that this occurs notwithstanding the indisputable fact that, under BITs, cases are not to be decided *ex aequo et bono*[137].

It goes without saying that this is precisely the opposite of the rule of law.[138] As noted, determinacy and legal certainty are essential conditions for any account of rule of law legitimacy.[139] By applying their own

[134] *ADC Affiliate Ltd et al v Hungary*, ICSID Case No ARB/03/16 (Kaplan, Brower, van den Berg), Award (2 October 2006), ¶ 445. See also, *Desert Line Projects LLC v The Republic of Yemen*, ICSID Case No ARB/05/17 (Tercier, Paulson, El-Kosheri), Award (6 February 2008), ¶ 192; *Biwater Gauff (Tanzania) Ltd v Tanzania*, ICSID Case No ARB/05/22 (Hanotiau, Born, Landau), Award (24 July 2008), ¶¶ 595, 603; *Rumeli Telekom AS et al v Kazakhstan*, ICSID Case No ARB/05/16 (Hanotiau, Boyd, Lalonde), Award (29 July 2008), ¶ 610; and, *Jan de Nul NV et al v Egypt*, ICSID Case No ARB/04/13 (Kaufmann-Kohler, Mayer, Stern), Award (6 November 2008), ¶ 185.

[135] *PSEG Global Inc et al v Turkey*, ICSID Case No ARB/02/05 (Orrego, Fortier, Kaufmann-Kohler), Award (19 January 2007), ¶ 239 [hereinafter PSEG Global] (emphasis added)

[136] *Sempra Energy International v Argentina*, ICSID Case No ARB/02/16 (Orrego, Lalonde, Morelli), Award (28 September 2007), ¶ 300 (emphasis added)

[137] See Schill, n 123, 2 (expressing the general and non-refutable understanding that 'the fair and equitable treatment undoubtedly constitutes a legal standard, not an empowerment of arbitral tribunals to render decisions *ex aequo et bono*').

[138] From an international law perspective, JG Merrills, *International Dispute Settlement*, 3rd edn (New York, CUP, 1998) 294, observes the precise characteristic of the rule of law that is not being achieved by these applications of the FET standard: 'A further aspect of adjudication, bound up with the issue of impartiality and hinted at above, is that the resolution of disputes by legal means employ a special sort of justification. For the reference of a dispute to arbitration or to the International Court demonstrates more than a desire for an impartial decision. It also shows that the parties want a decision which can be justified in a particular way, in terms of rules or principles rather than expediency or the judges' whim'.

[139] See Habermas, n 9, 143, who states that: 'The contribution of political power to the intrinsic function of law, hence to the stabilization of behavioral expectations, is to engender a *legal certainty* that enables the addressees of law to calculate the consequences of their own and other's behavior. From this point of view, legal norms must assume the form of comprehensible, consistent, and precise specifications, which normally are formulated in writing;

personal criteria, investment treaty tribunal members fail to respect and stabilise expectations, rendering norms illegitimate.[140]

Furthermore, because FET has emerged as the 'alpha and omega' of the BIT generation,[141] one of the most erosive situations concerning rule of law legitimacy derives from the interpretation that considers the FET standard to be autonomous or separate from international minimum standards (IMS).[142] As explained in chapter 1, IMS has traditionally been a dynamic standard,[143] embodying 'nothing more nor less than the ideas which are conceived to be essential to continuation of the existing social and economic order of European capitalistic civilization'.[144] This means that IMS traditionally provided two fundamental restraints upon adjudicators: those of general international law and those of comparative law. The *Restatement (Second) of Foreign Relations Law* explains this function of IMS:

> The international standard of justice . . . is the standard required for the treatment of aliens by: (a) the applicable principles of international law as established by international custom, judicial and arbitral decisions, and other recognized sources or, in the absence of such applicable principles,

they must be made known to all addressees, hence be public; they may not claim retroactive validity; and they must regulate the given set of circumstances or 'fact situation' in terms of general features and connect these with legal consequences in such a way that they can be applied to all persons and all comparable cases in the same way. These requirements are met by a codification that provides legal rules with a high degree of consistency and conceptual explication'. See also, Franck, n 79, 31–33.

[140] See Habermas, n 9, 198 ('Rational procedures for making and applying law promise to legitimate the expectations that are stabilized in this way; the norms deserve legal obedience. Such legitimacy should allow a law-abiding behavior that, based on respect for the law, involves more than sheer compliance'). See also, Esty, n 21, 1518, explaining this same aspect of the rule of law.

[141] See Charles H Brower, II, 'Fair and Equitable Treatment Under NAFTA's Investment Chapter' (2002) 96 *American Society of International Law Proceedings* 9, 9 (stating that Art 1105, which provides for the FET standard, 'has become the alpha and omega of investor-state arbitration under Chapter 11 of NAFTA'). See also, Robert Wisner, 'The Modern View of the 'Fair and Equitable Treatment' Standard in the Review of Regulatory Action by States' (2007) 20 *International Law Practicum* 129, 129 (noting that '[n]early every investor-state arbitration today involves an allegation of a breach of the 'fair and equitable treatment' obligation'); Peter Muchlinski, 'Policy Issues' in Peter Muchlinski et al (eds), *The Oxford Handbook of International Investment Law* (New York, OUP, 2008) 3, 24 (commenting that 'currently the most important standard, from the perspective of investor protection, is the fair and equitable treatment standard'). BITs tribunals are well aware of this fact; see *PSEG Global* ¶ 238 ('The standard of fair and equitable treatment has acquired prominence in investment arbitration as a consequence of the fact that other standards traditionally provided by international law might not in the circumstances of each case be entirely appropriate').

[142] See all cases and commentators cited in ch 6, 298–299.

[143] See eg Edwin Borchard, 'The 'Minimum Standard' of Treatment of Aliens' (1940) 38 *Michigan Law Review* 445, 457–58, and all other sources cited in ch 1, 69–71.

[144] Frederick Sherwood Dunn, 'International Law and Private Property Rights' (1928) 28 *Columbia Law Review* 166, 175.

(b) analogous principles of justice generally recognized by States that have reasonably developed legal systems.[145]

Comments (d) and (e) in that paragraph are even more precise:

> The test for determining whether conduct attributable to a state complies with the international standard is two fold. It must, in the first place, comply with the requirements specified by international law as established by the usual sources of such law . . . However, where authority from such sources is conflicting or absent, international law adopts, in this as in many other areas, analogous principles from reasonably developed legal countries . . . Reference to the international standard of justice as the standard of 'civilized states' is customary in the literature of international law, and the Statute of the International Court of Justice lists among the sources of law to be applied by the Court those derived from 'the general principles of law recognized by civilized nations'. Article 38(1)(c).[146]

The correct interpretation—that is, the one connecting FET with IMS—has been discredited through a 'straw man': the *Neer* case (1926).[147] In *Neer*, the Commission concluded that the treatment of an alien, in order to be a violation of international law, 'should amount to an outrage, to bad faith, to wilful neglect of duty, or to an insufficiency of governmental action so far short of international standards that every reasonable and impartial man would readily recognize its insufficiency'.[148] That holding has been used today to falsely identify IMS—and even the FET standard[149]—with 'bad faith', 'wilful neglect of duty' and 'outrage'.[150]

However, those attacking the FET-IMS connection fail to see that *Neer* is a 'denial of justice' case. *Neer* constitutes an allegation of judicial malfunctioning, consisting of the failure to apprehend and punish.[151] The decision rendered in that case would probably still be good law for a denial of

[145] See *Restatement of the Law, Second: Foreign Relations Law of the United States, as Adopted and Promulgated by the American Law Institute, May 26, 1962* (St Paul, American Law Institute, 1965) 501, ¶165.2.

[146] ibid 502.

[147] *LFH Neer and Pauline Neer (USA) v United Mexican States* (1926) 4 RIAA 60 (available at http://www.un.org/law/riaa/) (hereinafter, *Neer*).

[148] ibid 61–62.

[149] In *Siemens AG v Argentina*, ICSID Case No ARB/02/8 (Rigo, Brower, Bello), Award (6 February 2007), ¶ 293, the Tribunal wrongly stated that the Commission in *Neer* applied the FET standard itself; the Tribunal also failed to see that the *Neer* case was a denial of justice case concerning the functioning of the criminal law system.

[150] See eg, Ioana Tudor, *The* Fair and Equitable Treatment Standard *in The International Law of Foreign Investment* (New York, OUP, 2008) 67, who made the following incorrect statement: 'The main problem with equalizing FET with IMS is that it limits the scope of FET. *The IMS provides for action only in extreme cases.* In other words, the rights of the foreign Investor have to be violated in a serious manner in order for the Investor to obtain reparation from the host State'. (emphasis added)

[151] The claim was, *Neer* at 61, that the 'Mexican authorities showed an unwarrantable lack of diligence or an unwarrantable lack of intelligent investigation in prosecuting the culprits' that killed Mr. Neer.

justice case based on improper execution of state prosecutorial functions (which are, typically, highly discretionary in nature). Indeed, the Mexican authorities had investigated the crime—albeit not as thoroughly as the claimant had desired—and, in consequence, the Commission reached probably the same conclusion that an investment treaty tribunal would reach today:

> [I]n the view of the Commission there is a long way between holding that a more active and more efficient course of procedure might have been pursued, on the one hand, and holding that this record presents such lack of diligence and of intelligent investigation as constitutes an international delinquency, on the other hand.[152]

The main point—which will be expanded in chapter 6—is that if FET is seen as an autonomous or separate standard, arbitrators will consider (as have already considered) themselves authorised to unleash their discretion and 'creativity' without restraint.[153] Spontaneous generation or *Creationism*—ie, the relatively free invention of new rules without proper methodological foundation—runs the risk of becoming a common practice in the BIT generation.[154] The inappropriate liberation of adjudicators from the *Darwinist* restraints imposed by general international law and comparative law is indeed *one of the most serious threats to the rule of law legitimacy* of the BIT generation.

A final source of concern from this perspective is the lack of attention paid to domestic law by many investment treaty tribunals. Indeed, there has been a regrettable tendency to adopt a completely outmoded stance of 'radical dualism' with respect to the relationship between international and domestic law. Douglas has previously noted this phenomenon.[155]

Yet, arbitral tribunals cannot ignore domestic constitutional and administrative law without compromising the legitimacy of the system. In fact, there are several essential dimensions of investment treaty adjudication that are directly impacted by considerations of domestic law. The content, extent and limits of property rights and assets—all essential elements of the notion of investment, as will be proven in chapter 5—are defined at the

[152] ibid 61.

[153] Brownlie, n 74, 503, comments acutely that '[a] source of difficulty has been the tendency of writers and tribunals to give the international standard a too ambitious content, ignoring the old standards observed in many areas under the administration of governments with a "Western" pattern of civilization within the last century or so'.

[154] For a clear example of spontaneous generation, see *Tecmed* ¶ 154, followed later in *MTD Equity Sdn Bhd v Chile*, ICSID Case No ARB/01/07, Award (25 May 2004), ¶ 114 [hereinafter, MTDI]. As correctly pointed out by Zachary Douglas, 'Nothing If Not Critical for Investment Treaty Arbitration: *Occidental, Eureko* and *Methanex*' (2006) 22 *Arbitration International* 27, 28, 'the quoted obiter dictum in that award [*Tecmed* ¶ 154], unsupported by any authority, is now frequently cited by tribunals as the *only* and therefore *definitive* authority for the requirements of fair and equitable treatment'.

[155] Zachary Douglas, 'The Hybrid Foundation of Investment Treaty Arbitration' (2004) 74 BYIL 151, 155. See ch 6, n 87, and accompanying text.

domestic level.[156] The legality or illegality of the regulatory state action that harms foreign investors—sometimes, but not always, a necessary factor in the application of the FET clause—is also defined pursuant to domestic law.[157]

In summary, the legitimacy of the rule of law does not lend a great deal of capital to the BIT generation. Adjudicative law-making based on excessively open-ended standards is far from being fully legitimised by the rule of law. If arbitrators continue to make every possible effort to unfetter their discretion from any potentially useful legal system, and fail to restrain themselves through general international law, comparative law, and domestic law, they will inevitably exhaust this potential basis of legitimacy.

E Institution-Building Legitimacy

BITs require developing countries to 'establish and maintain an appropriate legal, administrative, and regulatory framework', including an 'efficient and legally restrained bureaucracy'.[158] If the original purpose was that these achievements would benefit foreign investors, there was also a high expectation that this would spill over to the general population. Such an institution-building capacity on the part of the BIT generation represents, yet, another basis of legitimacy.[159]

As seen earlier, this optimistic view has a long history in international law. In 1959, in their comments to the Draft Convention on The International Responsibility of States for Injuries to Aliens (Harvard Convention), Sohn and Baxter affirmed that 'by the establishment of an international minimum standard, the law has not only protected aliens but has also suggested a desideratum for States in their relationships with their own nationals'.[160] In 1983, Lillich followed along the same lines.[161]

[156] See ch 5, 243–253. Note that, at this point in time, it is becoming clear that the determination of the nationality of the *investor* requires direct reference to domestic law. See *Soufraki v The United Arab Emirates*, ICSID Case No ARB/02/7 (Feliciano, Nabulsi, Stern), Decision of the *Ad Hoc* Committee on the application for annulment of Mr. Soufraki (5 June 2007), ¶¶ 83–114.

[157] See ch 6, 323–342.

[158] W Michael Reisman and Robert D Sloane, 'Indirect Takings and its Valuation in the BIT generation' (2003) 74 British Ybk Intl Law 115, 117.

[159] See Schill, n 123, 32 ff (exploring the relevance of the rule of law, economic growth, and development in the context of international investment treaties). For a description of what an institution-building dynamic would look like, and some preliminary empirical analysis in this regard—with results that certainly do not serve the BIT cause—see Tom Ginsburg, 'International Substitutes for Domestic Institutions: Bilateral Investment Treaties and Governance' (2005) *International Review of Law and Economics* 107, 118 ff.

[160] Louis B Sohn and R Baxter, *Convention on the International Responsibility of States for Injuries to Aliens. Preliminary Draft with Explanatory Notes* (Cambridge, Mass, Harvard Law School, 1959) 28.

[161] See Richard Lillich, 'The Current Status of the Law of State Responsibility for Injuries to Aliens' in Richard Lillich (ed), *International Law of State Responsibility for Injuries to Aliens* (Charlottesville, VA, University Press of Virginia, 1983) 1, 13.

More recently, Wälde has referred to this 'signaling effect,'[162] and the World Bank has claimed the existence of a 'halo effect'.[163]

Of course, this basis of legitimacy demands that, as extensively argued in chapter 1, the two requirements of the updated Calvo Doctrine be met. One the one hand, BIT jurisprudence should not crystallise in more protective terms than those applied by the courts of *developed countries* toward their own national investors. Instead, it should crystallise in what was referred as *the good case* or *BITs-as-developed-countries-constitutional-law-and-no-more*.

With this in mind, the second part of this book will analyse the current state of BIT jurisprudence. Although it is too early to come up with any definitive assessment, both good and bad decisions can be observed within the pool of awards that exist currently. Not surprisingly, the quality of the decisions is highly dependent upon the identity of the particular arbitrators that participate in each tribunal.

On the other hand, international investment law jurisprudence must permeate developing countries' legal regimes, improving the content of domestic constitutional and administrative law. Regarding this point, and aside from the preliminary work by Ginsburg—who, as noted, does not provide good evidence for the BIT cause[164]—I am not aware of any study that shows a correlation, or lack of, between BITs and institution-building effects. In any case, as was previously indicated, it is developing countries' responsibility to eliminate instances of *reverse discrimination*, and to extend BIT standards—provided they are crystallised according to *the good case*—to all citizens, foreign and nationals.[165]

III DIVERSIFYING RISKS IN THE BIT LOTTERY: WHY AN APPELLATE BODY OR AN INTERNATIONAL INVESTMENT COURT IS NOT THE SOLUTION

As seen, many of the most serious legitimacy problems of the BIT generation derive from the use of ad hoc international arbitral tribunals for resolving disputes between investors and states. The natural solution would seem to be the establishment of an appellate body—similar to the

[162] Thomas W Wälde, 'The "Umbrella" Clause in Investment Arbitration. A Comment on Original Intentions and Recent Cases' (2005) 6 *Journal of World Investment and Trade* 183, 188.

[163] World Bank, *World Development Report 2005* (Washington DC, World Bank–OUP, 2005) 179.

[164] Ginsburg, n 159, 118 ff. He, ibid 122, concludes that 'the impact on BITs on subsequent governance [i.e., governance levels after the BIT is concluded] is ambiguous, and the results here suggest that under some circumstances BITs may lead to lower institutional quality in subsequent years'.

[165] As Ginsburg notes, ibid 121, without the internalisation of the benefits of institutional quality, '[t]he availability of international alternatives, then, may perpetuate poor domestic institutions by allowing powerful actors to exit'.

WTO Appellate Body[166]—or an international investment court.[167] However, if such a reform is not accompanied by the conclusion of a more detailed, precise, and well-balanced 'model' BIT or equivalent multilateral agreement, it may do more harm than good.

To prove this assertion, we must first understand why investment treaty-makers decided to delegate power to ad hoc arbitral bodies pursuant to open-ended provisions. One classic but incomplete explanation is that it was to avoid the *ex ante* costs of having to specify more precise rules; that is, to avoid transactional costs.[168] For instance, according to one of NAFTA's negotiators:

> [We] tried for some time to consider putting a line in the text that would distinguish between legitimate regulation on the one hand, bona fide and nondiscriminatory, and a taking on the other hand. We quickly gave up that enterprise. If the U.S. Supreme Court could not do it in over 150 years, it was unlikely that we were going to do it in a matter of weeks with one exception. We wished to make clear that a measure, generally applicable, which merely had the effect of lessening the economic fortunes of a particular enterprise, such that that enterprise could not repay a debt and therefore it could not be argued to be an expropriation ... The parties were not able to agree upon more clarification than that.[169]

However, there are more nuanced explanations. According to Trachtman—who has studied this phenomenon in greater depth in international law—the incompleteness of treaties permits treaty-makers either '(i) to agree to disagree for the moment in order to avoid the political price that may arise from immediate hard decisions or (ii) to cloak the hard decisions in the false inevitability of judicial interpretation'.[170]

Trachtman's theory is consistent with public choice accounts of the 'delegation doctrine'. Aranson, Gellhorn and Robinson, in trying to explain why Congress delegates too broad an authority to administrative agencies, developed a 'responsibility-shifting' model based on 'credit-claiming, blaming avoiding' behaviour by legislators, and on a public-policy lottery

[166] ICSID presented the idea of an Appellate Body in the discussion paper 'Possible Improvement of the Framework of ICSID Arbitration', available at http://icsid.worldbank.org/ICSID/FrontServlet?requestType=CasesRH&actionVal=OpenPage&PageType=AnnouncementsFrame&FromPage=NewsReleases&pageName=Archive_+Announcement 14. See also, Franck, n 81, 1617–25, in favor of an Appellate Body.

[167] See Van Harten, n 6, 180–84, in favor of an international investment court.

[168] See Alvarez, n 12, 472–73.

[169] Daniel M Price, 'Chapter 11—Private Party vs Government, Investor–State Dispute Settlement: Frankenstein or Safety Valve?' (2000) 26 *Canada–United States Law Journal* 107, 111–12.

[170] Trachtman, n 53, 351. See also, Alvarez, n 12, 472–73, stating that: 'Treaty-makers opt for less precise standards that only give general guidance (e.g., calling for application of "due process" or banning "takings"), either to avoid the ex ante costs of specifying more precise rules more amenable to routine application, or as a result of a more explicitly political decision to "agree to disagree", or to "cloak the hard decisions in the false inevitably of judicial interpretation"'. (internal citations omitted).

model.[171] In the first case, when legislators realise that some potential regulation may benefit one group while harming another, they will approve a bill containing vague terms. This enables them to take credit for helping those who win, while shifting blame to those who lose, and therefore, sidestepping any opposition in the next election.

In the second case, when legislators confront opposing groups and cannot reach a policy agreement, they too will recur to vagueness. If action is preferable to the status quo, then legislators will pass a vague statute, even without knowing which concrete policy decision will ultimately be adopted. As explained by Aranson, Gellhorn and Robinson, 'legislators will accept risks over the range of possibilities, preferring the gamble implicit in delegated legislative authority—the regulatory lottery—to the equivalent *ex ante* regulatory certainty'.[172]

In the BIT system we can observe a similar lottery: the 'BIT lottery'. In this lottery, investment treaty negotiators preferred to leave the formation of actual rules of international investment law to *ad hoc* arbitral adjudication, avoiding the long and painstaking treaty-making process, including the costs deriving from the opposition by powerful domestic interest groups. By using broad provisions, BIT negotiators could, in Tracthman's words, 'agree to disagree for the moment in order to avoid the political price that may arise from immediate hard decisions'.[173]

Once the decision of adopting open-ended substantive provisions of investment treaties had been made, treaty-negotiators confronted the following two alternative institutional designs. They could choose ad hoc arbitral panels—as they ultimately did—and risk a lack of *coherence* in the system, or choose an appellate body or international investment court, and risk *coherence in the wrong direction*.[174] By the latter risk I mean, what in this work has been previously referred to as *the bad case* or *BITs-as-gunboat-arbitration*: a situation corresponding to a *Lochnerian* jurisprudence, that overprotects investment and property rights. Negotiators, then, faced a clear trade-off of risks: *lack of coherence* v *coherence in the wrong direction*.

[171] Peter H Aranson et al, 'A Theory of Legislative Delegation' (1982) 68 *Cornell Law Review* 1, 77, 55 ff.

[172] ibid 61. See also, Mashaw, n 117, 140–42.

[173] See n 170.

[174] In this sense, we should be aware of the crucial question posed by Asif H Qureshi and Shandana Gulzar Khan, 'Implications of an Appellate Body for Invstment Disputes from a Developing Country Point of View' in Karl Sauvant (ed), *Appeals Mechanisms in International Investment Law* (New York, OUP, 2008), 267, 277: '[I]s the justification for an appellate system on the basis of "consistency and coherence" in judicial outcomes not really an argument for moulding a particular kind of "consistency and coherence" into the disorganized international investment system—given that interpretation in an appellate process is a form of legislation? Is the objection of "inconsistency" not really a call for normative uniformity?'

My claim here is that even if countries were risk-takers to the extent of signing investment treaties and participating in the BIT lottery[175] they were not sufficient risk-takers to accept a single global body or court. Given the less than remote possibility that the wrong members might end up being appointed to the appellate body or court—that is, highly conservative judges willing to protect investments in higher terms than those typically accepted in developed countries[176]—it was and still is a rational choice for countries to adopt a case-by-case resolution structure like the one we see today in investment treaties.[177] The risk of *coherence in the wrong direction*—as Legum clearly observes here—is quite serious, and developing countries should remain alert:

> The wrong sort of appellate body for investment disputes could do a tremendous amount of damage. Imagine an appellate body that considered its role as a sort of constitutional court in investment matters, and consistently took an activist stand in favor of the investors / claimants in every case to come before it. This could be an economic disaster for developing countries, a political disaster

[175] Indeed, in their 'responsibility-shifting' model, Aranson et al n 171, 60, assume that legislators are risk-takers.

[176] Today, a relevant proportion of the existing arbitrators can be 'profiled' as pro-investor or pro-state. See Judith Gill, 'Inconsistent Decisions: An Issue to Be Addressed or a Fact of Life?' in Federico Ortino et al (eds), *Investment Treaty Law. Current Issues I* (London, The British Institute of International and Comparative Law, 2006) 23, 26: 'Particular arbitrators gain a reputation for being perhaps "pro jurisdiction" or "pro investor" and for every arbitrator with such a reputation, one can find someone who is perceived as taking a different and perhaps opposite view. We all know that this "profiling" is part of the process that parties and their legal representatives already engage in . . . The questions raised by these issues lead one to ask whether an appellate system would resolve the issue'.

See also, Howard Mann, 'Transparency and Consistency in International Investment Law: Can the Problems Be Fixed by Tinkering' in Karl Sauvant (ed), *Appeals Mechanisms in International Investment Law* (New York, OUP, 2008) 213, 220 ('Indeed, it is becoming increasingly clear that some major law firms have a chosen group of arbitrators they like to draw from, while others choose people they know have rather fixed views on the law, or what the law should be'); and Katia Yannaca-Small, 'Improving the System of Investor-Dispute Settlement: The OECD Governments' Perspective' in Karl Sauvant (ed), *Appeals Mechanisms in International Investment Law* (New York, OUP, 2008) 223, 225–26 (noting how an appellate body could 'politicize the system'). Even Van Harten, n 6, 181, who advocates a single court, recognises that '[p]erhaps the most difficult question is how to appoint members of the court in a manner that balances representation of the different interests at stake in regulatory disputes between international business and states'. Later, ibid 183, he notes that '[m]ore difficult is the question of how this authority [to appoint] should be allocated among different groups of states'.

[177] See also, Michael Schneider, 'Does the WTO Confirm the Need for a More General Appellate System in Investment Disputes?' in Federico Ortino et al (eds), *Investment Treaty Law. Current Issues I* (London, The British Institute of International and Comparative Law, 2006) 103, 104, who similarly notes that 'it is preferable to let these systems develop in parallel, sort out the possible contradictions as the system develop rather than building on clay feet a system which does not have proper foundation for the harmonization function of an appellate body'. More generally, Martinez, n 8, 434, argues that, in international law, 'a high degree of centralization of power at the international level is not only infeasible in light of political reality but is undesirable normatively because it would have adverse effects in terms of democratic accountability'.

for developed countries, and a generalized disaster for the future of international investment law.[178]

Of course, the risk of *coherence in the wrong direction* remains present in the current decentralised setting. The body of international investment law that is slowly forming may also end up in *the bad case* or *as gunboat arbitration*. Nevertheless, case-by-case arbitration allows countries to diversify that risk.[179] It also permits them to react against bad cases, and to take defensive measures against arbitrators that exhibit too clear a pro-investor stance (and vice-versa).

The situation has not changed and will not change, until countries are able to sit at the table to produce an extensive and detailed treaty, that reduces the adjudicative discretion available to arbitrators under the current overly broad investment treaty standards.[180] Lawyers place too much emphasis on *coherence*, without realising how much is at stake politically. Kalb asks: 'can we live with these increasing inconsistencies?';[181] I would ask instead: 'can we live with an appellate body dominated by the wrong people?'. *Lack of coherence* is undoubtedly preferable to *coherence in the wrong direction*. The premature establishment of an appellate body or international investment court could prove disastrous for the system's legitimacy.

CONCLUSIONS: FUTURE OF THE BIT GENERATION

After reviewing the main possible sources of legitimacy for the BIT network, it appears to be too early to reach any kind of unified conclusion, overall. Definitive answers on these matters depend on information not yet available to us, mainly the correlation between BITs and FDI, and how investment treaty jurisprudence will crystallise the actual content of the no

[178] Barton Legum, 'Options to Establish an Appellate Mechanism for Investment Disputes' in Karl Sauvant (ed), *Appeals Mechanisms in International Investment Law* (New York, OUP, 2008) 231, 238.

[179] Asif Qureshi, 'Development Perspectives on the Establishment of an Appellate Process in the Investment Sphere' in Federico Ortino et al (eds), *Investment Treaty Law. Current Issues I* (London, The British Institute of International and Comparative Law, 2006) 99, 102, makes an observation that points somewhat in the same direction: 'An appellate process without an organized normative system would lead to the multilateralization of bilaterally negotiated agreements. An appellate process that is set up against the background of a disorganized normative framework in the investment sphere will also be set against a soft doctrine of precedent. It will inevitably fan out the normative sphere of what are essentially bilaterally negotiated arrangements'.

[180] Kalb, n 81, 203, recognises that '[c]reating an appellate mechanism would not necessarily correct this problem [the lack of coherence]. If these unresolved political conflicts between states are the source of the incoherence, the appellate body would likely continue to reflect them'. See also, Jan Paulsson, 'Avoiding Unintended Consequences' in Karl Sauvant (ed), *Appeals Mechanisms in International Investment Law* (New York, OUP, 2008), 258–62.

[181] Kalb, n 81, 196.

expropriation without compensation and FET standards. Developing countries should pay close attention to the evolution of that jurisprudence. The BIT network is still in the process of defining a consistent body of law.[182] Although I remain optimistic about the network's future, capital-importing countries should remain cognisant of the level of protection of property rights and investments that the network tends to achieve. Many BIT (and FTA) tribunals have expressed the truism that investment treaty law does not provide insurance against all risks to foreign investors.[183] Others have gone further, expressing the view that BITs (and investment chapters in FTAs) do not limit reasonable regulation.[184] More recently, a BIT tribunal has notably stated that:

> It is each State's undeniable right and privilege to exercise its sovereign legislative power. A State has the right to enact, modify or cancel a law at its own discretion. Save for the existence of an agreement, in the form of a *stabilisation* clause or otherwise, there is nothing objectionable about the amendment brought to the regulatory framework existing at the time an investor made its investment. As a matter of fact, any businessman or investor knows that laws will evolve over time.[185]

But cases such as the latter are not necessarily representative of the current pool of investment treaty decisions. In parallel to these, it is possible to find several others that point *in the wrong direction* (that is, *gunboat arbitration*). If an equilibrium is finally reached at a level consistently higher than that of the major legal traditions of Western capital exporting countries, then developing countries should seriously consider abandoning the BIT network.

[182] Commenting on NAFTA ch 11, Jack J Coe Jr, 'Taking Stock of NAFTA Chapter 11 in Its Tenth Year: An Interim Sketch of Selected Themes, Issues, and Methods' (2003) 36 *Vanderbilt Journal of Transnational Law* 1381, 1385, notes that '[t]hough a mature jurisprudence has by no means emerged, substantive trends have been established and several of Chapter 11's distinctive features, strengths, and weaknesses have been illuminated'. A similar comment may be made, more generally, with respect to the key substantive provisions of BITs.

[183] See *CMS Gas Transmission Co v Argentina*, ICSID Case No ARB/01/08 (Orrego, Lalonde, Rezek), Award (12 May 2005), ¶ 248; *MTD I*, ¶ 178; *Waste Management Inc v Mexico*, ICSID Case No ARB(AF)/00/3 (Crawford, Civiletti, Magallón), Award (30 April 2004), ¶ 177; *Maffezini v España*, ICSID Case No ARB/97/7 (Orrego, Buergenthal, Wolf), Award (13 November 2000), ¶ 64; and, *Azinian v Mexico*, ICSID Case No ARB(AF)/97/2 (Paulsson, Civiletti, von Wobeser), Award (1 November 1999), ¶ 83. There is an older precedent for this truism in *Barcelona Traction, Light and Power Co Ltd* (Belgium v Spain) (Second Phase) [1970] ICJ Rep. 4 ¶ 87: 'When a State admits into its territory foreign investments or foreign nationals it is, as indicated in paragraph 33, bound to extend to them the protection of the law. However, it does not thereby become an insurer of that part of another State's wealth which these investments represent. Every investment of this kind carries certain risk'.

[184] See eg *Marvin Feldman v Mexico*, ICSID Case No ARB(AF)/99/1 (Kerameus, Covarrubias, Gantz), Award (16 December 2002), ¶¶ 103, and 112; and *Methanex Corporation v US*, UNCITRAL Ad Hoc Arbitration (Veeder, Rowley, Reisman) Final, Award (9 August 2005), Pt IV, Ch D, at 4, ¶ 7, and Pt IV, Ch D, at 5, ¶ 9.

[185] *Parkerings-Compagniet v Lithuania*, ICSID Case No ARB/05/08 (Lévy, Lalonde, Lew), Award (11 September 2007), ¶ 332.

Considering an exit strategy is an essential dimension of the legitimacy supporting the BIT network. One partial alternative that developing countries should certainly consider, is the creation of a new model BIT, whose content is more complete and well-balanced than that of current treaties.[186] This new treaty, while protecting investment and investors through the same basic standards—that is, no expropriation without compensation, FET, full protection and security, etc.—would be designed to curtail the excesses of current BIT jurisprudence. This would include the provision for a clearer definition of the relationship between property rights and the public interest, and the establishment of standards of review for arbitrariness in state action. The strategy should therefore follow the US's lead—ie, 2004 US Model BIT[187] and most recent FTAs[188]—as well as Norway's example—that is, the 2008 Norway Model BIT.[189] A wholesale repudiation of BITs—in the form of full exit—may be unnecessary, if the network benefits can be preserved under a new and better-crafted treaty.

If the BIT generation is to continue to play any role in the future, capital-exporting countries should follow the examples set by the US and Norway, and refrain from pressing BIT protection beyond a reasonable level for protection of investments. Otherwise, as van Aaken has noted, they run the long-term risk of weakening investment protection in general.[190] Following Breyer's observation, the *lack of modesty* that characterised the failing of the *Lochner* era in US constitutional law history, should be repudiated in the BIT generation.[191]

[186] See Joachim Karl, 'International Investment Arbitration: A Threat to State Sovereignty' in Wenhua Shan et al (eds), *Redefining Sovereignty in International Economic Law* (Portland, Hart Publishing, 2008) 225, 238 (calling for the clarification of BIT standards, as the US and Canada have already done).

[187] Available at www.state.gov/documents/organization/117601.pdf.

[188] See *United States–Chile Free Trade Agreement* (Chile–US) (6 June 2003) (available at www.ustr.gov/Trade_Agreements/Bilateral/Chile_FTA/Section_Index.html); *United States–Singapore Free Trade Agreement* (Singapore–US) (6 May 2003) (available at www.ustr.gov/Trade_Agreements/Bilateral/Singapore_FTA/Section_Index.html).

[189] A description of this new model can be found in *Investment Treaty News* (25 March 2008) (available at http://www.iisd.org/pdf/2008/itn_mar27_2008.pdf).

[190] See Anne van Aaken, 'Perils of Success? The Case of International Investment Protection' (2008) *European Business Organization Law Review* 1, 4, observing the possibility that: ' "[O]verprotection" of foreign investment may lead to reactions that in the long run will weaken investment protection. In other words, international investment law has possibly passed a threshold of protection for FDI in the long run'. See also, ibid 21 (concluding that '[i]nternational investment law may become too successful from the viewpoint of States, which may lead to less protection in the long run').

[191] See Stephen G Breyer, *Active Liberty. Interpreting Our Democratic Constitution* (New York, Knopf, 2005) 41.

Second Part

An Assessment of the Present State of Investment Treaty Arbitration Jurisprudence

The Second Part of this work—in keeping with the normative focus of the First Part, particularly the updated Calvo Doctrine—assesses the present state of investment treaty jurisprudence in terms of the two most important treaty standards: no expropriation without compensation and fair and equitable treatment. The central question that lies behind the discussion throughout this Second Part is whether investment treaty law is protecting foreign investors to a greater extent than constitutional and administrative law in developed countries.

Addressing this question, the Second Part analyses state liability in domestic public law and international investment law. In regulatory capitalist systems, investors must usually but not always bear the negative consequences of government action and inaction. To properly determine the contents and limits of state liability in such systems, this Second Part relies heavily upon two different rationales. From a corrective justice perspective, for damages to be acceptable and bearable to citizens and investors, they must have resulted from a diligent, rational and legitimate exercise of power by public authorities. In addition, from a distributive justice perspective, the resulting allocation of burdens and benefits, even when legally and legitimately decided, must also be reasonable and proportionate.

With this dual framework in mind, chapter 4 analyses, from a comparative law perspective, the modern regulatory state and its power to harm citizens and investors. The main objective is to establish a benchmark for rules and principles governing state liability, including expropriations. Chapters 5 and 6 then analyse the current state of investment treaty jurisprudence regarding expropriations and the fair and equitable treatment, respectively, juxtaposing it with the comparative benchmarks presented in chapter 4.

4

Property Rights v the Public Interest: A Comparative Approach to a Global Puzzle

INTRODUCTION: RISKS AND BENEFITS OF BUILDING A COMPARATIVE PATCHWORK

THE REGULATORY STATE in which we live today has the constitutional power, recognised by international law, to harm citizens, including investors. This does not mean that citizens and investors must always bear the consequences of state action or inaction. Yet, neither does it mean that all injuries must be compensated.[1]

Most constitutional systems face the considerable normative hurdle of separating compensable harms from the burdens that represent the necessary price of living in society. International investment law—the global legal system of protection of investment—is no exception. Given the lack of content which characterises investment treaties, as well as the low density of general international law in this area, a comparative study of developed countries' legal systems is essential to understand not only what arbitral tribunals must do, but also to assess what they are actually doing.

As indicated in the First Part of this work, a desirable normative goal for the BIT generation is that investment treaty tribunals crystallise a jurisprudence that does not protect property rights beyond what can be found today in developed countries. This goal does not deny the right and capacity of developing countries to establish stricter standards of investment protection when concluding individual concession contracts or agreements with investors. States are sophisticated parties; as such there are no

[1] A thorough defense of the idea that governments should pay compensation for (almost) every damage incurred by regulation can be found in Richard A Epstein, *Takings: Private Property and the Power of Eminent Domain* (Harvard Cambridge, CUP, 1985), in particular, Sections 4.19–4.25, and more recently, in Richard A Epstein, *Supreme Neglect. How to Revive Constitutional Protection for Private Property* (New York, OUP, 2008) 46, where he summarises his position succinctly: '[I]magine the bundle of rights in a piece of land—in space, over time, and against neighbors—is a salami. Any slice of that salami is still salami, so that the state has to pay for each slice of the salami it cuts for itself, no matter how thin. The more it takes, the more it pays'.

a priori reasons to limit the specific commitments that they may conclude with foreign investors. However, concepts as broad and open-textured as the key substantive standards contained in BITs should not be unduly expanded beyond comparative law benchmarks.[2]

With this agenda in mind, this chapter will attempt, at a high level of abstraction, to structure the different comparative rationales that normally play relevant roles in the general division between compensable harms and non-compensable burdens. In short, the purpose is to produce a brief comparative survey of the relationship between property rights and the public interest.

Since, as the US Supreme Court has noted, 'comparison of systems is slippery business',[3] my aim here is not ambitious. I do not attempt to produce a complete and detailed comparative law analysis of expropriations and state liability. Such a study is well beyond the scope of this work, and can be found elsewhere.[4] Instead, at the risk of being overly general, I will present a more limited but workable patchwork—usually a counterpoint between two transatlantic national or supra-national systems, including references to general and human rights international law—in an attempt to shed light on some of the relevant methodological and political problems that arise when determining state liability.

I am aware of the inherent risks of this kind of selective comparison work, whereby reference is made to foreign legal systems and international courts that are often poorly understood.[5] Even if I was able to successfully overcome that obstacle, Judge Leventhal's powerful image remains: 'the equivalent of entering a crowded cocktail party and looking over the heads of the guest for one's friends'.[6] But the existence of these dangers does not preclude the need for this endeavor. Investment treaty jurisprudence must be nourished and inspired by reliable sources, not according to the whims of arbitrators.

[2] As the Permanent Court of International Justice held in *The Oscar Chinn Case* (*UK v Belgium*) [1934] PCIJ Rep Series A/B No 63, 84, 'it cannot be supposed that the contracting Parties adopted new provisions with the idea that they might lend themselves to a broad interpretation going beyond what was expressly laid down'.

[3] *Intel Corp v Advanced Micro Devices, Inc* (2004) 542 US 241, 263 fn 15.

[4] See eg Duncan Fairgrieve, *State Liability in Tort. A Comparative Law Study* (New York, OUP, 2003); and, Duncan Fairgrieve et al (eds), *Tort Liability of Public Authorities in Comparative Perspective* (London, The British Institute of International and Comparative Law, 2002); and John Bell and Anthony W Bradley (eds), *Governmental Liability: A Comparative Study* (London, UKNCCL, 1991).

[5] See Carol Harlow, *State Liability. Tort Law and Beyond* (New York, OUP, 2004) 62, citing P Atiyah, *The Damages Lottery* (Oxford, Hart Publishing, 1997).

[6] Cited by Patricia Wald, 'Some Observations on the Use of Legislative History in the 1981 Supreme Court Term' (1983) 68 *Iowa Law Review* 195, 214. For the application of Judge Leventhal's critique to the use of comparative law, see the dissenting opinion of Justice Scalia in *Roper v Simmons* (2005) 543 US 551, 617 (observing that 'all the Court has done today, to borrow from another context, is to look over the heads of the crowd and pick out its friends', referring to his concurring opinion in *Conroy v Aniskoff* (1993) 507 US 511, 519, where he cited Judge Leventhal).

Such a patchwork, even if moderately successful, carries both methodological and normative value. Although judges and arbitrators are not political philosophers, they usually have strong views when it comes to investments and state powers.[7] Yet, because of the nature of legal argumentation, those views are usually buried within legal doctrines of allegedly neutral character. The point is that a comparative enterprise like the one developed here should help us to highlight the value-laden doctrines where normative views hide, and thus clarify the roles that political or philosophical stances have actually been playing in the concrete resolution of cases.

This chapter proceeds as follows. Section I analyses the intertwined relationship between property rights and regulation. It reviews the nature and function of constitutional protection of property rights in democratic regimes, where majorities have the power to enact regulatory programs that redistribute resources among the population. It then explains how constitutional systems attempt to resolve the tension between democracy and property rights by relying on the familiar concept of vested rights, as well as the distinction between the core and periphery of property rights.

Section II explores the limits that the core, or essence, of property rights imposed on state behaviour. In principle—and subject to exceptions—property rights at the core cannot be freely sacrificed when pursing the public interest. The basic rule—established in order to avoiding complex balancing—dictates that when governments impact rights at their core, compensation should be paid regardless of circumstance. However, the determination of when property rights are truly affected at their core has proven extremely difficult to reduce to a simple, mechanical test.

Section III studies the periphery of property rights and its relation with the public interest. This outer dimension of property rights is generally dispensable in the process of regulatory reform, although only if proper tests of non-arbitrariness are satisfied. This includes the following four general tests: first, 'arbitrariness as illegality', which reviews the legality of the process and substance of the adopted measures; second, 'arbitrariness as irrationality', which scrutinises rationality, and, particularly, the presence of a proper relationship between means and ends; third, 'arbitrariness as special sacrifice', which assesses considerations of equality in the allocation of burdens among affected citizens and the general population; and, fourth, 'arbitrariness as lack of proportionality', which weighs and compares the harm suffered against the benefits derived as a consequence of state action or omission.

[7] According to Michael Abramowicz, 'En Bank Revisited' (2000) 100 *Columbia Law Review* 1600, 1605, '[e]ven if judges are not consciously seeking to advance their political agendas, law is indeterminate, and a judge who is liberal or conservative cannot always escape her personal philosophy in balancing competing arguments'. More in general, see William N Eskridge Jr and Kevin S Schwartz, 'Chevron and Agency Norm-Entrepreneurship' (2006) 115 *Yale Law Journal* 2623, 2630–31, and James J Brudney and Corey Ditslear, 'Canons of Construction and the Elusive Quest for Neutral Reasoning' (2005) 58 *Vanderbilt Law Review* 1.

The conclusions stress the existing tension between democracy and property rights. Such a tension accounts for the fact that, in mature regulatory capitalist nations, a strong conception of property rights is unnecessary, and even normatively problematic. As Rose-Ackerman and Rossi note, '[a] state that has a strong underlying commitment to the market economy need not be overly worried about establishing sweeping constitutional protections against government actions'.[8] The comparative overview presented in this chapter demonstrates that in protecting property rights and the rule of law, judges of developed nations show considerable deference toward the political branches of the state.

I THE INTERTWINED RELATIONSHIP OF PROPERTY RIGHTS AND REGULATION

This section explores the following set of ideas. In regulatory capitalist regimes, marked by pervasive regulation, the value of assets depends on present and future legal rules. Given this endogenous relationship between rights and norms, majorities—who, in democratic regimes, are empowered to adopt new rules—constantly redistribute value among different groups. To place a limit on the power of majorities to effectuate non-voluntary redistributions, constitutions usually (but not always) define property rights as fundamental rights. However, in the absence of a generally accepted account of property rights as fundamental rights, any such constitutional limitations face a problem of circularity; as Singer asks, '[h]ow can the state both define property rights and be limited by them?'.[9] Two concepts help us to partially escape the latter problem: acquired rights, and the distinction between the core and the periphery of property rights.

In the regulatory state, the existence, content, and limits of property rights depend on the exercise of public powers by legislatures and administrative agencies.[10] From an economic perspective, the initial premise is straightforward. What assets are worth depends on, among other things, present and future legal norms. According to Kaplow, 'a substantial portion of all statutes, regulations, and court decisions—even those that are nominally prospective—alter the value of prior investments simply because the future value of such investments will depend upon what rules

[8] Susan Rose-Ackerman and Jim Rossi, 'Disentangling Deregulatory Takings' (2000) 86 *Virginia Law Review* 1435, 1479.

[9] Joseph William Singer, *Property Law: Rules, Policies, and Practices* (Boston, Little, Brown and Company, 1993) 1174.

[10] See DJ Galligan, *Discretionary Powers: A Legal Study of Official Discretion* (New York, OUP, 1986) 183 ff.

are then in force';[11] '[a]lmost any change in legal rules or market conditions that is not fully anticipated will affect the value of firms, assets, or other investments that are directly targeted, as well as that of many others—such as those competing with the targeted investments'.[12]

From a political economy perspective, all regulatory changes, whether or not intended to be restrictive or expansive towards economic rights and freedoms, generate both winners and losers. In Dahl's opinion, '[w]e can take it as axiomatic that virtually all decisions by any government, including a democratic government, are disadvantageous to some people. If they produce gains, they also result in costs'.[13] Similarly, Joskow and Noll remark that 'with any major change in government regulation that has important impacts on price, market structure, cost, and product quality, some groups will gain while others lose'.[14]

While regulatory changes *may* be Pareto-superior—that is, where at least one party is better off and no one else is worse off—the reality demonstrates to us that this is rarely the case. The standard state of affairs is that new regulations are efficient in the Kaldor-Hicks sense—ie, winners win more than what losers lose, the test being whether winners *could* compensate losers—or that they are simply inefficient—that is, losers lose more than what winners win. The key point is that '*losses* are *ubiquitous*: any legal change restricts someone's opportunity set, that is, engenders losses'.[15]

Democratic constitutions do not and cannot require all new regulations to be Pareto-superior. By definition, democratic constitutions design the collective choice functioning of legislatures according to the majority rule (or more complex versions, which are more or less equivalent). This means that majorities can adopt legislation that imposes costs on defeated minorities. The constitutional structure of all Western democratic countries, therefore, permits the regulatory state to harm citizens to a certain degree.[16]

[11] Louis Kaplow, 'An Economic Analysis of Legal Transitions' (1986) 99 *Harvard Law Review* 509, 515. See also, Michael Graetz, 'Legal Transitions: The Case of Retroactivity in Income Tax Revision' (1977) 47 *University of Pennsylvania Law Review* 47.

[12] Kaplow, n 11, 517.

[13] Robert A Dahl, 'Can International Organizations Be Democratic? A Skeptic's View' in Ian Shapiro and Casiano Hacker-Cordón (eds), *Democracy's Edges* (New York, CUP, 1999) 19, 25.

[14] Paul L Joskow and Roger C Noll, 'Regulation in Theory and Practice: An Overview' in Gary Fromm (ed), *Studies in Public Regulation* (Cambridge, Mass, MIT Press, 1981) 1, 8. As pointed out by Jerry L Mashaw, *Greed, Chaos, and Governance. Using Public Choice to Improve Public Law* (New Haven, Yale University Press, 1997) 34, '[s]tatutes always shift rights or expectations'.

[15] Steven G Medema, 'Making Choices and Making Law: An Institutional Perspective on the Taking Issue' in Nicholas Mercuro (ed), *Taking Property and Just Compensation: Law and Economics Perspectives of The Takings Issue* (Boston, Kluwer Academic, 1992) 45, 46.

[16] See Eduardo García De Enterría, *La Responsabilidad Patrimonial Del Estado Legislador* (Madrid, Civitas, 2005) 35 (commenting that '[*u*]*na democracia no podría existir, simplemente, si cualquier cambio en el orden jurídico tuviese que ser indemnizado a los* beati possidentis *instalados en la legislación anterior*').

It must be noted that the only collective decisionmaking mechanism that can assure that nobody—even a single individual—will pay the costs of policy changes, is the rule of unanimity. As Buchanan and Tullock have explained before:

> To our knowledge little or nothing has been said about the external costs imposed on the individual by collective action. Yet the existence of such external costs is inherent in the operation of any collective decision-making rule other than that of unanimity. Indeed, the essence of the collective-choice process under majority voting rules is the fact that the minority of voters are forced to accede to actions which they cannot prevent and for which they cannot claim compensation for damages resulting.[17]

Obviously, democratic constitutions neither follow the unanimity rule, nor require that all regulatory losers receive compensation (a condition which would indeed be functionally equivalent to the unanimity rule[18]). From a US perspective, Rose-Ackerman accurately observes that 'the United States Constitution, in permitting policies to be adopted by majority votes in representative assemblies and approved by the President, did not contemplate that all statutes would meet with unanimous approval. Some people would suffer losses while others benefited'.[19]

This general overview of the tension between democracy and property interests is a well-known fact in domestic public law. Indeed, courts from a variety of traditions demonstrate awareness of what is really at stake when deciding damages actions against the government, and therefore do not equate harm with the duty to pay compensation. In the US, the Supreme Court has held that 'government regulation—by definition—involves the adjustment of rights for the public good. Often this adjustment curtails some potential for the use or economic exploitation of private property. To require compensation in all such circumstances would effectively compel the government to regulate by *purchase*'.[20] Similarly, the European Court of Justice (ECJ) has expressed that:

> Although these principles vary considerably from one member state to another [principles concerning state liability as a consequence of damage caused by

[17] James M Buchanan and Gordon Tullock, *The Calculus of Consent* (Ann Arbor, Michigan University Press, 1965) 89–90 .

[18] See ibid 91 ('The unanimity test is, in fact, identical to the compensation test if compensation is interpreted as that payment, negative or positive, which is required to secure agreement'.).

[19] Susan Rose-Ackerman, 'Against Ad Hocery: A Comment on Michelman' (1988) 88 *Columbia Law Review* 1697, 1708.

[20] *Andrus v Allard* (1979) 444 US 51, 65 (hereinafter, *Andrus*). Justice Holmes held something similar in *Pennsylvania Coal Co v Mahon* (1922) 260 US 393, 413 (hereinafter, *Mahon*): 'Government hardly could go on if to some extent values incident to property could not be diminished without paying for every such change in the general law'. See also, *Connelly v Pension Ben Guaranty Corp* (1986) 475 US 211, 225; and, Laurence Tribe, *Constitutional Choices* (Harvard, Cambridge, Mass, CUP, 1985) 167.

legislative measures], it is however possible to state that the public authorities can only exceptionally and in special circumstances incur liability for legislative measures which are the result of choices of economic policy . . . *It follows from these considerations that individuals may be required, in the sectors coming within the economic policy of the Community, to accept within reasonable limits certain harmful effects on their economic interests as a result of a legislative measure without being able to obtain compensation from public funds.* (emphasis added)[21]

It is important to highlight that the conflict between property rights and the public interest is inherent to any collective decisionmaking process that deviates from the unanimity rule. This conflict is not the result of a clash between the 'liberal state' and the 'social state', as sometimes depicted in the continental law world, although certainly the expansion of what constitutes acceptable public interests during the last one hundred years has exacerbated this tension.[22]

For the very same reasons explored before, constitutions do not leave citizens and investors to the mercy of majorities.[23] Property rights are usually but not always defined as a fundamental right,[24] that is, they provide redistributive limits to the collective decisionmaking processes. At a minimum, property rights as a fundamental right forbids *naked* transfers—that is, transfers lacking any public interest justification.[25] In Mashaw's terms, '[a]ny citizen should be entitled to an explanation of why her private harm is at least arguably outweighed by some coherent and plausible conception of the public good'.[26]

But, of course, that is less than sufficient protection. The next step, however, requires us to have recourse to a theory of rights. In Dworkin's account—one of the most popular existing theories—rights are conceived as trumps that defeat competing policy considerations. In his view, '[r]ights are best understood as trumps over some background justification

[21] Case 83/76 *Bayerische HNL and Others v Council and Commission* [1978] ECR 1209 ¶¶ 5–6 (hereinafter, *HNL*).

[22] See eg Gregory S Alexander, *The Global Debate over Constitutional Property. Lessons from American Takings Jurisprudence* (Chicago, The University of Chicago Press, 2006) 104–13 (exploring the reconciliation between the *Rechtsstaat* and the *Sozialsstaat*). See also, AJ van der Walt, *Constitutional Property Clauses. A Comparative Analysis* (Cambridge, Kluwer Law International, 1999) 122.

[23] See John Hart Ely, *Democracy and Distrust: A Theory of Judicial Review* (Harvard, Cambridge, Mass, CUP, 1980) 7.

[24] Alexander, n 22, 23 (noting that 'the constitutions of most democracies throughout the world do contain property clauses, but several advanced democracies with written constitutions or a charter of rights do not').

[25] See Cass R Sunstein, 'Naked Preferences and the Constitution' (1984) 84 *Columbia Law Review* 1689, 1730 (commenting that '[m]any of the provisions of the Constitution are aimed at a single evil: the distribution of resources to one person or group rather than another on the sole ground that those benefited have exercised the raw political power needed to obtain government assistance'). See also, ibid 1692, and Tribe, n 20, 165–66.

[26] Mashaw, n 14, 68. According to Mashaw, ibid 80, '[c]itizens have a constitutional right to demand that public law be public-regarding. Otherwise, their private harms are constitutionally inexplicable'.

for political decisions that states a goal for the community as a whole'.[27] In other words, even if the majority favours the adoption of a political decision that is properly seen to represent the public interest, it cannot do so because the fundamental rights of certain minority groups—here, property rights—would be sacrificed.

Yet, the application of this theory to property rights is problematic. We have already noted that property rights do not and cannot receive absolute protection in democratic regimes. As a consequence, we need some intermediate conception of property rights that, while recognising compensation in some cases, does not freeze the operation of the majority rule. But, *how do we choose among the alternative intermediate theories that compete to provide a solution to this problem*?

Following on that question—which applies more generally to all fundamental rights—Waldron has formulated a critique of Dworkin's theory that is particularly relevant in the context of property rights. He argues that in the presence of disagreement about the content of rights, as well as the trumping capacity of those rights, we require of a theory of authority. By this, he refers to a theory properly articulating the idea that on frequent occasions, we may end up with an outcome or policy that is undesirable or unfavourable to us:

> [A] substantive theory of rights is not itself the theory of authority that is needed in the face of disagreement about rights. An adequate answer to the question of authority must really settle the issue. It is no good saying that when people disagree about rights, the view which should prevail is *the truth about rights* or *the best account of the rights we have*. Each theorist regards his own view as better than any of the others ... [W]e cannot say that the whole *point* of rights is to 'trump' or override majority decisions. Rights may be the very thing that the members of the society are disagreeing about, the very issue they are using a system of voting to settle. If we say, in a situation in which people disagree about rights, that rights may 'trump' a majority decision, it is incumbent on us to announce which of the competing conceptions of rights is to do the trumping, and how that is to be determined. But to make such an announcement in the name of the whole society is of course to beg the very question at issue.[28]

So, following Waldron, we should change the question posed above and ask instead: who is the authority to decide the extent to which property rights are protected when they conflict with a valid public interest? The initial and partial answer to this question is that this authority is the legislature. Indeed, in contrast to other fundamental rights such as due process, free speech, life, etc., property rights are not created by constitutions.[29] The

[27] Ronald M Dworkin, 'Rights as Trumps' in Jeremy Waldron (ed), *Theories of Rights* (New York, OUP, 1984) 153, 153.

[28] Jeremy Waldron, *Law and Disagreement* (New York, OUP, 1999) 245–46 .

[29] David A Dana and Tomas W Merrill, *Property. Takings* (New York, Foundation Press, 2002) 62, observe that 'private property is not itself a right created by the Constitution'. In

general situation, paraphrasing Fischel, is that 'there is little constitutional property law'.[30] Property rights are creatures of civil and common law in particular, and of legislation in general.[31]

Therefore, although it is true that property rights constitute a limit to the majority, it is the same majority who defines, at least *ab initio*, those limits.[32] This does not mean that legislatures have the power to determine the definition of property rights for constitutional purposes, but rather that they define the extent and characteristics of the interests that later come under constitutional scrutiny. In other words, legislatures have few constitutional limitations when creating, *ex novo*, general rules that define categories of property rights. Although constitutional interpretation may establish some outer limits that curb the possibility of either 'too little' or 'too much' property rights relative to other values,[33] legislatures are given

Germany, Otto Kimminich, 'Property Rights' in Christian Starck (ed), *Rights, Institutions and Impact of International Law according to the German Basic Law* (Baden-Baden, Nomos Verlagsgesellschaft, 1987) 75, 82, notes that '[s]ince the Basic Law does not define the notion of property, legislation and jurisdiction are called upon to elaborate this definition within the framework of the Constitution'.

[30] William A Fischel, *Regulatory Takings: Law, Economics And Politics* (Harvard, Cambridge, Mass, CUP, 1995) 66. Fischel, ibid, continues by noting that '[w]hat constitutes property for the purposes of the Takings Clause must be established mainly by state sources of law, including common law, statutes, and state constitutions'. Tribe, n 20, 169, notes also that 'property and contracts, the Supreme Court has recognized, are for the most part what the state says they are'. See also, Carol M Rose, '*Mahon* Reconstructed: Why the Takings Issue is Still a Muddle' (1984) 57 *Southern California Law Review* 561, 594. For the German case, see Otto Kimminich '*La Propiedad en la Constitución Alemana*', in Javier Barnés (ed), *Propiedad, Expropiación y Responsabilidad. Derecho Comparado Europeo* (Madrid, Tecnos, 1995) 151, 151–52. In Spain, see Javier Barnés, 'El Derecho de Propiedad en la Constitución Española de 1978' in Javier Barnés (ed), *Propiedad, Expropiación y Responsabilidad. Derecho Comparado Europeo* (Madrid, Tecnos, 1995) 25, 27, who remarks the same point: '*El apartado 2.° del art. 33 CE constituye la clave de bóveda del precepto y es el que plantea mayores problemas interpretativos y más incertidumbres, tanto en nuestro sistema constitucional como en los occidentales, pues al tiempo que reconoce el derecho de propiedad le atribuye al legislador la delimitación de su contenido: ¿cómo protegerlo frente al legislador cuando es éste el llamado a definir su contenido, siendo así que su ámbito de protección no se determina fácilmente por la imagen que de la propiedad tenga la conciencia jurídica al margen de lo que las normas establezcan —como pudiera ocurrir con la idea de «familia» o de «matrimonio»—, sino que resulta precisamente del concreto régimen jurídico atribuido por el legislador respecto de cada manifestación dominical? O, en otros términos, ¿hasta dónde está obligado el propietario a soportar sin indemnización el menoscabo de su derecho?*'

[31] In the US, see eg *Phillips v Washington Legal Foundation* (1998) 524 US 156, 164 ('Because the Constitution protects rather than creates property interests, the existence of a property interest is determine by reference to "existing rules or understandings that stem from an independent source such as state law"'.) (internal citation omitted).

[32] Other fundamental rights, while to a lesser degree than property rights, also share this paradoxical relationship with legislatures. In Germany, see Christian Starck, 'Constitutional Definition and Protection of Rights and Freedoms' in Christian Starck (ed), *Rights, Institutions and Impact of International Law according to the German Basic Law* (Baden-Baden, Nomos Verlagsgesellschaft, 1987) 19, 25.

[33] See Thomas W Merrill, 'The Landscape of Constitutional Property' (2000) 86 *Virginia Law Review* 885, 916–54 (analysing the puzzle of 'pure positivism', including the 'positivist trap', which refers to the complete relinquishment of control that comes with positivism, and which leads 'to either too little or too much property relative to other [constitutional] value commitments'). For Germany, see Gunnar Folke Schuppert, 'The Right of Property' in Ulrich

ample discretion, including, in certain circumstances, the power to revoke rights without paying compensation.[34]

The legislative authority, however, is not complete. Otherwise, we will confront a circular problem, where property rights would determine limits to the state, although defined at will by the state itself. In this regard, one of the traditional attempts to solve to this problem of circularity relies on the notion of *acquired rights*.[35] While legislatures enjoy an almost unbridled power when it comes to defining property rights, that does not extend to the modification or extinction of existing rights. The limitations imposed by property rights over majorities function, hence, as principles of *coherence, consistency,* and *expectations*.[36] This is, indeed, the medieval notion of *iura quaesita* or vested rights.

The notion of vested rights forces us to rephrase the question of authority: Who is to decide the extent of vested right when they conflict with valid public interests? This is one of the central constitutional questions concerning the protection of property rights, and the absence of a doctrinal or scientific answer is the clearest demonstration that the notion of acquired rights does not solve the problem of circularity mentioned above.

In any case, to the extent that courts throughout the world strike down statutes and regulations, or provide for the payment of compensation, we witness that, as constitutional interpreters of last resort, they do display some degree of authority concerning the protection of acquired rights against ex post modifications or limitations.[37] Yet, due to the countermajoritarian objection,[38] courts show considerable but certainly less than

Karpen (ed), *The Constitution of the Federal Republic of Germany* (Baden-Baden, Nomos Verlagsgesellschaft, 1988) 107, 108–11, and van der Walt, n 22, 129–33 (explaining the concept of *Institutsgarantie*, which provides limitations to the legislature's discretion when defining property rights' content (*Inhalt*)).

[34] In the US, in *David H Lucas v South Carolina Coastal Council* (1992) 505 US 1003, 1029 (hereinafter, *Lucas*), the Supreme Court noted that '[a]ny limitation so severe cannot be newly legislated or decreed (without compensation), *but must inhere in the title itself*'. (emphasis added) In the continental world, this situation is known as administrative *precarius*. See Santiago Montt, 'La cláusula de precario y la utilización del dominio público: límites constitucionales a una institución leonina'. (2002) 212 *Revista de Derecho* 507.

[35] In Spain, Barnés, n 30, 28, follows this position: '*Ahora bien, ello no significa que el* dominus *quede por completo abandonado a su suerte, puesto que, una vez que el ordenamiento jurídico reconoce determinadas situaciones jurídicas de contenido patrimonial o regula una concreta forma de propiedad, el art. 33 CE asegura su conservación y mantenimiento frente al poder político y, desde luego, su conversión en su equivalente económico en caso de privación* (Art 33.3 CE)'. For Germany, see van der Walt, n 22, 153 (observing that the constitution protects 'only those rights that have already vested or been acquired, and not mere expectancies').

[36] RY Jennings, *State Contracts in International Law* (1961) 37 British Ybk of Intl Law 156, 174, from an international law perspective, remarks that the concept of acquired rights 'prevents the municipal law from going back on what it has itself created'.

[37] As Alexander, n 22, 31, observes, '[c]onstitutionalizing property does not mean that property rights become trumps, to use Ronald Dworkin's term, but it does mean that majoritarian politics does not always get its way'.

[38] The two classic texts in this regard are Alexander M Bickel, *The Least Dangerous Branch: The Supreme Court at The Bar Of Politics* (Indianapolis, Bobbs-Merrill, 1962), and Ely, n 23.

total deference towards legislatures' conceptions of property rights. Again, this division of authority between legislatures and courts reflects the great degree of tension also existing between property rights and democracy.[39]

From a comparative perspective, there is an important doctrinal framework that, while not resolving this tension (and the circularity problem), helps us to understand the dilemmas raised by this division of authority. In order to avoid either an overprotection of the status quo, or the evisceration of acquired rights through an overreliance on legislatures, constitutional interpretation usually follows a two-tiered strategy: a strong protection is provided to property rights at their *core* or essence, and a weak protection is granted to them at their *periphery*.

In the cases of some countries, this dual treatment receives explicit constitutional recognition, as, for example, in Germany,[40] Spain[41] and

[39] Exploring the tension between democracy and property, see Frank Michelman, 'Takings, 1987' (1988) 88 *Columbia Law Review* 1600, 1625–26. For a longer citation of Michelman on this tension, see n 313. For an overview of the topic, see Rose, n 30, 596, according to whom: 'The takings dilemma is thus not simply a confusion over legal terms, to be solved by adopting a scientific policy. Like the dilemma over state action, the takings dilemma is a legal manifestation of a much deeper cultural and political argument about the civic nature of what Holmes would have called the "human animal". This impasse is particularly unfortunate because both views of property have considerable commonsensible appeal. The argument for protecting acquisitiveness rests on the intuitive propositions that human beings act to further their own material well-being, that it is fruitless to attempt to suppress this characteristic entirely, and that the ability of individuals to act in their own best interest may have substantial social benefits. The civic arguments rests on the equally intuitive propositions that any community—including one that protects private property—must rely on some moral qualities of public spiritedness and mutual forbearance in its individual members to bond the community together, and that a democracy may be particularly dependent on these qualities because it relies not on force, but on voluntary compliance with the norms of the community'.

[40] This distinction is made explicit in two articles of the German Constitution (*Grundgesetz* (GG) or Basic Law (BL)): 'Art 14(2) [Property, inheritance, expropriation]: (1) Property and the right of inheritance shall be guaranteed. *Their content and limits shall be defined by the laws.* (2) Property entails obligations. Its use shall also serve the public good. (3) Expropriation shall only be permissible for the public good. It may only be ordered by or pursuant to a law that determines the nature and extent of compensation. Such compensation shall be determined by establishing an equitable balance between the public interest and the interests of those affected. In case of dispute respecting the amount of compensation, recourse may be had to the ordinary courts'. (emphasis added)

Art 19(2) [Constitution] [Restriction of basic rights]: (1) Insofar as, under this Basic Law, a basic right may be restricted by or pursuant to a law, such law must apply generally and not merely to a single case. In addition, the law must specify the basic right affected and the Article in which it appears. (2) *In no case may the essence of a basic right be affected.* (3) The basic rights shall also apply to domestic artificial [juridical] persons to the extent that the nature of such rights permits. (4) Should any person's rights be violated by public authority, he may have recourse to the courts. If no other jurisdiction has been established, recourse shall be to the ordinary courts. The second sentence of paragraph (2) of Article 10 shall not be affected by this paragraph. (emphasis added): available at www.iuscomp.org/gla/statutes/GG.htm.

According to Kimminich, n 29, 86, '[Art 14(2)] forms the constitutional basis for legislative acts restricting the exercise of property rights without compensation to the owner'.

[41] Concepts similar to those of the German Constitution appear in Arts 33(2) and 53(1) of the Spanish Constitution, written under German influence.

Chile.[42] In other cases, such as the US, it has been introduced through constitutional jurisprudence.[43] In France, leading constitutional scholars characterise property as *le droit artichaut* (the artichoke right): 'Even if many of its attributes are withdrawn from it, it remains the same, except if its heart is touched, case in which it disappears'.[44]

This means that democratic adjustments of rights and redistributions of wealth cannot, in principle, destroy the core of the interests that the legal system has accepted and recognised in the past as acquired rights. Moreover, even when those adjustments and redistributions do not affect the core, they still must be carried out in accordance with principles and values such as legality, equality, proportionality, democratic legal process, and legitimate expectations.

This dual classification embodies a popular division of labour between courts and legislatures. Courts tend to claim *more* authority—though short of monopoly—in cases concerning the destruction of property rights at their core, and conversely, show a *higher* degree of deference towards legislatures and executive agencies' decisions in cases affecting property rights' periphery. The 'gateway' question regarding the definition of the core remains a highly contingent one; non-interventionist courts struggle—not very successfully—to find objective parameters that will help them to support the claim that they do not arbitrarily bring cases within their own zone of authority.

The rest of this chapter will analyse the relationship between property rights and the public interest using the core/periphery dichotomy. However, an additional clarification is needed. In all major legal systems, state responsibility is comprised of two different categories: state

[42] Again, the same two concepts appear in Art 19 No 24 and No 26 of the Chilean Constitution, written under Spanish and German influence.

[43] Jed Rubenfeld, 'Usings' (1993) 102 *Yale Law Journal* 1077, 1097, critically explains the nature of this essentialism or fundamentalism in US constitutional law: 'Thus the question for *takings* doctrine ineluctably must be: when is a taking of property not a taking of property? To which the Court's consistent answer has been: when the property taken isn't really property in some *fundamental* sense, or when the taking isn't really so *fundamental* a deprivation that it counts for constitutional purposes. The logic that has structured takings has not been the logic of fundamental contradiction, but that of *fundamental rights*. The harm principle, the *Loretto* rule, and the economic-viability test all are predictable outgrowths of an effort to define those incidents of ownership that are fundamental to property holding, either because they involve "treasured" freedoms of ownership or because they are somehow implicit in the very concept of an individual having property'.

For example, in *Hodel v Irving* (1987) 481 US 704, 716 (hereinafter, *Hodel*), and *Kaiser Aetna v US* (1979) 444 US 164, 176, the Court analysed whether regulation destroyed 'one of the most essential sticks in the bundle of rights that are commonly characterized as property—the right to exclude others'.

[44] Bertrand Mathieu and Michel Verpeaux, *Contentieux Constitutionnel des Droits Fondamentaux* (Paris, LGDJ, 2002) 585, citing Louis Favoreu (*'Même si on lui retire un série d'attributs, il reste lui-même, sauf si l'on toucheau cœur, auquel cas il disparaît'*).

liability in tort and expropriations. Together, they constitute what the Germans referred to as *staatliche Ersatzleistungen* or 'public indemnifications'.[45] Although torts tend to cover situations that fall under the conceptual scope of corrective justice—mainly fault and negligence, including illegality and irrationality—and expropriations situations that fall under the conceptual scope of both corrective and distributive justice, they can overlap. Indeed, it is not infrequent for fact-patterns to qualify as expropriations in one country, while in others to fall within the realm of state liability in tort. The critical consideration here is to not cede to the temptation to focus solely on expropriations without paying attention to state liability in tort.

II THE CORE V THE PUBLIC INTEREST: HOPELESS ATTEMPTS TO ESCAPE FULLY FROM BALANCING

This section explores the tension between property rights at their core and the public interest. It begins analysing how the core of property rights functions as a fundamental right. Then it tackles the gateway question of what defines the core, discussing the related normative puzzles of conceptual severance and the denominator problem. Finally, it reviews those situations in which acquired rights completely cede to the public interest without compensation.

A Property Rights-at-the-Core as Fundamental Rights

If legal systems are not prepared to accept either of two extreme solutions—absolute protection of property rights, or no protection of those rights at all—then they will face the hurdles of *fundamentalism* or *essentialism*. This means that property rights exert their main protective force

[45] In Germany, *staatliche Ersatzleistungen* is the general concept which includes all types of compensations/damages that the State may have to pay to citizens, particularly: (1) torts or state responsibility *stricto sensu* (*Amtshaftung*); (2) various legal concepts linked to expropriation, including: (a) expropriation *stricto sensu*; (b) state interventions tantamount to expropriation of illegitimate character (unlawful quasi-expropriatory encroachments) (*enteignungsgleicher Eingriff*); (c) state interventions tantamount to expropriation of legitimate character (*enteignender Eingriff*), now included in the more modern concept of 'limitation of rights that requires payment of compensation' (*ausgleichspflichtige Inhaltsbestimmung*) and, (d) unequal burdens or special sacrifices in relation to non-patrimonial rights (*Aufopferungsanspruch*). See Mahendra P Singh, *German Administrative Law in Common Law Perspective*, 2nd edn (Springer, Berlin 2001) 244 ff; Oriol Mir Puigpelat, *La responsabilidad patrimonial de la Administración. Hacia un nuevo Sistema* (Madrid, Civitas, 2002) 71 ff; and Wolfgang Rüfner, 'Basic Elements of German Law on State Liability' in John Bell and Anthony W Bradley (eds), *Governmental Liability: A Comparative Study* (London, UKNCCL, 1991) 249.

only when the majority intends to sacrifice what actual legal rules and principles recognise as the core of acquired property.

Property rights can be compared to balloons. Upon their initial creation, legislatures decide how much to inflate them. Once this inflation has taken place, the same legislatures cannot deflate them beyond a threshold determined by the core of the balloon according to its original inflation (that is, the time at which property rights were acquired). Or, using the metaphor of the artichoke, we might say that legislatures decide its original size, but once the artichoke has been acquired, the state cannot touch its heart.

Property rights at their core stand out among other fundamental rights, because they are, at the same time, stronger and weaker than the latter. On the one hand, they are stronger because, except in rare circumstances, they cannot be fully sacrificed against the public interest. While most fundamental rights can be suppressed when the proper tests are satisfied, property rights cannot: the owner is generally entitled to claim compensation.

In the US regulatory takings jurisprudence, the stronger nature of property rights is reflected in the so-called *Lucas* categorical rule. This rule mandates compensation when property rights have been emptied out of all economically beneficial uses. In the court's words, 'when the owner of real property has been called upon to sacrifice *all* economically beneficial uses in the name of the common good, that is, to leave his property economically idle, he has suffered a taking'.[46] A more favourable rule, still somewhat related to the idea of total deprivation, is applied in cases dealing with price regulation of public utilities (*see* eg *Hope Natural Gas*[47] and *Duquesne Light*[48]). As summarised by Rose-Ackerman and Rossi, the

[46] *Lucas* 505 US 1019. See also, ibid 1015.

[47] *Federal Power Commission v Hope Natural Gas Co* (1944) 320 US 591, 602.

[48] *Duquesne Light Co v Barasch* (1989) 488 US 299. In this case, the plaintiffs had invested more than $40 million in projects to build nuclear plants that were later cancelled. When setting rates, the regulator did not agree to include those expenses in the rate base. Given that the rates fixed by the regulator nevertheless permitted the utilities to obtain a reasonable rate of return, the court dismissed the case. It held, ibid 312, that: '[T]he overall impact of the rate orders, then, is not constitutionally objectionable. No argument has been made that these slightly reduced rates jeopardize the financial integrity of the companies, either by leaving them insufficient operating capital or by impeding their ability to raise future capital. Nor has it been demonstrated that these rates are inadequate to compensate current equity holders for the risk associated with their investments under a modified prudent investment scheme'.

In the field of telecommunications, in a case of 'deregulatory takings', *Verizon Communications Inc v FCC* (2002) 535 US 467, 523–24, the Court insisted that to qualify as takings, the new rates should threaten the 'incumbent's "financial integrity"'. See *generally*, J Gregory Sidak and Daniel F Spulberg, *Deregulatory Takings and the Regulatory Contract* (New York, CUP, 1997); William J Baumol and Thomas W Merrill, 'Deregulatory Takings, Breach of the Regulatory Contract, and the Telecommunications Act of 1996' (1997) 72 *New York University Law Review* 1037; and Herbert Hovenkamp, 'The Takings Clause and Improving Regulatory Bargains' (1999) 108 *Yale Law Journal* 801.

Supreme Court has held that only when 'regulators threaten the financial integrity of a utility or provide inadequate compensation to current equity owners for the risks associated with their investment, they may effectuate a taking'.[49]

At the international level, the core's stronger nature can be observed in the jurisprudence of the European Court of Human Rights (ECHR), particularly in the application of the *second rule* of Article 1 of Protocol 1 of the European Convention on the Protection of Human Rights.[50] According to the ECHR jurisprudence, Article P1-1 contains three different rules: the *first rule* (Article P1-1 first paragraph, first sentence test), that covers the protection of the peaceful enjoyment of property; the *second rule* (Article P1-1 first paragraph, second sentence test), that covers the protection against deprivations of 'possessions'; and, the *third rule* (Article P1-1 second paragraph test), that recognises the 'right of a State to enforce such laws as it deems necessary to control the use of property in accordance with the general interest or to secure the payment of taxes or other contributions or penalties'.[51]

Article P1-1 first paragraph, second sentence—the second rule—provides that 'no one shall be deprived of his possessions except in the public interest and subject to the conditions provided for by law and by the general principles of international law'. According to the ECHR, this rule protects property right—or 'possessions', in the Convention nomenclature[52]—only against total deprivations. That is, the second rule requires that

[49] Rose-Ackerman and Rossi, n 8, 1456. See also, Richard Goldsmith, 'Utility Rates and 'Takings' (1989) 10 *Energy Law Journal* 241, and Dana and Merrill, n 29, 164–68.

[50] *Convention for the Protection of Human Rights and Fundamental Freedoms* (adopted 4 November 1950, entered into force 3 September 1953) 213 UNTS 221; and, *Protocol [No 1] to the Convention for the Protection of Human Rights and Fundamental Freedoms* (adopted 20 March 1952; entered into force 18 May 1954) 213 UNTS 262.

[51] The ECHR frequently explains the structure of Art P1–1. For instance, in *Antonetto v Italy* (App no 15918/89) (2003) 36 EHRR (10) 120, 127, ¶ 33, the ECHR held that: 'According to the Court's case law, Article 1 of Protocol No 1 which in substance guarantees the right of property, contains three distinct rules: the first rule, set out in the first sentence of the first paragraph, is of a general nature and enunciates the principle of the peaceful enjoyment of property; the second rule, contained in the second sentence of the first paragraph, covers deprivations of possessions and subjects it to certain conditions; the third rule, stated in the second paragraph, recognises that the Contracting States are entitled, amongst other things, to control the use of property in accordance with the general interests'. See also, See eg *Sporrong and Lönnroth v Sweden* (Apps no. 7151/75, 7152/75) (1983) 5 EHRR 35, ¶ 61 (hereinafter, *Sporrong*).

[52] The broad concept of 'possessions' encompasses rights '*in rem*' and '*in personam*', immovable and movable property, interests in property, shares, securities, patents, contractual rights, licences, etc. See Claire Weir and Richard Moules, 'Article 1 of Protocol No 1: Protection of Property' in Jessica Simor and Ben Emmerson, *Human Rights Practice* (rev 13 February 2007) (London, Sweet and Maxwell, 2008) ch 15, 15.004–15.

government must have taken away *'all meaningful use of the property in question'*,[53] in which case compensation must be paid.[54]

This stronger protection of the core can also be found in the Iran–US Claims Tribunals case law. The text of the Claims Settlement Declaration[55] distinguishes between 'expropriations', and other types of interference referred to as 'measures affecting property rights'.[56] In this framework, to find a compensable expropriation, the Tribunal requires a 'sufficient degree of interference', where sufficient means that it represents a 'deprivation'.[57]

According to the summary provided by Pellonpää, expropriation cases decided by this Tribunal 'have used somewhat varying general formulations, with certain awards speaking of "unreasonable interference" in the use of property, while other awards require more than just "ephemeral" deprivation of "fundamental rights of ownership" or of rendering the

[53] Ali Riza Çoban, *Protection of Property Rights within the European Convention On Human Rights* (Burlington, Ashgate, 2004) 176 (emphasis added) See also, Weir and Moules, n 52, 15.016–20. The leading case in this regard is *Sporrong* ¶ 63, in which the court held that: 'In the absence of a formal expropriation, that is to say a transfer of ownership, the Court considers that it must look behind the appearances and investigate the realities of the situation complained of . . . [I]t has to be ascertained whether that situation amounted to a de facto expropriation, as was argued by the applicants. In the Court's opinion, all the effects complained of stemmed from the reduction of the possibility of disposing of the properties concerned. Those effects were occasioned by limitations imposed on the right of property, which right had become precarious, and from the consequences of those limitations on the value of the premises. *However, although the right in question lost some of its substance, it did not disappear. The effects of the measures involved are not such that they can be assimilated to a deprivation of possessions'*. (internal references omitted and emphasis added).

[54] See Weir and Moules, n 52, 15.015 (observing that '[a] deprivation . . . necessarily gives rise to a right to compensation save in the most exceptional circumstances').

[55] See *The Declaration of the Government of the Democratic and Popular Republic of Algeria concerning the Settlement of Claims by the Government of the United States of America and the Government of the Islamic Republic of Iran*, reprinted in (1981) 75 *American Journal of International Law* 422.

[56] Art II.1 of the Claims Settlement Declaration, ibid 423, establishes that: 'An International Arbitral Tribunal (the Iran–United States Claims Tribunal) is hereby established for the purpose of deciding claims of nationals of the United States against Iran and claims of nationals of Iran against the United States, and any counterclaim which arises out of the same contract, transaction or occurrence that constitutes the subject matter of that national's claim, if such claims and counterclaims are outstanding on the date of this Agreement, whether or not filed with any court, and arise out of debts, contracts (including transactions which are the subject of letters of credit or bank guarantees), *expropriations* or *other measures affecting property rights*' (emphasis added)

[57] See Iran–US Claims Tribunal *Otis Elevator Co v Islamic Republic of Iran* (1987) 14 Iran–US Claims Trib Rep 283, 293 ¶ 29 ('The Tribunal must . . . examine the acts of interference Otis complains of and determine . . . whether any or all, by themselves or collectively, constitute *a sufficient degree of interference* to warrant a finding that deprivation of property has occurred') (emphasis added) See also, Matti Pellonpää, 'Compensable Claims Before the Tribunal: Expropriation Claims' in Richard B Lillich and Daniel Barstow Magraw (eds), *The Iran–United States Claims Tribunal: Its Contribution to the Law Of State Responsibility* (Irvington-on-Hudson, Transnational Publishers, 1998) 185, 257–58; and, Allahyar Mouri, *The International Law of Expropriation as Reflected in the Work of the Iran–US Claim Tribunals* (Boston, M Nijhoff, 1994) 100 ff.

property "useless" to the owner'.[58] In any case, a review of the relevant decisions shows that the Tribunal has generally required substantial, not ephemeral, deprivation.[59]

Yet, as mentioned before, while property rights are stronger than other fundamental rights in the respects discussed above, they are also weaker. This relative weakness stems from the fact that the core can be easily converted into compensation. Public officers enjoy a relatively great amount of discretion in determining whether to deprive owners of property if compensation is paid. The US Supreme Court has elaborated upon this point, noting that the protection of property rights does not constitute 'a substantive or absolute limit on the Government's power to act. The Clause operates as a conditional limitation, permitting the Government to do what it wants so long as it pays the charge'.[60]

[58] Pellonpää, n 57, 223. See eg Iran–US Claims Tribunal *International Technical Products Corp et al v Islamic Republic of Iran* (1985) 9 Iran–US Claims Trib Rep 206, 238, 240 ('unreasonable interference' and 'more or less irreversible deprivation of property').

[59] In one of the more recent decisions, Iran–US Claims Tribunal *Saghi v Islamic Republic of Iran* (1993) 29 Iran–US Claims Trib Rep 20, 44, the Tribunal summarised its practice in this field: 'The assumption of control over property by a government—for example, through the appointment of 'temporary management'—does not, *ipso facto*, mean that the property has been taken by the government, thus requiring compensation under international law. The appointment of such managers is, however, an important factor in finding a taking. If the appointments were part of a process by which *the owner of the property was deprived of fundamental rights of ownership and if the deprivation is not ephemeral,* then one must conclude that compensation is required'. (emphasis added)

See also the following cases: *Tippetts, Abbett, McCarthy, Stratton v TAMS-AFFA Consulting Engineers of Iran et. el.* (1984) 6 Iran–US Claims Trib Rep 219, 225 (hereinafter, *Tippetts*) (defining takings as a case in which 'the owner was deprived of fundamental rights of ownership and it appears that this deprivation is not merely ephemeral', that is, 'interference by a state in the use of that property with the enjoyment of its benefits, even where legal title to the property is not affected'); *Foremost Tehran, Inc and Islamic Republic of Iran* (1986) 10 Iran–US Claims Trib Rep 228, 247 (stating that the deprivation of declared cash dividends did not amount to expropriation of the company's property interests, 'when set against the background of Foremost's continued, albeit circumscribed, participation in the affairs of the company'); *Phelps Dodge Corp v Islamic Republic of Iran* (1986) 10 Iran–US Claims Trib Rep 121, 130 ¶ 22 (finding an expropriation in a case in which a company has been deprived of 'virtually all of the value of its property rights', a situation that was 'likely to continue indefinitely'); *Dames and Moore v Islamic Republic of Iran* (1983) 4 Iran–US Claims Trib Rep 212, 223 (observing that 'unilateral taking of possession of property and the denial of its use to the rightful owners may amount to an expropriation even without a formal decree regarding title to the property'); *Harza Engineering Co v Islamic Republic of Iran* (1981–82) 1 Iran–US Claims Trib Rep 499, 504 (noting that 'a taking of property may occur under international law . . . if a government has interfered unreasonably with the use of property'); *Sea-Land Service, Inc v Islamic Republic of Iran* (1984) 6 Iran–US Claims Trib Rep 149, 166 (stating that '[a] finding of expropriation would require, at the very least, that the Tribunal be satisfied that there was deliberate governmental interference with the conduct of the use and benefit of its investment'). Other relevant cases are *Starret Housing Corp v Islamic Republic of Iran* (1983) 4 Iran–US Claims Trib Rep 122, 154–57 (hereinafter, *Starret*); *SEDCO Inc et al v National Iranian Oil Co et al* (1985) 9 Iran–US Claims Trib Rep 248, 278 (hereinafter, *SEDCO*); *Thomas Earl Payne v Islamic Republic of Iran*, 12 Iran–US Claims Trib Rep 3, 9–11 (1986); and, *Sola Tiles Inc v Islamic Republic of Iran* (1987) 14 Iran–US Claims Trib Rep 223, 230–34.

[60] *Eastern Enterprises v Apfel* (1998) 524 US 498, 545. See also, *First English Evangelical Lutheran Church v County of Los Angeles* (1987) 482 US 304, 315 (hereinafter, *First English*

Following the nomenclature of the Calabresi and Melamed's *Cathedral*,[61] Fischel highlights this aspect of property rights by pointing out that, regarding owners' relationship with the state, property confers only liability-rule protection but no property-rule protection (that is, it does not include the right to 'just say no'[62]). Moreover, the general unwillingness of constitutional and supreme courts to review the public interest requirement for takings accentuates this liability-rule character of property rights.[63]

There are multiple reasons for protecting the core of property rights in such a dichotomous, strong/weak manner.[64] Following a division used throughout this work, I group these reasons in two: corrective and distributive justice rationales. The corrective justice rationale has a lengthy historical pedigree (in the Spanish legal tradition, since at least the thirteenth century[65]). The protection of the core of property rights insulates citizens and investors from their political enemies, including unscrupulous bureaucrats and their associated friends. Property may neither be *appropriated* by the state or third parties, nor illegally destroyed, without paying compensation.[66]

Evangelical Lutheran Church) (holding that the Fifth Amendment 'is designed not to limit the governmental interference with property rights per se, but rather to secure compensation in the event of otherwise proper interference amounting to a taking').

[61] See Guido Calabresi and Douglas Melamed, 'Property Rules, Liability Rules and Inalienability: One View of the Cathedral' (1972) 85 *Harvard Law Review* 1089.

[62] See Fischel, n 30, 67–68, who notes that: 'A homeowner has *property-rule protection* against the demands of other private parties, but only *liability-rule protection* against the demands of government or others endowed with the power of eminent domain . . . The property rule/liability shows that the Takings Clause is less protective of private property than it is sometimes made out to be. The Takings Clause dictates that private property is protected only by a liability rule with respect to the government or some other party granted the power of eminent domain. It allows property to be taken without consent'.

[63] In the US, the Supreme Court is reluctant to review the public interest invoked by the state. See *Kelo v City of New London* (2005) 545 US 469 (2005) (hereinafter, *Kelo*), and *Hawaii Housing Authority v Midkiff* (1994) 467 US 229 (hereinafter, *Hawaii Housing Authority*). According to Alexander, n 22, 65, '[t]he Court's approach has been highly deferential to legislative judgments about what uses satisfy the public-use requirement'. For the French case, Louis Favoreau and Loïc Philip, *Les Grandes Décisions du Conseil Constitutionnel*, 7th edn (Paris, Sirey, 1993) 283, observe that there is also a very weak constitutional control over this requirement. Germany seems to be an exception in this regard; according to Kimminich, n 30, 168, the Federal Constitutional Court controls the public interest condition more strictly.

[64] Dana and Merrill, n 29, 33 (observing that 'the practice of providing compensation for government takings of property has multiple rationales').

[65] See *Las Siete Partidas* in *Los Códigos Españoles Concordados y Anotados* (Madrid, Imprenta de la Publicidad, 1848). See ch 1, nn 129–130 and accompanying text.

[66] See Andrew Newcombe, 'The Boundaries of Regulatory Expropriation in International Law' (2005) 20 *ICSID Review—Foreign Investment Law Journal* 1, 8, who provides the following explanation: 'Looking at expropriation as a question of appropriation is consistent with the primary rationale for international protection of property rights: to ensure states do not take acquired rights without compensation. The classic international decisions on expropriation refer to the principle of respect for acquired rights. Respect for acquired rights finds expression in the principles of corrective justice and unjust enrichment'.

On the other hand, citizens and investors receive protection by virtue of their having to bear an unequal share of the public burden. This is also a classic rationale for the payment of compensation, based on the notion of distributive justice. Building an important highway is indisputably a public interest, and the highway must necessarily cross some properties. Nevertheless, those unfortunate owners whose properties are required for this public purpose have the right to claim that the community as a whole should bear the cost of building a new highway.

The emergence of the regulatory state, and its unlimited interventionist and redistributive pretensions, have led to an emphasis on this second rationale.[67] Sometimes these regulatory activities, even when not constituting an apropriation, wipe out the substantial value of the rights of citizens and investors. This reality poses a key normative question to constitutional systems: Should the rule of compensation for physical appropriations be extended to these new scenarios? Or, should regulations be considered mere 'risks', that investors bear just as they do 'natural' ones?

If we were certain that the state truly acted in the public interest, we would probably make no distinction between the risk of expropriaton and other natural risks (fires, hurricanes, floods, etc.).[68] But we are not. This is why, in the end, as Dana and Merrill point out, 'takings theory is ultimately about political theory—specifically, about how much faith one has in government'.[69] In this regard, the literature on economic regulation teaches us two lessons.[70] On the one hand, as Kenneth Arrow has demonstrated, we lack a rational, non-dictatorial way of aggregating private preferences in order to determine what the public interest really is; thus, there is no simple way of knowing whether any piece of regulation truly pursues the public interest.[71] On the other hand, even if we overcame the theoretical social choice barriers just mentioned, we must also recognise that

[67] As pointed out by Bruce Ackerman, *Private Property and the Constitution* (New Haven, Yale University Press, 1977) 1, the state is no longer a night-watchman, and, '[a]rmed with a prodigious array of legal tools, it sets about improving upon the invisible hand—taxing here, subsidizing there, regulating everywhere'.

[68] Not everybody agrees with this proposition. For example, Frank I Michelman, 'Property, Utility, and Fairness: Comments on the Ethical Foundations of "Just Compensation" Law' (1967) 80 *Harvard Law Review* 1165, 1214 ff, argues that the destruction of property right without compensation because of governmental action—in contrast of natural causes—creates 'demoralization costs'. Others have claimed that the problems of adverse selection and moral hazard can be more severe in the case of the risk of expropriation. See Lawrence Blume and Daniel L Rubinfeld, 'Compensation for Takings: An Economic Analysis' (1984) 72 *California Law Review* 569, 592–97.

[69] Dana and Merrill, n 29, 57.

[70] A good survey of theories of regulation can be found in Steven Croley, 'Theories of Regulation: Incorporating the Administrative Process' (1999) 98 *Columbia Law Review* 1.

[71] See Michael E Levine and Jennifer L Forrence, 'Regulatory Capture, Public Interest, and the Public Agenda: Towards a Synthesis' (1990) 6 *Journal of Law, Economics and Organization* 167 (1990).

empirically, as the Chicago and Virginia Schools remind us, the state does not always pursue the public interest; indeed, a considerable component of the state's activity is the result of regulatory capture.[72]

Hence, in a world of pervasive economic regulation, our agnosticism about the public interest and our suspicions about regulatory capture, which exists alongside our ideal of a democratic government pursuing the common good, lead us to conclude pragmatically that we cannot place courts or tribunals in the position of deciding, with strict rigor, whether or not regulatory programs are public-regarding. It is simply unwise to allow the entire field of expropriation to depend on judicial review of regulatory goals.[73] Apart from the intellectual challenge of such a mission, assigning it to courts is simply too dangerous. It would lead to the substitution of judges for the people when it comes to making policy decisions, not to mention the prospect of judicial capture.

So, as in the earlier history of physical takings, we see today how corrective and distributive justice rationales converge in the justification of a simple rule—a rule of thumb—that commands the payment of compensation for non-appropriatory destructions of property rights. In the age of the regulatory state, the corrective justice rationale alerts us to the overwhelming likelihood that regulations are not truly public-regarding. The distributive justice rationale insists that citizens should not be excessively or disproportionedly burdened, at least to the point that their acquired interests are destroyed.

Many constitutional traditions, therefore, have concluded that it makes sense to retain the traditional protection against direct physical expropriations, and expand it to the modern scenario, in which full deprivations of property derive from regulatory activity. That is, *in principle*, and regardless of any purpose of intent, if the government destroys certain property rights when pursuing the public interest, then it must pay compensation to the owner.

B The Gateway Question of the Core

As previously explained, courts generally claim the authority of having the last word on the protection of property rights in cases where their core has been destroyed. By contrast, outside that domain, they tend to recognise the authority of legislatures and executive agencies. This raises two

[72] In his excellent, recent study on regulation and the public interest, Steven P Croley, *Regulation and the Public Interest. The Possibility of Good Regulatory Government* (Princeton, Princeton University Press, 2008) 306, concludes that '[s]ome regulation has undermined social welfare; much important regulation has not. Empirical studies goes both ways'.

[73] For a more general case against judicial review, see Jeremy Waldron, 'The Core of the Case Against Judicial Review' (2006) 115 *Yale Law Journal* 1346.

questions: How should the core or essence of property rights be defined? And, who should be the final authority in this characterisation?

There are two contending methodologies that attempt to provide the necessary clues to these questions: those of lawyers, and those of economists.[74] The first methodology, which is probably more influential, reflects the wisdom of the old school of thought of private law. In most Western legal traditions that, to a certain extent, are tributaries of Roman law, property is associated with the essential bundles of *jus utendi* and *jus abutendi*. In this classic account, property is the 'sole and despotic dominion which one man claims and exercises over the external things of the world, in total exclusion of the right of any other individual in the universe'.[75]

The legal 'sciences' have long striven to pinpoint the essential elements of property, and this has resulted in a kind of 'privatisation' of the constitutional notion of property. Indeed, older legal teachings have ended up playing prominent roles in the constitutional definition of the core of property. In Germany, for example, Kimminich comments that 'the starting point for the determination of the concept of property [in the Constitution] continues to be civil [private] law';[76] and in the US, Alexander notes that '[t]he private law meaning of property invariably anchors the constitutional meaning'.[77]

As noted, the legal methodology is not alone in this endeavor. In light of the critiques of formalism made by legal realists and their successors, coupled with the growing importance of economics among the social sciences, considerations of value, profit and cash flows are challenging the traditional dominance of legalistic considerations. In a nutshell, economists

[74] Jeremy Paul, 'The Hidden Structure of Takings Law' (1991) 64 *Southern California Law Review* 1393, 1416–29 presents two 'property models': physicalism and the market model. His idea of physicalism is different from what I refer to here as the lawyers' approach, although of course physicalism plays a relevant role in the traditional legal conception of property.

[75] William Blackstone, *Commentaries on the Laws of England* (New York, From the 19th London Edition, WE Dean, 1847) Vol I Book 2, 1. Compare Blackstone's with Art 544 of the French Civil Code (*'La propriété este le droit de jouir et disponer des choses de la manière la plus absolute, pourvu qu'on n'en fas pas un usage prohibé par les lois our par les règlaments'*), and with Art 582 of the Chilean Civil Code (written by Andrés Bello) (*'El dominio (que se llama también propiedad) es el derecho real en una cosa corporal, para gozar y disponer de ella arbitrariamente; no siendo contra la ley o contra derecho ajeno'*).

[76] Kimminich, n 30, 125. Certainly, the constitutional concept of property is not determined by private law; as Kimminich notes, it only constitutes *'a starting point'*. Van der Walt, n 22, 127, observes also that the constitutional property concept is 'appreciably wider than the civil-law concept', but also, ibid 152, that 'the development of a specifically constitutional property concept nevertheless used the private-law property concept as its point of departure'. See also, Hanri Mostert, *The Constitutional Protection and Regulation of Property and its Influence on the Reform of Private Law and Landownership in South Africa and Germany. A Comparative Analysis* (New York, Springer, 2002) 247–48; and, Donald P Kommers, *The Constitutional Jurisprudence of the Federal Republic of Germany*, 2nd edn (Durham, NC, Duke University Press, 1997) 254.

[77] Alexander, n 22, 60. He also notes, ibid, that '[e]ven if the constitutional concept of property is formally uncoupled from the traditional private law concept, the latter will continue to influence the former. The constitution's concept may have its own life, but that life begins in the private law concept'.

approach the problem of the core through valuation techniques, all of which generally focus on market value and the present value of discounted future cash flows.

Unfortunately, economics as a science does not provide normative criteria to decide which diminutions in value impact the core. More critically, it cannot even distinguish between those cash flows to which the owner is or is not entitled.[78] Nor does economics respond to even more basic questions, such as which kind of losses should be compensated. Should compensation occur for losses of more than 50 per cent of the original value, or more than 90 per cent? Or, should it apply to changes that bring company figures from blue to red?[79]

In light of this confrontation between lawyers and economists, two accounts of the core have typically been employed. First, there is a 'pure' legal account, whereby the core protects against *total* or *substantial legal deprivations*, that is, interferences that destroy or neutralise all or substantially all of the owner's legal powers and capacities. For example, this seems to be the case of the demanding test that the ECHR uses in its Article P1-1 first paragraph, second sentence jurisprudence (the second rule).[80]

Second, there is a blended approach, whereby decisionmakers adopt a pragmatic and undefined combination of economic and legal methodologies in order to decide whether or not the core was affected. This appears to be the case, for instance, with the Iran–United States Claims Tribunal's jurisprudence. The case law, that sometimes refers to lawyers and sometimes to economists, makes it difficult to conclude whether this Tribunal has opted for one criterion over the other.

[78] This distinction can be highly complicated. For example, in the US, the Supreme Court has distinguished between government action that interferes with interests that are sufficiently bound up with the owner's expectation, and action that does not interfere with such interests. See eg *Penn Central Transportation Co v New York City* (1978) 438 US 104, 124–25 (hereinafter, *Penn Central*), where the Court noted that '[it] has dismissed 'taking' challenges on the ground that, while the challenged government action caused economic harm, it did not interfere with interests that were *sufficiently bound up* with the reasonable expectations of the claimant to constitute "property" for Fifth Amendment purposes'. (emphasis added)

[79] For an analysis of the conceptual and practical difficulties that arise when approaching the problem from an economic perspective, see Burns H Weston, ' "Constructive Takings" under International Law: A Modest Foray into the Problems of "Creeping Expropriations" ' (1975) 16 *Virginia Journal of International Law* 103, 119–20.

[80] As noted above, in *Sporrong*, n 53, 5 EHRR 51 ¶ 63, the ECHR held that the test for proving a de facto expropriation is a very strict one. Similarly, in *Matos E Silva Lda v Portugal* (App no 15777/89) (1997) 24 EHRR 573, 600–01 ¶ 85, the ECHR held that: '[T]here was no formal or de facto expropriation in the present case. The effects of the measures are not such that they can be equated with deprivations of possessions . . . The restrictions on the right to property stemmed from the reduced ability to dispose of the property and from the damage sustained by reason of the fact that expropriation was contemplated. *Although the right in question has lost some of its substance, it had not disappeared.* The Court notes, for example, that all reasonable manner of exploiting the property had not disappeared seeing that the applicants continued to work the land'. (emphasis added). See also, Çoban, n 53, 176, and Weir and Moules, n 52, 15.016–20.

The US Fifth Amendment jurisprudence also follows this blended approach. While the Supreme Court followed an economic approach in one of the categorical rules—the *Lucas* rule—in the other categorical rule—*Loretto*[81]—the Court held that any permanent physical occupation requires the payment of compensation, regardless of whether the economic impact is negligible.[82] Indeed, in *Loretto*, the court found a taking in spite of the fact that the case involved only a few square feet in the roof of a building for the setup of a TV cable box. The language used by the court deserves closer attention:

> The historical rule that a permanent physical occupation of another's property is a taking has more than tradition to commend it. Such an appropriation is perhaps the most serious form of invasion of an owner's property interests . . . [T]he government does not simply take a single 'strand' from the 'bundle' of property rights: it chops through the bundle, taking a slice of every strand. Property rights in a physical thing have been described as the rights 'to possess, use and dispose of it.' To the extent that the government permanently occupies physical property, it effectively destroys *each* of these rights. First, the owner has no right to possess the occupied space himself, and also has no power to exclude the occupier from possession and use of the space. The power to exclude has traditionally been considered one of the most treasured strands in an owner's bundle of property rights. Second, the permanent physical occupation of property forever denies the owner any power to control the use of the property; he not only cannot exclude others, but can make no nonpossessory use of the property . . . Finally, even though the owner may retain the bare legal right to dispose of the occupied space by transfer or sale, the permanent occupation of that space by a stranger will ordinarily empty the right of any value, since the purchaser will also be unable to make any use of the property.[83]

In the end, it seems difficult for sophisticated legal systems to avoid the blending of both approaches. The unavoidable outcome is a jurisprudence that combines economic and legal readings of the core in unpredictable ways. This is indeed one of the reasons that explains why the law of takings and state liability in tort is in doctrinal disarray worldwide, and why cases are resolved not in accordance with pre-established rules, but according to ad hoc tests that grant tribunals considerable discretion over the matter.[84]

[81] *Loretto v Teleprompter Manhattan CATV Corp* (1982) 458 US 419 (hereinafter, *Loretto*).

[82] A summary of the per se takings rules can be found in *Lingle v Chevron USA Inc* (2005) 544 US 528, 538: 'Our precedents stake out two categories of regulatory action that generally will be deemed È takings for Fifth Amendment purposes. First, where government requires an owner to suffer a permanent physical invasion of her property—however minor—it must provide just compensation. A second categorical rule applies to regulations that completely deprive an owner of "*all* economically beneficial use" of her property'. (internal citations omitted).

[83] *Loretto*, 458 US 435–36 (internal citations omitted).

[84] See Rose-Ackerman, n 19. Similarly, in Spain, see Mir, n 45, 293, and Ferrán Pons Cànovas, *La Incidencia de las Intervenciones Administrativas en el Derecho de Propiedad. Perspectivas Actuales* (Madrid, Marcial Pons, 2004) 83–84.

This leads us to the second question posed earlier: Who should define what is the core in particular instances, courts or legislatures/executive agencies? Chronologically speaking, legislatures and executive agencies decide first. By labeling measures as 'regulation' instead of 'expropriation', and refusing to compensate those harmed by the decisions adopted, they implicitly define the effects of those measures as not affecting the core.

Yet, to the extent that courts generally protect the core of acquired rights, this means that the authority to define the core lies in the hands of the judiciary, as well.[85] Otherwise, there would be no judicial review and expropriatory control of regulation. In other words, courts follow previous legal and economic doctrinal understandings of the core of property rights, even at the cost of choosing paths that are unacceptable to the political branches of government.

Because the entire question of whether compensation is due is substantially determined by the way in which the core is characterised, courts show a substantial degree of deference towards legislatures and executives agencies. In the absence of deference, courts could easily neutralise the policy judgments of legislatures and executives by the simple recourse of using strict conceptions of the core of property rights, an outcome that is evidently inappropriate for any democratic system.

C The Denominator Problem and Conceptual Severance

The distinction between the core and the periphery, and by implication, the prospect of any rule-of-thumb determination of property rights encroachments that necessitate the payment of compensation, experience a number of 'unexpected' difficulties. Two of them are particularly serious, and place the entire distinction between the core and periphery at risk: the 'denominator problem', and 'conceptual severance'.[86] Not surprisingly, both of them are central to many takings cases.[87]

The main issue here is that the meanings of 'total' and 'substantial' deprivations are relative. A comparison between two figures must always

[85] Concerning Germany, Alexander, n 22, 123, notes that 'Article 19(2) [of the German Constitution] enjoins the legislature against encroaching upon the "essence" of the property rights. It is the Federal Constitutional Court's task to determine what that essence is'.

[86] The latter term was coined by Margaret Jane Radin, 'The Liberal Conception of Property: Cross Currents in the Jurisprudence of Takings' (1988) 88 *Columbia Law Review* 1667, 1677.

[87] Epstein, *Supreme Neglect . . .*, n 1, 124, notes that '[w]ith regulations, however, the threshold question is whether the fraction in value lost is large enough to require compensation. *Now denominators are everything*'. (emphasis added). See eg, *Penn Central*, 438 US 104, and *Keystone Bituminous Coal Assn v DeBenedictis* (1987) 480 US 470 (hereinafter, *Keystone*), where the denominator problem determined the difference in positions between the majority and the dissenting members of the Court.

be made. In mathematical terms, this involves a fraction, where the numerator represents the harm suffered by the citizen or investor, and the denominator the referential unity of property. But, which denominator? In *Keystone*, the US Supreme Court described the denominator problem in the following terms:

> Because our test for regulatory taking requires us to compare the value that has been taken from the property with the value that remains in the property, one of the critical questions in determining how to define the unit of property 'whose value is to furnish the denominator of the fraction'.[88]

This question is essentially linked to the concept of property that is to be ultimately adopted. *Grosso modo*, the referential unity of property rights may be set at one of several levels: (a) the whole set of the claimant's assets; (b) each asset or a certain subset of assets, including the case of a contract as a whole; (c) one or more of the bundles of rights that are the constituent parts of an asset or a contract; (d) the same bundles of rights, but divided into spatial units—eg air rights over property—or divided into time units—eg, days, months or years. The idea of 'conceptual severance' refers to the logical step of setting the denominator at levels (c) or (d).

The battles over the denominator are very similar to those over the definition of markets' scope in certain antitrust cases (that is, monopolisation and horizontal mergers). If the market is broadly defined, then the defendant has a smaller market share. This smaller market share means that he/she has a higher chance of winning the case. In contrast, if the market is narrowly defined, then the defendant will have a higher share of the market, and the odds will be against him/her.[89] In our case, if property rights are defined in broad terms—that is, with no conceptual severance—then the state will tend to win the case; if property is severed, the state's chances of winning the case decrease.[90] In the extreme case, if property rights are always conceptually severed up to level (d), then the state will always lose takings cases using the rule of thumb of protecting the core—every regulation would amount to a taking.

A comparative approach indicates, for example, that neither US courts—except in cases of physical takings, ie, the *Loretto* rule—nor German courts, nor the ECHR, accept the idea of 'conceptual severance'. Indeed, the US Supreme Court has held that, 'where an owner possesses a

[88] *Keystone*, 480 US 497, citing Michelman, n 68, 1192.

[89] See Jonathan B Baker, 'Market Definition: An Analytical Overview' (2007) 74 *Antitrust Law Journal* 129, 129 (noting that 'the outcome of more [antitrust] cases has surely turned on market definition than on any substantive issue. Market definition is often the most critical step in evaluation market power').

[90] See Merrill, n 33, 899, who notes that 'conceptual severance makes it more likely that a court will find a government regulation is a taking'. Therefore, as Alexander, n 22, 78, points out, '[t]he bundle-of-rights theory supplies the foundation for a technique that has become the primary theoretical device for an aggressive, indeed, activist, interpretation of the taking clause'.

full "bundle" of property rights, the destruction of one "strand" of the bundle is not a taking, because the aggregate must be viewed in its entirety'.[91] In *Penn Central* it also held that:

> 'Taking' jurisprudence does not divide a single parcel into discrete segments and attempt to determine whether rights in a particular segment have been entirely abrogated. In deciding whether a particular governmental action has effected a taking, this Court focuses rather both on the character of the action and on the nature and extent of the interference with rights in the parcel as a whole.[92]

In his comparative constitutional law study of property clauses, van der Walt comments that German courts do not divide property rights into minor subdivisions or bundles of rights when assessing whether they have been inappropriately interfered with:

> [P]roperty is regarded as a unitary right rather than a bundle of entitlements, with the result that the separate protection of specific entitlements becomes more difficult than in some other jurisdictions. This does not mean that specific, traditional limited real rights (such as servitudes) cannot be distinguished and regarded as separate, independent property rights for purposes of the [constitutional] guarantee, but it does mean that entitlements cannot be split up in terms of what is sometimes referred to as 'conceptual severance'.[93]

Similarly, the ECHR has rejected the 'bundle of rights' theory.[94] In *Tre Traktörer Aktiebolag*, the Court held that a licence to sell alcohol should not be separated from the restaurant to which it was attached:

> Severe though it may have been, the interference at issue did not fall within the ambit of the second sentence of the first paragraph [i.e., the second rule]. The applicant company, although it could no longer operate Le Cardinal as a restaurant business, kept some economic interests represented by the leasing of the premises and the property assets contained therein, which it finally sold in June 1984 . . . There was accordingly no deprivation of property in terms of Article 1 of the Protocol (P1-1).[95]

It should be noted that the denominator problem reminds us of the reality that legal distinctions and doctrines cannot be fully replaced by

[91] *Andrus*, 444 US 65–66. More recently, see eg *Keystone*, 480 US 498, and *Tahoe-Sierra Preservation Council, Inc v Tahoe Regional Planning Agency* (2002) 535 US 302, 327.

[92] *Penn Central*, 438 US 130. In *Concrete Pipe and Prods v Construction Laborers Pension Trust* (1993) 508 US 602, 644, the Court stated that 'a claimant's parcel of property could not first be divided into what was taken and what was left for the purpose of demonstrating the taking of the former to be complete and hence compensable'.

[93] Van der Walt, n 22, 155.

[94] See Çoban, n 53, 175–76, who explains that '[t]he Court does not accept the bundle of rights theory of property. Accordingly it does not accept different rights arising from property as different property rights but use of property'. See eg *Chassagnou and Others v France* (App nos 25088/94, 28331/95 and 28443/95) (1999) 29 EHRR 615, 674 ¶ 74.

[95] *Tre Traktörer Aktiebolag v Sweden* (App no 10873/84) (1989) 13 EHRR 309 ¶ 55. See also, *Fredin v Sweden* (App no 12033/86) (1991) 13 EHRR 784 ¶¶ 44–45.

economic analysis. Even those jurisdictions that that have moved towards a more economic approach to property rights—such as the US under the *Lucas* rule—are irresistibly drawn back to legal doctrines. Indeed, in *Lucas* itself, the US Supreme Court held that:

> Regrettably, the rhetorical force of our 'deprivation of all economically feasible use' rule is greater than its precision, since the rule does not make clear the 'property interest' against which the loss of value is to be measured. When, for example, a regulation requires a developer to leave 90% of a rural tract in its natural state, it is unclear whether we would analyze the situation as one in which the owner has been deprived of all economically beneficial use of the burdened portion of the tract, or as one in which the owner has suffered a mere diminution in value of the tract as a whole ... Unsurprisingly, this uncertainty regarding the composition of the denominator in our 'deprivation' fraction has produced inconsistent pronouncements by the Court ... *The answer to this difficult question may lie in how the owner's reasonable expectations have been shaped by the State's law of property—i.e., whether and to what degree the State's law has accorded legal recognition and protection to the particular interest in land with respect to which the takings claimant alleges a diminution in (or elimination of) value.* (emphasis added)[96]

The importance of legal doctrines derives not only from the fact that courts are presided by lawyers, but more importantly, from the fact that it is law that provides the focal points around which reasonable expectations form. Economic and financial analyses come after the law.

In the end, conceptual severance and the denominator problem demonstrate that courts and tribunals cannot avoid balancing when resolving expropriation cases. Judges and arbitrators must have recourse to values and conceptions that transcend an automatic application of legal rules. For precisely the same reason, judges in different legal traditions use the discretion inherent in the protection of the core of property rights in a deferential way towards political branches of government.

D Termination of Property Rights without Compensation

As previously explained, the distinction between the core and the periphery allows courts to claim authority in certain circumstances, and to apply a rule of thumb: full destruction of property rights should entitle citizens and investors to receive compensation. With this strategy, all explicit complex balancing—including a very deferential stance towards legislatures and executives—is related to the protection of the periphery.

However, if this distinction is obscured by the legal and economic approaches to property, as well as the denominator problem and conceptual severance, then any possibility of a mechanical approach to expropriations

[96] *Lucas*, 505 US 1016 fn 7

is completely undermined by what the US constitutional lawyers refer to as the *nuisance exception*, or, what their French colleagues call *pre-eminent public interests*.

To understand these latter concepts, the relationship between property and the law must first be explored. For purposes of takings, this relationship can be classified as 'internal' or 'external'. By 'internal', I refer to the process of determining whether we are dealing with property rights in the very first place, including their original content and limits. For example, if an investor starts an illegal business—drug traffic, prostitution, gambling, etc—that is later closed by the government, he cannot claim that a taking has occurred. The internal relation tells us that property rights never existed, or, at least, that those rights never had the scope argued by the investor.

The relationship between property rights and the law can also be external. This relationship tells us whether or not the extinction or further restriction of pre-existing entitlements is appropriate. For example, an investor has an alcohol licence that is subsequently revoked in accordance with the law, because he sold beer to minors. If that revocation is legal and non-arbitrary, he cannot claim an expropriation. His property was 'taken', but not expropriated. Similar conclusions can be reached with respect to forfeiture or confiscation of property involved in crimes.

Although the test of 'arbitrariness as illegality' will be analysed in more detail below, an important point to note is that the specific nature of the relationship between property rights and the law explains why several cases involving destruction of property *in accordance with the law* are not expropriations.

Starting with international law, it has traditionally been recognised that states are not responsible for the full destruction of property rights, when they have properly followed the applicable legal rules. For example, 'an alien could not complain if explosives or arms which were in his possession in violation of the law of the State concerned were destroyed by the police or by the military authorities'.[97] This situation is clearly recognised and articulated in general terms in Sohn and Baxter's *Draft Convention on the International Responsibility of States for Injuries to the Economic Interests of Aliens* (Harvard Draft):

> Article 9.2: A destruction of the property of an alien resulting from the judgment of a competent tribunal or from the action of the competent authorities of the State in the maintenance of public order, health, or morality shall not be considered wrongful, provided there has not been: (a) a clear and discriminatory

[97] Louis B Sohn and Richard Baxter, 'Draft Convention on the International Responsibility of States for Injuries to the Economic Interests of Aliens' (1961) 55 *American Journal of International Law*, 545, 552 (hereinafter, Sohn and Baxter's Draft Articles). See also, 2 *Restatement of the Law (Third): The Foreign Relations Law of the United States* (St Paul, MN, American Law Institute Publishers, 1987) 201, §712, Comment g ('A state is not responsible for loss of property or for other economic disadvantage resulting from . . . forfeiture for crime') (hereinafter, *Restatement (Third) of Foreign Relations Law*).

> violation of the law of the State concerned; (b) a violation of any provision of Article 6 to 8 of this Convention [denial of justice]; (c) an unreasonable departure from the principles of justice recognized by the principal legal systems of the world; or (d) an abuse of the powers specified in this paragraph for the purpose of depriving an alien of his property.[98]

Similarly, Brownlie observes that '[j]urists supporting the compensation rule recognize the existence of exceptions, the most widely accepted of which are as follows: . . . confiscations as a penalty for crimes; seizure by way of taxation or other fiscal measures'.[99] The caselaw of various international tribunals and courts supports this position. In the *SEDCO* case, the Iran–United State Claims Tribunal held that 'forfeiture for crime' is an exception to the rule of expropriation, in the sense that the 'person(s) affected do not rightfully possess title to the property in question'.[100] Along similar lines, the ECHR held in *AGOSI* that:

> The forfeiture of the coins [which applicant AGOSI had sought to import into the United Kingdom against the law] did, of course, involve a deprivation of property, but in the circumstances the deprivation formed a constituent element of the procedure for the control of the use in the United Kingdom of gold coins [finding therefore that the claimant was not entitled to compensation].[101]

The relationship between property and the law does not always fall into these neat categories. There is one particular dimension of this relationship that leads us directly into muddied waters: property rights are conferred or recognised by the legal system under the explicit or implicit condition of not causing harm to third parties.[102] As Higgins remarks, 'international law, like municipal law, has come to affirm that property rights be exercised in a manner that is not dangerous and does not harm others'.[103] From a domestic law perspective, Ogus comments that in Swiss law, 'the enjoyment of property rights is subject to the implied reservation that they do not cause harm in terms of public health, safety, or order'.[104]

[98] Sohn and Baxter's Draft Articles, n 97, 551. See also, Art 10.5, ibid 554.

[99] See also, Ian Brownlie, *Principles of International Law*, 6th edn (New York, OUP, 2003) 511–12.

[100] See also, *SEDCO*, 9 Iran–US Claims Trib Rep 275. For US law, see *Bennis v Michigan* (1996) 516 US 442, where the court upheld the forfeiture of an automobile used in a crime.

[101] *AGOSI v UK* (App no 9118/80) (1986) 9 EHRR 1 ¶ 51 (hereinafter, *AGOSI*). In *Ryder v UK* (App 12360/86) (1987) 11 EHRR 80, the court held that the cessation of unlawful activities was not subject to the payment of compensation.

[102] See Laura S Underkuffler, *The Idea of Property: Its Meaning and Power* (New York, OUP, 2003) 20 ('It is an established legal principle that landowners cannot engage in activities that constitute a nuisance to the land use of others'). See also, *Lucas*, 505 US 1030–31 ('Principles of nuisance and [state] property law are part of a landowner's title').

[103] Rosalyn Higgins, 'The Taking of Property by the State: Recent Developments in International Law' in Académie de Droit International, 176 *Recueil des Cours. Collected Courses of the Hague Academy of International Law, 1982-III* (The Hague, M Nijhoff, 1983) 259, 275–76.

[104] Anthony Ogus, 'Property Rights and Freedom of Economic Activity' in Louis Henkin and Albert Rosenthal (eds), *Constitutionalism and Rights. The Influence of the United States Constitution Abroad* (New York, Columbia University Press, 1990) 125, 133.

In many cases involving compelling public interests, we have no way of really knowing whether the new regulation simply 'clarified' pre-existing limits of property rights, or imposed ex post restrictions on the scope of existing rights. This becomes a serious problem for constitutional law in at least two instances. The first is when new scientific evidence shows us that previous uses of property, that were at the time considered normal and proper, are, in fact harmful to valuable public interests (health, environment, etc.). The second case is represented by changes in people's preferences, which can cause certain public interests to be much more sensitive today than they had been in the past. In some cases, this may require the complete banning of previously accepted entitlements. Of course, these two scenarios may be quite connected: because we have more scientific evidence, we change our preferences.

Those cases introduce us to what Americans refer to as the *nuisance exception*. In common law traditions, a *nuisance* is a harmful interference with the rights of others or the interests of the general public. Describing this exception to expropriations in the American constitutional jurisprudence, Rose-Ackerman explains that:

> Compensation should not be paid when the complainant cannot legitimately claim to be entitled to the benefits that are lost when the government acts. For example, courts have found that individuals do not have the right to create a nuisance. Thus, if the state imposes regulations or confiscates a nuisance, the owner has no right to claim compensation. Nothing has been taken that the individual had a right to claim as his own.[105]

In the US, one of the leading nuisance exception cases is *Mugler v Kansas* (1887).[106] Peter Mugler had owned and operated a brewery in the state of Kansas since 1877. In 1880, reflecting a change in morality, the Kansas Constitution was amended, providing the following new article: 'The manufacture and sale of intoxicating liquors shall be forever prohibited in this state, except for medical, scientific, and mechanical purposes'. When deciding the expropriation case brought by Mr Mugler, the US Supreme Court held that:

> The principle, that no person shall be deprived of life, liberty, or property, without due process of law, was embodied, in substance, in the constitutions of nearly all, if not all, of the States at the time of the adoption of the Fourteenth Amendment; and it has never been regarded as incompatible with the principle, equally vital, because essential to the peace and safety of society, that all property in this country is held under the implied obligation that the owner's use of it shall not be injurious to the community.[107]

[105] Rose-Ackerman, n 21, 1708.

[106] *Mugler v Kansas* (1887) 123 US 623 (hereinafter, *Mugler*). Another famous case along these same lines is *Miller v Schoene* (1928) 276 US 272.

[107] *Mugler*, 123 US 665. The court cited, among others, *Patterson v Kentucky* (1878) 97 US 501, 504: 'By the settled doctrines of this court the police power extends, at least, to the protection of the lives, the health, and the property of the community against the injurious

This holding continues to be valid law in the US. 100 years later, in *Keystone*, the Supreme Court insisted again that risks taken by private individuals 'cannot estop the Commonwealth from exercising its police power to abate activity akin to a public nuisance'.[108]

This does not mean that any regulation that effects a deprivation without compensation passes constitutional muster. The crucial point is that US courts must be satisfied that the destructive exercise of the police powers is aimed at abating a *nuisance*. In other words, the scope of police powers is not 'coterminous' with the nuisance exception; the former is much broader than the latter.[109] As Underkuffler points out, the public interest involved in these cases must be 'of unusual urgency',[110] which ensures that these cases 'remain (most certainly) rarities'.[111]

In France, the jurisprudence of the *Conseil d'État* distinguishes between two types of public interests: *classic* public interests—requiring the payment of compensation in the case of expropriation—and *superior* or *pre-eminent* public interests—which do not require such payment. According to Moderne, the latter may be admitted in cases in which 'statutes forbid certain kinds of activities that can jeopardize the public health, public security, the security of the children, public morality, etc'.[112]

The situation in France and the US is structurally similar: property rights do not entitle the owner to harm others, so, in certain extreme circumstances where the state exercises its police powers and forbids harming uses, the destruction of entitlements is not technically an expropriation. It is worth observing how two commentators from two disparate legal traditions arrive at similar conclusions. In France, Moderne affirms

exercise by any citizen of his own rights. State legislation, strictly and legitimately for police purposes, does not, in the sense of the Constitution, necessarily intrench upon any authority which has been confided, expressly or by implication, to the national government. The Kentucky statute under examination manifestly belongs to that class of legislation. It is, in the best sense, a mere police regulation, deemed essential to the protection of the lives and property of citizens'.

108 *Keystone*, 480 US 488.

109 In a dissenting opinion, Justice Rehnquist reminds us that '[t]he nuisance exception to the taking guarantee is not coterminous with the police power itself. The question is whether the forbidden use is dangerous to the safety, health, or welfare of others' (*Penn Central*, 438 US 145).

110 Underkuffler, n 102, 89.

111 ibid.

112 Frank Moderne, '*La Responsabilidad por Actos del Legislador y por los Tratados Internacionales en Francia*' in Javier Barnés (ed), *Propiedad, Expropiación y Responsabilidad. Derecho Comparado Europeo* (Madrid, Tecnos, 1995) 955, 965. He cites the following cases of the Conseil d'État, in which pre-eminent public interests were recognised: (1) *Compagnie général de la Grande Pêche*, 14 January 1938 (Statute forbidding the exportation of alcohol to the US); (2) *Société Charron et cie*, 10 March 1940 (Statute forbidding the manufacture of a product harmful to health); (3) *Ste. des Ets Aupinel et autres*, 8 January 1965 (Statute forbidding fraud in alcohol); (4) *Ste. Stambouli*, 11 July 1990 (Statute forbidding gambling machines in the interest of public health); and, (5) *Rouillon*, 14 December 1984 (Statute entrenching property in order to protect the environment).

that 'we found out, then, a curious dichotomy of the public interest, which operates at two levels: at the superior level, it results in the absence of State responsibility; at the inferior one, it allows for the establishment of State liability, if damages suffered are abnormal'.[113] In the US, in the context of land-use regulation, Michelman points out that:

> [T]he Court seems by implication to sort the class of regulatory public purposes into two subclasses. One subclass includes regulations restricting or preventing nuisance-like uses—roughly meaning those that a court will recognize as harmful to legitimate and significant interests of the community or its members. The other subclass contains regulations affirmatively securing whatever other public benefits the device of land-use regulation may legitimately be used to secure.[114]

Germany seems to follow a somewhat similar path, yet some particular characteristics of its legal system require a more detailed analysis. The German Constitution protects owners against uncompensated destruction of the core of property rights.[115] However, the Federal Constitutional Court has attempted—with only partial succes, as will be explained later—to limit the remedies available in cases of violation of this norm only to nullification.[116] According to the court, expropriations are only those which the legislature and executive so define;[117] the judiciary cannot convert inappropriate interferences with the core of property rights—which are null and void—into valid expropriations by providing compensation.[118]

This different remedial structure has resulted in a constitutional adjudicative process that is more focused on proportionality—particularly, on the principle of prohibition against regulatory excess (*Übermaßverbot*)[119]—than on defining a rule of thumb centered around the core or essence of property rights.[120] Yet, this framework does not imply an outcome different from the one just observed in the cases of the US and France. According to the Federal Constitutional Court, in extreme instances, the core of rights may be completely destroyed without violating the Constitution:

[113] ibid 966.

[114] Michelman, n 39, 1603.

[115] See Arts 14(1) and 19(2), n 40. See also, Mostert, n 76, 220, 278–79, 308–10, and Alexander, n 22, 123.

[116] See Van der Walt, n 22, 141–45.

[117] See Alexander, n 22, 120 (explaining that in the *Naßauskiesung* case, the Federal Constitutional Court held that '[r]egulatory intention, not impact . . . was the basis for determining whether the restriction was a regulation or an expropriation').

[118] See Van der Walt, n 22, 149 (noting that, in Germany, 'excessive regulation is invalid and cannot be transformed into an expropriation through an award of compensation'). See also, Alexander, n 22, 116–17, 121.

[119] See Van der Walt, n 22, 133, 135; Mostert, n 76, 290.

[120] See Van der Walt, n 22, 160–61 (observing that '[Art 19(2)] has played a very limited part in the decisions of the Federal Constitutional Court with regard to property', and explaining that this was due to the 'impact of the proportionality principle').

Even the total abolition of previously existing rights protected by the property guarantee [of the Constitution] can be permissible under certain circumstances . . . The violation of rights that came into existence under previous law must be justified by public interest considerations, taking account of the principle of proportionality . . . The public interest considerations favouring such a violation *must be so significant* that they ought to be given preference over the citizen's trust in the continuing existence of his right which is protected by the guarantee contained in Art. 14(1)(1) BL [Basic Law or *Grundgesetz*] . . . *The legislator does not always have to mitigate the transformation or abolition of a right by the means of compensation or temporary regulations. The complete abolition of a right without a transition period and without compensation, however, may only be considered under special circumstances.* (emphasis added)[121]

General international law appears to be consistent with this comparative trend. For example, Article 10.5 of Sohn and Baxter's Draft Articles declares that public order, health and morality can be pre-eminent public interests:

An uncompensated taking of property of an alien or a deprivation of the use or enjoyment of property of an alien which results . . . *from the action of the competent authorities of the State in the maintenance of public order, health or morality*; or from the valid exercise of belligerent rights; or *is otherwise incidental to the normal operation of the laws of the State* shall not be considered wrongful. (emphasis added)[122]

Similarly, Article 11(a)(ii) of the MIGA Convention exempts from expropriation and its compensatory rules 'non-discriminatory measures of general application which governments normally take for the purpose of regulating economic activity in their territories'.[123] The *Restatement (Third) of Foreign Relations Law* affirms, as well, that '[a] state is not responsible for loss of property or for other economic disadvantage resulting from bona fide general taxation, regulation . . . or other action of the kind that is commonly accepted as within the police power of states'.[124] And, in *Greater Modesto Insurance*, the Iran–US Claims Tribunal affirmed that:

A State is not responsible for loss of property or for other economic disadvantage resulting from bona fide general taxation or any other action that is commonly accepted as within the police power of States, provided it is not

[121] *Right of Pre-Emption Case*, BVerGE 83, 201, 212–213 (1991) (cited in Sabine Michalowski and Lorna Woods, *German Constitutional Law. The Protection of Civil Liberties* (Brookfield, Ashgate/Dartmouth, 1999) 328).

[122] Sohn and Baxter's Draft Articles, n 97, 554.

[123] *Convention Establishing the Multilateral Investment Guarantee Agency* (entered into force 12 April 1988) 1508 UNTS 181, reprinted *in* 24 ILM 1605, Art 11: 'Covered Risks: . . . Expropriation and Similar Measures: any legislative action or administrative action or omission attributable to the host government which has the effect of depriving the holder of a guarantee of his ownership or control of, or a substantial benefit from, his investment, with the exception of non-discriminatory measures of general application which the governments normally take for the purpose of regulating economic activity in their territories'.

[124] 2 *Restatement (Third) of Foreign Relations Law*, n 97, 200–01, §712, Comment g.

> discriminatory and is not designed to cause the alien to abandon the property to the State or to sell it at a distress price.[125]

The rationale behind the nuisance exception and pre-eminent public interests is the same everywhere. Corrective and distributive justice considerations, that command the state to pay for entitlements sacrificed while pursuing the public interest, do not apply when the state deprives a party of assets or entitlements that are harmful to legitimate interests of the community. Of course, the key question remains: How are judges supposed to determine which public interests give owners and investors the right to claim compensation?

Instead of trying to answer this question, I will merely conclude here by noting how difficult it is—sometimes impossible—to escape from balancing, even at the core. The original purpose of distinguishing the core and the periphery was, in theory, to simplify the courts' decisionmaking process. The need to define pre-eminent public interests or nuisance exceptions contradicts such simplicity, though in truth the real-world implications of this fact should not be exaggerated, since these special interests apply only in rare circumstances.

III THE PERIPHERY V THE PUBLIC INTEREST: THE MUDDIED WATERS OF COMPLEX BALANCING

The power of the regulatory state to harm citizens and investors is particularly notorious in the periphery of property rights. As Craig points out, 'legislation is constantly being passed which is explicitly or implicitly aimed at benefiting one section of the population at the expense of another. It is a matter of conscious legislative policy'.[126] Of course, as previously noted, this does not mean that investors or citizens must always bear the negative consequences of the state's actions and omissions.

In the periphery of property rights—that is, in the area of non-destructive limitations to pre-existing entitlements—the tension between contradictory goals such as stability and flexibility, expectations and change, and individual autonomy and public welfare, proves to be

[125] *Too v Greater Modesto Insurances Associates* (1989) 23 Iran–US Claims Trib Rep 378, 387 ¶ 26. See also, *SEDCO*, 9 Iran–US Claims Trib Rep 275 (holding that 'it is also an accepted principle of international law that a State is not liable for economic injury which is a consequence of bona fide "regulation" within the accepted police power of states') (internal citations omitted).

[126] Paul P Craig, 'Compensation in Public Law' (1980) 96 LQR 413, 450. See also Henry G Schemers, 'Introduction' in Henry G Schemers et al (eds), *Non-Contractual Liability of the European Communities* (Boston, M Nijhoff, 1988) xii; and Søren J Schønberg, *Legitimate Expectations in Administrative Law* (New York, OUP, 2000) 11.

irreducible.[127] Here, there is no space for rules of thumb; on the contrary, it is indeed recognised that it is impossible to avoid the application of explicit and complex balancing tests, where both the quantity and quality of the harm suffered by the investor, and the nature of government action, are compared and assessed.

This Section will provide a brief description of the protection of property rights' periphery, and then examine four general tests used both in judicial review and damages actions settings: 'arbitrariness as illegality', which focuses on the unlawful or ultra vires behaviour of state agencies; 'arbitrariness as irrationality', which reviews the absence of a rationally acceptable means-ends relationship; 'arbitrariness as special sacrifice', which is concerned with the unequal imposition of burdens over certain groups or individuals; and 'arbitrariness as lack of proportionality', which centres attention on whether the burdens imposed are disproportionate in the light of the ends sought. Finally, it will review the specific case of 'legitimate expectations'.

A The Protection of Property Rights' Periphery: Expropriations and *Responsabilité de l'État*

From a comparative perspective, the protection of the periphery is carried out through more than one legal institution. Apart from judicial review (that is, nullification), the periphery is typically protected by either expropriation or state liability in tort. For instance, in the US the concept of expropriation protects the periphery, as in the *Penn Central* rule of regulatory takings; in contrast, in France the concept of *responsabilité de l'État*, including the case of the *responsabilité du fait des lois*, appears to be used for that same purpose.[128]

As already explained, in Germany, in cases of property rights violations, the Federal Constitutional Court has expressly limited available remedies to judicial review. However, the older practice by regular courts of recognising quasi-expropriatory encroachments on the basis of state liability in tort has proven resilient.[129] This practice includes the following categories: state interventions tantamount to expropriation of illegitimate character (*enteignungsgleicher Eingriff*); state interventions tantamount to expropriation of legitimate character (*enteignender Eingriff*); and, the more modern

[127] See Rose-Ackerman and Rossi, n 8, 1441 (observing that '[t]he key legal and policy issue is how to draw the line between the preservation of "investment-backed expectations" and the preservation of government flexibility'). For an equivalent comment in Spain, see Gaspar Ariño Ortiz, *El Nuevo Servicio Público* (Madrid, Marcial Pons, 1997) 52–53.

[128] See René Chapus, *1 Droit Administratif Général*, 15th edn (Paris, Montchrestien, 2001) 1227 ff, 1363–85.

[129] See Van der Walt, n 22, 143, 160; Mostert, n 76, 282–83.

concept of 'equalisation right' or delimitation of rights that requires the payment of compensation (*ausgleichspflichtige Inhaltsbestimmung* or *Ausgleichsanspruch*).[130] These categories have usually been inspired by the doctrines of special sacrifice (*Sonderopfertheorie*) and intensity of sacrifice (*Schweretheorie*).[131] In addition, state liability in tort (*Amtshaftung*) also protects citizens and investors against improper behaviour of public officers[132].

In international law, the institution that typically applies to the core—ie, expropriation—does not protect the periphery. For instance, in the case of the ECHR, the concept of expropriation protects property rights against total deprivations (that is, the so-called *second rule*, which appears in article P1-1 first paragraph, second sentence). Yet, a 'fair balance' test protects property against excessive individual burdens amounting to less than total deprivations.[133] Similarly, in the case of the Iran–United States Claims Tribunals, the periphery is protected under the heading of 'measures affecting property rights', and not that of 'expropriations'.[134]

Nevertheless, beyond the specific labels or concepts used to protect property rights' periphery, the award of damages typically follows one (or both) of the following rationales. One the one hand, the rationale of corrective justice demands that governmental interferences be conducted in a legal and rational manner; wrongful encroachment must therefore be accompanied by the payment of compensation. On the other hand, the rationale of distributive justice requires that the process of allocating burdens be conducted in an equal and proportionate way; otherwise, the payment of compensation is required.

B Arbitrariness as Illegality

The regulatory state is a *Rechtsstaat*, meaning a state-under-law, or *law-state*.[135] In this type of state, as MacCormick points out, 'the question what exercises of executive power are valid is a question of law; the political power of the executive is restrained under the authority of law'.[136] In the realm of property rights, this means that the regulatory state must act lawfully in order to impose burdens and limitations. In other words, because

[130] See Singh, n 45, 244 ff; van der Walt, n 22, 141–43; Mostert, n 76, 281–82.

[131] See Mostert, n 76, 311–12, and Kimminich, n 29, 87.

[132] See Art 839 of the German Civil Code and Art 34 of the German Constitution. See also, Singh, n 45, 246; Alexander, n 22, 117–18,

[133] See Weir and Moules, n 52, 15.030/1–31.

[134] See nn 55 and 56.

[135] Neil MacCormick, *Questioning Sovereignty. Law, State, And Nation in The European Commonwealth* (New York, OUP, 1999) 9.

[136] ibid.

'[h]arm alone cannot therefore be sufficient to establish liability',[137] then—as Caranta reminds us—'[i]llegality is going to be a most relevant issue'.[138] The test of arbitrariness as illegality is unquestionably more relevant and intense when judges confront administrative agencies' measures, than when they challenge legislative' statutes. The constitution gives ample discretion to legislatures, so the finding of hard-edged unlawfulness (in contrast to soft-edged unconstitutionality) is rare. In the end, arbitrariness as illegality is mainly about judges reviewing administrative agencies' fulfillment of the substantive and procedural requirements established by law. As the German Federal Constitutional Court explains, the objective is indeed to verify compliance with the rule of law:

> The rule of law requires that the administration can interfere with the rights of an individual only with the authority of law and that the authorisation must be clearly limited in its content, subject-matter, purpose and extent so that the interference is determinable and to a certain extent is foreseeable and calculable by the citizen.[139]

The relationship between harm, illegality and liability does not receive the same treatment in all legal systems. As a matter of public policy, many systems have decided to restrict the use of this corrective justice rationale to judicial review, and not extend it to expropriations or state liability in tort. Usually, in those countries, it is assumed that the state's obligation to abide by the principle of legality does not imply a duty of care toward citizens.

Indeed, common law countries, to a certain degree, still seem to follow the premise from the Middle Ages that 'the king can do no wrong'. This means that, in those countries, 'the principle of sovereignty immunity still survives'.[140] For instance, in the UK, as the House of Lords has held, '[i]llegality without more does not give rise to a cause of action'.[141] An unlawful decision 'does not give rise to a prima facie right to damages'.[142] The basic position is that 'governmental bodies may be sued and held liable in tort in the same way and to the same extent as private individuals and corporations'.[143] As Caranta notes, '[s]*omething more* than an

[137] Roberto Caranta, 'Public Law Illegality and Governmental Liability' in Duncan Fairgrieve et al (eds), *Tort Liability Of Public Authorities In Comparative Perspective* (London, The British Institute of International and Comparative Law, 2002) 271, 272.

[138] ibid.

[139] Cited by Singh, n 45, 153.

[140] ibid 244.

[141] *Three Rivers District Council v Bank of England (No 3)* [2000] 2 WLR 1220 (HL) 1220, 1268 (Lord Hobhouse).

[142] Schønberg, n 126, 183.

[143] Peter Cane, *Introduction to Administrative Law*, 3rd edn (New York, OUP, 1996) 241. See Anthony W Bradley and John Bell, 'Governmental Liability: A Preliminary Assessment' in John Bell and Anthony W Bradley (eds), *Governmental Liability: A Comparative Study* (London, UKNCCL, 1991) 1, 12–13.

illegality is thus needed to hold a public organisation liable. What more depends on each specific tort'.[144]

Hence, a plaintiff in the UK must prove the existence of a private law tort, which may come under one of three headings: breach of statutory duty, negligence, and misfeasance.[145] Under British jurisprudence, these torts impose several difficult requirements, which are indeed 'rarely satisfied'.[146] Among others, there must exist a particularised duty of care on the part of the official in favour of the individual plaintiff, which should also be considered 'just and reasonable', as well as compatible with the statute that was allegedly breached.[147] Schønberg explains the policy considerations that underpin this restricted approach:

> Modern English case law is imbued with the view that damages liability is an improper response to the problems caused by unlawful administrative decision-making ... The courts fear that liability will lead officials to approach their duties in an over-cautious manner (the chilling effect), that great volumes of—mostly hopeless—litigation will be created (the floodgates effects), that the courts are not able to set appropriate standards of care for difficult decisions and should not get involved in second-guessing such decisions (the justiciability issue), and that damages actions will erode more suitable administrative remedies.[148]

Similarly, in US federal law, a plaintiff seeking damages must prove that the measure under scrutiny would have caused liability if committed by a private person; again, there must be a private law tort. But the plaintiff's case is even more difficult than in the UK: discretionary powers are expressly immunised. According to the *Federal Tort Claims Act* (FTCA), the private tort law rule does not apply to:

[144] Caranta, n 138, 288 (emphasis added), referring also to *X (Minors) v Bedfordshire County Council*, [1995] 2 AC 633 (HL) 730, where Lord Wilkinson stated that '[t]he breach of a public law right by itself rise to no claim for damages. A claim for damages must be based on a private law cause of action'.

[145] The tort of *negligence* imposes requirements that are difficult to assert and prove. According to Cane, n 143, 242, in the negligence tort, 'the defendant ought to have foreseen that the plaintiff might suffer injury or damage if the defendant acted negligently; that there was a sufficient relationship of proximity between the plaintiff and the defendant; and that it would be just and reasonable to impose a duty of care on the defendant'. Similarly, as Peter Cane, *Responsibility in Law and Morality* (Oxford, Hart Publishing, 2002) 260, explains, the tort of *misfeasance* demands that the public agents know that 'their conduct was unlawful or, at least was aware that their conduct created a risk of harm. In other words, this is a mens rea tort, requiring either intention or recklessness in relation both to the quality of the conduct in question and to the harm caused'. See also, Peter Leyland and Gordon Anthony, *Administrative Law*, 5th edn (New York, OUP, 2005) 502–17.

[146] Schønberg, n 126, 183

[147] See Schønberg, n 126, 188 ('The modern approach to "just, fair, and reasonable" and justiciability means that public authorities rarely owe a duty of care towards persons affected by unlawful administrative decisions'). See also, ibid 189 ('It emerges that, due to the strictly limited duty of care and the requirement of *Wednesbury* unreasonableness, all but a grossly delinquent authority is effectively accorded an immunity for the negligent exercise of a statutory discretion').

[148] ibid 182–83.

> Any claim based upon an act or omission of an employee of the Government, exercising due care, in the execution of a statute or regulation, whether or not such statute or regulation be valid, or based upon the exercise or performance or the failure to exercise or perform a discretionary function or duty on the part of a federal agency or an employee of the Government, whether or not the discretion involved be abused.[149]

The purpose of this restriction is none other than to impede courts from reviewing discretionary powers. As stated by the US Supreme Court, 'Congress wished to prevent judicial "second-guessing" of legislative and administrative decisions grounded in social, economic, and political policy through the medium of an action in tort'.[150]

Another existing remedial alternative in the US is the so-called *Bivens* cause of action. Since *Bivens v Six Unknown Named Agents of The Federal Bureau of Narcotics*,[151] the Supreme Court has accepted damages as a possible remedy in cases involving violation of constitutional rights. But given the expansive potential of this legal action, 'the Court has been alert, however, to restrict *Bivens*-style actions in ways that would avoid wholesale transformation of tort actions against officials into constitutional causes of action'.[152] Here, the restrictive rationale of the Court is not very different from that revealed earlier: 'administrative review mechanisms crafted by Congress [provide] meaningful redress and thereby foreclosed the need to fashion a new, judicially crafted cause of action'.[153]

By contrast, in France, *faute* is the general condition for state liability in tort, and illegalities constitute *fautes* almost by definition.[154] Indeed, mere illegality 'is in itself a fault capable of giving rise to liability without more'.[155] In other words, no extra 'something more' is required. As Chapus explains, '*si la décision est illégale, elle est par là même fautive. La commission d'une illégalité est toujours une faute*'.[156] The same principle applies to a certain degree in countries such as Belgium, Italy and Spain.[157] The

[149] Federal Tort Claim Act 1946, 28 USC §2680(a).

[150] *US v SA Empresa de Viacao Aerea Rio Grandense (Varig Airlines)* (1984) 467 US 797, 814.

[151] (1971) 403 US 388.

[152] Jerry L Mashaw et al, *Administrative Law: The American Public Law System: Cases and Materials*, 5th edn (St Paul, MN, Thomson/West, 2003) 1153. See eg *Collins v Harker Heights* (1992) 503 US 115.

[153] *Correctional Services Corp v Malesko* (2001) 534 US 61, 68.

[154] See Schønberg, n 126, 171 (explaining that 'unlawfulness is equated with fault in French law (*illegalité = faute*). A decision which is unlawful, in the sense that it may be annulled in judicial review proceedings, always constitutes a service fault (*faute de service*) which is capable of making the administration liable in damage'). See also, Fairgrieve, n 4 (*State Liability in Tort . . .*), 28 ff.

[155] L Neville Brown and John S Bell, *French Administrative Law*, 5th edn (Oxford, Clarendon Press, 1998) 190.

[156] Chapus, n 128, 1295.

[157] See Bradley and Bell, n 143, 13; and, Luciano Parejo Alfonso, *Derecho Administrativo: Instituciones Generales: Bases, Fuentes, Organización y Sujetos, Actividad y Control* (Barcelona, Ariel, 2003) 867 ff (explaining that illegality qualifies as 'abnormal functioning of public services', which is one of the grounds for State liability in tort).

underlying rationale is that 'subjects have a genuine right to legality and can claim damages for the harmful consequences of the breach of this right'.[158]

Germany occupies a middle position, of a sort. Although in principle any unlawful infringement of property rights can give rise to tortious governmental liability,[159] the jurisprudence has required an additional element, known as the *Schutznormtheorie*.[160] This doctrine requires that the legal system must have established the breached norm for the purpose of safeguarding the plaintiff's interests; the mere public interest is not sufficient.[161] However, because this requirement is usually interpreted in flexible terms, the equilibrium of this system of liability seems to be closer to France than the UK.

In EU law, the rules governing torts caused by the European Union institutions have been established by taking into consideration general principles common to the laws of member states (as required by Article 288 of the EC Treaty).[162] The resulting system clearly resembles those of Germany and France. Indeed, on the one hand, when liability is imposed as a consequence of community 'legislation', the German structure seems to predominate. In such cases, claimants must meet two strict requirements: first, the illegality must be sufficiently serious and it must stem from the breach of a superior rule of law—the *Schöppenstedt* formula;[163] and, second, the infringed law must have the intent of conferring rights on individuals or safeguarding their interests (*Schutznormtheorie*).[164] These

[158] Brown and Bell, n 155, 190, citing Gentot's comments to the *Ville de Paris c Driancourt* decision (*Conseil d'État*, 26 January 1973). In other words, as Schønberg, n 126, 194, explains, in France 'the administration owes a duty of care towards *all* physical and legal persons. That is, the requirement of a duty of care does not limit the scope of liability as in English law'.

[159] Rüfner, n 45, 254–55.

[160] The German *Schutznormtheorie* is explained by Eberhard Grabitz, 'Liability for Legislative Acts' in Henry G Schermers et al (eds), *Non-Contractual Liability of the European Communities* (Boston, M Nijhoff, 1988) 1, 6, in the following terms: 'According to this theory, the State is liable for only when, in addition to causing an injury, it breaches a *Schutznorm*, which is a legal norm protecting a subjective public right of the injured party and which is intended not only to protect individuals in general, but also to protect a specific circle of individuals to which the injured party belongs. The requirement of protection of a specific circle of individuals has often been liberally interpreted'.

[161] As Bachof explains, '[w]hether the power of an authority to act also implies a corresponding duty towards a private persons depends on whether the power is given to the authority exclusively in the interests of the general public or also in the interests of a specific person' (cited by Singh, n 45, 254).

[162] *Treaty Establishing the European Community* (2006 OJ C321 29 December 2006 E/37), Art 288 establishes that: 'In the case of non-contractual liability, the Community shall, in accordance with the general principles common to the laws of the Member States, make good any damage caused by its institutions or by its servants in the performance of their duties' (available at www.ecb.int/ecb/legal/pdf/ce32120061229en00010331.pdf).

[163] See Harlow, n 5, 58–59.

[164] See eg Case 5/71 *Aktien-Zuckerfabrik Schöppenstedt v Council* [1971] ECR 975 ¶ 11; *HNL*, fn 21, ¶¶ 4–8; and, Case 238/78 *Ireks-Arkady GmbH v Council and Commission* [1979] ECR 2955 ¶ 9.

conditions are strictly applied, so that 'whatever reasons the European Court or the Court of First Instance may give, they usually end up denying recovery'.[165]

On the other hand, when liability derives from administrative behaviour, the standard for damages is less strict, and the ECJ tends to follow the French principle of *illégalité = faute*.[166] Indeed, as Schønberg explains, '[t]he fact that a decision was or could be annulled in judicial review proceedings is normally sufficient to establish that the administration was at fault'.[167]

In the jurisprudence of the ECHR, the situation does not greatly differ from that of countries following the French model. Because interferences with property rights are possible only 'if national law permits [it]',[168] illegal interferences may lead the court to grant compensation. In the *Iatridis* case, the ECHR held that:

> [T]he first and most important requirement of Article 1 of Protocol No 1 is that any interference by a public authority with the peaceful enjoyment of possessions should be lawful . . . [T]he rule of law, one of the fundamental principles of a democratic society, is inherent in all the Articles of the Convention and entails a duty on the part of the State or other public authority to comply with judicial orders or decisions against it. *It follows that the issue of whether a fair balance has been struck between the demands of the general interest of the community and the requirements of the protection of the individual's fundamental rights becomes relevant only once it has been established that the interference in question satisfied the requirement of lawfulness and was not arbitrary.*[169] (internal citations omitted and emphasis added)

Among all tests of arbitrariness, the one focusing on illegality is the least demanding in terms of balancing. This does not mean that the reviewing of illegality is merely a mechanical exercise. Assessing it in difficult cases, and defining the relationship between illegality and liability—including the 'something more' elements that restrict liability—are far from simple or neutral matters. In any case, the more objective nature of this test is a good reason to review illegality before conducting any of the other more demanding balancing tests, as the ECHR has recognised.[170]

165 Trevor C Hartley, *European Union Law in a Global Context* (New York, CUP, 2004) 389.

166 See Schønberg, n 126, 205–06. See eg Case C-395/95 *Geotronics SA v Commission* [1997] ECR I-2271 ¶ 57, and Case T-108/94 *Elena Candiotte v Council* [1996] ECR II-87 ¶ 54.

167 Schønberg, n 126, 206.

168 Çoban, n 53, 196.

169 *Iatridis v Greece* (App no 31107/96) (2000) 30 EHRR 97 ¶ 58. See also, *The Former King of Greece and Ors v Greece* (App no 25701/94) (2001) 33 EHRR 516 ¶ 79; and, *Carbonara and Ventura v Italy* (App no 24638/94) ECHR 2000-VI 93 ¶ 63 (hereinafter, *Carbonara*).

170 See *Carbonara* ¶ 62 ('Furthermore, the issue of whether a fair balance has been struck "becomes relevant only once it has been established that the interference in question satisfied the requirement of lawfulness and was not arbitrary" '). See also, *Belvedere Alberghiera SRL v Italy* (App no 31524/96) ECHR 2000-VI 135 ¶ 62; *Beyeler v Italy* (App no 33202/96) (2001) 33 EHRR 1224, 1258 ¶¶ 107–08 (hereinafter, *Beyeler*); and *Antonetto* ¶ 35.

C Arbitrariness as Irrationality

The government has the power to harm citizens, but only when exercising that power in a rational or reasonable manner. In the traditional constitutional law account:

> [A]ll legislation must embody reasonable legislative means in the pursuit of some constitutionally acceptable legislative purpose. *This promise of nonarbitrariness helps make acceptable the inevitable sacrifice of private interests in the pursuit of collective ends.* Therein lies the constitutional necessity of a review of nonarbitrariness. (emphasis added)[171]

In this regard, one of the central questions concerning the protection of property rights, as Singer notes, is whether regulatory burdens and limitations are 'justified by sufficiently strong reasons to overcome the presumption of legitimacy [of property rights]'.[172] Given the more general framework followed in this chapter, I locate the test of 'arbitrariness as irrationality' within the scope of the corrective justice rationale, because a strict or pure assessment of the means-ends relation does not include the gravity and specificity of the harm suffered by citizens or investors. The inquiry is regarding the *wrongful* character of state action because of the absence of rationality; either the goal is not a public one, or the means chosen does not fit the purpose sought.

The first dimension of the arbitrariness as irrationality test is the review of the public interest. A comparative overview shows that in cases of economic regulation, courts display a huge degree of deference towards the ends invoked by the government. Because a substantial theory of the public interest has been and still is one of the greatest challenges in political philosophy, as well as a highly disputed field in our political practice,[173] there is little doubt that the democratic branches of government should take precedence.

In the US, in the post-*Lochner* era, the Supreme Court has almost completely abdicated the review of the public interest nature of regulation. According to Mashaw, US courts live today under a 'reverse-Lochner, no review policy'.[174] This is particularly true in the takings jurisprudence,[175] where the Supreme Court has recently stated—in a case that turned on

[171] Mashaw, n 14, 52.

[172] Joseph William Singer, *Entitlement: The Paradox of Property* (New Haven, Yale University Press, 2000) 4.

[173] For a summarised survey, see Aileen McHarg, 'Reconciling Human Rights and the Public Interest: Conceptual Problems and Doctrinal Uncertainty in the Jurisprudence of the European Court of Human Rights' (1999) 62 *Modern Law Review* 671. For a sceptical view on the concept of public interest, see Levine and Forrence, n 71, 167.

[174] Mashaw, n 14, 60.

[175] See eg Epstein, n 1 (*Supreme Neglect . . .*), 76 (characterising the public use requirement of takings in US federal constitutional law as a 'toothless doctrine'); Thomas W Merrill, 'The Economics of Public Use' (1986) 72 *Cornell Law Review* 61, 61 (noting that 'most observers today think the public use limitation is dead letter'); and, Alexander, n 22, 65 (see n 62).

the question of whether a City's development plan 'serves a "public purpose"'—that '[w]ithout exception, our cases have defined that concept broadly, *reflecting our longstanding policy of deference to legislative judgments in this field*'.[176]

In international law, the ECHR has adopted a similar stance. On the one hand, the court has recognised that the Convention requires a public interest for state action to interfere with property rights.[177] But, on the other hand, the court uses an extremely deferential test in reviewing this requirement, that is, the *manifestly without reasonable foundation* test:

> The Court recalls that the national authorities enjoy a certain margin of appreciation in determining what is 'in the public interest', because under the Convention system it is for them to make the initial assessment both of the existence of a problem of public concern warranting measures of deprivation of property rights and of remedial action to be taken. Furthermore, the notion of 'public interest' is necessarily extensive . . . The Court, finding it natural that the margin of appreciation available to the legislature in implementing social and economic policies should be a wide one, will respect the legislature's judgment as to what is 'in the public interest' unless that judgment be *manifestly without reasonable foundation*. (emphasis added)[178]

Once the public interest at stake has passed muster, questions of means-ends relations come into play. These include—following the nomenclature of the first and second prong of the German and EU proportionality (broad sense) tests[179]—questions of *suitability*, that is, whether the measure is capable of achieving the desired public interest;[180] and, questions of

[176] *Kelo* 545 US 480. See n 63.

[177] See eg, *Beyeler* ¶ 111.

[178] *Pressos Compania Naviera SA and Others v Belgium* (App no 17849/91) (1996) 21 EHRR 301 ¶ 37 (hereinafter, *Pressos*). See also, *James* ¶¶ 39–45, particularly ¶ 40, and *Chassagnou* ¶¶ 76–79. According to Camilo B Schutte, *The European Fundamental Right of Property* (Deventer, Kluwer, 2004) 56, 'the Court is easily satisfied that the general interest was the aim of measures interfering with someone's property under the "manifestly without reasonable foundation" test'. Similarly, according to Helen Mountfield, 'Regulatory Expropriations in Europe: The Approach of the European Court of Human Rights' (2002) 11 *New York University Environmental Law Journal* 136, 140–41, '[t]he Court affords signatory governments a very significant area of judgment as to what is in the public interest. There is no case in which it has rejected a government's submission that a measure was in the public interest'.

[179] The third prong—proportionality in the narrow sense—falls under the distributive justice rationale, and will be analysed below. It is important to note, however, as indicated by Richard Gordon QC, *EC Law in Judicial Review* (New York, OUP, 2007) 292, that 'the ECJ seems, in practice, to have adopted a relatively pragmatic approach without seeking to distinguish the various possible elements [of proportionality]'.

[180] See George Gerapetritis, *Proportionality in Administrative Law: Judicial Review in France, Greece, England and in the European Community* (Athens, Sakkoulas, 1997) 54. See also, Evelyn Ellis (ed), *The Principle of Proportionality in the Laws of Europe* (Oxford, Hart Publishing, 1999); Yutaka Arai-Takahashi, *The Margin of Appreciation Doctrine and the Principle of Proportionality in the Jurisprudence of the ECHR* (Antwerp, Intersentia, 2002); and, Carlos Bernal Pulido, *El Principio de Proporcionalidad y los Derechos Fundamentales: El Principio de Proporcionalidad como Criterio para Determinar el Contenido de los Derechos Fundamentales Vinculantes para el Legislador*, 2nd edn (Madrid, Centro de Estudios Políticos y Constitucionales, 2005).

necessity, that is, whether 'there are alternative means, less restrictive of the individual's interests but equally effective for the realisation of the public objective'.[181] According to the ECJ:

> The Court has consistently held that the principle of proportionality is one of the general principles of Community law. By virtue of that principle, the lawfulness of the prohibition of an economic activity is subject to the condition that the prohibitory measures are appropriate and necessary in order to achieve the objectives legitimately pursued by the legislation in question; when there is a choice between several appropriate measures recourse must be had to the least onerous.[182]

When approaching such questions, constitutional and supreme courts must unavoidably formulate opinions that touch upon policy design and implementation. Their answers are not value neutral. If the control is too strict, courts will replace the policy considerations embodied in the regulation with their own, an outcome potentially contradictory to constitutional separation of powers and democratic principles. For that same reason, courts that apply the arbitrariness as irrationally test tend to show different levels of deference depending on the nature of the body under review.[183] The more democratic it is, the more deference it deserves (that is, legislatures v administrative agencies).

In the United States, the arbitrariness as irrationality test for legislation is insurmountable to plaintiffs. Since the 'switch in time that saved nine' in 1937,[184] there has not been a single case in which the Supreme Court struck down economic legislation on the basis of violations of the substantive due process clause.[185] In addition, it must be noted that this test does not permit plaintiffs to receive compensation; remedies are limited to judicial review. Recently, the Supreme Court clarified that the 'substantially advances a legitimate state interest' test mentioned in previous taking cases can only be applied as a stand-alone rationality test in the context of the

[181] Robert Thomas, *Legitimate Expectations and Proportionality in Administrative Law* (Portland, Hart Publishing, 2000) 77.

[182] Case 331/88 *R v MAFF, ex p Fedesa* [1990] ECR I-4023 ¶ 13.

[183] As pointed out by Thomas, n 181, 79, proportionality is applied 'on a sliding scale of review'.

[184] See William E Leuchtenburg, 'The Origins of Franklin D Roosevelt's 'Court-Packing' Plan' (1966) 1966 *Supreme Court Review* 347; Michael E Parrish, 'The Great Depression, the New Deal, and the American Legal Order' (1984) 59 *Washington Law Review* 723; Richard D Friedman, 'Switching Time and Other Thought Experiments: The Hughes Court and Constitutional Transformation' (1994) 142 *University of Pennsylvania Law Review* 1891; and, Leonard Baker, *Back to Back: The Duel Between FDR and the Supreme Court* (New York, Macmillan, 1967).

[185] As the Supreme Court held in *Williamson v Lee Optical of Oklahoma Inc* (1955) 348 US 483, 488, '[t]he day is gone when this Court uses the Due Process Clause of the Fourteenth Amendment to strike down state laws, regulatory of business and industrial conditions, because they may be unwise, improvident, or out of harmony with a particular school of thought'.

substantive due process clause.[186] This means that the review in regulatory takings cases should always focus on the citizen's or investor's harm, and cannot therefore function as a 'pure' abstract review of rationality.[187]

In the US, the rationality review of administrative actions—although not conducive to expropriations or state liability in tort—deserves a short mention here. Courts certainly show much less deference towards administrative agencies than towards legislatures, while still leaving plenty of room for agencies' discretion. Regarding questions of law, the courts tend to respect legal interpretations that properly reflect agencies' implementation of policy. In the famous *Chevron* case, the Supreme Court held that:

> When a challenge to an agency construction of a statutory provision, fairly conceptualized, really centers on the wisdom of the agency's policy, rather than whether it is a reasonable choice within a gap left open by Congress, the challenge must fail. In such cases, federal judges—who have no constituency—have a duty to respect legitimate policy choices made by those who do.[188]

Regarding questions of fact and policy, courts use different tests when reviewing agencies' findings.[189] Among them, the most important is the 'arbitrary and capricious' test contained in the *Administrative Procedure Act* (APA) section 706(2)(A).[190] The deferential nature of this test has changed over time, becoming more intrusive.[191] Since at the last two decades, the

[186] See *Lingle v Chevron USA Inc* (2005) 544 US 528. The Court, ibid 542, explained the difference between the substantial due process and expropriation tests in the following terms: 'The "substantially advances" formula suggests a means–ends test: It asks, in essence, whether a regulation of private property is *effective* in achieving some legitimate public purpose. An inquiry of this nature has some logic in the context of a due process challenge, for a regulation that fails to serve any legitimate governmental objective may be so arbitrary or irrational that it runs afoul of the Due Process Clause . . . But *such a test is not a valid method of discerning whether private property has been "taken" for purposes of the Fifth Amendment.* In stark contrast to the three regulatory takings tests discussed above [*Loretto, Lucas,* and *Penn Central* tests], *the "substantially advances" inquiry reveals nothing about* the magnitude or character of the burden *a particular regulation imposes upon private property rights. Nor does it provide any information about how any regulatory burden is* distributed *among property owners.* In consequence, this test does not help to identify those regulations whose effects are functionally comparable to government appropriation or invasion of private property'. (emphasis added) (hereinafter, *Lingle*).

[187] However, according to some commentators, the difference between the substantive due process and the *Penn Central* test continues to be unclear. See Nestor M Davidson, 'The Problem of Equality in Takings' (2008) 102 *Northwestern University Law Review* 1, 31–35; and, Steven J Eagle, 'Property Tests, Due Process Tests, and Regulatory Takings Jurisprudence' (2007) 87 *Brigham Young University Law Review* 899 (asserting that, even after *Lingle,* the *Penn Central* tests is a due process test).

[188] *Chevron, USA Inc v Natural Resources Defense Council, Inc* (1984) 467 US 837, 866.

[189] All these tests are established by the APA, esp 5 USC §706.

[190] 5 USC §706(2)(A) (providing that '[t]he reviewing court shall . . . hold unlawful and set aside agency action, findings, and conclusions found to be . . . arbitrary, capricious, an abuse of discretion, or otherwise not in accordance with law').

[191] As Stephen Breyer, 'Judicial Review of Questions of Law and Policy' (1986) 38 *Administrative Law Review* 363, 384, comments, '[t]he language in several important cases decided in the last two decades suggests an increasingly less hesitant judiciary, courts that

test has stabilised as a heightened form of rationality review.[192] As explained by Justice Breyer, the 'hard look' review 'require[s] that the agency examine all relevant evidence, to explain its decision in detail, to justify departures from past practices, and to consider all reasonable alternatives before reaching a final policy decision'.[193] According to the Supreme Court, a decision is arbitrary under this test if:

> [T]he agency has relied on factors which Congress has not intended it to consider, entirely failed to consider an important aspect of the problem, offered an explanation for its decisions that runs counter to the evidence before the agency, or is so implausible that it could not be ascribed to a difference in view or the product of agency expertise.[194]

Yet, four contextual observations are essential to a proper understanding of the comparatively high level of intrusiveness characterising the US 'hard look' test of review. First, the relationship between courts and agencies is seen as a collaborative enterprise;[195] in remedial terms, this means that courts either uphold the decision or remand the case back to the agency for further considerations, without awarding damages.[196] Secondly, high levels of intrusiveness are partially justified by the need to control *independent* agencies, that is, administrative bodies that are theoretically beyond the reach of Congress and the President.[197] Thirdly, the test, in principle, has a strong procedural element:[198] the court must

are more ready to overturn agency policy decisions that they consider unreasonable'. See also, William Funk, 'Rationality Review of State Administrative Rulemaking' (1991) 43 *Administrative Law Review* 147, 149, and the more recent empirical study of Thomas J Miles and Cass R Sunstein, 'The Real World of Arbitrariness Review' (2008) 75 *University of Chicago Law Review* 761.

[192] See Sidney A Shapiro and Richard E Levy, 'Heightened Scrutiny of the Fourth Branch: Separation of Powers and the Requirement of Adequate Reasons for Agency Decisions' (1987) 1987 *Duke Law Journal* 387, 388.

[193] Breyer, n 191, 383. See also, Stephen G Breyer et al, *Administrative Law and Regulatory Policy. Problems, Texts, and Cases*, 4th edn (New York, Aspen Law and Business, 1998) 346.

[194] *Motor Vehicle Manufacturers Association v State Farm Auto Mutual Insurance Co* (1983) 463 US 29, 43.

[195] Judge Leventhal, in *Greater Boston Television Corp v FCC* (1970) 444 F.2d 841, 851–52 (DC Circuit), expressed this collaborative relationship between agencies and courts in the following terms: 'The process thus combines judicial supervision with a salutary principle of judicial restraint, an awareness that agencies and courts together constitute a "partnership" in furtherance of the public interest, and are "collaborative instrumentalities of justice." The court is in a real sense part of the total administrative process, and not a hostile stranger to the office of first instance. This collaborative spirit does not undercut, it rather underlines the court's rigorous insistence on the need for conjunction of articulated standards and reflective findings'.

[196] Breyer et al, n 193, 347 ('Under the "hard look" or "adequate consideration" approach, the court usually does not condemn the agency's policy choices as irremediably faulty, but simply concludes that the agency has not adequately justify its choice. The normal remedy is a remand for further proceedings').

[197] See Shapiro and Levy, n 192, 388, 440.

[198] As Alfred C Aman Jr. and William T Mayton, *Administrative Law*, 2nd edn (St Paul, MN, West Group, 2001) 522, point out, 'Judge Leventhal did not see this doctrine in power terms. Nor did he see it necessarily as a substantive doctrine. Leventhal viewed it as a part of a decision-making process, a process in which courts played an integral part'.

review whether the agencies took a 'hard look' at the problem, though courts sometimes take a 'hard look' on their own.[199] Fourthly, the most intrusive versions of the test are subject to vigorous academic criticism;[200] for instance, according to Justice Breyer, courts should apply the 'arbitrary and capricious' standard 'with traditional attitude of "deference" to agency expertise'.[201]

In the United Kingdom, judicial review of statutes and damage actions stemming from legislative acts has been traditionally barred as a consequence of the sacred principle of Parliamentary sovereignty. At the administrative level, as mentioned before, a plaintiff claiming damages must prove the existence of a private law tort. In cases dealing with discretionary powers—the general case in economic regulation—the new test of proportionality (broad sense), sometimes used in the context of judicial review, is not sufficient to prove a tort.[202]

British courts, as Lord Keith has clearly stated, are particularly aware of 'the danger of judges wrongly though unconsciously substituting their own views for the view of the decision-maker who alone is charged and authorised by Parliament to exercise discretion'.[203] So, in order to prove a tort against the government in cases concerning improper exercise of discretionary powers, the measure at stake must be '*Wednesbury* unreasonable'.[204] This test—which, according to Thomas, 'has come to represent judicial restraint'[205]—is summarised by Lord Diplock in the following terms:

> By 'irrationality' I mean what can by now be succinctly referred to as '*Wednesbury* unreasonableness'. It applies to a decision which is so outrageous in its defiance of logic or of accepted moral standards that no sensible person who had applied his mind to the question to be decided could have arrived at it.[206]

[199] See Breyer et al, n 193, 346.

[200] For example, Sidney A Shapiro and Richard W Murphy, 'Eight Thing Americans Can't Figure Out About Controlling Administrative Power' (2009) 60 *Administrative Law Review* ___ (forthcoming) (available at http://papers.ssrn.com/sol3/papers.cfm?abstract_id=1162872) affirms that '[j]udicial review of the rationality of agency policies . . . has a regrettably strong political component of dubious legitimacy'.

[201] Breyer, n 191, 394.

[202] The test of proportionality has been gaining momentum in the UK See William Wade and Christopher Forsyth, *Administrative Law*, 9th edn (New York, OUP, 2004) 371 ff; Paul P Craig, *Administrative Law*, 5th edn (London, Sweet and Maxwell, 2003) 609 ff; and, Thomas, n 181, 86 ff.

[203] Lord Keith in *R v Secretary of State for Trade and Industry ex p Lonrho Plc*, [1989] 1 WLR 525, 535. See Wade and Forsyth, n 202, 362–63.

[204] See Cane, n 143, 246. See also, Cane, 145, 260.

[205] Thomas, n 181, 86.

[206] Lord Diplock in *Council of Civil Service Unions v Minister for the Civil Service* [1985] AC 374, 410 (internal citations omitted). See also, SA De Smith, L Woolf, and K Jowell, *Judicial Review of Administrative Action*, 5th edn (London, Sweet and Maxwell, 1995) 293.

In France, at the constitutional level, there is no tradition of ex post judicial review of legislation. Before the constitutional reform of 2008,[207] citizens did not have standing to challenge the validity of statutes.[208] Notwithstanding this limitation, the *Conseil d'État* developed an alternative means of awarding damages in cases where the Parliament had itself violated the principle of *l'égalité devant les charges publiques*. The resulting scheme is not technically an expropriation, but instead a form of no-fault state liability which applies only in extreme cases.[209]

In cases concerning administrative agencies' discretionary powers, the test of arbitrariness as irrationality, as an instance of unlawfulness and fault, *can* trigger state liability. However, in practice, the traditional French conception is that courts should not delve into policy matters. *L'opportunité*—as opposed to *la legalité*—is for the administration, not for the judge.[210] To temper the excesses of this overly deferential stance,[211] the *Conseil d'État* also developed the doctrine of 'manifest error of assessment of the facts'.[212] According to this doctrine, 'the administrator has the right to err, to decide wrongly, but not to make a *manifestly* wrongly decision'.[213] Moreover, under certain circumstances even more stringent tests of irrationality apply. If the state measure is an administrative regulation, the fault must be *gross* (*faute lourde*).[214] Finally, it must also be noted that, under the influence of European law, the proportionality test has expanded the potential scope of review of rationality for state action or inaction.[215]

[207] See Federico Fabbrini, 'Kelsen in Paris: France's Constitutional Reform and the Introduction of a Posteriori Constitutional Review of Legislation' (2008) vol 09 no 10 *German Law Journal* 1297 (available at www.germanlawjournal.com/article.php?id=1020).

[208] See John Bell, *French Constitutional Law* (Oxford, Clarendon Press, 1994) 32.

[209] This is the famous *arrêt La Fleurette* (*Société anonyme des produits laitiers 'La Fleurette'*, *Conseil d'État*, Jan 14, 1938, req n° 51704: Rec, p 25). See Brown and Bell, n 155, 199–200.

[210] According to Brown and Bell, ibid 261, this cause of action is 'a safety valve to enable justice to be done in extreme cases'.

[211] ibid.

[212] As the *Conseil d'État* held *Institut technique de Dunkerque* (*Conseil d'État*, 25 April 1980), cited by Chapus, n 128, 1061: ' "*Si l'autorité administrative compétente exerce en opportunité" ses attributions lorsque'elle dispose du pouvior discrétionnaire, 'la décision qu'elle prend ne doit pas reposer sur des faits matériellement inexacts, sur une erreur de droit,* sur une erreur manifeste d'appréciation *ou être entachée de détournement de pouvoir*'. (emphasis added)

[213] Brown and Bell, n 155, 262.

[214] See ibid 191–92. See also, Fairgrieve, n 154, 108, who explains this deferential stance in the following terms: 'Traditionally, the courts have taken a restrictive view of liability actions against public authorities exercising a regulatory function. So, *faute lourde* has been required for claims in respect of diverse regulatory activities including the supervision of public companies, social security offices, and friendly societies. In many areas of regulatory activity, the standard of *faute lourde* applied by the courts has been very high: seriously negligent conduct has been required. Regulatory bodies have rarely been found to have been negligent enough to have committed a gross fault'. The policy basis for this distinction, ibid 115, is that 'judicial intervention on restricted grounds accords a certain "margin of manoeuvre" to public authorities'.

[215] See ibid 263. See also, W van Gerven, 'Mutual Permeation of Public and Private Law at the National and Supranational Level' (1998) 5 *Maastricht Journal of European and Comparative Law* 7, 15 (commenting that '[i]n France, it [the principle of proportionality] is particularly

D Arbitrariness as Special Sacrifice

The distributive justice rationale helps to explain two tests of arbitrariness that play key roles in both expropriations and state liability in tort.[216] Because these tests do not involve wrongful action, in the continental world they are sometimes grouped under the label of 'liability for lawful action'.[217] One is the test of arbitrariness as special sacrifice, which reviews the egalitarian nature of the burden imposed on the citizen or investor. The other—which will be analysed in the next subsection—is arbitrariness as lack of proportionality (*stricto sensu*), which weights the harm suffered and the benefits derived from the regulatory measures, accordingly.

From a comparative perspective, the principle of equality is undoubtedly one of the classical bases used to find expropriations and liability in tort.[218] In the United States regulatory taking jurisprudence, the Supreme Court has repeatedly stated that the protection against takings of private property without just compensation 'was designed to bar Government from forcing some people alone to bear public burdens which, in all fairness and justice, should be borne by the public as a whole'.[219]

The French recognise a constitutional principle of *de l'égalité devant les charges publiques* (equality before public burdens). This principle can give way to state liability in tort not only in cases of administrative regulation or adjudication,[220] but even in the case where the Parliament establishes unequal burdens.[221] According to Moderne, state liability in this case is 'objective, without fault, and arises from the principle of equality of public burdens'.[222]

In Germany, as noted, ordinary courts have resisted the Federal Constitutional Court attempt to eliminated damage awards from the set of remedial alternatives in cases of property rights violations. In the

relevant as an extension of the '*principe de légalité*' in testing the lawfulness of administrative action in areas in which the authorities have been granted large discretionary powers, such as maintenance of public order, economic intervention measures and disciplinary sanctions').

[216] See Hanoch Dagan, 'Takings and Distributive Justice' (1999) 85 *Virginia Law Review* 741, 742–43 (noting that distributive justice 'requires that we consider what distributive criteria should guide the distribution of the burden of the public project, activity, or regulation between the landowner and the community that benefits from this public use').

[217] See Raymond Schlössels, 'Liability for Lawful Administrative Action. Observations on Common Principles of Law, Judicial Lawmaking and National Courts' in F Stroink and E van der Linden (eds), *Judicial Lawmaking and Administrative Law* (Antwerp, Intersentia, 2005) 181, 196 (noting that '[t]he principle of *égalité devant les charges publiques* can be seen as a *justice ideal* of the democratic *Rechtsstaat*. Applicable here is the notion of *justitia distributiva*, distributive justice').

[218] See Dana and Merrill, n 29, 33–41.

[219] *Armstrong v US* (1960) 364 US 40, 49. See also eg, *Lingle* 544 US 537; *Pennel v City of San Jose* (1988) 485 US 1, 9; and, *First English Evangelical Lutheran Church* 482 US 318–19.

[220] See Caranta, n 138, 276, and Schlössels, n 217, 187.

[221] See Fairgrieve, n 154, 144 ff.

[222] Moderne, n 112, 961. See also, Schlössels, n 217, 186–88.

jurisprudence of the High Court of Justice for Civil Matters, legitimate and illegitimate quasi-expropriations (*enteignender Eingriff* and *enteignungsgleicher Eingriff*) and the more modern concept of 'equalisation right' (*ausgleichspflichtige Inhaltsbestimmung* or *Ausgleichsanspruch*) are inspired, among other things, by the doctrine of special sacrifice (*Sonderopfertheorie*).[223] According to Rüfner, '[t]he most important element of a claim based on quasi-expropriatory encroachment is the 'special sacrifice' which is to be made good through the compensation'.[224]

The ECJ, drawing upon principles of law common to the member states, has extended the potential scope of European institutions' liability in tort to cases that go beyond the general rule of unlawfulness.[225] It has indeed implicitly relied on the French principle of *égalité devant les charges publiques* and the German *Sonderopfertheorie*. In the *Boer Buizen* case, the ECJ advanced the idea that compensation may be awarded for an unequal or disproportionate burden.[226] More recently, in the *Dorsch Consult* case, the Court held that 'in the event of the principle of Community liability for a lawful act being recognised in Community law, *a precondition for such liability would in any event be the existence of 'unusual' and 'special' damage*'. (emphasis added)[227]

One version of equality deserves particular attention as a rationale for finding expropriations/liability. Following the so-called process-based constitutional theories—which constitute an effort to overcome the counter-majoritarian difficulty of judicial substantive review[228]—courts sometimes control the democratic quality of the process used to reach the

[223] See nn 130 and 132. See also, Kommers, n 76, 253.

[224] Rüfner, n 45, 263. See also, van der Walt, n 22, 141–42.

[225] Although, the general rule, as Paul Craig and Gráinne de Búrca, *EC Law: Text, Cases, and Materials* (New York, OUP, 1995) 514, explain, continues to be that of illegality: 'in general, the Court has, however, demanded proof of some wrong before imposing liability on the Community'.

[226] See Case C-81/86, *De Boer Buizen BV v Council and Commission* [1987] ECR 3677 ¶ 17, in which the court held that: 'The foregoing considerations do not mean that, when establishing a licensing scheme for the exportation of tubes and pipes to one of the largest markets, the Community Institutions did not bear a degree of responsibility with regard to the particular circumstances of undertakings specializing in the distribution of such products, as indeed they acknowledged by providing for the possibility of such licences being transferred to distributive undertakings. *If it transpired that those undertakings, as a category, had to bear a disproportionate part of the burden attributable to the restrictions on export markets, it would be for the Community Institutions to provide a remedy by adopting the appropriate measures*'. (emphasis added)

[227] Case C-237/1998 *Dorsch Consult v Council and Commission* [2000] ECR I-4549 ¶ 19. Recently, in Cases C-120/2006 P and C-121/2006 P *Fabbrica italiana accumulatori motocarri Montecchio SpA* (*FIAMM*) *et al* [2008] ECR ___ ¶ 184, the ECJ restrictively noted that there is no regime of state liability for lawful conduct. However, it also recognised, ibid ¶ 184, that 'a Community legislative measure whose application leads to restrictions of the right to property and the freedom to pursue a trade or profession that impair the very substance of those rights in a *disproportionate and intolerable manner* . . . could give rise to non-contractual liability on the part of the Community'. (emphasis added)

[228] See Bruce Ackerman, 'Beyond Carolene Products' (1985) 98 *Harvard Law Review* 713, 715.

decision at stake. A classic discussion of this position can be found in Ely's *Democracy and Distrust*,[229] which Fischel has more recently promoted in the context of regulatory takings.[230]

In essence, as summarised by Tribe, 'governmental action that burdens groups effectively excluded from the political process is constitutionally suspect. In its most sophisticated form, the resulting judicial scrutiny is seen as a way of invalidating governmental classifications and distributions that turn out to have been motivated either by prejudiced hostility or by self-serving stereotypes'.[231] In the US, the original source of this doctrine is footnote four of the *Carolene Products* case, where the Supreme Court decided to focus its attention on encroachments to 'discrete and insular minorities'.[232] Today, with the hindsight provided by social sciences, commentators have also proposed extending this rationale to protecting diffused majorities from organised minorities.[233]

This criterion is particularly relevant because it has also been considered at the international level.[234] In fact, in *James*, the ECHR referred to it when explaining why the general international law rule of prompt, adequate, and effective compensation (the Hull Rule), applies only to foreigners and not to nationals (that is, it is not part of the fundamental right of property):

> Finally, the applicants pointed out that to treat the general principles of international law as inapplicable to a taking by a State of the property of its own nationals would permit differentiation on the ground of nationality . . . As to Article 1 (art. 1) of the Convention, it is true that under most provisions of the Convention and its Protocols nationals and non-nationals enjoy the same protection but this does not exclude exceptions as far as this may be indicated in a particular text . . . Especially as regards a taking of property effected in the context of a social reform, there may well be good grounds for drawing a distinction between nationals and non-nationals as far as compensation is concerned. To begin with, non-nationals are more vulnerable to domestic legislation: unlike nationals, they will generally have played no part in the election or designation of its authors nor have been consulted on its adoption. Secondly, although a taking of property must always be effected in the public interest, different

[229] Ely, n 23.

[230] See Fischel, n 30, 100, where he 'invoke[s] the authority of John Hart Ely's theory of constitutional interpretation in support of a selective enforcement of the regulatory takings doctrine'. See ibid 139.

[231] Laurence H Tribe, 'The Puzzling Persistence of Process-Based Constitutional Theories' (1980) 89 *Yale Law Journal* 1063, 1073.

[232] *US v Carolene Prods Co* (1938) 304 US 144, 152 n.4. According to Mashaw, n 14, 68, '[n]onlawyers will perhaps be amused to know that the post-Lochner edifice of judicial review has been built almost wholly on a footnote in *United States v Carolene Products, Inc*'. See also, Ackerman, n 228, 713.

[233] See Richard A Posner, 'Democracy and Distrust Revisited' (1991) 77 *Virginia Law Review* 641, 646; Ackerman, n 228, 745–46; and Mashaw, n 14, 68–69.

[234] It seems that John Basset Moore first presented this argument before the Spanish Treaty Claims Commission in the *Constancia Sugar Case*. See Edwin Borchard, 'The "Minimum Standard" of the Treatment of Aliens' (1940) 38 *Michigan Law Review* 445, 453.

considerations may apply to nationals and non-nationals and there may well be legitimate reason for requiring nationals to bear a greater burden in the public interest than non-nationals.[235]

The quality of the democratic process is a form of participatory and procedural equality. As a 'neutral' rationale of political and legislative control—'neutral', at least, when compared with other review mechanisms such as means-end relations, special sacrifice and proportionality—it will continue to attract the attention of domestic and international adjudicators and commentators.[236]

E Arbitrariness as Lack of Proportionality (*stricto sensu*)

The second test grounded in distributive justice is the arbitrariness as lack of proportionality (*stricto sensu*) test. This second instance of 'liability for lawful action'—which, in the European and German tradition constitutes the third prong of the proportionality (broad sense) test—asks 'whether the advantages of the measure outweigh the financial, social or other costs for the citizens or the community'.[237] The main point, in ECJ's words, is that '[the] disadvantages caused [by the measure] must not be disproportionate to the aims pursued'.[238]

The test of arbitrariness as lack of proportionality represents a definitive, although necessary, judicial intrusion into policy grounds. Broadly speaking, it is a form of cost-benefit analysis that, if unrestrained, has the potential to challenge the wisdom of the policy being reviewed. Beneath the words used to dress it up as a rule of law device, its application is neither neutral nor formal. For the same reason, although most systems

[235] *James and Others v UK* (App no 8793/79) (1986) 8 EHRR 123 ¶ 63 (hereinafter, *James*). Along the same lines, Judge Higgins, n 103, 370, in her well-known monograph work on expropriations (written before the *James* decision), also justified special treatment by international law in favor of aliens relying on this rationale.

[236] For instance, in the EU law context, Miguel Poiares Maduro, *We The Court: The European Court of Justice and the European Economic Constitution. A Critical Reading of Article 30 of the EC Treaty* (Oxford, Hart Publishing, 1998) 173, when studying the relationship between articles 28 and 30 of the EC Treaty, suggests that 'the Court of Justice should not second-guess national regulatory choices, but should instead ensure that there is no under-representation of the interests of nationals of other Member States in the national political process'. In the WTO context, Gráinne de Búrca and Joanne Scott, 'The Impact of the WTO on EU Decision-Making' in Gráinne de Búrca and Joanne Scott (eds), *The EU and the WTO. Legal and Constitutional Issues* (Portland, Hart Publishing, 2001) 1, 27, interpret the famous Shrimp/Turtle decision under the same light: '[T]he kind of procedural values highlighted by the AB [Appellate Body] in the Shrimp/Turtle report may be viewed as operating to promote more "inclusive" political processes, whereby "outsiders" in national or other terms may secure access to previously closed sites of political authority within states'.

[237] Gerapetritis, n 180, 54. See also, Mads Andena and Stefan Zleptnig, 'Proportionality: WTO Law: in Comparative Perspective' (2007) 42 *Texas International Law Journal* 371.

[238] Case C-331/88 *R v Ministry of Agriculture, Fisheries and Food, ex parte Fedesa* [1990] ECR I-4023 ¶ 13.

use this kind of tests in order to structure a proper balance between property rights and the public interest, they also require that constitutional and supreme courts apply them in a substantially deferential manner. Even in Germany, a country where courts are comparatively more interventionists, it is recognised—as Mostert notes—that:

> It must still be possible for the legislature to be creative in order to be functional. This so-called *Gestaltungsspielraum* of the legislature is of the utmost importance in the context of the limitation of property rights in the public interest, and should therefore always be taken into account by the courts when considering whether or not a specific regulation of property is constitutionally justifiable. The assessments of the legislature cannot simply be thrown overboard and be replaced at whim and fancy when constitutional interpretation is at stake.[239]

In the US, the well-known *Penn Central* test of regulatory takings may be located within the scope of the principle of proportionality.[240] In federal law, the *Penn Central* test represents the catch-all category that covers all regulatory takings not falling under the two categorical rules of deprivation of all value—the *Lucas* rule—and physical encroachment—the *Loretto* rule.[241] Formally, it includes the following three prongs:

> In engaging in these essentially ad hoc, factual inquiries, the Court's decisions have identified several factors that have particular significance. *The economic impact of the regulation on the claimant* and, particularly, the extent to which the regulation has *interfered with distinct investment-backed expectations* are, of course, relevant considerations. So, too, is the *character of the governmental action*. A 'taking' may more readily be found when the interference with property can be characterized as a physical invasion by government, than when interference arises from some public program adjusting the benefits and burdens of economic life to promote the common good. (emphasis added)[242]

[239] Mostert, n 76, 299.

[240] The Supreme Court has only adopted an explicit proportionality test in cases of *exactions* (ie, takings occurring when the government grants development permissions subject to the condition that the owner donates certain money or property to the government; see Dana and Merrill, n 29, 210–27). See *Nollan v Californian Coastal Commission* (1987) 483 US 825, and *Dolan v City of Tigard* (1994) 512 US 374. In the latter, ibid 391, the Court affirmed that: 'We think a term such as 'rough proportionality' best encapsulates what we hold to be the requirement of the Fifth Amendment. No precise mathematical calculation is required, but the city must make some sort of individualised determination that the required dedication is related both in nature and extent to the impact of the proposed development'. In any case, the difference between the *Penn Central* balancing test and proportionality may be merely theoretical; as Alexander, n 22, 203, notes, '[t]he actual processes of balancing and proportionality review substantially overlap and often yield the same result'.

[241] See Dana and Merrill, n 29, 127.

[242] *Penn Central* 438 US 124 (internal citations omitted) In *Anthony Palazzolo v Rhode Island* (2001) 533 US 606, 607 (hereinafter, *Palazzolo*), the Supreme Court provided a summarised version of the *Penn Central* test: 'Where a regulation places limitations on land that fall short of eliminating all economically beneficial use, a taking nonetheless may have occurred, depending on a complex of factors including the regulation's economic effect on the landowner, the extent to which the regulation interferes with reasonable investment-backed expectations, and the character of the government action'.

This essentially ad hoc and fact-intensive test requires the decision-maker to assess whether the regulation imposes an 'unduly harsh impact upon the owner's use of the property'.[243] Indeed, both the first and third prongs take into account the interests and harm suffered by the citizen or investor. The former—'diminution in value'—is conceptually straightforward, and can be characterised as a soft version of the *Lucas* categorical rule.[244] The latter—'investment-backed expectations'—is a complex amalgam of elements such as vested interests, retroactivity, historical understanding of the legal system, and specific individualised governmental assurances.[245] Its essence, as put by Alexander, is the protection of 'the owner's reliance interest'.[246]

On the other hand, the second prong, that is, the character of the government action, performs two separate functions. First, it operates as a weakened version of the categorical *Loretto* rule of physical invasions.[247] As Singer writes, '[t]he 'character of the government action' concerns the issue of whether the regulation is more closely analogous to a physical invasion or seizure of a core property right or to a general regulatory program affecting numerous parcels'.[248] Second, it allows the court to inquire into 'the relationship between the government's goal and the claimant's activities'.[249] In particular, the weight that the court gives to the public interest can play a pivotal role in the case's outcome.[250]

In addition to these three prongs, the Supreme Court noted in *Penn Central* that the rationality of the regulation should be taken into account.[251] This includes 'whether the challenged restriction can reasonably be deemed to promote the objectives of the [regulation]'[252] and whether it is 'reasonably necessary to the effectuation of a substantial public purpose'.[253] Moreover, considerations of equality and special sacrifice are particularly explicit in this hyper-balancing test, as the court also indicated that it 'will include consideration of the treatment of similar parcels [of property]'.[254] This is sometimes referred to as the 'reciprocity

243 Penn Central 438 US 127. See Paul, n 74, 1430.

244 See Dana and Merrill, n 29, 132, 135.

245 See ibid 156–64.

246 Alexander, n 22, 71. As he explains, ibid, '[a] taking is more likely to be found where the regulation interferes with an investment that the owner has already made, relying on some pre-existing regulatory arrangement rather than some future investment opportunity'.

247 See Dana and Merrill, n 29, 132, 139.

248 Singer, n 9, 1228. See also, Paul, n 74, 1433–92.

249 Paul, n 74, 1436.

250 See ibid 1438.

251 As mentioned before, nn 186 and 187 and accompanying text, the review of rationality in regulatory taking cases is not pure, but forms an integral part of the three-prong test explained above.

252 *Penn Central* 438 US 133 (internal citations omitted).

253 ibid 127.

254 ibid 133. In *Palazzolo* 533 US 607, the Supreme Court stated that the *Penn Central* test encompassed the review of equal distribution of public burdens: '[T]hese inquiries [those of

of advantages',[255] meaning that the 'owner has not been singled out for adverse treatment, but instead is simply being required to abide by a reasonably general requirement of widespread applicability'.[256]

In the end, the *Penn Central* test is not a proportionality test per se, but rather, an overly broad test that includes almost all versions of arbitrariness analysed in this chapter: irrationality, special sacrifice, and proportionality *stricto sensu* (including, in particular, the *gravity* or *intensity* of the damage suffered by the owner). The result, not surprisingly, is *conceptual* uncertainty. In the words of Dana and Merrill, '[a]ll one can say for certain is that the method is *ad hoc*, meaning that a variety of factors of uncertain priority or weight are potentially relevant, and there is no fixed method or procedure for relating these factors to each other or to the final determination whether a regulation is a taking'.[257] Yet, because of the deference usually applied by the courts, the *final outcome* is not unpredictable;[258] as Alexander notes, '[c]onstitutional challenges to property regulations rarely win. In the vast majority of taking cases where the extant balancing approach applies, the outcome is nearly always in favor of the government'.[259]

In Germany, as previously indicated, the principle of proportionality is understood to be a prohibition against regulatory excesses (*Übermaßverbot*). Its function, as van der Walt observes, is 'to ensure that the regulation starts with but also ends with the public interest, and that it respects and protects both the public interest and the individual interests equally'.[260] More concretely, proportionality *stricto sensu* ensures that the regulatory burdens are not disproportionate with respect to the benefits, and with respect to the individual situation of interest *in concreto* (*unverhältnismäßig*, also *unzumutbar*).[261]

In the realm of state liability, the Federal Administrative Court, in contrast to the High Court of Justice for Civil Matters, has applied the categories of legitimate and illegitimate quasi-expropriations (*enteignender*

the *Penn Central* test] are informed by the purpose of the Taking Clause, which is to prevent the government, from "forcing some people alone to bear public burdens which, in all fairness and justice, should be borne by the public as a whole" '. See also, Dana and Merrill, n 29, 152–56.

[255] See *Keystone* 480 US 491, where the court explains that: 'The Court's hesitance to find a taking when the State merely restrains uses of property that are tantamount to public nuisances is consistent with the notion of 'reciprocity of advantage' that Justice Holmes referred to in *Pennsylvania Coal*. Under our system of government, one of the State's primary ways of preserving the public weal is restricting the uses individuals can make of their property. While each of us is burdened somewhat by such restrictions, we, in turn, benefit greatly from the restrictions that are placed on others'.

[256] Dana and Merrill, n 29, 153.

[257] ibid 131.

[258] See Alexander, n 22, 217.

[259] ibid 206.

[260] Van der Walt, n 22, 135.

[261] See ibid 135; and Mostert, n 76, 289.

Eingriff and *enteignungsgleicher Eingriff*) and 'equalisation right' (*ausgleichspflichtige Inhaltsbestimmung* or *Ausgleichsanspruch*), with a special emphasis on the intensity of the damage and not its specialness (*Schweretheorie*).[262] For the jurisprudence of the administrative courts 'it is the *intensity* of the administrative measure directed against the property and the *weight of the burden* placed upon the owner which makes it transgress the borderline of the social obligation of property and enter the area of expropriation'. (emphasis added)[263]

A brief overview of the ECHR jurisprudence also demonstrates the relevance of the proportionality principle and the deferential manner in which is applied. Both the *first rule*—Article P1-1 first paragraph-first sentence test, that covers the protection of the peaceful enjoyment of property—and the *third rule*—Article P1-1 second paragraph test—that recognises the right of a State to control the use of property—protect property rights in the periphery. When reviewing alleged violations to both rules, the ECHR applies a 'fair balance' test.[264]

According to the Court, what must be assessed is whether 'a fair balance was struck between the demands of the general interests of the community and the requirements of the protection of the individual's fundamental rights'.[265] This test explicitly controls the proportionality that must exist between the means employed and ends sought in the decision under review.[266] The emphasis is usually placed on the excessive individual burden.[267]

[262] See nn 130 and 132. See also, Kommers, n 76, 253; and, Mostert, n 76, 311.

[263] Kimminich, n 29, 87.

[264] See nn 133, and 169, and accompanying text.

[265] *Sporrong* ¶ 69 (applying the fair balance test in the context of the *first* rule). See also, *AGOSI* ¶ 52 (applying the fair balance test in the context of the *third* rule): 'In determining whether a fair balance exists, the Court recognises that the State enjoys a wide margin of appreciation with regard both to choosing the means of enforcement and to ascertaining whether the consequences of enforcement are justified in the general interest for the purpose of achieving the object of the law in question'.

[266] See eg *James* ¶ 50 (requiring a 'a reasonable relationship of proportionality between the means employed and the aim sought to be realized'); *Pressos* ¶ 38 (establishing that compensation is due if the measure 'imposes a disproportionate burden on the applicants'); and, *Beyeler* ¶ 114 (holding that the fair balance test controls whether there exists 'a reasonable relationship of proportionality between the means employed and the aim sought to be realised'). See also, Marc-André Eissen, 'The principle of proportionality in the case-law of the European Court of Human Rights' in R St J Macdonald et al (eds), *The European System for the Protection of Human Rights* (Boston, M Nijhoff, 1993) 125, and Jeremy McBride, 'Proportionality and the European Convention of Human Rights' in Evelyn Ellis (ed), *The Principle of Proportionality in the Laws of Europe* (Portland, Hart Publishing, 1999) 23.

[267] See eg *Sporrong* ¶ 73: 'Being combined in this way, the two series of measures created a situation which upset the fair balance which should be struck between the protection of the right of property and the requirements of the general interest: the Sporrong Estate and Mrs. Lönnroth bore *an individual and excessive burden*'. (emphasis added). See also, *Inmobiliare Saffi v Itally* (1999) 30 EHRR 756 ¶ 59 (hereinafter, *Inmobiliare Saffi*) (finding a violation of the property rights of the claimant because it suffered an 'excessive burden').

The deferential stance of the Court is reflected in the well-known doctrine of the 'margin of appreciation'.[268] According to the ECHR, states deserve respect and recognition with respect to their determination of both the ends and the means-ends relation chosen.[269] However, if the court does not wish to abdicate its functions, it must achieve a delicate equilibrium between deference and the need to review state action in order to protect property rights; this is a concern that was made explicit in the *Sporrong* case:

> [The Court] finds it natural that, in an area as complex and difficult as that of the development of large cities, the Contracting States should enjoy a wide margin of appreciation in order to implement their town-planning policy. Nevertheless, the Court cannot fail to exercise its power of review and must determine whether the requisite balance was maintained in a manner consonant with the applicants' right to 'the peaceful enjoyment of [their] possessions', within the meaning of the first sentence of Article 1 (P1-1).[270]

In sum, a comparative view shows that most courts guarding the protection of property rights must perform some version of the proportionality test. This means that they must measure the intensity of the harm, and evaluate it in terms of the 'compelling-ness' of the public interest invoked by the state. The political branches of government do not have *carte blanche* to implement redistributive programs that disproportionately affect property rights; after all, we have traditionally understood property rights as possessing anti-redistributive strength.[271] Yet, legislatures and executive agencies do have the discretion or 'margin of appreciation' to define political and policy goals, and dictate how they should

[268] See eg, *AGOSI* ¶ 52: 'In determining whether a fair balance exists, the Court recognises that the State enjoys a wide margin of appreciation with regard both to choosing the means of enforcement and to ascertaining whether the consequences of enforcement are justified in the general interest for the purpose of achieving the object of the law in question'. The general grounds for the margin of appreciation can be found in *Handyside v UK* (1976) 1 EHRR 737 ¶ 48.

[269] Regarding the ends, *see* eg, *James* ¶ 46: 'Because of their direct knowledge of their society and its needs, the national authorities are in principle better placed than the international judge to appreciate what is 'in the public interests'. Under the system of protection established by the Convention, it is thus for the national authorities to make the initial assessment both of the existence of a problem of public concern warranting measures of deprivation of property and of the remedial action to be taken'. Regarding the means-ends relation, see eg, *Inmobiliare Saffi* ¶ 49: 'There must be a reasonable relationship of proportionality between the means employed and the aim pursued. In determining whether this requirement is met, the Court recognises that the State enjoys a wide margin of appreciation with regard both choosing the means of enforcement and to ascertaining whether the consequences of enforcement are justified in the general interest for the purpose of achieving the object of the law in question'.

[270] *Sporrong* ¶ 69.

[271] See Frank I Michelman, 'Possession vs. Distribution in the Constitutional Ideal of Property' (1987) 72 *Iowa Law Review* 1319, 1319 (noting that 'we primarily understand property in its constitutional sense as an antiredistributive principle, opposed to governmental interventions into the extant regime of holdings for the sake of distributive ends').

be implemented in society. The bottom line is always the same: a proper democracy is not a government of judges, but rather, one of the people.

F Legitimate Expectations

Finally, particular attention must be paid to a relatively recent development in public law: the protection of legitimate expectations. The basic idea here—following the general theme of property rights protection—is to 'ensure that the administration achieves its objectives while, so far as possible, protecting the individual's expectations'.[272]

The rationales underpinning legitimate expectations are the ideals of the rule of law, and individual fairness and autonomy. The rule of law presupposes formal equality and a certain level of consistency, certainty and stability in the application of the law.[273] Individual fairness and autonomy demands, as Schønberg explains, that individuals 'must, at least, be able to plan ahead and therefore foresee with some degree of certainty the consequences of their actions'.[274]

The concept of legitimate expectations encompasses two different ideas. On the one hand, legitimate expectations-weak sense is just another label for property rights' periphery, including sometimes interests that go beyond the periphery (that is, interests that 'have not traditionally been characterised as rights'[275]). For the same reason, legitimate expectations-weak sense only tells us that there are interests which deserve some protection against collective action, but not that those interests should prevail over the public interest. Legitimate expectations-weak sense thus refers to one side of the conflict, not to its solution.

On the other hand, legitimate expectations-strong sense does describe interests that defeat competing public interests, or, equivalently, interests that require compensation if sacrificed in the pursuit of collective goals. However, the concept proves to be highly circular in nature.[276] As previously explained, the general rule is that to be compensable, harm received in the periphery of property rights (or beyond) must be the product of arbitrary state action. Now, legitimate expectations-strong sense tries to

[272] Thomas, n 181, 42.

[273] See Schønberg, n 126, 13–14 (observing that '[t]he legal protection of expectations by administrative law principles is a way of giving expression to the requirements of predictability, formal equality, and constancy inherent in the Rule of Law').

[274] ibid 12.

[275] Paul Craig, 'Legitimate Expectations: A Conceptual Analysis' (1992) 108 LQR 79, 97. In Germany, see Kimminich, n 30, 161.

[276] This has been recognised in international investment law. See Newcombe, n 66, 48 (observing that '[t]he difficulty with the concept of legitimate expectations is its circularity'). See also, Rudolf Dolzer, 'Indirect Expropriations: New Developments?' (2002) 11 *New York University Environmental Law Journal* 64, 78.

affirm, at the same time, that a state measure may be arbitrary if it affects the periphery (or beyond).

Such circularity makes legitimate expectations vulnerable to activist judges, who may wish to impose their own political visions and considerations regarding the value of individual autonomy and property. The concept can be improperly extended to require the compensation of all harms, overcoming the democratic rule according to which legislatures and executive agencies have the power to allocate burdens and benefits among the population.[277]

Not surprisingly, nearly all well-structured regulatory capitalist legal systems require a fair number of restrictions when protecting expectations.[278] For the comparative purposes of this chapter, I will only review EU law, which is in itself a distillation of member states' common principles of law.[279] The first observation worth making here is that, even though EU law has established a 'generous' standard for the protection of expectations,[280] the resulting threshold is still very high.[281] As Thomas notes, 'relatively few arguments based on legitimate expectations have succeeded'.[282]

According to Schønberg, when assessing the strength of legitimate expectations under EU law, four scenarios are identified: (1) revocations of formal individualised decisions, as in the case of revocations of licences; (2) departures from individualised assurance previously obtained by citizens or investors; (3) departures from general policy statements or representations in particular cases; and (4) departures from general policy statements or representations because of a general shift of policy.[283] In scenarios (1) and (2) there is an individuated component; in scenarios (3) and (4) there is not.

The general rule for scenarios (3) and (4) is that, in principle, expectations do not receive protection. Legitimate expectations 'arise as a result of administrative conduct and operate only in the context of a specific relationship between an individual, or a specific class of people, and the administration'.[284] In EU law, 'the individual must be able to point either to a

[277] See Javier García Luengo, *El Principio de la Protección de la Confianza Legítima en el Derecho Administrativo* (Madrid, Civitas, 2002) 220–21.

[278] See *generally*, García Luengo, n 277, and Schønberg, n 126.

[279] It is interesting to note that the principle of legitimate expectations has not gained approval in French courts. See Elizabeth Snodgrass, 'Protecting Investors' Legitimate Expectations: Recognizing and Delimiting a General Principle' (2006) 21 *ICSID Review—Foreign Investment Law Journal* 1, 27.

[280] See Schønberg, n 126, 232 (commenting that 'the Community judicature . . . has developed a fairly generous approach to breach of legitimate expectations created by (correct) administrative measures').

[281] See Thomas, n 181, 46.

[282] ibid 46.

[283] See Schønberg, n 126, 5, 8–9.

[284] Thomas, n 181, 45–46.

bargain of some form which has been entered into between the individual and the authorities, or to a course of conduct or assurance on the part of the authorities which can be said to generate the legitimate expectation'.[285]

This means that the rules and principles contained in regulatory programs do not give away to legitimate expectations. According to Schønberg, 'policies should be, and are known to be, impermanent, they cannot reasonably be expected to remain fixed forever. Policies do not bear the mark of finality to the same extent as decisions and individualised representations'.[286] In this regard, the ECJ has held that:

> Since Community institutions enjoy a margin of discretion in the choice of the means needed to achieve their policies, traders are unable to claim that they have a legitimate expectation that an existing situation which is capable of being altered by decisions taken by those institutions within the limits of their discretionary power will be maintained.[287]

Only in extreme circumstances, such as abrupt policy changes without transitional measures,[288] or past regulations that clearly encouraged certain courses of action,[289] can citizens or investors claim legitimate expectation in the absence of a specific relationship with the administration.

In scenarios (1) and (2), expectations need to meet several conditions in order to obtain legal protection. First, the expectations must be *legitimate*, that is, they cannot be *contra legem*. The ECJ 'has refused to admit the

[285] Paul P Craig, 'Substantive Legitimate Expectations in Domestic and Community Law' (1996) 55 *Cambridge Law Journal* 289, 307.

[286] Schønberg, n 126, 15. See also, ibid 142, noting that: 'It is well-recognized principle, in English, French, and EC law that authorities have the power to change their policies from time to time. Without such a power, authorities would not be able to act effectively in the public interest. Individuals can therefore not legitimately expect that a favourable policy or practice will be maintained, and the mere fact that a person is disadvantaged by a change normally does not give rise to any cause for complaint'. In Spain, see García de Enterría, n 16, 42.

[287] Case 245/81 *Edeka Zentrale AG v Germany* [1982] ECR 2745 ¶ 27. See also, Case 52/81 *W Faust v Commission* [1982] ECR 3762 ¶ 27; Case C-296 and 307/93 *France and Ireland v Commission* [1996] ECR I-795 ¶ 59; Case C-375/96 *Galileo Zaninotto v Ispettorato Centrale Repressione Frodi and Others* [1998] ECR I-6629 ¶ 50; and Case C-284–94 *Kingdom of Spain v Council* [1998] ECR I-7309 ¶ 43.

[288] See Case 74/74 *CNTA v Commission* [1975] ECR 533 ¶ 43, where the ECJ stated that: 'The Community is therefore liable if, in the absence of an overriding matter of public interest, the Commission abolished with immediate effect and without warning the application of compensatory amounts in a specific sector without adopting transitional measures which would at least permit traders either to avoid the loss which would have been suffered in the performance of export contracts, the existence and irrevocability of which are established by the advance fixing of the refunds, or to be compensated for such loss'.

[289] See eg Case 120/86 *J Mulder v Minister van Landbouw en Visserij* [1988] ECR 2321 ¶ 24, where the court held that: 'Where such a producer, as in the present case, has been encouraged by a Community measure to suspend marketing for a limited period in the general interest and against payment of a premium he may legitimately expect not to be subject, upon the expiry of his undertaking, to restrictions which specifically affect him precisely because he availed himself of the possibilities offered by the Community provisions'. In any case, according to Schønberg, n 126, 145, decisions such as *CNTA* and *Mulder* are quite rare in EU law.

possibility of protecting expectations which have arisen as a consequence of unlawful administrative activity'.[290] In the *Air France* case, the First Instance Court held that 'a Community institution cannot be forced, by virtue of the principle of the protection of legitimate expectations, to apply Community rules contra legem'.[291]

Second, legitimate expectations require the applicant to have acted in good faith and in a diligent and reasonable manner. In the *SNUPAT* case, the ECJ held that an illegal measure can be revoked without paying compensation if it 'was adopted on the basis of false or incomplete information provided by the beneficiaries'.[292] According to Schønberg, '[a]n expectation is reasonable if a reasonable person acting with diligence would hold it in the relevant circumstances'.[293] The test here, the 'knowledge of a prudent trader', is not an easy one to survive. The ECJ, indeed, has established that:

> [A]ny trader in regard to whom an institution has given rise to justified hopes may rely on the principle of the protection of legitimate expectation. On the other hand, if a prudent and discriminating trader could have foreseen the adoption of a Community measure likely to affect his interests, he cannot plead that principle if the measure is adopted.[294]

Third, expectations that derive from formal decisions—scenario (1)—receive more protection than those emanating from assurances—scenario (2). Regarding the latter, it must be noted that while the form in which written assurances are given—letters, faxes, agreements, circulars, reports, communications, codes of conduct, white paper, etc[295]— does not matter, they must be still be 'specific, precise, unambiguous, and unqualified'.[296] Oral statements and consistent, prolonged conduct, though still capable of creating legitimate expectations, receive weaker protection than formal assurances.[297]

[290] Thomas, n 181, 57. See eg Case 5/82 *Hauptzollamt Krefeld v Maizena GmbH* [1982] ECR 4602 ¶ 22 (stating that '[a] practice of a member state which does not conform to Community rules may never give rise to legal situations protected by Community Law'). See also, Rob Widdershoven, 'European Administrative Law' in René Seerden and Frits Stroink (eds), *Administrative Law of the European Union and the United States. A Comparative Analysis* (Antwerp, Intersentia, 2002) 259, 284 ('[T]he ECJ has, to date, consistently rejected the application of the principle [of legitimate expectations] *contra legem*').

[291] Case T-2/93 *Societe Anonyme A Participation Ouvriere Compagnie Nationale Air France v Commission* [1994] ECR II-323 ¶101.

[292] Case 42 and 49/1959 *Société nouvelle des usines de Pontlieue—Aciéries du Temple (SNUPAT) v High Authority of the European Coal and Steel Community* [1961] ECR 53 (English special edition) ¶ 10.

[293] Schønberg, n 126, 6.

[294] Case 265/85 *Van den Bergh en Jurgens v Commission* [1987] ECR 1155 ¶ 44.

[295] See Schønberg, n 126, 120.

[296] Schønberg, n 126, 125. See also Case T-123/89 *Jean-Louis Chomel v Commission* [1990] ECR II-131 ¶ 26; Case T-465/93 *Consorzio gruppo di azione locale 'Murgia Messapica' v Commission* [1994] ECR II-361 ¶ 67; Case T-571/93 *Lefebvre v Commission* [1995] ECR II-2379 ¶ 72–74; and, Case T-521/93 *Atlanta AG and Others v Council* [1996] ECR II-1707 ¶ 57.

[297] See Schønberg, n 126, 121–22.

Finally, and most importantly, once the applicant has been able to show that his / her expectations are legitimate, he / she still must prove that those expectations outweigh the public interest. Only in that case will the citizen or investor be entitled to claim compensation. Here is where the dual notions of public and private interests finally confront one another. This is where the Court must take a position, without too much legal help, somewhere between the two values that lie at stake in every hard case of property rights protection: legal certainty / rule of law and policy flexibility / democracy. In Craig's words, '[l]egal certainty is expressive of the individual's perspective; legality, as manifested through the non-fettering doctrine, captures the needs of the public body to develop policy'.[298]

Consequently, legitimate expectations force the court, to involve itself with policy considerations, and even political evaluations.[299] When must private expectations overcome the public interests? What constitutes sufficient weight for those purposes? And more important, what level of deference must courts show towards previous determinations by legislatures and administrative agencies explicitly or implicitly affirming that the public interest must prevail without the payment of compensation?

In EU law, the ECJ recognises that 'the initial balance is therefore a task for the administration'.[300] The Court is clear in its understanding that it should not 'substitute its view of the desired public interest for that of the administrator, but to determine whether the disappointment of an expectation was indispensable for the attainment of that objective'.[301]

Ultimately, the concept of legitimate expectations comes back to the test of proportionality (broad sense), particularly to considerations of *necessity* and proportionality *stricto sensu*. Indeed, 'the Court will examine whether the infringement of the expectation was indispensable for the achievement of the public interest objective by looking at all relevant circumstances and the availability of alternative measures'.[302] For example, in *Dürbeck*, the Court held that in the absence of alternative means of achieving a certain public interest, the individual expectations must give way.[303] In other cases, Community courts will only interfere in situations of '*significant imbalance* between expectations and countervailing policy considerations'.[304]

In sum, under EU law, obtaining compensation on the basis of an alleged frustration of expectations is far from easy. The concept of legit-

[298] Craig, n 285, 303.

[299] See Thomas, n 181, 71 (noting that '[d]etermining the legitimacy of an expectation inevitably involves striking some balance between competing interests').

[300] ibid 63.

[301] ibid. See also, Schønberg, n 126, 158 (concluding that 'the study of EC law has shown that the principle of legitimate expectations does not lead to substitution of judgment').

[302] Thomas, n 181, 68.

[303] See Case 112/80, *Firma Anton Dürbeck v Hauptzollamt Frankfurt am Main-Flughafen* [1981] ECR 1095 ¶ 50.

[304] Schønberg, n 126, 158.

imate expectations is not used to override policy programs implemented by national or community institutions, nor to demand compensation when political branches of government have decided not to do so. Given that EU law—already the product of a comparative law effort—is more generous than other legal systems in this regard,[305] the level of protection it confers should serve as a benchmark for any newcomers to the concept of legitimate expectations.

CONCLUSIONS: THREE LESSONS FROM COMPARATIVE LAW FOR INTERNATIONAL INVESTMENT LAW

This chapter has presented a comparative patchwork describing the relationship of property rights and the public interest in major Western legal traditions. Such an endeavor is highly important to international investment law; as mentioned in the First Part of this work, only by examining the comparative experiences of developed countries can arbitral tribunals crystallise rules of protection for investors' rights and interests that are properly grounded in the legitimacy that the rule of law provides.

There are essentially three general lessons that we can draw from this comparative patchwork. First, there is an inherent tension between democracy and the protection of private rights and interests. In democratic regimes, dominant coalitions are empowered to design and implement policies and regulations that better fit their preferences. Democracy, in

[305] In the US, the Supreme Court takes seriously commitments that rise to the level of regulatory contracts, including explicit or implicit stabilisation clauses; see *US v Winstar Corp* (1996) 518 US 839, and *Mobil Oil Explorations and Producing Southeast Inc v US* (2000) 534 US 604. However, in the absence of contracts, the prospect of damage claims seems to be quite modest. For example, in *American Pelagic Fishing Co LP v US* (2004) 379 F.3d 1363, the Court of Appeals for the Federal Circuit rejected a taking claim based on the revocation of a fish permit; the court concluded, ibid 1374, that the plaintiff 'did not and could not possess a property interest in its fishery permits'. In *Conti v US* (2001) 48 Fed Cl 532, 537, the Court of Appeals for the Federal Circuit indicated that '[a]lthough mere 'participation in a heavily regulated industry' does not bar a plaintiff from ever prevailing on a takings claim, it does greatly reduce the reasonableness of expectations and reliance on regulatory provisions'. (internal citations omitted). In *Allied-General Nuclear Services v US* (1988) 839 F.2d 1572, the same court rejected a taking claim brought by companies that had built nuclear electricity plants relying on government assurances (with investments up to $200,000,000). The court held, ibid 1577–78, that: 'We find the absence of a contract count in the complaint to be dispositive . . . [T]he assertions about "inducement" in this case are not such as would support a good faith count pled along the line suggested. We think the hypothetical is the nearest to our actual case the law would go—if it went that far—in attaching significance to "inducement" by the government to private parties to invest their capital in a business enterprise. After all, when the government desires reluctant private capital to invest in risky enterprises, it is accustomed to make express contracts to "induce" by reducing or sharing the risk. *The constitutional control of Congress over the public fisc is an adverse factor against liability for mere "jawboning" by government employees not authorized to commit it to legal liability*'. (emphasis added)

other words, does not permit a freezing of the status quo.[306] Elected authorities, and administrative agencies acting by delegation, 'must be able to change policy in the public interest, even if this causes some harm to individuals'.[307]

At the same time, property and investments are and continue to be recognised as limits to the discretion of those dominant coalitions. As a result, constitutionalism is placed in the position of *aspiring* to 'reconcile private property (or, more generally, limited government) with democracy'.[308] Even beyond constitutionalism, as Harlow notes, 'the balance between the Rule of Law doctrine and principles of political and democratic supremacy may be hard to attain and is a subject of controversy'.[309]

Second, even though public law judges are institutionally located at the centre of this tension between democracy and property rights, the standard judicial attitude in all major Western legal traditions is that of restraint and deference to the political branches of government. Public law judges are generally aware that in democratic regimes, the proper government is that of the people, and not of courts. Judges, as the US Supreme Court has held, 'have a duty to respect legitimate policy choice made by those who [have constituencies]'.[310] If unrestrained, the noble ideal of the rule of law is, as Harlow warns us, 'capable of degenerating into an ideology of law courts'.[311] The result, as Michelman reminds us, is 'troubled and limited judicial protection of property'[312]:

> Limited, and probably destined to remain so, because the claims of popular sovereignty and classical property cannot, in truth, be stably reconciled at a very high level of abstraction or generality. Carried on, because the country's sense of constitutional freedom—of how we are both popularly self-governing and yet not under democratic tyranny—still motivates and demands respect for the idea of a rule of law imaginatively supported, in part, by the classical idea of property. Troubled, because the rule-of-law idea still pushes towards the high

[306] In Spain, this is also the opinion of García de Enterría, n 16, 54–55: '*La democracia, que es la que ha creado enteramente el concepto mismo de Legislación sobre el que hoy vivimos, no tolera la invocación de ninguna confianza, o comodidad, o interés de nadie en mantener la situación existente y que pueda justificar la imposibilidad de que el Legislador pueda cambiar la Ley a su arbitrio . . . «La libre configuración», como facultad necesaria del Legislador, resulta insoslayable y echa por tierra definitivamente cualquier intento de condicionarla invocando la confianza que cualquie cualquiera pudiera haber puesto en una estabilidad normativa cualquiera o gravando su ejercicio con cargas indemnizatorias en favor de quienes invoquen un perjuicio derivado del cambio normativo*'. See also, Carlos Bernal Pulido, *El Principio de Proporcionalidad y los Derechos Fundamentales*, 2nd edn (Madrid, CEPC, 2005) 204–05.

[307] Schønberg, n 126, 11. See also, Mountfield, n 178, 140, and 146.

[308] Michelman, n 39, 1625.

[309] Carol Harlow, 'Francovich and the Problem of the Disobedient State' (1996) 2 *European Law Journal* 199, 200.

[310] See n 188.

[311] Harlow, n 309, 222.

[312] Michelman, n 39, 1628.

formality of a few, simple, abstract rules; and the price of such high formality, in a dynamic and impacted world, is obtuseness.[313]

Third, judicial deference toward the state does not mean that citizens and investors are left to fend for themselves. Even if the judicial protection of property is 'troubled and limited', it does provide certain defenses against illegal state action, appropriations and redistribution. Indeed, citizens and investors are usually entitled to claim damages when negatively impacted by wrongful government behaviour, including physical appropriations, and also when the burdens allocated to them in the course of legitimate regulatory reform have been unequal or disproportionate. As noted, in contrast to private law, state liability is explained and justified by a much more complex mixture of corrective and distributive justice rationales: not every intentional harm caused by the state is a wrong, not even prima facie; and, the state may be required to pay compensation even in the absence of wrongdoing.

In the end, an explicit or implicit strategy used in many countries to reconcile property rights and democracy can be found in the use of a two-layered system. In the first layer, excepting unusual circumstances, full destruction of property rights demands the payment of damages; in the second layer, non-destructive interferences are permitted without compensation unless the state acted in an illegal, irrational, unequal, or disproportionate manner (arbitrariness, broad sense). When following this structure, courts claim authority over the political branches of government when the owner's entitlements have been suppressed, but show a high degree of deference when assessing the alleged arbitrary character of state measures that have only interfered with the exercise of rights and expectations.

313 ibid.

5

Investments, Indirect Expropriations and the Regulatory State

INTRODUCTION: WHY IS RECOGNISING INDIRECT TAKINGS SO DIFFICULT?

There are certain areas of the law that are in a permanent state of doctrinal disarray. It should come as no surprise that the field of expropriations is one of them. Mere doctrines cannot resolve the deeper political and philosophical questions dividing people over issues such as the proper balance between property rights and the public interest. This is a situation in which, as Posner has noted, '[y]ou will not be able to choose among these interpretations on semantic or conceptual grounds'.[1]

In the case of non-physical and non-direct takings, the disarray begins with issues of nomenclature. There are several labels competing to describe deprivations that are not easily identifiable: de facto expropriations, creeping expropriations, regulatory takings, indirect expropriations, and situations tantamount to expropriations, just to name a few.[2] Here, I will use the rubric of *indirect expropriations* to encompass all these terms.

[1] Richard A Posner, 'Democracy and Distrust Revisited' (1991) 77 *Virginia Law Review* 641, 650.

[2] Because treaties sometimes mention more than one of those labels, there exists some level of dispute regarding the relative applicability of each label. For instance, in the context of NAFTA Chapter 11, there has been some controversy regarding the relative scope of the terms 'indirect expropriations' and 'situations tantamount to expropriation'. While at least two tribunals have held that they are the same—*Feldman v Mexico*, ICSID Case No ARB(AF)/99/1 (Kerameus, Covarrubias, Gantz), Award (16 December 2002), ¶ 100 (hereinafter, *Feldman*), and, *SD Myers Inc v Canada*, UNCITRAL Ad Hoc Arbitration (Hunter, Schwartz, Chiasson), Partial Award (13 November 2000), ¶¶ 285–86 (hereinafter, *SD Myers I*)—on the other hand, one tribunal has held that the term 'situations tantamount to expropriation' is wider than 'indirect expropriations'—see eg *Waste Management v Mexico*, ICSID Case N°ARB(AF)/00/3 (Crawford, Civileti, Magallón), Award (30 April 2004), ¶ 144 (hereinafter, *Waste Management II*). Outside the realm of NAFTA, the Tribunal in *Telenor Mobile Communications AS v Hungary*, ICSID Case No ARB/04/15 (Goode, Allard, Marriott), Award (13 September 2006), ¶ 63 (hereinafter, *Telenor*), held that '[p]hrases such as "equivalent to expropriation" and "tantamount to expropriation" do not expand the concept of expropriation'; and, in at least two other cases, tribunals have applied 'indirect expropriations' and 'measures tantamount to expropriations' as equivalent categories: *Link-Trading v Moldova*, UNCITRAL Ad Hoc Arbitration (Herzfeld, Buruiana, Zykln), Award on jurisdiction (16 February 2001), ¶ 8 (hereinafter, *Link-Trading*); and *Middle East Cement Shipping and Handling*

But beyond words and semantics,[3] determining what is and is not an expropriation is a difficult enterprise. There are at least three reasons that explain, from a very general perspective, why this is the case, and they deserve immediate clarification. First, the regulatory state has the legitimate power, recognised by international law, to harm citizens and investors, without paying compensation.[4] At the same time, international law does not accept generally that investors should bear all kinds of burdens.[5] This means that the equilibrium must lie somewhere in between, and defining it is a complicated enterprise.[6]

Those who tend to overexpand the protective scope of investment treaties should be aware that these treaties do not modify the background of general international law. Investment treaties do not define expropriations,[7] so that arbitral tribunals must necessarily have recourse to general

Co SA v Egypt, ICSID Case NoARB/99/6 (Böckstiegel, Bernardini, Wallace), Award (12 April 2002), ¶¶ 105, 107 (hereinafter, *Middle East Cement*).

3 After all, as pointed out by Jack Coe Jr and Noah Rubins, 'Regulatory Expropriations and the TECMED Case: Context and Contributions' in Todd Weiler (ed), *International Investment Law and Arbitration: Leading Cases from the ICSID, NAFTA, Bilateral Investment Treaties and Customary International Law* (London, Cameron May, 2005) 597, 604, 'the multiplicity and overlap in terms and the lack of an agreed-upon typology probably results in little harm'.

4 As stated in *Azurix Corp v Argentina*, ICSID Case No ARB/01/12 (Rigo, Lalonde, Martins), Award (14 July 2006), ¶ 310 (hereinafter, *Azurix*), '[i]n the exercise of their public policy function, governments take all sorts of measures that may affect the economic value of investments without such measures giving rise to a need to compensate'. See also, Ian Brownlie, *Principles of Public International Law*, 6th edn (New York, OUP, 2003) 509 ('[S]tate measures, prima facie a lawful exercise of powers of goverments, may affect foreign interests considerably without amounting to expropriation'); and, Organisation for Economic Co-operation and Development (OECD), *'Indirect Expropriation' and the 'Right to Regulate' in International Investment Law*, Working Papers on International Investment No 2004/4 (2004) 4 ('[U]nder international law, not all state measures interfering with property are expropriations').

5 As Judge Anzilotti observed in his Individual Opinion in the *Oscar Chinn* case (*UK v Belgium*) (1934) PCIJ Rep Ser A/B No 63, 65, 112, '[i]t is clear that international law would be merely an empty phrase if it sufficed for a State to invoke the public interest in order to evade the fulfillment of its engagements'.

6 See Christoph H Schreuer, *The Concept of Expropriation under the ETC and other Investment Protection Treaties*, 28, ¶ 78 (available at www.univie.ac.at/intlaw/pdf/csunpublpaper_3.pdf), who also implicitly recognises that the equilibrium must lie somewhere in between the two extremes: 'Regulatory measures that are taken by States authorities in the exercise of their public order functions frequently have negative effects on private property rights including those of foreign investors. It is impossible to compensate a foreign investor for every measure taken by the host State that has some adverse effect, however minimal, on its business operation. Such a requirement would severely impair the State in its sovereign functions. On the other hand, the fact that a regulatory measure serves some legitimate public purpose cannot automatically lead to the conclusion that no expropriation has occurred and that, therefore, no compensation is due'.

7 This was also recognised by the Iran–United States Claims Tribunals. See Iran–US Claims Tribunal *Sea-Land Service Inc v Islamic Republic of Iran* (1984) 6 Iran–US Claims Trib Rep 149, 169 (hereinafter, *Sea-Land*): 'There is nothing in either Article II or Article IV of the Treaty which extends the scope of either State's international responsibility beyond those categories of acts already recognised by international law as giving rise to liability for a taking. *The concept of taking is the same in the Treaty as in international law, and, though the Treaty might, arguably, affect the level of compensation payable, it does not relieve a Claimant of the burden of*

international law when deciding about them.[8] In the words of the *Saluka* Tribunal, '[i]t is clear that the notion of deprivation, as that word is used in the context of Article 5 of the Treaty, *is to be understood in the meaning it has acquired in customary international law*'. (emphasis added)[9]

Secondly, the concept of expropriation must necessarily be defined as something less extensive than 'unlawful harm caused by the government'. Otherwise, we would over-expand expropriations to the point of being virtually equal to 'state liability for injuries to investors'. In reality, expropriation represents only one of the existing causes of action for obtaining damages; treaties also include other standards such as fair and equitable treatment (FET), full protection and security (FPS), and national treatment (NT), among others.

Concerning the separation of these different causes of action of state liability for injuries to investors, there is a long tradition in international law—and accepted in the BIT generation—of reserving the concept of expropriation for cases dealing with full or substantial deprivations of

establishing the breach of an international obligation. Accordingly, on the basis of its conclusions with regard to Sea-Land's assertion of expropriation, the Tribunal does not consider that any benefit can be derived in this case from reliance on the provisions of the Treaty'. (emphasis added)

Explaining the Iran–US Claims Tribunals, Matti Pellonpää, 'Compensable Claims Before the Tribunal: Expropriation Claims' in Richard B Lillich and Daniel Barstow Magraw (eds), *The Iran–United States Claims Tribunal: Its Contribution to the Law of State Responsibility* (Irvington-on-Hudson, Transnational Publishers, 1998) 185, 187, expresses a similar opinion: 'In many cases the Treaty of Amity between Iran and the United States has been regarded as the *lex specialis* to be followed. Nevertheless, as regards the questions of expropriation at issue here, there is no indication that the Tribunal conceives the Treaty standards to differ from standards of customary international law. Rather, there is positive proof to the contrary, in that the Tribunal has emphasized, for example, that the Treaty does not add anything to the general rules of international law insofar as concerns the concept of a taking'.

[8] See Coe and Rubins, n 3, 601, who make this precise observation: '[r]ather than setting forth a definition for "expropriation," investment protection treaties leave the specific contours of the concept (like many others) to customary international law'.

[9] *Saluka Investments BV v Czech Republic*, UNCITRAL Ad Hoc Arbitration (Watts, Fortier, Behrens), Partial Award (17 March 2006), ¶ 261 (hereinafter, *Saluka*). See also, *LG&E Energy Corp et al v Argentina*, ICSID Case No ARB/02/01 (de Maekelt, Rezek, van den Berg), Decision on Liability (3 October 2006), ¶ 185 (hereinafter, *LGandE*). Several commentators share this idea: see Campbell McLachlan et al, *International Investment Arbitration. Substantive Principles* (New York, OUP, 2007) 286; Rudolf Dolzer, 'The Impact of International Investment Treaties on Domestic Administrative Law' (2005) 37 *New York University Journal of International Law and Politics* 953, 958; and, Barry Appleton, 'Regulatory Takings: The International Law Perspective' (2002) 11 *New York University Environmental Law Journal* 35, 40. Moreover, recent US BITs and FTAs make this point explicit; indeed, the *2004 US Model BIT*, 'Annex B Expropriations,' at 38 (available at www.state.gov/documents/organization/117601.pdf) (hereinafter, *2004 US Model BIT*), states that '[t]he Parties confirm their shared understanding that: 1. Article 6 [expropriation clause] (1) is intended to reflect customary international law concerning the obligation of States with respect to expropriation'. See also, *United States-Chile Free Trade Agreement* (Chile–US) (6 June 2003) (available at www.ustr.gov/Trade_Agreements/Bilateral/Chile_FTA/Section_Index.html) (hereinafter, *US–Chile FTA*); and, *United States–Singapore Free Trade Agreement* (Singapore–US) (6 May 2003) (available at www.ustr.gov/Trade_Agreements/Bilateral/Singapore_FTA/Section_Index.html) (hereinafter, *US-Singapore FTA*).

property rights.[10] This permits us to follow a rule of thumb: in principle, if destruction of property rights occurs, this lies within the jurisdiction of the expropriation clause, and compensation must be paid. By contrast, non-destructive harm, which usually falls under the scope of other investment treaty clauses—mainly the FET standard—requires the adjudicator to focus on the arbitrary character of the state action.[11] Yet, however simple this distinction may look in the abstract, the exercise of identifying full or substantial deprivations turns out to be fraught with difficulty.

The third reason concerns the nature and function of indirect takings. It is generally said that 'indirect takings' demarcates the line separating regulation from expropriation.[12] For example, some commentators find it necessary to draw 'the dividing line between legitimate regulation and compensable indirect expropriation,'[13] or 'the line between, on the one hand, legitimate regulatory measures imposed by governments on foreign business and, on the other hand, illegitimate interference with the rights and interests of foreign investors'.[14]

Still, this is not entirely precise. The line we are really trying to draw—which continues to be a highly complicated task—divides regulation that effects a taking from regulation that does not. This means that the determination of this boundary is not an *ontological* enterprise, but a more pragmatic one: it is simply the *ex-post* effects of regulation on one or more investors, that causes it to be expropriatory; and it is not expropriatory per se, but only with respect to that or those investors.

A key obstacle in this regard stems from the fact that regulations causing deprivation to one or more investors may be *ex-ante* legitimate. In most cases, when the government labels a measure as regulation, and that measure ends up amounting to an expropriation, it means that the government did not properly assess the regulatory benefits and burdens and

[10] As noted in ch 4, 179–181, international law has followed a conceptual division that matches expropriations with destructive harm. Interferences that do not amount to deprivations are left to the scope of clauses worded in terms such as 'measure affecting property rights' (Iran–US Claims Settlement Agreements) and 'peaceful enjoyment of his possessions' and 'use of property in accordance with the general interest' (European Convention on Human Rights). See *The Declaration of the Government of the Democratic and Popular Republic of Algeria concerning the Settlement of Claims by the Government of the United States of America and the Government of the Islamic Republic of Iran*, reprinted in (1981) 75 *American Journal of International Law* 422, 423; and *Convention for the Protection of Human Rights and Fundamental Freedoms*, 4 November 1950, 213 UNTS 221, 223, and Protocol [No 1] to the Convention for the Protection of Human Rights and Fundamental Freedoms, 20 March 1952, 213 UNTS 262.

[11] See Vaughan Lowe, 'Regulation or Expropriation' (2002) 55 *Current Legal Problems* 447, 459. For full quotation, see n 86.

[12] See *Link-Trading* ¶ 8 (noting that 'commentators on the subject of "indirect expropriations" have noted how difficult is to draw the line between non-confiscatory regulation and indirect expropriation').

[13] Jan Paulsson and Zachary Douglas, 'Indirect Expropriation in Investment Treaty Arbitrations' in Norbert Horn and Stefan Kröll (eds), *Arbitrating Foreign Investment Disputes* (The Hague, Kluwer Law International, 2004) 145, 145.

[14] Lowe, n 11, 447. See also, *Saluka* ¶ 264.

their allocation among citizens and investors. It is only in rare instances that governments purposely deprive investments under the guise of regulation with the purpose of not paying compensation, and those cases, in contrast, represent actual instances of direct expropriations.

The clarification of these three aspects of indirect expropriation provides us with a starting point for this chapter, by placing the role of indirect takings within the larger scheme of state liability. Not all possible harms caused by state action or inaction, are compensable. And, even among compensable harms, expropriation is not always the proper cause of action. At the same time, regulation—a category in which I include acts and omissions emanating from all branches of the regulatory state—can be the source of compensable full and substantial deprivations, even when the state is pursuing a legitimate public interest.

The main objective of this chapter is to understand expropriations as they function in the BIT generation. Although doctrines and legal analysis alone cannot resolve political and philosophical disputes, they can help us to pinpoint and articulate the precise nature and scope of our disagreements. In addition, it attempts to assess how intensively investment treaty tribunals are protecting, and should protect, foreign investors in the specific case of complete or substantial deprivations.

This chapter proceeds as follows. Section I begins the analysis from a fairly obvious assumption: in order to determine the existence of an expropriation, the decision-maker must first establish that an investment exists. Investments and expropriations form a symbiotic relationship, very much resembling the one between property rights and expropriations in domestic constitutional law. In addition, this section explores the idea that the investment treaty arbitration regime constitutes a form of Global Constitutional Law (GCL). The core of investments, as with the core of property rights, *in principle* cannot be sacrificed when pursuing the public interest. Investments, thus, impose a new limit on the state's police powers, which derives from international law. The standards adopted by investment treaty tribunals for these purposes may be more protective of investments than those in domestic constitutional law. If that is the case, then—at the global level—BIT jurisprudence will be redefining the limits of what governments and people can decide and implement in their own territory.

Section II scrutinises the *rule of thumb* for expropriation in the BIT generation: complete or substantial deprivations of investments that demand the payment of compensation. This first step in the analysis—which attempts to avoid any complex balancing process—is fairly simple. Beyond that, however, two unexpected challenges are encountered: first, the definition of what constitutes the threshold for 'substantial'; and second, the determination of the proper unit of reference to be used when assessing full or substantial deprivations (the 'denominator problem').

Section III examines the potential *exceptions* and *counter-exceptions* that full and substantial deprivations may encounter before they can be legally qualified as compensable expropriations. Ultimately, the goal is to determine whether there are total or substantial deprivations that fail to meet the criteria for compensable expropriations in the BIT generation.

This section suggests that we should use a *three-step reasoning test* when analysing compensable expropriations.[15] The three steps are: first, the general rule stated earlier which defines the prima facie case as total or substantial deprivations; second, the *exceptions*, which refer to those situations in which the state, recognising that it has deprived the owner, can still successfully defend itself based on the application of domestic law, or the invocation of *pre-eminent* public interests; and, third, the *counter-exceptions*, which include those claims by investors that the exceptions of step two were improperly and arbitrarily applied in their particular case.

The conclusions provide a general assessment of the current state of BIT jurisprudence on the issue of indirect expropriations. In contrast to other, more alarmist voices, I consider the overall picture to show neither a radical nor abusive application of the expropriation clause. As used today, the expropriation clause is indeed a very moderate instrument of protection for investors against state measures. However, there is one other source of serious concern: the ad hoc manner in which the expropriation clause tends to be applied, which makes the adjudication process highly uncertain, unpredictable, and overy dependent upon the personal biases of individual arbitrators.

I INVESTMENTS AND INDIRECT EXPROPRIATIONS AS GLOBAL CONSTITUTIONAL LAW: NEW LIMITS FOR STATES' POLICE POWERS

This section proceeds from an idea previously explored in the First Part of this work: international investment law as Global Constitutional Law. It analyses the symbiotic relationship that exists, conceptually speaking, between investments and expropriations. Then, it touches upon the respective roles of domestic and international law in determining whether an investment was taken, defending the thesis that investments shouldbe conceived according to a 'patterning definition' approach.[16]

[15] Paulson and Douglas, n 13, 148, have previously identified a two-step analysis for finding indirect expropriations. Although I agree with them in essence, two important observations must be added: first, as I will try to prove in this chapter, the analysis is not two-step, but three-step; second, it is better to think of this analysis as comprising the prima facie case of expropriation (step one), followed by the 'exceptions' (step two), and then the 'counter-exceptions' (step three).

[16] The term was coined by Thomas W Merrill, 'The Landscape of Constitutional Property' (2000) 86 *Virginia Law Review* 885, 927.

Finally, it proposes a residual substantive role for the concept of investments.

A The Investment—Expropriation Relationship in Investment Treaties as a Global Constitutional Law Problem

As noted earlier in this work, few commentators appear to be have noticed the 'constitutional' character of the BIT generation.[17] Wälde and Kolo, referring to multilateral investment treaties, point out that 'one can view such international treaties as steps towards a proto-constitutional order of the global economy'.[18] Yet, given the network effects that characterise the BIT system,[19] the situation is not very different from multilateral treaties in this respect. The BIT network possesses the same proto-constitutional character that would, in theory, be present in a multilateral treaty.

I have already provided several reasons demonstrating why investment treaties can generally be characterised as GCL.[20] Those reasons apply with particular force to the principle of no expropriation without compensation. The obligation to pay compensation for the deprivation of investments constitutes a limit to states' police powers within their own territory. When applying the expropriation clause, arbitral tribunals limit the range of policy choices that would otherwise be open to states' collective decisionmaking processes.[21]

The concept of expropriation is a GCL matter, not because expropriation norms typically appear *printed* in many constitutions at the domestic level (which, certainly, could serve as evidence in this regard). It is such a matter because it constitutes an external redefinition of the proper relationship between property rights and regulatory powers. If we substitute the phrase 'individual's fundamental rights' for 'investor's investment', the mission identified by the European Court of Human Rights (ECHR) is

[17] See David Schneiderman, *Constitutionalizing Economic Globalization. Investment Rules and Democracy's Promise* (New York, CUP, 2008) 3 (commenting that 'the investment rules regime can be seen as disciplining and reshaping the constitutional law of various states across the globe'). See also, Vicki Been and Joel C Beauvais, 'The Global Fifth Amendment? NAFTA's Investment Protections and the Misguided Quest for an International "Regulatory Takings" Doctrine' (2003) 78 *New York University Law Review* 30, 120; and, Horacio A Grigera Naón, 'Arbitration in Latin America: Progress and Setbacks' (2005) 21 *Arbitration International* 127, 172.

[18] Thomas Wälde and Abba Kolo, 'Environmental Regulation, Investment Protection and "Regulatory Taking" in International Law' (2001) 50 ICLQ 811, 814.

[19] See ch 2, 96–115.

[20] See Introduction, pp 12–17.

[21] See more generally, Gus Van Harten, *Investment Treaty Arbitration and Public Law* (New York, OUP, 2007) 10 (observing that investment treaty arbitration, as a form of public law adjudication, 'uses rules and structures of international law and private arbitration to make governmental choices regarding the regulatory relationship between individuals and the state').

fully applicable to investment treaty tribunals: They 'must determine whether a fair balance was struck between the demands of the general interest of the community and the requirements of the protection of the individual's fundamental rights'.[22] Arbitral tribunals have already expressly recognised this reality.[23]

The precise GCL-character of the principle of no expropriation without compensation can be grasped through the lenses of corrective and distributive justice.[24] The corrective justice rationale covers situations in which the government appropriates investments in pursuit of their economic value (and because of it). Here, we are within the realm of corrective justice because we generally accept that property confers the right to reject appropriations attempted by citizens, and also by the state.[25]

Sax proposed an earlier classification that should be revisited to help us understand the corrective and distributive justice rationales. Although he was trying to separate compensable and non-compensable deprivation[26]—a division that certainly should not be accepted in the BIT generation—he made the valid distinction between the government acting 'as an enterprise', and the government mediating the different conflicts existing between private claims.[27] The former category—identified here with the corrective justice rationale—refers to those cases in which the government functions 'as a participant in the competition for the use of various

[22] *Sporrong and Lönnroth v Sweden* (Apps no. 7151/75 and 7152/75) (1983) 5 EHRR 35 ¶ 69 (hereinafter, *Sporrong*).

[23] See *LG&E* ¶ 189 ('In order to establish whether State measures constitute expropriation under Art IV(1) of the Bilateral Treaty, the Tribunal must balance two competing interests: the degree of the measure's interference with the right of ownership and the power of the State to adopt its policies').

[24] See eg *Continental Casualty Co v Argentina*, ICSID Case No ARB/03/9 (Sacerdoti, Veeder, Nader), Award (5 September 2008), ¶ 276 (hereinafter, *Continental Casualty*), which, in principle, follows a classification that—as I read it—does not seem very different from the corrective/distributive justice division I use in this chapter: '[There are] two types of encroachments by public authorities on private property: (i) On the one hand, there are certain types of measures or state conduct that are considered a form of expropriation because of their material impact on property . . . (ii) On the other hand, there are limitations to the use of property in the public interest that fall within typical government regulations of property entailing mostly inevitable limitations imposed in order to ensure the rights of others or of the general public (being ultimately beneficial also to the property affected) . . . These restrictions [the latter] are not therefore considered a form of expropriation and do not require indemnification, provided however that they do not affect property in an intolerable, discriminatory or disproportionate manner'.

[25] As Ernest J Weinrib, *The Idea of Private Law* (Harvard, Cambridge, Mass, CUP, 1995) 78, remarks, '[c]orrective justice presupposes the existence of entitlements, which, presumably, are the creation not of corrective justice itself but of distributive justice'. So, as discussed above, we accept that property, as a matter of entitlements, includes the right of protection against state's appropriation.

[26] The original purpose that Joseph Sax had in mind when developing this division was to distinguish compensable and non-compensable takings. See Joseph Sax, 'Takings and the Police Powers' (1964) 74 *Yale Law Journal* 36.

[27] See Sax, n 28, 150.

resources'[28]:

> Government as enterpriser operates in a host of areas, requiring money, equipment and real estate. It maintains an army which must be fed and clothed and supplied; it builds and maintains bridges and roads and buildings, and for these it must have land and other economic resources; it operates schools and offices and must have money to staff and equip them . . . [T]he concept of government in its enterprise capacity as used here describes the economic function of providing for and maintaining the material plant, whether that be the state capitol or a retail liquor store. In this capacity, government must acquire economic resources, which, by one means or another, it must get from the citizenry. It is to be noted that in the performance of this enterprise capacity, government is very much like those who function in the private sector of the economy, and indeed is in its resource-acquiring job a competitor with private enterprisers; it is a consumer of land, machines, clothing, and the like.[29]

The protection of investments under the corrective justice rationale—which largely corresponds to the category of 'direct expropriations'—has deep historical roots. As indicated, most constitutional and private law traditions have long recognised a degree of corrective-justice 'strength' in the concept of property rights. Property rights—or, at the international law level, investments[30]—behave as a rule-of-liability against the government: when acting as an enterprise, the state must pay for the citizens' properties/investments if a public interest requires their appropriation.

The millenary wisdom behind the corrective justice rationale is straightforward. Because there is no operative way of knowing what the public interest is or whether it is present in each instance, we cannot treat the use of the eminent domain the way we do with other natural risks, which fall under the burden of each individual owner. Moreover, we do not wish to empower judges or arbitrators with such a function, except in very limited instances (that is, egregiously manifest cases). Therefore, we simply assume a priori that it is *wrong* for the government to appropriate the full value of property rights or investments, and not pay for them.[31]

By contrast, the distributive justice rationale for protecting property rights and investments—that is, the anti-redistributive strength of such property rights and investments—is more problematic from a constitutional perspective. Here, following Sax, the state pursues the public interest by mediating 'the disputes of various citizens and groups within

[28] Joseph Sax, 'Takings, Private Property and Public Rights' (1971) 81 *Yale Law Journal* 149, 150.

[29] Sax, n 26, 62.

[30] International investment law protects 'investments' as defined in treaties. The relationship between property rights and interests in domestic law, and investments in international law, is explained below through the concept of 'patterning'. See Section I B, 243–251.

[31] According to Jules Coleman, *Risks and Wrongs* (New York, OUP, 1993) 329, '[t]here are two essential components in the concept of corrective justice. These are wrongfulness and responsibility. Only wrongful losses fall within the ambit of corrective justice'.

the society . . . [and resolving] conflict among competing and conflicting alternatives'.[32] So, if no appropriation is involved, should compensation be paid if property is fully or substantially destroyed?

This is the main issue in 'indirect expropriation', which more or less corresponds to the distributive justice dimension of the protection of property and investments: the environment should be preserved, thus the investor's polluting plant must be shut down. The investor's chicken industry endangers the public health, so the state health agency commands the killing of those birds and halting of further production. New, more stringent and more rational banking and financial regulation is necessary, and maybe one or more investors will be unable to operate profitably under the new rules. There are thousands of similar examples, and in all of them the overriding question is the same: is the investor entitled to claim compensation?

From our earlier review of constitutional law traditions, we know that property rights, almost everywhere, possess anti-redistributive strength. As explained in chapter 4, *in principle*—while subject to several exceptions and distinctions—property rights *at their core* can be sacrificed when pursuing the public interest only after compensation is paid. This means, in essence, that the same reasons justifying compensation under the corrective justice rationale are extended to the realm of distributive justice. The pervasive uncertainty surrounding any effort to determine the public interest justifies a simple approach, according to which, if property is fully or substantially destroyed, compensation must be paid.[33]

However, not all commentators agree that the concept of investment should carry this anti-redistributive function in international investment law. From a GCL perspective, as indicated, the distributive justice rationale is considerably more complicated than the traditional corrective justice rationale. For instance, Newcombe has expressly argued against the former's use in the application of expropriation clauses. In his opinion, 'the role of international expropriation law is to provide a minimum standard of protection to foreign investors against expropriatory measures. It need not, and should not, attempt to find the optimal balance between state interests and property protection'.[34]

In my own view, that position may excessively constrict the natural

[32] Sax, n 26, 62.

[33] Wälde and Kolo, n 18, 826, provide a 'public choice' justification of this rule that is not equivalent to the explanation I rely upon: 'The duty to pay compensation because of a finding of "regulatory taking" is here part of the normal function of a constitutional guarantee: to protect the minority's right against the majority, to make the majority pause and consider the cost of its action—rather than shift the cost to the minority. This applies particularly so where there is often no well-reflected and supported action by a true majority, but rather the capturing of the government machinery by well-organised interest groups. The constitutional (or treaty-based) duty to pay compensation means that the cost of such capture of the machinery of government should be made transparent'.

[34] Andrew Newcombe, 'The Boundaries of Regulatory Expropriation in International Law' (2005) 20 *ICSID Review—Foreign Investment Law Journal* 1, 7. As he further explains, ibid

scope of indirect expropriation and denies the GCL-dimension of expropriations in the BIT generation. If any public interest invoked by the regulatory state can successfully trump the core of investments, then protection under investment treaties will be useless, leaving foreign investors unprotected. Moreover, as a matter of treaty interpretation, we need to take into account the traditional legal meaning of the terms in question. By using the words *investments* and *expropriations,* parties signing investment treaties explicitly recognise—as in municipal law—that these concepts include a distributive justice component. As Michelman reminds us, 'we primarily understand property in its constitutional sense as an anti-redistributive principle, opposed to governmental interventions into the extant regime of holdings for the sake of distributive ends'.[35] Therefore, we cannot claim that that the concept of investment has no anti-redistributive strength.

The question is really one of degree. This is evident when we examine the main traditions of constitutional law. Note that, by invoking the word *expropriation* without defining it, and given the thinnes of customary international law in this regard,[36] investment treaties force us to have recourse to comparative law. As claimed ealier in this work—as a matter of treaty interpretation—investment treaties cannot end up recognising a higher level of protection of investments at their core than that usually accepted in most developed countries. Mann put forth this idea long ago:

> No state can be fixed with responsibility for expropriation unless the act complained of can fairly be said to involve the taking of property within the meaning attributed to that conception by the general principles of law recognized by civilized nations. These principles cannot be ascertained otherwise than by comparative law . . . This point requires emphasis. It is unfortunate that no international lawyer discussing expropriation, confiscation or nationalization has as yet to any appreciable extent investigated the municipal law on such

54–57, international investment law should only require the payment of compensation in three situations, which, as I undestand his argument, seems to fall under the corrective justice rationale: '(i) direct or indirect appropriations; (ii) arbitrary deprivations that cannot be justified by the exercise of state police powers to protect public order, morals, human health or the environment; and (iii) abrogation or destruction of contractual commitments or authorizations upon which an investor has relied'.

[35] Frank I Michelman, 'Possession vs. Distribution in the Constitutional Ideal of Property' (1987) 72 *Iowa Law Review* 1319, 1319.

[36] The history of international law, and in particular the precedents of claims commissions, is of small value when controlling the regulatory state in the BIT generation, since these precedents were almost exclusively occupied with the corrective justice dimension of takings. It is remarkable that, in 1983, in her influential study of expropriations, Rosalyn Higgins, 'The Taking of Property by the State: Recent Developments in International Law' in Académie de Droit International, 176 *Recueil des Cours. Collected Courses of the Hague Academy of International Law, 1982-III* (The Hague, M Nijhoff, 1983) 259, 269, observed that the question, 'do interventions by the State that leave title untouched in the hands of plaintiff, but nonetheless occasion him loss, give rise to a right of compensation?' was a 'somewhat newer theme'.

> fundamental matters as the conception of property, the conception of taking, the ambit of the duty to compensate and so forth. This is the principal reason why most studies of the international law relating to the taking of property are so unsatisfactory.[37]

Summarising the architecture laid out in chapter 4, investment treaties' recognition of the protection of investments against indirect expropriations can be defined and measured along the following five *doctrinal* comparative dimensions: first, whether the concept of taking is circumscribed to full and substantial deprivations, or, conversely, whether it is extended to lesser interferences; second, how to draw the line distinguishing substantial deprivations from mere interferences when the latter are excluded from the scope of expropriations; third, how to resolve the denominator problem, that is, how to determine the unit of reference of the fraction to be used when finding a total or substantial deprivation; fourth, whether the invocation of pre-eminent public interests, as well as the termination of rights in accordance with the rules, is allowed under the category of acceptable deprivations without compensation; and, fifth, how intensive the review of rationality and proportionality should be.

Investment treaties themselves do not themselves provide answers to any of these doctrinal questions.[38] Although the treaties define with certainty what *investments* are, the five questions are essentially left open to jurisprudential development. Investment treaties are 'incomplete contracts', in which treaty negotiators and drafters deliberately avoided confronting the difficulties posed by takings and the regulatory state. They instead preferred to use broad clauses, delegating arbitral panels the task of making them more specific.[39]

Investment treaty tribunals, in answering these five doctrinal questions, thus redefine the relationship between property rights and the public interest, effectively determining new limits for state police powers within the state's territory. Because *investments*—as defined in investment treaties—do possess a variable and uncertain degree of anti-redistributive strength, arbitral tribunals must control the equilibrium between property rights and the public interests that governments have chosen when assessing indirect expropriations. In this way, international investment tribunals are charged with the mission of developing GCL.

[37] Francis A Mann, 'State Contracts and State Responsibility' (1960) 54 *American Journal of International Law* 572, 583 and fn 51.

[38] In the context of NAFTA, see *Feldman* ¶ 98, where the Tribunal stated that 'the Article 1110 language is of such generality as to be difficult to apply in specific cases'.

[39] See Joel P Trachtman, 'The Domain of WTO Dispute Resolution' (1999) 40 *Harvard International Law Journal* 333, 346 ff. See Daniel M Price, 'Chapter 11—Private Party vs, Government, Investor-State Dispute Settlement: Frankenstein or Safety Valve?' (2000) 26 *Canada–United States Law Journal* 107, 111–12 (for full citation, see ch 3, n 169).

B A 'Patterning Definition' Approach to the Concept of Investment

This section defends a 'patterning definition' approach to the concept of investment. First, it analyses the problem of circularity that was previously identified in chapter 4—ie, that property rights are limits to the state's powers, yet are determined by the state itself—in the context of general international law. Then, it argues that the concept of investment found in investment treaties do not overcome this problem of circularity. Consequently, as explained here, a 'patterning definition' approach represents the best understanding of the concept of investment: treaties determine which 'patterns' deserve protection—as opposed to others that do not rise to the level of investment, such as rights arising from mere trade relations—but then, municipal law determines, *in concreto*, whether the claimant possesses an interest which satisfies the pattern's criteria.[40]

To begin, we must recall the problem of circularity explored in chapter 4.[41] To find an expropriation in international law, the existence of an entitlement must first be demonstrated. As the German Constitutional Court has expressed—an observation that can certainly be generalised—'[t]he examination of whether a legal event has to be characterised as expropriation initially requires the determination of whether or not the individual concerned, at the time of the encroachment [of his property], had a legal position that was susceptible to an expropriation'.[42]

Given this symbiotic relation between expropriations and entitlements, the problem of circularity arises because property rights set a limit on state's powers that is nevertheless defined by the state itself. As observed, we can only *partially* escape this circularity through recourse to the concept of acquired or vested rights (*iura quaesita*). Property rights, as a fundamental right, protect the core *of what has been acquired by the owner*. The anti-redistributive strength of property rights exerts its power only where

[40] I am literally following Merrill, n 16, 893, according to whom, in US constitutional law, the relationship between constitutional law and state property law should proceed along to the following lines: 'Under this strategy [the patterning definition approach], courts would proceed in two steps. First, they would identify, as a matter of federal constitutional law, general criteria that distinguish constitutional property from other interests or expectancies that do not rise to the level of property. Second, they would canvas sources of nonconstitutional law (most prominently but not exclusively state law) to determine whether the claimant has a legally recognized interest that satisfies these criteria and hence constitutes constitutional property'. See also, ibid 927: 'Federal constitutional law precribes the set of criteria an interest must have to qualify as property; whether the claimant has an interest that fits the pattern is then determined by examining independent sources such as state law'.

[41] See ch 4, 168–177.

[42] The *Gravel* Decision, BVerGe 58, 300, 336–38 (1981), cited by Sabine Michalowski and Lorna Woods, *German Constitutional Law. The Protection of Civil Liberties* (Brookfield, Ashgate/Dartmouth, 1999) 326. See also, Otto Kimminich, 'La Propiedad en la Constitución Alemana' in Javier Barnés (ed), *Propiedad, Expropiación y Responsabilidad. Derecho Comparado Europeo* (Madrid, Tecnos, 1995) 151, 163.

the majority intends to sacrifice what *actual legal rules and principles* recognise as the core of *acquired property*.

We should be aware that general international law does not overcome this problem of circularity.[43] On the one hand, general international law does not provide the decision-maker with a substantive body of rules that defines rights, their nature, extent and characteristics. As the PCIJ held in the *Panevezys-Saldutiskis* case, 'in principle, the property rights and the contractual rights of individuals depend in every State on municipal law';[44] or, as explained by the *Restatement (Second) of Foreign Relations Law*, '[r]ights of ownership in property located in the territory of a state are normally determined by the law of the state'.[45] On the other hand, the reliance of international law on the concept of acquired rights should not be exaggerated, because it only represents a partial solution.[46]

The relevance of domestic law in international adjudication concerning the definition and content of rights and interests—and therefore, the emergence of the problem of circularity discussed here—was brilliantly exposed by Judge Morelli in his separate opinion in the *Barcelona Traction*

[43] Exceptionally, and theoretically, there may be cases in which domestic rules define interests in so egregiously and arbitrary a way as to constitute a breach to public international law principles. The ECHR seems to have pointed out this exception in *Pressos Compania Naviera SA and Others v Belgium* (App no 17849/91) (1996) 21 EHRR 301 ¶ 31. See also Claire Weir and Richard Moules, 'Article 1 of Protocol No 1: Protection of Property' in Jessica Simor and Ben Emmerson, *Human Rights Practice* (rev 13 February 2007) (London, Sweet and Maxwell, 2008) ch 15, 15.005: 'For a claim to constitute a 'possession' within the meaning of Art 1 of Prot No 1, the applicant must be able to show a legal entitlement to the economic benefit at issue, or a legitimate exectation that the entitlement will materialise. *In most cases, this involves establishing an entitlement in domestic law, unless that law runs counter to the object and purpose of Art 1 of Prot. No 1*'. (emphasis added)

[44] *Panevezys-Saldutiskis Railway* (*Estonia v Lithuania*) [1939] PCIJ Rep Ser A/B No 76, 4, 18. See also, *Aguilar-Armory and Royal Bank of Canada Claims* (UK v Costa Rica) (1923) 1 RIAA 369, 399 (available at www.un.org/law/riaa/), where the Arbitrator—former President and US Supreme Court Chief Justice, William H Tafts—concluded that the invalidation of a contract in accordance with domestic law was not an internationally wrongful act (in this case, ibid 372, the applicable law was 'Agreements, [and] the principles of Public and International Law'): 'My award further is that the Law of Nullities in decreeing the invalidity of the Amory concession worked no injury to the Central Costa Rica Petroleum Company, Ltd., the assignee of the concession, and the British Controlled Oil Fields, Ltd., its sole stockholder, of which Great Britain can complain, *because the concession was in fact invalid under the Constitution of 1917*'. (emphasis added). For a traditional analysis of *ultra vires* contracts, see Theodor Meron, 'Repudiation of *Ultra Vires* State Contracts and the International Responsibility of States' (1957) 6 ILQ 273.

[45] *Restatement of the Law, Second: Foreign Relations Law of the United States, as Adopted and Promulgated by the American Law Institute, 26 May 1962* (St Paul, MN, American Law Institute, 1965) § 185, Comment (f).

[46] In his study of breaches of contracts and international law, RY Jennings, 'State Contracts in International Law' (1961) 37 BYIL 156, 174, remarks that: '[T]he principle of acquired rights provides an instructive way of asking the question which rights international law will protect, because it expresses so well the nature of that link between international law and municipal law which is at the heart of the problem that arises wherever a right, initially created and subsisting within municipal law, is protected by international law'.

case. According to the Italian Judge, the protection of international law applies 'to rights as conferred by the municipal legal order'.[47] In other words, '[i]t is on the hypothesis that the municipal order has adopted this attitude, optional in international law [i.e., creation of rights], that the international rule imposes certain obligations on the State'.[48] In his opinion,

> [T]he international rules of which I now speak refer to that same legal order for the purpose of performing a preliminary task, that of determining what interests are to be the subject of the protection envisaged. This is so in that the international rule postulates a certain attitude on the part of the State legal order, inasmuch as it has regard solely to interests which, within that legal order, have already received some degree of protection through the attribution of rights or other advantageous personal legal situations (faculties, legal powers or expectations): an attitude on the part of the State legal order which in itself is not obligatory in international law.[49] . . . [T]he fact that the rules of international law in question envisage solely such interests of foreigners as already constitute rights in the municipal order is but the necessary consequence of the very content of the obligations imposed by those rules; obligations which, precisely, presuppose rights conferred on foreigners by the legal order of the State in question.[50]

As Judge Morelli observed, we should not be surprised or concerned by this *renvoi* to domestic law:

> There is nothing abnormal in this reference of an international rule to the law of a given State. It is wholly untenable to object, as the Belgian Government has done, that in this way the international responsibility of the State is made to depend upon categories of municipal law, thus enabling a State to set up the provisions of its own legal order as a means of evading the international consequences of its acts. In reality, no subordination of international responsibility, as such, to the provisions of municipal law is involved; *the point is rather that the very existence of the international obligation depends on a state of affairs created in municipal law, though this is so not by virtue of municipal law but, on the contrary, by virtue of the international rule itself, which to that end refers to the law of the State.* (emphasis added)[51]

So, given this 'weak' background of international law, are investment treaties' broad definitions of investments not precisely intended to escape

[47] *Barcelona Traction, Light and Power Co Ltd (Belgium v Spain)* (Second Phase) [1970] ICJ Rep 4, 234 (Judge Morelli, Separate Opinion) (hereinafter, *Barcelona Traction*). That is, international law protects aliens' interests, ibid 233–34, 'if those interests already enjoy a certain degree of protection within the municipal legal system. This means that the international rule refers to the municipal legal order in that, to impose upon a State a particular obligation, it presupposes a certain freely adopted attitude on the part of the legal order of that State'.

[48] ibid 234–35.

[49] ibid 233.

[50] ibid.

[51] ibid 234.

the use of domestic law in investment disputes?[52] The answer, as indicated before, is no. Following a 'patterning definition' approach, the reference to domestic law continues to be essential. Following Judge Morelli, and adapting Merrill's words, under this approach municipal law is consulted not to discover the definition of investments, but to determine whether the claimant possesses interests that correspond to the international law criteria for the identification of investments.[53]

At first glance, a distinction should be made between treaties that refer to municipal law—typically, through an 'in accordance with domestic law' clause—and those that do not.[54] If investment treaties contain such a

[52] Certainly, tribunals and commentators have noted the 'broad' nature of the definition of investments. See *Occidental Exploration and Production Co*, LCIA Case No UN3467 (Orrego, Brower, Barrera), Award (1 July 2004), ¶ 85 ('It is also noticeable that bilateral investment treaties contain broad definitions of investments that can encompass many kinds of assets'). (hereinafter, *OEPC*); *Fedax NV v Venezuela*, ICSID Case No ARB/96/3 (Orrego, Heth, Owen), Decision on Jurisdiction (11 July 1997), ¶ 32 ('This definition evidences that the Contracting Parties to the Agreement intended a very broad meaning for the term "investment" '); and, L Yves Fortier and Stephen L Drymer, 'Indirect Expropriation in the Law of International Investment: I Know It When I See It, or Caveat Investor' (2004) 19 *ICSID Review–Foreign Investment Law Journal* 293, 296 fn 9.

[53] See Merrill, n 16, 952 (stating that, in the 'patterning definition' approach, 'state law is consulted not to discover the definition of property; it is reviewed to determine if interests have been created that corresponds to the federal criteria for the identification of constitutional property').

[54] Compare, for example, Art 1139 of NAFTA, and Article 1(1)-(2) of the *Agreement concerning the promotion and reciprocal protection of investments* (Chile–Denmark) (28 May 1993) 1935 UNTS 247. The former establishes the following: 'Investment means: (a) an enterprise; (b) an equity security of an enterprise; (c) a debt security of an enterprise (i) where the enterprise is an affiliate of the investor, or (ii) where the original maturity of the debt security is at least three years, but does not include a debt security, regardless of original maturity, of a state enterprise; (d) a loan to an enterprise (i) where the enterprise is an affiliate of the investor, or (ii) where the original maturity of the loan is at least three years, but does not include a loan, regardless of original maturity, to a state enterprise; (e) an interest in an enterprise that entitles the owner to share in income or profits of the enterprise; (f) an interest in an enterprise that entitles the owner to share in the assets of that enterprise on dissolution, other than a debt security or a loan excluded from subparagraph (c) or (d); (g) real estate or other property, tangible or intangible, acquired in the expectation or used for the purpose of economic benefit or other business purposes; and (h) interests arising from the commitment of capital or other resources in the territory of a Party to economic activity in such territory, such as under (i) contracts involving the presence of an investor's property in the territory of the Party, including turnkey or construction contracts, or concessions, or (ii) contracts where remuneration depends substantially on the production, revenues or profits of an enterprise'.

The latter establishes that: '(1) "Investment" means every kind of asset irrespective of the legal form provided that the investment has been made *in accordance with the laws and regulations of that Contracting Party* and shall include in particular, but not exclusively: (a) shares, parts or any other firm of participation in companies, (b) returns, reinvested, debentures, claims to money or any performance having an economic value, (c) movable and immovable property, as well as any other rights such as mortgages, liens, pledges, privileges and guarantees, (d) industrial and intellectual property rights, including copyrights, patents, trade names, technology, trade marks, goodwill, know-how and any other similar rights, (e) concessions conferred by law or under contract, including concessions to search for, extract or exploit natural resources. (2) "Returns" means the amounts yielded by an investment and in particular though not exclusively, includes profit, interest, capital gains, dividends, royalties

clause, then the *renvoi* to municipal law is beyond doubt.[55] The investment, in order to receive the protection of the treaty, must have been conducted according to the laws of the host state. A different question, however, is whether the issue should be treated as a jurisdictional matter (as has generally been the case[56]). A literal interpretation may seem to lead to that position.[57] Nevertheless, in my opinion, concluding lack of jurisdiction from domestic illegality—except under outrageous circumstances such as an overall illegality of the business scheme[58]—would result in the unjust enrichment of states, an outcome that does not mesh well with the object and purpose of investment treaties.[59]

Treating domestic illegality as an issue of merit constitutes, in my opinion, a more balanced approach.[60] In principle, deprivation of 'legal' investments

or fees. Such amounts, and in case of reinvestment amounts yielded from the reinvestment, shall be given the same protection as the investment'. (emphasis added)

[55] That was the case in *Fraport AG Frankfurt Airport Services Worldwide v Philippines*, ICSID Case No ARB/03/25 (Fortier, Reisman, Cremades), Award (16 August 2007), ¶ 394 (hereinafter, *Fraport*), and the Tribunal stated that '[t]he BIT is, to be sure, an international instrument, but its Articles 1 and 2 and ad Article 2 of the Protocol effect a *renvoi* to national law . . . A failure to comply with the national law to which a treaty refers will have an international legal effect'.

[56] See the following cases treating this issue as a jurisdictional matter: *Rumeli Telekom AS et.al. v Kazakhstan*, ICSID Case No ARB/05/16 (Hanotiau, Boyd, Lalonde), Award (29 July 2008), ¶ 319; *Desert Line Projects LLC v The Republic of Yemen*, ICSID Case No ARB/05/17 (Tercier, Paulsson, El-Kosheri), Award (6 February 2008), ¶ 97–123 (hereinafter, *Desert Line*); *Tokios Tokelės v Ukraine*, ICSID Case No ARB/02/18 (Mustill, Bernardini, Price), Award (26 July 2007), ¶ 97 (hereinafter, *Tokios Tokelės (Merits)*); *Fraport* ¶ 340; *Saipem SpA v Bangladesh*, ICSID Case No ARB/05/07 (Kaufmann-Kohler, Schreuer, Otton), Decision on Jurisdiction and Recommendation on Provisional Measures (21 March 2007), ¶ 79 n.11; *Mytilineos Holdings SA v The State Union of Serbia and Montenegro and the Republic of Serbia*, UNCITRAL Ad Hoc Arbitration Case (Reinisch, Koussoulis, Mitrović), Partial Award on Jurisdiction (8 September 2006), ¶¶ 147–57; *Inceysa Vallisoletana SL v El Salvador*, ICSID Case No ARB/03/26 (Oreamuno, Landy, von Wobeser), Award (2 August 2006), ¶ 203 (hereinafter, *Inceysa*); *LESI SpA et al v Algeria*, ICSID Case No ARB/05/3 (Tercier, Faurès, Gaillard), Decision on Jurisdiction (12 July 2006), ¶ 83(iii) (hereinafter, *LESI (Jurisdiction)*); *Bayindir Insaat Turizm Ticaret Ve Sanayi AŞ v Pakistan*, ICSID Case No Arb/03/29 (Kaufmann-Kohler, Berman, Böckstiegel), Decision on Jurisdiction (14 November 2005), ¶ 109; *Salini Costruttori SPA and Other v Morocco*, ICSID Case No ARB/00/4 (Briner, Cremades, Fadlallah), Decision on Jurisdiction (23 July 2001), ¶ 46.

[57] See eg *Inceysa* ¶ 203 ('[I]t is clear that the only correct interpretation of said article must be in the sense that any investment made against the laws of El Salvador is outside the protection of the Agreement and, therefore, from the competence of this Arbitral Tribunal').

[58] As was the case, eg, in *Inceysa* and *Fraport*.

[59] See eg *The General Finance Corporation* case (*US v Mexico*) (1942), cited by Meron, n 44, 282, where the United States Commission held that, notwithstanding the invalidity of the contracts, 'the Government of Mexico, under international law, must reimburse claimant to the extent that it has been unjustly enriched'.

[60] See Cremades, Disseting Opinion, *Fraport* ¶ 38, where he notes that '[a]s a matter of principle, therefore, the legality of the investor's conduct is a merit issue', and ibid ¶ 14, where he correctly observes that '[i]llegal conduct by the investor might well excuse or limit any liability of the State Party in an arbitration pursuant to the BIT, depending on the circumstances'. Note that, in *Fraport* ¶ 345, the Tribunal concluded that illegalities committed by the investor after the time of the investment's inception could also constitute a merit issue. A middle ground may be found in *Vanessa Ventures Ltd v Venezuela*, ICSID Case No ARB(AF)/04/6 (Briner, Stern, Brower), Decision on Jurisdiction (22 August 2008), ¶ 3.3.4., where the Tribunal joined the jurisdictional question to the merits.

should fall under the expropriation clause, but deprivation of 'illegal' investments under the FET standard, with a refutable presumption against liability in the latter case. This solution provides a remedy against the problem of states' unjust enrichment. Moreover, the complexities of assessing domestic illegality, and the prudential considerations that have been recently created to temper its draconian effect—see, for example, decisions demanding more than 'minor errors',[61] 'bureaucratic formalities',[62] and 'mere formalism(s)',[63] or requiring 'breach of fundamental legal principles of the host country,'[64] or conduct that is 'illegal per se'[65]—fit better with the FET standard than with the more formal jurisdictional analysis.[66]

In any case, even in those situations where the relevant treaty does not contain an 'in accordance with domestic law' clause, the concept of investment should still be understood as a 'patterning definition'. Investment treaties do not create an autonomous concept of *investments*, that is, an international notion of substantive rights and interests that does not depend on the domestic rules of property law broad sense.[67] To reiterate, under the approach defended here, treaties determine which 'patterns'—ie, investments— deserve protection, but then municipal law determines, *in concreto*, whether the claimant possesses an interest satisfying the requirements prescribed by the pattern.

Several commentators share the intuitions behind the 'patterning definition' approach. According to Dolzer, 'no one doubts, in principle, that each state has the right to set its own rules of property which the foreigner accepts when investing'.[68] Similarly, Newcombe stresses that '[w]hen foreign nationals invest in a state, they acquire rights subject to the existing domestic regulatory framework. International law looks to domestic law to determine the scope of acquired rights'.[69] Douglas—who also approves of Judge Morelli's position[70]—makes one of the strongest cases in favour of this approach:

[61] *Tokios Tokelės v Ukraine*, ICSID Case No ARB/02/18 (Weil, Bernardini, Price), Decision on Jurisdiction (29 April 2004), ¶ 86 (hereinafter, *Tokios Tokelòs (Jurisdiction)*).

[62] *Tokios Tokelės (Merits)*, ¶ 97.

[63] *Desert Line* ¶ 106.

[64] See eg *LESI (Jurisdiction)*, ¶ 83(iii); *Desert Line* ¶ 104; and, *Rumeli Telekom* ¶ 319.

[65] *Tokios Tokelės (Jurisdiction)*, ¶ 86.

[66] See the considerations that the Tribunal pointed out in *Fraport* ¶ 396.

[67] Broad sense is opposed here to property law as a right *in rem, stricto sensu*. Note that this is not new. In the past, as well, the concept of property in international law did not refer exclusively to domestic property law. See Jennings, n 46, 173, who observes that, 'there is good authority for the view that acquired rights are not confined to the notion of property in its narrowest sense, but also include rights derived from contract or concession'.

[68] Rudolf Dolzer, 'Indirect Expropriations: New Developments?' (2002) 11 *New York University Environmental Law Journal* 64, 78.

[69] Newcombe, n 34, 28.

[70] See Zachary Douglas, 'The Hybrid Foundation of Investment Treaty Arbitration' (2004) 74 British Ybk of Intl Law 151, 201 (2004) ('The statement of Judge Morelli in the *Barcelona Traction Case* is good law for the investment treaty regime').

Investment disputes are about investments, investments are about property, and property is about specific rights over things cognisable by the municipal law of the host State. Customary international law contains no substantive rules of property law. They cannot be a source of rights in property. Nor do investment treaties purport to lay down rules for acquiring rights *in rem* that are exercisable against the world at large. It is therefore the municipal law of the host state that determines whether a particular right *in rem* exists, the scope of that right, and in whom it vests. It is the investment treaty, however, that supplies the classification of an investment and thus prescribes whether the right *in rem* recognised by the municipal law is subject to the protection afforded by the investment treaty.[71]

Tribunals have also recognised the relevance of domestic law, as claimed here under the 'patterning definition' conception of investments. The decision rendered in *EnCana* represents a perfect example.[72] The Tribunal began its analysis with the premise that, for purposes of the BIT, a VAT refund was a proper investment.[73] But the decision as to whether this particular claimant—here, the EnCana Corporation's indirectly wholly owned subsidiaries—was entitled to VAT refunds in the light of the concrete facts of the case, was primarily an issue of Ecuadorian law. Even though the BIT did not contain an 'in accordance with domestic law' clause, the Tribunal correctly concluded that:

The relevant clause, Article XIII(7) of the BIT [Canada-Ecuador], provides only a tribunal exercising jurisdiction under the BIT 'shall decide the issues in dispute in accordance with this Agreement and applicable rules of international law'. *Unlike many BITs there is no express reference to the law of the host State. However for there to have been an expropriation of an investment or return (in a situation involving legal rights or claims as distinct from the seizure of physical assets) the*

[71] ibid 197–98. See also, ibid 198–99. Paulsson and Douglas, n 13, 157–58, raise the point again: '[O]ne must consider the nature and extent of the property interests of the investor as recognized by the *lex situs* (in the case of tangible property) and determine whether acts attributable to the Host State have interfered with these interests in such a manner as to constitute a taking'. Similarly, McLachlan et al, n 9, 69–70, explicitly follow Douglas on this point: 'The fact that the interpretation of BITs is governed by public international law does not exclude domestic law from consideration by investment treaty tribunals. The main role of domestic law is in defining the scope of the investment protected . . . The investments of non-State actors are creatures of private law and tribunals cannot avoid addressing issues arising under the law pursuant to which investments owe their existance in adjudicating treaty questions. It is only once a right has been created and recognized by domestic law that standards of investment protection under the treaty take over in regulating a State's behaviour towards those rights'. See also, ibid 181–83.

[72] *Encana Corporation v Ecuador*, UNCITRAL Ad Hoc Arbitration (Crawford, Grigera, Thomas), Award (3 February 2006) (hereinafter, *EnCana*).

[73] See ibid ¶¶ 180–83. Interestingly, in a sibling-case, the *OEPC* Tribunal reached the opposite conclusion on this point. See *OEPC* ¶ 86: 'The Tribunal, however, is not persuaded by the Claimant's arguments that in this case there has been an expropriation. It is not tenable to argue that there can be "no doubt that under the Treaty the Refund Claim is an investment *per se*". However broad the definition of investment might be under the Treaty it would be quite extraordinary for a company to invest in a refund claim'.

> *rights affected must exist under the law which creates them, in this case, the law of Ecuador.* The effect of the opening words of Article XII(4) [which says 'Article VIII may be applied to a taxation measure'] is to permit this Tribunal to *determine and apply the taxation law of Ecuador to the extent that it is necessary to do so in order to deal with a claim under Article VIII.* (emphasis added)[74]

In *Plama*, the Tribunal concluded that an investment obtained by fraud and misrepresentation on the part of the investor could not receive protection under the Energy Charter Treaty (ECT):

> The investment in Nova Plama was, therefore, the result of a deliberate concealment amounting to fraud, calculated to induce the Bulgarian authorities to authorize the transfer of shares to an entity that did not have the financial and managerial capacities required to resume operation of the Refinery . . . [T]he Tribunal is of the view that this behaviour is contrary to other provisions of Bulgarian law and to international law and that it, therefore, precludes the application of the protections of the ECT.[75]

The Tribunal expressly noted that the absence of language in the ECT connecting the definition of investments to domestic law did not alter the conclusion:

> Unlike a number of Bilateral Investment Treaties, the ECT does not contain a provision requiring the conformity of the Investment with a particular law. This does not mean, however, that the protections provided for by the ECT cover all kinds of investments, including those contrary to domestic or international law. . . . [T]he ECT should be interpreted in a manner consistent with the aim of encouraging respect for the rule of law. The Arbitral Tribunal concludes that the substantive protection of the ET cannot apply to investments that are made contrary to law.[76]

In *Kardassopoulos*, the Tribunal adopted a middle ground, whereby illegalities committed by the investor—but not those committed by the State—were relevant to determining whether to deny treaty protection.[77] The Tribunal noted that municipal law was relevant, even if there was no explicit reference to such a law in the relevant treaties:

> There is no doubt that a choice of international law by the Parties either in conjunction with a national law or on its own is valid and has to be respected by our

[74] *EnCana* ¶ 184.

[75] *Plama Consortium Ltd* v *Bulgaria*, ICSID Case No ARB/03/24 (Salans, van den Berg, Veeder), Award (27 August 2008), ¶ 135 (hereinafter, *Plama*).

[76] ibid ¶¶138–39.

[77] *Ioannis Kardassopoulos v Georgia*, ICSID Case No ARB/05/18 (Fortier, Orrego, Watts), Decision on Jurisdiction (6 July 2007), ¶ 182 (hereinafter, *Kardassopoulos*). This solution should be criticised. State's illegalities are investor's illegalities as well. So, the correct consideration is whether the state is prevented from raising its own illegality as a defense, but not whether the illegalities must come from the state's side. Besides, from a comparative perspective, we must remind ourselves that illegal acts generally do not give rise to legitimate expectations or acquired rights.

Tribunal. *While this Tribunal is not authorized to apply Georgian Law, it is well established that there are provisions of international agreements that can only be given meaning by reference to municipal law. In the present case, Georgian law is relevant as a fact to determine whether or not Claimant's investments is covered by the terms of the ECT and the BIT*. (emphasis added)[78]

In sum, investment treaties define, in broad terms, the categories of assets and interests that qualify as investments. They establish 'patterns' that control which interests are protected as a matter of international law. In consequence, a state cannot invoke its own domestic law to assert that such interests do not qualify as property or investments. However, by *renvoi*, it is domestic law—ie, the municipal norms regulating each of those categories of assets and rights encompassed by the 'pattern'—that ultimately determines whether the investor possesses those rights and interests qualifying as investments, *in concreto*.[79]

C Does the Definition of Investment Play a Substantive Role?

During the formative years of the BIT system, the notion of investment was usually thought of in jurisdictional terms.[80] Today, there is full consensus that the concept of investment, from a *ratione materia*/jurisdictional perspective, requires the commitment of capital, or at least some similar constraints that distinguish investments from interests created by trade relations (that is, the investment v trade debate).[81] Taking this a step

[78] *Kardassopoulos* ¶¶ 145–46. In the context of NAFTA Chapter 11, the Tribunal in *Bayview Irrigation District et al v Mexico*, ICSID Case No ARB(AF)05/1 (Lowe, Gómez-Palacio, Meese), Award (19 June 2007), had to answer to the question of whether the treaty protected 'national' investments, that is, investor's investments in his/her home state. In its analysis, ibid ¶ 98, it pointed out that: 'While this Tribunal does not purport to lay down a comprehensive and definitive test of what constitutes an investment covered by the protections of NAFTA Chapter Eleven, *it is evident that a salient characteristic will be that the investment is primarily regulated by the law of a State other than the State of the investor's nationality*, and that this law is created and applied by that State which is not the State of the investor's nationality'. (emphasis added)

[79] In the end, the situation in investment treaties to a certain extent resembles that of Protocol 1 of the European Convention of Human Rights, whose Art 1 protects 'possessions', a broader concept than property under the domestic laws of European countries. See Camilo B Schutte, *The European Fundamental Right of Property* (Deventer, Kluwer, 2004) 58.

[80] See Rudolf Dolzer, 'The Notion of Investment in Recent Practice' in Steve Charnovitz et al (eds), *Law in the Service of Human Dignity: Essays in Honour of Florentino Feliciano* (New York, CUP, 2005) 261, 263 ff (explaining the discussion of the notion of investment in the negotiation of the ECT and of ICSID).

[81] An exception may be found in *Petrobart Ltd v Kyrgyz*, SCC Case No 126/2003 (Danelius, Bring, Smets), Award (29 March 2005) at 69–72 (concluding that rights deriving from a sales of goods contract are investments). However, in my opinion, the case was wrongly decided. For a critique of the decision, see Galina Zukova, 'The Award in Petrobart Limited v Kyrgyz Republic' in Guillermo Aguilar Alvarez and W Michael Reisman (eds), *The Reasons Requirement in International Investment Arbitration: Critical Case Studies* (eds), (Leiden, M Nijhoff, 2008) 323.

further, this section asks whether the definition of investments plays any substantive role that goes beyond the patterning function previously identified.

The answer is no. As mentioned before, general international law does not contain a body of law concerned with property and investments. Similarly, the definition of investments in investment treaties does not establish such rules and principles. The substantive dimension of this concept extends only as far as its 'patterning ' function. Otherwise, it would mean that arbitral tribunals had been given the mandate to create a new global law of property and investments, a conclusion that is obviously wrong.

Moreover, the idea of a substantive function for investment is normatively problematic, for at least two reasons. First, states would be forced to have substantive regulation in place for each category that investment treaties recognise as investments. By not *creating* rights for each of these categories, states would permanently expose themselves to liability. However, as Douglas has previously observed, '[i]nvestment treaties do not oblige the contracting states to protect intangible property rights that are not recognized in the legal order of the contracting state'.[82]

Second, investment treaties would convert 'weak property' into 'strong property'. Real-life situations provide us with interesting cases of 'weak property', by which I refer to entitlements that can be revoked by the state more or less freely, at any moment, without paying compensation. For example, in the US, several major airports use a system of slots, which airlines must own in order to land or to take off. Slots have market value, and are bought and sold quite frequently. Nevertheless, the regulation that creates them establishes that 'slots do not represent a property right but represent an operating privilege subject to absolute FAA control. Slots may be withdrawn at any time to fulfill the Department's operational needs'.[83]

The underpinning logic is clear. Regulatory programs that allocate scarce resources, such as access to common pools, are usually designed and implemented to be provisional. Therefore, the implicit policy decision is to reserve the state's right to withdraw all titles in order to reallocate them in the future, hopefully according to a more rational plan. So, what happens when this moment arrives, and the regulator, in accordance with domestic law, withdraws the airport slots? Can the investor claim compensation? Assuming appropriate procedures and timing, I think not, nor do I think that investor can claim legitimate expectations in those circumstances. Domestic law must continue to have a voice in this matter; its definition of rights and interests has not been trumped by investment treaties' definition of investment.

[82] Douglas, n 70, 201.
[83] 14 CFR 93.223(a).

The fact that the concept of investment does not play a substantive role need not be a concern. On the one hand, the 'patterning function' does not imply that domestic law can serve as a defense in the face of an international law breach (as it, similarly, cannot serve that purpose when determining the nationality of the investor[84]). In the case of investments, domestic law plays a role in determining the existence of the breach, not defining a defense against an existing breach.[85]

On the other hand, the concept of investment does not and should not play a critical role in investment disputes. Indeed, apart from the jurisdictional requirement of possessing an investment—which is typically satisfied, unless outrageous circumstances vitiate the entire investor's business scheme—in most BIT clauses, particularly the FET clause, the decision-maker should assess the legitimate or illegitimate nature of the *harm* suffered by the investor, not the investment as such.[86] By contrast, it is only when applying the expropriation clause—which protects against *full* and *substantial* deprivations—that the decision-maker must focus almost exclusively on the precise content of investments.

II THE RULE OF THUMB: INDIRECT EXPROPRIATIONS AS TOTAL OR SUBSTANTIAL DEPRIVATIONS

This section reviews the first-step of the expropriation analysis, the prima facie case of expropriation claims, that is, the so-called 'sole effects doctrine', according to which indirect expropriations are defined as total or substantial deprivations.[87] As will be explored here, the prima facie case presents at least three problems that makes the finding of an indirect taking a difficult enterprise: the divergence between legal and economic approaches to assessing what is a substantial deprivation; the denominator

[84] See *Waguih Elie George Siag and Clorinda Siag v Egypt*, ICSID Case No ARB/05/15 (Williams, Pryles, Orrego), Decision on Jurisdiction (11 April 2007), ¶ 153; and *Soufraki v The United Arab Emirates*, ICSID Case No ARB/02/7 (Feliciano, Nabulsi, Stern), Decision on Annulment (5 June 2007), ¶¶ 83–102.

[85] See James Crawford (ed), *The International Law Commission's Articles on State Responsibility: Introduction, Text, and Commentaries* (CUP, Cambridge 2002) 61, Art 3 (hereinafter, *ILC's Draft Articles and Commentaries*): 'The characterization of an act of a State as internationally wrongful is governed by international law. Such characterization is not affected by the characterization of the same act as lawful by internal law'. See also, Art 27 of the Vienna Convention on the Law of Treaties: 'A party may not invoke the provisions of its internal law as justification for its failure to perform a treaty'.

[86] See Lowe, n 11, 459, who has previously observed that: 'One can do so very much more easily, however, by focusing not upon what rights the investor has, but upon what the government does, and by asking, not whether any right of the investor has been infringed by government action, but rather whether the government has or has not acted fairly'.

[87] The debate concerning whether there can be full or substantial deprivations that do not entitle investors to claim compensation is postponed to section III of this chapter.

problem; and, the role played by the categories of enterprises, investments, rights and legitimate expectations in the determination of the denominator.

A The 'Sole Effects' Doctrine in Indirect Expropriations: Total or Substantial Deprivations

In investment treaty law, the expropriation clause provides a relatively simple principle for the protection of investments: when the state effects a total or substantial deprivation, compensation must be paid, even if compelling public interests had justified adopting the measures at stake.[88] Non-destructive harms are left to be dealt with under the scope of other treaty standards.

In the history of BITs, this structural 'division of labour' was recognised as early as 1967. The official commentary to the influential OECD Draft Convention of 1967 makes very clear that 'the taking of property, within the meaning of the Article [3], must result in a *loss* of title or substance—otherwise a claim will not lie'.[89] Indeed, 'Article 3 [takings] deals with *deprivation* of property. Protection against wrongful *interference* with its use by unreasonable or discriminatory measures is, in principle, provided in Article 1 [the FET standard]'.[90]

As mentioned before, investment treaty jurisprudence is not alone in following this structural division. Both the Iran–United States Claims Tribunal and ECHR accept indirect expropriations only when full or substantial deprivations are present. Lesser interferences not constituting deprivations are left to the scope of other clauses.[91] In *Starrett Housing Corporation v Islamic Republic of Islam*—a case frequently cited in BIT awards—the Iran–United States Claims Tribunal stated that:

[88] The definition of investments as full or substantial deprivations has been widely adopted by arbitral tribunals; see eg the following recent cases: *Plama* ¶ 193 ('substantially complete deprivation'); *Metalpar SA and Buen Aire SA v Argentina*, ICSID Case No ARB/03/5 (Oreamuno, Cameron, Chabaneix), Award (6 June 2008), ¶ 172–73 (hereinafter, *Metalpar*) (*'todo o casi todo el valor económico de la inversión'*); *BG Group Plc. v Argentina*, UNCITRAL Ad Hoc Arbitration (Aguilar Alvarez, van den Berg, Garro), Award (24 December 2007), ¶ 271 (hereinafter, *BG Group*) ('substantial deprivation'); *Compañía de Aguas del Aconquija SA et al v Argentina*, Case No ARB/97/3 (Rowley, Kaufmann-Kohler, Bernal), Award (20 August 2007), ¶ 7.5.11 (hereinafter, *Vivendi III*) (summarising case law as requiring 'complete or near complete deprivation of value'); *Fireman's Fund Insurance Co v Mexico*, ICSID Case No ARB(AF)/02/1 (van den Berg, Lowenfeld, Saavedra), Award (17 July 2006), ¶ 176 ('substantially complete deprivation'). See also below n 108 ff and accompanying text. Among commentators, see the recent article by Ursula Kriebaum, 'Partial Expropriation' (2007) 8 *Journal of World Investment and Trade* 69, 69 (observing that '[i]t is widely accepted that an intereference with property, in order to amount to an expropriation, must lead to a total or at least substantial deprivation').

[89] *OECD Draft Convention On the Protection of Property, Adopted by the Council in its 150th Meeting on 12 October 1967* (1968) 7 ILM 117, 126.

[90] ibid 125 .

[91] See n 10.

> [I]t is recognised in international law that measures taken by a state can *interfere with property rights to such an extent that these rights are rendered so useless that they must be deemed to have been expropriated,* even though the state does not purport to have expropriated them and the legal title to the property formally remains with the original owner. (emphasis added)[92]

Similarly, in one of most prominent cases of the ECHR jurisprudence on the matter, *Sporrong and Lönnroth v Sweden*, the Court did not find an expropriation because 'although the right in question lost some of its substance, it did not *disappear. The effects of the measures involved are not such that they can be assimilated to a deprivation of possessions*'. (emphasis added)[93]

In the BIT generation, Dolzer has referred to this understanding of indirect expropriations as the 'sole effects' doctrine.[94] In principle, investment treaty tribunals should centre their assessments around the effects of government measures.[95] If these measures effect a complete or substantial deprivation of an investment, then an expropriation should be found and compensation paid.[96] In the words of the *Impregilo* Tribunal, 'the *effect* of the measures taken must be of such importance that those measures can be considered as having an *effect* equivalent to expropriation'. (emphasis added)[97]

[92] Iran–US Claims Tribunal *Starret Housing Corp v Islamic Republic of Iran* (1983) 4 Iran–US Claims Trib Rep 122, 154.

[93] *Sporrong* ¶ 63. See also, *Matos E Silva Lda v Portugal* (App no 15777/89) (1997) 24 EHRR 573 ¶ 85 ('In the Court's opinion, there was no formal or de facto expropriation in the present case. The effects of the measures are not such that they can be equated with deprivation of possessions'). According to Ali Riza Çoban, *Protection of Property Rights within the European Convention on Human Rights* (Burlington, Ashgate, 2004) 176, 'deprivation of one or some of the distinct use or disposal rights does not amount to deprivation in the meaning of the second sentence of the first paragraph of P1-1 unless the interference took away *all meaningful use of the property in question*'. (emphasis added)

[94] See Dolzer, n 68, 79. Newcombe, n 34, 10, refers to this doctrine—the 'orthodox approach'—which he recognises to be the dominant conception in international law. In *Archer Daniels Midland Co et al v Mexico*, ICSID Case No ARB(AF)/04/05 (Cremades, Rovine, Siqueiros), Award (21 November 2007), ¶ 240 (hereinafter, *Archer Daniels*), the Tribunal refers to it as the 'effect test'.

[95] See Paulsson and Douglas, n 13, 148.

[96] See Dolzer, n 68, 79–80: 'No one will seriously doubt that the severity of the impact upon the legal status, and the practical impact on the owner's ability to use and enjoy his property, will be a central factor in determining whether a regulatory measure effects a taking. What is much more controversial, however, is the question of whether the focus on the effect will be the only and exclusive relevant criterion ('sole effect doctrine'), or whether the purpose and the context of the governmental measure may also enter into the takings analysis'. See also, Schreuer, n 6, 28–29, ¶ 81: 'Judicial practice indicates that the severity of the economic impact is the decisive criterion when it comes to deciding whether an indirect expropriation or a measure tantamount to expropriation has taken place. An expropriation occurs if the interference is substantial and deprives the investor of all or most of the benefits of the investment. The deprivation would have to be permanent or for a substantial period of time'.

[97] *Impregilo SpA v Pakistan*, ICSID Case No ARB/03/3 (Guillaume, Cremades, Landau), Decision on Jurisdiction (22 April 2005), ¶ 279 (hereinafter, *Impregilo*). See also, *LESI (Merits)*, ¶ 132.

At this point in the development of investment treaty law, there is little doubt that the 'sole effects' doctrine dominates the prima facie case of expropriations (though, as will be seen below, this dominance does not extend to step two of the analysis, the *exceptions*[98]). It should be noted that at this stage—step one of the analysis—the 'sole effects' doctrine had already competed against a more restrictive position, which argued that investors must also prove an expropriatory 'purpose'.[99] The former represents, then, a specific alternative to that obsolete approach; Judge Holtzmann went to the heart of this matter in his dissenting opinion in the *Sea-Land* case, when noting that 'the critical question is the objective effect of a government's acts, not its subjective intentions. Acts by a government which have the effect of depriving an alien of his property are considered expropriatory in international law, whatever the government's intentions'.[100]

Although today there is a relatively universal acceptance of the 'sole effects' doctrine, that consensus is not in itself sufficient to fully resolve the first step of the expropriatory analysis. There are still several issues that confuse tribunals, commentators and practitioners in understanding the proper scope of the prima facie case for expropriations. Among them, two deserve special attention: the regulation/expropriation distinction, and the threshold necessary for a substantial deprivation.

The first is a labeling issue: can a *regulation* effect an *expropriation*? To properly answer this question, we must be aware that the word *regulation* is typically used in two different respects—one formal, another substantive. The formal usage refers to the highly important state power of label-

[98] This is the case because the position that completely rejects any *exceptions* to the rule of compensation in full and substantial deprivation is not generally accepted. Paulsson and Douglas, n 13, 148, have already observed the confusion that arises when applying this doctrine at these two different levels: 'Investment treaty awards sometimes appear to confuse two distinct analytical steps for a finding of expropriation by conflating the questions as to whether there has been a taking attributable to the Host State and whether the Host State is under an obligation to compensate that taking. The first stage of the analysis should focus on the nature or magnitude of the interference to the investor's property interests in its investment caused by measures attributable to the Host State to determine whether those acts amount to a taking. The second stage should determine whether this taking or interference rises to the level of an expropriation by reference to the relevant treaty standard'.

[99] See eg *Técnicas Medioambientales Tecmed v Mexico*, ICSID Case N°ARB(AF)/00/2 (Grigera, Fernández, Bernal), Award (29 May 2003), ¶ 114 ('Although these forms of expropriation do not have a clear or unequivocal definition, it is generally understood that they materialize through actions or conduct, which do not explicitly express the purpose of depriving one of rights or assets, but actually have that effect') (hereinafter, *Tecmed*); and, *Vivendi III* ¶ 7.5.20 ('There is extensive authority for the proposition that the state's intent, or its subjective motives are at most a secondary consideration. While intent will weigh in favour of showing a measure to be expropriatory, it is not a requirement, because the *effect* of the measure on the investor, not the state's intent, is the critical factor'). See also W Michael Reisman and Robert D Sloane, 'Indirect Takings and Its Valuation in the BIT Generation' (2003) 74 British Ybk of Intl Law 115, 130–31; Coe and Rubins, n 3, 615; GC Christie, 'What Constitutes a Taking of Property Under International Law?' (1962) 38 British Ybk of Intl Law 307, 311; and, Schreuer, n 6, ¶ 80.

[100] *Sea-Land* ¶ 207.

ing measures as regulation (and not expropriation), and thereby ensuring that compensation is not due, at least without further intervention of courts or tribunals. The substantive usage refers to measures that interfere with investments, but do not fully or substantially deprive them.

There are investment treaty awards, such as *CME*[101] and *SD Myers I*[102], which seem to confuse these two different meanings. Yet it is possible to read both the *CME* and *SD Myers I* awards as simply saying that, in most cases, there is a correspondence between regulations in the formal and in the substantive sense. This means that, most of the time, the state properly labels as regulations measures that do not produce total or substantial deprivation of investments. As the *SD Myers I* tribunal puts it, '[e]xpropriations *tend* to involve the deprivation of ownership rights; regulations a lesser interference'.[103]

However, the correspondence between regulation-formal sense and regulation-substantive sense is not merely a statistical matter. From a normative perspective, the regulatory state deserves deference when making a characterisation of measures as regulation or expropriations. As Weston remarks, there should be a refutable presumption in favour of finding that measures labeled as regulations do not amount to expropriation:

> At the outset of the 'taking'–'regulation' problem at the international level, therefore, is the necessary presumption that States are 'regulating' when they say they are 'regulating,' and they are especially to be honored when they are explicit in this regard. Community harmony and goodwill require no less. But like all presumptions, this one, too, is rebuttable.[104]

The fact that this is just a presumption implies that regulations *can*, from the perspective of their consequences, cause full or substantial deprivations. In fact, arbitral tribunals have been rightly clear on this issue. In *Tecmed*, the Tribunal found there is 'no principle stating that regulatory administrative actions are *per se* excluded from the scope of the Agreement . . . particularly if the negative economic impact of such actions on the financial position of the investor is sufficient to neutralize in full the value, or economic or commercial use of its investment'.[105] Similarly, in the context of NAFTA Chapter 11, the *Pope and Talbot* Tribunal held that:

[101] *CME Czech Republic BV v Czech Republic*, UNCITRAL Ad Hoc Arbitration (Kühn, Schwebel, Hándl), Partial Award (13 September 2001), ¶ 603 (hereinafter, *CME I*).

[102] *SD Myers I* ¶ 281.

[103] *SD Myers I* ¶ 282 (emphasis added) That seems to be the case also in *Telenor* ¶ 64: 'It is well established that the mere excercise by government of regulatory powers that create impediments to business or entails the payment of taxes or other levies does not of itself constitute expropriation. Any investor entering into a concession agreement must be aware that investment involves risks and that in some degrees the investor's activities are likely to be regulated and payments made for which the investor will not receive compensating advantages'.

[104] Burns H Weston, ' "Constructive Takings" under International Law: A Modest Foray into the Problems of "Creeping Expropriations" ' (1975) 16 *Virginia Journal of International Law* 103, 121.

[105] *Tecmed* ¶ 121. See also, ibid ¶¶ 114–15.

> While the exercise of police powers must be analyzed with special care, the Tribunal believes that Canada's formulation [that regulation cannot amount to expropriation] goes too far. Regulation can indeed be exercised in a way that would constitute creeping expropriation . . . Indeed, much creeping expropriation could be conducted by regulation, and a blanket exception for regulatory measures would create a gaping loophole in international protection against expropriation.[106]

On this point, the analysis here is neither ontological nor formal, but essentially empirical. Tribunals must centre attention upon the effects of regulation on recognised specific investments. This means that the evaluation is *relative*, in the sense of being performed from the claimant's perspective. The same measure can serve as regulation for the entire community, and yet remain expropriatory exclusively with respect to one particular investor.

The second and more complicated issue refers to the proper *quantum* threshold of the interferences. The extreme case is easy: full deprivations qualify, prima facie, as indirect expropriations.[107] For example, in *Tecmed*, the tribunal expressed no reservations in deciding that a total destruction of value would be considered an expropriation:

> To establish whether the Resolution is a measure equivalent to an expropriation under the terms of section 5(1) of the Agreement, it must be first determined if the Claimant, due to the Resolution, was *radically deprived of the economical use and enjoyment of its investments*, as if the rights related thereto—such as the income or benefits related to the Landfill or to its exploitation—had ceased to exist. In other words, if due to the actions of the Respondent, *the assets involved have lost their value or economic use for their holder and the extent of the loss*. This determination is important because it is one of the main elements to distinguish, from the point of view of an international tribunal, between a regulatory measure, which is an ordinary expression of the exercise of the state's police power that entails a decrease in assets or rights, and a de facto expropriation that deprives those assets and rights of any real substance. (emphasis added)[108]

Similarly, the *Lauder* Tribunal identified indirect expropriations with full deprivations when affirming that the former 'is a measure that does

[106] *Pope & Talbot Inc v Canada*, UNCITRAL Ad Hoc Arbitration (Dervaird, Greenberg, Belman), Interim Award (26 June 2000), ¶ 99 (hereinafter, *Pope & Talbot I*). Similarly, ibid ¶ 96, the Tribunal held that, 'the scope of that Article [Art 1110 of NAFTA] does cover non-discriminatory regulation that might be said to fall within an exercise of a state's so-called police powers'.

[107] As noted in ch 4, 178–179, in the US, one of the categorical rules of regulatory takings, the *Lucas rule*, strictly requires full destruction of economic value. See *David H Lucas v South Carolina Coastal Council* (1992) 505 US 1003 (hereinafter, *Lucas*).

[108] *Tecmed* ¶ 115. Coe and Rubins, n 3, 651, note a parallel between *Tecmed* and the *Lucas* decision in the US: 'Indeed, the *Tecmed* standard it is far closer to the jurisprudence of the U.S. Supreme Court, according to which a regulatory expropriation can only occur where there is "deprivation of all economic benefit ot he property . . . [and if] there was some other use available for the property, there was no compensable taking" '. [refering to *Lucas v SC Coastal*].

not involve an overt taking, but that *effectively neutralizes the enjoyment of the property*'.[109] The *Pope & Talbot* Tribunal seems to have moved in the same direction, when applying a test that asks 'whether that interference is sufficiently restrictive to support a conclusion that the property has been "taken" from its owner'.[110]

At the same time, it has been accepted that cases involving less than full deprivation may also qualify as indirect expropriations. Investment treaty tribunals 'have given support for the proposition that *partial* destruction of the value may be tantamount to an expropriation',[111] that is, that 'in some contexts and circumstances, it would be appropriate to view a deprivation as amounting to an expropriation, even if it were partial or temporary'.[112]

This means that in investment treaty law, the threshold is less strict than the *Lucas* rule in US constitutional law. Still, interferences, as Coe and Rubins point out, 'must *approach* total impairment';[113] they must wipe out 'all or almost all' the investor's investments.[114] In *Metalclad*, a seminal case on this matter, the Tribunal held that:

> Thus, expropriation under NAFTA includes not only open, deliberate and acknowledged takings of property, such as outright seizure or formal or obligatory transfer of title in favour of the host State, but also covert or incidental interference with the use of property *which has the effect of depriving the owner, in whole or in significant part*, of the use or reasonably-to-be-expected economic benefit of property even if not necessarily to the obvious benefit of the host State.[115] (emphasis added)

After this decision—frequently invoked by arbitral tribunals[116]—nobody seems to put into question the fact that, along with full deprivations,

[109] *Lauder v Czech Republic*, UNCITRAL Ad Hoc Arbitration (Briner, Cutler, Klein), Award (3 September 2001), ¶ 200 (emphasis added) (hereinafter, *Lauder*). See also, *CME I* ¶ 604, which uses similar language.

[110] *Pope and Talbot* I ¶ 102. See also, *GAMI Investment Inc v Mexico*, UNCITRAL Ad Hoc Arbitration (Paulsson, Lacarte, Reisman), Award (15 November 2004), ¶ 125 (hereinafter, *GAMI*) (quoting this passage of *Pope and Talbot I*); see also, *Compañía del Desarrollo Santa Elena SA v Costa Rica*, ICSID Case No ARB/96/1 (Weil, Fortier, Lauterpacht), Award (17 February 2000), ¶ 77 (hereinafter, *Santa Elena*); and, *Goetz v Burundi*, ICSID Case No ARB/95/3 (Weil, Bedjaoui, Bredin), Award (10 February 1999), ¶ 124.

[111] *GAMI* ¶ 131. Note, however, that the GAMI Tribunal did not decide this point: 'This Tribunal need not decide whether *partial* destruction of shareholding interests may be tantamount to an expropriation'. (*GAMI* ¶ 132).

[112] *SD Myers I* ¶ 283.

[113] Coe and Rubins, n 3, 621.

[114] *LG&E* ¶ 191: 'In many arbitral decisions, the compensation has been denied when it had not affected all or amost all the investment's economic value. Interferente with the investment's ability to carry on its business is not satisfied where the investment continues to operate, even if profits are diminished. The impact must be substantial in order that compensation may be claimed for the expropriation'. Following this decision, see *Metalpar* ¶¶ 172–73 (requiring that interferences destroy 'all or almost all the investment's economic value') (*'todo o casi todo el valor económico de la inversión'*).

[115] *Metalclad Corporation v Mexico*, ICSID Case No ARB(AF)/97/1 (Lauterpacht, Civiletti, Siqueiros), Award (30 August 2000), ¶ 103 (hereinafter, *Metalclad*).

[116] See eg *CME I* ¶ 606; *OEPC* ¶¶ 86–89, and *CMS Gas Transmission Co v Argentina*, ICSID Case No ARB/01/08 (Orrego, Lalonde, Rezek), Award (12 May 2005), ¶ 262 (hereinafter, *CMS*).

'significant part-deprivations' also constitute prima facie indirect takings.[117] As summarised by the Tribunal in *Telenor*, '[t]hough different tribunals have formulated the test in different ways, they are all agreed that the interference with the investor's rights must be such as *substantially to deprive* the investor of the economic value, use or enjoyment of its investment'. (emphasis added)[118]

One exception to this general consensus comes from the Canadian Court that entertained the challenge against the *Metalclad* award. Adopting a critical position toward this definition of indirect takings, Justice Tysoe held that '[t]he Tribunal gave an extremely broad definition of expropriation for the purposes of Article 1110 . . . This definition is sufficiently broad to include a legitimate rezoning of property by a municipality or other zoning authority'.[119]

Yet, this critique is inaccurate and unfair. We know already that, as a matter of step one of the expropriatory analysis—and not of step two, the *exceptions*—the notion of *substantial* deprivation limits and not expands the notion of indirect expropriation. Given that the idea is to apply a rule of thumb for finding expropriations, this limitation is simply saying, 'if the interferences do not destroy or substantially destroy an investment, no expropriation can be claimed'. To that extent, as Paulsson and Douglas have also recognised, *Metalclad* is good law.[120]

So, in the end, the 'sole effects' doctrine is simultaneously restrictive and expansive as a prima facie theory of indirect expropriations. The doctrine, properly understood to operate at step one of the analysis, asserts that to find prima facie expropriation, the claimant must prove a full or substantial deprivation. It is therefore expansive in the sense of not requiring proof of any ulterior motive on the government's part. But at the same time, by requiring proof of 'full and substantial deprivation?, it is more restrictive than those theories that equate any interference—regardless of magnitude—with an expropriation.

[117] See August Reinisch, 'Expropriation' in Peter Muchlinski et al (eds), *The Oxford Handbook of International Investment Law* (New York, OUP, 2008) 407, 438–39 (noting that '[t]here is a broad consensus that a certain degree or level of interference is required in order to qualify as expropriation. What is required is at least a "substantial loss of control or value" or "severe economic impact" '). (internal citations omitted).

[118] *Telenor* ¶ 65. See also, *Bogdanov et al v Moldova*, SCC Case (Cordero), Award (22 September 2005), at 17, ¶ 4.2.5.

[119] *The United Mexican States v Metalclad Corp* (2001) 89 BCLR 359, ¶ 99.

[120] According to Paulsson and Douglas, n 13, 149, *Metalclad* should be read as what I refer here to as step-one of the taking analysis: 'Rather than *defining* expropriation, the intention of this statement [*Metalclad* ¶ 103] may well have been to simply list the type of takings that expropriation might encompass, subject to a subsequent determination that the taking in question rises to the level of an expropriation for which Mexico was under a duty to compensate in accordance with Article 1110 of NAFTA. In other words, the Tribunal might not have been suggesting that a diminution of value caused by actions of the Host States without more constitutes a breach of Article 1110 of the NAFTA'.

B What is Substantial Deprivation?

Because substantial deprivations qualify as indirect expropriations, we are therefore forced to draw a line separating mere interferences from takings.[121] The attempt to define this line is, as Wälde and Kolo note, one of the most contentious issues in international investment law.[122] That difficulty stems primarily from the fact that legal and economic analyses do not converge in their conclusions.[123]

Indeed, lawyers and economists provide different criteria for separating mere interferences from substantial deprivations. The former refer to concepts such as *uti, frui* or *abuti*, and the latter to notions of discounted future cash flows and other techniques of valuation. Lawyers with a sophisticated understanding of these issues tend to recognise in principle that economics should prevail over legal doctrines with respect to this matter, but stop short of fully abdicating those doctrines.[124]

In any case, the more traditional legal stance continues to be very influential to the BIT generation. In her seminal work on expropriations, Judge Higgins noted that the international law tradition follows what I refer to here as the trend of lawyers:

> International tribunals have in the main preferred to look and see whether various government interferences have left these essential rights intact at the end of the day, rather than to see whether they have occasioned a diminution in value. *The tendency is for a diminution in value to remain uncompensated, so long as rights of use, exclusion and alienation remain.* (emphasis added)[125]

In the BIT generation, several tribunals have followed this legalistic stance. For example, in *Lauder*, the Tribunal held that a 'a *"formal"* expropriation is a measure aimed at a *"transfer of property"*, while a *"de facto"* expropriation occurs when a state deprives the owner of his *"right to use,*

[121] See Reinisch, n 117, 439.

[122] Wälde and Kolo, n 18, 837–38.

[123] See the general treatment of this matter in ch 4, 185–188.

[124] Wälde and Kolo, n 18, 835 ('[I]n modern understanding, the key function of property is less the tangibility of "things", but rather the capability of a combination of rights in a commercial and corporate setting and under a regulatory regime to earn a commercial rate of return'). See also, Paulsson and Douglas, n 13, 152–53, according to whom: '[R]ather than restricting the analysis to the effect of the state measures in question on the triad of ownership rights to the investor's property, a more expansive definition of property interest should be employed. The "modern understanding" of property advocated by Professor Waelde and Dr Kolo is a good starting point . . . Professor Weston's early study of "constructive takings" suggested an alternative, putting the emphasis solely on the economic interests embodied by the property through the use of the concept "wealth deprivation"'. See also, Kriebaum, n 88, 71 ('The decisive point for an expropriation is the destruction of the capability to make use of the investment *in an economic sense*. The investor . . . has to be deprived of the *economic benefit* of the investment'). (emphasis added)

[125] Higgins, n 36, 271.

let or sell (his) property"'.[126] In *Nykomb Synergetics*—a case in which the investment became allegedly worthless—the Tribunal nevertheless held that '[t]he decisive factor for drawing the border line towards expropriation must primarily be the degree of possession taking or control over the enterprise the disputed measures entail'.[127]

More unambiguously, in *Biwater Gauff*, the Tribunal expressly stated that the determination of 'substantial deprivation' is a legal issue, and that all economic considerations should be relegated to questions of causation and damage:

> Equally, whilst accepting that effects of a certain severity must be shown to qualify an act as expropriatory, *there is nothing to require that such effects be economic in nature*. A distinction must be drawn between (a) interference with rights and (b) economic loss. A substantial interference with rights may well occur without actually causing any economic damage which can be quantified in terms of due compensation. In other words, the fact that the effect of conduct must be considered in deciding whether an indirect expropriation has occurred, does not necessarily import an economic test. In the Arbitral Tribunal's view, the absence of economic loss or damage is primarily a matter of causation and quantum—rather than a necessary ingredient in the cause of action of expropriation itself. Thus, the suffering of substantive and quantifiable economic loss by the investor is not a pre-condition for the finding of an expropriation under Article 5 of the BIT. There may have been a substantial interference with an investor's rights, so as to amount to an expropriation, even if that interference has been overtaken by other events, such that no economic loss actually results, or the interference simply cannot be quantified in financial terms. (emphasis added—underlined in the original)[128]

Most arbitral decisions seem to follow the legal approach, while also integrating certain economic elements. This typically means a focus on the impairment and neutralisation of the control, enjoyment and use of investments.[129] In this regard, an important trend was initiated by *Pope & Talbot I*, where the Tribunal stated that:

[126] *Lauder* ¶ 200.

[127] *Nykomb Synergetics Technology Holding AB v Latvia*, SCC Case No 118/2001 (Haug, Schütze, Gernandt), Award (16 December 2003), ¶ 4.3.1. Immediately after, the Tribunal added that, in that case, 'there is no possession taking of Windau [the investment] or its assets, no interference with the shareholder's rights or with the management's control over and running of the enterprise'.

[128] *Biwater Gauff (Tanzania) Ltd v Tanzania*, ICSID Case No ARB/05/22 (Hanotiau, Born, Landau), Award (24 July 2008), ¶¶464–65 (hereinafter, *Biwater Gauff*).

[129] See eg *Société Général v Dominican Republic*, LCIA Case No 7927 (Orrego, Bishop, Cremades), Decision on Jurisdiction (19 September 2008), ¶ 64; *Metalpar* ¶ 174; *Sempra Energy International v Argentina*, ICSID Case No ARB/02/16 (Orrego, Lalonde, Morelli), Award (28 September 2007), ¶¶ 284–85 (hereinafter, *Sempra*); *BG Group* ¶ 271; *Archer Daniels* ¶¶ 240–45; *MCI Power Group LC et al v Ecuador*, ICSID Case No ARB/03/6 (Vinuesa, Greenberg, Irarrázabal), Award (31 July 2007), ¶ 300; *LG&E* ¶¶ 188, and 190; *Waste Management II* ¶ 159; *Consortium RFCC v Morocco*, ICSID Case No ARB/00/6 (Briner, Cremades, Fadlallah), Award (22 December 2003), ¶ 68 (hereinafter, *Consortium RFCC*); *CME I* ¶ 609, and, *Wena*

The Investor's (and the Investment's) Operation Controller testified at the hearing that the Investor remains in control of the Investment, it directs the day-to-day operations of the Investment, and no officers or employees of the Investment have been detained by virtue of the Regime. Canada does not supervise the work of the officers or employees of the Investment, does not take any of the proceeds of company sales (apart from taxation), does not interfere with management or shareholders' activities, does not prevent the Investment from paying dividends to its shareholders, does not interfere with the appointment of directors or management and does not take any other actions ousting the Investor from full ownership and control of the Investment.[130]

One of the decisions to follow this precedent,[131] *CMS*, displays an outstanding formalist character and demonstrates how legal analysis prevails over economic considerations in these more 'blended' approaches. The Tribunal assessed the economic harm caused by the host state in the amount of US$133,200,000,[132] and the residual value of the investment, in US$7,443,700.[133] Notwithstanding that fact, the Tribunal concluded that those figures did not prove the existence of an expropriation:

Substantial deprivation was addressed in detail by the tribunal in the *Pope & Talbot* case. The Government of Argentina has convincingly argued that the list of issues to be taken into account for reaching a determination on substantial deprivation, as discussed in that case, is not present in the instant dispute. In fact, the Respondent has explained, the investor is in control of the investment; the Government does not manage the day-to-day operations of the company; and the investor has full ownership and control of the investment.[134]

By contrast, other arbitral tribunals have expressly favoured the economic approach. The *Telenor* Tribunal required '*a major adverse impact on the economic value of the investment*', (emphasis added)[135] and the *Parkerings* Tribunal, 'a *substantial decrease of the value of the investment*'. (emphasis added)[136] Similarly, in *Tecmed*, the Tribunal held that the deprivation analysis should be focused on '*economical* use and enjoyment of its investments, as if the rights related thereto—such as the *income* or *benefits* related to the Landfill or to its exploitation—had ceased to exist'. (emphasis

Hotels Ltd v Egypt, ICSID Case No ARB/98/4 (Leigh, Fadlallah, Wallace), Award (8 December 2000), ¶ 99 (hereinafter, *Wena*).

[130] *Pope & Talbot I* ¶ 100.

[131] Other decisions following *Pope & Talbot I* are: *Enron Corporation et al v Argentina*, ICSID Case No ARB/01/3 (Orrego, van den Berg, Tschanz), Award (22 May 2007), ¶ 245 (hereinafter, *Enron*); *PSEG Global Inc et al v Turkey*, ICSID Case No ARB/02/5 (Orrego, Fortier, Kaufmann-Kohler), Award (19 January 2007), ¶ 278; and, *Feldman* ¶ 152.

[132] *CMS* ¶ 468.

[133] ibid ¶ 466.

[134] ibid ¶ 263.

[135] *Telenor* ¶ 64

[136] *Parkerings-Compagniet AS v Lituania*, ICSID Case No ARB/05/8 (Lévy, Lew, Lalonde), Award (11 September 2007), ¶ 455.

added)[137] In *Metalclad*, the Tribunal held that substantial deprivation refers to 'the use or reasonably-to-be-expected economic benefit of property even if not necessarily to the obvious benefit of the host State'.[138] In *Vivendi III*, the Tribunal summarised its view of the existing case law in the following manner:

> Numerous tribunals have looked at the *diminution of the value of the investment* to determine whether the contested measure is expropriatory. The weight of authority (further discussed below) appears to draw a distinction between only a partial deprivation of value (not an expropriation) and a complete or near complete deprivation of value (expropriation). (emphasis added)[139]

Yet, even though these tribunals correctly emphasise the relevance of the economic approach,[140] we should not overreact against legal doctrines. Economics as a science may provide us valuable information about the real world, but it does not answer the normative questions that arise in expropriation cases. As the Tribunal pointed out in *Archer Daniels*, 'the test for expropriation . . . cannot be considered in the abstract or based exclusively on the Claimants' loss of profits, which is not necessarily a sufficient sole criterion for an expropriation'.[141] A 'modern' economic conception of property cannot escape the need to refer back to legal doctrines.[142]

Whether we follow lawyers or economists, the key question remains open: how to draw the line between mere interferences and substantial deprivations? In the world of legal doctrines this difficulty is familiar,[143] and is reflected in continental law's old 'property-core' v 'property-periphery' debate. If we decide to move toward an economic conception of property, the challenges of determining this boundary, far from disappearing, increase. Is substantial deprivation a diminution in value that surpasses a certain threshold? If so, which threshold?: 50 per cent, 70 per cent, 90 per cent? Should this threshold always be the same, or should it change to reflect the particular importance of the public interest pursued

[137] *Tecmed* ¶ 115.

[138] *Metalclad* ¶ 103. See also, *Azurix* ¶ 316, but see ¶ 322.

[139] See also, *Vivendi III* ¶ 7.5.11. Note, however, that later, ibid ¶ 7.5.24., the Tribunal also incorporated legal elements into the analysis.

[140] A balanced and well-articulated blended approach can be found in *Plama* ¶ 193: 'The Arbitral Tribunal considers that the decisive elements in the evaluation of Respondent's conduct in this case are therefore the assessment of (i) substantially complete deprivation of the economic use and enjoyment of the rights to the investments, or of indentifiable, distinct parts thereof (*i.e.*, approaching total impairment); (ii) the irreversibility and permanence of the contested measures (*i.e.*, not ephemeral or temporary); and (iii) the extent of the loss of economic value experienced by the investor'.

[141] *Archer Daniels* ¶ 248.

[142] Ultimately, as Rudolf Dolzer and Christoph Schreuer, *Principles of International Investment Law* (New York, OUP, 2008) 107–08, point out, '[a]ny attempt to define an indirect expropriation on the basis of one factor alone will not lead to a satisfactory result in all cases'.

[143] See Christie, n 99, 330–36.

by the state?[144] Should we, instead, focus on whether the investment went from being profitable to one causing losses to the investor?[145]

Arbitral decisions have not yet provided any conclusive answer to these questions. *GAMI* and *Tokios Tokelės* only described the problem.[146] *Bognavod* confronted the matter, but arrived at a trivial answer because that particular case was an *easy* one on this dimension:

> [T]he Arbitral Tribunal does not find Article 6 of the BIT [the expropriation clause] applicable, because the concept of indirect expropriation applies only to measures having the effect of expropriation that affect the totality or a substantial part of the investment. In the instant case, the value of the Transferred Assets, upon which the parties agree, corresponds to less than 7% of the nominal value of the Privatized Company at the moment of the Privatization Contract, and circa 3% of the total investment carried out by the Local Investment Company. This is not sufficient to turn the lack of compensation for the Transferred Assets into a measure affecting the totality or a substantial part of the investment. (internal citations omitted)[147]

There is no automatic way to draw the line telling us when a loss is so great as to constitute a *substantial* deprivation. The *Feldman* Tribunal's observation, six years ago, that 'it is fair to say that no one has come up with a fully satisfactory means of drawing this line',[148] continues to be valid. This will continue to be the case, because, as Weston pointed out earlier, the regulation-taking dilemma 'cannot be defined, let-alone resolved, by "rules of decisions" which look only to one or two of its diverse aspects'. (internal citations omitted)[149]

C The Denominator Problem in Investment Treaty Disputes

The rule of thumb for expropriations is thus not as simple as we expected it to be, even in the simpler setting of full deprivations. The deprivation

144 See Weston, n 104, 119.

145 See Coe and Rubins, n 3, 623. In *Telenor* ¶¶ 77 and 79, the Tribunal seemed persuaded that an expropriation had not occurred because the investment remained a profitable enterprise.

146 See *GAMI* ¶ 133. See esp *Tokios Tokelės (Merits)*, ¶ 120: 'A critical factor in the analysis of an expropriation claim is the extent of harm caused by the government's actions. For any expropriation—direct or indirect—to occur, the state must deprive the investor of a "substantial" part of the value of the investment. Although neither the relevant treaty text nor existing jurisprudence have clarified the precise degree of deprivation that will qualify as "substantial", one can reasonably infer that a diminution of 5% of the investment's value will not be enough for a finding of expropriation, while a diminution of 95% would likely be sufficient. The determination in any particular case of where along that continuum an expropriation has occurred will turn on the particular facts before the tribunal'.

147 *Bognavod*, at 17, ¶ 4.2.5.

148 *Feldman* ¶ 100.

149 Weston, n 104, 120. See also ibid 121, where he concludes that '[t]he multidimensional "constructive taking" problem simply cannot be handled satisfactorily by unidimensional methods. To achieve any commonsense clarity, we must acknowledge the complexity of the real world in which we live'.

must be total, but total with respect to what? This quantitative relationship between the harm suffered and a theoretical unit of reference constitutes the so-called denominator problem.[150]

The denominator problem has not been given much express recognition in the BIT generation.[151] Among arbitral awards, the closest it has come to receiving explicit attention was in *GAMI*, where the Tribunal asked the central question but provided a circular answer:

> Should *Pope & Talbot* be understood to mean that property is taken only if it is so affected in its entirety? That question cannot be answered properly before asking: *what property?* The taking of 50 acres of a farm is equally expropriatory whether that is the whole farm or just a fraction. The notion must be understood as this: *the affected property* must be impaired to such an extent that it must be seen as "taken".[152]

Such lack of recognition does not mean that the problem has been absent, or that arbitral tribunals have not provided at least implicit answers. The denominator problem is unavoidable; it is consubstantial to the definition of expropriations from the perspective of the *effects* of measures on investments (that is, full or substantial deprivations). Several arbitral decisions confirm this observation.

In *Feldman*, the Tribunal confronted the question of whether the right to export cigarettes—strict definition—or the right to export goods in general, as the company had done in the past—broad definition—constituted the proper denominator. The Tribunal opted for the latter, and therefore, did not find an expropriation:

> Given that the Claimant here has lost the effective ability to export cigarettes, and any profits derived therefrom, application of the *Pope & Talbot* standard might suggest the possibility of an expropriation . . . [H]ere, as in *Pope & Talbot*, the regulatory action (enforcement of long-standing provisions of Mexican law) has not deprived the Claimant of control of the investment, CEMSA, interfered directly in the internal operations of CEMSA or displaced the Claimant as the controlling shareholder. The Claimant is free to pursue other continuing lines of export trading, such as exporting alcoholic beverages, photographic supplies, or other products for which he can obtain from Mexico the invoices required under Article 4, although he is effectively precluded from exporting cigarettes. Thus, this Tribunal believes there has been no 'taking' under this standard articulated in *Pope & Talbot*, in the present case.[153]

The problem appeared again in *Waste Management II*. The question in that instance was whether the Tribunal should analyse the expropriation of the whole enterprise, or of one set of assets (in this case, an unpaid debt):

150 See the general treatment of this matter in ch 4, 188–191.

151 An exception can be found in Kriebaum, n 88.

152 *GAMI* ¶ 126.

153 *Feldman* ¶ 152.

> The Claimant argued that Acaverde's entire enterprise in Acapulco was expropriated . . . Although the Claimant did not put it in these terms, it could also be argued that the persistent failure of the City to pay the amounts due under the Concession Agreement was tantamount to an expropriation at least of the amount unpaid. In the Tribunal's view the latter claim is encompassed within the former, and is *infra petita*. It is open to the Tribunal to find a breach of Article 1110 in a case where certain facts are relied on to show the wholesale expropriation of an enterprise but the facts establish the expropriation of certain assets only. Accordingly the Tribunal will consider first the standard set by Article 1110, in particular for conduct tantamount to an expropriation, then whether the enterprise as a whole was subjected to conduct in breach of Article 1110, and finally whether (even if there was no wholesale expropriation of the enterprise as such) the facts establish a partial expropriation. [154]

Here, the Tribunal decided to use both denominators, proceeding first to analyse the alleged expropriation of the whole enterprise, and then, to analyse the alleged expropriation of a small subset of assets (referring to it as a 'partial expropriation'). Note that this smaller denominator was applied even though the claimant had not characterised its claim in that way.

The denominator problem can be fully recognised in two sibling cases: *OEPC*—where the Tribunal did not find an expropriation—and *EnCana*—where the Tribunal considered the possibility of a full deprivation, but dismissed the claim on other grounds. In both cases, there was no doubt that the enterprise as a whole had not been subject to expropriation. The central aspect of the dispute was, instead, whether or not the denominator should be determined using the value of VAT refunds that Ecuador had denied (which would have led to the numerator's exactly matching the denominator, that is, a perfectly full deprivation).

In *OEPC*, the Tribunal did not accept this position. First, it held—wrongly in my opinion—that a VAT refund should not be considered an investment under the BIT.[155] Then, it observed that 'even if a refund claim is considered to be included in the claims to money and other rights mentioned in the definition, *still the expropriation has to meet the standards required by international law*'. (emphasis added)[156] Finally, without explaining precisely how it had arrived at such a conclusion while using a denominator equal to the VAT refund under dispute, the Tribunal simply stated that 'there has been no deprivation of the use or reasonably expected economic benefit of the investment, let alone measures affecting a significant part of the investment'.[157]

[154] *Waste Management II* ¶ 141.

[155] *OEPC* ¶ 86 ('However broad the definition of investment might be under the Treaty it would be quite extraordinary for a company to invest in a refund claim').

[156] ibid.

[157] ibid ¶ 89.

In *EnCana,* the Tribunal adopted a different position. Following the lead of the *Waste Management II* Tribunal—which had been presided over by the same arbitrator, James Crawford—the *EnCana* Tribunal set the denominator at two different levels: that of the enterprise, and that of the VAT refund. Then, it proceeded to analyse the first version of the expropriation claim—in which the denominator had been set using the enterprise—dismissing it as clearly meritless.[158] Regarding the second version of the claim, the Tribunal accepted *arguendo* that had the Ecuadorian government canceled valid existing debts under Ecuadorian law, an expropriation of VAT refunds would have been found.[159] Nevertheless, it rejected the expropriation claim because of the lack of certainty in Ecuadorian law on the question of the existence of the VAT refunds.

Of course, the key question for this section still lies unanswered: how should arbitral tribunals set the denominator when assessing indirect expropriation claims? In following order of size, they may select the enterprise as a whole, certain investments, rights within investments—particularly in contractual settings—or legitimate expectations. The time dimension should also be taken into consideration: tribunals may measure against a lifespan, or a shorter unit of time. The more that the tribunals engage in 'conceptual severance'—that is, chopping the denominator along parameters of space, time, and legal nature[160]—the easier is to find an expropriation.

Investment treaty tribunals have not treated the denominator problem uniformly. Some of them have refused to include denominators smaller than the enterprise as a whole. For example, in *Telenor,* the Tribunal adopted a categorical position: 'the investment must be viewed as a whole and that the test the Tribunal has to apply is whether, *viewed as a whole,* the investment has suffered substantial erosion of value'. (emphasis added)[161] In this non-derivative claim case,[162] the claimant's wholly owned subsidiary was 'a very successful and profitable company',[163] and therefore

[158] *EnCana* ¶¶ 172–178.

[159] ibid ¶¶ 183, 188, 189 and 193. In particular, see ibid ¶ 183: 'In the Tribunal's opinion, a law which cancels a liability the State already has to an investor . . . is capable of amounting to an expropriation'.

[160] See ch 4, 188–191.

[161] *Telenor* ¶ 67.

[162] See nn 179-184 and accompanying text. The distinction derivative/non-derivative is highly relevant. If the claim is derivative the enterprise as a whole is the only denominator that the tribunal can adopt. But in this case, the domestic vehicle, *Pannon,* was a wholly owned subsidiary of Telenor, a situation that gave the claim a direct character. Indeed, according to the Tribunal, ibid ¶ 27: 'Though claims based purely on breaches of contract are outside the Tribunal's mandate—a point discussed in detail later—the concession agreement between Pannon and Hungary is obviously of central importance in determining the nature and extent of the investment. Strictly speaking, *Telenor's investment is in Pannon, not in Pannon's right under the agreement, but since Pannon is Telenor's wholly owned subsidiary the Tribunal considers that in practical terms this can be regarded as a distinction without difference, and it is common ground that this is not an issue in the case*'. (emphasis added). See also, ibid ¶ 60.

[163] ibid ¶ 77.

the effect of the State measures complaint by Telenor fell 'far short of the substantial economic deprivation of its investment required to constitute expropriation'.[164]

At the other extreme, tribunals have also agreed to use a small subset of rights as denominators. *Eureko* is probably the most pronounced example, where mere breaches of contract ended up being equated with indirect expropriations.[165] In that case, the Tribunal found that the contractual right to buy additional shares in a privatised insurance company (PZU) served as the proper denominator, even considering that the shares already owned by the investor were not affected at all[166]:

> The Tribunal has found in an earlier section of the present Award that Eureko, under the terms of the First Addendum, acquired rights in respect of the holding of the IPO and that these rights are 'assets'. Since the RoP [Republic of Poland] deprived Claimant of those assets by conduct which the Tribunal has found to be inadmissible, it must follow that Eureko has a claim against the RoP under Article 5 of the Treaty [the expropriation clause].[167]

These two extreme cases illustrate that the definition of investments in BITs and other treaties, while establishing the starting point of the analysis, does not really solve the denominator problem. This is because investments cover the full range of potential denominators: from 'enterprises' to 'every kind of asset', 'claims to money' and 'any performance having an economic value'.[168] So, which 'investment', then, among all those indicated in the treaty, should be used when determining the denominator? Should tribunals 'conceptually sever' the larger units—typically enterprises or concession contracts as a whole—into the smallest possible units contemplated under the treaty, as was the case in *Eureko*?[169]

Before explaining why the idea of 'conceptual severance' should be rejected in the BIT generation, it is worth noting that economic approaches to investments on these questions—including the idea of 'reasonably-to-be-expected economic benefit of property'[170]—lead us no further. Economic analysis cannot distinguish between legitimate and mere expectations.

164 ibid ¶ 79.

165 *Eureko BV v Poland*, Ad Hoc Arbitration (Fortier, Schwebel, Rajski), Partial Award (19 August 2005) (hereinafter, *Eureko*). What it is controversial in this case is that the Tribunal set the denominator using a subset of rights under the contract, rather than the accepted idea that contracts can be expropriated.

166 ibid ¶ 239 ('It is plain that Respondent has not deprived Eureko of its shares in PZU which it continues to hold and on which it receives dividend').

167 ibid ¶ 240.

168 See the definitions of investments quoted in n 54.

169 Interestingly, in *Ioan Micula et al v Romania*, ICSID Case No ARB/05/20 (Lévy, Alexandrov, Ehlermann), Decision on Jurisdiction and Admissibility (24 September 2008), ¶ 128, the Tribunal halted its *jurisdictional* analysis at the larger unit of possible investments, and did not determine whether a smaller unit, some *incentives* according to domestic law, also qualified as investment, leaving the question open for a later expropriatory analysis.

170 *Metalclad* ¶ 103.

Furthermore, economic worth can always be divided into single dollars, the absolute extreme of 'conceptual severance'.

The point is that any operative notion of 'reasonably-to-be-expected economic benefit' cannot exist analytically independent of legal entitlements. We are forced to rely on those focal points generally accepted as denominators, which are provided by the legal system and business culture. Indeed, this has traditionally been one of the main functions of property law: to specify the units that are considered valid focal points for the denominator problem. The US Supreme Court has noted the relevance of the applicable background law in this regard:

> Unsurprisingly, this uncertainty regarding the composition of the denominator in our 'deprivation' fraction has produced inconsistent pronouncements by the Court . . . *The answer to this difficult question may lie in how the owner's reasonable expectations have been shaped by the State's law of property—i.e., whether and to what degree the State's law has accorded legal recognition and protection to the particular interest in land with respect to which the takings claimant alleges a diminution in (or elimination of) value.* In any event, we avoid this difficulty in the present case, since the 'interest in land' that Lucas has pleaded (a fee simple interest) is an estate with *a rich tradition of protection at common law.* (emphasis added)[171]

Similarly, the law of contracts (and public contracts)—as well as the rules applicable to assurances and representations—are critical factors. Contracts, assurances and representations may create not only entitlements but also denominators where otherwise non would exist. Perhaps air rights over land do not qualify as an autonomous denominator—as was the case in *Penn Central*[172]—but if the investor receives a public contract or specific authorisation to build a skyscraper on that 'space', it may later claim an indirect expropriation of those air rights.[173]

Let us now return to the main issue under discussion, and address the question of how the denominator should be set. Following the considerations expressed by the US Supreme Court in *Lucas*, my view is that arbitral tribunals should avoid the extremes represented by *Telenor* and *Eureko*. Instead, they should look for denominators which, properly grounded in the applicable law, represent generally shared business expectations concerning groups of rights that are accepted as autonomous entities. This can be supported by the fact that those rights are 'identifiable *distinct* parts' of the investors' enterprises, (emphasis

[171] *Lucas* (1992) 505 US 1016 n 7.

[172] See *Penn Central Transportation Co v New York City* (1978) 438 US 104 (hereinafter, *Penn Central*).

[173] See Paulsson and Douglas, n 13, 157, where they present an example that seems to refer to both the entitlement and the denominator.

added)[174] or that they are 'capable of *economic exploitation independently of the remainder of the investment*'.[175]

So, if an investor owns three buildings, he or she owns three separate entities that can be individually expropriated.[176] Infrastructure and other long-term contracts or concessions—but not bundles of rights within those agreements—are also generally autonomous entities, and therefore individually capable of being expropriated.[177] Administrative authorisations and licences, to the extent that separate business units depend on them for their own operation, are equally appropriate for use in the determination of a proper denominator.[178] As expected, this determination is dependent in each case on the nature and characteristics of the investor's business organisation.

As exception, there are two situations in which the decision-maker must necessarily adopt the full enterprise as the proper denominator: derivative claims and disputes involving liabilities and public utility rates. As is well known, derivative claims are those brought by investors in their capacity as shareholders of domestic companies, citing 'personal' indirect damage. These 'derivative' claims should not be confused with those situations in which domestic vehicles have standing to sue—as in Article 25(2)(b) of the ICSID Convention[179]—or when investors can sue on behalf of the domestic vehicles—as in NAFTA Article 1117.[180] If the domestic vehicle does not have standing to sue but is a wholly owned subsidiary of the investor, then

[174] *Fireman's Fund Insurance Co v Mexico*, ICSID Case No ARB(AF)/02/1 (van den Berg, Lowenfeld, Saavedra), Award (17 July 2006), ¶ 176. The complete holding is as follows: 'The taking must be a substantially complete deprivation of the economic use and enjoyment of the rights to the property, or of identifiable distinct parts thereof (i.e., it approaches total impairment)'.

[175] Kriebaum, n 88, 83. The complete solution this author proposes, ibid, is the following: '[U]nder this proposed solution, a partial expropriation should be accepted if the following requirements are fulfilled:—the overall investment project can be disassembled into a number of discrete rights;—the State has deprived the investor of a right which is covered by one of the items in the definition of 'investment' in the applicable investment protection treaty;—*this right is capable of economic exploitation independently of the remainder of the investment'*. (emphasis added). This reminds us of the requirements that David A Dana and Tomas W Merrill, *Property. Takings* (New York, Foundation Press, 2002) 68–85, advocate in the context of US constitutional law: discrete assets, possessing the right to exclude, *which might be available for exchange on a stand-alone basis.*

[176] See *GAMI* ¶¶ 126–128.

[177] The proposition that contracts can be subject to expropriation is uncontroverted in international law; see eg *LESI SpA et al v Algeria*, ICSID Case No ARB/05/3 (Tercier, Hanotiau, Gaillard), Award (12 November 2008), ¶ 131 (hereinafter, *LESI (Merits)*); *Sempra* ¶ 281; *Vivendi III* ¶7.5.4; *Siemens AG v Argentina*, ICSID Case No ARB/02/8 (Rigo, Brower, and Bello), Award (6 February 2007), ¶ 267; *Azurix* ¶ 314; *Eureko* ¶ 241; and, *Consortium RFCC* ¶ 60. A complete analysis of this issue can be found in Reinisch, n 117, 410–20, and Dolzer and Schreuer, n 142, 115–18.

[178] See *Middle East Cement* ¶¶ 101–65.

[179] *Convention on the Settlement of Investment Disputes between States and Nationals of Other States* (adopted 18 March 1965, entered into force 14 October 1966) 575 UNTS 159.

[180] *NAFTA* (1993) 32 ILM 605, 643.

the latter's claim may not be treated as a derivative claim (as was the case in *Telenor*)[181].

GAMI provides an excellent example. GAMI, the foreign investor and minority shareholder in GAM, the investment, had to prove an indirect expropriation of its shares, a condition equivalent to setting the denominator at the level of the full enterprise (instead of setting it at the level of assets owned by the investment).[182] In the Tribunal's words, 'GAMI's investment in GAM is protected by Article 1110 only if its shareholding was "taken"'.[183] GAM owned five sugar mills, all of which were expropriated; but later, after the arbitral proceedings were initiated, Mexican Courts reversed the expropriation, and returned three mills to GAM. Confronting this scenario, the Tribunal held that:

> GAM's own case would thus not have been affected in principle if only one mill had been expropriated. GAM's property rights in that single mill would have been 'taken' because GAM was formally dispossessed of those rights . . . But this Tribunal is not seised by GAM. GAMI's case is more difficult. The notions developed by *Pope & Talbot* may suggest that the 'impairment' of the value of its property (i.e. GAMI's shares in GAM) would not be equivalent to a 'taking' of that property if only one of five equally valuable GAM mills had been expropriated without compensation. The impairment might on the other hand have been *total* if that single mill was the only one having a positive value.[184]

The second situation involves state measures that, without destroying *assets*, augment the *liabilities*—for example, new taxes—or diminish the company's future income over which there are no formal entitlements. This is the case, for instance, with public utilities, when regulators set the cash inflow rate at too low a level. So, in cases involving taxation or utility rates, it will tend to be difficult for investors to win an indirect expropriation case. It should be noted that this is a normatively desirable outcome. Following the US Supreme Court's example, investment tribunals should avoid a 'piecemeal' review of ratemaking when entertaining expropriation claims;[185] that is, they should reject expropriation claims when the measure under scrutiny does not threaten the 'financial integrity' of the company.[186]

[181] See n 162.

[182] *GAMI* ¶ 123 ('GAMI's shares in GAM have not been expropriated. GAMI must therefore say that its *investment* in GAM has suffered something tantamount to expropriation').

[183] ibid ¶ 129.

[184] ibid ¶¶ 127–28.

[185] See *Duquesne Light Co v Barasch* (1989) 488 US 299, 314.

[186] See *Verizon Communications Inc v FCC* (2002) 535 US 467, 523–24, where the Court held that: 'At the outset, it is well to understand that the incumbent carriers do not present the portent of a constitutional taking claim in the way that is usual in ratemaking cases. They do not argue that any particular, actual TELRIC rate is "so unjust as to be confiscatory," that is, as threatening an incumbent's "financial integrity"'. (internal citations omitted).

Ultimately, the denominator problem is probably the most difficult normative assessment that decisionmakers face in determining whether a state measure effects a full or substantial deprivation. The respective ideological backgrounds of these decisionmakers—hidden amidst legal technicalities—can easily end up playing an outsised role if denominators are set either too small or too large. When too small, the very possibility of limiting the prima facie case of indirect expropriation to total or substantial deprivations is destroyed; when too high, investors are deprived of the protection of one of the key provisions of investment treaties. As with many other serious legal problems, the challenge is to find a solution representing a prudent middle ground.

III ARE THERE TOTAL OR SUBSTANTIAL DEPRIVATIONS THAT DO NOT QUALIFY AS EXPROPRIATIONS?

Are there total or substantial deprivations that do not qualify as indirect expropriations? This section addresses this question, presenting the *exceptions* and *counter-exceptions*, that is, step two and -three of the expropriatory analysis, respectively. The *exceptions* essentially refer to situations in which the state recognises that it has fully or substantially deprived the foreign investor, but still argues that compensation is not due. The *counter-exceptions* includes those cases where, in the presence of a total or substantial deprivation as well as a theoretically valid *exception*, the investor claims that the measures were applied in an unlawful or illegitimate manner.

An important terminological clarification must be made before delving into these issues. 'Interferences', 'deprivations', 'takings' and 'expropriations' all compete, from different sides of the semantic spectrum, descriptively and normatively, to dictate when a tribunal must find state liability. Given the confusion of these different labels,[187] several commentators have tried to identify them with different steps of the expropriatory analysis.[188] I take issue with such emphasis being made on the terminology problem, believing, like García-Amador, that this 'is not the crux of the matter'.[189] Words take on a life of their own. Therefore, we should avoid the attempt to resolve analytical problems by redefining old labels.

[187] According to Weston, n 104, 110, one of the factors that contributes to the 'lack of systematic appraisal of the international ' "taking"–"regulation" problem' stems precisely 'from ambiguous and imprecise language'.

[188] See eg Paulsson and Douglas, n 13, 148, and Weston, n 104, 112–13.

[189] FV García-Amador, 'Draft articles on the responsibility of the State for injuries caused in its territory to the person or property of aliens' in FV Garcia-Amador, Louis B Sohn and RR Baxter (eds), *Recent Codification of the Law of State Responsibility for Injuries to Aliens* (Dobbs Ferry, NY, Oceana Publications, 1974) 1, 47.

This section hence confronts the key question posed by Newcombe: 'How can we justify that a certain subset of state measures that result in substantial deprivations give rise to a right of compensation while others, with a similar effect from the perspective of the investor, do not?'.[190] To answer this question, the discussion of *exceptions* is organised around the two basic rationales of state liability used in this work: corrective and distributive justice. The discussion of *counter-exceptions* focuses on how considerations of arbitrariness that fall within the scope of the FET standard, become entangled in the expropriatory analysis.

A Exceptions I: Termination of Investment in Accordance with the Law

This first group of *exceptions* refers to those situations in which a state intentionally deprives the investor of his or her investment, but does so in accordance with the domestic law rules and principles regulating the extinction of such investment. The forfeiture of property involved in illegal activities and the general prohibition of such illegal activities, are probably the most extreme cases of this type of exceptions.

It is well established that customary international law does not treat either of those cases as compensable takings.[191] Relevant decisions may be found in the case law of the Iran–United States Claims Tribunal,[192] and also the European Court of Human Rights.[193] Similarly, Article 9.2. of Sohn and Baxter's *Draft Convention on the International Responsibility of States for Injuries to Aliens* (Harvard Draft) affirms that '[a] destruction of the property of an alien resulting from the judgment of a competent tribunal or from the action of the competent authorities of the State in the maintenance of the public order . . . shall not be considered wrongful',[194] and Comment 'g' of Section 712 of the *Restatement (Third) of the Foreign*

190 Newcombe, n 34, 26.

191 See Brownlie, n 4, 511–12.

192 *SEDCO Inc et al v National Iranian Oil Co et al* (1985) 9 Iran–US Claims Trib Rep 248, 275 (hereinafter, *SEDCO*), where the Tribunal held that 'forfeiture for crime' was an exception to the rule of expropriation, in the sense that the 'person(s) affected do not rightfully possess title to the property in question'.

193 *AGOSI v UK* (App no 9118/80) (1986) 9 EHRR 1 ¶ 51 (hereinafter, *AGOSI*): 'The forfeiture of the coins [which applicant AGOSI had sought to import into the United Kingdom against the law] did, of course, involve a deprivation of property, but in the circumstances the deprivation formed a constituent element of the procedure for the control of the use in the United Kingdom of gold coins such as Kruegerrands [finding therefore that the claimant was not entitled to compensation]'.

194 Louis B Sohn and Richard Baxter, 'Draft Convention on the International Responsibility of States for Injuries to the Economic Interests of Aliens' (1961) 55 *American Journal of International Law* 545, 551 (hereinafter, *Sohn and Baxter's Draft Articles*). In the commentaries to this Article, ibid 552, they provide a clear example: 'an alien could not complain if explosive or arms which were in his possession in violation of the law of the State concerned were destroyed by the police or by the military authorities'.

Relations Law indicates that '[a] state is not responsible for loss of property or for other economic disadvantage resulting from . . . forfeiture for crime'.[195]

Commentators in the BIT generation do not seem to dispute this rule of customary international law. According to UNCTAD, 'those takings that can be characterized as criminal law penalties, resulting from the violation of laws of a host State, are not compensable under customary international law'.[196] Similarly, Coe and Rubins comment that:

> An enterprise that is found through proper criminal proceedings to have used its investment property for unlawful activities presumably has no claim for compensation when that property is forfeited to the state . . . [A]ssuming that no denial of justice or other independent international wrong has occurred, the loss is, in a sense, self-inflicted.[197]

A representative case among investment treaty awards may be found in *Thunderbird*.[198] The investor was engaged in the business of operating gaming facilities. The Mexican Government, following a full investigation, closed all of the investor's facilities and seised its machines because they constituted illegal gaming equipment under Mexican law. When deciding the expropriation claim, the Tribunal held that, 'compensation is not owed for regulatory takings where it can be established that the *investor or investment never enjoyed a vested right in the business activity that was subsequently prohibited*'. (emphasis added)[199]

In addition, *exceptions* can also be found in those situations where the state annuls, cancels, or revokes a contract or concession, if it does so in accordance with the conditions established in the same agreement or in the applicable rules of domestic law. If the *ex ante* definition of those conditions does not fall below international minimum standards, then the appropriate termination of investments should not force the state to pay compensation.

As Vagts points out, there may be a violation of an international obligation in cases involving 'cancellation of the franchise, permit, or authorization to do business in which the investor relies, *except in accordance with its terms*'.[200] More recently, Newcombe has argued that state responsibility

[195] 2 *Restatement of the Law (Third): The Foreign Relations Law of the United States* (St Paul, MN, American Law Institute Publishers, 1987) 201, §712, Comment g (hereinafter, *Reinstatement (Third) of Foreign Relations Law*).

[196] United Nations Conference on Trade and Development (UNCTAD), *Taking of Property* (New York, United Nations, 2000) 41.

[197] Coe and Rubins, n 3, 637.

[198] *International Thunderbird Gaming v Mexico*, UNCITRAL Ad Hoc Arbitration (van den Berg, Wälde, Portal), Award (26 January 2006) (hereinafter, *Thunderbird*).

[199] ibid ¶ 208.

[200] Detlev F Vagts, 'Coercion and Foreign Investment Re-Arrangements' (1978) 72 *American Journal of International Law* 17, 35. The Tribunal in *CME I* ¶ 526, cited with approval this opinion.

does not arise 'for every permit, licence or concession cancellation. The rights arising under any form of government authorization will depend on the specific regulatory and legislative framework governing the right in question'.[201]

There are already several cases on record. In *Azinian*,[202] the Mexican Municipality of Naucalpan terminated the investor's concession on two grounds: original invalidity and investor's failure of performance. The Municipality took the invalidity case to Mexican courts, which, applying Mexican laws, upheld the claim. Confronting this scenario, the NAFTA Chapter 11 Tribunal concluded that:

> [T]he Claimants have not even attempted to demonstrate that the Mexican court decisions constituted a fundamental departure from established principles of Mexican law. The Respondent's evidence as to the relevant legal standards for annulment of public service contracts stands unrebutted. Nor do the Claimants contend that these legal standards breach NAFTA Article 1110. The Arbitral Tribunal finds nothing in the application of these standards with respect to the issue of invalidity that appears arbitrary or unsustainable in light of the evidentiary record. To the contrary, the evidence positively supports the conclusions of the Mexican courts.[203]

In *Saluka*, the Tribunal had to decide whether the termination of an investment using bankruptcy-type proceedings was an indirect expropriation (technically, the banking regulator put the company under 'forced administration'). After observing that 'Saluka has been deprived of its investment'[204]—ie, step one of the analysis—the Tribunal proceeded to review the *exceptions*, concluding that the behaviour of the defendant state was justified under domestic law:

> As will be seen, the CNB's decision is fully motivated. Having reviewed the totality of the evidence which the CNB invoked in support of its decision, the Tribunal is of the view that the CNB was justified, under Czech law, in imposing the forced administration of IPB and appointing an administrator to exercise the forced administration. The Czech State, in the person of its banking regulator, the CNB, had the responsibility to take a decision on 16 June 2000. It enjoyed a margin of discretion in the exercise of that responsibility. In reaching its decision, it took into consideration facts which, in the opinion of the Tribunal, it was very reasonable for it to consider. It then applied the pertinent Czech legislation to those facts—again, in a manner that the Tribunal considers reasonable. In the absence of clear and compelling evidence that the CNB erred or acted otherwise improperly in reaching its decision, which evidence has not been presented to

201 Newcombe, n 34, 19.

202 *Azinian et al v Mexico*, ICSID Case N° ARB(AF)/97/2 (Paulsson, Civiletti, von Wobeser), Award (1 November 1999), ¶¶ 93 ff. (hereinafter, *Azinian*).

203 ibid ¶ 120. See also, Newcombe, n 34, 19–20.

204 *Saluka* ¶ 267.

the Tribunal, the Tribunal must in the circumstances accept the justification given by the Czech banking regulator for its decision.[205]

Note that these *exceptions* do not require redistributive or balancing exercises. The Tribunal must only check whether the investor acted within the scope of legality given by the formal terms of its investment, and whether the state exercised its powers without incurring any wrong. The analysis is essentially bilateral, focused on the wrongfulness of each party's actions. For the same reason, the decision-maker should pay special attention to domestic law,[206] the body of law that generally defines what is legal or illegal in the defendant's state territory, and which also defines the conditions for termination of contracts, concessions, and, more generally, investments.[207]

B Exceptions II: Pre-eminent Public Interests

A second group of *exceptions* refers to those situations in which the state invokes what Moderne refers to as 'pre-eminent-public interests',[208] that is, public ends that justify the sacrifice of private interests without paying compensation.[209] The existence of these pre-eminent public interests in investment treaty arbitration leads us directly into the realm of distributive justice and global constitutional law, and to the question: what qualifies as a pre-eminent public interest in the BIT generation? In other

[205] ibid ¶¶ 271–73. See also, ibid ¶ 275: 'The CNB's decision is, in the opinion of the Tribunal, a lawful and permissible regulatory action by the Czech Republic aimed at the general welfare of the State, and does not fall within the ambit of any of the exceptions to the permissibility of regulatory action which are recognised by customary international law. Accordingly, the CNB's decision did not, fall within the notion of a "deprivation" referred to in Article 5 of the Treaty, and thus did not involve a breach of the Respondent's obligations under that Article.'

[206] See eg Santiago Montt, 'The Award in *Thunderbird v Mexico*' in Guillermo Aguilar Alvarez and W Michael Reisman (eds), *The Reasons Requirement in International Investment Arbitration: Critical Case Studies* (M Nijhoff, Leiden 2008) 261 (criticising the award in *Thunderbird* for not giving proper attention to Mexican law).

[207] The relevant law here is usually the domestic law of public contracts. See eg *Biwater Gauff*, ¶¶399–470, where the investor argued that the repudiation of a lease was an indirect expropriation. When deciding the expropriation claim, the Tribunal started by noting, ibid ¶ 469, that its role was not to decide contractual issues. However, it then observed, ibid ¶ 470, that 'in determining the treaty claims as between BGT and the Republic, it is impossible to disregard the way in which the Lease Contract was concluded, performed, renegotiated and terminated'. Later, it stated clearly, ibid ¶ 471 that because it 'can only discharge its mandate by considering issues relevant to the contractual relationship, it obviously has jurisdiction to do so'. See also, Meron, n 44, 275 (noting in this regard that 'an international tribunal, whose normal function is to administer international law, may find it necessary to apply a certain domestic law').

[208] Frank Moderne, '*La Responsabilidad por Actos del Legislador y por los Tratados Internacionales en Francia*' in Javier Barnés (ed), *Propiedad, Expropiación y Responsabilidad. Derecho Comparado Europeo* (Madrid, Tecnos, 1995) 955, 965.

[209] See ch 4, 193–198.

words, does the state pursue goals of such compelling character that they can justify full deprivations without paying compensation?[210]

It should be stressed, as explained in chapter 4,[211] that the efforts by commentators to reduce the problem of pre-eminent public interests to the logic of corrective justice have been fruitless. According to this argument, property rights do not entitle owners to harm others; therefore, in cases involving pre-eminent public interests the government is simply updating the original limits of those property rights. In United States' constitutional law, this is the function of the 'nuisance exception'.[212] However, the distinction between regulations that avoid harm and those that fosters welfare is virtually impossible to maintain, reflecting the fact that the problem touches really upon the distribution of burdens and benefits across society.[213]

In general international law—however surprising—the existence and validity of pre-eminent public interests have traditionally been accepted. For example, Article 10.5 of Sohn and Baxter's *Draft Convention on the International Responsibility of States for Injuries to Aliens* (Harvard Draft) declares that the public order, health, and morality may be such kind of ends.[214]

Similarly, Brownlie lists among the exceptions to the compensation rule 'loss caused indirectly by health and planning legislation and the concomitant restrictions on the use of property'.[215] The *Restatement (Third) of Foreign Relations Law* affirms as well that '[a] state is not responsible for loss of property or for other economic disadvantage resulting from bona

[210] See Coe and Rubins, n 3, 598, who pose similar questions: 'In particular, do non-discriminatory measures of a regulatory nature enjoy, simply by virtue of their regulatory character, an exemption from the normal operation of expropriation doctrine? If not as a general matter, are there nevertheless certain circumstances, or kinds of regulation, that attract preferential treatment?' Later, ibid 638, they also ask 'whether some public purposes are so compelling that a State pursuing such an end should be absolved of the duty to compensate adversely affected foreign investors'. Similarly, Newcombe, n 34, 3, asks: 'what is a *legitimate* and *bona fide* exercise of state police powers that justifies a complete deprivation of property with no corresponding obligation to pay compensation?'.

[211] See ch 4, 191–198.

[212] As explained by Susan Rose-Ackerman and Jim Rossi, 'Disentangling Deregulatory Takings' (2000) 86 *Virginia Law Review* 1435, 1445, '[e]ven in total deprivation cases' the nuisance exception allows 'for deference to government action intended to address key public health, safety, and welfare concerns'.

[213] See Frank Michelman, 'Property, Utility, and Fairness: Comments on the Ethical Foundations of 'Just Compensation' Law' (1967) 80 *Harvard Law Review* 1165, 1197 (noting that the method of distinguising between the prevention of harms and the extraction of benefits 'will not work unless we can establish a benchmark of "neutral" conduct which enables us to say where refusal to confer benefits (not reversible without compensation) slips over into readiness to inflict harms (reversible without compensation)'; and, Jeremy Paul, 'The Hidden Structure of Takings Law' (1991) 64 *Southern California Law Review* 1393, 1440–41 (noting that '[g]overnment regulators will always be able to characterize specific restrictions as harm-preventing').

[214] *Sohn and Baxter*'s *Draft Articles*, n 194, 554. For full citation, see ch 4, n 122, and accompanying text.

[215] See Brownlie, n 191, 511–12.

fide general taxation, regulation . . . or other action of the kind that is commonly accepted as within the police power of states'.[216]

In the BIT generation, recent US BITs and FTAs have explicitly stated that not all instances of full and substantial deprivations represent expropriations.[217] Moreover, even in the absence of express treaty provisions, tribunals have recognised the existence and validity of pre-eminent public interests.[218] In *Methanex*, a Canadian investor challenged the legitimacy of a Californian regulation that banned the use of MTBE—a methanol-based product used as oxygenate for gasoline—forcing the use of a competing ethanol-based product. As a consequence, the investor argued that a substantial portion of its investment—defined as its share of the California market and the corresponding goodwill—had been deprived. Although the Tribunal did not appear persuaded of the existence of a total or substantial deprivation, it decided the taking question against the investor on more general terms, holding that:

> In the Tribunal's view, Methanex is correct that an intentionally discriminatory regulation against a foreign investor fulfils a key requirement for establishing expropriation. *But as a matter of general international law, a non-discriminatory regulation for a public purpose, which is enacted in accordance with due process and, which affects, inter alios, a foreign investor or investment is not deemed expropriatory and compensable unless specific commitments had been given by the regulating government to the then putative foreign investor contemplating investment that the government would refrain from such regulation.* (emphasis added)[219]

Later, in *Saluka*, the Tribunal made a similarly categorical statement: 'It is now established in international law that States are not liable to pay compensation to a foreign investor when, in the normal exercise of their regulatory powers, they adopt in a non-discriminatory manner *bona fide* regulations that are aimed at the general welfare'.[220]

It should be noted that there is a huge difference between concluding that *some* public interests are pre-eminent—rare, indeed[221]—and stating that all

[216] 2 *Reinstatement of the Law of Foreign Relations (Third)*, n 195, 200–01, §712 Comment g.

[217] See eg *US–Singapore FTA*, n 9; *US–Chile FTA*, n 9; and, the *2004 US Model BIT*, n 9. The latter, see No 4(b) of Annex B, provides the following: 'Except in rare circumstances, nondiscriminatory regulatory actions by a Party that are designed and applied to protect legitimate public welfare objectives, such as public health, safety, and the environment, do not constitute indirect expropriations'. More recently, the *Australia–Chile Free Trade Agreement* (signed 27 May 2008, entered into force on 6 March 2009), Annex 10-B, No 3(b), provides exactly the same exception (available at http://www.austlii.edu.au/au/other/dfat/treaties/2009/6/10.html#Heading677) (hereinafter, *Australia–Chile FTA*).

[218] The *Santa Elena* case ¶ 72, is sometimes cited to support the opposite proposition that there are no pre-eminent public interests in the BIT generation. However ¶ 72 is mere *dicta*. The dispute submitted to the *Santa Elena* Tribunal included only the amount of compensation, not the expropriation itself (see ibid ¶¶18, 54).

[219] *Methanex Corporation v US*, UNCITRAL Ad Hoc Arbitration (Veeder, Rowley, Reisman), Award (9 August 2005), Pt IV, Ch D, at 4, ¶ 7 (hereinafter, *Methanex*).

[220] *Saluka* ¶ 255. See also, ibid ¶ 262.

[221] From the perspective of U.S constitutional law, Justice Rehnquist reminds us that '[t]he

bona fide and non-discriminatory regulation permits states to evade the duty of paying compensation.[222] To affirm otherwise would have the effect of completely erasing the protective scope of investment treaties; states could always justify their behaviour by invoking some public interest.[223]

Public interests are typically non-pre-eminent, and this should also be the operative presumption in investment treaty disputes. The distributive justice rationale at work reminds us—as Paulsson and Douglas observe—that the state should not make a practice of invoking its police powers to radically overburden investors:

> Where the value of an investment has been *totally* destroyed by *bona fides* regulation in the public interest, it may well be that international law does not allow the Host State to place such a high individual burden on an investor for the pursuit of a regulatory objective for the benefit of the community at large without the payment of compensation.[224]

Of course, we cannot generate two rigid lists of public interests, one encompassing those that are standard and the other, pre-eminent. Public interests come in all types and varieties, covering the full spectrum from the most weak and ordinary, to the most serious, such as 'essential interests' that must be safeguarded against 'grave an imminent peril(s)' (which, under certain circumstances, precludes wrongfulness in international law).[225] Although the expropriation logic forces us into a *summa divisio*, the decision making process does not work in an all-or-nothing fashion. Here, we encounter a complex process of balancing, whereby the decision-maker must review the means-ends relationship and proportionality of the state's measures. This means that, on this dimension, step two and -three of the expropriatory analysis cannot, in practice, truly be separated.[226]

nuisance exception to the taking guarantee is not coterminous with the police power itself. The question is whether the forbidden use is dangerous to the safety, health, or welfare of others' (*Penn Central* (1978) 438 US 145 (Rehnquist J dissenting)), and that the nuisance exception is a 'narrow exception allowing the government to prevent "a misuse or illegal use"' (*Keystone Bituminous Coal Assn et al v DeBenedictis, Secretary, Pennsylvania Dept of Environmental Resources et al* (1987) 480 US 470, 512 (Rehnquist J dissenting) (internal citation omitted)). See Ethan Shenkman, 'Could Principles of Fifth Amendment Takings Jurisprudence Be Helpful in Analyzing Regulatory Expropriation Claims under International Law' (2002) 11 *New York University Environmental Law Journal* 174, 187.

[222] In this sense, in *Saluka* ¶ 263, the Tribunal does not seem to consider that all public interests are pre-eminent: 'That being said, international law has yet to identify in a comprehensive and definitive fashion precisely what regulations are considered 'permissible' and 'commonly accepted' as falling within the police or regulatory power of States and, thus, noncompensable. In other words, it has yet to draw a bright and easily distinguishable line between non-compensable regulations on the one hand and, on the other, measures that have the effect of depriving foreign investors of their investment and are thus unlawful and compensable in international law'.

[223] See Coe and Rubins, n 3, 639.

[224] Paulsson and Douglas, n 13, 158. As cited in ch 4, n 121, the German Constitutional Court offers arbitral tribunals a convenient path for further exploration.

[225] Art 25(1)(a) of the *ILC's Draft Articles and Commentaries*, n 85, 178.

[226] Weston, n 104, 123, proposes an holistic approach which I found too abstract and,

Nevertheless, in chapter 4 I advanced a distinction—general policy changes based on new scientific evidence or technology v general policy changes based on change in polities' preferences—that may be useful in discerning when compensation must be paid.[227] When new evidence or technology shows us that previously acceptable uses of property are indeed harmful, the prohibition or radical regulatory reform of those uses should not, *in principle*, be considered a compensable expropriation. On the contrary, when changes in the preferences of polities (or politicians) give place to regulatory reform, then, *in principle*, compensation must be paid. I am aware that it can be difficult to distinguish between these two situations; new scientific knowledge can produce changes in polities' preferences, and the latter may be masked or justified by allegedly new scientific information. But this dichotomy, at least, provides an analytical starting point from which to approach the difficult issue of pre-eminent public interests.

Finally, how much deference do states deserve in their consideration of certain public interests as pre-eminent? I would suggest here that states deserve little deference; investment treaty tribunals must review with heightened scrutiny the pre-eminent character of public interests in accordance with international law, though with a comparative law benchmark in mind.[228] The bottom line is that, following the German Constitutional Court, only 'special circumstances' justify the complete destruction of property without paying compensation.[229] In the BIT generation, pre-eminent public interests should remain 'rarities'.[230]

C Counter-Exceptions: Arbitrariness and Fair and Equitable Treatment Considerations in Expropriation Claims

An investor who faces the termination of an investment in accordance with the law or the state's invocation of a pre-eminent public interest, may

consequently, difficult to apply to concrete cases: 'Thus, to resolve the "taking"–"regulation" dilemma in the international realm—to decide when compensation should or should not be paid for the "regulatory" deprivation of foreign wealth—one should look to see whether, *in total context*, the "regulations" under challenge do or do not advance a world public order which holds of at least the prospect of universal security and abundance, the *desideratum* of compensatory decision generally. If so, then deference should be accorded the necessary State competence presumption mentioned above and the deprivative intervention held liability-free. If not, then the reverse is true, and compensation should be paid'.

[227] I am only interested here in general legislation or regulation. Specific instances of administrative action, such as revocations of permits, are analysed in more detail in ch 6, 323–366.

[228] As explained in more detail in ch 6, 303–310, international minimum standards serve as the 'transmission belt' beween international and comparative law.

[229] *Right of Pre-Emption Case*, BVerGE 83, 201, 212–213 (1991), cited in ch 4, n 121.

[230] Laura S Underkuffler, *The Idea of Property. Its Meaning and Power* (New York, OUP, 2003) 89 (noting, from a US perspective, that 'we may *overcome* the power of title claims . . . with public interests of unusual urgency. However, such instances are very controversial in law, and remain (most certainly) rarities').

counter argue that the depriving measure was illegally or arbitrarily imposed. As Coe and Rubins explain, '[a]ssuming a legitimate objective, it remains possible that under the guise of otherwise unobjectionable pre-screening or supervising of investment activity, officials may act with such arbitrariness and disproportionality that the original objective is besides the point'.[231] This statement represents a demand that tribunals review—as acknowledged in *Archer Daniels*—'whether the measure was proportionate or necessary for a legitimate purpose; whether it discriminated in law or in practice; whether it was not adopted in accordance with due process of law; or whether it interfered with the investor's legitimate expectations when the investment was made'.[232]

Step-three of the analysis—the *counter-exceptions*—thus focuses on all the forms of arbitrariness that generally comprise an important part of the FET standard (and all of which are carefully studied in the next chapter): 'arbitrariness as illegality', 'administrative due process', 'arbitrariness as irrationality', 'arbitrariness as special sacrifice', and 'arbitrariness as lack of proportionality'.[233] It is at this stage of the analysis that we observe some degree of conceptual overlap between the expropriation and FET clauses.[234] (Discrimination, which usually gives way to a separate national treatment claim, also plays an equivalent role in the expropriatory analysis[235]).

The function and character of the *counter-exceptions* depends on the *exceptions* being invoked by the state. For deprivations allegedly justified under corrective justice rationales—ie, termination of investments in accordance with the law[236]—counter-exceptions are typically grounded in illegality and lack of due process. Also, given that the termination of such rights usually function as a sanction, as a matter of retributive justice these

[231] Coe and Rubins, n 3, 642.

[232] *Archer Daniels Midland Co et al v Mexico*, ICSID Case No ARB(AF)/04/05 (Cremades, Rovine, Siqueiros), Award (21 November 2007), ¶ 250.

[233] See ch 6, 323–366.

[234] This raises a methodological question. Should the *counter-exceptions* or step-three of the analysis be part of the expropriation clause, or should it be confined to the application of the FET clause? In my opinion, when duly claimed, the 'counter-exceptions'—legality, rationality, proportionality, due process, etc.—are proper elements of the no expropriation without compensation standard. In other words, there is no monopoly by the FET clause cases over such elements, and no dogmatic reason that forbids their consideration in step-three of the expropriatory analysis. The main issue is, after all, as pointed out by Yoram Dinstein, 'Deprivation of Property of Foreigners under International Law' in Nisuke Ando et al (eds), 2 *Liber Amicorum Judge Shigeru Oda* (New York, Kluwer Law International, 2002) 849, 852, that 'whereas the extent of ordinary governmental activities cannot be precisely defined, the emphasis must be placed on good faith and reasonableness'.

[235] See 2 *Restatement (Third) of Foreign Relations Law*, n 195, 201, §712. See also, Arts 9.2 and 10.5 of *Sohn and Baxter*'s *Draft Articles*, n 194, 551, and 553, both of which require a series of 'negative' conditions for non-compensable deprivations, ie, non-discriminatory application of domestic law, no denial of justice, no departure from the general principles of the law, and no abuse of power (for full citation, see ch 4, n 98, and accompanying text).

[236] See nn 191–207, and accompanying text.

counter-exceptions may be grounded in a lack of proportionality. The point is that fines, forfeitures and revocations of contracts and authorisations are permissible only when the state proceeds in a manner that is legal, procedurally appropriate, and proportionate.

Metalclad constitutes an interesting example of such a case, in which illegality played—at least implicitly—a key role. In *Metalclad*, the Tribunal concluded that by illegally denying a permit (ultra vires), a Mexican Municipality destroyed the investor's investment, bringing a compensable expropriation:

> A central point in this case has been whether, in addition to the above-mentioned permits, a municipal permit for the construction of a hazardous waste landfill was required.[237] . . . [T]he Municipality denied the local construction permit in part because of the Municipality's perception of the adverse environmental effects of the hazardous waste landfill and the geological unsuitability of the landfill site. *In so doing, the Municipality acted outside its authority.* As stated above, the Municipality's denial of the construction permit without any basis in the proposed physical construction or any defect in the site, and extended by its subsequent administrative and judicial actions regarding the *Convenio, effectively and unlawfully prevented the Claimant's operation of the landfill* (emphasis added).[238]

In addition, as noted, the lack of *due process* can transform a lawful seizure into an indirect expropriation. In *Middle East Cement*,[239] the Tribunal concluded that due to a failure to properly notify the investor of the seizure and auction of its vessel *Poseidon*, the latter 'was taken by a "measure the effects of which would be tantamount to expropriation" and that the Claimant is entitled to a compensation'.[240] In *Rumeli*, the termination of a contract without having properly followed its established procedure was held to be a violation of the FET standard, and also part of a larger-scale *creeping expropriation*.[241]

Finally, as a matter of retributive justice, arbitral tribunals may review whether the seizure of property, termination of contracts or licences, and other administrative fines and punishments constitute proportionate sanctions that take into account the wrong committed by the investor and its consequences. This review should give particular deference to sanctions that are defined *ex ante* within legal or contractual norms, and be slightly more intrusive for sanctions that are imposed pursuant administrative discretionary powers.

237 *Metalclad* ¶ 79.

238 ibid ¶ 106.

239 *Middle East Cement* ¶¶ 139–44. Note the conceptual overlap between the expropriation and the FET clauses in ¶ 143.

240 ibid ¶ 144.

241 *Rumeli Telekom* ¶¶ 612–18, 708. Note, again, the conceptual overlap between the expropriation and FET standards in ¶ 708.

On the other hand, for deprivations allegedly justified under distributive justice rationales—ie, the invocation by the state of a pre-eminent public interest[242]—counter-exceptions are typically grounded in 'arbitrariness as irrationality', and 'arbitrariness as lack of proportionality'. With regards to irrationality—which, as a counter-exception, tries to discredit the honesty of the state's distributive effort—*Methanex* constitutes an important decision. In this case, the claimant challenged the rationality and means-ends relationship of certain California environmental measures, arguing that the regulator's real purpose was not the protection of the environment, but to benefit the American ethanol industry.

The *Methanex* Tribunal recognised the need to perform some form of rationality review. However, it chose to follow a review that was process-based, exhibiting a high level of deference with respect to the findings of facts and substantive reasons invoked by the state to justify the new measures:

> Methanex entered a political economy in which it was widely known, if not notorious, that governmental environmental and health protection institutions at the federal and state level, operating under the vigilant eyes of the media, interested corporations, non-governmental organizations and a politically active electorate, continuously monitored the use and impact of chemical compounds and commonly prohibited or restricted the use of some of those compounds for environmental and/or health reasons. Indeed, the very market for MTBE in the United States was the result of precisely this regulatory process. Methanex appreciated that the process of regulation in the United States involved wide participation of industry groups, non-governmental organizations, academics and other individuals, many of these actors deploying lobbyists. Methanex itself deployed lobbyists. Mr Wright, Methanex's witness, described himself as the government relations officer of the company.[243]

It should be noted that in the context of rationality review, states' *purposes* do matter. In the BIT generation (and prior), commentators and tribunals have inquired as to the proper place for *purposes*.[244] In the context of indirect expropriations, the answer should now be clear: if the state invokes a pre-eminent public interest (an exception), the investor may argue (as a counter-exception) that this interest plays no meaningful role in the actual conflict at stake.[245] This is the archetypal pattern of the *détournement de pouvoir*, where the real purpose of the state is to deprive the foreign investor, and not to pursue the interest invoked as pre-eminent. This also

242 See nn 209–230, and accompanying text.

243 *Methanex*, Pt IV, Ch D, at 5, ¶ 9.

244 See eg Schreuer, n 6, 28, ¶ 80; Newcombe, n 34, 25; and, Coe and Rubins, n 3, 616.

245 As Christie, n 99, 332, explains in his classic work on the matter: ' "Purpose", however, is a much abused word in international law. It is impossible to read many of the authors who have written widely on the subject of expropriation and nationalization without coming to suspect that, at least some of the time, they are not talking about the purpose which a State actually gives for its action but rather about some 'real' purpose, some subjective purpose, which motivates the State or, rather, the persons who have the supreme power in a State.

occurs when the public interest in question is an ordinary one, disguised as pre-eminent.

This rare instance of review of states' purposes should not be confused with another scenario in which that review is inappropriate. Some tribunals and commentators are stating—incorrectly from my perspective[246]—that 'lawful expropriations' and 'unlawful expropriations' should receive different treatment in terms of the amount of compensation.[247] Expropriations' lawful or unlawful character would depend on compliance with the list of conditions that investment treaties typically establish for expropriations: a public interest, due process, non-discrimination, and payment of compensation. In this context—as effectively occurred in *ADC*—tribunals would be authorised to dictate whether the goal invoked by the state qualifies as a public interest (including ordinary public interests).[248]

Yet, contrary to how it may appear, these four requirements listed in investment treaties are of virtually no interest to the expropriatory analysis (unless one accepts—which I do not—that remedies different from compensation may be adopted and enforced against states[249]). The effects of lawful or unlawful expropriations are the same. As the *Feldman* Tribunal held, '[i]f there is a finding of expropriation, *compensation is required, even if* the taking is for public purpose, non-discriminatory and in accordance with due process and Article 1105(1)'. (emphasis added)[250]

[246] Arguing against this distinction, see Manuel A Abdala and Pablo Spiller, 'Chorzów's Standard Rejuvenated—Assessing Damages in Investment Treaty Arbitration' (2008) 25 *Journal of International Arbitration* 103, 107 ('[T]he loss in value of the investment is the same regardless of the legality of the act . . . [W]e discard any interpretation that presupposes a distinction, from an economic perspective, between lawful and unlawful expropriation').

[247] See eg *Biwater Gauff* ¶ 775 (stating that unlawful expropriation entitles investor to consequential damages); and, *ADC Affiliate Ltd et al v Hungary*, ICSID Case No ARB/03/16 (Kaplan, Brower, van den Berg), Award (2 October 2006), ¶¶ 483–500 (hereinafter, *ADC*) (holding that compensation in cases of unlawful expropriations should follow the rules of customary international law, and not the rules provided in the BIT for expropriations; this lead the Tribunal to assess market value as at the date of the award instead of market value as at the date of the expropriation). See also, Dolzer and Schreuer, n 142, 124.

[248] In *ADC* ¶ 429, the Tribunal concluded that it 'can see no public interest being served by the Respondent's depriving actions of the Claimants' investments in the Airport Project'. Then, ibid ¶¶ 432–33, it added that: 'In the Tribunal's opinion, a treaty requirement for *"public interest"* requires some genuine interest of the public. If mere reference to *"public interest"* can magically put such interest into existence and therefore satisfy this requirement, then this requirement would be rendered meaningless since the Tribunal can imagine no situation where this requirement would not have been met. With the claimed *"public interest"* unproved and the Tribunal's curiosity thereon unsatisfied, the Tribunal must reject the arguments made by the Respondent in this regard. In any event, as the Tribunal has already remarked, the subsequent privatization and the agreement with BAA renders this whole debate somewhat unnecessary'.

[249] See ch 3, nn 66–69 and accompanying text. In theory, restitution is an admissible remedy, but, in practice, it should be converted into damages for those cases in which the state does not choose to voluntary restitute the taken property or re-establish a certain regulatory regime.

[250] *Feldman* ¶ 98. But see, August Reinisch, 'Legality of Expropriations' in August Reinisch, *Standards of Investment Protection* (New York, OUP, 2008) 171, 199–203.

The key question—whether a compensable expropriation has really occurred at all—not only comes prior to any consideration of those requirements,[251] but exhausts essentially all relevant discussions concerning the application of the expropriation clause. There are no punitive damages against states in international investment law; in addition, tribunals should avoid an interventionist review of the public interest under the guise of controlling unlawful expropriations.

Lack of proportionality can also serve as a counter-exception in cases involving deprivations that have been justified under the distributive justice rationale. As previously noted, step two and -three of the expropriatory analysis become intertwined at this point. The claimant would argue that, even if the public interest invoked by the state is theoretically preeminent, in the light of the circumstances, that goal does not carry sufficient normative weight to justify a complete elimination of his or her investment. Similarly, the claimant may argue that the imposition of that burden may constitute a situation of excessive special sacrifice as compared with the rest of society.

Several tribunals have recognised the relevance of proportionality in expropriation disputes.[252] In *Tecmed*, the Tribunal provided a long explanation which deserves full citation:

> After establishing that regulatory actions and measures will not be initially excluded from the definition of expropriatory acts, in addition to the negative financial impact of such actions or measures, the Arbitral Tribunal will consider, in order to determine if they are to be characterized as expropriatory, whether such actions or measures are proportional to the public interest presumably protected thereby and to the protection legally granted to investments, taking into account that the significance of such impact has a key role upon deciding the proportionality . . . There must be a reasonable relationship of proportionality between the charge or weight imposed to the foreign investor and the aim

[251] This was recognised in *Fireman's Fund Insurance Co v Mexico*, ICSID Case No ARB(AF)/02/1 (van den Berg, Lowenfeld, Saavedra), Award (17 July 2006), ¶ 174: 'In determining whether a State Party to the NAFTA has violated its obligations under Article 1110 of the NAFTA, an arbitral tribunal has to start with the analysis whether an expropriation has occurred. Mexico correctly points out that one cannot start an inquiry into whether expropriation has occurred by examining whether the conditions in Article 1110(1) of the NAFTA for avoiding liability in the event of an expropriation have been fulfilled. That would indeed be putting the cart before the horse (*'poner la carreta delante de los caballos'*). Paragraphs (a) through (d) do not bear on the question as whether an expropriation has occurred. Rather, the conditions contained in paragraphs (a) through (d) specify the parameters as to when a State would not be liable under Article 1110'.

[252] This confirms that the 'sole effects' doctrine does not extend beyond step-one of the expropriatory analysis. Otherwise, there would be no need to discuss whether or not the measures at stake are proportional. As Coe and Rubins, n 3, 653, note in relation to the consideration of proportionality in the *Tecmed* case, '[t]he Tribunal's analysis did not end with the finding that there had been a near-total deprivation of Tecmed's enjoyment of its investment as a result of the permit revocation. Rather, the burden shifted to Mexico, to show that the expropriation was justified as falling within the State's police power'.

sought to be realized by any expropriatory measure. To value such charge or weight, it is very important to measure the size of the ownership deprivation caused by the actions of the state and whether such deprivation was compensated or not.[253]

In *Link-Trading*, the Tribunal held that taxes can be expropriatory if they are applied unfairly and inequitably, by which it seems to refer to lack of proportionality and special sacrifice:

> As a general matter, fiscal measures only become expropriatory when they are found to be an abusive taking. Abuse arises where it is demonstrated that the State had acted unfairly or inequitable towards the investment, where it has adopted measures that are arbitrary or discriminatory in character or in their manner of implementation, or when the measure taken violate an obligation undertaken by the State in regard to the investment.[254]

Similarly, in *LG&E*, the Tribunal observed that an initial situation of non-compensable deprivation might be transformed into a compensable expropriation if the measure is disproportionate to the end sought:

> With respect to the power of the State to adopt its policies, it can generally be said that the State has the right to adopt measures having a social or general welfare purpose. In such a case, the measure must be accepted without any imposition of liability, except in cases where the State's action is obviously disproportionate to the need being addressed.[255]

Finally, before ending our discussion about step two and -three of the expropriatory analysis, a brief remark should be made about the confusion that some of the newest BITs and FTAs have created by importing the US *Penn Central* regulatory takings test. For example, the Chile–United States FTA establishes that:

> The determination of whether an action or series of actions by a Party, in a specific fact situation, constitutes an indirect expropriation, requires a case-by-case, fact-based inquiry that considers, among other factors: (i) the economic impact of the government action, although the fact that an action or series of actions by a Party has an adverse effect on the economic value of an investment, standing alone, does not establish that an indirect expropriation has occurred; (ii) the extent to which the government action interferes with distinct, reasonable investment-backed expectations; and (iii) the character of the government action.[256]

The introduction of the *Penn Central* test to investment treaty arbitration has a disruptive effect. The *Penn Central* test is used in the US in order to

[253] *Tecmed* ¶ 122.

[254] *Link-Trading* ¶ 64. Note, again, the conceptual overlap between the expropriation and FET standards in the language used by the Tribunal.

[255] *LG&E* ¶ 195.

[256] *US–Chile FTA*, n 9, ch 10, Annex D, No 4(a). See also, *2004 US Model BIT*, n 9, Annex B, and, *Australia–Chile FTA*, n 217, Annex 10-B, No 3(a).

expand the excessively restrictive *Lucas* and *Loretto* categorical tests, which require, respectively, full economic deprivations and physical occupations. Yet, paradoxically, it seems that in investment treaties the *Penn Central* test has been introduced to restrict the extent of indirect expropriations, not to expand them.

How can we find a rational solution to this contradictory regulation of expropriations in investment law? The most important point is that the *Penn Central* test should not be used to expand the prima facie case of expropriations beyond full and substantial deprivations. We must keep in mind that these US treaties also state that they intend 'to reflect customary international law concerning the obligation of States with respect to expropriation'.[257]

In my opinion, the *Penn Central* balancing test should be applied at step two and -three of the expropriatory analysis, that is, to the assessment of potential exceptions and counter-exceptions. But the test should also be used as a guide, when appropriate, for FET claims. In international investment law, the proper context for considering non-destructive harm is not expropriations—as in US constitutional law—but the FET clause. That clause is the more appropriate context for the type of balancing and proportionality exercises that the *Penn Central* test invites tribunals to perform.

CONCLUSIONS: FEARING AD HOCISM MORE THAN AN EXCESSIVELY EXTENSIVE CONCEPT OF EXPROPRIATIONS

In accordance with the normative framework developed in the first part of this work, the main objective of these conclusions is to assess whether international investment law is crystallising rules and principles for protection of investments that go beyond those recognised by supreme and constitutional courts of mature regulatory capitalist countries with respect to their own national investors.

In the BIT generation, the expropriation clause's potential for hyper expansion has been an issue of constant concern.[258] For example, Dolzer has affirmed that 'it is not unreasonable to assume that the legal issues in the foreign investment context may, for the time being, be dominated by the definition of expropriation'.[259] In 2003, Been and Beauvais made a preliminary, and 'speculative' analysis,[260] concluding that compared to

[257] *US–Chile FTA*, n 9, ch 10, Annex D, No 1. See also, *2004 US Model BIT*, n 9, Annex B, No 1 ('The parties confirm their shared understanding that: 1. Article 6 [Expropriation and Compensation] is intended to reflect customary international law concerning the obligation of States with respect to expropriation').

[258] See eg Been and Beauvais, n 17, 34.

[259] Dolzer, n 68, 66. See also, Fortier and Drymer, n 52, 298.

[260] Been and Beauvais, n 17, 37.

the US takings jurisprudence, '[BIT] tribunals' nascent interpretation of Chapter 11 broaden the definition of compensable property interests in several significant ways'.[261]

However, I disagree with their conclusions. This chapter has reviewed each of five doctrinal dimensions identified in section I,[262] and the overall outcome appears reasonable when compared to the constitutional traditions studied in chapter 4. At least three general observations can be mentioned in this regard. First, expropriations are defined to exclude mere interferences. Therefore, in the BIT generation, expropriations must be considered to protect the core but not the periphery of investments. Not surprisingly, then, the general adjudicative tension between the private and the public interest has been transferred from the expropriatory clause to the FET clause, which must be considered the key provision of investment treaties today.

Secondly, though BIT case law has not yet found clear or uniform answers for the definition of substantial deprivation and the denominator problem, at least several tribunals have resisted the temptation to move toward 'conceptual severance'. In other words, there is no dominant trend among investment treaty tribunals of chopping up investment to the point that the damage suffered coincides with the unit of rights representing the proper denominator of the fraction. To accept that practice would lead tribunals to conclude that any type of regulation is, indeed, an expropriation.

Thirdly, there have already been important arbitral decisions recognising that the invocation of pre-eminent public interests and the termination of rights in accordance with the rules, are acceptable deprivations that do not require payment of compensation. This means that bona fide and non-discriminatory regulation, even when fully destroying the value of investment, *may* not require the payment of compensation. In addition, the intensity with which arbitral tribunals have reviewed rationality and proportionality in step three of the expropriatory analysis does not seem excessively interventionist.

The result is that today, even in the absence of a crystallised case law on the matter, the general picture of the expropriation clause shows, on average, a considerable degree of deference towards the regulatory state. Of course, it does not follow that the same conclusions must be drawn for the FET clause. But in expropriations, it is possible to find several holdings and dicta proving that tribunals are aware of the potentially disruptive effect of an excessively expansive notion of takings. Here, the *Feldman* tribunal deserves a longer quotation:

> [G]overnments must be free to act in the broader public interest through protection of the environment, new or modified tax regimes, the granting or withdrawal

[261] ibid 37.
[262] See 242.

> of government subsidies, reductions or increases in tariff levels, imposition of zoning restrictions and the like. Reasonable governmental regulation of this type cannot be achieved if any business that is adversely affected may seek compensation, and it is safe to say that customary international law recognizes this.[263]

The issue of labels—that is, the fact that the state has the power to characterise its own measures as regulations, and not as expropriations—also reveals a significant level of deference toward states. As the *SD Myers I* Tribunal expressed, '[t]he general body of precedent usually does not treat regulatory action as amounting to expropriation. *Regulatory conduct by public authorities is unlikely to be the subject of legitimate complaint under Article 1110 of the NAFTA*' (emphasis added).[264] If the state affirms that a measure is regulation and not expropriation, arbitral tribunals should show deference to that characterisation. But of course, this is only a presumption, which the investor can rebut.

Ultimately, one can summarise this assessment of the BIT generation by saying that the hyper-expansion of the expropriation clause is of much lesser concern than the ad hoc characterisation of its application. Indeed, this ad hoc process can easily end up transforming the clause into an instrument for double (or even multiple) standards. Similarly, it may allow arbitrators to use their personal views and preferences to prevail over any possible pattern-based application of the law, a result that—as explored in chapter 3[265]—clearly undermines the rule of law legitimacy of the BIT generation.

I am not claiming that the expropriation clause should be applied in a mechanical way.[266] However, it is one thing is to recognise that a certain amount of flexibility and balancing is unavoidable when resolving expropriatory clause cases, and yet a very different thing to celebrate the ad hoc nature of expropriatory adjudication.[267] Praising the latter's alleged virtues serves as a general means of obfuscating the true reasoning behind the decision, including its political and philosophical underpinnings.[268]

More important is the fact that, as Rose-Ackerman points out, '[w]hatever the merits of ad hoc balancing in other areas of law, it has special difficulties in the takings area because of the important role of

[263] *Feldman* ¶ 103. In *Pope & Talbot* ¶ 99, the Tribunal held that 'the exercise of police powers must be analyzed with special care'.

[264] *SD Myers I* ¶ 281. See also, ibid ¶ 282. Similarly, in *CME I* ¶ 603, the Tribunal expressed that '*Regulatory measures are common in all types of legal and economic systems in order to avoid use of private property contrary to the general welfare of the (host) State*' (emphasis added).

[265] See ch 3, 146–154.

[266] See Christie, n 99, 336 (observing that '[t]here are some guiding principles in deciding what kind of interference will constitute a taking, but they apply only to a certain degree').

[267] See Fortier and Drymer, n 52, 314, and 326–27.

[268] Examples of decisions praising 'ad hocery' can found in *Lauder* ¶ 200; *Tecmed* ¶ 114; and, *Generation Ukraine, Inc v Ukraine*, ICSID Case No ARB/00/9 (Paulsson, Salius, Voss), Award (16 September 2003), ¶ 20.29.

investment-backed expectations'.[269] Ultimately, to glorify the ad hoc quality of indirect takings, leading to the unconstrained application of a poorly defined concept—even when that concept is understood to be relatively limited—presents a more dangerous threat than the potentially excessive reach of expropriation. Attention should be therefore directed toward the task of locating and identifying the hidden patterns of behaviour among arbitrators who claim to be performing ad hoc adjudication.

[269] Susan Rose-Ackerman, 'Against Ad Hocery: A Comment on Michelman' (1988) 88 *Columbia Law Review* 1697, 1697.

6

Controlling Arbitrariness through the Fair and Equitable Treatment Standard

INTRODUCTION: ARBITRARINESS IN INTERNATIONAL INVESTMENT LAW

AS PREVIOUS CHAPTERS have demonstrated, the protection of investment and property rights in the BIT generation is following a pattern that is not new to international law. Implicitly following the template used by the official commentary of the influential OECD Draft of 1967, international investment caselaw has reduced the scope of the expropriation clause to destruction of investments—ie, deprivation of investments in whole or in significant part[1]—and expanded that of the fair and equitable standard (FET) to non-destructive harm.[2]

Because state interferences do not generally involve total or substantial deprivations in regulatory capitalist nations, the FET standard has become the most relevant cause of action in international investment arbitration. It has superseded in prominence the expropriation clause, which was traditionally regarded as the most important provision of investment treaties.[3]

[1] See *Metalclad Corporation v Mexico*, ICSID Case No ARB(AF)/97/1 (Lauterpacht, Civiletti, Siqueiros), Award (30 August 2000), ¶ 103 (hereinafter, *Metalclad*). In sum, as stated by the Tribunal in *Occidental Exploration and Production Co*, LCIA Case No UN3467 (Orrego, Brower, Barrera), Award (1 July 2004), ¶ 88, to qualify as expropriations, deprivations 'must affect at least a significant part of the investment' (hereinafter, *OEPC*).

[2] See *OECD Draft Convention On the Protection of Property, Adopted by the Council in its 150th Meeting on 12 October 1967* (1968) 7 ILM 117, 125, Notes and Comments to Art 3 No 4(b) ('Article 3 [takings] deals with *deprivation* of property. Protection against wrongful *interference* with its use by unreasonable or discriminatory measures is, in principle, provided in Article 1 [fair and equitable treatment]. Yet such interference may amount to *indirect* deprivation. Whether it does, will depend on its extent and duration' (emphasis underlined in the original) (hereinafter, *OECD Draft of 1967*).

[3] See eg Rudolf Dolzer, 'Indirect Expropriations: New Developments?' (2002) 11 *New York University Environmental Law Journal* 64, 66; and L Yves Fortier and Stephen L Drymer, 'Indirect Expropriation in the Law of International Investment: I Know It When I See It, or Caveat Investor' (2004) 19 *ICSID Review–Foreign Investment Law Journal* 293, 298.

The FET standard has thus become the 'alpha and omega'[4] of the BIT generation.[5]

International law recognises the regulatory state's power to harm citizens and investors. To express this in more subtle terms, not all regulation requires the paymentof compensation to those who suffer damages.[6] Such a firm commitment to the status quo would render public governance impossible, and completely frustrate the essential public goals of coordination, cooperation, and redistribution.[7] Arbitral tribunals have not disputed this very basic assumption.[8] Its clearest articulation can be found in*Tecmed*, where the Tribunal expressely statedthat '[t]he principle that the State's exercise of its sovereign powers within the framework of its police power may cause economic damage to those subject to its powers as

[4] See Charles H Brower, II, 'Fair and Equitable Treatment Under NAFTA's Investment Chapter' (2002) 96 *American Society of International Law Proceedings'* 9, 9 (stating that Art 1105, which provides for the FET standard, 'has become the alpha and omega of investor–state arbitration under Chapter 11 of NAFTA').

[5] See eg Campbell McLachlan, 'Investment Treaties and General International Law' (2008) 57 ICLQ 361, 375 (observing that the FET standard has been 'outcome-decisive in many such cases, eclipsing in the result the more established right of protection against expropriation'); Peter Muchlinski, 'Policy Issues' in Peter Muchlinski et al (eds), *The Oxford Handbook of International Investment Law* (New York, OUP, 2008) 3, 24 (noting that 'currently the most important standard, from the perspective of investor protection, is the fair and equitable treatment standard'); Surya P Subedi, *International Investment Law. Reconciling Policy and Principle* (Portland, Hart Publishing, 2008) 63 (stating that the concept of FET 'is a major, if not the most important, principle of foreign investment law'); Christoph Schreuer, 'Introduction: Interrelationship of Standards' in August Reinisch, *Standards of Investment Protection* (New York, OUP, 2008) 1, 2 (commenting that 'FET is currently the most promising standard of protection from the investor's perspective'); and, Christoph H Schreuer, 'Fair and Equitable Treatment in Arbitral Practice' (2005) 6 *Journal of World Investment and Trade* 357, 357 (commenting also that the FET standard 'is currently the most important standard in investment disputes'). In the case law, see eg *PSEG Global Inc et al v Turkey*, ICSID Case No ARB/02/5 (Orrego, Fortier, Kaufmann-Kohler), Award (19 January 2007), ¶ 238 (hereinafter, *PSEG Global*) (commenting on the 'prominence' of the FET standard in investment arbitration).

[6] See Vaughan Lowe, 'Regulation or Expropriation' (2002) 55 *Current Legal Problems* 447, 460 (noting that '[i]t is more helpful to accept that the State has the right to regulate its economy'); and, Francisco Orrego Vicuña, 'From Preston to Prescott: Globalizing Legitimate Expectations' in Steve Charnovitz et al (eds), *Law in the Service of Human Dignity. Essays in Honour of Florentino Feliciano* (Cambridge, CUP, 2005) 301, 302 (observing that the state's right to adopt regulatory measures 'has not been questioned, nor could it be unless one is aiming at the total dissolution of state functions').

[7] See Thomas Waelde and Abba Kolo, *Environmental Regulation, Investment Protection and 'Regulatory Taking' in International Law* (2001) 50 ILCQ 811, 839.

[8] See eg *Methanex Corporation v US*, UNCITRAL Ad Hoc Arbitration (Veeder, Rowley, Reisman), Award (9 August 2005), Pt IV, Ch D, at 4, ¶ 7 (hereinafter, *Methanex*); *CME Czech Republic BV v Czech Republic*, UNCITRAL Ad Hoc Arbitration (Kühn, Schwebel, Hándl), Partial Award (13 September 2001), ¶ 603 (hereinafter, *CME I*); *SD Myers Inc v Canada*, UNCITRAL Ad Hoc Arbitration (Hunter, Schwartz, Chiasson), Partial Award (13 November 2000), ¶¶ 281–82 (hereinafter, *SD Myers I*); and, *Azinian et al v Mexico*, ICSID Case N° ARB(AF)/97/2 (Paulsson, Civiletti, von Wobeser), Award (1 November 1999), ¶ 83 (hereinafter, *Azinian*).

administrator without entitling them to any compensation whatsoever is undisputable'.[9] Similarly, in *Feldman*, the Tribunal observed that 'governments must be free to act in the broader public interest . . . *Reasonable governmental regulation . . . cannot be achieved if any business that is adversely affected may seek compensation, and it is safe to say that customary international law recognizes this*'.[10] (emphasis added)

Given this division of labour found among investment treaties' provisions, Judge Higgins' key question for contemporary international investment law—'[d]o interventions by the State that leave title untouched in the hands of plaintiff, but nonetheless occasion him loss, give rise to a right of compensation?'[11]—must be narrowed down when confronting the FET standard. Specifically, we should ask the following: Which are the conditions that non-destructive harm must meet in order to trigger state liability pursuant to the FET standard?

Although there are no simple answers, it is possible to provide a somewhat tautological response: state liability arises when *arbitrary* governmental conduct causes damage to investors. The key question, obviously, remains open: What action counts as 'arbitrary governmental conduct'? Yet, the apparent tautology is not completely useless. By focusing on arbitrariness, this approach reminds us that state liability in the context of the FET standard depends mostly on the character of the regulatory state's actions and omissions (instead of the content of investors' investments).

More importantly, looking at the FET standard through the lens of arbitrariness allows us to re-examine international investment law from a Global Administrative Law (GAL) perspective. The problem of arbitrariness in the behaviour of state entities when regulating the activity of private parties, has resided at the core of the administrative law enterprise across legal cultures since at least the nineteenth century. When comparing France and the US, Edley comments that 'the project of administrative law has been the same: control of illegal and abusive discretion'.[12] A similar point is made by Mashaw, according to whom one of the central questions of American public law is 'how actively should judges review . . . *administrative judgments for arbitrariness*?' (emphasis added)[13]

[9] See *Técnicas Medioambientales Tecmed v Mexico*, ICSID Case N°ARB(AF)/00/2 (Grigera, Fernández, Bernal), Award (29 May 2003) ¶ 119 (hereinafter, *Tecmed*).

[10] *Feldman v Mexico*, ICSID Case No ARB(AF)/99/1 (Kerameus, Covarrubias, Gantz), Award (16 December 2002), ¶ 103 (hereinafter, *Feldman*) (for the full quote, see Ch 5 n 263 and accompanying text). See also, ibid ¶ 112.

[11] Rosalyn Higgins, 'The Taking of Property by the State. Recent Developments in International Law' in Académie de Droit International, 176 *Recueil des Cours. Collected Courses of the Hague Academy of International Law, 1982-III* (The Hague, M Nijhoff, 1983) 259, 269.

[12] Christopher F Edley, *Administrative Law. Rethinking Judicial Control of Bureaucracy* (New Haven, Yale University Press, 1990) 245.

[13] Jerry L Mashaw, *Greed, Chaos, and Governance. Using Public Choice to Improve Public Law* (New Haven, Yale University Press, 1997) 199.

Questions of arbitrariness abound in international investment arbitration. This comes as no surprise. Investment treaties' clauses in general, and the FET standard in particular, require arbitral tribunals to focus their attention on the reasonableness, rationality, fairness, non-discrimination, and generally, non-arbitrariness of state's behaviour. More than any other, the FET standard—as correctly captured by the *Continental Casualty* Tribunal—'is aimed at assuring that the normal law-abiding conduct of the business activity by the foreign investor is not hampered *without good reasons* by the host government and other authorities'. (emphasis added)[14]

This chapter builds on the basic idea that the application of the FET standard involves and commands the formation of a new body of Global Administrative Law.[15] The saliency that the executive and its agencies hold in the regulatory state, coupled with the waiver of the local remedies rules in investment arbitration, has led administrative actions and omissions to occupy a prominent position in the BIT generation.[16] Of course, this descriptive observation is not intended to cast any doubt on the reviewability of judicial or legislative measures under the FET standard; the point is simply that in the BIT generation, the FET standard primarily serves the purpose of controlling the administrative state.[17]

Following the ideas presented in the Introduction of this work, and continuing with the same framework adopted in chapters 4 and 5, this chapter explores two different rationales that help us to frame questions of arbitrariness in the context of GAL: first, a corrective justice rationale that examines the legality and rationality of the regulatory state's behaviour (fault/negligence, and more generally, wrongfulness); and, second, a distributive justice rationale that assesses the equality, fairness, and proportionality of the relative allocation of benefits and burdens among regulatory winners and losers.

[14] *Continental Casualty Co v Argentina*, ICSID Case No ARB/03/9 (Sacerdoti, Veeder, Nader), Award (5 September 2008), ¶ 254. (hereinafter, *Continental Casualty*).

[15] For previous connections between investment treaty arbitration and global and domestic administrative law, see eg Thomas W Wälde, 'The Present State of Research Carried Out by the English-Speaking Section of the Centre for Studies and Research' in Centre for Studies and Research in International Law and International Relations, *New Aspects of International Investment Law* (Leiden, Nijhoff, 2006) 63, 84; Gus Van Harten and Martin Loughlin, 'Investment Treaty Arbitration as a Species of Global Administrative Law' (2006) 17 *European Journal of International Law* 121; Rudolf Dolzer, 'The Impact of International Investment Treaties on Domestic Administrative Law' (2005) 37 *New York University Journal of International Law and Politics* 953; and Thomas W Wälde, 'The "Umbrella" Clause in Investment Arbitration. A Comment on Original Intentions and Recent Cases' (2005) 6 *Journal of World Investment and Trade* 183, 204 fn 78.

[16] See Antonin Scalia, 'Judicial Deference to Administrative Interpretations of Law' (1989) *1989 Duke Law Journal* 511, 516 (commenting that '[b]road delegation to the Executive is the hallmark of the modern administrative state').

[17] Note also, that the review of judicial measures is to be conducted pursuant to the old and distinctive customary norms of 'denial of justice', which, in my opinion, do not present great challenge to the BIT generation.

The main purpose of this chapter is to provide a general structure from which to make the first steps toward building a new GAL approach to the FET standard. With that background in mind, the chapter proceeds as follows. Section I delves into what has become the current debate in international investment law: whether FET is an autonomous standard, or whether it reflects general international law (GIL), including customary international law (CIL) and international minimum standards (IMS).

Section II analyses the general relationship of domestic and international law. The regulatory state, almost everywhere, is a *Rechsstaat*. Because domestic law continues to define many of the limits of state action in the BIT generation, a careful consideration of the roles of both domestic and international law is essential to properly capture the scope and breath of the FET standard. In that context, this section formulates the four crucial questions that structure and organise the GAL approach to the FET standard into its *three* different dimensions, outlined below.

Section III explores the first dimension of the GAL approach to the FET standard: whether the legal system falls above or below the FET standard. This is the first and most basic question that investment treaty tribunals should ask. If the legal system fails to measure up to international standards, then the case, in theory, is over, and a decision should be rendered in favour of the foreign investor. But this is rarely the case; after all, states enjoy a high level of discretion when deciding how to regulate economic activities within their own territory.

Section IV develops the second dimension of the GAL approach to the FET standard: domestic illegalities as the basis of international wrongful acts. States enjoy regulatory freedom, but they must abide by their own legal programs. Of course, this does not make a domestic illegality in itself an international wrongful act; 'something more' is needed. Still, these two conditions—domestic illegality plus 'something more'—define a second set of problems different in character from those posed by the first dimension.

Section V reviews the third dimension of the GAL approach. The main question here is how to assess arbitrariness in state behaviour, when the measures at stake were issued in accordance with the domestic legal system, and when such a system does not fall below the FET standard. The main theme explored here is the importance of general principles of law, and by implication, of comparative law. Investment treaty tribunals should be aware of the level of intrusiveness they display when applying any test of arbitrariness; they should avoid imposing their own visions regarding policy matters over those of administrative agencies and legislatures.

The conclusions touch upon common aspects of the GAL approach to the FET standard that can be observed throughout its three dimensions. The FET standard can be characterised as encompassing two different subsets of rules and principles: one comprising a body of substantive norms that define the scope and depth of arbitrariness review in international investment law;

and, another made up of conflict-of-laws norms that establish the proper basis for application of domestic law and judicial review in accordance with that law. The former reminds arbitral tribunals that they must follow the guidance of comparative law faithfully when the creation of new substantive rules of GAL is required; the latter, that they should largely avoid resolving disputes without taking into consideration domestic law issues.

I THE CURRENT DEBATE IN INTERNATIONAL INVESTMENT LAW: THE ALLEGED AUTONOMOUS CHARACTER OF THE FET STANDARD

One of the hottest debates in international investment law during the last few years has been whether the FET standard is autonomous ('FET-autonomous'), or whether it embodies international minimum standards ('FET-IMS').[18] This section starts by explaining the 'nature' of the FET

[18] For general recent references, see Ioana Tudor, 'The Fair and Equitable Treatment Standard' in *The International Law of Foreign Investment* (New York, OUP, 2008) 53–104; Rudolf Dolzer and Christoph Schreuer, *Principles of International Investment Law* (New York, OUP, 2008) 124–130; Katia Yannaca-Small, 'Fair and Equitable Treatment Standard: Recent Developments' in August Reinisch (ed), *Standards of Investment Protection* (New York, OUP, 2008) 111, 113–18; Campbell McLachlan et al, *International Investment Arbitration. Substantive Principles* (New York, OUP, 2007); Todd J Grierson-Weiler and Ian A Laird, 'Standards of Treatment' in Peter Muchlinski et al (eds), *The Oxford Handbook of International Investment Law* (New York, OUP, 2008) 259, 264–72. To sum up, I classify the international investment case law according to the following three positions (the list is not exhaustive, and only comprises cases, outside NAFTA, in which tribunals have adopted a clear stance):

(a) *Decisions adopting the FET-autonomous position*: (1) *Sempra Energy International v Argentina*, ICSID Case No ARB/02/16 (Orrego, Lalonde, Morelli), Award (28 September 2007), ¶ 302 (hereinafter, *Sempra*); (2) *Compañía de Aguas del Aconquija SA et al v Argentina*, Case No ARB/97/3 (Rowley, Kaufmann-Kohler, Bernal), Award (20 August 2007), ¶¶ 7.4.1–7.4.9 (hereinafter, *Vivendi III*); (3) *Enron Corporation et al v Argentina*, ICSID Case No ARB/01/3 (Orrego, van den Berg, Tschanz), Award (22 May 2007), ¶ 258 (hereinafter, *Enron*); (4) *PSEG Global* ¶ 239.

(b) *Decisions adopting the FET-IMS position*: (1) *MCI Power Group LC et al v Ecuador*, ICSID Case No ARB/03/6 (Vinuesa, Greenberg, Irarrázabal), Award (31 July 2007), ¶ 369 (hereinafter, *MCI Power Group*); and, (2) *Alex Genin et al v Estonia*, ICSID Case No ARB/99/2 (Fortier, Heth, van den Berg), Award (25 June 2001), ¶ 367 (hereinafter, *Genin*).

(c) *Decisions that, either adopting the FET-autonomous position or nor, pragmatically converge toward recognizing the existence of only one standard:* (1) *Duke Energy Electroquil Partners and Electroquil SA v Ecuador*, ICSID Case No ARB/04/19 (Kaufmann-Kohler, Gómez, van den Berg), Award (18 August 2008), ¶ 337 (hereinafter, *Duke Energy Electroquil*); (2) *Rumeli Telekom AS et al v Kazakhstan*, ICSID Case No ARB/05/16 (Hanotiau, Boyd, Lalonde), Award (29 July 2008), ¶ 611 (hereinafter, *Rumeli Telekom*); (3) *Biwater Gauff (Tanzania) Ltd v Tanzania*, ICSID Case No ARB/05/22 (Hanotiau, Born, Landau), Award (24 July 2008), ¶¶ 591–92 (hereinafter, *Biwater Gauff*); (4) *BG Group Plc. v Argentina*, UNCITRAL Ad Hoc Arbitration (Aguilar Alvarez, van den Berg, Garro), Award (24 December 2007), ¶ 291 (hereinafter, *BG Group*); (5) *Azurix Corp v Argentina*, ICSID Case No ARB/01/12 (Rigo, Lalonde, Martins), Award (14 July 2006), ¶¶ 361–372 (hereinafter, *Azurix*); (6) *Saluka Investments BV v Czech Republic*, UNCITRAL Ad Hoc Arbitration (Watts, Fortier,

standard, which is conceived as a textual formulation inviting the development of a new operative test of arbitrariness in international law. It then argues that, as a matter of treaty interpretation, the literalist approach defending the FET-autonomous position is incorrect. Finally, it clarifies the meaning of the correct position, FET-IMS standard—which has been wrongly associated with the *Neer* case[19]—and argues that the FET-autonomous position is incompatible with the rule of law.

A The Challenge of the FET Standard: Defining a New Standard of Review

The FET standard, as stated by the *Saluka* Tribunal, prohibits the regulatory state from acting in a way that is 'manifestly inconsistent, non-transparent, unreasonable (i.e. *unrelated to some rational policy*)' (emphasis added).[20] At its core, this standard calls for the establishment of an appropriate test for review of 'arbitrariness' (broad sense, including illegality, irrationality, special sacrifice, and lack of proportionality).[21] To a greater extent than all other treaty provisions, international investment law places the FET standard in the role of deciding what constitutes a reasonably well-behaved regulatory state.[22]

The starting point is clear: the FET standard lacks a clear content, either in treaties or in general international law.[23] BITs are terse and vague in their textual expression, and reveal little in the way of specific guidance. *More importantly*, general international law has hitherto not had to deal

Behrens), Partial Award (17 March 2006), ¶ 291 (hereinafter, *Saluka*); (7) *CMS Gas Transmission Co v Argentina*, ICSID Case No ARB/01/08 (Orrego, Lalonde, Rezek), Award (12 May 2005), ¶ 282–84 (hereinafter, *CMS*); and, (8) *OEPC* ¶¶ 189–90.

19 *LFH Neer and Pauline Neer (USA) v United Mexican States* (1926) 4 RIAA 60 (available at http://www.un.org/law/riaa/) (hereinafter, *Neer*).

20 *Saluka* ¶ 309.

21 See eg *Rumeli Telekom* ¶ 609; *Parkerings-Compagniet AS v Lituania*, ICSID Case No ARB/05/8 (Lévy, Lew, Lalonde), Award (11 September 2007), ¶¶ 300, and 315 (hereinafter, *Parkerings*); *GAMI Investment Inc v Mexico*, UNCITRAL Ad Hoc Arbitration (Paulsson, Lacarte, Reisman), Award (15 November 2004), ¶ 94 (hereinafter, *GAMI*); *Waste Management v Mexico*, ICSID Case N°ARB(AF)/00/3 (Crawford, Civileti, Magallón), Award (30 April 2004), ¶ 98 (hereinafter, *Waste Management II*). Among commentators, see eg Barnali Choudhury, 'Evolution or Devolution? Defining Fair and Equitable Treatment in International Investment Law' (2005) 6 *Journal of World Investment and Trade* 297, 311.

22 See Stephan W Schill, 'Fair and Equitable Treatment under Investment Treaties as an Embodiment of the Rule of Law' IILJ Working Paper 2006/6, Global Administrative Law Series (2006) at 4 (available at <http://www.iilj.org/publications/documents/2006-6-GAL-Schill-web.pdf>, accessed 8 November 2008), who has already pointed out the essence of this matter: '[The FET standard possesses] a quasi-constitutional function that serves as a yardstick for the exercise of host states' administrative, judicial or legislative activity vis-à-vis foreign investors. In this perspective, the arbitral jurisprudence does not appear as a fragmented and disordered aggregate of awards but as an expression of the continuous emergence of a global regime that governs foreign investment and the conduct of host states relating to it'.

23 See ch 3, 129–154. See also, n 60.

with questions related to control of the regulatory state, and thus lacks a coherent doctrinal basis for consistent and rational decision making.[24] Weil clearly anticipated the challenge ahead when noting that '[t]he standard of "fair and equitable treatment" is certainly no less operative than was the standard of "due process of law", and it will be for future practice, jurisprudence and commentary to impart specific content to it'.[25]

International investment law, then, must articulate a new standard of review.[26] But what does this mean? The essence of any standard of review lies in the level of deference, including both procedural and substantive elements, that the reviewing body gives to the reviewed entity.[27] However, as the comparative experience of domestic administrative law demonstrates, establishing a standard of review, in the abstract, is far from sufficient. The complexities and intricacies of the process of judicial review require the establishment of a 'dense' argumentative framework that structures and determines the way in which parties present their claims, and the manner in which the reviewing body reasons and is persuaded.

It is naïve to think that such a goal can be achieved through a literal approach to concepts such as 'fair' and 'equitable', probably two of the more general and abstract ideas found in the human enterprise known as the law. Using Ackerman's notable phrase, the FET standard is so open-ended as to 'strike terror in the hearts of the literalists'.[28] In such a context, no guidance can be expected from dictionaries.[29] Moreover, such a stance not only provides no meaningful help, but produces the opposite result from that generally expected when using a literalist approach to treaty interpretation: instead of constraining decision makers' discretion, it over-expands it[30].

[24] As McLachlan, n 5, 376, explains, '[i]n the field of administrative decision-making, tribunals have had to develop the scope of the standard without specific guidance from the old law on the treatment of aliens'.

[25] Prosper Weil, 'The State, the Foreign Investor, and International Law: The No Longer Stormy Relationship of a *Mènage à Trois*' (2000) 15 *ICSID Review–Foreign Investment Law Journal* 401, 415.

[26] See Grierson-Weiler and Laird, n 18, 299 (observing that 'what we are collectively searching for here is an international standard of review for the regulatory treatment of foreign nationals').

[27] According to Tudor, n 18, 149, '[a]t the end of the day, *the main issue concerning the FET standard is the determination of the level of treatment* that will breach or, on the contrary, respect the international obligation of the State'. (emphasis added)

[28] Bruce Ackerman, *Private Property and the Constitution* (New Haven, Yale University Press, 1977) 6 (referring to the concept of takings in the US Constitution Fifth Amendment).

[29] See Rudolf Dolzer, 'Fair and Equitable Treatment: A Key Standard in Investment Treaties' (2005) 39 *International Lawyer* 87, 88 (commenting on the 'circular character of such definitions [of famous dictionaries]'). Moreover, as McLachlan, n 5, 369, notes, 'in the case of the general test for fair and equitable treatment, it [the ordinary meaning approach] may result in little more than exchange of synonyms'.

[30] Non-literal elements are the ones typically associated with the over-expansion of discretion. See eg Ian Sinclair, *The Vienna Convention on the Law of Treaties*, 2nd edn (Dover, Manchester University Press, 1984) 131 (commenting that '[t]here is also the risk that the placing of undue emphasis on the "object and purpose" of a treaty will encourage teleological methods of interpretations').

The most serious dilemmas that investments treaties place before us cannot be addressed through dictionaries. On the contrary, the development of an appropriate new standard of review requires that the international legal community agree upon some essential policy objectives for international investment law. In McLachlan's words, 'the legal protection afforded by the guarantee of fair and equitable treatment cannot be understood without a conception of the proper *function* of international law in assessing the standards of justice achieved by national systems of law and administration'.[31]

The interpretation espoused in this work argues that international investment law must define minimum thresholds determining what is expected from a 'reasonably well-behaved regulatory state'.[32] More than 80 years ago, the Mexican–US General Claims Commission provided a formulation that should still be considered authoritative today: state liability should be the consequence of the '*failure to maintain the usual order which it is the duty of every state to maintain within its territory*'. (emphasis added)[33] This means—as the updated Calvo Doctrine reminds us[34]—that investment law jurisprudence should not crystallise rules of protection of investments that go beyond the standards of arbitrariness that courts of *developed countries* recognise in favour of their own investors.

Not only is the literalist stance inadequate for developing the FET standard as a test of arbitrariness, but it actually obfuscates this essential challenge of international investment law. A demonstration can be found in those situations where BITs expressly include the concepts of 'arbitrariness' or 'reasonableness', typically within the same clause containing the FET standard.[35] The literalist camp searches here for a different standard contained within that expression (that is, different from FET),[36] and typically claims support for such approach in the *ELSI* case.[37]

[31] McLachlan, n 5, 381.

[32] As noted in the Introduction of this work, this comes from Freeman's idea of 'well-administered government'. See Alwyn V Freeman, 'Responsibility of States for Unlawful Acts of Their Armed Forces' in Académie de Droit International, 88 *Recueil des Cours—1955 II* (Leyde, AW Sijthoff, 1956) 263, 277–78. Freeman's concept was relied on by the Tribunal in *Asian Agricultural Products Ltd v Sri Lanka*, ICSID Case No ARB/87/3 (El Kosheri, Goldman, Asante), Award (27 June 1990), ¶ 77 (referring to the idea of a 'reasonably well organized modern State').

[33] *George Adams Kennedy (USA) v United Mexican States* (1927) 4 RIAA 194, 198, ¶ 7 (available at http://www.un.org/law/riaa/.

[34] ch 1, 74–80.

[35] See Veijo Heiskanen, 'Arbitrary and Unreasonable Measures' in August Reinisch, *Standards of Investment Protection* (New York, OUP, 2008) 87.

[36] See eg *Plama Consortium Ltd* v *Bulgaria*, ICSID Case No ARB/03/24 (Salans, van den Berg, Veeder), Award (27 August 2008), ¶ 184 (hereinafter, *Plama II*); *Sempra* ¶ 318; *Enron* ¶ 281; *Siemens AG v Argentina*, ICSID Case No ARB/02/8 (Rigo, Brower, and Bello), Award (6 February 2007), ¶ 318 (hereinafter, *Siemens*); *LG&E Energy Corp et al v Argentina*, ICSID Case No ARB/02/01 (de Maekelt, Rezek, van den Berg), Decision on Liability (3 October 2006), ¶¶ 156–63 (hereinafter, *LG&E*); *Azurix* ¶ 391–92; *Noble Ventures, Inc v Romania*, ICSID Case No ARB/01/11 (Böckstiegel, Lever, Dupuy), Award (12 October 2005), ¶¶ 175–83 (hereinafter, *Noble Ventures*); *OEPC* ¶¶ 159–66; *Lauder v Czech Republic*, UNCITRAL Ad Hoc Arbitration

However, the arbitrariness standard referred to in the *ELSI* case is a relic from the pre-BIT generation era, a time when the international law for protection of aliens was focused on judicial behaviour.[38] That low standard is certainly less demanding than the FET standard, and, in all situations not dealing with the judicial branch of government, has in reality become irrelevant to international investment law. Not surprisingly, as Heiskanen concludes in his study on the subject, '[t]he case law . . . shows that the non-impairment standard rarely plays a dispositive role in international arbitral awards'.[39]

The proper understanding of the FET standard as a test of arbitrariness rejects the recognition of separate standards of 'arbitrariness' or 'reasonableness'.[40] As decided by the *PSEG Global* Tribunal, 'there is no ground for a separate heading on liability based on account of arbitrariness'.[41] As the *Biwater Gauff* Tribunal held, citing *Saluka,* 'the standard of "reasonableness" has no different meaning than the 'fair and equitable treatment' standard "*with which it is associate*" [*sic*]'.[42]

B A New Standard Under Traditional Methods: FET and Treaty Interpretation under Articles 31 and 32 of the Vienna Convention

In my view, the literalist view of the FET standard that underlies the 'autonomous' thesis is incorrect as a matter of treaty interpretation. As is well known, Article 31 of the Vienna Convention on the Law of Treaties defines a *single rule* of treaty interpretation, which comprises various elements.[43] Notwithstanding the existence of a complex *single rule*, the literalist camp has insisted upon ending the analysis at Article 31(1)—with a special emphasis on ordinary meaning—while completely disregarding

(Briner, Cutler, Klein), Award (3 September 2001), ¶¶ 214–88 (hereinafter, *Lauder*); and, *Genin* ¶ 368.

[37] See eg *Siemens* ¶ 318; *LG&E* ¶ 157; *Azurix* ¶ 391–92; and, *Noble Ventures* ¶ 176.

[38] See *Elettronica Sicula SpA* (ELSI) (US v Italy) [1989] ICJ Rep 15, ¶ 129 (hereinafter, *ELSI*). In that paragraph, one may see the rationale of the denial of justice age at work, particularly when the ICJ stated that 'the Mayor's order was consciously made in the context of an operating system of law and of appropriate remedies of appeal, and treated as such by the superior administrative authority and the local court. These are not at all the marks of an "arbitrary" act'.

[39] Heiskanen, n 35, 109.

[40] Note that the full protection and security (FPS) standard is a different standard mainly for historical reasons: FPS predates FET. As befits its nineteenth century roots, the FPS standard has a more restrictive scope, determined by the idea of *due diligence,* which typically applies in the context of physical violence.

[41] *PSEG Global* ¶ 261.

[42] *Biwater Gauff* ¶ 692, citing *Saluka* ¶ 460. See also, *CMS* ¶ 290; *MTD Equity Sdn Bhd et al v Chile,* ICSID Case No ARB/01/07 (Rigo, Lalonde, Oreamuno), Award (25 May 2004) ¶ 196 (hereinafter, *MTD I*); and *Rumeli Telekom* ¶ 679.

[43] See Richard K Gardiner, *Treaty Interpretation* (New York, OUP, 2008) 1–50.

Article 31(3)(c)—'relevant rules of international law applicable in the relations between the parties'—and 31(4)—'special meaning'. Furthermore, to the extent that 'fair' and 'equitable' are highly ambiguous concepts, Article 32 has also been improperly set aside.

Recently, McLachlan has brilliantly argued that BITs are not self-contained regimes but creatures of international law, which governs them.[44] Consequently, BITs follow the presumption that the parties to a treaty have not contracted out of general international law.[45] The full argumentation can be found in McLachlan's work; here, I will just cite two of his conclusions:

> (1) *The investment treaty as a creature of international law*: The primary obligations assumed by States towards foreign investors and enshrined in investment treaties are governed by public international law. This flows from the elementary fact that such treaties are themselves creatures of international law . . . (2) *International law as a whole applicable to treaty obligations*: Thus, when, by virtue of Article 42 of the ICSID Convention or otherwise, tribunals are directed that the applicable law to the particular issue before them is international law, that is a reference to the whole of international law, and not merely the specific treaty before them.[46]

The point, then, is that the FET standard cannot be presummed to be 'autonomous' from general international law.[47] In the words of the *Desert Line Projects* Tribunal, 'general international law . . . forms the context in which the BIT is called upon to operate'.[48] Hence, in my opinion, explicit

[44] McLachlan, n 5, 369 ff. See also, McLachlan et al, n 18, 15, and Annie Leeks, 'The Relationship Between Bilateral Investment Treaty Arbitration and the Wider Corpus of International Law: The ICSID Approach' (2007) 65 *University of Toronto Faculty of Law Review* 1, 35–36 (noting that 'investment law exists within the wider corpus of international law and should be interpreted in this context . . . There is no reason to suppose that the network of BITs creates a self-contained regime. BITs do not exclude other rules of international law').

[45] As Joost Pauwelyn, *Conflict of Norms in Public International Law: How WTO Law Relates to Other Rules of International Law* (CUP, Cambridge 2003) 212–13, explains: '[G]iven the presumption against conflict . . . and, hence, against "contracting out", it is for the party claiming that a treaty has "contracted out" of general international law to prove it. In other words, the party claiming that there should *not* be "fall-back" on general international law bears the burden of proof'. See also, Campbell McLachlan, 'The Principle of Systemic Integration and Article 31(3)(c) of the Vienna Convention' (2005) 54 ICLQ 279, 311, arguing that a 'principle of systemic interpretation', embedded in Art 31(3)(c) of the Vienna Convention, includes two presumptions: '(a) *negatively* that, in entering into treaty obligations, the parties intend not to act inconsistenly with generally recognised principles of international law or with previous treaty obligations towards third states; and, (b) *positively* that the parties are to have taken "to refer to general principles of international law for all questions which [the Treaty] does not itself resolve in express terms or in a different way"'. (internal citations omitted).

[46] McLachlan, n 5, 398–99.

[47] Sinclair, n 30, 139, in his canonic book on treaties, observes that '[e]very treaty provision must be read not only in its own context, but in the wider context of general interational law'.

[48] See *Desert Line Projects LLC v Yemen*, ICSID Case No ARB/05/17 (Tercier, Paulsson, El-Kosheri), Award (6 February 2008), ¶ 106 (hereinafter, *Desert Line Projects*). Interestingly, Dolzer and Schreuer, n 18, 5, two prominent defenders of the FET-autonomous position, recognise that '[t]he treaty-based rules on investments have to be understood and

phrases like 'in accordance with international law', and other similar constructions that can be found in certain treaties, do not add any additional content to the FET standard. In this sense, the *Siemens* Tribunal correctly affirmed that:

> There is no reference [in the BIT] to international law or to a minimum standard. However, in applying the Treaty, the Tribunal is bound to find the meaning of these terms under international law bearing in mind their ordinary meaning, the evolution of international law and the specific context in which they are used.[49]

In the context of the Vienna Convention, Article 31(3)(c),[50] which dictates the '*systematic integration* within the international legal system',[51] rules out the idea of an autonomous FET standard. There is generally no language in BITs by which the parties had indicated their intention to be exempted from the background rules of general international law.[52] This means that the development of FET as a test of arbitrariness cannot escape reference to IMS and the 'general principles of the law common to civilized nations' (Article 38(1)(c) of the ICJ Statute[53]). Citing McLachlan again:

interpreted, like all treaties, in the context of the general rules of international law. This includes not only customary law but also general principles of law within the meaning of Article 38(1) lit. c of the ICJ Statute'.

[49] *Siemens* ¶ 291.

[50] Recently, arbitral tribunals have begun paying attention to Art 31(3)(c) of the Vienna Convention. In *Ioan Micula et al v Romania,* ICSID Case No ARB/05/20 (Lévy, Alexandrov, Ehlermann), Decision on Jurisdiction and Admissibility (24 September 2008), ¶ 87 (hereinafter, *Micula*), the Tribunal correctly held that 'in interpreting the BIT, i.e., an instrument between two sovereign States, it [the Tribunal] may take into account, as directed by Article 31(3)(c) of the Vienna Convention on the Law of Treaties, any relevant rule of international law'. Similarly, in *Vladimir Berschader et al v Russian Federation,* SCC Case No 080/2004 (Sjövall, Lebedev, Weiler), Award (21 April 2006), ¶ 95 (hereinafter, *Berschader*), the Tribunal held that '[i]nsofar as the terms of the Treaty are unclear or require interpretation or supplementation, the Vienna Convention requires the Tribunal to consider "the relevant rules of international law applicable in relations between the parties"'. See also, *Enron* ¶ 257 (referring to Art 38(1)(c) of the ICJ Statute).

[51] McLachlan, n 45, 280. See also, Gardiner, n 43, 260, and 284–87.

[52] General international law includes general principles of both international law and national legal systems. According to the International Law Commission, 'Fragmentation of International Law: Difficulties Arising from the Diversification and Expansion of International Law, Report of the Study Group of the International Law Commission' (Martti Koskenniemi) UN Doc A/CN.4/L.682, 13 April 2006, at 254 (available at http://untreaty.un.org/ilc/guide/1_9.htm): ' "General international law" clearly refers to general customary law as well as "general principles of law recognized by civilized nations" under article 38(1)(c) of the Statute of the International Court of Justice. But it might also refer to principles of international law proper and to analogies from domestic laws, especially principles of the legal process (*audiatur et altera pars, in dubio mitius,* estoppel and so on). In the practice of international tribunals, including the Appellate Body of the WTO or the European and Inter-American Courts of Human Rights reference is constantly made to various kinds of "principles" sometimes drawn from domestic law, sometimes from international practice but often in a way that leaves their authority unspecified'.

[53] See Alain Pellet, 'Article 38' in Andreas Zimmerman et al (eds), *The Statute of the International Court of Justice: A Commentary* (New York, OUP, 2006) 677, 764–73.

> Where the investment treaty poses new questions not previously addressed by custom (as, for example, in the application of the fair and equitable treatment standard to administrative decision-making), reference to general international law may still illuminate the rule to the extent that it reveals general principles which guide the application of the rule.[54]

Article 31(4) of the Vienna Convention reinforces the previous points. As a matter of practice, when parties to a BIT decide to include a FET clause, they neither discuss nor negotiate the concepts of 'fair' and 'equitable'. Instead, the decision they make is whether to include a universally known module of meaning associated with that specific textual formulation. That module of meaning—repeated in almost 2,500 treaties, with roots in earlier twentieth- and even nineteenth-century international documents,[55] including Article 23(e) of the League of Nations Covenant[56]—does not depend, in principle, on minor variations of textual formulation, but on general international law.

Thus, FET—like other closely related principles, such as no expropriation without compensation, and full protection and security[57]—is a 'special meaning' term.[58] As Judge Higgins noted in her separate opinion in the *Oil Platforms* case, 'the key terms "fair and equitable treatment to nationals and companies" and "unreasonable and discriminatory measures" are *legal terms of art* well known in the field of overseas investment protection'. (emphasis added)[59]

Finally, Article 32 of the Vienna Convention *confirms*, generally, what has been said earlier. There should be no doubt that reference to this supplementary means of interpretation is granted when dealing with terms as vague and ambiguous as 'fair' and 'equitable'.[60] Then, having recourse to

[54] McLachlan, n 5, 400.

[55] As explained by Rudolf Dolzer, 'Comment' in Federico Ortino et al (eds), *Investment Treaty Law. Current Issues II. Nationality and Investment Treaty Claims. Fair and Equitable Treatment in Investment Treaty Law* (London, The British Institute of International and Comparative Law, 2007) 141, 142: '[T]he classical FCN treaties which of course have a very long tradition, century old tradition, referred to just and equitable and someone discovered the other day, apparently in the US department of commerce, a document from 1799 that talks about fair and equitable commerce among all nations, *so the term has a long tradition*'. (emphasis added)

[56] See ch 1, 51–52, and 66–74.

[57] The prospect of interpreting what an expropriation is, or what constitutes full protection and security, using dictionaries looks similarly inappropriate. It must also be noted that, concerning the FPS standard, drawing conclusions from different textual formulations such 'protection and security', 'full protection and security', and 'the most constant protection and security', among others, is similarly wrong; the standard is the same and its meaning must be found in general international law. The following tribunals should be criticised for their overemphasis on the ordinary meaning in this regard: *Azurix* ¶ 408 and *Biwater Gauff* ¶ 729.

[58] See McLachlan et al, n 18, 223–24.

[59] See *Oil Platforms (Iran v US)* [1996] ICJ Rep 803, 858 (Judge Higgins, Separate Opinion).

[60] Of course, tribunals have noted the vagueness, ambiguity, 'non clearness', and/or open-ended nature of the FET standard; see eg *Sempra* ¶ 296; *Enron* ¶ 256; *Saluka* ¶ 284; and,

the 'circumstances' of BITs conclusion,[61] including the 'historical background' of BITs,[62] allows us to see that the idea of an autonomous FET standard, more demanding than IMS, is far too dismissive of the history of state responsibility in international law.

As chapter 1 explored,[63] the confrontation between the standards of national treatment on the one hand, and IMS on the other, endured for nearly a century and half. By the second half of the twentieth century, developing countries had essentially won this battle by transforming protection of aliens abroad into a heated and volatile field. Then, over the course of several decades, by signing BITs—originally designed to function in the classic state-by-state setting—developing countries surrendered their sacrosanct position on national treatment, and accepted the IMS proposed by developed countries.

Yet, one must ask how could it be the case that the FET clause ended up providing a standard that went beyond IMS, when the latter was the monolithic position of developed countries at the time that the FET standard was originally included in BITs? The answer, in this regard, is quite clear: a careful historical analysis demonstrates that the two key core non-contingent standards in BITs—no expropriation without compensation and FET—do not provide for treatment that extends beyond GIL.[64] After all, the main achievements of modern BITs which explain their popularity are, not the attempt to escape international law in favour of an 'autonomous' new law, but the re-enactment of pre-New International Economic Order standards of treatment as espoused by developed countries (that is, IMS), and the establishment of investor–state arbitration to resolve investment disputes without needing previous recourse to domestic remedies.

Genin ¶ 367. Among commentators, see eg Andrea K Bjorklund, 'Investment Treaty Arbitral Decisions as *Jurisprudence Constante*' in Colin B Picker et al (eds), *International Economic Law. The State and Future of the Discipline* (Portland, Hart Publishing, 2008) 265, 265, and 269; Schill, n 22, 5, and 37; Matthew C Porterfield, 'An International Common Law of Investor Rights' (2006) 27 *University of Pennsylvania Journal of International Economic Law* 79, 80; Schreuer, n 5, 385; Dolzer, n 29, 87; and, Carlos G Garcia, 'All the Other Dirty Little Secrets: Investment Treaties, Latin America, and the Necessary Evil of Investor-State Arbitration' (2004) 16 *Florida Journal of International Law* 301, 350.

[61] As Gardiner, n 43, 343, explains: 'What is meant by the circumstances of conclusion is not indicated in the Vienna Convention. The circumstances that cause a treaty to be drawn up, affect its content and attach to its conclusion are all factors which are in practice taken into account'.

[62] See Sinclair, n 30, 141, who remarks upon the need of the interpreter 'to bear constantly in mind the historical background against which the treaty has been negotiated'. According to Special Rapporteur Humphrey Waldock, 2 *Yearbook of the International Law Commission 1964* (New York, United Nations, 1965) at 59 ¶ 22, '[t]his broad phrase [circumstances surrounding the conclusion of the treaty] is intended to cover the contemporary circumstances and the historical context in which the treaty was concluded'.

[63] See ch 1, 62–74.

[64] As McLachlan, n 5, 372, observes, '[t]he treaty framers often consciously sought not to go beyond obligations which were thought to reflect the current state of international law'.

C IMS as a Methodological Constraint over Arbitral Tribunals

Even though the challenge ahead involves the creation of a new standard of review of arbitrariness, this does not mean that the standard to be developed must be 'autonomous'. Above all, adjudication under international law must continue to be guided by the rule of law. This principle demands the constraints of not only a proper set of pre-existing norms—which may not always exist, as is frequently the case in international law—but also of the *methods* and *sources* of general international law.[65] The central tenet of the view of the FET standard as embodying IMS is hence no other that the demand for a jurisprudence anchored in general international law, and grounded on the rule of law.

Yet, to understand the content of IMS, we should first explore what they are not. This is necessary because the literalist camp has presented a distorted view of what such standards entail. Contrary to the common assumption, IMS *do not* reflect the legal sensitivities of the nineteenth century (the 'frozen in amber' argument); these minima have always been considered to have a dynamic character. Indeed, IMS bear a direct relationship to the 'general principles of law recognised by civilized nations',[66] which, undoubtedly, had an evolutionary nature. As Borchard explains, '[t]he international standard is compounded of general principles recognized by the domestic law of practically every civilized country, and it is not to be supposed that any normal state would repudiate it or, if able, fail to observe it'.[67] Similarly, according to the *Restatement (Second)of Foreign Relations Law*:

> The international standard of justice . . . is the standard required for the treatment of aliens by: (a) the applicable principles of international law as established by international custom, judicial and arbitral decisions, and other recognized sources or, in the absence of such applicable principles, (b) *analogous principles of justice generally recognized by States that have reasonably developed legal systems*. (emphasis added).[68]

[65] See JC Thomas, 'Reflections on Article 1105 of NAFTA: History, State Practice and the Influence of Commentators' (2002) 17 ICSID *Review—Foreign Investment Law Journal* 21, 28 (stating that the FET and FPS standard 'are to be interpreted not as independent and autonomous standards, but rather as elements of conduct that international law has required of states. In other words, they acquire their meaning from international law').

[66] Art 38(1)(c) of the ICJ Statute.

[67] See eg Edwin Borchard, 'The 'Minimum Standard' of Treatment of Aliens' (1940) 38 *Michigan Law Review* 445, 458.

[68] *Restatement of the Law, Second: Foreign Relations Law of the United States, as Adopted and Promulgated by the American Law Institute, 26 May 1962* (St Paul, MN, American Law Institute, 1965) 501, ¶ 165.2. Then Comments (d) and (e), ibid 503, note that: 'The test for determining whether conduct attributable to a state complies with the international standard is two fold. It must, in the first place, comply with the requirements specified by international law as established by the usual sources of such law . . . However, where authority from such sources is conflicting or absent, international law adopts, in this as in many other areas, analogous

It should be noted that the association of IMS with the *Neer* case—as explained in detail in chapter 3[69]—is misguided. That conflation serves to falsely identify IMS with 'bad faith', 'wilful neglect of duty', and 'outrage'.[70] Yet, those espousing this connection fail to see how narrow a case *Neer* was. Not only was it one out of thousands of decisions rendered by mixed commissions, but more importantly, *Neer* was a denial of justice case based on the alleged *failure to apprehend and punish* those who killed Mr Neer.[71] Considered in terms of its factual background, the decision in *Neer* proves to be good law for a denial of justice case based on improper execution of state prosecutorial functions.

However, given the low density of general international law in this field, what is the exact meaning of FET-IMS as a standard of review of arbitrariness? And what is it that makes it different from the autonomous version of the FET standard? As claimed here, the FET-IMS must be understood, essentially, as a methodological constraint over arbitral tribunals' discretion.[72] FET-IMS reminds arbitrators that they should not decidecases according to their own whims or sense of justice, but should make decisions consistent with the proper *methods* and *sources* of international law.[73] The *ADF* Tribunal, finding a precedent in *Mondev*, has already pointed in this direction:

> We understand *Mondev* to be saying—and we would respectfully agree with it—that any general requirement to accord 'fair and equitable treatment' and 'full protection and security' must be disciplined by being based upon State practice and judicial or arbitral case law or other sources of customary or general international law.[74]

principles from reasonably developed legal countries . . . Reference to the international standard of justice as the standard of 'civilized states' is customary in the literature of international law, and the Statute of the International Court of Justice lists among the sources of law to be applied by the Court those derived from "the general principles of law recognized by civilized nations".: Article 38(1)(c)'.

[69] See ch 3, 152–153.

[70] See eg, Tudor, n 18, 67 (incorrectly stating that 'IMS provides for action only in extreme cases').

[71] The claim was, *Neer* at 61, that the 'Mexican authorities showed an unwarrantable lack of diligence or an unwarrantable lack of intelligent investigation in prosecuting the culprits'.

[72] Surprisingly, in *PSEG Global* ¶ 239, the Tribunal stated that the FET standard 'is sometimes not as precise as would be desirable', and therefore, 'allow[s] for justice to be done'. In *Sempra* ¶ 300, the Tribunal noted that it '*serves the purpose of justice*'. (emphasis added)

[73] As noted before in this work, the official commentary to the *OECD Draft of 1967*, above n 2, 120, Comment 4(a) to Art 1, notes that the FET standard is 'customary in relevant bilateral treaties', and observes that '[t]he standard required conforms in effect to the "minimum standard" which forms part of international law'.

[74] *ADF Group Inc v US*, ICSID Case No ARB(AF)/00/1 (Feliciano, deMestral, Lamm), Award (9 January 2003), ¶ 184 (hereinafter, *ADF Group*). The reference is to *Mondev International Ltd v US*, ICSID Case No ARB(AF)/99/2 (Stephen, Crawford, Schwebel), Award (11 October 2002), ¶ 120 (hereinafter, *Mondev*): 'The Tribunal has no difficulty in accepting that *an arbitral tribunal may not apply its own idiosyncratic standard in lieu of the standard laid down in Article 1105 (1)* . . . It also makes it clear that the standard of treatment, including fair and equitable treatment and full protection and security, *is to be found by reference to*

This approach also alerts us to the fact that the FET-autonomous position is inconsistent with rule of law principles. An autonomous standard—methodologically independent from general international law—does not qualify as a system of objective and accessible commands, commands 'which can be seen to flow from collective agreement rather than from the exercise of discretion or preferences by those persons who happens to be in position of authority'.[75] Such a standard—as observed by Habermas—does not permit the legitimacy of the adjudicative process to be shifted to that of the pre-existing norms being applied.[76] Instead, that conception—which lies dangerously near of conferring arbitrators the power to decide *ex aequo et bono*—can only lead back to the discretion of the arbitral panel.

It is certainly comforting to observe that most arbitral tribunals have lately arrived at the conclusion that the FET standard, whether or not it is 'autonomous', does not go de facto beyond IMS.[77] Yet, from the position defended here, that may not be enough. Arbitral tribunals should remain alert to the methodological constraints that in here in the application of IMS.[78] The key lesson offered by IMS is that tribunals should be *Darwinists*, and not *Creationists* in rendering awards; in other words, the constraints of general international law, including general principles of law, forbid arbitral tribunals from simply creating well-intended norms of 'almost perfect' governance that lack roots in any currently existing legal tradition.[79]

Note that under the position defended here, the NAFTA Free Trade Commission properly *interpreted* NAFTA Article 1105—and did not amend it—in its Note of 31 July 2001.[80] Since then, NAFTA Chapter 11 tribunals have demonstrated that a well-articulated FET-IMS standard, one that is evolutionary in character[81] and establishes a high threshold for its

international law, i.e., by reference to the normal sources of international law determining the minimum standard of treatment of foreign investors'. (emphasis added)

75 Mashaw, n 13, 138–39.

76 Jürgen Habermas, *Between Facts and Norms* (Cambridge, Mass, MIT Press, 1996) 261–62.

77 See cases listed in n 18 under the letter c).

78 It is surprising to see the misperceptions surrounding the concept of IMS. See eg *Enron* ¶ 257, where Tribunal correctly understood the FET standard as demanding recourse to the general principles of the law, but did not wish to associate the FET standard with IMS.

79 Among all, Zachary Douglas, 'Nothing If Not Critical for Investment Treaty Arbitration: *Occidental*, *Eureko* and *Methanex*' (2006) 22 *International Arbitration* 27, 28, has presented the strongest arguments against what I refer to as *Creationism* in international investment law: 'The *Tecmed* "standard" is actually not a standard at all; it is rather a description of perfect public regulation in a perfect world, to which all states should aspire but very few (if any) will ever attain'.

80 See the NAFTA Free Trade Commission, *Notes of Interpretation of Certain Chapter 11 Provisions* (31 July 2001) ¶ B.1 (available at http://www.sice.oas.org/TPD/NAFTA/Commission/CH11understanding_e.asp).

81 See eg, *International Thunderbird Gaming v Mexico*, UNCITRAL Ad Hoc Arbitration (van den Berg, Wälde, Portal), Award (26 January 2006), ¶ 194 (hereinafter, *Thunderbird*); *ADF*

application,[82] can properly fulfill the key policy goals of international investment law. For the same reason, it is inappropriate to negate that *interpretation* outside of the context of NAFTA, and reading BITs—which generally apply to developing countries—as establishing a FET standard more demanding that the one that applies to the US and Canada.[83] Such a haphazard and discriminatory system of state responsibility is offensive to the equality of nations.[84]

II A GENERAL FRAMEWORK OF ANALYSIS: FINDING THE ESSENTIAL DIMENSIONS OF A GAL APPROACH TO THE FET STANDARD

The previous section argued that the main function of the FET standard is to serve as a standard of review of arbitrariness pursuant to the methods and sources of general *international* law (that is, IMS). In this section, I claim that in the BIT generation, any meaningful test of arbitrariness must also consider the legal or illegal character of state behaviour in accordance with *domestic* law. Placing domestic law in its proper role in investment disputes, I present here the three essential dimensions of the GAL approach to the FET standard, which be expanded later in this chapter.

The regulatory state is, everywhere, a *Rechsstaat*. This means that to legitimately impose burdens on investors, state authorities must act in accordance with the domestic legal programs, as pre-established by constitutions and legislatures.[85] However, arbitral tribunals have tended to overlook this essential characteristic of modern government.[86] By

Group ¶ 179; *Mondev* ¶¶ 119–25; and, *Pope & Talbot Inc v Canada*, UNCITRAL Ad Hoc Arbitration (Dervaird, Greenberg, Belman), Award on Damages (31 May 2002) ¶ 59 (hereinafter, *Pope & Talbot III*).

82 See eg *Thunderbird* ¶ 194.

83 See Robert Wisner, 'The Modern View of the 'Fair and Equitable Treatment' Standard in the Review of Regulatory Action by States' (2007) 20 *International Law Practicum* 129, 130 (observing that '[i]t is unlikely that they [NAFTA members] sought to negotiate a different standard of treatment to apply among themselves').

84 The Tribunal in *Biwater Gauff* ¶ 599, correctly held that 'the description of the general threshold for violations of this standard [NAFTA Art 1105] is appropriate in the context of Article 2(2) of the BIT'.

85 See Carol Harlow, 'Global Administrative Law: The Quest for Principles and Values' (2006) 17 *European Journal of International Law* 187, 190 (observing that '[e]very Western administrative law system is founded on the rule of law').

86 In an article of descriptive character, Meg Kinnear, 'Treaties as Agreements to Arbitrate: International Law as the Governing Law' in Albert van den Berg (ed), *International Arbitration 2006: Back to Basis?* (Alphen aan den Rijn, Kluwer Law International, 2007) 401, 442–43, summarises the current situation in the following terms: 'There is a very strong preference for international law to be applied as the governing law of treaties, either because it is expressly stated to govern by the State Parties to the treaty or because tribunals find it is the appropriate substantive law in the circumstances of the case. Even where municipal law is stated to be a possible governing law, tribunals rarely refer to municipal law other than to set the facts upon which the treaty violation will be assessed'.

adopting a somewhat radical dualist stance, some tribunals have interpreted the FET standard as being completely autonomous from any domestic law considerations. Douglas, one of the few commentators to pay attention to this trend, observes that:

> Many of the awards of investment treaty tribunals—and the pleading of parties to these disputes—proceed on the basis of a dogmatic distinction between 'international' or 'treaty' versus 'municipal' or 'contractual' spheres, as if the two can be strictly dissociated one from the other. Thus, by characterising the status of an investment treaty tribunal as 'international', arbitrators have professed to occupy a position of supremacy in a 'hierarchy' of legal orders, and thereby have dismissed the relevance on any competing law or jurisdiction. The principle of international law that is used to buttress this approach, whether expressly or implicitly, is the rule of state responsibility that a state cannot invoke provisions of its own law to justify a derogation from an international obligation.[87]

The basic premises that inform any analysis of the relationship between international and domestic law are already universally accepted. In the absence of either an umbrella clause or a sufficiently broad definition of jurisdiction, investment treaty tribunals only have jurisdiction over treaty breaches.[88] Such claims thus must be assessed in accordance with public international law. As the ICJ stated in the *ELSI* case, '[c]ompliance with municipal law and compliance with the provisions of a treaty are different questions. What is a breach of treaty may be lawful in the municipal law and what is unlawful in the municipal law may be wholly innocent of violation of a treaty provision'.[89]

Using this basic framework, we can now draw the following table combining the two legal systems (Figure 8). This table matches domestic legality/illegality, on rows, with international legality/illegality, on columns. Hence, for example, the pair (legal, illegal), which corresponds to the North East (NE) position of the table, represents a measure that is legal under domestic law and wrongful under international law:

[87] Zachary Douglas, 'The Hybrid Foundation of Investment Treaty Arbitration' (2004) 74 British Ybk of Intl Law 151, 154–55. An example of 'radical dualism' can be found in *Wena Hotels Ltd v Egypt*, ICSID Case No ARB/98/4 (Kerameus, Bucher, Orrego), Decision on Annulment (5 February 2002), ¶ 35 (hereinafter, *Wena II*) (rejecting the idea of 'amalgamation of different legal instruments').

[88] See Jörn Griebel, 'Jurisdiction over "Contract Claims" in Treaty-Based Investment Arbitration on the Basis of Wide Dispute Settlement Clauses in Investment Agreements', 4(5) *Transnational Dispute Management* (September 2007).

[89] *ELSI* ¶ 73. In the BIT generation, see the much cited equivalent holding of the Tribunal in *Compañía de Aguas del Aconquija SA and Vivendi Universal v Argentina*, ICSID Case No ARB/97/3 (Fortier, Crawford, Fernández), Decision on Annulment (3 July 2002), ¶¶ 95–96 (hereinafter, *Vivendi II*).

Figure 8

		International Law	
		Legal	Illegal
Domestic Law	Legal	(legal, legal)	(legal, illegal)
	Illegal	(illegal, legal)	(illegal, illegal)

The radical dualist reading of these basic premises is mistaken regarding a very important point. The fact that a state cannot use its internal law 'as a means of escaping international responsibility'[90] does not imply that domestic law is irrelevant to international adjudication. As a matter of general international law, such a conclusion is incorrect. As Brownlie points out, '[c]ases in which a tribunal dealing with issues of international law has to examine the municipal law of one or more states are by no means exceptional'.[91] This is due to the fact that, as the PCIJ held in the Advisory Opinion in *Exchange of Greek and Turkish Populations* (1925), the parties may incorporate domestic law by 'express or implicit reference'.[92]

Only radical dualists can confuse the correct reading that domestic illegality is neither a necessary nor a sufficient condition of an internationally wrongful act, with the incorrect claim that domestic lawfulness does not matter at all. Radical dualists may purport to find support in the traditional stance of international law towards domestic law. However, as the Introduction of this work explained, the success of dualism in the 'denial of justice' age was due to two structural elements that are absent in the BIT generation: the lack of standing among individuals in international law, and the rule of exhaustion of domestic remedies. As Jenning explained in 1961:

> Whatever might be the position today it is certain that an individual was not [in the past] a subject of traditional international law. International law was therefore incapable by reason of its very structure of accommodating any notion of reciprocal obligations arising at international law between a State and an

[90] Comment No 1 to Art 3 of the ILC's Draft Articles on State Responsibility, in James Crawford (ed), *The International Law Commission's Articles on State Responsibility: Introduction, Text, and Commentaries* (CUP, Cambridge 2002) 89 (hereinafter, *ILC's Draft Articles and Commentaries*). See eg *Treatment of Polish Nationals and Other Persons of Polish Origin or Speech in the Danzig Territory* [1932] PCIJ Rep Series A/B No 44, 4, and 24–25.

[91] Ian Brownlie, *Principles of Public International Law*, 6th edn (New York, OUP, 2003) 36.

[92] *Exchange of Greek and Turkish Populations* [1925] PCIJ Rep Ser B No10, 19. See also, Georg Schwarzenberger, 1 *International Law* (Stevens and Sons, London 1957) 68 (explaining that 'parties to international disputes are free, either expressly or by way of implication, to authorise international judicial institutions to apply rules which, in substance, are rules of municipal law').

individual from their contract. For the protection of the individual, the introduction of the protecting State was necessary; and, *therefore, there had to be a transformation of the claim out of the realm of obligations fixed by the parties in contract, to the realm of general duties owed by one State to another. And this is precisely a transformation from the realm of contract to the realm of tort or delict.* (emphasis added)[93]

The radical dualist understanding of the relationship between international and domestic law has become outmoded. Today, investment treaty tribunals must control the regulatory state, and mainly the behaviour of administrative agencies, without previous intervention by domestic courts. In this context, the proper stance for investment treaty tribunals is *moderate dualism*. A moderate dualist recognises, as the ICJ did in the *ELSI* decision, that 'the qualification given to the impugned act by a municipal authority *may be a valuable indication* [of arbitrariness at the international plane]'. (emphasis added)[94] The point is, as the ILC's commentaries to the *Draft Articles on State Responsibility* remark, that 'there are many cases where issues of internal law are relevant to the existence or otherwise of responsibility . . . [I]n such cases it is international law which determines the scope and limits of any reference to internal law'.[95]

The *Vivendi* saga is the best demonstration of what I refer to as moderate dualism. In *Vivendi I*, although the Tribunal mistakenly dismissed the claims, it correctly noted the 'impossibility, on the facts of the instant case, of separating potential breaches of contract claims from BIT violations without interpreting and applying the Concession Contract'.[96] This observation—which, incidentally, can be found 40 years earlier in Jennings' own writings[97]—was not rejected by the Annulment

[93] RY Jennings, 'State Contracts in International Law' (1961) 37 British Ybk of Intl Law 156, 164.

[94] *ELSI* ¶ 124.

[95] *ILC's Draft Articles and Commentaries*, n 90, 89, Art 3, Comment No 8. See also, ibid, Art 3, Comment No 7 (affirming that '[e]specially in the fields of injury to aliens and their property and of human rights, *the content and application of internal law will often be relevant to the question of international responsibility'.*) (emphasis added)

[96] *Compañía de Aguas del Aconguija SA and Vivendi Universal v Argentina*, ICSID Case No ARB/97/3 (Rezek, Buergenthal, Trooboff), Award (21 November 2000), ¶ 81 (hereinafter, *Vivendi I*).

[97] Jennings, n 93, 165, observed in 1961, that 'it is impossible for a court to decide whether there has been an "arbitrary" interference with a particular contract without looking at the actual terms of the contract'. His lucid contractual analysis deserves to be quoted at length: 'What was agreed between the parties in the contract is inescapably a factor in deciding whether there has been an arbitrary interference with the expected course of the contractual relationship or not. The result may be in form "an international tort of the traditional type"; but it is also in substance at least partly contractual because the delict is not here independent of the terms of the contract'. (ibid 165) . . . 'The claim may even involve a necessary consideration of the local law; for it is not possible to say there has been arbitrary termination of the contract except after looking at the contract; and to look at the contract is to look at the local law in which it has its being'. (ibid 168).

Committee. In *Vivendi II*, the Tribunal reaffirmed the decision makers' obligations to take domestic law into account to the extent necessary to resolve an international claim:

> [I]t is one thing to exercise contractual jurisdiction (arguably exclusively vested in the administrative tribunals of Tucumán by virtue of the Concession Contract) and *another to take into account the terms of a contract in determining whether there has been a breach of a distinct standard of international law, such as that reflected in Article 3 of the BIT*. (emphasis added)[98]

Later, in *Vivendi III*, the Tribunal insisted that it had to take 'the contractual background into account in determining whether or not a breach of the Treaty has occurred',[99] and that it was permissible for it 'to consider such alleged contractual breaches, not for the purpose of determining whether a party has incurred in liability under domestic law, but to the extent necessary to analyse and determine whether there has been a breach of the Treaty'.[100] The same situation can be seen, more recently, in *Biwater Gauff*, where the Tribunal adopted a clear and transparent position that deserves to be cited in full:

> 469. It is not the role of this Arbitral Tribunal to decide contractual issues as between City Water and DAWASA, for example whether the Lease Contract was duly performed, whether the Lease Contract was rightly or wrongfully terminated and what would be the consequences of a wrongful termination . . .
>
> 470. On the other hand, *in determining the treaty claims as between BGT and the Republic, it is impossible to disregard the way in which the Lease Contract was concluded, performed, renegotiated and terminated*. The Lease Contract was, after all, the principal asset in question in this dispute. Both sides' cases entailed the presentation of extensive evidence on all aspects of the contractual position. *None of the acts of the Republic about which BGT complains can be evaluated in the abstract, without considering the precise circumstances in which they occurred, which in turn necessarily involves consideration of the contractual position*. . .
>
> 471. Since this Arbitral Tribunal can only discharge its mandate by considering issues relevant to the contractual relationship, it obviously has jurisdiction to do so. Equally, however, any findings this Arbitral Tribunal may make in respect of the Lease Contract could only be binding as between BGT and the Republic, and in the context of the treaty claims. Such findings cannot be binding as

[98] *Vivendi II* ¶ 105. See also ¶ 101 ('At most, it [domestic law] might be relevant—*as municipal law will often be relevant*—in assessing whether there has been a breach of the treaty') (emphasis added); and ¶ 110 ('[T]he Tribunal had jurisdiction to base its decision upon the Concession Contract, *at least so far as necessary* in order to determine whether there had been a breach of the substantive standards of the BIT') (emphasis added).

[99] *Compañía de Aguas del Aconquija et al v Argentina*, ICSID Case No ARB/97/3 (Rowley, Kaufmann-Kohler, Bernal), Award (20 August 2007) ¶ 7.3.9 (hereinafter, *Vivendi III*).

[100] ibid ¶ 7.3.10.

> between City Water and DAWASA, in the context of their separate contract dispute. (emphasis added)[101]

Moderate dualism can be broken down into three general considerations that will be explored throughout this chapter. First, domestic legality exerts a pull from NE (legal, illegal) to NW (legal, legal) (see Figure 8); in other words, it is more difficult, though still possible, to conclude that an international wrongful act exists when executive bodies have acted in accordance with domestic law.[102] Second, domestic illegality—including breaches of contract—pulls in the opposite direction, from SW (illegal, legal) to SE (illegal, illegal); once a 'measure' under scrutiny has been found illegal under domestic law, the additional distance required in order to find a breach to the BIT is significantly reduced. Third, the resolution of NE (legal, illegal) or SE (illegal, illegal) claims follow such different reasoning processes that it is highly convenient to distinguish one from the other.

The pull that domestic law exerts from SW (illegal, legal) to SE (illegal, illegal), as well as from NE (legal, illegal) to NW (legal, legal), was first identified more than seventy years ago, also in cases where local remedies had been waived. In his study of the Mexican–US General Claims Commission's jurisprudence, De Beus observed:

> Experience shows, and this is readily understandable, that an act at variance with municipal law is seldom deemed to come up to international standards . . . In the great majority of cases conduct towards a foreigner which does not conform with local law, is also at variance with the law of nations . . . *The only value which can under the law of nations be attributed to domestic law as a standard is, on the one hand, that if the behaviour complained of shows a pronounced departure from that law to the prejudice of a foreigner, there is an international delinquency, and, on the other hand, that if the action is in accordance with that law, international commissions will perhaps hesitate to declare that the national law is below international standards of civilization. But it should always be kept in mind, that compliance with local prescriptions is not in itself a conclusive test.*[103]

Certainly, not all investment treaty tribunals have based their decisions on radical dualism. Many of them have been well aware of the pull that

[101] *Biwater Gauff* ¶¶ 469–71. See also, *Helnan International Hotels A/S v Egypt*, ICSID Case No ARB/05/19 (Derains, Dolzer, Lee), Award (3 July, 2008), ¶ 103 (hereinafter, *Helnan International Hotels*).

[102] See also, Dolzer, n 29, 100–04 (explaining that 'the state of the law of the host state which was in force at the time at which the foreigner acquired his investment' is relevant for the operation of the FET standard, and noting also the existence of a 'chronological anchoring of the operation of the standard' with respect to domestic law as it existed at the time of the investment).

[103] JG de Beus, *The Jurisprudence of the General Claims Commission United States and Mexico Under The Convention of September 8, 1923* ('s-Gravenhage, M Nijhoff, 1938) 140.

domestic law exerts when deciding international claims[104] (particularly in recent awards).[105] Spiermann, in a recent article on applicable law, reached a similar conclusion:

> While treaty claims are obviously to be decided on the basis of international law, national law still has a role to play.[106] . . . Deciding 'preliminary' or 'incidental' questions of national law does not convert the arbitral tribunal into a court of appeal of national proceedings; this is inherent jurisdiction necessary in order to give effect to the investor's right to international arbitration as well as the object and purpose of most, if not all, investment treaties.[107]

At this point, let us move forward to establish a more ambitious analytical framework for parsing the relationship between international and domestic law in investment disputes. Such a framework is essential in order to better grasp the exact meaning and scope of the FET standard, as applied under a moderated dualist approach. Inspired by de Beus's earlier exercise,[108] I claim that an appropriate methodological structure should be organised around the following four basic questions: (Q1), whether the defendant state's legal system—ie, not the specific measure in dispute itself, but the legal norms that serve as its basis—falls below IMS; (Q2), whether the particular measure under scrutiny is illegal under domestic law; (Q3), if the measure is illegal, which extra requirements would make it wrongful in the international context; and (Q4), if the measure is legal and the legal system is above IMS, how to assess it directly pursuant to IMS.

Applying these four questions (Q1–Q4) with the table presented in Figure 8, it is possible to develop the following 'reasoning chart', describing the analytical framework for a GAL approach to the FET standard (Figure 9):

[104] See eg *MTD Equity Sdn Bhd et al v Chile*, ICSID Case No ARB/01/07 (Guillaume, Crawford, Ordóñez), Decision on Annulment (21 March 2007), ¶¶ 72, and 75 (hereinafter, *MTD II*); *GAMI* ¶ 91; *MTD I* ¶¶ 187, 204; *Waste Management II* ¶ 73; *Loewen v US*, ICSID Case No ARB(AF)/98/3 (Mason, Mikva, Mustill), Award (26 June 2003), ¶ 135 (hereinafter, *Loewen*); and, *Tecmed* ¶ 120.

[105] See eg, *Helnan International Hotels* ¶¶ 103, and 125; and, *Limited Liability Company AMTO v Ukraine*, SCC Case No 080/2005 (Cremades, Runeland, Soderlund), Award (26 March 2008), ¶ 99.

[106] Ole Spiermann, 'Applicable Law' in Peter Muchlinski et al (eds), *The Oxford Handbook of International Investment Law* (New York, OUP, 2008) 89, 110.

[107] ibid 112. See also, Choudhury, n 21, 314 (observing that '[a] clear demonstration of a violation of the fair and equitable treatment standard can also be shown by demonstrating that the host State, or its agent, acted beyond the scope of its legal authority').

[108] De Beus, n 103, 144, in 1938, considered the following questions: '*First Question*: Is act in itself, quite apart from its accordance with municipal law, below minimum standards? *Second Question*: a. If so, there is an international delinquency, and no second question is needed. b. If not, is act at variance with municipal law in such a way as to constitute an international delinquency by that single fact?'

Figure 9

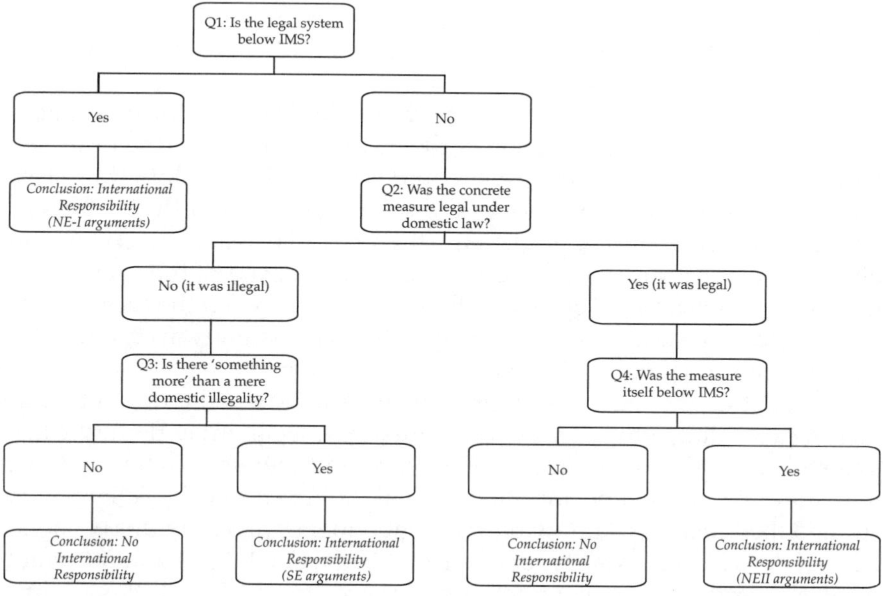

As indicated by the chart, these four questions, in the order presented, lead to three possible favourable outcomes for investors. These outcomes serve as the foundation around which the three constituting parts of the GAL enterprise are organised, each of which describes a different and distinctive set of problems: first, the NE-I arguments (legal, illegal),which put into question the legal system of the defendant state; second, the SE arguments (illegal, illegal), which require some level of domestic law judicial review on the part of investment treaty tribunals, and which also require a definition of the 'something more' needed to prove a treaty violation; and third, the NE-II arguments (legal, illegal), which demand the development of substantive tests of arbitrariness at the international level.

I certainly do not argue here that this three-part structure constitutes an exhaustive and exclusive reading of the FET standard. This is only a preliminary GAL attempt to resolve the doctrinal disarray that characterises this field of the law. While I do attempt to cover most relevant scenarios, I recognise that the considerable flexibility of the FET standard represents a natural limit to any ambitious project such as the one developed here.

III THE FIRST DIMENSION OF THE GAL APPROACH TO THE FET STANDARD: THE LEGAL SYSTEM FALLING BELOW IMS AS THE BASIS OF INTERNATIONAL WRONGFULNESS

This section analyses what should be the initial question for investment treaty tribunals in the application of the FET standard: Does the legal system serving as basis for the measure under scrutiny fall below IMS? This question represents the essence of the NE-I arguments. If the regulatory state must obey domestic public law, then any discussion concerning an objectionable measure must be preceded by an analysis of the compatibility of that domestic legal system with international law. If the former does not comply with IMS, then, in principle, the discussion is over, and arbitral tribunals must decide in favour of the plaintiff.[109]

The fact that the legal system may fall below IMS is the most obvious reason explaining why a certain measure can be legal under domestic law and still wrongful under international law, and therefore, why domestic law may be irrelevant in international adjudication.[110] Feller—who studied the Mexican Claims Commissions—makes precisely this observation: 'It does not necessarily follow [from the fact that the claimant cannot recover based on the contract under Mexican law] that the Claims Commission may not make an award. *The provisions of Mexican law in question may be beneath the international standard of justice*'. (emphasis added)[111] Similarly, in the *Norwegian Shipowners' Claim* (1922), the Arbitral Tribunal held that '[it] cannot ignore the municipal law of the Parties, *unless that law is contrary to the principle of the equality of the Parties, or to the principles of justice which are common to all civilised nations*'. (emphasis added)[112]

In the BIT generation—particularly in the context of NAFTA Chapter 11—several cases have already proven that it may be necessary to assess whether the domestic legal system passes muster under IMS (and not only in FET claims, but also expropriation claims). For instance, in *Azinian*, the Tribunal held that the termination of a contract by a Mexican municipality, in accordance with a domestic law not falling below IMS, could not be

[109] As Jan Paulsson, *Denial of Justice in International Law* (New York, CUP, 2005) 4, remarks, '[i]nternational law provides standards by which national systems can be judged from the outside'.

[110] See Art 3 of the ILC's Draft Articles, in *ILC's Draft Articles and Commentaries*, n 90, 86. See also, Art 27 of the Vienna Convention on the Law of Treaties.

[111] AH Feller, *The Mexican Claims Commissions 1923–1934; A Study In the Law and Procedure of International Tribunals* (New York, The Macmillan Company, 1935) 179. See also, Jennings, n 93, 168 (commenting that 'the international claim will not be dependent on showing that there was a breach of contract in the sense of the local law (which might simply be untrue) but that *the local law is not in accord with the requirements of international law*'). (emphasis added)

[112] *Norwegian Shipowners' Claim* (Norway v US) (1922) 1 RIAA 307, 331 (available at http://www.un.org/law/riaa/). See also Hersch Lauterpacht's Separate Opinion in *Certain Norwegian Loans* (*France v Norway*) [1957] ICJ Rep 9, 37.

considered an expropriation. In performing this analysis, the Tribunal appropriately separated the determination of whether the legal system passes muster under IMS, from the same determination for the concrete measure at issue:

> [T]he Claimants have not even attempted to demonstrate that the Mexican court decisions constituted a fundamental departure from established principles of Mexican law. *The Respondent's evidence as to the relevant legal standards for annulment of public service contracts stands unrebutted. Nor do the Claimants contend that these legal standards breach NAFTA Article 1110.* The Arbitral Tribunal finds nothing in the application of these standards with respect to the issue of invalidity that appears arbitrary or unsustainable in light of the evidentiary record. To the contrary, the evidence positively supports the conclusions of the Mexican courts. (emphasis added)[113]

Similarly, in *Thunderbird*, the Tribunal, before analysing the particular measure under scrutiny, proceeded to implicitly assess Mexican gambling laws with IMS, concluding that no violation had occurred at that level.[114] The Tribunal correctly concluded that the Mexican government possessed a broad regulatory discretion concerning the content of its own legal system:

> Mexico has in this context a wide regulatory 'space' for regulation; in the regulation of the gambling industry, governments have a particularly wide scope of regulation reflecting national views on public morals. Mexico can permit or prohibit any forms of gambling as far as the NAFTA is concerned. It can change its regulatory policy and it has a wide discretion with respect to how it carries out such policies by regulation and administrative conduct. [115]

This recognition of states' regulatory space—that is, the discretion to define their own legal systems and policies—can also be found in *SD Myers I*. In its decision, the Tribunal remarked upon the 'high measure of deference that international law generally extends to the right of domestic authorities to regulate matters within their own borders'.[116]

In *GAMI*, the Tribunal went even further, noting that '[t]he duty of NAFTA tribunals is rather to appraise whether and how preexisting laws and regulations are applied to the foreign investor',[117] and that '[i]nternational law does not appraise the content of a regulatory programme extant before an investor decides to commit'.[118] The Tribunal showed, hence, a high level of deference towards the domestic legal system—in that case, economic regulation of the sugar industry—as it existed at the time of the

113 *Azinian* ¶ 120. See also, ibid ¶¶ 93 ff.

114 *Thunderbird* ¶ 123 (recognising, in principle, 'the right of a Contracting Party to regulate conduct that it considers illegal').

115 ibid ¶ 127.

116 *SD Myers I* ¶ 263.

117 *GAMI* ¶ 94.

118 ibid ¶ 91. See also ibid ¶ 93 ('To repeat: NAFTA arbitrators have no mandate to evaluate laws and regulations that predate the decision of a foreigner to invest').

investment. The principle is clear: unless there are extreme circumstances, investors cannot complain about the content of the legal system that they voluntarily entered into.[119]

Another NAFTA Chapter 11 case that deserves particular attention is *Mondev*. In that case, the Tribunal considered whether the legal system of the commonwealth of Massachusetts may have been below IMS as a consequence of providing immunity to administrative agencies (in particular, to the Boston Redevelopment Authority, BRA). In its decision, the Tribunal referred to the broad regulatory space of states, in this instance with a focus on tort law and immunities:

> [Mondev] argued that for a NAFTA Party to confer on one of its public authorities immunity from suit in respect of wrongful conduct affecting an investment was in itself a failure to provide full protection and security to the investment, and contravened Article 1105(1).[120] . . . [W]ithin broad limits, the extent to which a State decides to immunize regulatory authorities from suit for interference with contractual relations is a matter for the competent organs of the State to decide.[121]

Cases such as *Mondev*, *GAMI* and *Thunderbird* remind us how difficult it is for a claimant to win a case based on NE-I arguments (that is, where the legal system falls below IMS). As de Beus observed in 1938, '[e]xperience shows, and this is readily understandable, that . . . still less often a national law is deemed to be below international standards of civilization'.[122] The reason, as noted, is quite simple: states enjoy great regulatory latitude in determining the content of domestic law regarding economic matters. Stated another way, the actual content of IMS with respect to economic regulation is very thin, and, as a consequence, investors are forced to take host state law as they find it.[123]

This brings us to one of the central questions of this chapter: How will investment treaty tribunals construe and develop IMS, in order to assess the domestic legal systems of defendant states? Considering international law's lack of experience in this regard, is there any other way of accomplishing this that might avoid comparative law references and assessments? I will return to these questions when discussing the third dimension of the GAL approach to the FET standard.

For the moment, I only wish to note that arbitral tribunals have already stressed the role that a comparative law approach must have in determin-

[119] In *Plama II* ¶ 220, the Tribunal stated that the 'Claimant was, of course, aware of, or should have been aware of, the state of Bulgarian law when it invested in Nova Plama'.

[120] *Mondev* ¶ 140.

[121] ibid ¶ 154 (emphasis added) The Tribunal went even further on this point, ibid ¶ 143, and affirmed that 'there are difficulties in reading Article 1105(1) so as in effect to create a new substantive civil right to sue BRA for tortious interference with contractual relations'.

[122] De Beus, n 103, 140.

[123] See McLachlan et al, n 18, 236–37, and 245, and Dolzer, n 102.

ing whether a particular piece of legislation or general policy falls above or below IMS. In *Mondev,* the Tribunal gave attention to comparative experiences on the issue of immunity of public authority in domestic public law.[124] Similarly, in *ADF Group,*[125] *Noble Ventures Romania*[126] and *Link-Trading,*[127] tribunals rendered their decisions based on the belief that domestic policy was consistent with that of 'many states', 'all legal systems', and 'many countries in the world'.

Even though winning a case based on NE-I arguments requires that claimants meet a high threshold, today we can witness an exception to this in the emergence of a certain line of argument that may carry implications for NE-I claims. Some investment treaty tribunals have interpreted the FET standard as establishing a principle that can be referred to as 'almost perfect governance'. This systemic principle, applicable to legal systems as a whole, would supposedly include elements of transparency, consistency, non-ambiguity, stability, and predictability.[128]

At least four awards belong to the trend of decisions that have given the FET standard 'a life of its own':[129] *Metalclad, Tecmed, OEPC* and *LG&E*. The *Metalclad* Tribunal initiated matters with the following concept of transparency:

> Prominent in the statement of principles and rules that introduces the Agreement is the reference to 'transparency' *(NAFTA Article 102(1))*. The Tribunal understands this to include the idea that all relevant legal requirements for the purpose of initiating, completing and successfully operating investments made, or intended to be made, under the Agreement should be capable of being readily known to all affected investors of another Party. There should be no room for doubt or uncertainty on such matters. Once the authorities of the central government of any Party (whose international responsibility in such matters has been identified in the preceding section) become aware of any scope for misunderstanding or confusion in this connection, it is their duty to ensure that the correct position is promptly determined and clearly stated so that investors can proceed with all appropriate expedition in the confident belief that they are acting in accordance with all relevant laws.[130]

[124] *Mondev* ¶¶ 149–150.

[125] *ADF Group* ¶ 188.

[126] *Noble Ventures* ¶178.

[127] *Link-Trading Join Stock Co v Moldova*, UNCITRAL Ad Hoc Arbitration (Hertzfeld, Buruiana, Zykin), Award (18 April 2002), ¶ 72 (hereinafter, *Link-Trading*).

[128] Several studies of investment law are taking notice of this trend. See eg, Muchlinski, n 5, 25, who summarises this view: 'In the light of the contemporary perspective, it is now reasonably well settled that the standard [FET] requires a particular approach to governance, on the part of the host country, that is encapsulated in the obligations to act in a consistent manner, free from ambiguity and in total transparency, without arbitrariness and in accordance with the principle of good faith'.

[129] Lowe, n 6, 455.

[130] *Metalclad* ¶ 76.

In *Tecmed*, the already demanding concept created in *Metalclad* was augmented with the notions of consistency and non-ambiguity. In what has been ironically referred to as the '*TecMed* programme for good governance',[131] or more simply the 'no standard at all',[132] the Tribunal held that:

> [The BIT] requires the Contracting Parties to provide to international investments treatment that does not affect the basic expectations that were taken into account by the foreign investor to make the investment. The foreign investor expects the host State to act in a consistent manner, free from ambiguity and totally transparently in its relations with the foreign investor, so that it may know beforehand any and all rules and regulations that will govern its investments, as well as the goals of the relevant policies and administrative practices or directives, to be able to plan its investment and comply with such regulations. Any and all State actions conforming to such criteria should relate not only to the guidelines, directives or requirements issued, or the resolutions approved thereunder, but also to the goals underlying such regulations.[133]

In *OEPC*, the Tribunal again expanded the standard, this time with references to stability and predictability:

> However, it is that very confusion and lack of clarity [of the Ecuadorian tax legal system] that resulted in some form of arbitrariness, even if not intended by the SRI.[134] . . . It is also evident that the Respondent's treatment of the investment falls below such standards [of international law] . . . The relevant question for international law in this discussion is . . . whether the legal and business framework meets the requirements of stability and predictability under international law.[135]

The final stage of this creative trend can be seen in *LG&E*,[136] where the Tribunal synthesised this principle of 'almost perfect governance' as follows:

> [T]his Tribunal, having considered, as previously stated, the sources of international law, understands that the fair and equitable standard consists of the host State's consistent and transparent behaviour, free of ambiguity that involves the obligation to grant and maintain a stable and predictable legal framework necessary to fulfill the justified expectations of the foreign investor.[137]

131 Chile's Annulment Reply, quoted in *MTD II* ¶ 66. As indicated there, '[t]he *TecMed* dictum is also subject to strenuous criticism from the Respondent's experts, Mr. Jan Paulsson and Sir Arthur Watts'.

132 See Douglas, n 79.

133 *Tecmed* ¶ 154.

134 *OEPC* ¶ 163. Before *OEPC*, see *Maffezini v España*, ICSID Case No N°ARB/97/7 (Orrego, Buergenthal, Wolf), Award (13 November 2000), ¶ 83.

135 *OEPC* ¶ 190–91. See also, *CMS* ¶ 274.

136 I should mention here the extreme version of consistency as ' "unity of the state" vis-à-vis foreign investors' adopted in *MTD I* ¶¶ 163–66; see also, *MTD II* ¶ 81.

137 *LG&E* ¶ 131. See also, ibid ¶ 125. It is far from clear which 'sources of international law' the Tribunal considered, apart from citing various previous *creationist* awards (although, not all decisions cited there are *creationist*).

In any case, this trend—which already includes a fair number of decisions[138]—is not only inappropriate as matter of treaty interpretation—for the reasons given in section I—but also undesirable from a normative perspective. Which is the proper standard of transparency, consistency, non-ambiguity, stability, and predictability that legal systems must comply with in the BIT generation? What would serve as the benchmark for comparison? Is there any legal system in the world that could pass muster the 'almost perfect' standard of governance that these arbitral tribunals are currently imposing on defendant states in investment arbitration?[139]

The expansive potential of these components when unrestricted, and their illegitimacy when improperly applied, proves once more the need for a deferential attitude among arbitral tribunals when applying IMS and the FET standard.[140] Fortunately, the recent decisions in *Continental Casualty Co*, *Plama* and *Parkerings* offer hope that a more prudent stance, which takes the realities of public administration and domestic politics seriously into account, is beginning to form among investment treaty tribunals.[141]

IV THE SECOND DIMENSION OF THE GAL APPROACH TO THE FET STANDARD: DOMESTIC ILLEGALITIES AS THE BASIS OF INTERNATIONAL WRONGFUL ACTS

Even if the domestic legal system passes muster under IMS, investors can still recover damages based on SE arguments (that is, (illegal, illegal) in Figure 8). In SE claims, according to Figure 9 above, two conditions must be met: the measure must be illegal under domestic law, and it must meet the 'something more' required as a matter of international law. As will be

[138] See eg *Duke Energy Electroquil* ¶¶ 338–39 (expressly following LG&E ¶ 131); *Biwater Gauff* ¶602 (transparency, consistency); and, *Enron* ¶ 260 (stability).

[139] According to Douglas, n 79, the answer seems to be 'very few (if any)'.

[140] The Tribunal in *Saluka* ¶ 304, observes rightly that 'while it subscribes to the general thrust of these and similar statements [i.e., including investor's expectations and legal stability], it may be that, if their terms were to be taken too literally, they would impose upon host States' obligations which would be inappropriate and unrealistic'.

[141] Indeed, in *Continental Casualty* ¶ 258, the Tribunal held that: '[I]t would be unconscionable for a country to promise not to change its legislation as time and needs change . . . Such an implication as to stability in the BIT's Preamble would be contrary to an effective interpretation of the Treaty; reliance on such an implication by a foreign investor would be misplaced and, indeed, unreasonable'. In *Plama II* ¶ 219, the Tribunal noted that the FET standard is not equivalent to a stabilisation clause: 'However, the Tribunal believes that the ECT does not protect investors against any and all changes in the host country's laws. Under the fair and equitable treatment standard the investor is only protected if (at least) reasonable and justifiable expectations were created in that regard. It does not appear that Bulgaria made any promises or other representations to freeze its legislation on environmental law to the Claimant or at all'. In *Parkerings* ¶ 306, the Tribunal went even further, stating that 'it would have been foolish for a foreign investor in Lithuania to believe, at that time, that it would be proceeding on stable legal ground, as considerable changes in the Lithuanian political regime and economy were undergoing'.

explained further, this means that international investment law must refine two different sets of norms: a conflict-of-laws body, that sets forth the rules for the application of domestic law; and a substantive law body, that defines the precise nature of the 'more' required in addition to domestic illegality.

A The Non-Courts of Appeal Doctrine

As we have seen, domestic law exerts a pull from SW (illegal, legal) to SE (illegal, illegal) (see Figure 8). This pulling effect, which is the essence of the second dimension of the GAL approach to the FET standard, demands that arbitral tribunals conduct some form of domestic judicial review.

However, several tribunals have evaded any such judicial review by repeating that they are not courts of appeal. Probably the clearest formulation of this 'doctrine' can be found in *ADF Group*, where the Tribunal held that it 'has no authority to review the legal validity and standing of the U.S. measures here in question under *U.S. internal administrative law*. We do not sit as a court with appellate jurisdiction with respect to the U.S. measures'.[142] Other tribunals that have advanced similar propositions include *Thunderbird,*[143] *EnCana,*[144] *Generation Ukraine*[145] and *CME.*[146]

But is this 'doctrine'—or more precisely, the most extreme versions of it—correct under general international law? Should investment treaty tribunals only apply international law to decide investment disputes, avoiding all issues of domestic law? The answer is no, and section II has already argued, at length, why radical dualism—which usually lies behind this non-courts of appeal doctrine—is wrong as a matter of general international law. It must be added here that this doctrine also cannot find support in the traditional concept of reserved domain (*domaine réservé*), which has always been a relative concept in international law; the extent of the *domaine réservé* 'depends *on International Law* and varies according to its development',[147] not vice versa.

[142] *ADF Group* ¶ 190. See also, ibid fn 182.

[143] *Thunderbird* ¶ 125 ('It is not the Tribunal's function to act as a court of appeal or review').

[144] *Encana v Ecuador*, UNCITRAL Ad Hoc Arbitration (Crawford, Grigera, Thomas), Award (3 February 2006), ¶ 145 ('[T]his Tribunal is not a court of appeal') (hereinafter, *Encana*).

[145] *Generation Ukraine Inc v Ukraine*, ICSID Case No ARB/00/9 (Paulsson, Salius, Voss), Award (16 September 2003), ¶ 20.33 ('This Tribunal does not exercise the function of an administrative review body') (hereinafter, *Generation Ukraine*).

[146] *CME I* ¶ 467 ('The Tribunal is not to decide on the Czech Administrative Law aspect of this question'). See also, ibid ¶ 590.

[147] The Institute of International Law, 45-II *Annuaire de l'Institut de Droit International* (Editions juridiques et sociologiques, Bale 1954) 299 (emphasis added). See also, Humphrey Waldock, 'General Course on Public International Law' in Académie de Droit International, 106 *Recueil des Cours—1962-II* (AW Sijthoff, Leyde 1963) 1, 179, and 183; and, *Nationality Decree in Tunis and Morocco* [1923] PCIJ Rep Ser B No 7, 23–24 ('The question whether a certain matter is or is not solely within the jurisdiction of a State is an essentially relative question; it depends upon the development of international relations').

In the BIT generation, tribunals must directly control acts and omissions by the regulatory state according to IMS, without the previous assistance of domestic courts. In many instances, this function cannot be carried out without applying domestic law, even in cases in which international law is the exclusive applicable law according to the pertinent treaty. Indeed, because of international law's low legal density, as well as the accepted policy space that states enjoy in matters of economic regulation, by *renvoi*, investment treaty tribunals *must* perform, to some extent, domestic law judicial review.[148]

The key point is that, as the *Waste Management II* Tribunal stated, domestic law, when necessary, becomes part of the 'incidental jurisdiction' of investment treaty tribunals.[149] Consequently, as noted in *Tecmed*, arbitral tribunals 'must consider such matters [grounds or motives of the measure at stake pursuant to domestic law] to determine if the Agreement [the BIT] was violated'.[150]

An example from *Metalclad* may help to clarify this pint. Here, the parties disputed whether or not a municipal construction permit was required to build a landfill, and whether the municipality of Guadalcazar had properly denied it. Clearly, those two key issues could only be answered with reference to Mexican public law. After conducting a review of Mexican public law—review that was neither explicit nor clear in terms of its reasoning regarding Mexican law—the Tribunal concluded that no permit was required and that, in addition, the municipality had illegally denied it.[151]

148 Feller, n 111, 178, in his study of the Mexico–US General Commission, where the rule of local remedies had also been waived, set a prophetic tone for today's international investment law: '[H]ow is such a claim [contractual claim] to be decided 'in accordance with the principles of international law'? International law contains no rules for the decision of controversies involving breach of such contracts. *All that can be found in international law is a reference back to municipal law.* Under the usual type of convention all the Commission could do would be to tell the claimant to take the controversy into the municipal courts, to exhaust his local remedies. Under this Convention it cannot do so [because local remedies were waived]. Therefore the Commission itself must apply a municipal, in this case Mexican, law. *It may either be said then that the Commission in this case acts as a Mexican tribunal, or that it acts as an international tribunal applying Mexican law which, for this purpose, has been incorporated into international law'.* (emphasis added)

149 See *Waste Management II* ¶ 73. See also the cases cited in nn 96, 98, 99, 104 and 105. Note that this may also be the case in expropriation claims; see *Feldman* ¶ 88 (explaining that the validity of certain tax assessments pursuant to Mexican law was relevant for deciding an Art 1110 claim—expropriation—and an Art 1102 claim—national treatment).

150 *Tecmed* ¶ 120.

151 See *Metalclad* ¶¶ 79, and 106 (for full citation, see ch 5, nn 237, and 238, and accompanying text). Another interesting example can be found in *Genin*, where the Tribunal had to determine the legitimacy of the revocation of a bank licence. In contrast to *Metalclad*, in *Genin* the Tribunal did properly and explicitly examine the law of Estonia. See *Genin* ¶¶ 348–73, particularly the summary provided in ¶ 363: 'In sum, the Tribunal finds that the Bank of Estonia acted within its statutory discretion when it took the steps that it did, for the reasons that it did, to revoke EIB's licence. Its ultimate decision cannot be said to have been arbitrary or discriminatory against the foreign investors in the sense in which those words are used in the BIT'.

As will be explored below, one of the essential missions of the second dimension of the GAL approach to the FET standard—that is, claims involving SE arguments—is to reduce the confusion that extreme versions of the non-courts of appeal doctrine have brought to international investment jurisprudence. Jenks's observation is more valid today than ever: 'it is desirable that there should be a franker and fuller recognition than there has been that in a variety of types of cases the functions of the Court necessarily include the interpretation and application of municipal law?[152]

B Extent of Domestic Judicial Review

When reviewing the regulatory state pursuant to the FET standard—which, most of the time, corresponds to administrative action—investment treaty tribunals confront one or more of the following three elements: facts, policy, and law. Which legal system—international or domestic law—should arbitral tribunals apply when reviewing each of them, and how much deference should be given to defendant states?

Traditionally, as explored in chapter 4 at length, domestic courts have been deferential in matters of policy, but not in matters of fact and law. Legal systems distinguish between administrative powers that are comprehensively defined by legislation and those that confer agencies a certain degree of freedom to decide between alternative policies. For example, French administrative law separates *compétence liée* from *pouvoir discrétionnaire*,[153] and Spanish and Latin American administrative law distinguishes *potestades regladas* from *potestades discrecionales*.[154] Similarly, legal traditions recognise situations labeled as *l'opportunité*, *Zweckmässigkeit*, or *policy considerations* that encompass areas in which administrative agencies enjoy high levels of autonomy.

These distinctions are important in comparative law because they structure the way in which judicial review is conducted. Tests of 'arbitrariness as illegality', which cover legal applications and interpretations by administrative agencies, tend to be substantially more intrusive than tests of 'arbitrariness as irrationality', 'special sacrifice' and 'lack of proportionality', which generally apply to the soft-edged questions of rationality, reasonableness and proportionality in policy-making.

A central matter with which the second dimension of the GAL approach to the FET standard must deal is the *extent* of domestic law review. That is,

[152] C Wilfred Jenks, 'The Interpretation and Application of Municipal Law by the Permanent Court of International Justice' (1938) 19 British Ybk of Intl Law 67, 99–100.

[153] René Chapus, 1 *Droit Administratif Général*, 15th edn (Paris, Montchrestien, 2001) 1055 and 1058.

[154] Eduardo García de Enterría and Tomás-Ramón Fernández, 1 *Curso de Derecho Administrativo*, 12th edn (Madrid, Civitas, 2004) 460 ff.

once we accept the relevance of domestic law to investment arbitration, then which group of tests—the hard-edged 'arbitrariness as illegality' and/or soft-edged 'arbitrariness as irrationality/special sacrifice/lack of proportionality'—must be included in the *renvoi* to domestic law?

Three theoretical positions emerge in this regard, which are explored immediately below. The first, which takes the non-courts of appeal doctrine more seriously, requires the remanding of cases to domestic tribunals before adjudicating at the international level. By contrast, the second position orders investment treaty tribunals to assume jurisdiction, and also to conduct all tests in accordance with domestic law. A third and middle position—which I will argue is the correct one—requires arbitral tribunals to assume jurisdiction only with respect to the test of 'arbitrariness as illegality'. The remaining tests—'arbitrariness as irrationality', 'arbitrariness as special sacrifice' and 'arbitrariness as lack of proportionality'—are matters to be reserved for substantive international investment law. They form a part of the third dimension of the GAL approach to the FET standard (NE-II arguments), and, consequently, no *renvoi* to domestic law is required.

i First Option: Remanding Cases to Domestic Courts: The Rebirth of the Local Remedies Rule

The *Vivendi I* case adopted the most extreme pro-state approach to the question of the extent of judicial review. In that case, the claimant argued breaches of the treaty based on facts and allegations that involved the interpretation and application of both a concession contract, and the applicable domestic law. The Tribunal dismissed the claim on the merits, implicitly remanding the case to domestic courts:[155]

> [T]he Tribunal holds that, *because of the crucial connection in this case between the terms of the Concession Contract and these alleged violations of the BIT, the Argentine Republic cannot be held liable unless and until Claimants have, as Article 16.4 of the Concession Contract requires, asserted their rights in proceedings before the contentious administrative courts of Tucumán and have been denied their rights, either procedurally or substantively.* [emphasis added][156] . . . The Tribunal emphasizes that this decision does not impose an exhaustion of remedies requirement under the BIT because such requirement would be incompatible with Article 8 of the BIT and Article 26 of the ICSID Convention. In this case, however, *the obligation to resort to the local courts is compelled by* the express terms of Article 16.4 of the private contract between Claimants and the Province of Tucumán and *the impossibility, on the facts of the instant case, of separating potential breaches of contract claims from*

[155] The Annulment Committee in *Vivendi II* annulled this award for adopting such a radical stance.

[156] *Vivendi I* ¶ 78.

> *BIT violations without interpreting and applying the Concession Contract, a task that the contract assigns expressly to the local courts.* (emphasis added)[157]

A similar, though more subtle, approach has been adopted by two tribunals presided over by James Crawford. In *Waste Management II*, the Tribunal explained this position in the following terms:

> The importance of a remedy, agreed on between the parties, for breaches of the Concession Agreements bears emphasis. It is true that in a general sense the exhaustion of local remedies is a procedural prerequisite for the bringing of an international claim, one which is dispensed with by NAFTA Chapter 11. But the availability of local remedies to an investor faced with contractual breaches is nonetheless relevant to the question whether a standard such as Article 1105(1) have been complied with by the State. Were it not so, Chapter 11 would become a mechanism of equal resort for debt collection and analogous purposes in respect of all public (including municipal) contracts, which does not seem to be its purpose.[158]

Later, the *EnCana* Tribunal expanded this approach to pure regulatory contexts (ie, non contractual). Although the Tribunal was entertaining an expropriation claim—the only one over which it had jurisdiction according to the relevant BIT—its reasoning appears sufficiently broad to be included, by analogy, in this present study of the FET standard:

> In terms of the BIT the executive is entitled to take a position in relation to claims put forward by individuals, even if that position may turn out to be wrong in law, provided it does so in good faith and stands ready to defend its position before the courts. Like private parties, governments do not repudiate obligations merely by contesting their existence. An executive agency does not expropriate the value represented by a statutory obligation to make a payment or refund by mere refusal to pay, provided at least that (a) the refusal is not merely wilful, (b) the courts are open to the aggrieved private party, (c) the courts' decisions are not themselves overridden or repudiated by the State.[159]

Recently, the *Parkerings* Tribunal has also endorsed such a thesis. While deciding a case under a 'fair and reasonable' standard contained in the treaty—which was correctly considered equivalent to the FET standard[160]—it held that:

> Under certain limited circumstances, a substantial breach of contract could constitute a violation of a treaty . . . In most cases, a preliminary determination by a competent court as to whether the contract was breached under municipal law is necessary. This preliminary determination is even more necessary if the par-

[157] *Vivendi I* ¶ 81.
[158] *Waste Management II* ¶ 116. Concerning the expropriation claim, see ibid ¶¶ 174–76.
[159] *EnCana* ¶ 194. See also ¶ 200 n.138.
[160] *Parkerings* ¶ 277.

ties to the contract have agreed on a specific forum for all disputes arising out of the contract.[161]

In my opinion, the position adopted in these cases is inconsistent with the legal architecture of investment treaties. In most cases, BITs waive the requirement of exhaustion of local remedies. The non-courts of appeal doctrine, if taken this far, may lead tribunals to compromise the protection that investors receive from treaties. That result is ultimately akin to a reinstalling of the local remedies requirement, an inappropriate and counter-intuitive move.[162]

Following such reasoning, the *CME* Tribunal provided a powerful critique of this position:

> A purpose of an international investment treaty is to grant arbitral recourse outside the host country's domestic legal system. The clear purpose is to grant independent judicial remedies on the basis of an international, accepted legal standard in order to protect foreign investments . . . As the Treaty is silent on the obligation of exhaustion of local remedies, the Claimant is entitled and in the position to substantiate its loss without being obligated to have its subsidiary âNTS obtain a final civil law court decision by the Czech Supreme Court.[163]

Along very similar lines, in *EnCana*, the dissenting arbitrator provided solid arguments against the majority decision.[164] Both of these critiques—to which the reader is referred—prove that the policy of remanding domestic law issues to domestic courts should be rejected.[165]

ii Second Option: Reviewing Illegality, Irrationality, Special Sacrifice, and Lack of Proportionality in Accordance with Domestic Law

The second position takes the opposite stance regarding all tests of arbitrariness. It completely dismisses the 'non-courts of appeal' doctrine and requires investment treaty tribunals to proceed with domestic law judicial review in full, as if they were domestic courts. As a matter of international law, this position may claim to find some basis in the *Brazilian Loans* case:

[161] ibid ¶ 316. See also ibid ¶¶ 448–52.

[162] See Christoph Schreuer, 'The Coexistence of Local and International Law Remedies (Panel)' in Federico Ortino et al (eds), *Investment Treaty Law. Current Issues I* (London, The British Institute of International and Comparative Law, 2006) 157, 158 (noting that '[o]ne of the purpose of investor–State arbitration is to avoid local courts').

[163] *CME I* ¶ 417.

[164] See *EnCana*, Partial Dissenting Opinion ¶¶ 8–10.

[165] See also, Christoph Schreuer, 'Calvo's Grandchildren: The Return of Local Remedies in Investment Arbitration' (2005) 4 *The Law and Practice of International Courts and Tribunals* 1, 13–16.

> Once the Court has arrived at the conclusion that it is necessary to apply the municipal law of a particular country, there seems no doubt that it must seek to apply it as it would be applied in that country. It would not be applying the municipal law of a country if it were to apply it in a manner different from that in which that law would be applied in the country in which it is in force. It follows that the Court must pay the utmost regard to the decisions of the municipal courts of a country, for it is with the aid of their jurisprudence that it will be enabled to decide what are the rules which, in actual fact, are applied in the country the law of which is recognized as applicable in a given case . . . [T]o compel the Court to disregard that jurisprudence would not be in conformity with its function when applying municipal law.[166]

This position does not differ significantly from the third position—explained in greater detail below—except in those situations in which tests for irrationality, special sacrifice, and proportionality under domestic law are *more demanding* than IMS. Note that if those tests are less demanding, then measures may be legitimate under domestic law but still constitute a breach of the FET standard. However, the situation presented here is the opposite: what to do if those tests are more demanding under domestic law, such that a concrete measure is not below IMS, but is illegitimate according to domestic law.

In my opinion, it is inappropriate and undesirable for investment treaty tribunals to find an international violation in such situations. If domestic law is 'better' than IMS, then a foreign investor should use domestic remedies. If there is some value in the idea that BIT tribunals are not courts of appeal, it is precisely in this regard. After all, the principle stated in Article 3 of the ILC's Draft Articles works both ways; as noted in the commentary, 'an act of a State cannot be characterized as internationally wrongful unless it constitutes a breach of an international obligation, *even if it violates a provision of the State's own law*'. (emphasis added)[167] The full argument in favour of a middle position—which in itself constitutes a refutation of this more extreme form of 'courts of appeal' doctrine—is provided immediately below.

iii Third Option: Reviewing Only Illegality in Accordance with Domestic Law

According to this third position, which I consider to be the correct one, investment treaty tribunals should review the hard-edged questions of

[166] *Payment in Gold* of *Brazilian Federal Loans Contracted in France* [1929] PCIJ Rep Ser A No 21, 124. See also, *Payment of Various Serbian Loans Issued in France* [1929] PCIJ Rep Ser A No 20, 46–47.

[167] *ILC's Draft Articles and Commentaries*, n 90, 86, Art 3, Comment No 1. See also, Feldman ¶ 78, where the Tribunal stated that 'an action deemed to be illegal or unconstitutional under Mexican law may not rise to the level of a violation of international law'.

domestic illegality in accordance with domestic law, but avoid the soft-edged questions of irrationality, special sacrifices and proportionality under that system. This latter group of questions should be dealt with pursuant to the rules and principles that constitute the third dimension of the GAL approach to the FET standard, that is, an international substantive set of rules of arbitrariness (NE-II arguments).

We cannot overlook the fact that investment treaty tribunals are the guardians of treaties, and not of domestic law in general. If domestic illegalities are critical to finding international breaches (as in cases involving SE arguments), arbitral tribunals nevertheless should not take the extreme approach of converting themselves into administrative law courts.[168] From a policy perspective, it does not seem wise to place arbitrators in the extremely awkward position of applying domestic public law soft-edged tests of irrationality, special sacrifices, and proportionality. These are usually quite embedded in the domestic legal culture, and characterised by nuances that a foreign lawyer would not be able to master in the course of a single arbitration.

Moreover, a closer look shows that there are powerful reasons to justify international tribunals' non-application of domestic law in these soft-edged tests. On the one hand, if irrationality, special sacrifices and proportionality tests are *stricter* under domestic law than IMS, then the illegitimate domestic act is not a breach of the FET standard because it lacks the 'something more' element required to characterise it as an international wrongful act. Put simply, more irrationality, more sacrifice or more lack of proportionality is needed. As noted, this gap should not concern BIT tribunals: investors can have recourse to domestic remedies if they wish to take advantage of higher levels of protection under domestic law.

On the other hand, if irrationality, special sacrifice and proportionality tests embedded in IMS are more demanding than those of domestic law, then, in principle, one might assume that in such cases the legal system falls below IMS. It would follow, then, that we need to assess them according to the prescriptions of the first dimension of the GAL approach to the FET standard (that is, NE-I arguments). However, under closer examination, those cases really fall under the scope of the third dimension—that is, the set of substantive standards of arbitrariness in international investment law (that is, NE-II arguments).

Soft-edged domestic law tests are minimum thresholds for state behaviour. They establish floors below which the regulatory state cannot fall.

[168] As appropriately stated in *Generation Ukraine* ¶ 20.33: 'This Tribunal does not exercise the function of an administrative review body to ensure that municipal agencies perform their tasks diligently, conscientiously or efficiently. That function is within the proper domain of domestic courts and tribunals that are cognisant of the minutiae of the applicable regulatory regime'.

Hence, on a case-by-case basis, administrative agencies can always behave in ways that reflect higher levels of rationality, special sacrifice and proportionality than those minima. Undoubtedly, international investment law does not take an academic interest in domestic administrative law and its minima. Rather, it is interested in the concrete outcomes that affect foreign investors. In the end, the relevant question on soft-edged matters is whether the specific measure passes muster under IMS and the substantive rules of arbitrariness of international law, regardless of the domestic legal system. As we will see, these are matters of the third dimension of the GAL approach.

C Standards of Review of Questions of Law

As explained, when deciding treaty claims, investment treaty tribunals must usually confront hard-edged questions of legality, and decide whether the regulatory state acted legally or illegally under domestic law (including violations of domestic public law in general and breaches of contract in particular). The regulatory state has the power to harm citizens and investors, but to do so, it must act in accordance with the program pre-established by domestic public law, including binding contractual norms.

The analysis must now focus on issues concerning standards of review of questions of law. From an administrative law perspective, these standards involve a fairly simple question: Who has the final word in interpreting the law, particularly in cases in which the legislature has not spoken clearly? As a matter of legal theory, some may claim that because there is only 'one correct legal answer', courts and tribunals should have the final voice in providing that answer. But others may claim that interpretation may sometimes yields genuine cases of strong discretion, and that therefore there may be more than one possible legal solution. Who decides here?

If tribunals adopt a strict standard of review, they will tend to have the final say on the matter. In contrast, if they adopt looser standards, administrative agencies will tend to have the final word. There are, of course, many positions in between. As Craig reminds us, 'judicial review can vary in intensity'.[169] I will now compare various alternatives that investment treaty tribunals face in this respect, and attempt to determine which should be considered the proper one.

[169] Paul P Craig, *Administrative Law*, 5th edn (London, Sweet and Maxwell, 2003) 552.

i First Option: Transposing Denial of Justice Age Standards to the BIT Generation: The 'Manifestly Unjust' Standard

This first alternative holds that investment treaty tribunals should continue to adopt standards of review resembling those used during the denial of justice age. Specifically, this would mean that tribunals should only admit a claim based on SE arguments—ie, domestic illegality plus 'something more'—when they find an egregious or manifest violation of domestic law.

The traditional standard of review for denial of justice *stricto sensu* was, and continues to be, extremely non-intrusive. Courts' errors in the application of domestic law do not generally qualify for international review. Furthermore, according to Paulsson, the standard is so deferential that its real nature is procedural.[170] A good example can be found in the *Martini* case (1930), where the Tribunal held that:

> [T]he question [under dispute] . . . belongs to those which, in any country, may easily give rise to different interpretations, in the absence either of detailed and precise legislative or contractual provisions, or of well-established jurisprudence. *It has not been proven that the interpretation of the Venezuelan Law in the matter, given by the Court of Caracas, was erroneous, much less that it was manifestly unjust.* (emphasis added)[171]

However, as explained in the Introduction of this work, we have moved from the denial of justice age to the BIT generation.[172] Today, when the state branch under review is most frequently the executive and not the judiciary, such deferential a standard of review with respect to questions of law is clearly inappropriate. As a point of reference, if international investment law were to adopt this position, the result would be that treaty protection in claims involving SE arguments would fall far below that of domestic administrative law.

There is an additional inconvenience. Considering, as previously shown, that claims involving NE-I arguments are difficult to prove, closing the door to SE arguments with such a demanding standard would force BIT jurisprudence to decide all cases under NE-II arguments (See Figures 8 and 9). That would, in turn, place all adjudicative pressure on the third dimension of the GAL approach to the FET standard, which focuses on substantive standards of arbitrariness. This is far from desirable. Given the low density of substantive rules and principles of arbitrariness in international investment law, the realm of NE-II arguments is precisely where

170 See Paulsson, n 109, 98.

171 *The Martini Case* (*Italy v Venezuela*) Award (3 May 1930) reprinted in (1931) 25 *American Journal of International Law* 554, 571–72. For another highly deferential case, see the *Lighthouses Case* (*France v Greece*) [1934] PCIJ Rep Ser A/B No 62, 22; see also the explanation provided by Jenks, n 152, 73.

172 See Introduction of this work, 17–20.

BIT tribunals run the risk of excessive subjectivity, risk that poses a serious threat to the legitimacy of the BIT generation.

In any case, it should be clarified that the 'manifestly unjust' standard continues to be the valid test for reviewing denial of justice cases in the BIT generation (which form part of the scope of the FET standard[173]). This means that, when the measure under scrutiny is a judicial decision, the process of review remains extremely deferential. In those circumstances, the standard of review has appropriately been described in the case law as '[m]anifest injustice in the sense of a lack of due process leading to an outcome which offends a sense of judicial propriety',[174] 'egregiously wrong', 'so patently arbitrary, unjust or idiosyncratic that it demonstrates bad faith',[175] 'clearly improper and discreditable [decision]',[176] and 'clear and malicious misapplication of the law'.[177]

ii Second Option: Municipal Law as Facts: De Novo *Review*

A second and wholly distinct approach, argues that investment tribunals should give no deference to legal determinations of executive agencies. This position may claim support in the traditional international law principle, according to which national law and its application are facts in international adjudication.[178]

Since according to this theory, any determination of this nature is merely factual, an investment treaty tribunal ends up with full powers and may show, if it wishes, zero deference to executive agencies' application of domestic law. Grigera Naón seems to have espoused this position in his separate opinion in *EnCana*:

> Consequently, the local laws, administrative acts and practices and other conduct attributable to the host State at the moment they had the effect of operating the deprivation of property, are *facts* to be freely evaluated by the arbitrators to

[173] See eg *Rumeli Telekom* ¶ 651 (recognising that 'the duty not to deny justice arises from customary international law and can also be considered to fall within the scope of treaty provisions provided for *"fair and equitable treatment"* ').

[174] *Jan de Nul NV et al v Egypt*, ICSID Case No ARB/04/13 (Kaufmann-Kohler, Mayer, Stern), Award (6 November 2008), ¶ 192 (hereinafter, *Jan de Nul*), citing *Loewen* ¶ 132.

[175] *Rumeli Telekom* ¶ 653. See also ¶ 619.

[176] *Mondev* ¶ 127.

[177] *Azinian* ¶ 103.

[178] See *Certain German Interests in Polish Upper Silesia* [1926] PCIJ Rep Ser A No 7, 19 ('From the standpoint of International Law and of the Court which is its organ, municipal laws are merely facts which express the will and constitute the activities of States, in the same manner as do legal decisions or administrative measures'). See *generally*, Brownlie, n 91, 38–40, and C Wilfred Jenks, *Prospects of International Adjudication* (Dobbs Ferry, NY, Oceana Publications, 1964) 548 ff (both discussing and criticising the premise of municipal laws as 'facts' before international courts and tribunals).

determine if the foreign investor's entitlement to protection under international law has been infringed at a specific moment in time or not.[179]

As paradoxical as it may sound, it is not rare for tribunals to simultaneously endorse both the zero-deference stance that results from the idea of municipal law as facts, and the allegedly deferential non-courts of appeal doctrine. In such cases, tribunals combine these two concepts in the following obfuscating manner. First, the non-courts of appeal doctrine is used to deny the need to formally resolve issues of domestic law. Then, when domestic law issues arise, tribunals degrade them to facts, and proceed to review them, in practical terms, *de novo*.

The *Thunderbird* case can be cited as an example.[180] In this NAFTA Chapter 11 controversy, the Mexican regulator closed the investor's gaming facilities and seized its machines, based on a domestic gambling law that did not fall below IMS.[181] Even though it was highly relevant to know whether the regulator had acted legally or illegally pursuant to that domestic law, the Tribunal evaded the issue, affirming that it was not a court of appeal.[182]

However, beyond that formal declaration, the Tribunal did review the agency's findings of fact, affirming that the operation of the investor's machines involved a considerable degree of chance.[183] Then, although the Tribunal never conceded that those machines were illegal equipment under Mexican law—the prohibited conclusion under the non-courts of appeal doctrine—that proposition appears implicit in several parts of the award (indeed, without that conclusion, the decision is difficult to understand).[184] The closest it comes to an explicit recognition can be found in the decision of the expropriation claim, where the Tribunal held that 'compensation is not owed for regulatory takings where it can be established that the *investor or investment never enjoyed a vested right* in the business activity that was subsequently prohibited'. (emphasis added)[185]

The lack of attention to and discussion of Mexican law in *Thunderbird* proves the point being made here. The Tribunal was ready to review the agency's findings of fact, while also cloaking the revision of legal

[179] *EnCana,* Partial Dissenting Opinion ¶ 12.

[180] A more detailed critical analysis of this award in Santiago Montt, 'The Award in Thunderbird v Mexico' in Guillermo Aguilar Alvarez and W Michael Reisman (eds), *The Reasons Requirement in International Investment Arbitration: Critical Case Studies* (Leiden, M Nijhoff, 2008) 261.

[181] See nn 114, 115 and accompanying text.

[182] See *Thunderbird* ¶ 125.

[183] See ibid ¶ 136.

[184] See ibid ¶¶ 164, 183, and 208.

[185] ibid ¶ 208. See also, ibid ¶ 183, where the Tribunal noted that 'it would be inappropriate for a NAFTA tribunal to allow a party to rely on Article 1102 of the NAFTA to vindicate equality of non-enforcement *within the sphere of an activity that a Contracting Party deems illicit*' (emphasis added).

determinations under the appearance of facts. It could not avoid expressing the position that the investor did not have vested rights, yet provided no legal discussion to prove that assertion. In the end, because the Tribunal's conclusions were the same as those of the administrative agency, we cannot know whether the review was conducted *de novo* or giving some deference to the administrative agency's determinations.

While not formally adhering to the non-courts of appeal doctrine, the *Metalclad* Tribunal also showed zero deference for the administrative entity subject to review. In that case, a central point was 'whether, in addition to the above-mentioned permits, a municipal permit for the construction of a hazardous waste landfill was required'.[186] The Tribunal proceeded to rule on this issue, holding that 'the Municipality denied the local construction permit . . . [and] [*i*]*n so doing, the Municipality acted outside its authority*'. (emphasis added)[187] *Metalclad* appears to be a *de novo* review because the Tribunal made no effort to demonstrate that, as a matter of Mexican law, no additional permit was required.

Such a *de novo* standard of review is clearly inappropriate in the BIT generation. If, from a conflict-of-laws perspective, investment treaty tribunals must apply domestic law to decide issues of illegality, that function cannot be understood as a mandate to review *de novo* the administrative agencies' legal findings. As a matter of legal theory, applying the law—even if that law requires proof, as is the case for legal systems with which the arbitrators are not familiar—is something substantially different from fact-finding.[188]

More importantly, international law carries ample authority to support the proposition that when applying domestic law, international tribunals cannot construe it themselves, but should follow the precedents of the highest state courts. In my opinion, this should be interpreted in the sense that, when confronting the issue of the proper level of deference towards legal applications of administrative agencies, investment treaty tribunals should follow the standards of review applied by domestic courts.

Therefore, if the domestic courts of the defendant state apply a certain level of deference—be it high or low—there is no clear reason why arbitral tribunals should not apply at least that same level of deference. Accepting *de novo* review in the BIT generation, when that review is not accepted domestically in the particular country under review, may transform arbitral tribunals into policymakers, a situation which is fraught with legitimacy problems, and certainly runs counter to the legal architecture of investment treaties.

186 *Metalclad* ¶ 79.

187 ibid ¶ 106.

188 Jenks, n 152, 552, provides a very powerful critique of the idea of municipal law as facts.

iii Third Option: The Same Level of Deference That is Generally Applied by Domestic Courts

As noted, the third alternative, which in my opinion is correct, affirms that investment treaty tribunals should apply at least the same level of deference that domestic courts show with respect to legal findings of executive bodies.

Under this approach, investment treaty tribunals should be prepared to declare the domestic illegality of the measure under scrutiny. This was the situation, for example, in the *OEPC* case. The Tribunal, interpreting Ecuadorian tax legislation, ruled against the position espoused by the Ecuadorian Tax Authority (SRI). Certainly, in a VAT reimbursement case, the determination of Ecuadorian tax law was essential to finding a treaty violation.[189] The Tribunal—in contrast to the *Encana* Tribunal, which remanded this issue to domestic courts[190]—did not hesitate to conduct judicial review, concluding that 'under Ecuadorian tax legislation the Claimant is entitled to such a refund, particularly as it has been held by the Ecuadorian courts that such a right pertains to exporters generally, whether involved in manufactures or in production'.[191]

The more complicated issue is what to do when confronting a domestic law that is confusing or contradictory, or simply does not provide clear answers. In my view, arbitral tribunals should consider the 'type' of country they are dealing with. This may either be one in which legal ambiguities are understood to be implicit delegations of power to administrative entities (and not to courts); or, one in which doubts and ambiguities relating to the application of the law are matters that fall within the jurisdiction of courts.

If, in the defendant state's legal system, administrative agencies have the last word on matters of legal interpretation, then investment treaty tribunals should lean toward showing deference to the agency. If, on the other hand, courts have the last word on matters of legal interpretation, arbitral tribunals may approach the issue from a fresh vantage point, although even then, they would not err by continuing to show a reasonable level of deference toward those interpretations.

[189] See ch 5, 249–250, for further explanations.

[190] See n 159, and accompanying text.

[191] *OEPC* ¶ 143. Previously, in ¶ 136, the Tribunal proceeded to conduct the following domestic law determination: 'The Tribunal agrees with the SRI that Article 69A grants the right to a tax refund to exporters of goods involved in activities such as mining, fishing, lumber, bananas and African palm oil. *The Tribunal does not, however, agree that the oil industry is excluded from the application of Article 69A, especially considering that Article 169 of the Tax Law Regulations establishes the right of a tax refund of VAT paid on purchases of goods and services for exporters irrespective of whether they be manufacturers or producers'*. (emphasis added)

D The 'Something More' Doctrine

As noted, in the absence of umbrella clause or jurisdictional provision that covers disputes beyond treaty violations, investment treaty tribunals are not guardians of domestic law and contracts. Thus, even if domestic illegalities may be important for the reasons mentioned above, they constitute only one element of what investors must satisfy when their claims corresponds to what I refer to here as SE arguments. Apart from domestic illegalities, the other element of the second dimension of the GAL approach to the FET standard is the so-called 'something more' doctrine.

This is particularly important in the context of contractual relations. International law has traditionally accepted what French private law calls the '*cumul des responsabilités*':[192] the existence of a contractual relation does not exclude the possibility of extra-contractual liability.[193] More precisely, as stated in *Bayindir*, 'when the investor has a right under both the contract and the treaty, it has a self-standing right to pursue the remedy accorded by the treaty'.[194] At the same time, however, a contractual breach is not sufficient to give rise to a treaty breach. As the commentaries to the ILC's Draft Articles note, 'the breach by a State of a contract does not as such entail a breach of international law. *Something further* is required before international law becomes relevant'.[195]

Among investment treaty tribunals, and concerning pure regulatory contexts, the clearest formulation of the 'something more' doctrine appears in the *ADF Group* case:

[192] In French Civil law, under the principle of '*non-cumul des responsabilités*', there cannot be a tort in the presence of a contract (as a general rule); the wrongfulness of the behavior must be assessed exclusively under the contractual frame. According to Christian von Bar and Ulrich Drobnig, *The Interaction of Contract Law and Tort and Property Law in Europe* (München, Sellier, 2004) 198–99, in Belgium and France 'liability in damages cannot be contractual and tortious at the same time. In cases of overlap and conflict, contractual law prevails'.

[193] See generally, Guido Santiago Tawil, 'The Distinction Between Contract Claims and Treaty Claims: An Overview' in Albert van den Berg (ed), *International Arbitration 2006: Back to Basics?* (Alphen aan den Rijn, Kluwer Law International, 2007) 492; Griebel, n 88; Michael D Nolan and Edward G Baldwin, 'The Treatment Of Contract-Related Claims In Treaty-Based Arbitration' (2006) 21(6) *Mealey's International Arbitration Report* 1; and, Christoph Schreuer, 'Investment Treaty Arbitration and Jurisdiction over Contract-Claims—The *Vivendi I* Case Considered' in Todd Weiler (ed), *International Investment Law and Arbitration: Leading Cases from the ICSID, NAFTA, Bilateral Treaties and Customary International Law* (London, Cameron May, 2005) 281.

[194] *Bayindir Insaat Turizm Ticaret Ve Sanayi Afi v Pakistan*, ICSID Case No ARB/03/29 (Kaufmann-Kohler, Berman, Böckstiegel), Decision on Jurisdiction (14 November 2005), ¶ 167 (hereinafter, *Bayindir*).

[195] *ILC's Draft Articles and Commentaries*, n 90, 96, Art 4, Comment No 6. See also Chittharanjan Felix Amerasinghe, 'State Breach of Contracts with Aliens and International Law' (1964) 58 *American Journal of International Law* 881, 884 (commenting that '[several writers] require *something more than a mere breach of contract* by the state to give rise to a breach of international law'(emphasis added)).

> [E]ven if the U.S. measures were somehow shown or admitted to be *ultra vires* under the internal law of the United States, that by itself does not necessarily render the measures grossly unfair or inequitable under the customary international law standard of treatment embodied in Article 1105(1). An unauthorized or *ultra vires* act of a governmental entity of course remains, in international law, the act of the State of which the acting entity is part, if that entity acted in its official capacity. *But something more than simple illegality or lack of authority under the domestic law of a State is necessary to render and act or measure inconsistent with the customary international law requirements of Article 1105(1).*(emphasis added)[196]

Similar holdings can also be found in the contractual context.[197] But what exactly is this 'something more' that is required? In the case law, a first approximation to that doctrine appears to revisit the standards of review problem by connecting to the idea of a deferential standard of review. For example, in *Waste Management II*, the Tribunal affirmed that:

> For present purposes it is sufficient to say that even the persistent non-payment of debts by a municipality is not to be equated with a violation of Article 1105, provided that it does not amount to *an outright and unjustified repudiation of the transaction* and provided that some remedy is open to the creditor to address the problem. In the present case the failure to pay can be explained, albeit not excused, by the financial crisis which meant that at key points the City could hardly pay its own payroll. There is no evidence that it was motivated by *sectoral or local prejudice*. (emphasis added)[198]

[196] *ADF Group* ¶ 190. See also, *Saluka* ¶ 442: 'The unlawfulness of a host State's measures under its own legislation or under another international agreement by which the host State may be bound, is neither necessary nor sufficient for a breach of Article 3.1 of the Treaty. The Treaty cannot be interpreted so as to penalise each and every breach by the Government of the rules or regulations to which it is subject and for which the investor may normally seek redress before the courts of the host State'. And *Eastern Sugar BV v The Czech Republic*, UNCITRAL Ad-Hoc Arbitration (Karrer, Volterra, Gaillard), Partial Award (27 March 2007), ¶ 272 (hereinafter, *Eastern Sugar*): 'A violation of a BIT does not only occur through blatant and outrageous interference. However, a BIT may also not be invoked each time the law is flawed or not fully and properly implemented by a state. Some attempt to balance the interests of the various constituents within a country, some measure of inefficiency, a degree of trial and error, a modicum of human imperfection must be overstepped before a party may complain of a violation of a BIT. Otherwise, every aspect of any legislation of a host state or its implementation could be brought before an international arbitral tribunal under the guise of a violation of the BIT. This is obviously not what BITs are for'. Among commentators, see Jan Paulsson, 'Avoiding Unintended Consequences' in Karl Sauvant (ed), *Appeals Mechanisms in International Investment Law* (New York, OUP, 2008) 241, 254.

[197] See eg the following recent decisions: *TSA Spectrum de Argentina SA v Argentina*, ICSID Case No ARB/05/5 (Danelius, Abi-Saab, Aldonas), Award (19 December 2008), ¶ 60 ('[N]ot all breaches of the CNC's obligations in the Concession Contract would qualify as breaches of the BIT'); *Duke Energy Electroquil* ¶ 342 ('[I]t is now a well-established principle that in and of itself the violation of a contract does not amount to the violation of a treaty'); *Parkerings* ¶ 289 ('[A] possible breach of an agreement does not necessarily amount to a violation of a BIT') and ¶ 315 ('[M]any tribunals have stated that not every breach of an agreement or of domestic law amounts to a violation of a treaty').

[198] *Waste Management II* ¶ 115.

Moving beyond that first approximation and towards a more substantive account, the 'something more' doctrine displays variable thickness.[199] This thickness depends mostly on whether the foreign investors suffered damages due to one discrete and highly relevant illegal act, or because of several repeated, lesser illegal acts, including failures to implement or enforce domestic regulations.

In the first scenario, the doctrine tends to be thin—that is, not much more is required, and tribunals tend to conclude relatively easily that a breach of the treaty has occurred as a consequence of the state's failure to abide by its own law. This particularly applies to cases in which the regulatory state illegally denies or revokes permits, licences, or concession contracts, as for example, in *Metalclad,* where the unlawful denial of a construction permit prevented the claimant's operation of a landfill.[200]

In the second scenario, by contrast, the 'something more' doctrine shows itself to be thicker. The leading case in this regard, which deserves closer attention here, is *GAMI*. In that case, the Tribunal explicitly confronted the problem of state's compliance with its own regulatory programs, providing a thoughtful and thorough analysis:

> The duty of NAFTA tribunals is rather to appraise whether and how preexisting laws and regulations are applied to the foreign investor. It is no excuse that regulation is costly. Nor does a dearth of able administrators or a deficient culture of compliance provide a defence. Such is the challenge of governance that confronts every country. Breaches of NAFTA are assuredly not to be excused on the grounds that a government's compliance with its own law may be difficult. Each NAFTA Party must to the contrary accept liability if its officials fail to implement or implement regulations in a discriminatory or arbitrary fashion.[201] . . . The key question is the extent to which an investor may rely on the implementation by the host state of laws in place before its investment is made. What efforts by a government to implement its regulatory programme suffice to fulfil the international standards requirement of Article 1105?[202]

The Tribunal advanced what can be referred to as *the record as a whole-four-part* test of the 'something more' doctrine, which includes the following four elements:

[199] As Horacio Grigera Naón noted in *EnCana,* Partial Dissenting Opinion ¶ 12, *gravity, permanence, irrevocability,* and *harmful effects* are relevant factors in this regard. See also, Thomas W Wälde, 'Investment Arbitration under the Energy Charter Treaty: An Overview of Selected Key Issues Based on Recent Litigation Experience' in Norbert Horn and Stefan Kröll (eds), *Arbitrating Foreign Investment Disputes* (The Hague, Kluwer Law International, 2004) 193, 210–11 (observing that '[a] simple breach of a rule is not enough: The "fair and equitable" standard is only then breached if there is an accumulation of breaches of relevant standards of sufficient severity, weight and impact to justify the intervention of the treaty in domestic governance').

[200] *Metalclad* ¶ 79.

[201] *GAMI* ¶ 94.

[202] ibid ¶ 100.

> (1) The failure to fulfil the objectives of administrative regulations without more does not necessarily rise to a breach of international law. (2) A failure to satisfy requirements of national law does not necessarily violate international law. (3) Proof of good faith effort by the Government to achieve the objectives of its laws and regulations may counter-balance instances of disregard of legal or regulatory requirements. (4) The record as a whole—not isolated events—determines whether there has been a breach of international law.[203]

With this holistic approach of 'the record as a whole' in mind, the *GAMI* Tribunal took astep further by providing a focal point for the identification of international law violations, the 'outright and unjustified repudiation' test:

> A claim of maladministration would likely violate Article 1105 if it amounted to an 'outright and unjustified repudiation' of the relevant regulations. There may be situations where even lesser failures would suffice to trigger Article 1105. It is the record as a whole—not dramatic incidents in isolation—which determines whether a breach of international law has occurred.[204]

Note that this test merely represents a focal point. The Tribunal did not deny that breaches of international law can still be found for lesser infractions of domestic law. Furthermore, when asking, '[w]ould something less than repudiation still be actionable under Article 1105?,'[205] the Tribunal accepted *arguendo* that 'an abject failure to implement a regulatory program indispensable for the viability of foreign investments that had relied on it'[206] may be a treaty breach. Note, in any case, that the line drawn by the *GAMI* Tribunal leaves no doubt that *bad faith* repudiations of domestic law and contracts would not pass muster.[207]

Additionally, in the contractual context, the 'something more' doctrine has adopted another very specific formulation. Several tribunals have required that the state must have acted as a *puissance publique,* and not merely as a private party.[208] The actions of the state, as noted in *Siemens,*

[203] ibid ¶ 97.
[204] ibid ¶ 103.
[205] ibid ¶ 105.
[206] ibid ¶ 108.
[207] See eg the following decisions dealing with such behavior: *Siemens* ¶ 308 ('initiation of the renegotiation of the Contract for the sole purpose of reducing its costs, unsupported by any declaration of public interest'); *Vivendi III* ¶ 7.4.39 (destructive campaign against the investor); and, *CME I* ¶ 611 ('*evisceration* of the arrangements in reliance upon which the foreign investor was induced to invest'). (emphasis added)
[208] See eg *Duke Energy Electroquil* ¶ 345 *Impregilo SpA v Pakistan,* ICSID Case No ARB/03/3 (Guillaume, Cremades, Landau), Decision on Jurisdiction (22 April 2005), ¶¶ 260–61; *Salini Costruttori SpA v Jordan,* ICSID Case No ARB/02/13 (Guillaume, Cremades, Sinclair), Decision on Jurisdiction (November 2004), ¶¶ 154–55; *Consortium RFCC v Morocco,* ICSID Case No ARB/00/6 (Briner, Cremades, Fadlallah), Award (22 December 2003), ¶ 65. This requirement can also be found in the application of the expropriation clause; see eg *Parkerings* ¶¶ 443–44; *Azurix* ¶¶314–15; *Waste Management II* ¶ 174; ; and *Consortium RFCC v Morocco,* ICSID Case No ARB/00/6 (Briner, Cremades, Fadlallah), Award (22 December 2003), ¶ 65.

'have to be based on its "superior governmental power"'.[209] As explained by the Tribunal in *Biwater Gauff*:

> [T]he critical distinction is between situations in which a State acts merely as a contractual partner, and cases in which it acts *'iure imperi'*, exercising elements of its governmental authority. These are often termed *'actes de puissance publique'*, where the use by the State of its public prerogatives or *imperium* is involved in the actions complained of.[210]

In summation, the second dimension of the GAL approach to the FET standard is essentially guided by a corrective justice rationale. Its purpose is to correct instances of negligence and fault exhibited by the regulatory state vis-à-vis foreign investors. Yet, the 'something more' doctrine—which reminds us of the more exact and proper meaning of the idea that investment treaty tribunals are not courts of appeal—introduces important restrictions on state liability. Although the content of this doctrine is still far from determined, it is at least clear that not every disappointment and illegality suffered by foreign investors at the hands of the regulatory state can constitute an international wrongful act.[211]

V THE THIRD DIMENSION OF THE GAL APPROACH TO THE FET STANDARD: ARBITRARINESS AND THE CONTROL OF DISCRETIONARY POWERS

The third dimension of the GAL approach to the FET standard—which corresponds to NE-II arguments in Figures 8 and 9 above—comes only after the other two. When making reference to this third dimension, the decision-maker, at least *arguendo*, must have already concluded two things: that the domestic legal system according to which the measure was issued does not fall below IMS—the first dimension—and that the measure under scrutiny was legal under domestic law—the second dimension. At its core, the task at hand here is none other than the control of the regulatory state's exercise of discretionary powers.

This section explores this last dimension of the GAL approach, where the regulatory state's measures come under the direct scrutiny of international standards of arbitrariness. It first defends the important role that comparative law should have in the development of these new substantive standards, and calls attention to the perils of process-based heightened scrutiny and object-and-purpose interpretation. It then analyses the case law on the most important instances of arbitrariness in investment treaty arbitration: administrative due process, 'arbitrariness as irrational-

[209] *Siemens* ¶ 253.
[210] *Biwater Gauff* ¶ 458.
[211] See n 196, and accompanying text.

ity', 'arbitrariness as special sacrifice' and 'lack of proportionality', and legitimate expectations.

A The Perils of Process-Based Heightened Scrutiny and Object and Purpose Interpretation

Section I argued that the FET standard should be interpreted as embodying IMS. It rejected the literalist approach that leads to an autonomous standard, where the terms 'fair' and 'equitable' are interpreted according to dictionaries. As explained, the true challenge for international investment law lies in the development of a well-defined standard of review, that properly identifies arbitrariness in the conduct of the regulatory state. The third dimension of the GAL approach to the FET standard—comprising NE-II arguments—is the most vulnerable to the potential over-expansion of arbitral tribunals' discretion. This is because it is at this point that investment treaty tribunals must develop the most relevant international tests of arbitrariness, which are independent of domestic law. To be effective, these standards must undoubtedly be less deferential than those of the first dimension of the GAL approach (that is, NE-I arguments concerning whether the domestic legal system falls below IMS).

International law's lack of experience with controlling the regulatory state means that in general we cannot rely too much on rules and principles created by public international law to assess inter-state conduct.[212] Wälde has spoken to this issue, and a long excerpt of his opinion is worthwhile:

> [I]nvestment treaties such as the NAFTA, deals with a significantly different context from the one envisaged by traditional public international law: At its heart lies the right of a private actor to engage in an arbitral litigation against a (foreign) government over governmental conduct affecting the investor. That is fundamentally different from traditional international public law, which is based on solving disputes between sovereign states and where private parties have no standing. Analogies from such inter-state international law have therefore to be treated with caution; more appropriate for investor–state arbitration are analogies with judicial review relating to governmental conduct—be it international judicial review (as carried out by the WTO dispute panels and Appellate Body, by the European- or Inter-American Human Rights Courts or the European Court of Justice) or national administrative courts judging the disputes of individual citizens' over alleged abuse by public bodies of their governmental powers . . . The issue is to keep a government from abusing its role as sovereign and regulator after having made commitments of a more

[212] See Dolzer, n 29, 105 (noting that the task entrusted to arbitral tribunals of giving content to the FET standard is 'formidable' because 'the standard had to be developed *ad novo* in the absence of any rule or precedent in any other field of international law').

formal character (contracts and licenses) or of a less formal character (i.e. the assurances by explicit communication or by meaningful conduct that form the basis of the legitimate expectations principle under Art. 1105 of the NAFTA).[213]

So, without the assistance of public international law, there is no other alternative than having recourse to comparative law.[214] This means that, pursuant to Articles 31(3)(c) of the Vienna Convention on Treaties and 38(1)(c) of the ICJ Statute, we must draw inspiration from the public law traditions of the main legal systems.[215] Note that this is not only true as a matter of treaty interpretation. As defended at length in chapter 3, from a policy perspective, we cannot conclude that by abiding to something as broad and general as the FET standard, developing countries could have agreed to something more demanding than the standards already prevailing in developed countries.[216]

In any case, the main function of having recourse to comparative law is to restrain arbitrators' discretion. In the main legal traditions around the world, courts show considerable deference toward administrative policy decisions; in the words of the US Supreme Court, the judiciary 'is not empowered to substitute its judgment for that of the agency'.[217] As evidenced by the comparative patchwork of chapter 4, courts generally move with caution when reviewing for arbitrariness, and that should also be the stance of arbitral tribunals in the BIT generation. Any proper understanding of democracy implies that the government is of the people and not of judges or arbitrators.

Yet, in international investment law, not everybody agrees that tribunals should be guided by such a deferential attitude. I have identified two rationales appearing in awards, both of which, in addition to the literalist approach to the FET standard that serves as an invitation for unrestrained discretion, advance the argument that arbitral tribunals should adopt a heightened review stance, in which ambiguities and doubts are borne by states, and not by investors.

The first is inspired by equality and 'process-based' theories, and views foreign investors—particularly those that are not multinational corpora-

[213] *Thunderbird*, Separate Opinion ¶ 13. See also, Douglas, n 87, 151 (observing that '[t]he analytical challenge presented by the investment treaty regime for the arbitration of investment disputes is that it cannot be adequately rationalised either as a form of public international or private transnational dispute resolution').

[214] See Waelde and Kolo, above note 7, 822 (commenting that '[c]omparative constitutional law seems to provide the most suitable analogy and precedent since treaties in effect set up a similar system of higher-ranked controls over domestic law-making').

[215] See Schill, n 22, 4 and 29.

[216] In *The Oscar Chinn* case [1934] PCIJ Rep Ser A/B No 63, 84, the Permanent Court held that '[i]t cannot be supposed that the contracting Parties adopted new provisions with the idea that they might lend themselves to a broad interpretation going beyond what was expressly laid down'.

[217] *Citizens to Preserve Overton Park, Inc v Volpe, Secretary of Transportation* (1971) 401 US 402, 416.

tions—as handicapped players in the domestic political game. Following the *James* case (European Court of Human Rights),[218] the *Tecmed* Tribunal was the first to espouse this idea:

> [T]he foreign investor has a reduced or nil participation in the taking of the decisions that affect it, partly because the investors are not entitle [sic] to exercise political rights reserved to the nationals of the State, such as voting for the authorities that will issue the decisions that affect such investors.[219]

This rationale faces two serious problems. On the one hand, from an empirical point of view and in the absence of concrete evidence, these generalisations are so broad that they cannot serve to expand the standards of review of arbitrariness. Moreover, the reality may be precisely the opposite: in capital-intensive industries foreign investors are usually powerful political players.

But, on the other hand, and more importantly, this theory overlooks the fact that the alleged political handicapping of foreign companies justifies the *existence* of the unique remedy of direct resort to international arbitration without the exhaustion of local remedies. That being that the case, these handicaps cannot be used a second time with the purpose of providing a rationale for applying a heightened standard of review of arbitrariness.

The second strategy employed to expand the intrusiveness of the tribunal's review is through the 'object and purpose' rule of treaty interpretation, which refers to the objects and purposes usually found in BITs' preambles. A perfect example can be found in the *MTD* case:

> As regards the object and purpose of the BIT, the Tribunal refers to its Preamble where the parties state their desire 'to create favourable conditions for investments by investors of one Contracting Party in the territory of the other Contracting Party', and the recognition of 'the need to protect investments by investors of both Contracting Parties and to stimulate the flow of investments and individual business initiative with a view to the economic prosperity of both Contracting Parties'. Hence, in terms of the BIT, fair and equitable treatment should be understood to be treatment in an even-handed and just manner, conducive to fostering the promotion of foreign investment. Its terms are framed as a pro-active statement—'to promote', 'to create', 'to stimulate'—rather than prescriptions for a passive behaviour of the State or avoidance of prejudicial conduct to the investors.[220]

[218] See ch 4, 214–216.

[219] *Tecmed* ¶ 122. See also, Wälde in *Thunderbird*, Separate Opinion ¶ 33.

[220] *MTD I* ¶ 113. See also, ibid ¶ 104. See also, *OEPC* ¶ 183; and *CMS* ¶ 274. When interpreting an umbrella clause, the Tribunal in *SGS Société Générale de Surveillance SA v Philippines*, ICSID Case No ARB/02/6 (El-Kosheri, Crawford, Crivallero), Decision on Jurisdiction (29 January 2004), ¶ 116, held that '[a]ccording to the preamble it [the BIT] is intended "to create and maintain favourable conditions for investments by investors of one Contracting Party in the territory of the other". *It is legitimate to resolve uncertainties in its interpretation so as to favour the protection of covered investments*' (emphasis added). Note that in

The problem with this approach is similar to that of the previous one. When signing BITs, developing countries took into consideration the objects and purposes contained in the preambles of the treaties, but only to the extent necessary to agree with the *actual expressed content of those treaties*. These objectives led countries to delegate sovereignty to arbitral tribunals for the adjudication of disputes in highly sensitive areas, such as those involving the balance between property rights and the public interest. So, as argued above, the same motives cannot be used a second time to justify a heightened degree of intrusiveness.

The overemphasis on BITs' 'object and purpose' is ultimately akin to the 'super-constitutionalisation' of the notion of investment. The latter—as a new version of property rights—already exists as a 'constitutional' concept that competes against the public interests in the various balancing processes used to assess arbitrariness.[221] Yet, under the rationale above, the notion of investments is raised to a prominent position, trumping all state interests and becoming the super-value of the BIT generation.

This is clearly wrong. As a matter of treaty interpretation, the *Saluka* Tribunal, among others, has noted that BITs' preambles contained statements that are more subtle than the simplistic view found in other arbitral awards:

> This [the preamble] is a more subtle and balanced statement of the Treaty's aims than is sometimes appreciated. The protection of foreign investments is not the sole aim of the Treaty, but rather a necessary element alongside the overall aim of encouraging foreign investment and extending and intensifying the parties' economic relations. That in turn calls for a balanced approach to the interpretation of the Treaty's substantive provisions for the protection of investments.[222]

More importantly, even though the protection of investment represents a key component of a well-organised capitalist society, such a goal does not deserve a priori to trump all other non-economic values. As repeatedly noted in the First Part of this work, neither efficiency nor any other commonly accepted social justice account or political philosophy justifies such an intense commitment to the status quo. Indeed, no Western capitalist

Ioannis Kardassopoulos v Georgia, ICSID Case No ARB/05/18 (Fortier, Orrego, Watts), Decision on Jurisdiction (6 July 2007), ¶¶ 178–79, the Tribunal observed that 'it is not only the ordinary meaning of the terms of a treaty which will resolve their interpretation. The object and purpose of the treaty must also be taken into consideration. It is obvious to the Tribunal that the object and purpose of this BIT do not support a literal interpretation'.

[221] In the words of the Tribunal in *Saluka* ¶ 306, '[t]he determination of a breach of [the fair and equitable treatment clause] . . . therefore requires a weighing of the Claimant's legitimate and reasonable expectations on the one hand and the Respondent's legitimate regulatory interests on the other'.

[222] *Saluka* ¶ 300. See also, *ADF Group* ¶ 147, and *Plama Consortium Ltd v Bulgaria*, ICSID Case No ARB/03/24 (Salans, van den Berg, Veeder), Decision on Jurisdiction (8 February 2005), ¶ 193.

country today takes such a strong normative view with respect to property rights and economic liberties.

In the end, there are sound normative justifications for adopting a non-intrusive standard of review, comparable to those usually applied in developed countries. One of the most important of these justifications—*global subsidiarity*—has been identified by Howse and Nicolaidis in the field of trade.[223] As they explain it, 'there needs to be prima facie recognition of outcomes from more democratically legitimate political and regulatory institutions'.[224] In the following quote, if one were to substitute the word 'investment' for 'trade', and 'investment tribunals 'for 'WTO', the concept of global subsidiarity would prove to be perfectly applicable to international investment law:

> In the case of WTO, we believe that *global subsidiarity* requires accepting the logic and development of a plural, decentralized, a multi-centered system of global socio-economic governance of which the trade organization would be one of many nodes. This, in turn, requires that WTO political agreements and judicial rulings display appropriate sensitivity to the superior credentials that other institutions of governance may have in deciding the substantive trade-offs entailed in domestic policies that the WTO dispute settlement organs are, necessarily, required to review from the perspective of WTO rules on trade. This includes, but need not start with, a presumption of deference to the states themselves. The WTO dispute settlement machinery cannot substitute itself for domestic democratic processes which have often painstakingly shaped fundamental trade-offs between economic, social, political cost-benefit considerations and values.[225]

The rest of this section will explore in detail the strategies that arbitral tribunals have adopted for reviewing arbitrariness in the context of discretionary powers. This includes procedural tests (administrative due process), corrective justice tests (arbitrariness as irrationality), distributive justice tests (arbitrariness as special sacrifice, and lack of proportionality), and the mix of rationales typically at play in the concept of 'legitimate expectations'.

[223] Robert Howse and Kalypso Nicolaidis, 'Legitimacy through 'Higher Law'? Why Constitutionalizing the WTO is a Step Too Far' in Thomas Cottier and Petros C Mavroidis (eds), *The Role of the Judge in International Trade Regulation. Experiences and Lessons for the WTO* (University of Michigan Press, Ann Arbor 2003) 307, 332. See also, Wälde, n 199, 210 (noting that investment treaties 'must also not be operated in order to become an excessively interventionist instrument. The EU Treaty's—so far quite theoretical—rule of 'subsidiarity' can help as some guidance').

[224] Howse and Nicolaidis, n 223, 334.

[225] ibid 332 . See also, Robert Howse, 'The Most Dangerous Branch? WTO Appellate Body Jurisprudence on the Nature and Limits of the Judicial Power' in Thomas Cottier and Petros C Mavroidis (eds), *The Role of the Judge in International Trade Regulation. Experiences and Lessons for the WTO* (Ann Arbor, University of Michigan Press, 2003) 11, 35.

B Due Process: Administrative Denial of Justice

The theoretical and practical complexities involved in defining substantive tests of arbitrariness in global law have lead several scholars to promote the control of legal process over substance. For instance, Howse and Nicolaidis observe that the WTO 'should emphasize procedural obligations rather than normative constraints on the conduct of lower level policies'.[226] This is not merely an academic phenomenon; the procedural approach is indeed a nascent trend in supra-national adjudication.[227]

In the context of international investment law, this means that arbitral tribunals should limit their review to whether the measures under scrutiny were adopted through a process that permitted all relevant players to voice and represent their interests adequately. From a general perspective, and as noted in chapter 5, *Methanex* seems to have been the first case in which 'process-based' theories played a prominent role.[228]

In any case, apart from this comprehensive role in the general scheme of global review of arbitrariness, the due process standard—which undoubtedly forms part of the FET standard[229]—continues to play an important function in controlling the quality of process. As a matter of judicial due process, there is consensus over the general conditions that must be present in order to have fair judicial proceedings.[230] In 1928, Eagleton noted that it was 'not to be doubted' that 'the community of nations has a standard for the administration of justice towards aliens'.[231]

[226] Howse and Nicolaidis, n 223, 311.

[227] See Gráinne de Búrca and Joanne Scott, 'The Impact of the WTO on EU Decision-Making' in Gráinne de Búrca and Joanne Scott (eds), *The EU and the WTO. Legal and Constitutional Issues* (Portland, Hart Publishing, 2001) 1, 28–29, who make the following observation concerning the experiences of the WTO and EU: 'The Appellate Body, against a backdrop of radical value pluralism, is adopting a "lighter" touch in terms of substantive review. In addition, however, it is scrutinising and evaluating the decision-making processes underpinning the contested measures adopted within the Member States . . . [I]t is readily apparent that there is something interesting and important happening here. At the same time as one non-state polity—the EU—is looking increasingly to procedural techniques as a means of circumscribing Member States autonomy in governance, against a backdrop of growing substantive flexibility, another (the WTO) is looking to procedural techniques to define the scope of residual Member State autonomy in a framework of market integration'.

[228] *Methanex*, Part IV, Ch D, at 5, ¶ 9. For full citation, see also, ch 5, n 243, and accompanying text.

[229] See eg *Jan de Nul* ¶ 187, *Rumeli Telekom* ¶ 609, and *Saluka* ¶ 308. According to Choudhury, n 21, 305, 'violation of due process rights is one of the least controversial and most often accepted grounds for demonstration of a failure to provide fair and equitable treatment'.

[230] See eg Louis B Sohn and Richard Baxter, 'Draft Convention on the International Responsibility of States for Injuries to the Economic Interests of Aliens' (1961) 55 *American Journal of International Law* 545, 550–51 (Arts 6, 7, and 8).

[231] Clyde Eagleton, *The Responsibility of States in International Law* (New York, New York University Press, 1928) 110.

However, we do not have a clear idea of what *administrative* due process means. We lack a commonly accepted theory that would help us in determining what attributes make an administrative decision-making process legitimate and non-arbitrary in international investment law. As a consequence, the initial premise regarding administrative denial of justice, as recognised by the *Thunderbird* Tribunal, is very modest; due process concerning administrative action is considerably less intense than the traditional judicial concept:

> Rather, the Tribunal cannot find on the record any administrative irregularities that were grave enough *to shock a sense of judicial propriety and thus give rise to a breach of the minimum standard of treatment . . . The administrative due process requirement is lower than that of a judicial process.* (emphasis added)[232]

Beyond this initial premise, arbitral tribunals have continued to indicate that the administrative due process test is not very demanding. In *Waste Management II*, the Tribunal required 'complete lack of transparency and candour in an administrative process'[233], and the *Thunderbird* Tribunal, 'manifest arbitrariness or unfairness'.[234]

In any case, if arbitral tribunals plan to establish somewhat higher thresholds, or simply to give a more concrete content to this standard, they should be aware that in administrative law, the main questions of due process are those concerning hearings and the minimum content of process in those hearings.[235] In this regard, a fundamental distinction must be made between rule-making and adjudication.

On the one hand, it is more or less evident that legislation and regulation *stricto sensu* cannot, and should not, be produced under judicial adversarial trial-type proceedings. Indeed, due process considerations rarely apply in legislative proceedings. In the case of executive rule-making—regulation *stricto sensu*—countries follow different traditions. As a point of reference, in the US—the country presenting one of the most sophisticated systems of procedural protection—the *Administrative Procedural Act* establishes, as a general rule, the relatively undemanding system of 'notice and comment'

[232] *Thunderbird* ¶ 200.

[233] *Waste Management II* ¶ 197.

[234] *Thunderbird* ¶ 197 ('As to the alleged failure to provide due process (constituting an administrative denial of justice) . . . the Tribunal cannot find sufficient evidence on the record establishing that the SEGOB proceedings were arbitrary or unfair, *let alone so manifestly arbitrary or unfair as to violate the minimum standard of treatment*'). (emphasis added)

[235] In the international sphere, the attention has been set on some of these issues at least since the WTO Appellate Body ruling in the *Shrimp-Turtle II* case, which made administrative due process a general topic of debate among global law commentators. See *United States—Import Prohibition of Certain Shrimp and Shrimp Products*, AB-1998-4, Report of the Appellate Body, WT/DS58/AB/R (12 October 1998), ¶ 143. See also, Sabino Cassese, 'Global Standards for National Administrative Procedure' (2005) 68 *Law and Contemporary Problems* 109, and Giacinto de la Cananea, 'Beyond the State: the Europeanization and Globalization of Procedural Administrative Law' (2003) 9 *European Public Law* 563.

rule-making.[236] In contrast, in the continental world, it is not unusual that administrative regulation come with almost no procedural guarantees.

On the other hand, administrative adjudication proves to be more complex. This is due to the fact that a wide range of administrative activities fall into this category, not all of which can be subject to the same due process requirements. Not even in the US does the law require full hearings in every kind of circumstance. On the matter of constitutional law minima, in *Matthews v Eldridge*, the US Supreme Court required hearings only when a three-pronged balancing test demanded it:

> [O]ur prior decisions indicate that identification of the specific dictates of due process generally requires consideration of three distinct factors: First, the private interest that will be affected by the official action; second, the risk of an erroneous deprivation of such interest through the procedures used, and the probable value, if any, of additional or substitute procedural safeguards; and finally, the Government's interest, including the function involved and the fiscal and administrative burdens that the additional or substitute procedural requirement would entail.[237]

The rationale of this balancing process is clear: 'structuring administrative adjudication confronts a crucial competition between bureaucratic management and individualized justice'.[238] As Mashaw explains:

> [C]urrent constitutional doctrine tends to proceed in two steps, one 'qualitative'—'Is this the type of government decisions for which the Constitution guarantees certain minimum procedures?'—; and the second 'quantitative'—'How much process is due, given the need to 'balance' the importance of the private party's interest, the government's need for expedition and informality, and the likelihood of erroneous decisions absent procedural protection sought?'[239]

So, should notice and comment be mandatory when passing new regulation? Should full hearings be required for adjudicatory decisions that interfere with foreign investors' investments? A tentative response would be as follows: With respect to rule-making, excepting extraordinary circumstances, investment treaty tribunals should refrain from establishing minima. With respect to adjudication, tribunals should follow a balancing test similar to the one adopted by the US Supreme Court in *Matthews v Eldridge*, and apply it with a deferential attitude.[240]

[236] See 5 USC §553.

[237] *Mathews v Eldridge* (1976) 424 US 319, 334–35.

[238] Jerry L Mashaw et al, *Administrative Law. The American Public Law System. Cases and Materials*, 5th edn (St Paul, MN, Thomson/West, 2003) 315.

[239] ibid 316.

[240] The decision in *Metalclad*, which held implicitly that a full hearing was needed in order for the administrative body to grant or reject a permit, must be criticised here as too extreme. See *Metalclad* ¶ 91 ('Moreover, the permit was denied at a meeting of the Municipal Town Council of which Metalclad received no notice, to which it received no invitation, and at which it was given no opportunity to appear').

There is one final point to be addressed here. Many legal traditions recognise and accept that in certain settings, 'post-deprivation procedures' satisfy the demands of due process.[241] Therefore, a balance or equation is adopted in domestic law, according to which ex-post administrative and judicial remedies are deemed sufficient for the demands of procedural fairness. But what happens, then, in the BIT generation, where those remedies are waived, and investors are immediately free to seek an international adjudicator? The answer is clear: if the original domestic institutional designs fulfill the requirements of due process, then the new investment treaty remedies should not alter the fairness of those arrangements (that is, more remedies cannot result in less due process).

C Arbitrariness as Irrationality

Apart from due process, the third dimension of the GAL approach to the FET standard forces investment treaty tribunals to determine whether measures harming foreign investors, that have already been deemed legal according to domestic laws that are above IMS, are irrational or unreasonable. The search here, as the *Thunderbird* Tribunal put it, is for 'arbitrariness in administration (constituting proof of an abuse of right)',[242] or, as the *MTD* Tribunal held in positive terms, for good faith and proportionality.[243]

As repeated throughout this work, the regulatory state has the power to harm investors, so harm alone cannot be the criteria for state liability. What matters in investment treaty disputes, and particularly for the third dimension discussed here, is, again, *arbitrary* impairment. The first test of arbitrariness, that of irrationality, comprises two general conditions that should be generally seen as falling under the realm of the corrective justice rationale: the regulatory state must act only in pursuit of the public interest—naked transfers from foreign investors to other groups are not allowed—and policy programs or decisions being implemented must demonstrate a proper means-ends relationship.[244]

i Ends and Legitimate State Interests

The regulatory state—a variety of the administrative state—pursues a broad range of goals considered acceptable and legitimate: public health, public order, public morals, the working place, the environment,

[241] See Mashaw, n 238, 316.
[242] *Thunderbird* ¶ 197.
[243] *MTD I* ¶ 109.
[244] See ch 4, 206–212.

consumer protection, efficiency, etc.[245] In both national and international orders, courts and tribunals display a high degree of deference towards the public interests invoked by states to justify their policies.[246]

In the BIT generation, two related forms of control of ends should be distinguished. On the one hand, tribunals confront the state's characterisation of certain interests as public ends, that is, the state's affirmation that certain interests justify having adopted one or more measures interfering with investors' property rights. In an exercise that, as noted, is exceptional, the tribunal reviews whether those precise interests are 'really' public ones; in other words, the tribunal controls the public-regarding character of the ends invoked by the state.

One of these rarely seen situations is exemplified by *Eastern Sugar*, in which the Tribunal concluded that the ends invoked by the Czech government for changing the regulatory regime of the sugar beet industry—in particular, for the adoption of a 'one-day production basis to allocate quota'[247]—was 'not persuasive'.[248] The Tribunal concluded that a violation of the FET standard had occurred,[249] because, among other reasons, '[m]oving to an entirely new basis *just for the sake of doing something different* simply makes no sense to the Arbitral Tribunal'. (emphasis added)[250]

On the other hand, tribunals confront the question of whether the public interests invoked are really the ones being pursued in the concrete measures at stake. This form of review, while still infrequent, is potentially more common than the previous one. It corresponds to what French law has traditionally referred to as *détournement de pouvoir*. In those cases, the analysis focuses on whether the public interest being invoked might be a mere cover or 'simulation' for a 'naked transfer', or a different public interest which may not carry sufficient weight. As noted in chapter 5,[251] this seems to have been the case in *ADC*, where the Tribunal, analysing an expropriation claim, held that it saw 'no public interest being served':[252]

> Although the Respondent repeatedly attempted to persuade the Tribunal that the Amending Act, the Decree and the actions taken in reliance thereon were necessary and important for the harmonization of the Hungarian Government's transport strategy, laws and regulations with the EU law, it failed to substanti-

[245] See eg Waelde and Kolo, n 7, 827–28.

[246] See ch 4, 206–207.

[247] *Eastern Sugar* ¶ 298. This case seems to fit the 'naked transference' story; as explained by the Tribunal ¶ 314, '[t]he only rational explanation is that the Government wished to appease the beet growers'.

[248] ibid ¶ 313.

[249] ibid ¶ 334–35.

[250] ibid ¶ 313.

[251] See ch 5, 285–286.

[252] *ADC Affiliate Ltd et al v Hungary*, ICSID Case No ARB/03/16 (Kaplan, Brower, van den Berg), Award (2 October 2006), ¶ 429.

ate such a claim with convincing facts or legal reasoning.[253] . . . In the Tribunal's opinion, a treaty requirement for *'public interest'* requires some genuine interest of the public. If mere reference to *'public interest'* can magically put such interest into existence and therefore satisfy this requirement, then this requirement would be rendered meaningless since the Tribunal can imagine no situation where this requirement would not have been met.[254]

Although the extreme character of the facts may explain the outcomes in *Eastern Sugar* and *ADC*, overturning the public character of the ends invoked by the states, in general, should be an exceptional occurrence in the BIT generation. The stance taken should always be highly deferential. This is, indeed, one of the main lessons that can be drawn from *SD Myers I*, even if in that case the Tribunal concluded that the contested measure did not serve the alleged environmental purposes claimed by the government:[255]

When interpreting and applying the 'minimum standard', *a Chapter 11 tribunal does not have an open-ended mandate to second-guess government decision-making.* Governments have to make many potentially controversial choices. In doing so, they may appear to have made mistakes, to have misjudged the facts, proceeded on the basis of a misguided economic or sociological theory, placed too much emphasis on some social values over others and adopted solutions that are ultimately ineffective or counterproductive.[256] . . . The Tribunal considers that a breach of Article 1105 occurs only when it is shown that an investor has been treated in such an unjust or arbitrary manner that the treatment rises to the level that is unacceptable from the international perspective. That determination must be made in the light of the *high measure of deference that international law generally extends to the right of domestic authorities to regulate matters within their own borders.* (emphasis added)[257]

There are good reasons to avoid having arbitral tribunals make interventionist revisions of the public nature of state goals. Apart from the argument of *global subsidiarity* explained above, we should be aware that there is virtually no such thing as an innocent regulation. As explained in chapter 4,[258] in every case there is a group of winners that strongly favoured—and probably lobbied for—the new measure. The result is that in both theory and practice, there is no simple way of knowing what the public interest is, and whether any one piece of regulation truly pursues that public interest.

[253] ibid ¶ 430.

[254] ibid ¶ 432.

[255] See *SD Myers I* ¶ 195 ('The Tribunal finds that there was no legitimate environmental reason for introducing the ban').

[256] ibid ¶ 261.

[257] ibid ¶ 263. See also, GC Christie, 'What Constitutes a Taking of Property Under International Law?' (1962) 38 BYIL 307, 338 (observing that 'if the reasons given are valid and bear some plausible relationship to the action taken, no attempt may be made to search deeper to see whether the State was activated by some illicit motive').

[258] See ch 4, 168–184.

ii Means and Their Relationship to Ends

Once the tribunal has accepted that the goals pursued by the state are legitimate, then it must assess whether the adopted measures are rationally related to those ends. Property rights compete against other public values. In their periphery—that is, in cases of non-destructive harm—rights must often yield to those other goals, but only under the condition that there is a rational connection between means and ends (including 'sound science').[259]

Given its corrective justice foundation, arbitrariness as irrationality focuses exclusively on the connection between means and ends, and not on the reasonableness and proportionality of the measures and harm suffered by the investor. Distributive justice considerations, meanwhile, generally are to be dealt with under tests of arbitrariness as special sacrifice and lack of proportionality *stricto sensu*. Although we should be aware that issues of rationality and reasonableness tend to be grouped together in the case law, this section focuses strictly on means–ends issues.

As always, when checking means–ends relations, the general stance of investment treaty tribunals should be deferential. Some tests can reach high levels of intrusiveness, such as the *least-restrictive alternative* test—where the tribunal inquires whether there is a less harmful means of accomplishing the same end—or the US 'hard look review'.[260] Those tests should be avoided in the BIT generation; intrusiveness on these issues has the effect of blurring the distinction between policy judgment and legal adjudication. The weak legitimacy foundation of dispute settlement under investment treaties only permits tribunals to adopt a modest attitude toward government policy decisions.

To date, the most important decision in this area is *Methanex*. In this case, the Tribunal held that, in the context of regulation *stricto sensu* (that is, rule-making), 'serious and objective' scientific work represented a sufficient justification for upsetting the status quo to the detriment of foreign investors:

> Having considered all the expert evidence adduced in these proceedings by both Disputing Parties, the Tribunal accepts the UC Report as reflecting a *serious, objective and scientific approach to a complex problem in California*. Whilst it is possible for other scientists and researchers to disagree in good faith with certain of its methodologies, analyses and conclusions, the fact of such disagreement, *even if correct*, does not warrant this Tribunal in treating the UC Report as part of a political sham by California. In particular, the UC Report was

[259] See Waelde and Kolo, n 7, 825.

[260] See Joel P Trachtman, 'The Agency Model of Judging in Economic Integration: Balancing Responsibilities' in Thomas Cottier and Petros C Mavroidis (eds), *The Role of the Judge in International Trade Regulation. Experiences and Lessons for the WTO* (Ann Arbor, University of Michigan Press, 2003) 135, 137.

> subjected at the time to public hearings, testimony and peer-review; and its emergence as a serious scientific work from such an open and informed debate is the best evidence that it was not the product of a political sham engineered by California, leading subsequently to the two measures impugned by Methanex in these arbitration proceedings. (emphasis added)[261]

Methanex represents a valuable precedent: It defined a threshold of scientific soundness that suffices to secure rationality in rule-making. In that decision, the threshold was set, in my opinion, at an appropriate level: An open regulatory process accompanied by serious scientific work, which demonstrates that no political sham has been orchestrated by the defendant state.

In closing, a brief comment must be made concerning the related topic of standards of rationality in situations where different agencies or branches of government behave inconsistently. In this regard, some tribunals have shown lower degrees of deference toward defendant states. In *MTD*, the Tribunal found reproachable 'the inconsistency of action between two arms of the same Government *vis-à-vis* the same investor even when the legal framework of the country provides for a mechanism to coordinate'.[262]

This case is of particular interest, because it constitutes an 'inverse' regulatory taking of sorts. The state lost the case not due to regulatory changes that harmed the investor, but for failing to change the regulation in order to make the investor's business viable. The Tribunal held that the State, Chile, 'has an obligation to act coherently and apply its policies consistently, independently of how diligent an investor is. Under international law . . . the State of Chile needs to be considered by the Tribunal as a unit'.[263]

Given the breadth and complexity of the regulatory state in the twenty-first century—and particularly, considering the fact that its various agencies and branches may be controlled by different political parties—such a standard of consistency and coherence appears unwise, unrealistic, and probably impossible to achieve for any developed or developing nation.

D Arbitrariness as Special Sacrifice and Lack of Proportionality (*Stricto Sensu*)

Investments enjoy a certain degree of anti-redistributive protection. This means that investors can resist—or validly claim compensation for—certain public policies that are detrimental to their interests, even in the

261 *Methanex*, Pt III, Ch A, p 51, ¶ 101.
262 *MTD I* ¶ 163.
263 ibid ¶ 165.

absence of *wrongful* state conduct. The FET standard, therefore, requires international investment law to draw a line, using Rose-Ackerman and Rossi's words, 'between the preservation of "investment-backed expectations" and the preservation of government flexibility'.[264]

Distributive justice considerations should only come into play at the very end of the process, once arbitral tribunals have found that the public interests invoked by the state are appropriate, and the means–ends relationships rational. At this point, the relevant question is whether the harm suffered by the investor, given its nature and extent, is fair, proportionate, and reasonable in the light of the ends pursued by the government. Discrimination has also been considered a relevant factor,[265] although, if informed by nationality, it is more naturally addressed under the national treatment or most favoured nation standards. A general formulation—presumably mixed with elements of rationality, as is always the case—can be found in *Saluka*:

> A foreign investor protected by the Treaty may in any case properly expect that the Czech Republic implements its policies *bona fide* by conduct that is, as far as it affects the investors' investment, reasonably justifiable by public policies and that such conduct does not manifestly violate the requirements of consistency, transparency, even-handedness and non-discrimination. In particular, any differential treatment of a foreign investor must not be based on unreasonable distinctions and demands, and must be justified by showing that it bears a reasonable relationship to rational policies not motivated by a preference for other investments over the foreign-owned investment.[266]

Special sacrifice and proportionality *stricto sensu*, although focusing on different aspects, are two tests that consider the harm suffered by the claimant in light of the public interest sought.[267] On the one hand, the test of special sacrifice asks whether the burden allocated to the investor—even if proportionate—should nevertheless be born by the community at large. This test's main concern is equality, or, in French terms, the principle of *l'égalité devant les charges publiques*.

For instance, in *Pope & Talbot II*, the Tribunal had to review the alleged special sacrifice nature of certain burdens allocated by the Canadian government among lumber producers when implementing the Softwood Lumber Agreement (SLA) of 1996 (including a 'settlement' of the 'BC stumpage' dispute with the US that resulted in an amendment of the

[264] Susan Rose-Ackerman and Jim Rossi, 'Disentangling Deregulatory Takings' (2000) 86 *Virginia Law Review* 1435, 1441 (concerning US administrative law). For Spanish administrative law, see Gaspar Ariño Ortiz, *El Nuevo Servicio Público* (Madrid, Marcial Pons, 1997) 52–53. We see here a confrontation between the two pillars of foreign investment law identified by Dolzer, n 29, 106: 'the respect for the host state's rights of economic sovereignty and the protection of the investor's legitimate expectations'.

[265] See eg, *Saluka* ¶¶ 309 ff. But see *Methanex*, Pt IV, Ch C, p 8, ¶ 16.

[266] *Saluka* ¶ 307. See ibid ¶ 309.

[267] See the detailed explanation of both tests in ch 4, 213–212.

treaty). The 'Super Fee'—one of these burdens—was part of a complicated quota / fee regime established for the export of softwood lumber to the US The Tribunal rejected the FET claim against the imposition of this fee, revealing its unwillingness to interfere with policy-making:

> The choice made to resolve the BC stumpage dispute through the Super Fee undoubtedly *required certain exporters to pay a price for a benefit accorded by B.C. to all producers in that province.* Therefore, Canada might have chosen another approach to settlement, *one that shared the burden more equitable across the range of B.C. producers that received the benefits of the stumpage reductions.* However, *it is not the place of this Tribunal to substitute its judgment on the choice of solutions for Canada's, unless that choice can be found to be a denial of fair and equitable treatment.* Given the *large number of B.C. producers affected* by the settlement as well as the hierarchical treatment of shipment levels under the SLA itself, the Tribunal cannot conclude that Canada's decision to apportion the costs as it did was a denial of fair and equitable treatment to the Investment. (emphasis added)[268]

On the other hand, proportionality *stricto sensu* is, loosely speaking, a form of cost-benefit analysis. As Trachtman explains, 'proportionality *stricto sensu* inquires whether the means are "proportionate" to the ends: whether the costs are excessive in relation to the benefits'.[269] In international investment law, the *LG&E* Tribunal has provided a general approach to this test:

> With respect to the power of the State to adopt its policies, it can generally be said that the State has the right to adopt measures having a social or general welfare purpose. In such cases, the measure must be accepted without imposition of liability, *except in cases where the State's action is obviously disproportionate to the need being addressed.* (emphasis added)[270]

Proportionality *stricto sensu* has emerged and will continue to emerge as an important consideration in cases involving penalties, fines and termination of licences and contracts. Note that these cases may involve either the expropriation or the FET standard, depending on the degree of damage suffered by the investor (the expropriation standard requires total or substantial deprivation). In either case, as mentioned in chapter 5, the analysis should be essentially equivalent as a matter of proportionality, and, therefore, we may deal with expropriation and FET cases together.[271]

A perfect example in this regard can be found in the *Tecmed* case, where the Tribunal reviewed, among other measures, the state's refusal to extend the authorisation to operate the investor's landfill:

> [I]n addition to the negative financial impact of such actions or measures, the Arbitral Tribunal will consider, in order to determine if they are to be

[268] *Pope & Talbot Inc v Canada*, UNCITRAL Ad Hoc Arbitration (Dervaird, Greenberg, Belman), Award on Damages (10 April 2001) ¶ 155 (hereinafter, Pope & Talbot II).

[269] *Trachtman*, n 260, 137.

[270] *LG&E* ¶ 195.

[271] See ch 5, 281–288.

> characterized as expropriatory, *whether such actions or measures are proportional to the public interest presumably protected thereby and to the protection legally granted to investments, taking into account that the significance of such impact has a key role upon deciding the proportionality.* (emphasis added)[272]

Following ECHR precedents, the *Tecmed* Tribunal recognised that the 'analysis starts at the due deference owing to the State when defining the issues that affect its public policy or the interests of society as a whole'.[273] Still, the mission of the Tribunal was to control whether there was 'a reasonable relationship of proportionality between the charge or weight imposed on the foreign investor and the aim sought to be realized by any expropriatory measure'.[274]

In that case, the Tribunal found that the deprivation of the claimant's landfill business—resulting from the refusal to renew the necessary authorisations—was not justified by breaches on the part of the claimant (as alleged by Mexico), but rather for 'socio-political' reasons, meaning the community opposition to the landfill's operation.[275] Measuring the proportionality of the revocation against these reasons, the Tribunal found that, in light of the relevant facts, the measures adopted by the Mexican government were not proportional, and that as a result, the investor had suffered a compensable expropriation.[276]

Beyond cases involving penalties, fines and cancellation of licences and contracts, there can be no doubt that regulatory reform in general—whether isued in times of emergency or in normal times—will be frequently brought to test under the concept of proportionality *stricto sensu*. Throughout the world, the history of administrative law has proven that the reasonableness and soundness of administrative conduct, and its relative weight compared to the burdens imposed on investors, are permanently pitted against the investors' expectation of legal stability and economic intangibility.

The case of the FET standard follows—and will continue to follow—the same pattern; in Dolzer's words, '[u]nderlying all of these applications of fair and equitable treatment are the basic themes of stability of the law and, seen from the investor's perspective, predictability of the requirements to be met and the rights to be granted'.[277] In this regard, the emergence of the new category of 'legitimate expectations' has concentrated many of the analytical considerations that corresponds to the test of proportionality *stricto sensu*. This next section will deal with it on a separate basis.

[272] *Tecmed* ¶ 122.
[273] ibid.
[274] ibid.
[275] ibid ¶¶ 128 ff.
[276] ibid ¶ 139.
[277] Dolzer, n 29, 104.

E Legitimate Expectations

The concept of legitimate expectations—which falls under the FET standard—has assumed a prominent role in international investment law.[278] In *Saluka*, the Tribunal went even further to note that 'the notion of legitimate expectations . . . is *the dominant element of that standard* [FET]'. (emphasis added)[279] A full consideration of this concept would justify a complete study in itself; the analysis here, therefore, barely qualifies as a summary.

As discussed in chapter 4,[280] the concept of legitimate expectations has two different meanings: legitimate expectations-weak sense, where expectations merely refer to interests that compete against the public interest; and legitimate expectations-strong sense, where expectations refer to interests that overcome the public interest (at least in the sense of requiring the payment of compensation if sacrificed). In its weak sense, the concept provides no new information; in the strong sense, it is substantially circular.

Legitimate expectations, if unqualified, can be one of the most dangerous factors weighting the net effects of the BIT generation improperly toward foreign investors. This is especially true because legitimate expectations protect not only property rights but also interests possessing a lesser status. So, the combination of the already expansive concept of 'investment' with that of legitimate expectations may end up producing a commitment to the status quo that goes beyond any 'expectation' that developing countries could have held at the time of concluding BITs.

At this point in the history of the BIT generation, investment treaty tribunals have specified various conditions that qualify the protection of investors' expectations. First of all, protectable expectations cannot be formed unilaterally on the investor's side. According to the *Parkerings* Tribunal, 'not every hope amounts to an expectation under international law'.[281] Similarly, the *MTD* Annulment Committee, criticising the *Tecmed* Tribunal, expressed that '[t]he obligations of the host State towards

[278] See eg *Biwater Gauff* ¶ 602; *Parkerings* ¶ 330; *Enron* ¶ 262; *LG&E* ¶ 127; *Thunderbird*, Separate Opinion ¶¶ 1, and 37; *Bogdanov et al v Moldova*, SCC Case (Cordero), Award (22 September 2005), at 16, ¶ 4.2.4; *CMS* ¶¶ 278–79; *OEPC* ¶¶ 180–187, and 191; *Waste Management II* ¶ 98; *Tecmed* ¶ 154; *Generation Ukraine* ¶ 20.37; *ADF Group* ¶ 189; and, *Metalclad* ¶ 89. Among commentators, see Dolzer and Schreuer, n 18, 133–140; Elizabeth Snodgrass, 'Protecting Investors' Legitimate Expectations: Recognizing and Delimiting a General Principle' (2006) 21 *ICSID Review—Foreign Investment Law Journal* 1; and, Schill, n 22, 15.

[279] *Saluka* ¶ 302.

[280] See ch 4, 222–227.

[281] *Parkerings* ¶ 344. See also, *MCI Power Group* ¶ 278 ('The legitimacy of the expectations for proper treatment entertained by a foreign investor protected by the BIT does not depend solely on the intent of the parties, but on certainty about the contents of the enforceable obligations'); and *LG&E* ¶ 130 ('[T]hey [legitimate expectations] may not be established unilaterally by one of the parties').

foreign investors derive from the terms of the applicable investment treaty and not from any set of expectations investors may have or claim to have'.[282]

Second, expectations, to receive protection in international investment law, must be *legitimate* and *reasonable*.[283] In particular, the *Saluka* Tribunal has created an important precedent concerning these requirements: '[T]he scope of the Treaty's protection of foreign investment against unfair and inequitable treatment *cannot exclusively be determined by foreign investors' subjective motivations and considerations*. Their expectations, in order for them to be protected, must rise to the level of *legitimacy and reasonableness in light of the circumstances*'. (emphasis added)[284]

Although the inclusion of these constraints in the case law should be applauded, legitimacy and reasonableness also remind us that, in the end, the protection of legitimate expectations depends on more basic questions of arbitrariness such as illegality, irrationality, special sacrifice and proportionality *stricto sensu*. In other words, conceptually speaking, not much is accomplished by introducing the concept of legitimate expectations.

In any case, in order to evaluate the actual degree of protection of legitimate expectations in the BIT generation, we should distinguish between those situations in which the investor was given specific assurances or representations, from those in which he was given none. The case law shows that this distinction—already explored in detailed in chapter 4[285]—has become the critical consideration in this field.

i Without Assurances

The weakest version of legitimate expectation is represented by those cases where there are no formal or informal assurances, but only legislation, regulation and / or case law. In these circumstances, and knowing, as Mashaw observes, that '[s]tatutes always shift rights or expectations'[286], can investors claim that they relied on a particular statute or regulation, and therefore, that the harm derived from policy changes should be compensated?

[282] *MTD II* ¶ 67.

[283] See eg *Jan de Nul* ¶ 186 ('Tribunals have considered that fair and equitable treatment was denied when the protection of the investor's expectations had not been warranted, provided that these were reasonable and legitimate'); *Duke Energy Electroquil* ¶ 340 ('To be protected, the investor's expectations must be legitimate and reasonable at the time the investor makes the investment'); *Rumeli Telekom* ¶ 609 ('The case law also confirms that to comply with the standard, the State must respect the investor's reasonable and legitimate expectations'); and, *Biwater Gauff* ¶ 602 (expectations must be 'reasonable and legitimate and have been relied upon by the investor to make the investment').

[284] *Saluka* ¶ 304.

[285] See ch 4, 223–225.

[286] Mashaw, n 13, 34.

Although open-ended concepts such as 'transparency', 'stability', 'predictability', 'no ambiguity'and others explored and criticised earlier (in the first dimension of the GAL approach to the FET standard) seem to point in this direction,[287] international investment law does not support such a conservative reading of treaties.[288] Even decisions that give expansive protection to legitimate expectations, such as *CMS*, make this clear:

> It is not a question of whether the legal framework might need to be frozen as it can always evolve and be adapted to changing circumstances, but neither is it a question of whether the framework can be dispensed with altogether when specific commitments to the contrary have been made. The law of foreign investment and its protection has been developed with the specific objective of avoiding such adverse legal effects.[289]

Moreover, any remaining doubts should be assuaged by the most recent case law, which has explicitly confronted this issue. In *Continental Casualty*, the Tribunal held that the legitimate expectations depended on 'the specificity of the undertaking allegedly relied upon',[290] and therefore, 'general legislative statements engender reduced expectations . . . Their enactment is by nature subject to subsequent modification'.[291] Even more clear, in *Parkerings*, the Tribunal noted first that '[t]he expectation is legitimate if the investor received an explicit promise or guaranty from the host-State, or if implicitly, the host-State made assurances or representation that the investor took into account in making the investment'.[292] Then, it emphatically held that:

> It is each State's undeniable right and privilege to exercise its sovereign legislative power. *A State has the right to enact, modify or cancel a law at its own discretion. Save for the existence of an agreement, in the form of a* stabilisation *clause or otherwise, there is nothing objectionable about the amendment brought to the regulatory framework existing at the time an investor made its investment.* As a matter of fact, any businessman or investor knows that laws will evolve over time. What is prohibited however is for a State to act unfairly, unreasonably or inequitably in the exercise of its legislative power. In principle, an investor has a right to a certain stability and predictability of the legal environment of the investment. The

[287] See nn 128–139, and accompanying text.

[288] See Waelde and Kolo, n 7, 824–25 (noting that '[o]ne cannot postulate that the environmental regimen should be absolutely frozen . . . The question is rather to identify the threshold of unexpected regulatory change and of its impact on the investor's legitimate expectation which require that the investor be paid compensation'); and Yoram Dinstein, 'Deprivation of Property of Foreigners under International Law' Nisuke Ando et al (eds), 2 *Liber Amicorum Judge Shigeru Oda* (New York, Kluwer Law International, 2002) 849, 853 (observing that 'a foreigner entering a local country for commercial purposes must take into account normal hazards and have no more than plausible expectations. He cannot rely on the local law standing still').

[289] *CMS* ¶ 277.

[290] *Continental Casualty* ¶ 261.

[291] ibid.

[292] *Parkerings* ¶ 331.

> investor will have a right of protection of its legitimate expectations provided it exercised due diligence and that its legitimate expectations were reasonable in light of the circumstances. *Consequently, an investor must anticipate that the circumstances could change, and thus structure its investment in order to adapt it to the potential changes of legal environment.* (emphasis added)[293]

In *EnCana*, the Tribunal also stated that '[i]n the absence of a specific commitment from the host State, the foreign investor has neither the right nor any legitimate expectation that the tax regime will not change, perhaps to its disadvantage, during the period of the investment'.[294] And, in *Saluka*, that '[n]o investor may reasonably expect that the circumstances prevailing at the time the investment is made remain totally unchanged'.[295]

Of course, this does not mean that the defendant state can arbitrarily change the regulatory framework, and that the investor can *never* claim legitimate expectations based on the legal system. The situation that the *PSEG Group* Tribunal refers to as the ' "roller-coaster" effect of the continuing legislative changes' may certainly constitute an improper frustration of the investor's legitimate expectations, even in the absence of assurances.[296] Similarly, structural modifications of the rules that govern an entire sector, without appropriate transitional periods, may also demand a more careful analysis.

We may conclude that, notwithstanding some initial false starts, international investment law is now moving in the right direction. In the absence of specific commitments and assurances, there is very little basis for protection of investors' expectations. In Schill's words, 'where a foreign investor merely relies on the general legal framework without any specific commitments or intention on behalf of the host state to attract foreign investors, the concept of legitimate expectations may only have a more marginal scope of application'.[297]

ii With Assurances

Legitimate expectations, in order to be protected, must arise from individualised assurances or 'specific undertakings'.[298] As indicated in *PSEG*

293 ibid ¶¶ 332–33. See also, ibid ¶ 336.

294 *EnCana* ¶ 173.

295 *Saluka* ¶ 305.

296 *PSEG Group* ¶ 250. As properly indicated then in ¶ 254, '[s]tability cannot exist in a situation where the law kept changing continuously and endlessly, as did its interpretation and implementation'.

297 Schill, n 22, 28. See also, Snodgrass, n 278, 56.

298 *Continental Casualty* ¶¶ 260. See also, *Duke Energy Electroquil* ¶ 340 ('[S]uch expectations must arise from the conditions that the State offered the investor and the latter must have relied upon them when deciding to invest'); and, LG&E ¶ 130 ('[Legitimate expectations] are based on the conditions offered by the host State at the time of the investment').

Global, '[l]egitimate expectations by definition require a promise of the administration on which the Claimants rely to assert a right that needs to be observed'.[299] Expectations should also be protected to the extent that the investor relies on them at the moment the investment is conducted ('inducements').[300] In the words of the *Enron* Tribunal, '[w]hat seems to be essential, however, is that these expectations derived from the conditions that were offered by the State to the investor at the time of the investment and that such conditions were relied upon by the investor when deciding to invest'.[301]

However, there is one aspect of the development of legitimate expectations that should be criticised. In principle, the concept should not be applied when there are contractual arrangements already in place between the parties. As Crawford has acutely observed, 'the doctrine of legitimate expectations should not be used as a substitute for the actual arrangements agreed between the parties, or as supervening and overriding source of the applicable law'.[302] Contractual rights and interests should be protected in the framework of the contract, and not pursuant to the international investment law principle of legitimate expectations.

In terms of the GAL structure of this chapter, where there are contractual relations, the case should be resolved under the rules and principles of the second dimension of the GAL approach to the FET standard (that is, SE arguments, which consists of domestic illegalities—including breaches of contract—plus 'something more'). Specific assurances should be assessed in the context of the contract, and their violation should be seen, at best, as a potential breach of contract (or of domestic law). It is difficult to understand, for example, how the *MTD* Tribunal could conclude that there was no breach of contract, but that the investor's expectations formed on the basis of that same contract were frustrated.[303]

It is worth noting that, in the caselaw, several of the strongest assertions concerning legitimate expectations have been expressed in the context of contractual rights, precisely the area where the concept should be less relevant. That was clearly the case in *OEPC*. The Tribunal—referring specifically to a contract clause—held that 'there is certainly an obligation not to alter the legal and business environment in which the investment

[299] *PSEG Global* ¶ 241. See *Metalpar SA and Buen Aire SA v Argentina*, ICSID Case No ARB/03/5 (Oreamuno, Cameron, Chabaneix), Award (6 June 2008), ¶ 186.

[300] See eg *Continental Casualty* ¶ 260; *Sempra* ¶ 298; *BG* ¶ 343; *Methanex*, Pt IV, Ch D, at 5, ¶ 10; and, *CME I* ¶ 611. Among commentators, see McLachlan et al, n 18, 237 (noting that '[t]he making of specific representations has been a material factor in the decision in favour of the investor in a number of the recent cases'); and, Choudhury, n 21, 316 (observing that 'fair and equitable treatment includes treatment which does not affect an investor's legitimate expectations which were relied upon in making the investment').

[301] *Enron* ¶ 262.

[302] James Crawford, 'Treaty and Contract in Investment Arbitration', available at http://www.lcil.cam.ac.uk/Media/lectures/pdf/Freshfields%20Lecture%202007.pdf).

[303] See *MTD I* ¶¶ 163, 188.

has been made. In this case it is the latter question that triggers a treatment that is not fair and equitable'.[304] The same can be said of the *CMS* case, where there was also a detailed concession contract binding the parties.[305]

As covered in chapter 4, legitimate expectations arising from representations typically receive protection in the presence of the following requirements: first, representations must be legal, or at least, not *contra legem*, and also must have been provided by a competent official acting within his or her jurisdiction; secondly, they must be specific, precise, unambiguous, and unqualified; thirdly, they must not have been adopted on the basis of false or incomplete information provided by the beneficiary; and, fourthly, they must outweigh the public interest. So, have investment treaty tribunals followed these four relatively common restrictions when giving protection to legitimate expectations?

In *Metalclad*, the Tribunal completely ignored the first of these rules. It decided to protect US investors' reliance on assurances given by Mexican *federal* officials to the effect that a *Municipal* construction permit would not be required, a permit that was later denied by the Municipality. The Tribunal did not carefully consider the permit's legality under Mexican public law, and, instead, concluded that 'Metalclad was entitled to rely on the representations of federal officials . . . In following the advice of these officials . . . Metalclad was merely acting prudently and in the full expectation that the permit would be granted'.[306]

The importance of this first requirement cannot be over-emphasised: If expectations are permitted *contra legem*, then public officials can derogate constitutions and statutes using merely informal (even oral) assurances.[307] By altering this basic rule, international investment law would inevitably erode the rule of law and help to establish a culture of corruption in the developing world.[308]

Concerning the second and third rules just mentioned, the *Thunderbird* case established extremely valuable norms in international investment law. Indeed, that Tribunal dismissed the claimant's allegations based on the fact that the claimant had provided false information to SEGOB in its *Solicitud*, particularly when affirming that the operation of its 'gaming' machines did not involve chance.[309] The Tribunal concluded:

304 *OEPC* ¶ 191.

305 See *CMS* ¶¶ 274–76. See also, *LG&E* ¶ 133.

306 *Metalclad* ¶¶ 89. See also, ibid ¶¶ 87–88.

307 Wälde, *Thunderbird*, Separate Opinion ¶ 93, has also stressed the importance of the idea that assurances cannot be *contra legem*. See also, ibid ¶ 21.

308 See Lowe, n 6, 465, who also notes that: 'If the State's own law does not permit the government to make such commitments, such a decision may easily appear to put the investor above the law, and to entail the conclusion that individuals within the government have given favours, beyond the limits of what the law allows, to the investor'. But see Snodgrass, n 278, 40 (concluding that '[a] reasonable position might be that *ultra vires* acts, while they may give rise to legitimate expectations, will do so less readily than would lawful acts').

309 See *Thunderbird* ¶¶ 152–53.

> The Tribunal is therefore of the opinion that the *Solicitud* is not a proper disclosure and that it puts the reader on the wrong track. The *Solicitud* creates the appearance that the machines described are video arcade games, designed solely for entertainment purposes.[310] . . . Thunderbird was the moving party presenting a '*Solicitud*' to the Mexican administration; one would therefore expect that the moving party supply adequate information and make a proper disclosure. In the Tribunal's view, the *Solicitud* did not give the full picture, even for an informed reader.[311]

Not only did the claimant's behaviour impede expectations to receive protection under international law, but also, the *Oficio*'s content was not sufficiently unambiguous and unqualified to give way to legitimate expectations. The Tribunal noted that any possible assurances contained in the *Oficio* were *expressly* conditioned and qualified by SEGOB as depending on the veracity of the information indicated by the claimant in its *Solicitud*.[312] So, if statements contained in the latter were not true, then the *Oficio* could not have raised any expectation on which the claimants could have relied.

This was one of the strongest points of opposition between the majority and the dissenting arbitrator in *Thunderbird*. In his separate opinion, Wälde explained why he thought that ambiguities in the legal treatment of foreign investors must be borne by the state and not by the investor: 'the risk of ambiguity falls square on the shoulders of the assurance-issuing public authority'.[313] The argument that ambiguous assurances trump previous interpretation of domestic law is an extreme one, and in my opinion, investment treaties offer no basis on which to infer such a pro-investor stance.[314]

Finally, the last rule demands that the decision-maker weigh the investor's frustrated expectations against the public interest sought by the state.[315] This important dimension of the protection of expectations has, with notable exceptions, been overlooked in international investment arbitration.[316] However, as noted, recent decisions have stressed the need

[310] ibid ¶ 155.

[311] ibid ¶ 159

[312] ibid ¶ 161.

[313] *Thunderbird*, Separate Opinion ¶ 50.

[314] Wälde's argument on this point, ibid ¶ 47, is unpersuasive: 'The implications of the obligation to be clear and avoid ambiguity is that the government agency has to bear the risk of its own ambiguity. This allocation of the risk of ambiguity requires that the investor did and could reasonably have confidence in the assurance'. Adopting regulation is substantially different from concluding contracts; the law and economics' conceptions on how to allocate risks through interpretation in the contractual setting cannot be imported wholesale into the interpretation of the law.

[315] See Snodgrass, n 278, 45.

[316] The most notable exception appears to be Wälde, in *Thunderbird*, Separate Opinion ¶ 30: 'Such protection is, however, not un-conditional and ever-lasting. It leads to a balancing process between the needs for flexible public policy and the legitimate reliance on in particular investment-backed expectations'. See also, *Tecmed* ¶ 122.

to check the *reasonableness* and *legitimacy* of the expectations. If international investment law is to develop an appropriate jurisprudence on the matter, those latter requirements should also serve the purpose of permitting arbitral tribunals to conduct a balancing process, pursuant to which expectations may be protected only when proportionality and special sacrifice authorise it.

CONCLUSIONS: THE HORIZONTAL AND VERTICAL CONSTRAINTS ON THE FET STANDARD

What we are witnessing today in the BIT generation is a demonstration that the exhaustion of local remedies rule was a far from merely procedural requirement.[317] Its removal has deeply impacted the way in which arbitral tribunals adjudicate investment claims, and made the relationship between international and domestic law especially interdependent and complex. Not many commentators have perceived this critical fact about the BIT generation.[318]

The denial of justice age, with its characteristic respect for state sovereignty, is over. In those years, under the dominance of dualist conceptions, international law was 'extremely reticent as regard the competence of States to govern their internal affairs'[319]. Domestic law and its application were considered matters of domestic jurisdiction, forming part of the *domaine réservé*.[320]

This ideology, which underpinned the denial of justice age, should not be carried over to the BIT generation. The bottom line of the GAL approach to the FET standard developed in this chapter is this: Arbitral tribunals always must bear in mind that international investment law lacks a fully mature set of rules of global constitutional and administrative law that would permit them to resolve investment disputes without any reference to domestic law or comparative law. Investment treaty tribunals should therefore refrain from 'inventing', from scratch, new norms that simply do not exist. Following Sunstein—who cites Justice Holmes—we

[317] This was a familiar and complex debate in international law during the denial of justice age. See JES Fawcett, 'The Exhaustion of Local Remedies: Substance or Procedure?' (1954) 31 *British Ybk Intl Law* 452.

[318] Among others, Douglas, n 87, 241, deserves special attention; he accurately remarks that '[t]he displacement of the local remedies rule in investment treaty arbitration has made it critical to examine the relationship between the municipal, transnational, and international legal orders'.

[319] Karl Joseph Partsch, 'International Law and Municipal Law' in Rudolf Bernhard (ed), 2 *Encyclopedia of Public International Law* (New York, North-Holland, 1992) 1183, 1185.

[320] According to Waldock, n 147, 123, 'nor can there be any doubt that the internal law of a State and the administration of its internal law are, in principle, matters of domestic jurisdiction'.

may observe here that the meaning of the FET standard is not a 'brooding omnipresence in the sky'.[321]

To determine the proper content and limits of a standard such as FET, we must step back for a larger perspective on the general tensions that exist throughout the field of international investment law. In this regard, as in any other mature regulatory capitalist legal system, international investment law, in Reisman's words, 'must balance claims for respect for the special requirements of national communities, which is one of its central postulates, against the need for sustaining the rule of law so that economic activity can continue to flow freely about the globe'.[322]

Moreover, beyond this tension, as noted earlier in this chapter, the development of appropriate new standards of review of arbitrariness demands that the members of the international community reach a basic consensus on some of the essential policy objectives for international investment law. As I argue here, the BIT generation must define minimum thresholds that determine what is expected from a reasonably well-behaved regulatory state; state liability, as a central tenet, should only be the consequence of the '*failure to maintain the usual order which it is the duty of every state to maintain within its territory*'. (emphasis added)[323]

In this general context, the GAL approach to the FET standard developed in this chapter demonstrates that international investment law must take seriously two general methodological constraints. First, there is a vertical constraint, represented by a conflict-of-laws set of rules and principles concerning the application of domestic law; and, second, a horizontal constraint, represented by a set of substantive norms of global character which are to be developed under the guidance of comparative law. These constraints are key to the fine-tuning of the relationship between democracy, rule of law, and investment protection in the BIT generation.

The vertical constraint highlights the dangers that radical versions of dualism pose and will continue to pose to the legitimacy of the BIT generation. The regulatory state continues to be a *Rechtsstaat*, that is, a state whose program of action is mainly commanded by domestic public law. That program, if not falling below IMS, continues to be effectively binding to foreign investors. What is fair and equitable under international law cannot overlook such a major component of the world's institutional structure. 'Respect for the integrity of the law of the host state', as stated in *Fraport*, 'is also a critical part of development and a concern of international investment law'.[324]

[321] Cass R Sunstein, 'Beyond Marbury: The Executive Power to Say What the Law Is' (2006) 115 *Yale Law Journal* 2580, 2583, citing *Southern Pacific Co v Jensen* (1917) 244 US 205, 222 (Holmes J dissenting).

[322] W Michael Reisman, 'International Arbitration and Sovereignty' (2002) 18 *Arbitration International* 231, 234–35.

[323] See n 33.

[324] *Fraport AG Frankfurt Airport Services Worldwide v Philippines*, ICSID Case No ARB/03/25 (Fortier, Reisman, Cremades), Award (16 August 2007), ¶ 402.

On the other hand, the relevance of the horizontal constraint can be seen throughout the three dimensions of the GAL approach to the FET standard. This is the case because a comparative perspective is required in every instance where IMS must be concretised. As noted above, we need such substantive standards to review the domestic legal systems as such—the NE-I arguments of the first dimension—to give content to the 'something more' doctrine—the SE arguments of the second dimension—and to define proper tests of arbitrariness as irrationality, special sacrifice, and proportionality *stricto sensu*, including the protection of legitimate expectations—the NE-II arguments of the third dimension.

Investment treaty tribunals must be aware of the inherent risks of furthering substantive international standards without taking into account the comparative experiences of the main legal systems of the world. In particular, the excesses of intrusiveness that sometimes can be found in international investment decisions represent a strong commitment to the status quo, which countries did not agree upon when signing BITs and other similar treaties. Arbitrators who are unfamiliar with judicial review in public law settings may not be aware that, as Breyer reminds us, 'one result of strict judicial review of agency policy decisions is a strong conservative pressure in favor of the status quo'.[325]

To sum up, any assessment of the current status of the FET jurisprudence should exhibit concern about the lack of seriousness with which investment treaty tribunals sometimes treat the aforementioned vertical and horizontal methodological constraints. It is not rare for arbitral tribunals to completely ignore them, and then, in the realm of 'pure' international law, feel free to devise new concretisations of what they understand to be fair and equitable. Yet those personal understandings, based on subjective impressions that surfaced during the arbitral processes, are unlikely to have any bearing on general international, nor on domestic law, nor on a comparative understanding of the legal systems of developed countries.

Tribunals such as those just described are not currently great in number, but enough of them exist to constitute a danger to the system. Both developing and developed countries should be aware of these risks, and press for a more transnational model of adjudication. The advent of the BIT generation compels us to re-conceive the relationship of international, domestic, and comparative law, and to recognise that radical dualism and extreme versions of the 'non-courts of appeal' doctrine cannot be reconciled with the contemporary state of global interdependence and governance.

[325] Stephen Breyer, 'Judicial Review of Questions of Law and Policy' (1986) 38 *Administrative Law Review* 363, 393.

Conclusions: Future of the BIT Generation: For a Global Legal Order Committed to the Rule of Law and Human Welfare

THIS WORK WAS divided into two parts. The First Part provided a framework of analysis, placing the BIT generation in its historical and normative context. One main purpose of this part was to give a closer reading of Latin America's traditional position toward foreign investors, in the hope of gaining further insight into the wisdom and foresight that guided the nineteenth century regional thinkers.

A key outcome of that research was the elaboration of an updated Calvo Doctrine, which embodies two minimal conditions of legitimacy for the BIT generation: first, that BIT jurisprudence resulting from the application of broad and open-ended treaty provisions crystallise in *the good case,* or *BITs-as-developed-countries-constitutional-law-and-no-more*; and, second, that international investment law be extended also to domestic investors in order to avoid the creation of 'legal enclaves' for foreign investors.

The Second Part explored the relationship between property rights, the public interest, and the regulatory state. It began by presenting and comparing this relationship, as it exists today in major Western legal systems and international regimes. Then, it analysed the existing case law for the two main standards of investment treaties—no expropriation without compensation, and fair and equitable treatment (FET)—under a comparative public law approach, the ultimate goal being to determine whether or not BIT jurisprudence today resembles *the good case*.

As has been argued at length, these two main investment treaty standards, if properly interpreted, do not provide higher standards than those of general international law (GIL). Indeed, the concept of 'expropriation' remains undefined in treaties, and the interpreter must have recourse to GIL. The same can be said of the FET standard, whose content must be understood to refer to international minimum standards (IMS), and therefore to GIL. If investors are not satisfied by these standards, they can always demand concession contracts or investments agreements that carry more stringent obligations for host states.

This observation might surprise some readers. They might ask: What is the purpose of having BITs and studying them in so much detail if they simply repeat the principles and rules of GIL? However, this question indicates a lack of awareness among commentators, and even investment treaty tribunals, regarding BITs' most powerful and remarkable tool: investor–state arbitration without exhaustion of legal remedies. As Wälde remarks, '[I]t is the ability to access a tribunal outside the sway of the host State which is the principle advantage of a modern investment treaty. This advantage is much more significant than the applicability to the dispute of substantive international law rules'.[1]

From the perspective of developing countries, this work has claimed that investment treaties' broad and open-texture standards not be, as such, the object of our concern. Standards such as no expropriation without compensation and FET are quite reasonable at first glance, and cannot be considered, by themselves, a serious threat to sovereignty and democratic self-determination. However, an unrestrained international investment jurisprudence based on those standards may constitute such a threat. There exists the real danger that international investment law jurisprudence could crystallise conservative rules that overprotect the status quo. In *the bad case* or *BITs-as-gunboat-arbitration*, treaties would be converted into a conservative system that over-protects foreign investments and the status quo, where most diminutions in value resulting from state action would entitle them to compensation. From a global governance perspective, this would be, in Keohane's terms, a 'nightmare scenario'.[2]

Yet another nightmare scenario, not explored in this work, but one that should be mentioned here, involves an international investment jurisprudence in which developed countries win when they should have lost,[3] and developing states lose when they should have won.[4] Such a situation, if repeated over time, would simply devastate the system's legitimacy.[5] The words written in 1875 by the Colombian writer and politician Torres Caicedo—the man who also invented the term 'Latin America'—still resonate:

[1] Thomas W Wälde, 'The "Umbrella" Clause in Investment Arbitration. A Comment on Original Intentions and Recent Cases' (2005) 6 *Journal of World Investment and Trade* 183, 190.

[2] Robert O Keohane, 'Governance in a Partially Globalized World. Presidential Address, American Political Science Association 2000' (2001) 95 *American Political Science Review* 1, 1.

[3] See eg *Loewen v US*, ICSID Case No ARB(AF)/98/3 (Mason, Mikva, Mustill), Award (26 June 2003).

[4] See eg *MTD Equity Sdn. Bhd. et al v Chile*, ICSID Case No ARB/01/07 (Rigo, Lalonde, Oreamuno), Award (25 May 2004).

[5] Compare, for instance, the lenient application of the national treatment standard in *United Parcel Services of America Inc v Canada*, UNCITRAL Ad-Hoc Arbitration (Keith, Cass, Fortier), Award (24 May 2007), ¶¶ 80 ff, with its over-expansive application in *Occidental Exploration and Production Petroleum Co v Ecuador*, UNCITRAL Ad-Hoc Arbitration (Orrego, Brower, Sweeny), Award (1 July 2004), ¶¶ 173 ff.

> *El sistema de indemnizaciones es la mina que se ha explotado hasta hoy con más fruto: con lo que han pagado las Repúblicas americanas en materia de indemnizaciones, habrian tenido para hacer buenos caminos carreteros, si no ferro-carriles, y hoy su industria y su comercio se hallarian muy desarrollados, y con ello habrian asegurado su paz y bienandanza.*[6]

Nevertheless, a proper understanding of international investment law should not lead to the scenario referred to as *the bad case*. To this end, this work has analysed two constraints that can help to crystallise BIT jurisprudence according to *the good case*. The first one is what should be described as the global version of the US *Erie* doctrine:[7] the vertical or conflict-of-laws dimension. The BIT generation demands a much richer and more complex dialogue between international and domestic law than what currently exists.

Indeed, following the example of the US Supreme Court in *Erie*—where, instead of creating an entirely new federal common law, the court decided to apply a conflict-of-laws approach which referred back to state law—arbitral tribunals should be more prepared to apply domestic law, and avoid the creation of new rules and principles that may lack basis in any formal source of law.[8] As explained, the predominant state in the world today is, and should continue to be, a *Rechtsstaat* or law-state, in which those who exercise public powers must primarily follow the program of action prescribed by domestic public law. More importantly, as Reisman explains, '[a] basic postulate of public international law is that every territorial community may organise itself as a State and, within certain basic limits prescribed by international law, organise its social and economic affairs in ways consistent with its own national values'.[9]

The second constraint is the horizontal dimension of comparative law. Investment treaty tribunals should refrain from leaping to any conclusion that might simply look 'equitable', 'just' or 'common sense', without taking into consideration the public law traditions of developed countries. The relevance of comparative law stems mainly from the fact that international law, which has traditionally been interstate, lacks experience in controlling the regulatory state. Only since the Second World War have international human right laws added an additional dimension directly

[6] JM Torres Caicedo, 2 *Mis Ideas y Mis Principios* (Paris, Imprenta Nueva, 1875) 260–61.

[7] *Erie Railroad Co v Tompkins* (1938) 304 US 64. See also, Lea Brilmayer and Jack Goldsmith, *Conflict of Laws: Cases and Materials*, 5th edn (New York, Aspen Law and Business, 2002) 565; and, Peter Hay et al, *Conflict of Laws: Cases and Materials*, 11th edn (New York, Foundation Press, 2000) 654. I am indebted to Professor Michael Levine for the idea of having a kind of *Erie* doctrine in international investment disputes.

[8] See Cass R Sunstein, 'Beyond *Marbury*: The Executive Power to Say What the Law Is' (2006) 115 *Yale Law Journal* 2580, 2583.

[9] W Michael Reisman, 'The Regime for *Lacunae* in the ICSID Choice of Law Provision and the Question of its Threshold' (2000) 15 *ICSID Review?Foreign Investment Law Journal* 362, 366.

linking the individual and state at the international level, but this is of limited use in international investment law.

Comparative law—whose application is relevant pursuant to Articles 31(3)(c) of the Vienna Convention on the Law of Treaties and 38(1)(c) of the ICJ Statute—provides general guidance, which investment treaty tribunals cannot and must not disregard. Property rights, like all fundamental rights, receive variable protection under nearly all legal traditions. The actual degree of protection depends on the weight assigned to the public interests that oppose those rights.[10]

More precisely, as a pragmatic comparative law synthesis demonstrates, in this balancing process the public interest tends to be divided into two discrete values: standard public interests and pre-eminent public interests. Meanwhile, the adverse effects on property rights tend as well to be divided into mere interferences and total/substantial deprivations. Combining these four variations, we can produce the following table:

<table>
<tr><td colspan="2"></td><td colspan="2">Nature of the public interest justifying the state measures</td></tr>
<tr><td colspan="2"></td><td>Standard Public Interest</td><td>Pre-eminent Public Interest</td></tr>
<tr><td rowspan="2">Degree of adverse effect on property rights</td><td>Mere Interference</td><td>Liability if the state acts arbitrarily</td><td>Liability if the state acts arbitrarily (highly unusual)</td></tr>
<tr><td>Total/Substantial Deprivation</td><td>Expropriation</td><td>No-Expropriation; liability if the state acts arbitrarily</td></tr>
</table>

Property rights at their core receive strong protection. This is why investors typically win total/substantial deprivations when the public interest is a standard one. Only rarely do states invoke pre-eminent public interests that trump property rights, and which result in investors losing their claims. In contrast, property rights at their periphery receive weak protection. In countries where property rights are traditionally respected, most investment disputes occurring over these rights tend to involve only the periphery, and investors frequently end up having to bear the burdens imposed by the regulatory state, unless arbitrariness is proven.

[10] See Laura S Underkuffler, *The Idea of Property. Its Meaning and Power* (New York, OUP, 2003) 133 (observing that 'we must understand that the presumptive power of property rights—like the presumptive power of all rights—depends upon the nature of the public interests that oppose them').

As I have attempted to show, investment treaty jurisprudence is currently following and should continue to follow this general structure. Restricting the scope of expropriations to claims involving total and substantial deprivations—global constitutional law—and assigning the FET clause to claims involving the periphery—global administrative law—serve as a proper and convenient interpretation of investment treaties. Not only are there sound methodological reasons for following this structure, but it also permits us to identify, separate and classify some of the most difficult questions to be raised amidst the dangerously value-laden realms of regulatory takings and state liability in tort.

So, after all these considerations, I must not evade what is considered to be the most important question in terms of assessing the BIT generation: Is investment treaty jurisprudence today crystallising according to the *good case* or to the *bad case*? As concluded in chapters 5 and 6, when compared with legal traditions in several developed countries, investment treaty jurisprudence shows mixed results. On the one hand, the expropriation clause has been reasonably applied, effectively silencing those alarmists who feared otherwise.

On the other hand, the real motive for concern is, and will continue to be, the interpretation and application of the FET clause, and consequently, the level of protection of property rights and investments in their periphery. Chapter 6's conclusion stated that one of the greatest threats to the BIT system's legitimacy is the process of reviewing arbitrariness without the horizontal constraints of comparative law, and the vertical constraints of domestic law.

It is not uncommon that arbitral tribunals, inspired by an ideology of *radical dualism*—ie, the drastic separation between domestic and international legal orders—utterly ignore the relevance of both comparative and domestic law to investment disputes. The result is that at the 'pure' international level, emboldened by the flexibility afforded by such an undefined standard of review of arbitrariness, they feel free to invent new concretisations of what they understand to be fair and equitable. The danger, thus, is clear: freed from any legal constraints that may be imposed by domestic law, and given the inherent lack of density that characterises the FET standards in international law, tribunals find a way of basing their decisions on whatever subjective impressions may have formed during the arbitral processes.

Without excessive prejudice toward these and other threats, I must state that my assessment is, ultimately, positive. I remain optimistic about the future of the BIT generation. The jurisprudence is still in the midst of defining a consistent body of law; the system has not yet crystallised clear definitions and concrete rules for indirect expropriations and fair and equitable treatment.

Consequently, capital-importing countries should remain alert to the level of protection of property rights and investments that the BIT jurisprudence defines in the coming years. If the final equilibrium reached is at a level consistently higher than the levels that the main legal traditions of Western capital exporting countries prescribed for their own domestic investors, then developing countries should seriously consider abandoning the BIT network. This option is, in fact, an essential piece of the 'exit legitimacy' supporting that same network.

My optimism regarding the future of the BIT generation is far from naïve. A BIT network equilibrium, like the one suggested here—that is, not higher than that of capital-exporting countries—should not be dismissed out of hand by foreign investors, nor by host States. The protection of property rights and economic liberties in developed countries has proven more than sufficient to sustain healthy and well-functioning capitalist societies. Indeed, essentially all of these societies are today committed to broader collective goals, such as the protection of health, safety and the environment, and, more broadly, personal autonomy and human welfare.

For developing countries, the benefits of a fair and equilibrated BIT network can be considerable. The successful creation and refinement of a global constitutional and administrative law that is truly functional may represent a substantial advance for the rule of law. Imposing those standards top-down from the international level—one of the consequences of trading sovereignty for credibility—may be an efficient means of bypassing local elites and special interest groups, whose abuse of power is largely responsible for the weak institutional foundations of developing countries. This, after all, is one of the most attractive features of global governance: the stabilising presence of an additional layer of checks and balances, that limits the political effectiveness of *factions*.[11]

Equality among nations and equality among investors and citizens, the two principles embodied in the Calvo Doctrine, are still valuable goals today. The BIT generation must work in tandem with the regulatory state—not against it. This regulatory state is a fundamental dimension of modern life; like it or not, it is a key player in the pursuit of collective goals that include, but also transcend, efficiency and maximisation of wealth.[12] A balanced body of law—one containing reasonable rules of global law, and fostering the rule of law and human welfare—constitutes a goal that we can and must demand from the BIT generation.

[11] See Mattias Kumm, 'The Legitimacy of International Law: A Constitutionalist Framework of Analysis' (2004) 15 *European Journal of International Law* 907, 919 (noting that '[i]nternational law *contributes to the check and balances of a constitutional system*, complementing domestic separation of powers and federalism as another means of achieving this').

[12] See Cass R Sunstein, *Free Markets and Social Justice* (New York, OUP, 1997).

Bibliography

Aulis Aarnio, *Philosophical Perspectives in Jurisprudence* (Helsinki, Philosophical Society of Finland, 1983).

Alden F Abbott, 'Latin America and International Arbitration Conventions: The Quandary of Non-Ratification' (1976) 17 *Harvard International Law Journal* 131.

Manuel A Abdala and Pablo Spiller, 'Chorzów's Standard Rejuvenated—Assessing Damages in Investment Treaty Arbitration' (2008) 25 *Journal of International Arbitration* 103.

Michael Abramowicz, 'En Bank Revisited' (2000) 100 *Columbia Law Review* 1600.

Bruce Ackerman, *Private Property and the Constitution* (New Haven, Yale University Press, 1977).

——, 'Beyond Carolene Products' (1985) 98 *Harvard Law Review* 713.

——, 1 *We the People. Foundations* (Cambridge, Mass, Belknap Press of Harvard University Press, 1991).

Guillermo Aguilar Alvarez and William W Park, 'The New Face of Investment Arbitration: NAFTA Chapter 11' (2003) 28 *Yale Journal of International Law* 365.

Robert B Ahdieh, 'Making Markets: Networks Effects and the Role of Law in the Creation of Strong Securities Markets' (2003) 76 *Southern California Law Review* 277.

Robert Alexy, *A Theory of Constitutional Rights* (New York, OUP, 2002).

Gregory S Alexander, *The Global Debate over Constitutional Property. Lessons from American Takings Jurisprudence* (Chicago, The University of Chicago Press, 2006).

Alan S Alexandroff (ed), *Investor Protection in the NAFTA and Beyond. Private Interest and Public Purpose* (CD Howe Institute, Toronto 2006).

Roger P Alford, 'The Proliferation of International Courts and Tribunals: International Adjudication in Ascendance' (2000) 94 *American Society of International Law Proceedings* 160.

Alejandro Alvarez, 'Latin American and International Law' (1909) 3 AJIL 269.

Alexander Alvarez, *Le Droit International Américain, Son Fondement—Sa Nature D'Après L'Histoire Diplomatique Des États du Nouveau Monde et Leur Vie Politique et Économique* (Paris, A Pedone, 1910).

Jose E Alvarez, 'Political Protectionism and United States Investment Obligations in Conflicts: The Hazards of Exon-Florio' (1989) 30 *Virginia Journal of International Law* 1.

——, 'Critical Theory and the North American Free Trade Agreement's Chapter Eleven' (1997) 28 *The University of Miami Inter-American Law Review* 303.

——, *International Organizations as Law Makers* (New York, OUP, 2005).

Joseph Alsop and Turner Catledge, *The 168 Days* (Doubleday, Doran, Garden City 1938).

Alfred C Aman Jr and William T Mayton, *Administrative Law*, 2nd edn (St Paul, MN, West Group, 2001).

Chittharanjan Felix Amerasinghe, 'State Breach of Contracts with Aliens and International Law' (1964) 58 *American Journal of International Law* 881.
——, *Local Remedies in International Law*, 2nd edn (New York, CUP, 2004).
American Law Institute, *Restatement of the Law, Second: Foreign Relations Law of the United States, as Adopted and Promulgated by the American Law Institute, May 26, 1962* (St Paul, MN, American Law Institute, 1965).
——, *Restatement of the Law (Third): The Foreign Relations Law of the United States* (St Paul, MN, American Law Institute Publishers, 1987).
Mads Andenas, 'An Introduction to the British Institute of International and Comparative Law's Investment Forum' in Federico Ortino et al (eds), *Investment Treaty Law: Current Issues I* (London, The British Institute of International and Comparative Law, 2006).
Mads Andena and Stefan Zleptnig, 'Proportionality: WTO Law: in Comparative Perspective' (2007) 42 *Texas International Law Journal* 371.
Gavin W Anderson, *Constitutional Rights after Globalization* (Portland, Hart Publishing, 2005).
Anglo-Chilean Tribunal of Arbitration, *Reclamaciones presentadas al Tribunal Anglo-Chileno* (Santiago de Chile, Imprenta i Libreria Ercilla, 1896).
Ricardo Anguita, *Leyes Promulgadas en Chile desde 1810 hasta el 1o de Junio de 1912* (Santiago de Chile, Imprenta Barcelona, 1912).
Barry Appleton, 'Regulatory Takings: The International Law Perspective' (2002) 11 *New York University Environmental Law Journal* 35.
Yutaka Arai-Takahashi, *The Margin of Appreciation Doctrine and the Principle of Proportionality in the Jurisprudence of the ECHR* (Antwerp, Intersentia, 2002).
Peter H Aranson et al, 'A Theory of Legislative Delegation' (1982) 68 *Cornell Law Review* 1.
Gaspar Ariño Ortiz, 'Derechos del Rey, Derechos del Pueblo' in *Actas del II Symposium Historia de la Administración* (Madrid, Instituto de Estudios Administrativos, 1971).
——, *El Nuevo Servicio Público* (Madrid, Marcial Pons, 1997).
Ian Ayres and John Braithwaite, *Responsive Regulation. Transcending the Deregulation Debate* (New York, OUP, 1992).
Douglas G Baird et al, *Game Theory and the Law* (Cambridge, Mass, Harvard University Press, 1994).
Leonard Baker, *Back to Back: The Duel Between FDR and the Supreme Court* (New York, Macmillan, 1967).
Jonathan B Baker, 'Market Definition: An Analytical Overview' (2007) 74 *Antitrust Law Journal* 129.
Christian von Bar and Ulrich Drobnig, *The Interaction of Contract Law and Tort and Property Law in Europe* (München, Sellier, 2004).
Javier Barnés, 'El Derecho de Propiedad en la Constitución Española de 1978' in Javier Barnés (ed), *Propiedad, Expropiación y Responsabilidad. Derecho Comparado Europeo* (Madrid, Tecnos, 1995).
William J Baumol and Thomas W Merrill, 'Deregulatory Takings, Breach of the Regulatory Contract, and the Telecommunications Act of 1996' (1997) 72 *New York University Law Review* 1037.
Richard R Baxter, 'Reflection on Codification in Light of the International Law of State Responsibility for Injuries to Aliens' (1965) 16 *Syracuse Law Review* 745.

Raj Bhala, 'Symposium: Global Trade Issues in the New Millenium: The Power of the Past: Towards de Jure Stare Decisis in WTO Adjudication (Part Three of a Trilogy)' (2001) 33 *George Washington International Law Review* 873.

Vicki Been and Joel C Beauvais, 'The Global Fifth Amendment? NAFTA's Investment Protections and the Misguided Quest for an International "Regulatory Takings" Doctrine' (2003) 78 *New York University Law Review* 30.

Abraham Bell and Gideon Parchomovsky, 'Givings' (2001) 111 *Yale Law Journal* 547.

John Bell, *French Constitutional Law* (Oxford, Clarendon Press, 1994).

Andrés Bello, *Principios de Derecho de Jentes*, 1st edn (Santiago de Chile, Imprenta de la Opinion, 1832).

——, *Principios de Derecho Internacional*, 2nd edn (JM De Rojas, Caracas 1844, printing of 1847).

Carlos Bernal Pulido, *El Principio de Proporcionalidad y los Derechos Fundamentales*, 2nd edn (Madrid, CEPC, 2005).

Raul Bertelsen et al, '*Informe en Derecho. Arbitrajes Internacionales por Inversiones Extranjeras en Chile*' in Roberto Mayorga and Luis Montt, *Inversión Extranjera en Chile. Marco Legal General Nacional e Internacional* (Santiago de Chile, Cono-Sur, 1993).

Americo Beviglia Zampetti and Pierre Sauvé, 'International Investment' in Andrew T Guzman and Alan O Sykes, *Research Handbook in International Economic Law* (Northampton, E Elgar, 2007).

Alexander Bickel, *The Least Dangerous Branch: The Supreme Court at the Bar of Politics* (Indianapolis, Bobbs-Merrill, 1962).

Doak Bishop, 'The Case for an Appellate Panel and Its Scope of Review' in Federico Ortino et al (eds), *Investment Treaty Law. Current Issues I* (London, The British Institute of International and Comparative Law, 2006).

Andrea K Bjorklund, 'Investment Treaty Arbitral Decisions as *Jurisprudence Constante*' in Colin B Picker et al (eds), *International Economic Law. The State and Future of the Discipline* (Portland, Hart Publishing, 2008).

Harold Blakemore, *British Nitrates and Chilean Politics 1886–1896* (London, Athlone Press for the Institute of Latin American Studies, 1974).

Lawrence Blume and Daniel L Rubinfeld, 'Compensation for Takings: An Economic Analysis' (1984) 72 *California Law Review* 569.

Lawrence Blume et al, 'The Taking of Land: When Should Compensation Be Paid?' (1984) 99 *Quarterly Journal of Economics* 71.

Armin von Bogdandy, 'Legitimacy of International Economic Governance: Interpretative Approaches to WTO law and the Prospects of its Proceduralization' in Stefan Griller (ed), *International Economic Governance and Non-Economic Concerns* (New York, Springer, 2003).

——, 'Globalization and Europe: How to Square Democracy, Globalization, and International Law' (2004) 15 *European Journal of International Law* 885.

Edwin M Borchard, *The Diplomatic Protection of Citizens Abroad; or, The Law of International Claims* (New York, The Banks Law Publishing, 1916).

——, 'Theoretical Aspects of the International Responsibility of States' (1929) 1 *Zeitschrift für ausländisches öffentliches Recht und Völkerrecht* 242.

——, ' "Responsibility of States", at the Hague Codification Conference' (1930) 24 *American Journal of International Law* 517.

Edwin M Borchard, 'The "Minimum Standard" of the Treatment of Aliens' (1939) 33 *American Society of International Law Proceedings* 51.

——, 'The "Minimum Standard" of Treatment of Aliens' (1940) 38 *Michigan Law Review* 445.

Roberto Bouzas and Daniel Chudnovsky, *Foreign Direct Investment and Sustainable Development. The Recent Argentine Experience*, Preliminary Version, 2004 (available at http://www.iisd.org/pdf/2004/investment_country_report_argentina.pdf).

Anthony W Bradley and John Bell, 'Governmental Liability: A Preliminary Assessment' in John Bell and Anthony W Bradley (eds), *Governmental Liability: A Comparative Study* (London, UKNCCL, 1991).

John Braithwaite, *Regulatory Capitalism. How it Works, Ideas for Making it Work Better* (Edward Elgar, Northampton 2008).

Stephen G Breyer, 'Judicial Review of Questions of Law and Policy' (1986) 38 *Administrative Law Review* 363.

——, *Active Liberty. Interpreting Our Democratic Constitution* (New York, Knopf Books, 2005).

—— et al, *Administrative Law and Regulatory Policy. Problems, Texts, and Cases*, 4th edn (New York, Aspen Law and Business, 1998).

Lea Brilmayer and Jack Goldsmith, *Conflict of Laws: Cases and Materials*, 5th edn (New York, Aspen Law and Business, 2002).

Bob Brouwer and PW Brouwer (eds), *Coherence and Conflict in Law: Proceedings of the 3rd Benelux-Scandinavian Symposium in Legal Theory, Amsterdam, January 3–5, 1991* (Boston, Kluwer Law and Taxation Publishers, 1992).

Charles N Brower and John B Tepe Jr, 'The Charter of Economic Rights and Duties of States: A Reflection or Rejection of International Law?' (1975) 9 *International Lawyer* 295.

Charles H Brower, II, 'Fair and Equitable Treatment Under NAFTA's Investment Chapter' (2002) 96 *American Society of International Law Proceedings* 9.

——, 'Structure, Legitimacy, and NAFTA's Investment Chapter' (2003) 36 *Vanderbilt Journal of Transnational Law* 37.

Chester Brown, *A Common Law of International Adjudication* (New York, OUP, 2007).

L Neville Brown and John S Bell, *French Administrative Law*, 5th edn (Oxford, Clarendon Press, 1998).

Ian Brownlie, 'Legal Status of Natural Resources in International Law (Some Aspects)' in Académie de Droit International, 162 *Recueil des Cours. Collected Courses of the Hague Acadamy of International Law* (Alphen aan den Rijn, Sijthoff and Noordhoff, 1980) 255.

——, *Principles of Public International Law*, 6th edn (New York, OUP, 2003).

James J Brudney and Corey Dtslear, 'Canons of Construction and the Elusive Quest for Neutral Reasoning' (2005) 58 *Vanderbilt Law Review* 1.

Ryan Bubb and Susan Rose-Ackerman, 'BITs and Bargains: Strategic Aspects of Bilateral and Multilateral Regulation of Foreign Investment' (2007) 27 *International Review of Law and Economics* 291.

James M Buchanan and Gordon Tullock, *The Calculus of Consent* (Ann Arbor, Michigan University Press, 1965).

Gráinne de Búrca and Joanne Scott, 'The Impact of the WTO on EU Decision-Making' in Gráinne de Búrca and Joanne Scott (eds), *The EU and the WTO. Legal and Constitutional Issues* (Portland, Hart Publishing, 2001).

Tim Büthe and Helen V Milner, *The Politics of Foreign Direct Investment into Developing Countries: Increasing FDI through Policy Commitment via Trade Agreements and Investment Treaties?*, Draft (available at http://nathanjensen.wustl.edu/me/files/ButheMilner.pdf).

Guido Calabresi and Douglas Melamed, 'Property Rules, Liability Rules and Inalienability: One View of the Cathedral' (1972) 85 *Harvard Law Review* 1089.

Carlos Calvo, *Derecho Internacional Teorico y Practico de Europa y America*, 1st edn (Paris, D'Amyot, 1869).

Carlos Calvo, *Le Droit International Théorique et Pratique; Précédé d'un Exposé Historique Des Progrès de la Science du Droit des Gens*, 5th edn (Paris, Arthur Rousseau, 1896).

Giacinto de la Cananea, 'Beyond the State: the Europeanization and Globalization of Procedural Administrative Law' (2003) 9 *European Public Law* 563.

Peter Cane, *Introduction to Administrative Law*, 3rd edn (New York, OUP, 1996).

——, *Responsibility in Law and Morality* (Oxford, Hart Publishing, 2002).

Roberto Caranta, 'Public Law Illegality and Governmental Liability' in Duncan Fairgrieve et al (eds), *Tort Liability of Public Authorities in Comparative Perspective* (London, The British Institute of International and Comparative Law, 2002).

A James Casner et al, *Cases and Text on Property*, 5th edn (New York, Aspen Publishers, 2004).

Deborah Z Cass, 'The 'Constitutionalization' of International Trade Law: Judicial Norm-Generation as the Engine of Constitutional Development in International Trade' (2001) 12 *European Journal of International Law* 39.

——, *The Constitutionalization of the World Trade Organization. Legitimacy, Democracy, and Community in the International Trading System* (New York, OUP, 2005).

Sabino Cassese, 'Global Standards for National Administrative Procedure' (2005) 68 *Law and Contemporary Problems* 109.

René Chapus, *Droit Administratif Général*, 15th edn (Paris, Montchrestien, 2001).

Jonathan I Charney, 'Is international law threatened by multiple international tribunals?' in Académie de Droit International, 271 *Recueil des Cours. Collected Courses of the Hague Academy of International Law, 1998* (The Hague, M Nijhoff, 1999) 101.

——, 'The Impact on the International Legal System of the Growth of International Courts and Tribunals' (1999) 31 *New York University Journal of International Law and Politics* 697.

Bin Cheng, *General Principles of Law: As Applied by International Courts and Tribunals* (Cambridge, Grotius Publications, 1987).

Tai Heng Cheng, 'Power, Authority, and International Investment Law' (2005) 20 *American University International Law Review* 465.

——, 'Precedent and Control in Investment Treaty Arbitration' (2007) 30 *Fordham International Law Journal* 1014.

Barnali Choudhury, 'Evolution or Devolution? Defining Fair and Equitable Treatment in International Investment Law' (2005) 6 *Journal of World Investment and Trade* 297.

GC Christie, 'What Constitutes a Taking of Property Under International Law?' (1962) 38 British Ybk Intl Law 307.

Adrian TL Chua, 'Precedent and Principles of WTO Panel Jurisprudence' (1998) 16 *Berkeley Journal of International Law* 171.

Amy L Chua, 'The Privatization–Nationalization Cycle: The Link Between Markets and Ethnicity in Developing Countries' (1995) 95 *Columbia Law Review* 223.

Jack J Coe Jr, 'Taking Stock of NAFTA Chapter 11 in Its Tenth Year: An Interim Sketch of Selected Themes, Issues, and Methods' (2003) 36 *Vanderbilt Journal of Transnational Law* 1381.

—— and Noah Rubins, 'Regulatory Expropriations and the TECMED Case: Context and Contributions' in Todd Weiler (ed), *International Investment Law and Arbitration: Leading Cases from the ICSID, NAFTA, Bilateral Investment Treaties and Customary International Law* (London, Cameron May, 2005).

Jules Coleman, *Risks and Wrongs* (New York, OUP, 1993).

——, *The Practice of Principle. In Defence of a Pragmatic Approach to Legal Theory* (New York, OUP, 2001).

Paul E Comeaux and Stephen Kinsella, 'Reducing Political Risk in Developing Countries: Bilateral Investment Treaties, Stabilization Clauses, and MIGA and OPIC Investment Insurances' (1994) 15 *New York Law School Journal of International and Comparative Law* 1.

John G Collier and Vaugham Lowe, *The Settlement of Disputes in International Law. Institutions and Procedures* (New York, OUP, 1999).

Jeffrey P Commission, 'Precedent in Investment Treaty Arbitration' (2006) 24 *Journal of International Arbitration* 129.

Thomas Cottier and Maya Hertig, 'The Prospects of 21st Century Constitutionalism' (2003) 7 *Max Planck Yearbook of United Nations Law* 261.

Paul P Craig, 'Compensation in Public Law' (1980) 96 *Law Quarterly Review* 413.

——, 'Legitimate Expectations: A Conceptual Analysis' (1992) 108 *The Law Quarterly Review* 97.

——, 'Substantive Legitimate Expectations in Domestic and Community Law' (1996) 55 CLJ 289.

——, 'Report on the United Kingdom' in Anne-Marie Slaughter et al (eds), *The European Court and National Courts, Doctrine and Jurisprudence: Legal Change in its Social Context* (Oxford, Hart Publishing, 1998).

——, *Administrative Law*, 5th edn (London, Sweet & Maxwell, 2003).

—— and Gráinne de Búrca, *EC Law. Text, Cases, and Materials* (New York, OUP, 1995).

James Crawford (ed), *The International Law Commission's Articles on State Responsibility: Introduction, Text, and Commentaries* (New York, CUP, 2002).

——, 'Treaty and Contract in Investment Arbitration', available at http://www.lcil.cam.ac.uk/Media/lectures/pdf/Freshfields%20Lecture%202007.pdf).

Bernardo Cremades, 'Disputes Arising Out of Foreign Direct Investment in Latin America: A New Look at the Calvo Doctrine and Other Jurisdictional Issues' (2004) 59 *Dispute Resolution Journal* 78.

Steven P Croley, *Regulation and the Public Interest: The Possibility of Good Regulatory Government* (Princeton, Princeton University Press, 2008).

—— and John H Jackson, 'WTO Disputes Procedures, Standards of Review, and Deference to National Governments' (1996) 90 *American Journal of International Law* 193.

John Crook, 'The 2002 Judicial Activity of the International Court of Justice' (2003) 97 *American Journal of International Law* 352.

Miguel Cruchaga Tocornal, *Nociones de Derecho International*, 3rd edn (Madrid, Reus, 1923).

Hanoch Dagan, 'Takings and Distributive Justice' (1999) 85 *Virginia Law Review* 741.

Robert A Dahl, 'Can International Organizations Be Democratic? A Skeptic's View' in Ian Shapiro and Casiano Hacker-Cordón (eds), *Democracy's Edges* (New York, CUP, 1999).

David A Dana and Thomas W Merrill, *Property: Takings* (New York, Foundation Press, 2002).

Ronald J Daniels, 'Defecting on Development: Bilateral Investment Treaties and the Subversion of the Rule of Law in the Developing World' (Draft) (available at www.unisi.it/lawandeconomics/stile2004/daniels.pdf).

Paul A David, *Path Dependence and the Quest for Historical Economics: One More Chorus of the Ballad of Qwerty*, University of Oxford, Discussion Papers in Economic and Social History No 20, November 1997 (available at http://www.nuffield.ox.ac.uk/economics/history/paper20/david3.pdf).

——, *Path Dependence, Its Critics and the Quest for 'Historical Economics'* (available at http://129.3.20.41/eps/eh/papers/0502/0502003.pdf).

——, 'Clio and the Economics of QWERTY' (1985) 75 *American Economic Review* 332.

Nestor M Davidson, 'The Problem of Equality in Takings' (2008) 102 *Northwestern University Law Review* 1.

Frank Griffith Dawson, 'International Law, National Tribunals and the Rights of Aliens: The Latin American experience' (1968) 21 *Vanderbilt Law Review* 712.

——, 'The Influence of Andres Bello on Latin-American perceptions of the non-intervention and State Responsibility' (1987) 57 British Ybk Intl Law 253.

—— and Ivan L Head, *International Law, National Tribunals, and the Rights of Aliens* (Syracuse University Press, Syracuse 1971).

JG de Beus, *The Jurisprudence of the General Claims Commission United States and Mexico Under The Convention of September 8, 1923* ('S-Gravenhage, M Nijhoff, 1938).

Brunno de Witte, 'Direct Effect, Supremacy, and the Nature of the Legal Order' in Paul Craig and Gráinne de Búrca (eds), *The Evolution of EU Law* (New York, OUP, 1999).

Eileen Denza and Shelagh Brooks, 'Investment Protection Treaties: United Kingdom Experience' (1987) 36 ICLQ 908.

Yoram Dinstein, 'Deprivation of Property of Foreigners under International Law' Nisuke Ando et al (eds), 2 *Liber Amicorum Judge Shigeru Oda* (New York, Kluwer Law International, 2002).

Colin S Diver, 'The Optimal Precision of Administrative Rules (1983) 93 *Yale Law Journal* 65.

Avinash Dixit and Barry Nalebuff, *Thinking Strategically* (New York, Norton, 1991).

Rudolf Dolzer, 'New Foundations of the Law of expropriation of Alien Property' (1981) 75 AJIL 553.

——, 'Indirect Expropriation of Alien Property' (1986) 1 *ICSID Review—Foreign Investment Law Journal* 41.

——, 'Indirect Expropriations: New Developments?' (2002) 11 *New York University Environmental Law Journal* 64.

——, 'The Notion of Investment in Recent Practice' in Steve Charnovitz et al (eds), *Law in the Service of Human Dignity. Essays in Honour of Florentino Feliciano* (New York, CUP, 2005).

Rudolf Dolzer, 'Fair and Equitable Treatment: A Key Standard in Investment Treaties' (2005) 39 *International Lawyer* 87.

——, 'The Impact of International Investment Treaties on Domestic Administrative Law' (2005) 37 *New York University Journal of International Law and Politics* 953.

——, 'Comment' in Federico Ortino et al (eds) *Investment Treaty Law. Current Issues II: Nationality and Investment Treaty Claims. Fair and Equitable Treatment in Investment Treaty Law* (London, The British Institute of International and Comparative Law, 2007).

—— and Christoph Schreuer, *Principles of International Investment Law* (New York, OUP, 2008).

—— and Margrete Stevens, *Bilateral Investment Treaties* (Boston, M Nijhoff, 1995).

—— and André von Walter, 'Fair and Equitable Treatment—Lines of Jurisprudence on Customary Law' in Federico Ortino et al (eds) *Investment Treaty Law. Current Issues II: Nationality and Investment Treaty Claims. Fair and Equitable Treatment in Investment Treaty Law* (London, The British Institute of International and Comparative Law, 2007).

Zachary Douglas, 'The Hybrid Foundation of Investment Treaty Arbitration' (2004) 74 British Ybk Intl Law 151.

——, 'Nothing If Not Critical for Investment Treaty Arbitration: *Occidental, Eureko* and *Methanex*' (2006) 22 *International Arbitration* 27.

Luis M Drago, 'State Loans in their Relation to International Policy' (1907) 1 *American Journal of International Law* 692.

Frederick Sherwood Dunn, 'International Law and Private Property Rights' (1928) 28 *Columbia Law Review* 166.

——, *The Diplomatic Protection of Americans in Mexico* (New York, Columbia University Press, 1933).

Pierre Duprey, 'Do Arbitral Awards Constitute Precedents? Should Commercial Arbitration Be Distinguished from Arbitration Based on Investment Treaties' in Emmanuel Gaillard (ed), *Towards a Uniform International Arbitration Law?* (Huntington, Juris Publishing, 2005).

David Dysenhaus, *Legality and Legitimacy. Carl Schmitt, Hans Kelsen and Herman Heller in Weimer* (New York, OUP, 1997).

Ronald M Dworkin, 'Rights as Trumps' in Jeremy Waldron (ed), *Theories of Rights* (New York, OUP, 1984).

——, *Law's Empire* (Cambridge, Mass, The Belknap Press of Harvard University Press, 1986).

Steven J Eagle, 'Property Tests, Due Process Tests, and Regulatory Takings Jurisprudence' (2007) 87 *Brigham Young University Law Review* 899.

Clyde Eagleton, *The Responsibility of States in International Law* (New York, New York University Press, 1928).

Christopher F Edley, *Administrative Law. Rethinking Judicial Control of Bureaucracy* (New Haven, Yale University Press, 1990).

Peter Egger and Micheal Pfaffermayr, 'The Impact of Bilateral Investment Treaties on Foreign Direct Investment' (2004) 32 *Journal of Comparative Economics* 788.

Marc-André Eissen, 'The principle of proportionality in the case-law of the European Court of Human Rights' in R St. J Macdonald, F Matscher and H Petzold (eds), *The European System for the Protection of Human Rights* (Boston, M Nijhoff, 1993).

Zachary Elkins, Andrew T Guzman and Beth Simmons, 'Competing for Capital: The Diffusion of Bilateral Investment Treaties, 1960–2000' (2006) 60 *International Organization* 811.

John Hart Ely, *Democracy and Distrust: A Theory of Judicial Review* (Cambridge, Mass, Harvard University Press, 1980).

Richard A Epstein, *Takings: Private Property and the Power of Eminent Domain* (Cambridge, Mass, Harvard University Press, 1985).

——, *Supreme Neglect. How to Revive Constitutional Protection for Private Property* (New York, OUP, 2008).

William N Eskridge, Jr and Kevin S Schwartz, '*Chevron* and Agency Norm-Entrepreneurship' (2006) 115 *Yale Law Journal* 2623.

Daniel C Esty, 'Good Governance at the Supranational Scale: Globalizing Administrative Law' (2006) 115 *Yale Law Journal* 1490.

Ulrich Everling, 'The Court of Justice as a Decisionmaking Authority' (1984) 82 *Michigan Law Review* 1294.

Duncan Fairgrieve, *State Liability in Tort. A Comparative Law Study* (New York, OUP, 2003).

Alireza Falsafi, 'The International Minimum Standard of Treatment of Foreign Investor's Property: A Contingent Standard' (2007) 30 *Suffolk Transnational Law Review* 317.

Daniel A Farber, 'Rights as Signals' (2002) 31 *Journal of Legal Studies* 83.

—— and Philip P Frickey, 'Jurisprudence of Public Choice' (1987) 65 *Texas Law Review* 873.

Alexander P Farichi, 'International Law and the Property of Aliens' (1929) 10 British Ybk Intl Law 32.

E Allan Farnsworth, *Contracts*, 4th edn (New York, Aspen Publishers, 2004).

Joseph Farrell and Garth Saloner, 'Standardization, Compatibility, and Innovation' (1985) 16 *RAND Journal of Economics* 70.

Louis Favoreau and Loïc Philip, *Les grandes décisions du Conseil constitutionnel*, 7th edn (Paris, Sirey, 1993).

JES Fawcett, 'The Exhaustion of Local Remedies: Substance or Procedure?' (1954) 31 British Ybk Intl Law 452.

Niall Ferguson, 'Sinking Globalization' (2005) 84(2) *Foreign Affairs* 64.

Stephen Fietta, 'Expropriation and the 'Fair and Equitable Treatment' Standard: The Developing Role of Investors' Expectations' (2006) 23 *Journal of International Arbitration* 375.

William A Fischel, 'Introduction: Utilitarian Balancing and Formalism in Takings' (1988) 88 *Columbia Law Review* 1581.

——, *Regulatory Takings: Law, Economics and Politics* (Cambridge, Mass, Harvard University Press, 1995).

—— and Perry Shapiro, 'Takings, Insurance, and Michelman: Comments on Economic Interpretations of 'Just Compensation' Law' (1988) 17 *Journal of Legal Studies* 269.

John Fischer Williams, 'International Law and the Property of Aliens' (1928) 9 British Ybk Intl Law 1.

GG Fitzmaurice, 'The Meaning of the Term 'Denial of Justice'' (1932) 13 British Ybk Intl Law 93.

Gunnar Folke Schuppert, 'The Right of Property' in Ulrich Karpen (ed), *The Constitution of the Federal Republic of Germany* (Baden-Baden, Nomos Verlagsgesellschaft, 1988).

L Yves Fortier and Stephen L Drymer, 'Indirect Expropriation in the Law of International Investment: I Know It When I See It, or Caveat Investor' (2004) 19 *ICSID Review–Foreign Investment Law Journal* 293.

Susan D Franck, 'The Legitimacy Crisis in Investment Treaty Arbitration: Privatizing Public International Law through Inconsistent Decisions' (2005) 73 *Fordham Law Review* 1521.

Thomas M Franck, *Fairness in International Law* (New York, OUP, 1995).

——, 'Can the United States Delegate Aspect of Sovereignty to International Regimes' in Thomas Franck (ed), *Delegating State Powers: The Effect of Treaty Regimes on Democracy and Sovereignty* (Ardsley, Transnational Publishers, 2000).

Alwyn V Freeman, *The International Responsibility of States for Denial of Justice* (New York, Longmans, Green and Co, 1938).

——, 'Recent Aspects of the Calvo Doctrine and the Challenge to International Law' (1946) 40 AJIL 121.

——, 'Responsibility of states for unlawful acts of their armed forces' in Académie de Droit International, 88 *Recueil des Cours—1955 II* (Leyde, AW Sijthoff, 1956) 263.

Lawrence M Friedman, 'Frontiers: National and Transnational Order' in Karl-Heinz Ladeur (ed), *Public Governance in the Age of Globalization* (Burlington, Ashgate, 2004).

Richard D Friedman, 'Switching Time and Other Thought Experiments: The Hughes Court and Constitutional Transformation' (1994) 142 *University of Pennsylvania Law Review* 1891.

William Funk, 'Rationality Review of State Administrative Rulemaking' (1991) 43 *Administrative Law Review* 147.

Greta Gainer, 'Nationalization: The Dichotomy Between the Western and Third World Perspectives in International Law' (1983) 26 *Howard Law Journal* 1547.

DJ Galligan, *Judicial Review and the Textbook Writers* (1976) 2 *Oxford Journal of Legal Studies* 257.

DJ Galligan, *Discretionary Powers: A Legal Study of Official Discretion* (New York, OUP, 1986).

Pamela B Gann, 'The US Bilateral Investment Treaty Program' (1985) 21 *Stanford Journal of International Law* 373.

Carlos G Garcia, 'All the Other Dirty Little Secrets: Investment Treaties, Latin America, and the Necessary Evil of Investor-State Arbitration' (2004) 16 *Florida Journal of International Law* 301.

Eduardo García de Enterría, *La lucha contra las inmunidades de poder en el derecho administrativo: poderes discrecionales, poderes de gobierno, poderes normativos*, 3rd edn (Madrid, Civitas, 2004).

——, *La Responsabilidad Patrimonial del Estado Legislador* (Madrid, Civitas, 2005).

—— and Tomás-Ramón Fernández, 1 *Curso de Derecho Administrativo*, 12th edn (Madrid, Civitas, 2004).

FV García-Amador, 'Draft articles on the responsibility of the State for injuries caused in its territory to the person or property of aliens' in FV García Amador, Lous B Sohn and RR Baxter, *Recent Codification of the Law of State Responsibility for Injuries to Aliens* (Dobbs Ferry, NY, Oceana Publications, 1974).

——, 1 *The Inter-American System. Treaties, Conventions and Other Documents* (New York, Oceana, 1983).

——, 1 *The Changing Law of International Claims* (New York, Oceana Publications, 1984).

——, *El Derecho Internacional del Desarrollo. Una Nueva Dimensión del Derecho Internacional Económico* (Madrid, Civitas, 1987).

——, 'Calvo Doctrine, Calvo Clause' in Rudolph Bernhardt (ed), 2 *Encyclopedia of Public International Law* (New York, North-Holland, 1992).

Javier García Luengo, *El Principio de la Protección de la Confianza Legítima en el Derecho Administrativo* (Madrid, Civitas, 2002).

Richard K Gardiner, *Treaty Interpretation* (New York, OUP, 2008).

Oscar M Garibaldi, *Carlos Calvo Redivivus:* 'The Rediscovery of the Calvo Doctrine in the Era of Investment Treaties', 3(5) *Transnational Dispute Management* 4 (2006).

Rainer Geiger, 'Regulatory Expropriations in International Law: Lessons from the Multilateral Agreement on Investment' (2002) 11 *New York University Environmental Law Journal* 94.

——, 'The Multifaceted Nature of International Investment Law' in Karl Sauvant (ed), *Appeals Mechanisms in International Investment Law* (New York, OUP, 2008).

George Gerapetritis, *Proportionality in Administrative Law: Judicial Review in France, Greece, England and in the European Community* (Sakkoulas, Athens 1997).

Andrea Giardina, 'International Investment Arbitration: Recent Developments as to the Applicable Law and Unilateral Recourse' (2006) 5 *The Law and Practice of International Courts and Tribunals* 29.

Antony Giddens, *Runaway World. How Globalisation is Reshaping Our Lives* (London, Profile, 2000).

Judith Gill, 'Inconsistent Decisions: An Issue to Be Addressed or a Fact of Life?' in Federico Ortino et al (eds), *Investment Treaty Law. Current Issues I* (London, The British Institute of International and Comparative Law, 2006).

Tom Ginsburg, 'International Substitutes for Domestic Institutions: Bilateral Investment Treaties and Governance' (2005) *International Review of Law and Economics* 107.

Julius Goebel Jr, 'The International Responsibility of States for Injuries Sustained by Aliens on Account of Mob Violence, Insurrections, and Civil Wars' (1914) 8 AJIL 802.

Richard Goldsmith, 'Utility Rates and 'Takings'? (1989) 10 *Energy Law Journal* 241.

Mario Góngora, *Ensayo Histórico sobre la Noción de Estado en Chile en los Siglos XIX y XX* (Santiago de Chile, Editorial Universitaria, 1986).

Richard Gordon QC, *EC Law in Judicial Review* (New York, OUP, 2007).

Eberhard Grabitz, 'Liability for Legislative Acts' in Henry G Schermers, Ton Heukels and Philip Mead (eds), *Non-Contractual Liability of the European Communities* (Boston, M Nijhoff, 1988).

Jörn Griebel, 'Jurisdiction over 'Contract Claims' in Treaty-Based Investment Arbitration on the Basis of Wide Dispute Settlement Clauses in Investment Agreements' 4(5) *Transnational Dispute Management* (September 2007).

Horacio A Grigera Naón, 'Arbitration in Latin America: Progress and Setbacks' (2005) 21 *Arbitration International* 127.

David Singh Grewal, 'Network Power and Global Standardization: The Controversy Over the Multilateral Agreement on Investment' (2005) 36 *Metaphilosophy* 128.

Robert E Grosse, *Multinationals in Latin America* (New York, Routledge, 1989).

K Scott Gudgeon, 'Arbitration Provisions of US Bilateral Investment Treaties' (1985) 20 *Studies in Transnational Legal Policy* 41.

——, 'United States Bilateral Investment Treaties: Comments on their Origin, Purposes, and General Treatment Standards' (1986) 4 *International Tax and Business Law* 105.

Andrew T Guzman, 'Why LDCs Sign Treaties That Hurt Them: Explaining the Popularity of Bilateral Investment Treaties' (1998) 38 *Virginia Journal of International Law* 639.

Guy Haarscher, 'Some Contemporary Trends in Continental Philosophy of Law' in Martin Golding and William A Edmundson (eds), *The Blackwell Guide to the Philosophy of Law and Legal Theory* (Malden, Blackwell, 2005).

Jürgen Habermas, *Between Facts and Norms* (Cambridge, Mass, MIT Press, 1996).

Green H Hackworth, 'Responsibility of States for Damages Caused in Their Territory to the Person or Property of Foreigners. The Hague Conference for the Codification of International Law' (1930) 24 AJIL 500.

——, *Digest of International Law* (US Government Printing Office, Washington 1940).

Andrea Hamann and Hélène Ruiz Fabri, 'Transnational Networks and Constitutionalism' (2008) 6 *International Journal of Constitutional Law* 481.

Veijo Heiskanen, 'Arbitrary and Unreasonable Measures' in August Reinisch, *Standards of Investment Protection* (New York, OUP, 2008).

Calvin A Hamilton and Paula I Rochwerger, 'Trade and Investment: Foreign Direct Investment Through Bilateral and Multilateral Treaties' (2005) 18 *New York International Law Review* 1.

Carol Harlow, 'Francovich and the Problem of the Disobedient State' (1996) 2 *European Law Journal* 199.

——, *State Liability. Tort Law and Beyond* (New York, OUP, 2004).

——, 'Global Administrative Law: The Quest for Principles and Values' (2006) 17 *European Journal of International Law* 187.

HLA Hart, *Concept of Law*, 1st edn (Oxford, Clarendon Press, 1961).

Trevor C Hartley, *European Union Law in a Global Context* (New York, CUP, 2004).

Harvard Law School (Research in International Law Series), *The Law of Responsibility of States for Damage Done in Their Territory to the Person or Property of Foreigners* (Cambridge, Mass, Harvard Law School, 1929).

——, *Nationality; responsibility of states; territorial waters. Drafts of conventions prepared in anticipation of the First Conference on the Codification of International Law* (Cambridge, Mass, Harvard Law School, 1930).

Peter Hay et al, *Conflict of Laws: Cases and Materials*, 11th edn (New York, Foundation Press, 2000).

Edward T Hayes, 'Changing Notion of Sovereignty and Federalism in the International Economic System: A Reassessment of WTO Regulation of Federal States and the Regional and Local Governments Within their Territories' (2004) 25 *Northwestern Journal of International Law and Business* 1.

David Held, 'The Transformation of Political Community: Rethinking Democracy in the Context of Globalization' in Ian Shapiro and Casiano Hacker-Cordón (eds), *Democracy's Edges* (New York, CUP, 1999).

Laurence R Helfer, 'Constitutional Analogies in the International Legal System' (2003) 37 *Loyola Los Angeles Law Review* 193.

Laurence R Helfer and Anne-Marie Slaughter, 'Toward a Theory of Effective Supranational Adjudication' (1997) 107 *Yale Law Journal* 273.

—— and Graeme B Dinwoodie, 'Designing Non-National Systems: The Case of the Uniform Domain Name Dispute Resolution Policy' (2001) 43 *William and Mary Law Review* 141.

Amos S Hershey, 'The Calvo and Drago Doctrines' (1907) 1 AJIL 26.

A Pearce Higgins, *The Hague Peace Conferences and Other International Conferences Concerning the Laws and Usages of War* (Cambridge, CUP, 1909).

Rosalyn Higgins, 'The Taking of Property by the State. Recent Developments in International Law' in Académie de Droit International, 176 *Recueil des Cours. Collected Courses of the Hague Academy of International Law, 1982-III* (The Hague, M Nijhoff, 1983) 259.

Albert O Hirschman, *Exit, Voice, and Loyalty. Responses to Decline in Firms, Organizations, and States* (Cambridge, Mass, Harvard University Press, 1970).

Paul Hirst and Grahame Thompson, 'Globalization and the Future of the Nation State' (1995) 24 *Economy and Society* 408.

Kaj Hobér, *Investment Arbitration in Eastern Europe. In Search of a Definition of Expropriation* (Huntington, JurisNet, 2007).

Herbert Hovenkamp, 'The Takings Clause and Improving Regulatory Bargains' (1999) 108 *Yale Law Journal* 801.

Jon Hovi, *Games, Threats and Treaties. Understanding Commitments in International Relations* (Washington, Pinter, 1998).

Robert Howse, 'The Most Dangerous Branch? WTO Appellate Body Jurisprudence on the Nature and Limits of the Judicial Power' in Thomas Cottier and Petros C Mavroidis (eds), *The Role of the Judge in International Trade Regulation. Experiences and Lessons for the WTO* (Ann Arbor, University of Michigan Press, 2003).

—— and Kalypso Nicolaidis, 'Legitimacy through 'Higher Law'? Why Constitutionalizing the WTO is a Step Too Far' in Thomas Cottier and Petros C Mavroidis (eds), *The Role of the Judge in International Trade Regulation. Experiences and Lessons for the WTO* (Ann Arbor, University of Michigan Press, 2003).

Charles Cheney Hyde, *International law: Chiefly as Interpreted and Applied by the United States* (Boston, Little, Brown, 1922).

International Law Commission, Study Group, *Fragmentation of International Law: Difficulties Arising from the Diversification and Expansion of International Law*, UN Doc A/CN.4/L.682, 13 April 2006.

John H Jackson, 'The Great 1994 Debate: United States Acceptance and Implementation of the Uruguay Round Results' (1997) 36 *Columbia Journal of Transnational Law* 157.

John J Jackson, 'Sovereignty-Modern: A New Approach to an Outdated Concept' (2003) 97 AJIL 782.

Subhash C Jain, *Nationalization of Foreign Property: A Study in North–South Dialogue* (New Delhi, Deep and Deep, 1983).

Ivan Jaksić, *Andrés Bello: Scholarship And Nation-Building in Nineteenth-Century Latin America* (New York, CUP, 2001).

——, *Andrés Bello: La Pasión Por el Orden* (Santiago de Chile, Editorial Universitaria, 2001).

Harold James, *The End of Globalization: Lessons From the Great Depression* (Cambridge, Mass, Harvard University Press, 2002).
C Wilfred Jenks, 'The Interpretation and Application of Municipal Law by the Permanent Court of International Justice', (1938) 19 British Ybk Intl Law 67 .
——, *The Prospects of International Adjudication* (Dobbs Ferry, NY, Oceana Publications, 1964).
RY Jennings, 'State Contracts in International Law' (1961) 37 British Ybk Intl Law 156.
Eduardo Jiménez de Aréchaga, 'State Responsibility for the Nationalization of Foreign Owned Property' (1978) 11 *New York University Journal of International Law and Politics* 179.
Emilio Jofré, *Boletín de Leyes y Decretos sobre Ferrocarriles dictados por la República de Chile desde 1848 hasta 1890* (Santiago de Chile, Imprenta 'Santiago', 1891).
Jacint Jordana and David Levi-Faur (eds), *The Politics of Regulation: Institutions and Regulatory Reform for the Age of Governance* (Edward Elgar, Northampton 2004).
Paul L Joskow and Roger C Noll, 'Regulation in Theory and Practice: An Overview' in Gary Fromm (ed), *Studies in Public Regulation* (Cambridge, MIT Press, 1981).
CN Kakouris, 'Use of the Comparative Method by the Court of Justice of the European Communities' (1994) 6 *Pace International Law Review* 267.
Johanna Kalb, 'Creating an ICSID Appellate Body' (2005) 10 *UCLA Journal of International Law and Foreign Affairs* 179.
Mark Kantor, 'Fair and Equitable Treatment: Echoes of FDR's Court-Packing Plan in the International Law Approach Towards Regulatory Expropriation' (2006) 5 *The Law and Practice of International Courts and Tribunals* 231.
Louis Kaplow, 'An Economic Analysis of Legal Transitions' (1986) 99 *Harvard Law Review* 509.
——, 'Rules versus Standards: An Economic Analysis' (1992) 42 *Duke Law Journal* 557.
Joachim Karl, 'International Investment Arbitration: A Threat to State Sovereignty' in Wenhua Shan et al (eds), *Redefining Sovereignty in International Economic Law* (Portland, Hart Publishing, 2008).
Michael Katz and Carl Shapiro, 'Network Externalities, Competition and Compatibility' (1985) 75 *American Economic Review* 424.
——, 'System Competition and Network Effects' (1994) 8 *Journal of Economic Perspectives* 93.
Helen Keller and Alec Stone Sweet, *A Europe of Rights. The Impact of the ECHR on National Legal Systems* (New York, OUP, 2008).
Robert O Keohane, 'Governance in a Partially Globalized World. Presidential Address, American Political Science Association, 2000' (2001) 95 *American Political Science Review* 1.
Theodore Kill, 'Don't Cross the Streams: Past and Present Overstatement of Customary International Law in Connection with Conventional Fair and Equitable Treatment Obligations', 106 *Michigan Law Review* 853 (2008).
Otto Kimminich, 'Property Rights' in Christian Starck, 'Constitutional Definition and Protection of Rights and Freedoms' in Christian Starck (ed), *Rights, Institutions and Impact of International Law according to the German Basic Law* (Baden-Baden, Nomos Verlagsgesellschaft, 1987).

——, '*La propiedad en la Constitución Alemana*' in Javier Barnés (ed), *Propiedad, Expropiación y Responsabilidad. Derecho Comparado Europeo* (Madrid, Tecnos, 1995).

Benedict Kingsbury, Nico Krisch and Richard B Stewart, 'The Emergence of Global Administrative Law' (2005) 68 *Law and Contemporary Problems* 15.

Meg Kinnear, 'Treaties as Agreements to Arbitrate: International Law as the Governing Law' in Albert van den Berg (ed), *International Arbitration 2006: Back to Basis?* (Alphen aan den Rijn, Kluwer Law International, 2007).

Michael Klausner, 'Corporations, Corporate Law, and Network of Contracts' (1995) 81 *Virginia Law Review* 757.

Marcela Klein Bronfman, 'Fair and Equitable Treatment: An Evolving Standard' (2006) 10 *Max Planck Yearbook of United Nations Law* 609.

Stephen J Kobrin, 'Foreign Enterprise and Forced Divestments in LCDs' (1980) 34 *International Organization* 65.

Harold H Koh, 'Review Essay: Why Do Nations Obey International Law?' (1997) 106 *Yale Law Journal* 2599.

Donald P Kommers, *The Constitutional Jurisprudence of the Federal Republic of Germany*, 2nd edn (Durham, NC, Duke University Press, 1997).

Thijmen Koopsman, 'The Birth of European Law at the Crossroads of Legal Traditions' (1991) 39 *American Journal of Comparative Law* 493.

RH Kreindler, 'Fair and Equitable Treatment—A Comparative International Law Approach' in 3(3) *Transnational Dispute Management* (June 2006).

——, 'The Law Applicable to International Investment Disputes' in Norbert Horn and Stefan Kröll (eds), *Arbitrating Foreign Investment Disputes* (The Hague, Kluwer Law International, 2004).

David M Kreps, 'Intrinsic Motivation and Extrinsic Incentives' (1997) 87(2) *American Economic Review* 359.

Ursula Kriebaum, 'Partial Expropriation' (2007) 8 *Journal of World Investment and Trade* 69.

Nico Krisch and Benedict Kingsbury, 'Introduction: Global Governance and Global Administrative Law in the International Legal Order' (2006) 17 *European Journal of International Law* 1.

Detlef Kröger, 'La Propiedad Privada como Derecho Fundamental de la Unión Europea', en Javier Barnés, *Propiedad, Expropiación y Responsabilidad. Derecho Comparado Europeo* (Madrid, Tecnos, 1995).

Mattias Kumm, 'The Legitimacy of International Law: A Constitutionalist Framework of Analysis' (2004) 15 *European Journal of International Law* 907.

Karl-Heinz Ladeur, 'Globalization and Public Governance—A contradiction?' in Karl-Heinz Ladeur (ed), *Public Governance in the Age of Globalization* (Burlington, Ashgate, 2004).

——, 'Globalization and the Conversion of Democracy to Polycentric Networks: Can Democracy Survive the End of the Nation State?' in Karl-Heinz Ladeur (ed), *Public Governance in the Age of Globalization* (Burlington, Ashgate, 2004).

Andrew Lang, 'Book Reviews: Deborah Cass. The Constitutionalization of the World Trade Organization' (2006) 17 *European Journal of International Law* 309.

Arthur Larson, 'Recipients' Rights Under an International Investment Code' (1960) 9 *Journal of Public Law* 172.

Las Siete Partidas (1256–1265) in *Los Códigos Españoles Concordados y Anotados* (Madrid, Imprenta de la Publicidad, 1848).

Hersch Lauterpacht, *The Development of International Law by the International Court* (New York, Praeger, 1958).

Annie Leeks, 'The Relationship Between Bilateral Investment Treaty Arbitration and the Wider Corpus of International Law: The ICSID Approach' (2007) 65 *University of Toronto Faculty of Law Review* 1.

Barton Legum, 'Options to Establish an Appellate Mechanism for Investment Disputes' in Karl Sauvant (ed), *Appeals Mechanisms in International Investment Law* (New York, OUP, 2008).

Mark A Lemley and David McGowan, 'Legal Implications of Network Economic Effects' (1998) 86 *California Law Review* 479.

William E Leuchtenburg, 'The Origins of Franklin D Roosevelt's "Court-Packing" Plan' (1966) 1966 *Supreme Court Review* 347.

David Levi-Faur, 'The Global Diffusion of Regulatory Capitalism' in David Levi-Faur (ed), *The Rise of Regulatory Capitalism: The Global Diffusion of a New Order* (Thousand Oaks, SAGE Publications, 2005).

Michael E Levine, 'Revisionism revised? Airline Deregulation and the Public Interest' (1981) 44 *Law and Contemporary Problems* 179.

—— and Jennifer L Forrence, 'Regulatory Capture, Public Interest, and the Public Agenda: Toward a Synthesis' (1990) 6 *Journal of Law, Economics and Organization* 167.

Claire L'Heureux-Dube, 'The Importance of Dialogue: Globalization and the International Impact of the Rehnquist Court' (1998) 34 *Tulsa Law Journal* 15.

Peter Leyland and Gordon Anthony, *Administrative Law*, 5th edn (New York, OUP, 2005).

SJ Liebowitz and Stephen Margolis, 'Path Dependence, Lock-in, and History' (1995) 11 *Journal Law Economics and Organization* 205.

Richard Lillich, 'The Current Status of the Law of State Responsibility for Injuries to Aliens' in Richard Lillich (ed), *International Law of State Responsibility for Injuries to Aliens* (Charlottesville, University Press of Virginia, 1983).

——, 'Duties of states regarding the civil rights of aliens' in Académie de Droit International, 161 *Recueil des Cours. Collected Courses of The Hague Academy of International Law, 1978-III* (Alphen aan den Rijn, Sijthoff and Noordhoff, 1980) 329.

Ulf Linderfalk, *On the Interpretation of Treaties. The Modern International Law as Expressed in the 1969 Vienna Convention of the Law of Treaties* (Dordrecht, Springer, 2007).

Peter L Lindseth, 'Democratic Legitimacy and the Administrative Character of Supranationalism: The Example of the European Community' (1999) 99 *Columbia Law Review* 628.

Pedro Lira Urqueta, *El Código Civil Chileno y Su Época* (Santiago de Chile, Editorial Jurídica, 1956).

Vaughan Lowe, 'Regulation or Expropriation' (2002) 55 *Current Legal Problems* 447.

Andreas F Lowenfeld, *International Economic Law* (New York, OUP, 2002).

William Lucy, *Philosophy of Private Law* (New York, OUP, 2007).

Neil MacCormick, *Questioning Sovereignty: Law, State, and Nation in the European Commonwealth* (New York, OUP, 1999).

Jonathan R Macey and Geoffrey P Miller, 'Toward an Interest-Group Theory of Delaware Corporate Law' (1987) 65 *Texas Law Review* 469.

Giandomenico Majone, 'The Rise of the Regulatory State in Europe' (1994) 17 *West European Politics* 77.

VS Mani, *International Adjudication: Procedural Aspects* (Boston, M Nijhoff, 1980).

Francis A Mann, 'State Contracts and State Responsibility' (1960) 54 AJIL 572.

——, 'British Treaties for the Promotion and Protection of Investments' (1981) 52 British Ybk Intl Law 241.

——, *Further Studies in International Law* (New York, OUP, 1990).

——, *The Legal Aspect of Money*, 5th edn (New York, OUP, 1992).

Howard Mann, 'Transparency and Consistency in International Investment Law: Can the Problems Be Fixed by Tinkering' in Karl Sauvant (ed), *Appeals Mechanisms in International Investment Law* (New York, OUP, 2008).

Denise Manning-Cabrol, 'The Imminent Death of the Calvo Clause and the Rebirth of the Calvo Doctrine: Equality of Foreign and National Investors' (1995) 26 *Law and Policy in International Business* 1169.

Jenny S Martinez, 'Toward an International Judicial System' (2003) 56 *Stanford Law Review* 429.

Jerry L Mashaw, *Greed, Chaos, and Governance. Using Public Choice to Improve Public Law* (New Haven, Yale University Press, 1997).

—— et al, *Administrative Law. The American Public Law System. Cases and Materials*, 5th edn (St Paul, MN, Thomson/West, 2003).

Bertrand Mathieu and Michel Verpeaux, *Contentieux Constitutionnel Des Droits Fondamentaux* (Paris, LGDJ, 2002).

Y Matsui, 'The Transformation of the Law of State Responsibility' (1993) 20 *Thesaurus Acroasium* 5.

Graham Mayeda, 'Playing Fair: The Meaning of Fair and Equitable Treatment in Bilateral Investment Treaties' (2007) 41 *Journal of World Trade* 273.

Jeremy McBride, 'Proportionality and the European Convention of Human Rights' in Evelyn Ellis (ed), *The Principle of Proportionality in the Laws of Europe* (Portland, Hart Publishing, 1999).

Brett H McDonnell, 'Getting Stuck' (2003) 31 *Hofstra Law Review* 681.

Myres S McDougal et al, *Human Rights and World Public Order. The Basic Policies of an International Law of Human Dignity* (New Haven, Yale University Press, 1980).

John O McGinnis and Mark L Movsesian, 'The World Trade Constitution' (2000) 114 *Harvard Law Review* 512.

Aileen McHarg, 'Reconciling Human Rights and the Public Interest: Conceptual Problems and Doctrinal Uncertainty in the Jurisprudence of the European Court of Human Rights' (1999) 62 *Modern Law Review* 671.

Campbell McLachlan, 'The Principle of Systemic Integration and Article 31(3)(c) of the Vienna Convention' (2005) 54 ICLQ 279.

——, 'Investment Treaties and General International Law' (2008) 57 ICLQ 361.

—— et al, *International Investment Arbitration. Substantive Principles* (New York, OUP, 2007).

Steven G Medema, 'Making Choices and Making Law: An Institutional Perspective on the Taking Issue' in Nicholas Mercuro (ed), *Taking Property and Just Compensation: Law and Economics Perspectives of the Takings Issue* (Boston, Kluwer Academic, 1992).

Theodor Meron, 'Repudiation of *Ultra Vires* State Contracts and the International Responsibility of States' (1957) 6 *International Law Quarterly* 273.

Thomas W Merrill, 'The Economics of Public Use' (1986) 72 *Cornell Law Review* 61.
——, 'The Landscape of Constitutional Property' (2000) 86 *Virginia Law Review* 885.
JG Merrills, *International Dispute Settlement*, 3rd edn (New York, CUP, 1998).
Mexico, 'Translation of Note from the Minister of Foreign Affairs of Mexico to the American Ambassador at Mexico City' (September 2, 1938)' (1938) 32 AJIL Supp. 201.
Iván Meznerics, 'Guarantees for Foreign Investors' in Zotan Peteri and Vanda Lamm (eds), *General Reports to the 10th International Congress of Comparative Law* (Budapest, Akadémiai Kiadó, 1981).
Sabine Michalowski and Lorna Woods, *German Constitutional Law. The Protection of Civil Liberties* (Brookfield, Ashgate/Dartmouth, 1999).
Frank Michelman, 'Property, Utility, and Fairness: Comments on the Ethical Foundations of 'Just Compensation' Law' (1967) 80 *Harvard Law Review* 1165.
——, 'Possession vs. Distribution in the Constitutional Idea of Property' (1987) 72 *Iowa Law Review* 1319.
——, 'Takings, 1987' (1988) 88 *Columbia Law Review* 1600.
Thomas J Miles and Cass R Sunstein, 'The Real World of Arbitrariness Review' (2008) 75 *University of Chicago Law Review* 761.
Arthur S Miller, 'Protection of Private Foreign Investment by Multilateral Convention' (1959) 53 AJIL 371.
Oriol Mir Puigpelat, *La responsabilidad patrimonial de la Administración. Hacia un nuevo Sistema* (Madrid, Civitas, 2002).
Frank Moderne, 'La Responsabilidad por Actos del Legislador y por los Tratados Internacionales en Francia' in Javier Barnés (ed), *Propiedad, Expropiación y Responsabilidad. Derecho Comparado Europeo* (Madrid, Tecnos, 1995).
Christoph Möllers, ''We are (afraid of) the People': Constituent Power in German Constitutionalism' in Martin Loughlin and Neil Walker, *The Paradox of Constitutionalism. Constituent Power and Constitutional Form* (New York, OUP, 2007).
Santiago Montt, 'La cláusula de precario y la utilización del dominio público: límites constitucionales a una institución leonina' (2002) 212(2) *Revista de Derecho* 507.
——, 'Aplicación de los tratados bilaterales de protección de inversiones por tribunales chilenos. Responsabilidad del estado y expropiaciones regulatorias en un mundo crecientemente globalizado' (2005) 32 *Revista Chilena de Derecho* 19.
——, 'The Award in *Thunderbird v Mexico*' in Guillermo Aguilar Alvarez and W Michael Reisman (eds), *The Reasons Requirement in International Investment Arbitration: Critical Case Studies* (Leiden, M Nijhoff, 2008).
——, *El Dominio Público* (Santiago, Conosur-Lexis, 2002).
Hanri Mostert, *The Constitutional Protection and Regulation of Property and its Influence on the Reform of Private Law and Landownership in South Africa and Germany. A Comparative Analysis* (New York, Springer, 2002).
Helen Mountfield, 'Regulatory Expropriations in Europe: The Approach of the European Court of Human Rights' 11 *New York University Environmental Law Journal* 136.
Allahyar Mouri, *The International Law of Expropriation as Reflected in the Work of the Iran-US Claim Tribunals* (Boston, M Nijhoff, 1994).
Peter Muchlinski, 'Policy Issues' in Peter Muchlinski et al (eds), *The Oxford Handbook of International Investment Law* (New York, OUP, 2008).

Eric Neumayer and Laura Spess, *Do Bilateral Investment Treaties Increase Foreign Direct Investment to Developing Countries?* (May 2005) 5 (available at http://ssrn.com/abstract=616242).

Mark K Neville Jr, 'The Present Status of Compensation by Foreign States for the Taking of Alien-Owned Property' (1980) 13 *Vanderbilt Journal of Transnational Law* 51.

Andrew Newcombe, 'The Boundaries of Regulatory Expropriation in International Law' (2005) 20 *ICSID Review—Foreign Investment Law Journal* 7.

Michael D Nolan and Edward G Baldwin, 'The Treatment Of Contract-Related Claims In Treaty-Based Arbitration' 21(6) *Mealey's International Arbitration Report* 1.

Douglas C North, *Understanding the Process of Economic Change* (Princeton University Press, Princeton 2005).

Thomas F O'Brien, *The Nitrate Industry and Chile's Crucial Transition, 1870–1891* (New York, New York University Press, 1982).

Organisation of Economic Co-Operation and Development (OECD), 'OECD Draft Convention On the Protection of Property, adopted by the Council in its 150th meeting on 12 October 1967' (1968) 7 ILM 117.

——, *Fair and Equitable Treatment Standard in International Investment Law*, Working Papers on International Investment No 2004/3 (2004) (available at http://www.oecd.org/dataoecd/22/53/33776498.pdf).

——, *'Indirect Expropriation' and the 'Right to Regulate' in International Investment Law*, Working Papers on International Investment No 2004/4 (2004) (available at http://www.oecd.org/dataoecd/22/54/33776546.pdf).

Matthias Oesch, *Standards of Review in WTO Dispute Resolution* (New York, OUP, 2003).

Anthony Ogus, 'Property Rights and Freedom of Economic Activity' in Louis Henkin and Albert Rosenthal (ed), *Constitutionalism and Rights. The Influence of the United States Constitution Abroad* (New York, Columbia University Press, 1990).

Marcus Olson, *The Logic of Collective Action: Public Goods and the Theory of Groups* (Cambridge, Mass, Harvard University Press, 1965).

Francisco Orrego Vicuña, 'Keynote Address: Carlos Calvo, Honorary NAFTA Citizen' (2002) 11 *New York University Environmental Law Journal* 19.

Francisco Orrego Vicuña, 'From Preston to Prescott: Globalizing Legitimate Expectations' in Steve Charnovitz et al (eds), *Law in the Service of Human Dignity. Essays in Honour of Florentino Feliciano* (Cambridge, CUP, 2005).

Lluís Paradell, 'The BIT Experience of the Fair and Equitable Treatment Standard' in Federico Ortino et al (eds) *Investment Treaty Law. Current Issues II. Nationality and Investment Treaty Claims. Fair and Equitable Treatment in Investment Treaty Law* (London, The British Institute of International and Comparative Law, 2007).

Luciano Parejo Alfonso, *Derecho Administrativo: Instituciones Generales: Bases, Fuentes, Organización y Sujetos, Actividad y Control* (Barcelona, Ariel, 2003).

Antonio R Parra, 'Applicable Substantive Law in ICSID Arbitration Initiated Under Investment Treaties' (2001) 16 *ICSID Review—Foreign Investment Law Journal* 20.

Michael E Parrish, 'The Great Depression, the New Deal, and the American Legal Order' (1984) 59 *Washington Law Review* 723.

Clive Parry, 'Some Considerations upon the Protection of Individuals in International Law' in Académie de Droit International, 90 *Recueil des Cours—1956-III* (Leyde, Sijthoff, 1957) 653.

Karl Joseph Partsch, 'International Law and Municipal Law' in Rudolf Bernhard (ed), 2 *Encyclopedia of Public International Law* (New York, North-Holland, 1992).

Jeremy Paul, 'The Hidden Structure of Takings Law' (1991) 64 *Southern California Law Review* 1393.

Jan Paulsson and Zachary Douglas, 'Indirect Expropriation in Investment Treaty Arbitrations' in Norbert Horn and Stefan Kröll (eds), *Arbitrating Foreign Investment Disputes* (The Hague, Kluwer Law International, 2004).

Jan Paulsson, *Denial of Justice in International Law* (New York, CUP, 2005).

——, 'Avoiding Unintended Consequences' in Karl Sauvant (ed), *Appeals Mechanisms in International Investment Law* (New York, OUP, 2008).

Joost Pauwelyn, *Conflict of Norms in Public International Law: How WTO Law Relates to other Rules of International Law* (CUP, Cambridge 2003).

Alain Pellet, 'Article 38' in Andreas Zimmerman et al (eds), *The Statute of the International Court of Justice: A Commentary* (New York, OUP, 2006).

Matti Pellonpää, 'Compensable Claims Before the Tribunal: Expropriation Claims' in Richard B Lillich and Daniel Barstow Magraw (eds), *The Iran–United States Claims Tribunal: Its Contribution to the Law of State Responsibility* (Irvington-on-Hudson, Transnational Publishers, 1998).

Roger Penrose, *The Road to Reality. A Complete Guide to the Laws of the Universe* (New York, AA Knopf, 2004).

Sol Picciotto, 'Constitutionalizing Multilevel Governance' in (2008) 6 *International Journal of Constitutional Law* 457.

Luis A Podesta Costa, '*La Responsabilidad Internacional del Estado*' in *Academia Interamericana de Derecho Comparado e Internacional*, 2 *Cursos Monográficos* 171 (La Habana, Cuba, 1952).

Miguel Poiares Maduro, 'Legal Travels and the Risk of Legal Jet-Lag. The Judicial and Constitutional Challenges of Legal Globalization' in Mario Monti et al (eds), *Economic Law and Justice in Times of Globalisation. Festschrift for Carl Baudenbacher* (Baden Baden, Nomos Verlagsgesellschaft, 2007).

Miguel Poiares Maduro, *We The Court. The European Court of Justice and The European Economic Constitution. A Critical Reading of Article 30 of the EC Treaty* (Oxford, Hart Publishing, 1998).

Matthew C Porterfield, 'An International Common Law of Investor Rights?' (2006) 27 *University of Pennsylvania Journal of International Economic Law* 79.

Ferran Pons Cànovas, *La incidencia de las intervenciones administrativas en el derecho de propiedad. Perspectivas actuales* (Madrid, Marcial Pons, 2004).

Richard A Posner, 'Democracy and Distrust Revisited' (1991) 77 *Virginia Law Review* 641.

——, *Economic Analysis of Law*, 5th edn (New York, Aspen Law and Business, 1998).

Robert Post, *Constitutional Domains. Democracy, Community, and Management* (Cambridge, Mass, Harvard University Press, 1995).

Roy Preiswerk, 'New Developments in Bilateral Investment Protection (With Special Reference to Belgian Practice)' (1967) 3 *Revue Belge du Droit International* 173.

Daniel M Price, 'Nafta Chapter 11– Investor-State-Dispute Settlement: Frankenstein or Safety Valve?' (2000) 26 *Canada–United States Law Journal* 107.

Carlos Bernal Pulido, *El Principio de Proporcionalidad y los Derechos Fundamentales: El Principio de Proporcionalidad como Criterio para Determinar el Contenido de los Derechos Fundamentales Vinculantes para el Legislador*, 2nd edn (Madrid, Centro de Estudios Políticos y Constitucionales, 2005).

Asif Qureshi, 'Development Perspectives on the Establishment of an Appellate Process in the Investment Sphere' in Federico Ortino et al (eds), *Investment Treaty Law. Current Issues I* (London, The British Institute of International and Comparative Law, 2006).

—— and Shandana Gulzar Khan, 'Implications of an Appellate Body for Invstment Disputes from a Developing Country Point of View' in Karl Sauvant (ed), *Appeals Mechanisms in International Investment Law* (New York, OUP, 2008).

Margaret Jane Radin, 'The Liberal Conception of Property: Cross Currents in the Jurisprudence of Takings' (1988) 88 *Columbia Law Review* 1667.

August Reinisch, 'Expropriation' in Peter Muchlinski et al (eds), *The Oxford Handbook of International Investment Law* (New York, OUP, 2008).

——, 'Legality of Expropriations' in August Reinisch, *Standards of Investment Protection* (New York, OUP, 2008).

Steven R Ratner, 'Regulatory Takings in Institutional Context: Beyond the Fear of Fragmented International Law' (2008) 102 AJIL 475.

Kal Raustiala, 'Rethinking the Sovereignty Debate in International Economic Law' (2003) 6 *Journal of International Economic Law* 841.

Dardo Regules, *La Lucha por la Justicia y por el Derecho. Apuntes sobre la IX Conferencia Reunida en Bogotá durante el Mes de Abril de 1948* (Montevideo, Barreiro y Ramos, 1949).

W Michael Reisman, 'International Law after the Cold War' (1990) 84 AJIL 859.

——, 'The Regime for *Lacunae* in the ICSID Choice of Law Provision and the Question of its Threshold' (2000) 15 *ICSID Review—Foreign Investment Law Journal* 362.

——, 'International Arbitration and Sovereignty' (2002) 18 *Arbitration International* 231.

—— and Mahnoush H Arsanjani, 'The Question of Unilateral Governmental Statements as Applicable Law in International Disputes' (2004) 19 *ICSID Review–Foreign Investment Law Journal* 328.

—— and Robert D Sloane, 'Indirect Takings and its Valuation in the BIT generation' (2003) 74 British Ybk Intl Law 115.

J Fred Rippy, 'The British Investment 'Boom' of the 1880's in Latin America' (1949) 29(2) *The Hispanic-American Historical Review* 281

Ali Riza Çoban, *Protection of Property Rights within the European Convention on Human Rights* (Burlington, Ashgate, 2004).

Mark J Roe, 'Delaware's Competition' (2003) 117 *Harvard Law Review* 588.

Jeffrey H Rohlfs, *Bandwagon Effects in High-Technology Industries* (Cambridge, Mass, MIT Press, 2001).

Cesare PR Romano, 'The Proliferation of International Judicial Bodies: The Pieces of the Puzzle' (1999) 31 *New York University Journal of International Law and Policy* 709.

Roberta Romano, 'Law as a Product' (1985) 1 *Journal of Law, Economic and Organization* 225.

Carol M Rose, '*Mahon* Reconstructed: Why the Takings Issue is Still a Muddle' (1984) 57 *Southern California Law Review* 561.

——, 'The Shadow of *The Cathedral*' (1997) 106 *Yale Law Journal* 2175.

Susan Rose-Ackerman, 'Against Ad Hocery: A Comment on Michelman' (1988) 88 *Columbia Law Review* 1697.

——, 'Regulatory Takings: Policy Analysis and Democratic Principles' in Nicholas Mercuro (ed), *Taking Property and Just Compensation: Law and Economics Perspectives of the Takings Issue* (Boston, Kluwer Academic, 1992).

—— and Jim Rossi, 'Disentangling Deregulatory Takings' (2000) 86 *Virginia Law Review* 1435.

—— and Jennifer Tobin, 'Do BITs Benefit Developing Countries?' in Roger P Alford and Catherine A Rogers (eds), *The Future of Investment Arbitration* (OUP, forthcoming, 2009)

Shabtai Rosenne (ed), *League of Nations Committee of Experts for the Progressive Codification of International Law (1925–1928)* (Dobbs Ferry, NY, Oceana Publications, 1972).

—— (ed), *League of Nations Conference for the Codification of International Law* (1930) (Dobbs Ferry, NY, Oceana Publications, 1975).

—— (ed), *The International Law Commission's Draft Articles on State Responsibility* (Boston, M Nijhoff, 1991).

Andreas H Roth, *The Minimum Standards of International Law Applied to Aliens* (Leiden, AW Sijthoff, 1949).

Andres Rozental, 'The Charter of Economic Rights and Duties of States and the New International Economic Order' (1976) 16 *Virginia Journal of International Law* 309.

Jed Rubenfeld, 'Usings' (1993) 102 *Yale Law Journal* 1097.

——, 'Unilateralism and Constitutionalism' (2004) 79 *New York University Law Review* 1971.

Noah Rubins, 'The Notion of 'Investment' in International Investment Arbitration' in Norbert Horn and Stefan Kröll (eds), *Arbitrating Foreign Investment Disputes* (The Hague, Kluwer Law International, 2004).

Wolfgang Rüfner, 'Basic Elements of German Law on State Liability' in John Bell and Anthony W Bradley (eds), *Governmental Liability: A Comparative Study* (London, UKNCCL, 1991).

Wayne Sachs, 'The 'New' US Bilateral Treaties' (1984) 2 *International Tax and Business Law* 192.

Jeswald W Salacuse, 'BIT by BIT: The Growth of Bilateral Investment Treaties and Their Impact on Foreign Investment in Developing Countries' (1990) 24 *International Lawyer* 655.

—— and Nicholas P Sullivan, 'Do BITs Really Work?: An Evaluation of Bilateral Investment Treaties and Their Grand Bargain' (2005) 46 *Harvard International Law Journal* 67.

Saskia Sassen, 'De-Nationalized State Agendas end Privatized Norm-Making' in Karl-Heinz Ladeur (ed), *Public Governance in the Age of Globalization* (Ashgate, Burlington 2004).

Joseph Sax, 'Takings and the Police Powers' (1964) 74 *Yale Law Journal* 36.

——, 'Takings, Private Property and Public Rights' (1971) 81 *Yale Law Journal* 149.

Antonin Scalia, 'Judicial Deference to Administrative Interpretations of Law' (1989) *1989 Duke Law Journal* 511.

Oscar Schachter, 'Compensation for Expropriation' (1984) 78 AJIL 121.
Fritz W Scharpf, *Governing in Europe: Effective and Democratic?* (New York, OUP, 1999).
Henry G Schemers, 'Introduction' in Henry G Schemers et al (eds), *Non-Contractual Liability of The European Communities* (Boston, M Nijhoff, 1988).
Stephan W Schill, *Fair and Equitable Treatment under Investment Treaties as an Embodiment of the Rule of Law*, IILJ Working Paper 2006/6, Global Administrative Law Series 5 (2006) (available at http://iilj.org/publications/documents/2006-6-GAL-Schill-web.pdf).
Hans-Jürgen Schlochauser, 'International Court of Justice' in Rudolph Bernhardt (ed) 1 *Encyclopedia of Public International Law* (New York, North-Holland Publishing, 1981).
Michael Schneider, 'Does the WTO Confirm the Need for a More General Appellate System in Investment Disputes?' in Federico Ortino et al (eds), *Investment Treaty Law. Current Issues I* (London, The British Institute of International and Comparative Law, 2006).
David Schneiderman, *Constitutionalizing Economic Globalization: Investment Rules and Democracy's Promise* (New York, CUP, 2008).
Raymond Schössels, 'Liability for Lawful Administrative Action. Observations on Common Principles of Law, Judicial Lawmaking and National Courts' in F Stroink and E van der Linden (eds), *Judicial Lawmaking and Administrative Law* (Antwerp, Intersentia, 2005).
Søren J Schønberg, *Legitimate Expectations in Administrative Law* (New York, OUP, 2000).
Christoph H Schreuer, 'Commentary on the ICSID Convention' (1999) 15 *ICSID Review—Foreign Investment Law Journal* 46.
——, *The ICSID Convention: A Commentary* (New York, CUP, 2001).
——, 'Fair and Equitable Treatment in Arbitral Practice' (2005) 6 *Journal of World Investment and Trade* 357.
——, 'Non-pecuniary Remedies in ICSID' (2004) 20 *Arbitration International* 325.
——, 'Calvo's Grandchildren: The Return of Local Remedies in Investment Arbitration' (2005) 4 *The Law and Practice of International Courts and Tribunals* 1.
——, 'Fair and Equitable Treatment in Arbitral Practice' (2005) 6 *Journal of World Investment and Trade* 357.
——, *The Concept of Expropriation under the ETC and other Investment Protection Treaties* (available at www.univie.ac.at/intlaw/pdf/csunpublpaper_3.pdf).
——, 'The Coexistence of Local and International Law Remedies (Panel)' in Federico Ortino et al (eds), *Investment Treaty Law. Current Issues I* (London, The British Institute of International and Comparative Law, 2006).
——, 'Introduction: Interrelationship of Standards' in August Reinisch, *Standards of Investment Protection* (New York, OUP, 2008).
Nico Schrijver, *Sovereignty Over Natural Resources: Balancing Rights and Duties* (New York, CUP, 1997).
Camilo B Schutte, *The European Fundamental Right of Property* (Deventer, Kluwer, 2004).
Georg Schwarzenberger, 'The Province and Standards of International Economic Law' (1948) 2 *International Law Quarterly* 402.
——, 1 *International Law* (London, Stevens and Sons, 1957).

Georg Schwarzenberger, *Foreign Investments and International Law* (New York, Praeger, 1969).

Colin Scott, 'Regulation in the Age of Governance: The Rise of the Post-Regulatory State' in Jacint Jordana and David Levi-Faur (eds), *The Politics of Regulation: Institutions and Regulatory Reform for the Age of Governance* (Edward Elgar, Northampton 2004).

James Brown Scott (ed), *The Hague Peace Conferences of 1899 and 1907. A Series of Lectures Delivered Before the John Hopkins University in the Year 1908* (John Hopkins University, Baltimore 1909).

James Brown Scott (ed), *The International Conferences of American States 1889–1928: A Collection of the Conventions, Recommendations, Resolutions, Reports, and Motions Adopted By the First Six International Conferences of the American States, and Documents Relating to the Organization of the Conferences* (New York, OUP, 1931).

Secretaría de Relaciones Exteriores (Mexicana), *Conferencias Internacionales Americanas. Segundo Suplemento 1945–1954* (México, Secretaría de Relaciones Exteriores, 1956).

Martin Shapiro, 'Administrative Law Unbounded: Reflection on Government and Governance' (2001) 8 *Indiana Journal of Global Legal Studies* 369.

Scott Shapiro, 'HLA Hart' in AP Martinich and David Sosa (eds), *A Companion to Analytic Philosophy* (Malden, Blackwell, 2001).

Sidney A Shapiro and Richard E Levy, 'Heightened Scrutiny of the Fourth Branch: Separation of Powers and the Requirement of Adequate Reasons for Agency Decisions' (1987) 1987 *Duke Law Journal* 387.

—— and Richard W Murphy, 'Eight Thing Americans Can't Figure Out About Controlling Administrative Power' (2008) 60 *Administrative Law Review* (forthcoming) (http://papers.ssrn.com/sol3/papers.cfm?abstract_id=1162872).

Malcolm N Shaw, *International Law*, 5th edn (New York, OUP, 2003).

Donald Richard Shea, *The Calvo Clause: A Problem of Inter-American and International Law and Diplomacy* (Minneapolis, University of Minnesota Press, 1955).

Ethan Shenkman, 'Could Principles of Fifth Amendment Takings Jurisprudence Be Helpful in Analyzing Regulatory Expropriation Claims under International Law?' (2002) 11 *New York University Environmental Law Journal* 174.

J Gregory Sidak and Daniel F Spulberg, *Deregulatory Takings and the Regulatory Contract* (New York, CUP, 1997).

Beth A Simmons, 'Money and the Law: Why Comply with the Public International Law of Money' (2000) 25 *Yale Journal of International Law* 323.

John Liddle Simpson and Hazel Fox, *International Arbitration. Law and Practice* (New York, Praeger, 1959).

Ian Sinclair, *The Vienna Convention on the Law of Treaties,* 2nd edn (Dover, Manchester University Press, 1984).

Joseph William Singer, *Property. Rules, Policies, and Practices* (Boston, Little, Brown and Company, 1993).

——, *Entitlement: The Paradoxes of Property* (New Haven, Yale University Press, 2000).

Mahendra P Singh, *German Administrative Law in Common Law Perspective*, 2nd edn (Berlin, Springer, 2001).

Robert H Sitkoff and Max M Schanzenbach, 'Jurisdictional Competition for Trust Funds: An Empirical Analysis of Perpetuities and Taxes' (2005) 115 *Yale Law Journal* 356.

Anne-Marie Slaughter, 'Judicial Globalization' (2000) 40 *Virginia Journal of International Law* 1103.

——, *A New World Order* (Princeton, Princeton University Press, 2004).

SA De Smith, L Woolf, and K Jowell, *Judicial Review of Administrative Action*, 5th edn (London, Sweet & Maxwell, 1995).

Elizabeth Snodgrass, 'Protecting Investors' Legitimate Expectations: Recognizing and Delimiting a General Principle' (2006) 21 *ICSID Review—Foreign Investment Law Journal* 1.

Earl Snyder, 'Protection of Foreign Investment, Examination and Appraisal' (1961) 10 ICLQ 469.

Louis B Sohn and R Baxter, *Convention on the International Responsibility of States for Injuries to Aliens. Preliminary Draft with Explanatory Notes* (Cambridge, Mass, Harvard Law School, 1959).

Louis B Sohn and Richard Baxter, 'Draft Convention on the International Responsibility of States for Injuries to the Economic Interests of Aliens' (1961) 55 AJIL 545.

——, 'Convention on the International Responsibility of States for Injuries to Aliens. Final Draft with Explanatory Notes' in FV Garcia-Amador, Louis B Sohn and RR Baxter (eds), *Recent Codification of the Law of State Responsibility for Injuries to Aliens* (Dobbs Ferry, NY, Oceana Publications, 1974).

M Sornarajah, *The International Law on Foreign Investment*, 1st edn (New York, CUP, 1994).

——, *The International Law on Foreign Investment*, 2nd edn (Cambridge, CUP, 2004).

Shane Spelliscy, 'Burning the Idols of Non-Arbitrability: Arbitrating Administrative Law Disputes with Foreign Investors' (2001) 12 *American Review of International Arbitration* 95.

Ole Spiermann, 'Applicable Law' in Peter Muchlinski et al (eds), *The Oxford Handbook of International Investment Law* (New York, OUP, 2008).

Marina Spinedi and Bruno Simma (eds), *United Nations Codification of State Responsibility* (New York, Oceana, 1987).

Christian Starck, 'Constitutional Definition and Protection of Rights and Freedoms' in Christian Starck (ed), *Rights, Institutions and Impact of International Law according to the German Basic Law* (Baden-Baden, Nomos Verlagsgesellschaft, 1987).

Eric Stein, 'International Integration and Democracy: No Love at First Sight' (2001) 95 AJIL 489.

Alexander Marie Stuyt, *Survey of International Arbitration, 1794–1989* (Boston, M Nijhoff Publishers, 1990).

Kathleen M Sullivan and Gerald Gunther, *Constitutional Law*, 14th edn (New York, Foundation Press, 2001).

Lionel M Summers, 'The Calvo Clause' (1933) 19 *Virginia Law Review* 459.

——, 'Arbitration and Latin America' (1972) 3 *California Western International Law Journal* 1.

Cass R Sunstein, 'Naked Preferences and the Constitution' (1984) 84 *Columbia Law Review* 1689.

——, *Free Markets and Social Justice* (New York, OUP, 1997).

——, 'Beyond *Marbury*: The Executive Power to Say What the Law Is' (2006) 115 *Yale Law Journal* 2580.

Surya P Subedi, *International Investment Law. Reconciling Policy and Principle* (Portland, Hart Publishing, 2008).

Alan C Swan and John F Murphy, *Cases and Materials on the Regulation of International Business and Economic Relations*, 2nd edn (New York, M Bender, 1999).

Alec Stone Sweet, *Governing with Judges. Constitutional Politics in Europe* (New York, OUP, 2000).

——, 'Path Dependency, Precedent, and Judicial Power' in Martin Shapiro and Alec Stone Sweet, *On Law, Politics, and Judicialization* (New York, OUP, 2002).

——, *The Judicial Construction of Europe* (New York, OUP, 2004).

Paul C Szasz, 'The Investment Disputes Convention and Latin America' (1970) 11 *Virginia Journal of International Law* 256.

Felipe Tena Ramírez (ed), *Leyes Fundamentales de México 1998–2002* (México, Editorial Porrúa, 2002).

Guido Santiago Tawil, 'The Distinction Between Contract Claims and Treaty Claims: An Overview' in Albert van den Berg (ed), *International Arbitration 2006: Back to Basis?* (Alphen aan den Rijn, Kluwer Law International, 2007).

Gunther Teubner, 'Global Private Regimes: Neo-Spontaneous Law and Dual Constitution of Autonomous Sectors?' in Karl-Heinz Ladeur (ed), *Public Governance in the Age of Globalization* (Burlington, Ashgate, 2004).

JC Thomas, 'Reflections on Article 1105 of NAFTA: History, State Practice and the Influence of Commentators' (2002) 17 ICSID *Review—Foreign Investment Law Journal* 21.

Robert Thomas, *Legitimate Expectations and Proportionality in Administrative Law* (Portland, Hart Publishing, 2000).

James Tobin, 'A Comment on Dahl's Skepticism' in Ian Shapiro and Casiano Hacker-Cordón (eds), *Democracy's Edges* (New York, CUP, 1999).

Jennifer Tobin and Susan Rose-Ackerman, *Foreign Direct Investment and the Business Environment in Developing Countries: The Impact of Bilateral Investment Treaties*, Yale Law School (May 2005) (available at http://ssrn.com/abstract=557121).

——, *Bilateral Investment Treaties: Do They Stimulate Foreign Direct Investment?*, Yale Law School (Draft, June 2006).

JM Torres Caicedo, *Mis Ideas y Mis Principios* (Paris, Imprenta Nueva, 1875).

Joel P Trachtman, 'The Domain of WTO Dispute Resolution' (1999) 40 *Harvard International Law Journal* 333.

——, 'The Agency Model of Judging in Economic Integration: Balancing Responsibilities' in Thomas Cottier and Petros C Mavroidis (eds), *The Role of the Judge in International Trade Regulation. Experiences and Lessons for the WTO* (Ann Arbor, University of Michigan Press, 2003).

——, 'The Constitutions of the WTO' (2006) 17 *European Journal of International Law* 623.

Laurence H Tribe, 'The Puzzling Persistence of Process-Based Constitutional Theories' (1980) 89 *Yale Law Journal* 1063.

——, *Constitutional Choices* (Cambridge, Mass, Harvard University Press, 1985).

Ioana Tudor, *The* Fair and Equitable Treatment Standard *in The International Law of Foreign Investment* (New York, OUP, 2008).

Laura S Underkuffler, *The Idea of Property. Its Meaning and Power* (New York, OUP, 2003).

United Nations Centre on Transnational Corporations, *Bilateral Investment Treaties* (Graham and Trotman, Boston 1988).

United Nations Conference on Trade and Development (UNCTAD), *Bilateral Investment Treaties in the Mid-1990s* (New York, United Nations, 1998).

——, *Fair and Equitable Treatment* (New York, United Nations, 1999).

——, *Bilateral Investment Treaties 1959–1999* (New York, United Nations, 2000).

——, *South-South Cooperation in International Investment Arrangements. UNCTAD Series on International Investment Policies for Development* (New York, United Nations, 2005) (available at www.unctad.org/en/docs/iteiit20053_en.pdf).

——, *World Investment Report* (New York, United Nations, 2005).

——, *World Investment Report* (New York, United Nations, 2006).

——, *World Investment Report* (New York, United Nations, 2007).

——, *Taking of Property* (New York, United Nations, 2000).

United States, 'The Secretary of State of the United States (Cordel Hull) to Mexican Ambassador at Washington DC' (1938) 32 AJIL Supp 181.

Detlev F Vagts, 'Coercion and Foreign Investment Re-Arrangements' (1978) 72 AJIL 17.

——, 'Protecting Foreign Direct Investment: An International Law Perspective' in Cynthia Day Wallace (ed), *Foreign Direct Investment in the 1990s: A New Climate in the Third World* (Boston, M Nijhoff, 1990).

Anne van Aaken, 'Perils of Success? The Case of International Investment Protection' (2008) *European Business Organisation Law Review* 1.

AJ van der Walt, *Constitutional Property Clauses. A Comparative Analysis* (Cambridge, Kluwer Law International, 1999).

W van Gerven, 'Mutual Permeation of Public and Private Law at the National and Supranational Level' (1998) 5 *Maastricht Journal of European and Comparative Law* 7.

Gus van Harten and Martin Loughlin, 'Investment Treaty Arbitration as a Species of Global Administrative Law' (2006) 17 *European Journal of International Law* 121.

——, *Investment Treaty Arbitration and Public Law* (New York, OUP, 2007).

Kenneth J Vandevelde, 'The Bilateral Investment Treaty Program of the United States' (1988) 21 *Cornell International Law Journal* 201.

——, 'The BIT Program: A Fifteen-Year Appraisal, in the Development and Expansion of Bilateral Investment Treaties' (1992) 86 *American Society of International Law Proceedings* 532.

——, 'US Bilateral Investment Treaties: The Second Wave' (1993) 14 *Michigan Journal International Law* 621.

——, 'The Political Economy of a Bilateral Investment Treaty' (1998) 92 AJIL 621.

VV Veeder, 'The Necessary Safeguards of an Appellate System' in Federico Ortino et al (eds), *Investment Treaty Law. Current Issues I* (London, The British Institute of International and Comparative Law, 2006).

William Wade and Christopher Forsyth, *Administrative Law*, 9th edn (New York, OUP, 2004).

Patricia Wald, 'Some Observations on the Use of Legislative History in the 1981 Supreme Court Term' (1983) 68 *Iowa Law Review* 195.

Thomas W Wälde, 'Investment Arbitration under the Energy Charter Treaty—From Dispute Settlement to Treaty Implementation' (1996) 12 *Arbitration International* 429.

Thomas W Wälde, 'Investment Arbitration as a Discipline for Good-Governance' in Todd Weiler (ed), *NAFTA Investment Law and Arbitration: Past Issues, Current Practice, Future Prospect* (Ardsley, Transnational Publishers, 2003) 475.

——, 'The "Umbrella" Clause in Investment Arbitration. A Comment on Original Intentions and Recent Cases' (2005) 6 *Journal of World Investment and Trade* 183.

——, 'Investment Arbitration under the Energy Charter Treaty: An Overview of Selected Key Issues Based on Recent Litigation Experience' in Norbert Horn and Stefan Kröll (eds), *Arbitrating Foreign Investment Disputes* (The Hague, Kluwer Law International, 2004)

——, 'The Present State of Research Carried Out by the English-Speaking Section of the Centre for Studies and Research' in Centre for Studies and Research in International Law and International Relations, *New Aspects of International Investment Law* (Leiden, Nijhoff, 2006).

—— and Abba Kolo, 'Environmental Regulation, Investment Protection and 'Regulatory Taking' in International Law' (2001) 50 ICLQ 811.

Humphrey Waldock, 'General Course on Public International Law' in Académie de Droit International, 106 *Recueil des Cours—1962-II* (Leyde, AW Sijthoff, 1963) 1.

Jeremy Waldron, *Law and Disagreement* (New York, OUP, 1999).

——, 'The Core of the Case Against Judicial Review' (2006) 115 *Yale Law Journal* 1346.

Christian Walter, 'Constitutionalizing (Inter)national Governance—Possibilities for and Limits to the Development of an International Constitutional Law' (2001) 44 *German Yearbook of International Law* 170.

Herman Walker Jr, 'Treaties for the Encouragement and Protection of Foreign Investment: Present United States Practice' (1956) 5 *American Journal of Comparative Law* 229.

——, 'Modern Treaties of Friendship, Commerce and Navigation' (1958) 42 *Minnesota Law Review* 805.

Neil Walker, 'The EU and the WTO: Constitutionalism in a New Key' in Gráinne de Búrca and Joanne Scott (eds), *The EU and the WTO. Legal and Constitutional Issues* (Portland, Hart Publishing, 2001).

——, 'Beyond Boundary Disputes and Basic Grids: Mapping the Global Disorder of Normative Orders' (2008) 6 *International Journal of Constitutional Law* 373.

Jason Webb Yackee, 'Conceptual Difficulties in the Empirical Studies of Bilateral Investment Treaties', Legal Studies Research Paper No 1053, October 2007 (available at http://ssrn.com/abstract=1015088).

Prosper Weil, 'The State, the Foreign Investor, and International Law: The No Longer Stormy Relationship of a *Mènage à Trois*' (2000) 15 *ICSID Review–Foreign Investment Law Journal* 401.

JHH Weiler, 'The Transformation of Europe' (1991) 100 *Yale Law Journal* 2403.

——, *Introduction: The Reformation of European Constitutionalism* in JHH Weiler, *The Constitution of Europe* (New York, CUP, 1999).

—— and Iulia Motoc, 'Taking Democracy Seriously: The Normative Challenges to the International Legal System' in Stefan Griller (ed), *International Economic Governance and Non-Economic Concerns* (New York, Springer, 2003).

Todd J Grierson-Weiler (ed), *Investment Treaty Arbitration and International Law* (Huntington, JurisNet, 2008).

—— and Ian A Laird, 'Standards of Treatment' in Peter Muchlinski et al (eds), *The Oxford Handbook of International Investment Law* (New York, OUP, 2008).

Ernest J Weinrib, *The Idea of Private Law* (Cambridge, Mass, Harvard University Press, 1995).

Claire Weir and Richard Moules, 'Article 1 of Protocol No 1: Protection of Property' in Jessica Simor and Ben Emmerson, *Human Rights Practice* (rev 13 February 2007) (London, Sweet & Maxwell, 2008).

Burns H Weston, ' "Constructive Takings" under International Law: A Modest Foray into the Problems of "Creeping Expropriations" ' (1975) 16 *Virginia Journal of International Law* 103.

——, 'The Charter of Economic Rights and Duties and the Deprivation of Foreign Owned Wealth' (1981) 75 AJIL 437.

Gillian White, *Nationalisation of Foreign Property* (New York, Praeger, 1961).

GM White, 'Wealth Deprivations: Creditor and Contract Claims' in Richard Lillich et al (eds), *International Law of State Responsibility for Injuries to Aliens* (Charlottesville, University Press of Virginia, 1983).

Clair Wilcox, *A Charter for World Trade* (New York, Macmillan Co, 1949).

George Winfield Scott, 'Hague Convention Restricting the Use of Force to Recover Contract Claims' (1908) 2 AJIL 78.

Robert Wisner, 'The Modern View of the 'Fair and Equitable Treatment' Standard in the Review of Regulatory Action by States' (2007) 20 *International Law Practicum* 129.

World Bank, *World Development Report 2005* (Washington DC, World Bank-OUP, 2005).

BA Wortley, *Expropriation in Public International Law* (Cambridge, CUP, 1959).

Richard W Wright, 'Right, Justice, and Tort Law' in David G Owen (ed), *Philosophical Foundations of Tort Law* (New York, OUP, 1995).

Katia Yannaca-Small, 'Improving the System of Investor-Disute Settlement: The OECD Governments' Perspective' in Karl Sauvant (ed), *Appeals Mechanisms in International Investment Law* (New York, OUP, 2008).

——, 'Fair and Equitable Treatment Standard: Recent Developments' in August Reinisch, *Standards of Investment Protection* (New York, OUP, 2008).

Ernest A Young, 'Institutional Settlement in a Globalizing Judicial System' (2005) 54 *Duke Law Journal* 1143.

H Peyton Young, *Individual Strategy and Social Structure* (Princeton University Press, Princeton 1998).

Galina Zukova, 'The Award in *Petrobart Limited v Kyrgyz Republic*' in Guillermo Aguilar Alvarez and W Michael Reisman (eds), *The Reasons Requirement in International Investment Arbitration: Critical Case Studies* (eds) (M Nijhoff, Leiden 2008).

Index